ENTREPRENEURSHIP

ENTREPRENEURSHIP

FIFTH EDITION

Robert D. Hisrich, Ph.D.

A. Malachi Mixon III Professor of Entrepreneurial Studies
Chair, Entrepreneurship and Policy Divisions
Weatherhead School of Management
Case Western Reserve University

Michael P. Peters, Ph.D.

Associate Professor of Marketing
Carroll School of Management
Boston College

Boston   Burr Ridge, IL   Dubuque, IA   Madison, WI   New York   San Francisco   St. Louis
Bangkok   Bogotá   Caracas   Kuala Lumpur   Lisbon   London   Madrid   Mexico City
Milan   Montreal   New Delhi   Santiago   Seoul   Singapore   Sydney   Taipei   Toronto

McGraw-Hill Higher Education ⚛

A Division of The **McGraw-Hill** *Companies*

ENTREPRENEURSHIP
Published by McGraw-Hill/Irwin, an imprint of The McGraw-Hill Companies, Inc., 1221 Avenue of the Americas, New York, NY, 10020. Copyright © 2002, 1998, 1995, 1992, 1989, by The McGraw-Hill Companies, Inc. All rights reserved. No part of this publication may be reproduced or distributed in any form or by any means, or stored in a database or retrieval system, without the prior written consent of The McGraw-Hill Companies, Inc., including, but not limited to, in any network or other electronic storage or transmission, or broadcast for distance learning.
Some ancillaries, including electronic and print components, may not be available to customers outside the United States.

This book is printed on acid-free paper.

2 3 4 5 6 7 8 9 0 CCW/CCW 0 9 8 7 6 5 4 3 2 1
2 3 4 5 6 7 8 9 0 CCW/CCW 0 9 8 7 6 5 4 3 2 1

ISBN 0-07-231406-0

Publisher: *John E. Biernat*
Sponsoring editor: *Marianne C. P. Rutter*
Editorial coordinator: *Tammy Higham*
Marketing manager: *Lisa Nicks*
Project manager: *Ruth Smith*
Production supervisor: *Susanne Riedell*
Coordinator freelance design: *Mary L. Christianson*
Associate supplement producer: *Joyce J. Chappetto*
Media technology producer: *Jenny R. Williams*
Cover freelance designer: *Didona Design*
Cover photograph: © *Stone*
Compositor: *Carlisle Communications, Ltd.*
Typeface: *10/12 Berling*
Printer: *Courier Westford*

Library of Congress Control Number: 2001090843

INTERNATIONAL EDITION ISBN 0-07-112351-2
Copyright © 2002. Exclusive rights by The McGraw-Hill Companies, Inc., for manufacture and export. This book cannot be re-exported from the country to which it is sold by McGraw-Hill. The International Edition is not available in North America.

www.mhhe.com

To our wives, Tina and Debbie,
and daughters Kary, Katy, Kelly, Christa, and Kimberly,
and their supportive entrepreneurial spirit

Preface

Starting and operating a new business involve considerable risk and effort to overcome the inertia against creating something new. In creating and growing a new venture, the entrepreneur assumes the responsibility and risks for its development and survival and enjoys the corresponding rewards. The fact that consumers, businesspeople, and government officials are interested in entrepreneurship is shown in the increasing research on the subject, the large number of college courses and seminars on the topic, the more than two million new enterprises started each year despite a 70 percent failure rate, the significant coverage and focus by the media, and the realization that this is an important topic for industrialized, developing, and once-controlled economies.

Who is the focus of all this attention—who is willing to accept all the risks and put forth the effort necessary to create a new venture? It may be a man or a woman, someone from an upper-class or lower-class background, a technologist or someone lacking technologic sophistication, a college graduate or a high school dropout. The person may have been an inventor, manager, nurse, salesperson, engineer, student, teacher, homemaker, or retiree. It is someone able to juggle work, family, and civic responsibilities while meeting payroll.

To provide an understanding of this person and the process of creating and growing a new venture, this fifth edition of *Entrepreneurship* is divided into four major sections. Part I—The Entrepreneurial Perspective introduces the entrepreneur and the entrepreneurial process from both a historical and a research perspective. The role and nature of entrepreneurship as a mechanism for creating new ventures and affecting economic development are presented, along with career aspects and future direction of entrepreneurship. The characteristics and background of entrepreneurs are discussed, as well as some methods for individual self-assessment and the various aspects of international entrepreneurship.

Part II—Creating and Starting the Venture focuses on all the elements in the entrepreneurial process that are a part of creating a new venture. After a discussion of creativity and obtaining the right business area, the legal issues—such as intellectual property protection and product safety and liability—are addressed. Important aspects of the business plan are then presented, and a chapter is devoted to each of the major components of the business plan: the marketing plan, the financial plan, and the organizational plan.

One of the most difficult aspects of creating and establishing a new venture is the focus of Part III—Financing the New Venture. After a discussion of the alternative sources of capital, specific attention is given to two primary financing mechanisms: informal risk capital and venture capital.

Part IV—Managing, Growing, and Ending the New Venture presents material related to establishing, developing, and ending the venture. Particular attention is paid to managing the new venture during growth, early operations, and expansion. Managerial skills that are important to the successful performance and growth of a new venture are included in this section. This part also addresses going public—the goal of many entrepreneurs when starting the entrepreneurial process—as well as methods for ending the venture. Specific topics examined include mergers and acquisitions, franchising, leveraged buyouts, negotiation, and time management.

To make *Entrepreneurship* as meaningful as possible, each chapter begins with a profile of an entrepreneur whose career is especially relevant to the chapter material. Chapter objectives follow, and numerous examples occur throughout. Important websites to assist the reader in getting started, as well as *Business Week* and Ethics boxes, are also included in this fifth edition. Each chapter concludes with discussion questions, a list of key terms, and selected readings for further information.

Many people—students, business executives, entrepreneurs, professors, and publishing staff—have made this book possible. Of great assistance were the detailed and thoughtful comments of our reviewers: Steve Dunphy (Northeastern Illinois University), Michael Gallagher (Mesa State College), Patricia Greene (Rutgers University), Robert Gulovsen (Washington University), Ram Kesavan (University of Detroit), Ralph Parrish (Colorado State University), Bryan Toney (Georgia Institute of Technology), Godwin Wong (Golden Gate University), and Frederick Young (Salem State College). Particular thanks go to Bill Wetzel for helpful comments on Chapter 12, "Informal Risk Capital and Venture Capital," and to Lynn Moore for comments on Chapter 16, "Going Public." Special thanks are given to Jennifer Baker and Teresa Kabat for preparing the manuscript so competently, and to Ines Troconis, Branko Bucar, and Bostjan Antoncic for providing research material and editorial assistance for this edition. Also thanks to our supplement authors—Gayle Ross, Alka Srivastva, and Steve Dunphy—for their wonderful work on the Instructor's Manual and PowerPoint slides, respectively.

We are deeply indebted to our spouses, Tina and Debbie, whose support and understanding helped bring this effort to fruition. It is to future entrepreneurs—our daughters Christa, Kary, Katy, Kelly, and Kimberly and the generation they represent—that this book is particularly dedicated. May you always beg forgiveness rather than ask permission.

Robert D. Hisrich
Michael P. Peters

Contents in Brief

Contents

𝄞

CASES FOR PART I

PART II   CREATING AND STARTING THE VENTURE *163*

8   The Marketing Plan   *252*

9   The Financial Plan   *284*

PART IV   MANAGING, GROWING, AND ENDING THE NEW VENTURE   *467*

I

THE ENTREPRENEURIAL PERSPECTIVE

1

The Nature and Importance of Entrepreneurs

LEARNING OBJECTIVES

1. To introduce the concept of entrepreneurship and its historical development.

2. To explain the entrepreneurial decision process.

3. To identify the basic types of start-up ventures.

4. To explain the role of entrepreneurship in economic development.

5. To discuss the ethics and racial responsibility of entrepreneurs.

TED TURNER

Ted Turner, founder of Turner Broadcasting System, is an entrepreneur who loves living life on the edge. Who else would buy an unprofitable Metro-Goldwyn-Mayer film studio for $1.6 billion? Who else would bet on producing the Goodwill Games with U.S. versus Soviet athletes at a cost of about $50 million? Who else would report that "the thrill of victory is everything we imagined it would be," following the triumph of Turner's Atlanta Braves in the 1995 World Series, after three consecutive, unsuccessful trips to the playoffs?

www.turner.com

Although Turner's unorthodox endeavors always contain an element of risk, they are not limited to his entrepreneurial pursuits. In 1999, he promised to donate $1 billion of his $7.8 billion fortune to the United Nations, declaring that he would "rather use [his wealth] for the benefit of mankind than spend it selfishly."

Robert Edward Turner, III, born in 1938, spent his boyhood primarily in Savannah, Georgia. As a boy, he was an enthusiastic reader of books about heroes, from Horatio Hornblower to Alexander the Great.

Unsuccessful in playing any of the major sports, he turned to one that required no special physical attributes, but rather relied on the ability to think, take chances, and compete—sailing. Turner became a fanatic sailor, using a method that earned him such nicknames as the Capsize Kid and Turnover Ted. He loved sailing's competitive frenzy.

Turner graduated from the second military school he attended and applied to Harvard for admission but was rejected. His father insisted that he attend an Ivy League college, so he went to Brown University to study Greek classics. Dismayed by this area of study, Turner's father eventually convinced him to change his major to economics. After two suspensions for infractions involving women, Turner was kicked out of Brown University for setting fire to his fraternity's homecoming float.

After a few years, Turner joined the family business. His father, R. E. Turner, Jr., was an ambitious businessman who had built a $1 million billboard business. However, in a short time, Turner's family disintegrated: his sister, Mary Jane, died; his parents were divorced; and his father killed himself.

Although his father's will left the Atlanta billboard company to Ted, a contract to sell the business had been signed before he died. Showing the deal-making ingenuity that has characterized his business activities, the young Turner convinced the buyers that, by shifting lease sites to another company he had inherited, he would be able to sabotage the company before the deal closed. The buyers backed down, and Turner's career moved forward. At the helm of the company, Turner began to expand, buying up billboard companies and radio stations. Since these constant acquisitions required huge outlays of cash and incurred debt, he learned to maintain a sufficient cash flow to cover payments.

In 1969, he took his company public with a merger that included a small Atlanta television station now called WTBS. In 1976, WTBS was the first station to become a network by beaming its signal to cable systems via satellite. By 1986, WTBS reached 36 million U.S. households and was cable television's most profitable advertising-supported network. The 1986 operating cash flow of the company was $70 million, and 1989 sales topped the $1 billion mark.

Turner did not sit back and watch the cash come in. He was, and is, always looking for ways to build his assets. Despite industry skepticism, Turner used the growing cash flow from WTBS to start the Cable News Network (CNN) in 1989. In spite of criticism from industry "experts," the 24-hour news channel was a success, catapulting into international success with the extensive coverage of the Gulf War in 1990. The success of CNN enabled Turner to create additional news networks domestically and internationally, including Headline News, CNN Financial News Network, and CNN International, as well as sites on the World Wide Web. By the end of 1995, the news division of Turner Broadcasting Systems posted revenues of $765 million and an operating cash flow of $281 million. Phenomenal public viewing of the coverage of the O. J. Simpson trial accounted for an increase of 45 percent in combined household viewing of CNN and Headline News on a 24-hour basis. Turner's success, however, also served to attract additional competition, with three of the four major networks launching news networks in 1996. Today, however, CNN sets the standard for hard-hitting news coverage; in 1998, cable viewers voted CNN their preferred news network. In 2000 it was reported to have more than 75 million subscribers in the United States. CNN is also America's number one distributed news network.

Turner's uncanny success in starting high-risk ventures is not accidental. A vigilant and relentless manager, Turner would often sleep on his office couch after working an 18-hour day. Even now, his commute to work is a matter of going "down" to the office; he lives in the penthouse apartment of one of the Turner towers in Atlanta. Until autumn 1986, when Turner established a five-man management committee consisting of veteran TBS executives, he personally supervised company tasks and decisions. One person familiar with Turner's management style was surprised at the formation of the committee: "He [Turner] would never even let the five go out and have a beer together, let alone run the company."

Turner's talents extend beyond the corporate boardroom. A high risk taker, he won the America's cup race in 1977. In 1979, he won the Fastnet race off England's southwest coast, during which 156 competitors died in the violent seas.

In his own view, Turner is a quintessential achiever. He says, "I've got more awards than anybody—anybody my age. I've probably got more debt than anyone in the world. That's something, isn't it?" What makes him keep pushing for more?

Not satisfied with his accomplishments, Turner has established a visionary goal: to use his power and network to influence world issues. He wants to concentrate on issues such as nuclear weapons, environmental abuse, and overpopulation. He speaks proudly of TBS specials, such as the one based on the life and works of Martin Luther King, Jr. When asked if he would want to be president of the United States, Turner said, "The United States is only five percent of the world's population. I'm in global politics already."

Turner's view is both global and long term; he is obsessed with both owning a U.S. television network and being the dominant figure in the international cable TV market. But at the end of 1989, gross profits were $631 million and sales were over $1 billion. Turner felt that the simple solution was either to increase buyer clout by taking over an existing network or to acquire his own program library.

Turner's attempt to take over CBS in 1985 failed, costing him $23 million in lawyer and investment banker fees. But Turner, an undaunted optimist and aggressive competitor, viewed this attempted hostile takeover defeat as a triumph, since CBS had to borrow heavily to acquire stock to stop the takeover. At the time, Turner felt that this set CBS back 10 years, while the event left him in a position to pursue his aggressive growth strategy.

Turner moved directly from his setback with CBS to the acquisition of MGM. In 1985, one CNN executive said, "Ted's mind is always 5 or 10 years down the road. Right now he's probably living in 1995." Turner's purchase of the MGM studio was motivated by rising licensing fees for old movies and television shows. Bill Bevins, TBS financial chief executive, projected that the higher fees would lower operating profits from 40 percent of sales in 1985 to 10 percent in 1990. The 3,650-film library offered Turner Broadcasting a solution to rising licensing fees. About 1,000 of these films have enduring commercial value and have been, and continue to be, aired on WTBS. Some analysts felt that the price paid—$1.6 billion—was too high, with the deal putting Turner heavily into debt. More debt for TBS resulted from Turner's decision to colorize about 10 percent of the films in this newly acquired library—at an average cost of $300,000 per film and a total cost of $22 million to $55 million.

Careful management of cash flows, however, permitted continued expansion, including expansion into additional networks (Turner Classic Movies and The Cartoon Network) as well as into motion picture production (Castle Rock Entertainment, New Line Cinema, and Turner Pictures). His original motion pictures combined yielded $400 million in box office receipts, a respectable 9.3 percent of the 1995 domestic box office market.

Today, Turner's entertainment networks—which now include TBS Superstation, TNT, Cartoon Network, and Turner Classic Movies—reflect the same level of excellence and resultant success that CNN embodies. In 1999, each of these networks was an industry leader in virtually every primary demographic segment. TBS Superstation is reported to draw a larger adult demographic audience than any other cable network, while TNT won landmark success in 1998 by setting a cable distribution record of 75 percent of U.S. television homes. This distribution was achieved within 10 years of TNT's inception, an industry record. The success of the entertainment networks is further augmented by Turner's deftness in global relations. Turner uses his international savvy to provide 15 localized versions of his entertainment networks to regions of Europe and Asia. Finally, Turner entertainment networks have more than 10 World Wide Web sites that complement regular programming and offer original content exclusive to the Web, an avenue that allows service to yet another contingent of viewers.

Turner's Home Box Office network has also gained renown as America's most successful premium television network. Home Box Office offers audiences two 24-hour services—HBO and Cinemax. At the end of 1999, these services reached 35.7 million U.S. subscribers. Turner's international finesse is again evident in HBO's servicing of 11 million subscribers in more than 40 countries in Latin America, Asia, and Central Europe. Home Box Office's success can be largely attributed to its powerful programming. Turner provides audiences with access to Hollywood's best movies, which in turn drives subscriber acquisition. In January 2000 HBO drew 7.6 million viewers for the second-season launch of the big hit program, The Sopranos.

Constant attention to his goals of expansion finally bore fruit with the merger of TBS and CBS. In a series of extremely complex and time-consuming negotiations that required the approval of the Justice Department and the Federal Trade Commission, this merger created the world's largest entertainment conglomerate, valued at between $6.2 billion and $8.5 billion. Under the terms of the agreement, each (TBS and CBS) is a wholly owned subsidiary of a new Time Warner Holding Company, of which Ted Turner is the vice chairman while remaining CEO of TBS. According to estimates, the effective sales for 1994 were $18.7 billion, with cash flows of $3.4 billion. In less than three decades, Turner leveraged a $1 million billboard company into a multi-billion-dollar entertainment conglomerate. He saw cable television ending the near-monopoly status of the Big Three television networks, saw the value in providing real-time international news coverage, saw the emerging entertainment market in international markets, and will most likely predict with accuracy the integration of the Internet with news coverage.

In spite of the frequent criticism of his obsessions by one of his major stockholders, and the high risk associated with doing things that were new and different, Turner maintained his focus. People who know Turner well will not bet against him. He has an entrepreneurial spirit that thrives on living on the edge and relishes challenging situations.

The saga of Ted Turner reflects the story of many entrepreneurs in a variety of industries and various-sized companies. The historical aspect of entrepreneurship, as well as the decision that Ted Turner and others have made to become entrepreneurs, is reflected in the following remarks of two successful entrepreneurs:

> Being an entrepreneur and creating a new business venture is analogous to raising children—it takes more time and effort than you ever imagine and it is extremely difficult and painful to get out of the situation. Thank goodness you cannot easily divorce yourself from either situation.
>
> When people ask me if I like being in business, I usually respond: On days when there are more sales than problems, I love it; on days when there are more problems than sales, I wonder why I do it. Basically, I am in business because it gives me a good feeling about myself. You learn a lot about your capabilities by putting yourself on the line. Running a successful business is not only a financial risk, it is an emotional risk as well. I get a lot of satisfaction from having dared it—done it—and been successful.

Do the profile of Ted Turner and these quotes fit your perception of the career of an entrepreneur? Both say a great deal about what it takes to start and operate a successful business. To understand this better, it is important to learn about the nature and development of entrepreneurship, the decision process involved in becoming an entrepreneur, and the role of entrepreneurship in the economic development of a country.

NATURE AND DEVELOPMENT OF ENTREPRENEURSHIP

Who is an entrepreneur? What is entrepreneurship? What is an entrepreneurial career path? These frequently asked questions reflect the increased national and international interest in entrepreneurs, who they are, and how they impact an economy. In spite of all this interest, a concise, universally accepted definition has not yet emerged. The development of the theory of entrepreneurship parallels to a great extent the development of the term itself (see Table 1.1). The word *entrepreneur* is French and, literally translated, means "between-taker" or "go-between."

entrepreneur   Individual who takes risks and starts something new

Earliest Period

An early example of the earliest definition of an entrepreneur as a go-between is Marco Polo, who attempted to establish trade routes to the Far East. As a go-between, Marco Polo would sign a contract with a money person (forerunner of today's venture capitalist) to sell his goods. A common contract during this time provided a loan to the merchant–adventurer at a 22.5 percent rate, including insurance. While the capitalist was a passive risk bearer, the merchant–adventurer took the active role in trading, bearing all the physical and emotional risks. When the merchant–adventurer

TABLE 1.1	Development of Entrepreneurship Theory and the Term *Entrepreneur*
Stems from French: means *between-taker or go-between*.	
Middle Ages:	actor and person in charge of large-scale production projects.
17th century:	person bearing risks of profit (loss) in a fixed-price contract with government.
1725:	Richard Cantillon—person bearing risks is different from one supplying capital.
1803:	Jean Baptiste Say—separated profits of entrepreneur from profits of capital.
1876:	Francis Walker—distinguished between those who supplied funds and received interest and those who received profit from managerial capabilities.
1934:	Joseph Schumpeter—entrepreneur is an innovator and develops untried technology.
1961:	David McClelland—entrepreneur is an energetic, moderate risk taker.
1964:	Peter Drucker—entrepreneur maximizes opportunities.
1975:	Albert Shapero—entrepreneur takes initiative, organizes some social and economic mechanisms, and accepts risks of failure.
1980:	Karl Vesper—entrepreneur seen differently by economists, psychologists, businesspersons, and politicians.
1983:	Gifford Pinchot—intrapreneur is an entrepreneur within an already established organization.
1985:	Robert Hisrich—entrepreneurship is the process of creating something different with value by devoting the necessary time and effort; assuming the accompanying financial, psychological, and social risks; and receiving the resulting rewards of monetary and personal satisfaction.

Source: Robert D. Hisrich, "Entrepreneurship and Intrapreneurship: Methods for Creating New Companies That Have an Impact on the Economic Renaissance of an Area." In *Entrepreneurship, Intrapreneurship, and Venture Capital.* ed. Robert D. Hisrich (Lexington, MA: Lexington Books, 1986), p. 96.

successfully sold the goods and completed the trip, the profits were divided with the capitalist taking most of them (up to 75 percent), while the merchant–adventurer settled for the remaining 25 percent.

Middle Ages

In the Middle Ages, the term *entrepreneur* was used to describe both an actor and a person who managed large production projects. In such large production projects, this individual did not take any risks, but merely managed the project using the resources provided, usually by the government of the country. A typical entrepreneur in the Middle Ages was the cleric—the person in charge of great architectural works, such as castles and fortifications, public buildings, abbeys, and cathedrals.

17th Century

The reemergent connection of risk with entrepreneurship developed in the 17th century, with an entrepreneur being a person who entered into a contractual arrangement with the government to perform a service or to supply stipulated products. Since the contract price was fixed, any resulting profits or losses were the entrepreneur's. One entrepreneur in this period was John Law, a Frenchman, who was allowed to establish a royal bank. The bank eventually evolved into an exclusive franchise to form a trading company in the New World—the Mississippi Company. Unfortunately, this monopoly on French trade led to Law's downfall when he attempted to push the company's stock price higher than the value of its assets, leading to the collapse of the company.

Richard Cantillon, a noted economist and author in the 1700s, understood Law's mistake. Cantillon developed one of the early theories of the entrepreneur and is regarded by some as the founder of the term. He viewed the entrepreneur as a risk taker, observing that merchants, farmers, craftsmen, and other sole proprietors "buy at a certain price and sell at an uncertain price, therefore operating at a risk."[1]

18th Century

Finally, in the 18th century, the person with capital was differentiated from the one who needed capital. In other words, the entrepreneur was distinguished from the capital provider (the present-day venture capitalist). One reason for this differentiation was the industrialization occurring throughout the world. Many of the inventions developed during this time were reactions to the changing world, as was the case with the inventions of Eli Whitney and Thomas Edison. Both Whitney and Edison were developing new technologies and were unable to finance their inventions themselves. Whereas Whitney financed his cotton gin with expropriated British crown property, Edison raised capital from private sources to develop and experiment in the fields of electricity and chemistry. Both Edison and Whitney were capital users (entrepreneurs), not providers (venture capitalists). A venture capitalist is a professional money manager who makes risk investments from a pool of equity capital to obtain a high rate of return on the investments.

19th and 20th Centuries

In the late 19th and early 20th centuries, entrepreneurs were frequently not distinguished from managers and were viewed mostly from an economic perspective:

> Briefly stated, the entrepreneur organizes and operates an enterprise for personal gain. He pays current prices for the materials consumed in the business, for the use of the land, for the personal services he employs, and for the capital he requires. He contributes his own initiative, skill, and ingenuity in planning, organizing, and administering the enterprise. He also assumes the chance of loss and gain consequent to unforeseen and uncontrollable circumstances. The net residue of the annual receipts of the enterprise after all costs have been paid, he retains for himself.[2]

Andrew Carnegie is one of the best examples of this definition. Carnegie invented nothing, but rather adapted and developed new technology in the creation of products to achieve economic vitality. Carnegie, who descended from a poor Scottish family, made the American steel industry one of the wonders of the industrial world, primarily through his unremitting competitiveness rather than his inventiveness or creativity.

entrepreneur as an innovator   An individual developing something unique

In the middle of the 20th century, the notion of an *entrepreneur as an innovator* was established:

> The function of the entrepreneur is to reform or revolutionize the pattern of production by exploiting an invention or, more generally, an untried technological method of producing a new commodity or producing an old one in a new way, opening a new source of supply of materials or a new outlet for products, by organizing a new industry.[3]

The concept of innovation and newness is an integral part of entrepreneurship in this definition. Indeed, innovation, the act of introducing something new, is one of the most difficult tasks for the entrepreneur. It takes not only the ability to create and conceptualize but also the ability to understand all the forces at work in the environment. The newness can consist of anything from a new product to a new distribution system to a method for developing a new organizational structure. Edward Harriman, who reorganized the Ontario and Southern railroad through the Northern Pacific Trust, and John Pierpont Morgan, who developed his large banking house by reorganizing and financing the nation's industries, are examples of entrepreneurs fitting this definition. These organizational innovations are frequently as difficult to develop successfully as the more traditional technological innovations (transistors, computers, lasers) that are usually associated with being an entrepreneur.

This ability to innovate can be observed throughout history, from the Egyptians who designed and built great pyramids out of stone blocks weighing many tons each, to the Apollo lunar module, to laser beams. Although the tools have changed with advances in science and technology, the ability to innovate has been present in every civilization.

DEFINITION OF ENTREPRENEUR

The concept of an entrepreneur is further refined when principles and terms from a business, managerial, and personal perspective are considered. In particular, the concept of entrepreneurship from a personal perspective has been explored in this century. This exploration is reflected in the following three definitions of an entrepreneur:

> In almost all of the definitions of entrepreneurship, there is agreement that we are talking about a kind of behavior that includes: (1) initiative taking, (2) the organizing and reorganizing of social and economic mechanisms to turn resources and situations to practical account, (3) the acceptance of risk or failure.[4]
>
> To an economist, an entrepreneur is one who brings resources, labor, materials, and other assets into combinations that make their value greater than before, and also one who introduces changes, innovations, and a new order. To a psychologist, such a person is typically driven by certain forces—the need to obtain or attain something, to experiment, to accomplish, or perhaps to escape the authority of others. To one businessman, an entrepreneur appears as a threat, an aggressive competitor, whereas to another businessman the same entrepreneur may be an ally, a source of supply, a customer, or someone who creates wealth for others, as well as finds better ways to utilize resources, reduce waste, and produce jobs others are glad to get.[5]
>
> Entrepreneurship is the dynamic process of creating incremental wealth. The wealth is created by individuals who assume the major risks in terms of equity, time, and/or career commitment or provide value for some product or service. The product or service may or may not be new or unique, but value must somehow be infused by the entrepreneur by receiving and locating the necessary skills and resources.[6]

Although each of these definitions views entrepreneurs from a slightly different perspective, they all contain similar notions, such as newness, organizing, creating, wealth, and risk taking. Yet each definition is somewhat restrictive, since entrepreneurs are found in all professions—education, medicine, research, law, architecture, engineering, social work, and distribution. To include all types of entrepreneurial behavior, the following definition of entrepreneurship will be the foundation of this book:

entrepreneurship   Process of creating something new and assuming the risks and rewards

Entrepreneurship is the process of creating something new with value by devoting the necessary time and effort, assuming the accompanying financial, psychic, and social risks, and receiving the resulting rewards of monetary and personal satisfaction and independence.[7]

This definition stresses four basic aspects of being an entrepreneur regardless of the field. First, entrepreneurship involves the creation process—creating something new of value. The creation has to have value to the entrepreneur and value to the audience for which it is developed. This audience can be (1) the market of buyers in the case of a business innovation, (2) the hospital's administration in the case of a new admitting procedure and software, (3) prospective students in the case of a new course or even college of entrepreneurship, or (4) the constituency for a new service provided by a nonprofit agency. Second, entrepreneurship requires the devotion of the necessary time and effort. Only those going through the entrepreneurial process appreciate the significant amount of time and effort it takes to create something new and make it operational. Assuming the necessary risks is the third aspect of entrepreneurship. These risks take a variety of forms, depending on the field of effort of the entrepreneur, but usually center around financial, psychological, and social areas. The final part of the definition involves the rewards of being an entrepreneur. The most important of these rewards is independence, followed by personal satisfaction. For profit entrepreneurs, the monetary reward also comes into play. For some of these entrepreneurs, money becomes the indicator of the degree of success.

For the person who actually starts his or her own business, the experience is filled with enthusiasm, frustration, anxiety, and hard work. There is a high failure rate due to such things as poor sales, intense competition, lack of capital, or lack of managerial ability. The financial and emotional risk can also be very high. What, then, causes a person to make this difficult decision? The question can be best explored by looking at the decision process involved in becoming an entrepreneur.

THE ENTREPRENEURIAL DECISION PROCESS

Many individuals have difficulty bringing their ideas to the market and creating a new venture. Yet entrepreneurship and the actual entrepreneurial decisions have resulted in several million new businesses being started throughout the world. Although no one knows the exact number, in the United States (which leads the world in company formation) estimates indicate that 1.1 to 1.9 million new companies have been formed each year in recent years.[8]

Indeed, millions of ventures are formed despite recession, inflation, high interest rates, lack of infrastructure, economic uncertainty, and the high probability of failure. Each of these ventures is formed through a very personal human process that, although unique, has some characteristics common to all. Like all processes, the *entrepreneurial decision process* entails a movement, *from* something *to* something—a movement from a present lifestyle to forming a new enterprise, as indicated in Table 1.2.

entrepreneurial decision process   Deciding to become an entrepreneur by leaving present activity

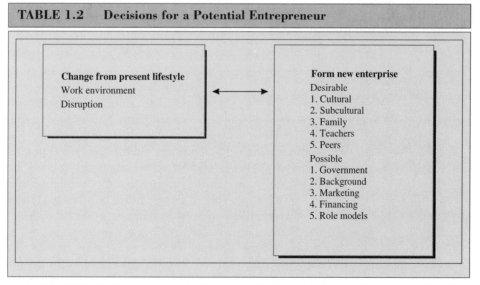

TABLE 1.2	Decisions for a Potential Entrepreneur
Change from present lifestyle Work environment Disruption	**Form new enterprise** Desirable 1. Cultural 2. Subcultural 3. Family 4. Teachers 5. Peers Possible 1. Government 2. Background 3. Marketing 4. Financing 5. Role models

Source: Robert D. Hisrich, "Entrepreneurship and Intrapreneurship: Methods for Creating New Companies That Have an Impact on the Economic Renaissance of an Area." In *Entrepreneurship, Intrapreneurship, and Venture Capital.* ed. Robert D. Hisrich (Lexington, MA: Lexington Books, 1986), p. 90

Change from Present Lifestyle

The decision to leave a career or lifestyle is not an easy one. It takes a great deal of energy and courage to change and do something new and different. Although individuals tend to start businesses in areas that are familiar, two work environments have been particularly good for spawning new enterprises: research and development, and marketing. While working in technology (research and development), individuals develop new product ideas or processes and often leave to form their own companies when these new ideas are not accepted by their employers. Similarly, individuals in marketing have become familiar with the market and customers' unfilled wants and needs, and they frequently leave to start new enterprises to fill these needs.

Perhaps an even stronger incentive to overcome the inertia and leave a present lifestyle to create something new comes from a negative force—disruption. A significant number of companies are formed by people who have retired, who are relocated due to a move by the other member in a dual-career family, or who have been fired. There is probably no greater force than personal dislocation to galvanize a person's will to act. A study in one major city in the United States indicated that the number of new business listings in the yellow pages increased by 12 percent during a layoff period. Another cause of disruption that can result in company formation is someone's completion of an educational degree. For example, a student who is not promoted after receiving an MBA degree may become frustrated and decide to leave and start a new company.

What causes this personal disruption to result in a new company being formed? The decision to start a new company occurs when an individual perceives that forming a new enterprise is both desirable and possible.

Desirability of New Venture Formation

The perception that starting a new company is desirable results from an individual's culture, subculture, family, teachers, and peers. A culture that values an individual who successfully creates a new business will spawn more venture formations than one that does not. The American culture places a high value on being one's own boss, having individual opportunities, being a success, and making money—all aspects of entrepreneurship. Therefore, it is not surprising to find a high rate of company formation in the United States. On the other hand, in some countries successfully establishing a new business and making money are not as highly valued, and failure may be a disgrace. Countries with cultures that more closely emulate this attitude do not have as high a business formation rate. It will be interesting to watch which of the once-controlled economies will develop a pro-entrepreneur culture.

desirability of new venture formation   Aspects of a situation that make it desirable to start a new company

No culture is totally for or against entrepreneurship. Many subcultures that shape value systems operate within a cultural framework. There are pockets of entrepreneurial subcultures in the United States. Although the more widely recognized ones include Route 128 (Boston), Silicon Valley (California), and the North Carolina Triangle, some less-known but equally important entrepreneurial centers are Los Angeles, Denver, Cleveland, and Austin. These subcultures support and even promote entrepreneurship—the forming of a new company—as one of the best occupations. No wonder more individuals actively plan new enterprises in these supportive environments.

There are also variations within these subcultures (such as Silicon Valley) caused by family traits. Studies of companies in a variety of industries throughout the world indicate that a very high percentage of the founders of companies had fathers and/or mothers who valued independence. The independence achieved by company owners, professionals, artists, professors, or farmers permeates their entire family life, giving encouragement and value to their children's company-formation activity.

Encouragement to form a company is further stimulated by teachers, who can significantly influence individuals to regard entrepreneurship as a desirable and viable career path. Schools with exciting courses in entrepreneurship and innovation tend to develop entrepreneurs and can actually drive the entrepreneurial environment in an economic area. For example, the number of entrepreneurship courses a person takes increases the probability of starting a venture. Both MIT and Harvard are located near Route 128; Stanford is in the Silicon Valley; the University of North Carolina, North Carolina State, and Duke are the points of the North Carolina Triangle; and Case Western Reserve University facilitates entrepreneurship in the Cleveland area. An area having a strong education base is a strong support factor for entrepreneurial activity and company formation.

Finally, peers are very important in the decision to form a company. An area with an entrepreneurial pool and a meeting place where entrepreneurs and potential entrepreneurs can discuss ideas, problems, and solutions spawns more new companies than an area where these are not available.

Possibility of New Venture Formation

Although the desire derived from the individual's culture, subculture, family, teachers, and peers needs to be present before any action is taken, the second feature necessary centers around this question: "What makes it possible to form a new company?" Several factors—government, background, marketing, role models, and finances—contribute to the creation of a new venture (see Table 1.2). The government contributes by providing the infrastructure to help and support a new venture. It is no wonder that more companies are formed in the United States—given the roads, communication and transportation systems, utilities, and economic stability—than in other countries. Even the U.S. tax rate for companies and individuals is better than in countries like Ireland, England, or Germany. Countries that have a repressive tax rate on businesses or individuals can suppress company formation, since companies will not have the money to start and grow and monetary gain cannot be achieved. However, the social, psychological, and financial risks are still present. The entrepreneur must also have the necessary background. Formal education and previous business experience give a potential entrepreneur the skills needed to form and manage a new enterprise. Although educational systems are important in providing the needed business knowledge, individuals will tend to be more successful in forming businesses in fields in which they have worked. Entrepreneurs are not born: They develop.

Marketing also plays a critical role in forming a new company. In addition to the presence of a market of sufficient size, there must also be a level of marketing know-how to put together the best total package of product, price, distribution, and promotion needed for successful product launching. A company is more easily formed when the driving force is more from market demand than a technology push.

A role model can be one of the most powerful influences in making company formation seem possible. To see someone else succeed makes it easier to picture yourself

possibility of new venture formation Factors making it possible to create a new venture engaged in a similar activity—of course, even more successfully. A frequent comment of entrepreneurs when queried about their motivations for starting their new venture is, "If that person could do it, so can I!"

Finally, financial resources must be readily available. Although most of the start-up money for any new company comes from personal savings, credit, friends, and relatives, there is often a need for additional seed capital. Risk-capital availability plays an essential role in the development and growth of entrepreneurial activity. More new companies form when seed capital is readily available.

TYPES OF START-UPS

What types of start-ups result from this entrepreneurial decision process? One very useful classification system divides start-ups into three categories: lifestyle firms, foundation companies, and high-potential ventures. A *lifestyle firm* is privately held and usually achieves only modest growth due to the nature of the business, the objectives of the entrepreneur, and the limited money devoted to research and development. This type of firm may grow after several years to 30 or 40 employees and have annual revenues of about $2 million. A lifestyle firm exists primarily to support the owners and usually has little opportunity for significant growth and expansion.

lifestyle firm   A small venture that supports the owners and usually does not grow

The second type of start-up—the *foundation company*—is created from research and development and lays the foundation for a new business area. This firm can grow in 5 to 10 years from 40 to 400 employees and from $10 million to $20 million in yearly revenues. Since this type of start-up rarely goes public, it usually draws the interest of private investors only, not the venture-capital community.

foundation company   A type of company formed from research and development that usually does not go public

The final type of start-up—the *high-potential venture*—is the one that receives the greatest investment interest and publicity. While the company may start out like a foundation company, its growth is far more rapid. After 5 to 10 years, the company could employ around 500 employees, with $20 million to $30 million in revenue. These firms are also called *gazelles* and are integral to the economic development of an area.

high-potential venture   A venture that has high growth potential and therefore receives great investor interest

Given that the results of the decision-making process need to be perceived as desirable and possible for an individual to change from a present lifestyle to a radically new one, it is not surprising that the type and number of new business formations vary greatly throughout the world. Some regions of the United States have more support infrastructure and a more positive attitude toward new business creation. For example, in 1997, compared with the previous year, 6 out of 10 SBA regions had increases in new business incorporations: the Southwest region (Arizona, California, Hawaii, and Nevada) had the largest increase (7.1 percent), followed by the Southeast (4.1 percent) and Mountain regions (3.3 percent). The new business incorporations in the New England states declined 5.8 percent, in the Northwest 1.9 percent, and in the East North Central region 1.4 percent.[9]

gazelles   Very high growth ventures

ROLE OF ENTREPRENEURSHIP IN ECONOMIC DEVELOPMENT

The role of entrepreneurship in economic development involves more than just increasing per capita output and income; it involves initiating and constituting change in the structure of business and society. This change is accompanied by growth and increased output, which allows more wealth to be divided by the various participants. What in an area facilitates the needed change and development? One theory of economic growth depicts innovation as the key, not only in developing new products (or services) for the market but also in stimulating investment interest in the new ventures being created. This new investment works on both the demand and the supply sides of the growth equation; the new capital created expands the capacity for growth (supply side), and the resultant new spending utilizes the new capacity and output (demand side).

In spite of the importance of investment and innovation in the economic development of an area, there is still a lack of understanding of the *product-evolution process*. This is the process through which innovation develops and commercializes through entrepreneurial activity, which in turn stimulates economic growth.

product-evolution process   Process for developing and commercializing an innovation

The product-evolution process illustrated in Figure 1.1 as a cornucopia, the traditional symbol of abundance, begins with knowledge in the base technology and science—such as thermodynamics, fluid mechanics, or electronics—and ends with products or services available for purchase in the marketplace.[10] The critical point in the product-evolution process is the intersection of knowledge and a recognized social need, which begins the product development phase (IV in Figure 1.1). This point, called *iterative synthesis*, often fails to evolve into a marketable inno-

iterative synthesis   The intersection of knowledge and social need that starts the product development process

vation and is where the entrepreneur needs to concentrate his or her efforts. The lack of expertise in this area—matching the technology with the appropriate market and making the needed adjustments—is an underlying problem in any technology transfer.

The innovation can, of course, be of varying degrees of uniqueness. Most innovations introduced to the market are *ordinary innovations*, that is, with little uniqueness or technology. As expected, there are fewer *technological innovations* and *breakthrough innovations*, with the number of actual innovations decreasing as the technology involved increases. Regardless of its level of uniqueness or technology, each innovation (particularly the latter two types) evolves into and develops toward commercialization through one of three mechanisms: the government, intrapreneurship, or entrepreneurship.

ordinary innovations   New products with little technological change

technological innovations   New products with significant technological advancement

breakthrough innovations   New products with some technological change

Entrepreneurship has assisted in revitalizing areas of the inner city. Individuals in inner-city areas can relate to the concept and see it as a possibility for changing their present situation. One model project in New York City changed a depressed area into one having many small entrepreneurial companies.

Government as an Innovator

The government is one conduit for commercializing the results of the synthesis of social need and technology. This is frequently called *technology transfer* and has been the focus of a significant amount of research effort. Despite this effort, relatively few inventions resulting from sound scientific government-sponsored research have reached (been transferred to) the commercial market. Most of the by-products of this

government as an innovator   A government active in commercializing technology

technology transfer   Commercializing the technology in the laboratories into new products

FIGURE 1.1   Product Evolution

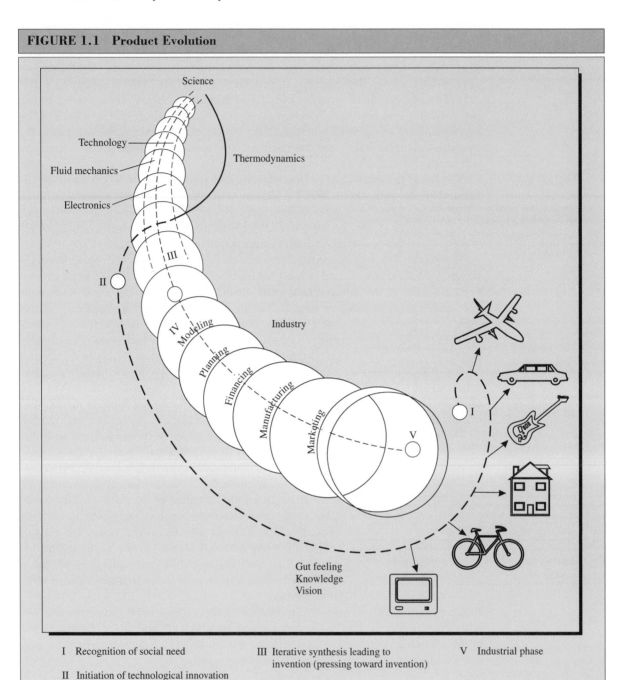

I	Recognition of social need	III	Iterative synthesis leading to invention (pressing toward invention)	V	Industrial phase
II	Initiation of technological innovation	IV	Development phase		

scientific research have little application to any social need. The few by-products that are applicable require significant modification to have market appeal. Though the government has the financial resources to successfully transfer the technology to the marketplace, it lacks the business skills, particularly marketing and distribution, necessary for successful commercialization. In addition, government bureaucracy and red tape often inhibit the business from being formed in a timely manner.

Recently, this problem has been addressed with federal labs being required to commercialize some of their technology each year. In order to help their scientists commercialize their technology and think more entrepreneurially, some labs are providing entrepreneurial training and are working with university entrepreneurial educators.

Intrapreneurship

Intrapreneurship (entrepreneurship within an existing business structure) can also bridge the gap between science and the marketplace. Existing businesses have the financial resources, business skills, and frequently the marketing and distribution systems to commercialize innovation successfully. Yet, too often the bureaucratic structure, the emphasis on short-term profits, and a highly structured organization inhibit creativity and prevent new products and businesses from being developed. Corporations recognizing these inhibiting factors and the need for creativity and innovation have attempted to establish an intrapreneurial spirit in their organizations. In the present era of hypercompetition, the need for new products and the intrapreneurial spirit have become so great that more and more companies are developing an intrapreneurial environment, often in the form of strategic business units (SBUs). Intrapreneurship is discussed in Chapter 2.

Intrapreneurship   Entrepreneurship within an existing organization

Entrepreneurship

The third method for bridging the gap between science and the marketplace is via entrepreneurship. Many entrepreneurs have a difficult time bridging this gap and creating new ventures. They may lack managerial skills, marketing capability, or financial resources. Their inventions are often unrealistic, requiring significant modification to be marketable. In addition, entrepreneurs frequently do not know how to interface with all the necessary entities, such as banks, suppliers, customers, venture capitalists, distributors, and advertising agencies.

Yet, in spite of all these difficulties, entrepreneurship is presently the most effective method for bridging the gap between science and the marketplace, creating new enterprises, and bringing new products and services to the market. These entrepreneurial activities significantly affect the economy of an area by building the economic base and providing jobs. Given its impact on both the overall economy and the employment of an area, it is surprising that entrepreneurship has not become even more of a focal point in economic development.

ENTREPRENEURIAL CAREERS AND EDUCATION

What causes an individual to take all the social, psychological, and financial risks involved in starting a new venture? At first there was limited research on this aspect of entrepreneurship, but since 1985 there has been an increased interest in entrepreneurial careers and education. This increased interest has been fostered by such factors as the recognition that small firms play a major role in job creation and innovation; an increase in media coverage of entrepreneurs; the awareness that there are more entrepreneurs than those heralded in the media, as thousands upon thousands of small cottage companies are formed; the view that most large organizational structures do not provide an environment for self-actualization; the shift in employment, as women become increasingly more active in the workforce and the number of families earning two incomes grows; and the formation of new ventures by female entrepreneurs at three times the rate of their male counterparts.

In spite of this increase, many people, particularly college students, do not consider entrepreneurship as a career. A conceptual model for understanding entrepreneurial careers, indicated in Table 1.3, views the career stages as dynamic ones, with each stage reflecting and interacting with other stages and events in the individual's life—past, present, and future. This *life-cycle approach* conceptualizes entrepreneurial careers in nine major categories: educational environment, the individual's personality, childhood family environment, employment history, adult development history, adult nonwork history, current work situation, the individual's current perspective, and the current family situation.[11]

Although there exists a common perception that entrepreneurs are less educated than the general population, this opinion has proved to be more myth than reality. Studies have found entrepreneurs overall, and female entrepreneurs in particular, to be far more educated than the general populace.[12] However, the types and quality of the education received sometimes do not develop the specific skills needed in the venture creation and management process. For example, some female entrepreneurs are at more of a disadvantage than their male counterparts in this respect, as they frequently do not take significant business or engineering courses.

Childhood influences have also been explored, particularly in terms of values and the individual's personality. The most frequently researched personality traits are the need for achievement, focus of control, *risk taking*, and gender identity. Since personality traits are more thoroughly discussed in Chapter 3, it is sufficient here to indicate that few firm conclusions can be drawn from all the research regarding any universal personality traits of entrepreneurs.

risk taking   Taking calculated chances in creating and running a venture

The research on the childhood family environment of the entrepreneur has had more definitive results. Entrepreneurs tend to have self-employed fathers, many of whom are also entrepreneurs. Many also have entrepreneurial mothers, although this

TABLE 1.3   A Framework for an Entrepreneur's Career Development

Life Space Areas	Childhood	Early Adulthood	Present Adulthood
Work/occupation	Education and childhood work experience I	Employment history IV	Current work situation VII
Individual/personal	Childhood influences on personality, values, and interests II	Adult development history V	Individual's current perspective VIII
Nonwork/family	Childhood family environment III	Adult family/nonwork history VI	Current family/nonwork situation IX

Source: Adapted from Donald D. Bowen and Robert D. Hisrich, "The Female Entrepreneur: A Career Development Perspective," *The Academy of Management Review II* (April 1986), pp. 393–407.

aspect did not receive much research attention until the last decade. This lack of research emphasis has limited the amount of information available on entrepreneurial mothers. The family, particularly the father or mother, plays an important role in establishing the desirability and credibility of entrepreneurship as a career path. As one entrepreneur said: "My father and mother always encouraged me to try new things and do everything very professionally. They wanted me to be the very best and have the freedom and independence of being my own boss."

Employment history also has an impact on entrepreneurial careers, in both a positive and a negative sense. On the positive side, entrepreneurs tend to have a higher probability of success when the venture created is in their field of work experience. This increased success rate makes the providers of risk capital particularly concerned when this work experience is not present. Negative displacement (such as dissatisfaction with various aspects of one's job, being fired or demoted, being transferred to an undesirable location, or having one's spouse take a new position in a new geographic area) encourages entrepreneurship, not only in the United States but in other cultures as well.

Although no definitive research has been done on the adult development history of entrepreneurs, it appears to also affect entrepreneurial careers. One's development history has somewhat more of an impact on women, since they tend to start businesses at a later stage in life than men, usually after having experienced significantly more job frustration.

There is a similar lack of data on adult family/nonwork history. Although there is some information on entrepreneurs' marital and family situations, the available data add little to our understanding of entrepreneurial career paths.

The impact of the current work situation has received considerably more research and attention. Entrepreneurs are known for their strong work values and aspirations, their long workdays, and their dominant management style. Entrepreneurs tend to fall in love with the organization and will sacrifice almost anything in order to ensure its survival. This desire is reflected in the individual entrepreneur's current career perspective and family/nonwork situation. The new venture usually takes the highest priority in the entrepreneur's life and is the source of the entrepreneur's self-esteem.

While in college, few future entrepreneurs realize that they will pursue entrepreneurship as their major life goal. Even among the minority that do, relatively few individuals will start a business immediately after graduation, and even fewer will prepare for a new venture creation by working in a particular position or industry. This mandates that entrepreneurs continually supplement their education through books, trade journals, seminars, or taking courses in weak areas. Generally, skills that need to be acquired through seminars or courses include creativity, financing, control, opportunity identification, venture evaluation, and deal making.

Entrepreneurship education is a fast growing area in colleges and universities in the United States and Europe. Many universities offer at least one course in entrepreneurship at the graduate or undergraduate level, and a few actually have a major or minor concentration in the area. Since the area is so new, the U.S. Department of Education has not yet separated entrepreneurship from small business, and the statistics associated with entrepreneurship are not as accurate as other educational statistics in more established educational areas.

While the courses in entrepreneurship vary by university, there is a great deal of commonality, particularly in the initial one or two courses in this field of study. These courses tend to reflect the overall objectives for a course in entrepreneurship. Sample

TABLE 1.4   Overall Objectives for a Course in Entrepreneurship

- Understand the role of new and smaller firms in the economy.
- Understand the relative strengths and weaknesses of different types of enterprises.
- Know the general characteristics of an entrepreneurial process.
- Assess the student's own entrepreneurial skills.
- Understand the entrepreneurial process and the product planning and development process.
- Know alternative methods for identifying and evaluating business opportunities and the factors that support and inhibit creativity.
- Develop an ability to form, organize, and work in interdisciplinary teams.
- Know the general correlates of success and failure in innovation and new venture creation.
- Know the generic entry strategies for new venture creation.
- Understand the aspects of creating and presenting a new venture business plan.
- Know how to identify, evaluate, and obtain resources.
- Know the essentials of
  - Marketing planning
  - Financial planning
  - Operations planning
  - Organization planning
  - Venture launch planning
- Know how to manage and grow a new venture.
- Know the managerial challenges and demands of a new venture launch.
- Understand the role of entrepreneurship in existing organizations.

Source: Robert D. Hisrich, "Toward an Organization Model for Entrepreneurial Education," *Proceedings*, International Entrepreneurship Conference, p. 29.

course objectives, indicated in Table 1.4, tend to center around skill identification and assessment; understanding entrepreneurial decision making and the entrepreneurial process; understanding the characteristics of entrepreneurs and their role in economic development on a domestic and, more recently, on an international basis; assessing opportunities and coming up with an idea for a new venture; writing and presenting a full-scale business plan; knowing how to obtain resources; managing and growing the enterprise; and understanding the role of entrepreneurship in an existing organization, that is, intrapreneurship.

The skills required by entrepreneurs can be classified into three main areas: technical skills, business management skills, and personal entrepreneurial skills (see Table 1.5). Technical skills involve such things as writing, listening, oral presentations, organizing, coaching, being a team player, and technical know-how.

Business management skills include those areas involved in starting, developing, and managing any enterprise. Skills in decision making, marketing, management, financing, accounting, production, control, and negotiation are essential in launching and growing a new venture. The final skill area involves personal entrepreneurial skills. Some of these skills differentiate an entrepreneur from a manager. Skills included in this classification are inner control (discipline), risk taking, innovativeness, persistence, visionary leadership, and being change oriented.

These skills and objectives form the basis of the modular approach to an entrepreneurship curriculum. By laying out the modules, a course or sequence of courses

TABLE 1.5   Types of Skills Required in Entrepreneurship

Technical Skills
- Writing
- Oral communication
- Monitoring environment
- Technical business management
- Technology.
- Interpersonal
- Listening
- Ability to organize
- Network building
- Management style
- Coaching
- Being a team player

Business Management Skills
- Planning and goal setting
- Decision making
- Human relations
- Marketing
- Finance
- Accounting
- Management
- Control
- Negotiation
- Venture launch
- Managing growth

Personal Entrepreneurial Skills
- Inner control/disciplined
- Risk taker
- Innovative
- Change oriented
- Persistent
- Visionary leader
- Ability to manage change

Source: Robert D. Hisrich, "Toward an Organization Model for Entrepreneurial Education," *Proceedings*, International Entrepreneurship 1992 Conference, Dortmund, Germany (June 1992), p. 29.

can be developed, depending on the needs, interests, and resources of the particular university. This modular approach helps ensure that the most important areas of the field are covered in the courses offered, whether on a quarter or semester basis or involving one or a series of courses.

As seen in *Business Week:*
Hi, I'm John, and I'm an entrepreneur . . .

Everybody knows about support groups to help overeaters, alcoholics, and smokers. But what about the well-being and self-esteem of entrepreneurs who must deal with office leases falling through and potential employees demanding way too many stock options?

Sometimes, only someone else who's got the bug can understand. It's not easy to be a headstrong twentysomething willing to risk everything for a shot at the next Amazon.com. That's why Aaron Ross, 27, chief executive of San Francisco–based upstart Equipment Leasing.com, founded Gotthebug.com last March. It's an online community devoted to helping executives at struggling start-ups deal with everything from finding an accountant to learning how to survive without a salary. The group has grown to about 60 entrepreneurs from Silicon Valley to New Hampshire.

Ross, a Stanford grad, got the idea after encountering the loneliness of starting a Net business. "Sometimes it feels like it's you against the world," he explains. "So anyplace you can find support helps reduce the stress." And for his next venture? Ross is considering a new site, Keepthefaith.com, for entrepreneurs ready to call it quits.

Source: Linda Himelstein, "Hi, I'm John, and I'm an Entrepreneur . . . " *Business Week*, October 25, 1999, p. 7.

An interesting trend in entrepreneurial education has evolved in the last five years with some entrepreneurs finding the need for and having the desire to obtain MBA degrees. Previously, for generations, entrepreneurs loathed everything about the MBA. But today's advanced technology sophistication, telecommunication, computer usage, and hypercompetition have changed that attitude. Entrepreneurs are recognizing the need to learn some of the "science" of management in an MBA program to compete and grow their businesses effectively in today's global environment. Take, for example, Dan Poston, founder and CEO of International HTC, Inc., who grew his firm until sales stagnated at about $6 million. Finding himself ill-equipped to remedy the situation, he decided he needed an MBA degree.

ETHICS AND SOCIAL RESPONSIBILITY OF ENTREPRENEURS

The life of the entrepreneur is not easy. An entrepreneur must take risks with his or her own capital in order to sell and deliver products and services while expending greater energy than the average businessperson in order to innovate. Faced with daily stressful situations and other difficulties, the possibility exists that the entrepreneur will establish a balance between ethical exigencies, economic expediency, and social responsibility, a balance that differs from the point at which the general business manager takes his or her moral stance.[13]

A manager's attitudes concerning corporate responsibility are related to the organizational climate perceived to be supportive of laws and professional codes of ethics. On the other hand, entrepreneurs with a relatively new company who have few role models usually develop an internal ethical code. Entrepreneurs tend to depend on their own personal value systems much more than other managers when determining ethically appropriate courses of action.

Although drawing more on their own value system, entrepreneurs have been shown to be particularly sensitive to peer pressure and general social norms in the community, as well as pressures from their competitors. The differences between entrepreneurs in different types of communities and in different countries reflect, to some extent, the general norms and values of the communities and countries involved. This is clearly the case for metropolitan as opposed to nonmetropolitan locations within a single country. Internationally, there is evidence to this effect about managers in general. U.S. managers seem to have more individualistic and less communitarian values than their German and Austrian counterparts.

The significant increase in the number of internationally oriented businesses has impacted the increased interest in the similarities and differences in business attitudes and practices in different countries. This area has been explored to some extent within the context of culture and is now beginning to be explored within the more individualized concept of ethics. The concepts of culture and ethics are somewhat related. Whereas ethics refers to the *"study of whatever is right and good for humans," business ethics* concerns itself with the investigation of business practices in light of human values. Ethics is the broad field of study exploring the general nature of morals and the specific moral choices to be made by the individual in his relationship with others. While business ethics has emerged as an important topic within popular and academic publications in the past few decades, to date it has been treated ahistorically and with an orientation dominated by the U.S. Protestant heritage.

business ethics   The study of behavior and morals in a business situation

Although the English word *ethics* is generally recognized as stemming from the Greek *êthos*, meaning "custom and usage," it is more properly identified as originating from *swëdhêthos*, in which the concepts of individual morality and behavioral habits are related and identified as an essential quality of existence.

Most Western authors credit the Greek philosophers Socrates (469–399 B.C.), Plato (427–347 B.C.), and Aristotle (384–322 B.C.) as providing the earliest writings upon which currently held ethical conceptions are based. Much earlier writings pertaining to moral codes and laws, however, can be found within both Judaism (1800 B.C.) and Hinduism (1500 B.C.).

American attitudes on ethics result from three principal influences: the Judeo-Christian heritage, a belief in individualism, and opportunities based upon ability rather than social status. The United States was formed by immigrants from other countries, frequently fleeing oppression in their homelands, dedicated to creating a society where their future and fortunes were determined by their abilities and dedication to work.

Research on business ethics can be broken down into four broad classifications: (1) pedagogically oriented inquiry, including both theory and empirical studies; (2) theory-building without empirical testing; (3) empirical research, measuring the attitudes and ethical beliefs of students and academic faculty; and (4) empirical research within business environments, measuring the attitudes and ethical views, primarily of managers within large organizations. Each of these areas offers insight into the ethical dimensions of entrepreneurs and managers. Some aspects of business ethics are indicated in the Ethics box. Ethics is not only a general topic for conversation but a deep concern of businesspeople as the survey results indicate.

THE FUTURE OF ENTREPRENEURSHIP

As evidenced by the many different definitions, the term *entrepreneurship* means different things to different people and can be viewed from different conceptual perspectives. However, in spite of the differences, there are some common aspects: risk taking, creativity, independence, and rewards. These commonalities will continue to be the driving force behind the notion of entrepreneurship in the future. One thing

RESOURCE The Study of Behavior and Morals in a Business Situation

What is "right," "proper," "just," and "fair" to an entrepreneur? These terms, and the question of how they are interpreted, are becoming increasingly important in today's competitive and technologically complex environment. Much has been written about ethics causing U.S. society to become much more sensitive regarding the responsibilities of the entrepreneur and businessperson—individuals whose decisions can affect people in ways that are outside of their direct control.

Business ethics, or the determination of what is "right" and "proper" and "just" and "fair" by an entrepreneur as reflected in his or her decisions and actions, extends far beyond the simple issues of theft, falsification, bribery, and collusion. At the core of business ethics is the issue of relationships. Beyond employees, investors, customers, creditors, suppliers, and distributors, it includes all of the members of the community, either by direct representation or by virtue of the products and services.

What should be done with one of the founding members of the firm when he is no longer needed?

Does an entrepreneur inform a supplier about a significant underbilling on a major purchase? Does the entrepreneur have a responsibility to purchasers of their products that have discovered a defect that may cause not only operational failure but potentially unsafe conditions? How does an entrepreneur relate to a distributor that provided assistance in establishing a beachhead within the market but has failed to maintain an efficiency level to permit market expansion? How should an entrepreneur react to a customer that offers to "show" a copy of the competitor's confidential proposal? How does an entrepreneur reconcile responsibilities to investors in light of societal duties and responsibilities?

This, then, is the central issue in business ethics: the very real and continual conflict between the economic performance of a venture (usually reflected by "bottom-line" performance of sales, costs, and profits) and the social responsibilities of individuals and collective members of society. There is no easy answer; social perfor-

is clear: The future for entrepreneurship appears to be bright. We are living in the age of the entrepreneur, with entrepreneurship endorsed by educational institutions, governmental units, society, and corporations. Entrepreneurial education has never been so important in terms of courses and academic research. The number of universities and colleges offering at least one course in entrepreneurship increased from 16 in 1970 to over 400 by 1995, with at least 50 universities offering four or more courses in the area of entrepreneurship that allow students to take concentrations, majors, and degrees.[14] A recent study examined demand and supply of entrepreneurship faculty between academic years 1989/90 and 1997/98. While total number of entrepreneurship positions during this period increased 253 percent, from 26 to 92, the total number of candidates applying for these positions increased by only 94 percent, from 35 to 68, a very encouraging situation for entrepreneurship faculty candidates.[15] There are some unique entrepreneurial programs as well, such as the master's program in entrepreneurial physics at Case Western Reserve University.

Entrepreneurship education in Europe is also growing. Many universities in the 24 countries surveyed had recently started a program in entrepreneurship. Most universities and associations in the countries did research on entrepreneurship, followed by training courses, and then education courses—courses for which degree credit was given. Very few of the sample were involved in the actual enterprise creation process where the university, faculty, and/or students shared in the sales and profits of the new venture.[16]

This increase in course offerings has been accompanied by an increase in academic research, endowed chairs in the area, entrepreneurship concentrations and majors, and centers of entrepreneurial activity. This trend will continue, supported by an increase in PhD activity, which will in turn provide the needed faculty and remance does not have clearly defined, "bottom-line" measurements. In most of the issues that will confront the entrepreneur, the individual must balance between economic and social performance: two dissimilar quantities, each having many possible outcomes.

Throughout this book, the issue of business ethics will be highlighted to provide specific guidelines for action, to instill an awareness of the issues, and to provide an opportunity for the individual to become familiar with the actual and potential issues and some methods for analyzing them.

A survey of 1,324 randomly selected workers, managers, and executives in multiple industries yielded the following results:

Top 10 factors that could trigger workers to act unethically or illegally:

- Balancing work and family
- Poor internal communications
- Poor leadership
- Work hours, workload
- Lack of management support
- Need to meet sales, budget, or profit goals
- Little or no recognition of achievements
- Company politics
- Personal financial worries
- Insufficient resources

Top 5 types of unethical/ illegal behavior that workers say they have engaged in over the past year because of pressure:

- Cut corners on quality control
- Covered up incidents
- Abused or lied about sick days
- Lied to or deceived customers
- Put inappropriate pressure on others

Overall, most workers felt some pressure to act unethically or illegally on the job (56 percent) and 48 percent said they actively made at least one unethical or illegal action in the past year. Do you belong to the 56 or 48 percent group?

Source: Adapted from Del Jones, "Doing the Wrong Thing," *USA Today*, April 4–6, 1997, pp. 1A and 2A.

search effort to support the future increases in course offerings, endowed positions, centers, and research efforts.

Various governments are taking an increased interest in promoting the growth of entrepreneurship. Individuals are encouraged to form new businesses and are provided such government support as tax incentives, buildings, roads, and a communication system to facilitate this creation process. Encouragement by the federal and local governments should continue in the future as more lawmakers understand that new enterprises create jobs and increase economic output in the area. Some state governments in the United States are developing their own innovative industrial strategies for fostering entrepreneurial activity and the timely development of the technology of the area. The impact of this strategy is seen in the venture-capital industry, which is always sensitive to government regulations and policies. Many states now have their own state-sponsored venture funds, where a percentage of the fund has to be invested in ventures in the state. The current level and growth in venture-capital money have resulted from a lowering of the capital gains tax in 1978 from 49 percent to 28 percent in the United States and the institution of more relaxed rules regarding pension fund investment. Pension funds now contribute about 30 percent of the venture-capital money raised each year in the United States.

Society's support of entrepreneurship will also continue. This support is critical in providing both motivation and public support. Never before have entrepreneurs been so revered by the general populace. Entrepreneurial endeavors in the United States are considered honorable and even, in many cases, prestigious pursuits. A major factor in the development of this societal approval is the media. The media has played, and will continue to play, a powerful and constructive role by reporting on the general entrepreneurial spirit in the United States and highlighting specific success cases of this spirit in operation. Major articles in such prestigious newspapers as the *New York Times*, the *Wall Street Journal*, and the *Washington Post* have focused on the pioneer spirit of today's entrepreneurs, describing how this spirit benefits society by keeping the United States in the lead in technology. General business magazines such as *Barron's*, *Business Week*, *Forbes*, and *Fortune* have provided similar coverage by adding special columns on entrepreneurship and venturing. Magazines such as *Black Enterprise*, *Entrepreneur*, *Inc.*, *Journal of Venturing*, and *Venture*—which focus on specific issues of the entrepreneurial process, starting new ventures, and small, growing businesses—have built solid and increasing circulation rates. Television on both a national and a local level has highlighted entrepreneurship by featuring specific individuals and issues involved in the entrepreneurial process. Not only have local stations covered regional occurrences, but nationally syndicated shows such as *The Today Show*, *Good Morning America*, and *20/20* have had special segments devoted to this phenomenon. This media coverage uplifts the image of the entrepreneur and growth companies, and focuses on their contributions to society.

Finally, large companies will continue to have an interest in their special form of entrepreneurship—intrapreneurship—in the future. These companies will be increasingly interested in capitalizing on their research and development (R&D) in the hypercompetitive business environment today. The largest 15 companies in the United States account for over 20 percent of the total U.S. R&D and over 40 percent of private-sector R&D. General Electric, for example, has created three $1 billion businesses internally in the last 15 years and is moving all their lighting research and development to Hungary in their joint venture, Tungstram. Other companies will want to create more new businesses through intrapreneurship in the future, particularly in light of the hypercompetition and the need for globalization.

IN REVIEW

Summary

The definition of an entrepreneur has evolved over time as the world's economic structure has changed and become more complex. Since its beginnings in the Middle Ages, when it was used in relation to specific occupations, the notion of the entrepreneur has been refined and broadened to include concepts that are related to the person rather than the occupation. Risk taking, innovation, and creation of wealth are examples of the criteria that have been developed as the study of new business creations has evolved. In this text, entrepreneurship is defined as the process of creating something new with value by devoting the necessary time and effort; assuming the accompanying financial, psychological, and social risks; and receiving the resultant rewards of monetary and personal satisfaction and independence.

The decision to start an entrepreneurial venture consists of several sequential steps: (1) the decision to leave a present career or lifestyle, (2) the decision that an entrepreneurial venture is desirable, and (3) the decision that both external and internal factors make new venture creation possible. Although the decision-making process is applicable to each of the three types of start-up companies, the emphasis in each one is certainly different. Because of their differing natures, foundation companies and high-potential ventures require a more conscious effort to reach a defensible decision on these points than do lifestyle firms.

There are both pushing and pulling influences active in the decision to leave a present career: the "push" of job dissatisfaction or even a layoff, and the "pull" toward entrepreneurship of seeing an unfilled need in the marketplace. The desirability of starting one's own company is strongly influenced by culture, subculture, family, teachers, and peers. Any of these influences can function as a source of encouragement for entrepreneurship, with support ranging from government policies that favor business to strong personal role models of family or friends. Beyond the stage of seeing entrepreneurship as a "good idea," the potential entrepreneur must possess or acquire the necessary education, management skills, and financial resources for launching the venture.

The study of entrepreneurship has relevance today, not only because it helps entrepreneurs better fulfill their personal needs but because of the economic contribution of the new ventures. More than increasing national income by creating new jobs, entrepreneurship acts as a positive force in economic growth by serving as the bridge between innovation and the marketplace. Although the government gives great support to basic and applied research, it has not had great success in translating the technological innovations to products or services. Although intrapreneurship offers the promise of a marriage of those research capabilities and business skills that one expects from a large corporation, the results so far in many companies have not been spectacular. This leaves the entrepreneur, who frequently lacks both technical and business skills, to serve as the major link in the process of innovation development, and economic growth and revitalization. The study of entrepreneurship and the education of potential entrepreneurs are essential parts of any attempt to strengthen this link so essential to a country's economic well-being.

Questions for Discussion

1. Why study entrepreneurship?
2. What is your definition of an entrepreneur? Which definition of *entrepreneurship* best describes Ted Turner? Marco Polo? List the strengths and weaknesses (as appropriate) of the various definitions highlighted in the text.
3. Give some reasons why an individual entrepreneur might succeed in bringing a product to the market where the government or a large corporation might fail.
4. Give some examples of each of the three types of start-up companies. Did any of your examples begin in one category and turn out to be something much smaller or larger than anticipated? How does the entrepreneur's vision for the future affect the decision to start the company?

Key Terms

breakthrough innovations	high-potential venture
business ethics	intrapreneurship
desirability of new venture formation	iterative synthesis
entrepreneur	lifestyle firm
entrepreneur as an innovator	ordinary innovations
entrepreneurial decision process	possibility of new venture formation
entrepreneurship	product-evolution process
foundation company	risk taking
gazelles	technological innovations
government as an innovator	technology transfer

More Information—Net Addresses in This Chapter

America Online (AOL)
www.AOL.com

Babson College
www.babson.edu

Cable News Network (CNN)
www.CNN.com

Cal State
www.extension.csuhayward.edu

Case Western Reserve University
www.cwru.edu

Castle Rock Entertainment
castle-rock.com/indexnet.htm

CBS
www.cbs.com

CNN Financial News Network
www.cnnfn.com

Duke
www.duke.edu

General Electric (GE)
www.ge.com

George Mason University
www.gmu.edu

Harvard
www.harvard.edu

Kellogg School at Northwestern University
www.kellogg.nwu.edu

Massachusetts Institute of Technology (MIT)
web.mit.edu

Metro-Goldwyn-Mayer
www.mgmua.com

NBC
nbc.com

New Line Cinema
www.newline.com

North Carolina State
www2.acs.ncsu.edu

Northeastern University–Mass.
www.neu.edu

St. Thomas
www.stthom.edu

Small Business Administration
www.sbaonline.sba.gov

Stanford
www.stanford.edu

The Cartoon Network
www.filmzone.com/SpaceGhost/cartoonnet.html

Turner Broadcasting System (TBS)
www.turner.com

Turner Classic Movies
www.turner.com/tcm

University of North Carolina
www.unc.edu

Selected Readings

Bechard, Jean-Pierre; and Jean-Marie Toulouse. (1998). Validation of a Didactic Model for the Analysis of Training Objectives in Entrepreneurship. *Journal of Business Venturing*, vol. 13, no. 4, pp. 317–32.

Entrepreneurship teaching programs are categorized according to three categories of objectives (general, teaching, and specific). A didactic model in entrepreneurship that includes these three dimensions is proposed and tested.

Bird, Barbara J.; David J. Hayward; and David N. Allen. (1993). Conflicts in Commercialization of Knowledge: Perspectives from Science and Entrepreneurship. *Entrepreneurship: Theory and Practice*, vol. 17, no. 4, pp. 57–77.

Faculty with entrepreneurial inclinations experience conflicts of interest and value. The study results indicate that the values and interest affect the relationships of the faculty member and his or her entrepreneurial activity.

Cameron, Alan; Claire Massey; and Daniel Tweed. (2000). Entrepreneurs—A Vital Force? *Chartered Accountants Journal of New Zealand*, vol. 79, no. 10, pp. 10–13.

Results from the Global Entrepreneurship Monitor project give new insights into the role entrepreneurs play in economic growth. It was found that the level of entrepreneurial activity (as measured by the numbers of new businesses) was positively correlated with the recent gains in GDP for the 10 countries in the study.

Chia, Robert. (1996). Teaching Paradigm Shifting in Management Education: University Business Schools and the Entrepreneurial Imagination. *Journal of Management Studies*, vol. 33, no. 4, pp. 409–28.

The cultivation of entrepreneurial imagination is the single most important contribution university business schools can make to the business community. This requires a radical shift in pedagogic priorities away from teaching analytical problem-solving skills to cultivating an innovative, paradigm-shifting mentality.

Gifford, Sharon. (1998). Limited Entrepreneurial Attention and Economic Development. *Small Business Economics*, vol. 10, no. 1, pp. 17–30.

Economic development depends on the allocation of entrepreneurial resources to efforts to discover new profit opportunities. Limited entrepreneurial attention is allocated between maintaining current activities and starting new activities. The problem of allocating limited entrepreneurial attention in a variety of contexts is addressed.

Harmon, Brian; Alexander Ardishvili; Richard Cardozo; Tait Elder; John Leuthold; John Parshall; Michael Raghian; and Donald Smith. (1997). Mapping the University Technology Transfer Process. *Journal of Business Venturing*, vol. 12, no. 4, pp. 423–34.

The study examined university-based technology transfer process at the University of Minnesota in a 10-year period. The technology transfer process was mapped according to three approaches (formal search, informal networking arrangements, and a hybrid approach). Five types of transfer process were identified: the technology is invented in the university lab and (1) sold to an already existing company, with which the lab had prior connection; (2) sold to an already existing company, with which the inventor did not have a prior relationship; (3) sold to a venture-capital company; (4) a new company is created specifically to sell the technology; and (5) the technology is initially developed by a private firm, but the firm seeks out the university assistance in areas where expertise is needed.

Osborne, Stephen W.; Thomas W. Falcone; and Prashanth B. Nagendra. (2000). From Unemployed to Entrepreneur: A Case Study in Intervention. *Journal of Developmental Entrepreneurship*, vol. 5, no. 2, pp. 115–36.

A summary is given of the entrepreneurial potential, training, and success of a group of recently unemployed workers from a wide spectrum of previous occupations and industries.

Ripsas, Sven. (1998). Towards an Interdisciplinary Theory of Entrepreneurship. *Small Business Economics*, vol. 10, no. 2, pp. 103–15.

The role of the entrepreneur in the history of economic thought is reviewed. An interdisciplinary approach to the development of entrepreneurship theory is proposed on the basis of contributions from economic decision theory, sociological system theory, psychoanalytical research, and behavioral studies.

Sage, Gary. (1993). Entrepreneurship as an Economic Development Strategy. *Economic Development Review*, vol. 2, no. 2, pp. 66–67.

Since future economic development strategy needs to promote an environment that is conducive to new business formation and growth, six factors need to be particularly addressed that correlate well with the stimulation of new business.

Sarfraz, Mian A. (1996). Assessing Value-Added Contributions of University Technology Business Incubators to Tenant Firms. *Research Policy*, vol. 25, no. 3 pp. 325–35.

In addition to providing a nurturing environment for new business start-ups, university technology business incubators provide value-added benefits to both the recipient firms and the universities.

Stearns, Timothy M. (1996). Entrepreneurship and New Firm Development: A Definitional Introduction. *Journal of Business Research*, vol. 36, no. 1, pp. 1–4.

Entrepreneurial activity has increased globally due to the erosion of the corporate ladder, the fall of communism, and increased economic globalization. Several entrepreneur model elements are presented and debated, including (1) the environment/economic system, (2) the persons engaged in entrepreneurship, (3) entrepreneurial behavior, (4) an organization, (5) opportunity, (6) innovation, (7) taking risks, (8) marshaling resources, and (9) creating and realizing value for individuals and society.

Wennekers, Sander; and Roy Thurik. (1999). Linking Entrepreneurship and Economic Growth. *Small Business Economics*, vol. 13, no. 1, pp. 27–55.

The concept of entrepreneurship is decomposed with the aim to explain the entrepreneurship role in the process of economic growth. By considering three levels on which entrepreneurship can be analyzed (individual, firm, and aggregate level) the relationship between entrepreneurship and economic growth is examined.

APPENDIX A   Should You Start Your Own Business?

Each day, thousands of individuals ask the difficult question, "Should I start my own business?" When queried, *85 percent of the populace* said they would like to be in business for themselves. The driving force behind this desire to start a new venture is the desire to be one's own boss, to be independent. Since there is no definitive measurement developed that allows an individual to determine if he or she can be a successful entrepreneur, each individual needs to carefully appraise his or her situation through several different methods and self-assessment models. One way to determine if you have what it takes to be an entrepreneur is to fill out the questionnaire in Table A.1 and check the answers at the end of this appendix. Keep in mind that the answers develop an average profile of an entrepreneur. There are many exceptions, and there is no such person as a typical entrepreneur.

According to the Small Business Administration, the creation of a new business is very risky. Over 1,000 small business firms, most less than five years old, fail each day. To help evaluate whether you have some of the abilities necessary to avoid this

---

TABLE A.1   Characteristics of an Entrepreneur
1. An entrepreneur is most commonly the _____ child in the family.
a. oldest   *c.* youngest   *b.* middle   *d.* doesn't matter
2. An entrepreneur is most commonly:
a. married   *c.* widowed   *b.* single   *d.* divorced
3. An entrepreneur is most typically a:
a. man   *c.* either   *b.* woman
4. An individual usually begins his or her first significant entrepreneurial business enterprise at what age?

a. teens   *d.* forties
    b. twenties   *e.* fifties
    c. thirties

TABLE A.1   Continued

5. Usually an individual's entrepreneurial tendency first appears evident in his or her:

    a. teens   *d.* forties
    b. twenties   *e.* fifties
    c. thirties

6. Typically, an entrepreneur has achieved the following educational attainment by the time the first significant business venture begins:

    a. less than high school   *d.* master's degree
    b. high school diploma   *e.* doctor's degree
    c. bachelor's degree

7. An entrepreneur's primary motivation for starting a business is:

    a. to make money   *d.* to create job security
    b. to be independent   *e.* to be powerful
    c. to be famous

8. The primary motivation for the entrepreneur's high ego and need for achievement is based upon a ralationship with:

    a. spouse   *c.* father
    b. mother   *d.* children

9. To be successful in an entrepreneurial venture, you need:

    a. money   *d.* a good idea
    b. luck   *e.* all of the above
    c. hard work

10. Entrepreneurs and venture capitalists:

    a. get along well   *c.* are cordial friends
    b. are the best of friends   *d.* are in conflict

11. A successful entrepreneur relies on which of the following for critical management advice?

    a. internal management team   *c.* financial sources
    b. external management   *d.* no one
        professionals

12. Entrepreneurs are best as:

    a. managers   *c.* planners
    b. venture capitalists   *d.* doers

13. Entrepreneurs are:

    a. high risk takers (big gamblers)   *c.* small risk takers (take few chances)
    b. moderate risk takers (realistic   *d.* doesn't matter
        gamblers)

14. Entrepreneurs:

    a. are the life of the party   *c.* will never go to parties
    b. are bores at a cocktail party   *d.* just fit into the crowd at a party

15. Entrepreneurs tend to "fall in love" with:

    a. new ideas   *d.* new financial plans
    b. new employees   *e.* all of the above
    c. new manufacturing ideas

16. Entrepreneurs typically form:

    a. service businesses   *d.* construction companies
    b. manufacturing companies   *e.* a variety of ventures
    c. financial companies

high failure rate and to be a successful entrepreneur, take the Entrepreneur Assessment Quiz in Table A.2 before reading further. Note that this quiz has not been validated statistically. If you score well, however, you may have the ability to be a successful entrepreneur. If you do not, do not be discouraged. Many entrepreneurs believe that passion for the idea and the desire to succeed are the most important ingredients for success.

After you have completed this quiz in Table A.2, count the number of Yes answers. Give yourself one point for each Yes. If you scored above 17 points, you have the drive to be an entrepreneur—the desire, energy, and adaptability to make a viable business venture a success. However, make sure any business venture you are contemplating is a good one.

If you scored from 13 to 17 points, your entrepreneurial drive is not apparent. While you may definitely have the ability to be an entrepreneur, make sure that you can accept all the problems and headaches that accompany the joy of being your own boss.

If you scored below 13 points, your entrepreneurial drive is even less apparent. Even though most people say they want to be entrepreneurs, in reality many of them are actually better off working for someone else.

Regardless of your score, take time to develop and gain experience in your present position or your industrial area of interest while evaluating your real interests and desires before you actually become involved in the entrepreneurial process. Again, keep in mind that the quiz is not a scientifically validated indicator of entrepreneurial drive. Such an instrument has not yet been developed.

Answers to Characteristics of an Entrepreneur Quiz (Table A.1)

1. *Oldest.* Although, indeed, entrepreneurs come from many different birth orders, there is a slight tendency for an entrepreneur to be the oldest child in the family, thereby having had time alone with parents without other siblings.
2. *Married.* While there has never been any statistical validation, most entrepreneurs are married when they start their first significant venture. The spouse plays an important support role.
3. *Man.* Although men still outnumber women entrepreneurs in terms of actual numbers, women entrepreneurs are presently forming new ventures at two to three times the rate of men.
4. *Thirties.* Although ventures may be started at any age, the first significant venture is usually started in the early thirties for men and late thirties for women.
5. *Teens.* An individual's ability to handle ambiguity, the drive for independence, and creativity (important characteristics for an entrepreneur) are evident early in life.
6. *Bachelor's Degree.* While the Horatio Alger story is indeed still possible, most entrepreneurs are college educated, like most of the general populace in the United States. Women entrepreneurs are even more educated, with many having a master's degree. This education is particularly important in securing financing and starting technology-based ventures. Although not as highly educated as those in the United States, entrepreneurs in foreign countries are at least as highly educated as the general populace.

TABLE A.2	Entrepreneur Assessment Quiz

1. Can you start a project and see it through to completion in spite of a myriad of obstacles?
   _____ Yes   _____ No

2. Can you make a decision on a matter and then stick to the decision even when challenged?
   _____ Yes   _____ No

3. Do you like to be in charge and be responsible?
   _____ Yes   _____ No

4. Do other people you deal with respect and trust you?
   _____ Yes   _____ No

5. Are you in good physical health?
   _____ Yes   _____ No

6. Are you willing to work long hours with little immediate compensation?
   _____ Yes   _____ No

7. Do you like meeting and dealing with people?
   _____ Yes   _____ No

8. Can you communicate effectively and persuade people to go along with your dream?
   _____ Yes   _____ No

9. Do others easily understand your concepts and ideas?
   _____ Yes   _____ No

10. Have you had extensive experience in the type of business you wish to start?
    _____ Yes   _____ No

11. Do you know the mechanics and forms of running a business (tax records, payroll records, income statements, balance sheets)?
    _____ Yes   _____ No

12. Is there a need in your geographic area for the product or service you are intending to market?
    _____ Yes   _____ No

13. Do you have skills in marketing and/or finance?
    _____ Yes   _____ No

14. Are other firms in you industrial classification doing well in your geographic area?
    _____ Yes   _____ No

15. Do you have a location in mind for your business?
    _____ Yes   _____ No

16. Do you have enough financial backing for the first year of operation?
    _____ Yes   _____ No

17. Do you have enough money to fund the start-up of your business or have access to it through family or friends?
    _____ Yes   _____ No

18. Do you know the suppliers necessary for your business to succeed?
    _____ Yes   _____ No

19. Do you know individuals who have the talents and expertise you lack?
    _____ Yes   _____ No

20. Do you really want to start this business more than anything else?
    _____ Yes   _____ No

7. *To Be Independent.* The need for independence (the inability to work for any-one else) is what drives the entrepreneur to take the risks to work all the hours necessary to create a new venture.

8. *Father.* Regardless of whether it is a love or hate relationship, entrepreneurs report a strong parental relationship, particularly with the father. This strong father relationship is particularly important for women entrepreneurs.

9. *Luck.* Hard work, money, and a good idea are necessary but not sufficient for a successful venture. The venture formation by the entrepreneur is characterized also as being "lucky"—being in the right place at the right time.

10. *Are in Conflict.* Venture capitalists and entrepreneurs have two different goals. The venture capitalist's goal is to make money and exit from the business within five years. The entrepreneur's goal is independence through survival of the organization.

11. *External Management Professionals.* This use of an external professional for advice often takes the form of a mentor or at least a good network system. The use of this individual(s) helps reduce the loneliness of being an entrepreneur.

12. *Doers.* Entrepreneurs take pride in creating and doing. They are definitely not managers and planners—the appropriate side of the entrepreneurial continuum. Rarely are they also good venture capitalists.

13. *Moderate Risk Takers.* The myth that entrepreneurs are high risk takers is nothing more than just a myth. The calculating decision to risk everything and perhaps fail reflects moderate risk taking.

14. *Just Fit into a Crowd.* Unless you knew that an individual was an entrepreneur, there would be no way to distinguish an entrepreneur from a manager based on external physical appearance.

15. *All of the Above. New* is an entrepreneurial magnet, as it implies creativity and venture creation, the drive of every entrepreneur.

16. *Variety of Ventures.* Entrepreneurs create a wide variety of ventures, depending on their field of experience and backgrounds. Women entrepreneurs, however, do tend to concentrate in the service sector.

Endnotes

1. Robert F. Herbert and Albert H. Link, *The Entrepreneur—Mainstream Views and Radical Critiques* (New York: Praeger Publishers, 1982), p. 17.
2. Richard T. Ely and Ralph H. Hess, *Outlines of Economics*, 6th ed. (New York: MacMillan, 1937), p. 488.
3. Joseph Schumpeter, *Can Capitalism Survive?* (New York: Harper & Row, 1952), p. 72.
4. Albert Shapero, *Entrepreneurship and Economic Development* (Wisconsin: Project ISEED, LTD., The Center for Venture Management, Summer 1975), p. 187.
5. Karl Vesper, *New Venture Strategies* (Englewood Cliffs, NJ: Prentice Hall, 1980), p. 2.
6. Robert C. Ronstadt, *Entrepreneurship* (Dover, MA: Lord Publishing Co., 1984), p. 28.
7. This definition is modified from the definition first developed for the woman entrepreneur. See Robert D. Hisrich and Candida G. Brush, *The Woman Entrepreneur: Starting, Financing, and Managing a Successful New Business* (Lexington, MA: Lexington Books, 1985), p. 18.
8. This material is taken from an article by the author in Robert D. Hisrich, ed., *Entrepreneurship, Intrapreneurship, and Venture Capital: The Foundation of Economic Renaissance* (Lexington, MA: Lexington Books, 1986), pp. 71–104.

9.   Small Business Economic Indicators, January–December 1997. Office of Advocacy, U.S. Small Business Administration, from data provided by the U.S. Department of Labor, Employment and Training Administration. Online: http://www.sba.org/ADVO.

10. This process is discussed in Yao Tzu Li, David G. Jansson, and Ernest G. Cravelho, *Technological Innovation in Education and Industry* (New York: Van Nostrand Reinhold, 1980), pp. 6–12.

11. Each of these categories is fully developed, particularly for the female entrepreneur, in D. D. Bowen and R. D. Hisrich, "The Female Entrepreneur: A Career Development Perspective," *Academy of Management Review* 2 (April 1986), pp. 393–407; and J. D. Brodzinski, R. F. Sherer, and F. A. Wiebe, "Entrepreneur Career Selection and Gender: A Socialization Approach," *Journal of Small Business Management* 27 (March 1989), pp. 37–43.

12. See R. D. Hisrich and C. G. Brush, *The Woman Entrepreneur: Starting, Financing, and Managing a Successful New Business* (Lexington, MA: Lexington Books, 1986).

13. A summary of the research on ethics displayed by entrepreneurs and managers and the material for this section can be found in Robert D. Hisrich and Emeric Solymossy, "Ethics in Entrepreneurship: The Present State of the Art," Unpublished Working Paper, 1996.

14. Karl H. Vesper and William B. Gartner, "Measuring Progress in Entrepreneurship Education," *Journal of Business Venturing*, (1997), vol. 12, pp. 403–21.

15. Todd A. Finkle and David Deeds, "Trends in the Market of Entrepreneurship Faculty during the Period 1989–1998," in press at the *Journal of Business Venturing*, 2000.

16. See Robert D. Hisrich and Barra O'Cinneida, "Research Trends in Entrepreneurship: The Potential in Expanding Europe and Transatlantic Perspectives," *Proceedings*, 7th Nordic Conference on Small Business Research (June 1992), pp. 1–9.

2

The Entrepreneurial and Intrapreneurial Mind

ℱ

LEARNING OBJECTIVES

1. To explain the aspects of the entrepreneurial process.

2. To explain the differences between the entrepreneurial and managerial domains.

3. To explain the organizational environment conducive for intrapreneurship.

4. To identify the general characteristics of an intrapreneur.

5. To explain the process of establishing intrapreneurship in an organization.

EWING MARION KAUFFMAN

Born on a farm in Garden City, Missouri, Ewing Marion Kauffman moved to Kansas City with his family when he was eight years old. A critical event in his life occurred several years later when Kauffman was diagnosed with a leakage of

the heart. His prescription was one year of complete bed rest; he was not even allowed to sit up. Kauffman's mother, a college graduate, came up with a solution to keep the active 11-year-old lying in bed—reading. According to Kauffman, he "sure read! Because nothing else would do, I read as many as 40 to 50 books every month. When you read that much, you read anything. So I read the biographies of all the presidents, the frontiersmen, and I read the Bible twice and that's pretty rough reading."

Another important early childhood experience centered on door-to-door sales. Since his family did not have a lot of money, Kauffman would sell 36 dozen eggs collected from the farm, or fish he and his father had caught, cleaned, and dressed. His mother was very encouraging during these formative school years, telling young Ewing each day, "There may be some who have more money in their pockets, but Ewing, there is nobody better than you."

During his youth, Kauffman worked as a laundry delivery person and was a Boy Scout. In addition to passing all the requirements to become an Eagle Scout and a Sea Scout, he sold twice as many tickets to the Boy Scout Roundup as anyone else in Kansas City, an accomplishment that enabled him to attend, for free, a two-week scout summer camp that his parents would not otherwise have been able to afford. According to Kauffman, "This experience gave me some of the sales techniques which came into play when subsequently I went into the pharmaceutical business."

Kauffman went to junior college from 8 to 12 in the morning, then walked two miles to the laundry where he worked until 7 P.M. Upon graduation, he went to work at the laundry full time for Mr. R. A. Long, who would eventually become one of his role models. His job as route foreman involved managing 18 to 20 route drivers, where he would set up sales contests, such as challenging the other drivers to get more customers on a particular route than he could obtain. Ewing says, "I got practice in selling and that proved to be beneficial later in life." R. A. Long made money not only at the laundry business but also on patents, one of which was a form fit for the collar of a shirt that would hold the shape of the shirt. He showed his young protégé that one could make money with brains as well as brawn. Kauffman commented, "He was quite a man and had quite an influence on my life."

Kauffman's sales ability was also useful during his stint in the Navy, which he joined shortly after Pearl Harbor on January 11, 1942. When designated as an apprentice seaman, a position that paid $21 per month, he responded, "I'm better than an apprentice seaman, because I have been a sea scout. I've sailed ships and I've ridden in whale boats." His selling ability convinced the Navy that he should instead start as a seaman first class, with a $54 monthly salary. Kauffman was assigned to the admiral's staff where he became an outstanding signalman (a seaman who transmitted messages from ship to ship), in part because he was able to read messages better than anyone else due to his previous intensive reading. With his admiral's encouragement, Kauffman took a correspondence navigator's course and was given a deck commission and made a navigation officer.

After the war was over in 1947, Ewing Kauffman began his career as a pharmaceutical salesperson after performing better on an aptitude test than 50 other applicants. The job involved selling supplies of vitamin and liver shots to doctors. Working on straight commission, without expenses or benefits, his pay was higher than the president's salary by the end of the second year; the president promptly cut the commission. Eventually, when Kauffman was made Midwest sales manager, he made 3 percent of everything his salespeople sold and continued to make more money than the president. When his territory was cut, he eventually quit and in 1950 started his own company—Marion Laboratories. (Marion is his middle name.)

When reflecting on founding the new company, Ewing Kauffman commented, "It was easier than it sounds because I had doctors whom I had been selling office supplies to for several years. Before I made the break, I went to three of them and said, 'I'm thinking of starting my own company. May I count on you to give me your orders if I can give you the same quality and service?' These three were my biggest accounts and each one of them agreed because they liked me and were happy to do business with me."

Marion Laboratories started by marketing injectable products that were manufactured by another company under their label. The company expanded to other accounts and other products, and then developed its first prescription item, Vicam, a vitamin product. The second pharmaceutical product they developed, oyster shell calcium, also sold well.

In order to expand the company, Kauffman borrowed $5,000 from the Commerce Trust Company. He repaid the loan, and the company continued to grow. After several years, outside investors could buy $1,000 worth of common stock if they loaned the company $1,000 to be paid back in five years at $1,250, without any intermittent interest. This initial $1,000 investment, if held until 1993, would have been worth $21 million.

Marion Laboratories continued to grow and reached over a billion dollars per year in sales, due primarily to the relationship between Ewing Kauffman and the people in the company, who were called associates, not employees. "They are all stockholders, they build this company, and they mean so much to us," said Kauffman. The concept of associates was also a part of the two basic philosophies of the company: those who produce should share in the results or profits, and treat others as you would like to be treated.

The company went public through Smith Barney on August 16, 1965, at $21 per share. The stock jumped to $28 per share immediately and has never dropped below that level, sometimes selling at a 50 to 60 price/earnings multiple. The associates of the company were offered a profit sharing plan, where each could own stock in the company. When Marion Laboratories merged with Merrill Dow in 1989, there were 3,400 associates, 300 of whom became millionaires as a result of the merger. The new company, Marion Merrill Dow, Inc., grew to 9,000 associates and sales of $4 billion in 1998 when it was acquired by Hoechst, a European pharmaceutical company. In late 1999 the company was again merged with Aventis Pharma.

Ewing Marion Kauffman's philosophies of associates, rewarding those who produce, and allowing decision making throughout the organization are the fundamental concepts underlying what is now called *intrapreneurship* in a company. He went even further and illustrated his belief in entrepreneurship and the spirit of giving back when he established the Kauffman Foundation. When fully funded, the foundation will have assets of over $1.2 billion and will equally support programs in two areas: youth development and entrepreneurship. Truly a remarkable entrepreneur, Mr. K, as he is affectionately called by his employees, will now produce many more successful "associate entrepreneurs."

intrapreneurship Entrepreneurship within an existing organization

Like Ewing Marion Kauffman, many other entrepreneurs and future entrepreneurs frequently ask themselves, "Am I really an entrepreneur or an intrapreneur? Do I have what it takes to be a success? Do I have sufficient background and experience to start and manage a new venture?" As enticing as the thought of starting and owning a business may be, the problems and pitfalls inherent to the process are as legendary as the success stories. The fact remains that more new business ventures fail than succeed. To be one of the few successful entrepreneurs requires more than just hard work and luck. It requires a hard, honest assessment both of the viability of the prospective business and, perhaps even more important, of one's own strength and weaknesses. There are similar requirements to be a successful intrapreneur.

THE ENTREPRENEURIAL PROCESS

The process of starting a new venture is embodied in the *entrepreneurial process*, which involves more than just problem solving in a typical management position.[1] An entrepreneur must find, evaluate, and develop an opportunity by overcoming the forces that resist the creation of something new. The process has four distinct phases: (1) identification and evaluation of the opportunity, (2) development of the business plan, (3) determination of the required resources, and (4) management of the resulting enterprise (see Table 2.1). Although these phases proceed progressively, none is dealt with in isolation or is totally completed before factors are being dealt with in a sequential phase. For example, to successfully identify and evaluate an opportunity (phase 1), an entrepreneur must have in mind the type of business desired (phase 4).

entrepreneurial process The process through which a new venture is created by an entrepreneur

Identify and Evaluate the Opportunity

Opportunity identification and evaluation is quite a difficult task. Most good business opportunities do not suddenly appear, but rather result from an entrepreneur's alertness to possibilities or, in some cases, the establishment of mechanisms that identify potential opportunities. For example, one entrepreneur asks at every cocktail party if

opportunity identification The process by which an entrepreneur comes up with the opportunity for a new venture

TABLE 2.1 Aspects of the Entrepreneurial Process			
Identify and Evaluate the Opportunity	**Develop the Business Plan**	**Determine the Resources Required**	**Manage the Enterprise**
Creation and length of opportunity	Title Page Table of Contents	Existing resources of entrepreneur	Management style
Real and perceived value of opportunity	Executive Summary	Resource gaps and available supplies	Key variables for success
Risk and returns of opportunity	1.0 Description of Business	Access to needed resources	Identification of problems and potential problems
Opportunity versus personal skills and goals	2.0 Description of Industry 3.0 Marketing Plan		Implementation of control systems
Competitive situation	4.0 Financial Plan 5.0 Production Plan 6.0 Organization Plan 7.0 Operational Plan 8.0 Summary		
	Appendices (Exhibits)		

anyone is using a product that does not adequately fulfill its intended purpose. This person is constantly looking for a need and an opportunity to create a better product. Another entrepreneur always monitors the play habits and toys of her nieces and nephews. This is her way of looking for any unique toy product niche for a new venture.

Although most entrepreneurs do not have formal mechanisms for identifying business opportunities, some sources are often fruitful: consumers and business associates, members of the distribution system, and technical people. Often, consumers, such as business associates purchasing products to fit a certain lifestyle, are the best source of ideas for a new venture. How many times have you heard someone comment, "If only there was a product that would . . . ." This comment occasionally results in the creation of a new business. One entrepreneur's evaluation of why so many business executives were complaining about the lack of good technical writing and word-processing services resulted in the creation of her own business venture to fill this need. Her technical writing service grew to include 10 employees in two years.

Due to their close contact with the end user, channel members of the distribution system also see product needs. One entrepreneur started a college bookstore after hearing all the students complain about the high cost of books and the lack of service provided by the only bookstore on campus. Many other entrepreneurs have identified business opportunities through a discussion with a retailer, wholesaler, or manufacturer's representative.

Finally, technically oriented individuals often conceptualize business opportunities when working on other projects. One entrepreneur's business resulted from seeing the application of a plastic resin compound in developing and manufacturing a new type of pallet while developing the resin application in another totally unrelated area—casket moldings.

Whether the opportunity is identified by using input from consumers, business associates, channel members, or technical people, each opportunity must be carefully screened and evaluated. This evaluation of the opportunity is perhaps the most critical element of the entrepreneurial process, as it allows the entrepreneur to assess whether the specific product or service has the returns needed for the resources required. As indicated in Table 2.1, this evaluation process involves looking at the creation and length of the opportunity, its real and perceived value, its risks and returns, its fit with the personal skills and goals of the entrepreneur, and its differential advantage in its competitive environment.

It is important for the entrepreneur to understand the cause of the opportunity. Is it technological change, market shift, government regulation, or competition? These factors and the resulting opportunity have a different market size and time dimension.

The market size and the length of the *window of opportunity* form the primary basis for determining risks and rewards. The risks reflect the market, competition, technology, and amount of capital involved. The amount of capital forms the basis for the return and rewards. The methodology for evaluating risks and rewards, the focus of Chapters 7 and 9, frequently indicates that an opportunity offers neither a financial nor a personal reward commensurate with the risks involved. The return and reward of the opportunity need to be viewed in light of any possible subsequent opportunities as well. One company that delivered bark mulch to residential and commercial users for decoration around the base of trees and shrubs added loam and shells to its product line. These products were sold to the same customer base using the same distribution (delivery) system. Similarly, follow-on products become very important for a company expanding or diversifying in a particular channel. A distribution channel such as Kmart, Service Merchandise, or Target prefers to do business with multiproduct, rather than single-product, firms.

window of opportunity   The time period available for creating the new venture

Finally, the opportunity must fit the personal skills and goals of the entrepreneur. It is particularly important that the entrepreneur be able to put forth the necessary time and effort required to make the venture succeed. Although many entrepreneurs feel that the desire can be developed along with the venture, typically it does not materialize, therefore dooming the venture to failure. An entrepreneur must believe in the opportunity so much that he or she will make the necessary sacrifices to develop and manage the organization.

Opportunity analysis, or what is frequently called an opportunity assessment plan, is not a business plan. Compared to a business plan, it should be shorter; focus on the opportunity, not the entire venture; and provide the basis for making the decision of whether or not to act on the opportunity.

An opportunity analysis plan includes the following: a description of the product or service, an assessment of the opportunity, an assessment of the entrepreneur and the team, specifications of all the activities and resources needed to translate the opportunity into a viable business venture, and the source of capital to finance the initial venture as well as its growth—first and second stage financing. The most difficult and critical aspect of opportunity analysis is the assessment of the opportunity. This requires answering the following questions:

- What market need does it fill?
- What personal observations have you experienced or recorded with regard to that market need?

- What social condition underlies this market need?
- What market research data can be marshaled to describe this market need?
- What patents might be available to fulfill this need?
- What competition exists in this market? How would you describe the behavior of this competition?
- What does the international market look like?
- What does the international competition look like?
- Where is the money to be made in this activity?

Develop a Business Plan

A good *business plan* must be developed in order to exploit the defined opportunity. This is perhaps the most difficult phase of the entrepreneurial process. An entrepreneur usually has not prepared a business plan before and does not have the resources available to do a good job. Although the preparation of the business plan is the focus of Chapter 7, it is important to understand the basic issues involved as well as the three major sections of the plan (see Table 2.1). A good business plan is not only important in developing the opportunity but also essential in determining the resources required, obtaining those resources, and successfully managing the resulting venture.

business plan   The description of the future direction of the business

Determine the Resources Required

The resources needed for the opportunity must also be determined. This process starts with an appraisal of the entrepreneur's present resources. Any resources that are critical must then be distinguished from those that are just helpful. Care must be taken not to underestimate the amount and variety of resources needed. The downside risks associated with insufficient or inappropriate resources should also be assessed.

Acquiring the needed resources in a timely manner while giving up as little control as possible is the next step in the entrepreneurial process. An entrepreneur should strive to maintain as large an ownership position as possible, particularly in the start-up stage. As the business develops, more funds will probably be needed to finance the growth of the venture, requiring more ownership to be relinquished. Every entrepreneur should give up an ownership position in the venture only after every other alternative has been explored. Alternative suppliers of these resources, along with their needs and desires, must be identified. By understanding resource supplier needs, the entrepreneur can structure a deal that enables the resources to be acquired at the lowest possible cost and the least cost control.

Manage the Enterprise

After resources are acquired, the entrepreneur must employ them through the implementation of the business plan. The operational problems of the growing enterprise must also be examined. This involves implementing a management style and structure, as well as determining the key variables for success. A control system must be identified so that any problem areas can be carefully monitored. Some entrepreneurs have difficulty managing and growing the venture they created. This is one difference between entrepreneurial and managerial decision making.

MANAGERIAL VERSUS ENTREPRENEURIAL DECISION MAKING

The difference between the entrepreneurial and managerial styles along five key business dimensions—strategic orientation, commitment to opportunity, commitment of resources, control of resources, and management structure—is summarized in Table 2.2.[2] Managerial styles are labeled in the table as *administrative domain*.

administrative domain The ways managers make decisions

TABLE 2.2   A Comparison of the Entrepreneurial and Administrative Domains

Entrepreneurial Domain				Administrative Domain
Pressures toward This Side		**Key Business Dimension**		**Pressures toward This Side**
Diminishing opportunity streams				Social contracts Performance measurement
Rapidly changing: Technology Consumer electronics Social values Political rules	Driven by perception of opportunity	Strategic orientation	Driven by resources currently controlled	Social contracts Performance measurement criteria Planning systems and cycle
Action orientation Short decision windows Risk management Limited decision constituencies	Revolutionary with short duration	Commitment to opportunity	Evolutionary of long duration	Acknowledgment of multiple constituencies Negotiation of strategy Risk reduction Management of fit
Lack of predictable resource needs Lack of long-term control Social need for more opportunity per resource unit International pressure for more efficient resource use	Multistaged with minimal exposure at each stage	Commitment of resources	Single-staged with complete commitment upon decision	Personal risk reduction Incentive compensation Managerial turnover Capital allocation systems Formal planning systems
Increased resource Long resource life compared to need Risk of obsolescence Risk inherent in any new venture Inflexibility of permanent commitment to resources	Episodic use or rent of required resources	Control of resources	Ownership or employment of required resources	Power, status, and financial rewards Coordination Efficiency measures Inertia and cost of change Industry structures
Coordination of key noncontrolled resources Challenge to legitimacy of owners' control Employees' desire for independence	Flat with multiple informal networks	Management structure	Formalized hierarchy	Need for clearly defined authority and responsibility Organizational culture Reward systems Management theory

Source: Adapted from Howard H. Stevenson and William Sahlman, "Importance of Entrepreneurship in Economic Development." In *Entrepreneurship, Intrapreneurship, and Venture Capital: The Foundations of Economic Renaissance,* ed. Robert D. Hisrich (Lexington, MA: Lexington Books, 1986), pp. 18–25.

Strategic Orientation

The entrepreneur's strategic orientation depends on his or her perception of the opportunity. This orientation is most important when other opportunities have diminishing returns accompanied by rapid changes in technology, consumer economies, social values, or political rules. When the use of planning systems as well as measuring performance to control current resources is the strategic orientation, there is more pressure for the administrative (managerial) domain to be operant, as is the case with many large multinational organizations.

Commitment to Opportunity

In terms of the commitment to opportunity, the second key business dimension, the two domains vary greatly with respect to the length of this commitment. The *entrepreneurial domain* is pressured by the need for action, short decision windows, a willingness to assume risk, and few decision constituencies and has a short time span in terms of opportunity commitment. The administrative (managerial) domain is not only slow to act on an opportunity, but once action is taken, the commitment is usually for a long time span, a span that is too long in some instances. There are often no mechanisms set up in companies to stop and reevaluate an initial resource commitment once it is made—a major problem in the administrative (managerial) domain.

entrepreneurial domain The ways entrepreneurs make decisions

Commitment of Resources

An entrepreneur is used to having resources committed at periodic intervals that are often based on certain tasks or objectives being reached. These resources, often acquired from others, are usually difficult to obtain, forcing the entrepreneur to achieve significant milestones using very few resources. This multistage commitment allows the resource providers (such as venture capitalists or private investors) to have as small an exposure as possible at each stage of business development and to constantly monitor the track record being established. Even though the funding may also be implemented in stages in the administrative domain, the commitment of the resources is for the total amount needed. Administratively oriented individuals respond to the source of the rewards offered and receive personal rewards by effectively administering the resources under their control.

Control of Resources

Control of the resources follows a similar pattern. Since the administrator (manager) is rewarded by effective resource administration, there is often a drive to own or accumulate as many resources as possible. The pressures of power, status, and financial rewards cause the administrator (manager) to avoid rental or other periodic use of the resource. The opposite is true for the entrepreneur who—under the pressures of limited resources, the risk of obsolescence, a need for flexibility, and the risks involved—strives to rent, or otherwise achieve periodic use of the resources, on an as-needed basis.

Management Structure

The final business dimension, management structure, also differs significantly between the two domains. In the administrative domain, the organizational structure is formalized and hierarchical in nature, reflecting the need for clearly defined lines of authority and the responsibility based on management theory and the reward system. The entrepreneur, true to his or her desire for independence, employs a flat organizational structure with informal networks throughout.

CAUSES FOR INTEREST IN INTRAPRENEURSHIP

These differences in the entrepreneurial and managerial domains have contributed toward an increased interest in intrapreneurship. This interest shown by existing organizations has intensified due to a variety of events occurring in the United States on social, cultural, and business levels. On a social level, there is an increasing interest in "doing your own thing" and doing it on one's own terms. Individuals who believe strongly in their own talents frequently desire to create something of their own. They want responsibility and have a strong need for individual expression and more freedom in their present organizational structure. When this freedom is not forthcoming, frustration can cause that individual to become less productive or even leave the organization to achieve self-actualization elsewhere. This new search for meaning, and the impatience involved, has recently caused more discontent in structured organizations than ever before. When meaning is not provided within the organization, individuals often search for an institution that will provide it. Intrapreneurship is one method of stimulating, and then capitalizing on, individuals in an organization who think that something can be done differently and better.

Most people think of Xerox as a large bureaucratic Fortune 100 company. Although, in part, this may be true of the $15 billion giant company, Xerox has done something unique in trying to ensure that its creative employees do not leave like Steve Jobs did to form Apple Computer, Inc. In 1989, Xerox set up Xerox Technology Ventures (XTV) for the purpose of generating profits by investing in the promising technologies of the company, many of which would have otherwise been overlooked.[3] Xerox hopes to avoid mistakes of the past by having "a system to prevent technology from leaking out of the company," according to Robert V. Adams, president of XTV.

The $30 million fund has supported a dozen start-ups thus far, only two of which have failed. XTV is run as a classic venture-capital operation, providing seed capital and finding outside investors when needed. The story of the 12 companies is much like that of Quad Mark, the brainchild of Dennis Stemmle, a Xerox employee of 25 years. Stemmle's idea was to make a battery-operated, plain paper copier that would fit in a briefcase along with a laptop computer. For 10 years, the idea was not approved by Xerox's operating committee. The idea was funded by XTV and Taiwan's Advanced Scientific Corporation, which now controls 20 percent of Quad Mark for its $3.5 million investment. As is the case with all the companies funded by XTV, 20 percent of each company is owned by the founder and key employees. This provides an incentive for employees like Dennis Stemmle to take the risk, leave Xerox, and form a technology-based venture.

The payoffs can be substantial, as was the case with the first company funded by XTV, Advanced Workstations Products, Inc. The company developed the idea of its founder, Tony Domit. The idea was an add-in circuit board that allowed an inexpensive IBM personal computer to perform like a $10,000 Xerox workstation. Xerox decided it needed to buy back the company for $15 million (of which the company's founders and employees received $2 million) and market the product itself. Dennis Stemmle hopes to reap similar monetary returns with his new product, perhaps by taking his company public.

XTV provides both financial and nonfinancial benefits to its parent, Xerox. The funded companies will return profits for the parent company as well as the founders and employees, and now Xerox managers pay closer attention to employees' ideas as well as internal technologies. Is XTV a success? Apparently so, if replication is any indication. The XTV concept contains an element of risk in that Xerox employees forming new ventures are not guaranteed a management position if the new venture fails. This makes XTV different from most intrapreneurship ventures in companies. This aspect of risk and no guaranteed employment is the basis for AT&T Ventures, a two-year-old fund modeled on XTV.

What Xerox recognized is what hundreds of executives are also becoming aware of in their organizations: It is important to keep, or instill, the entrepreneurial spirit in an organization in order to innovate and grow. This realization promises to revolutionize American management thinking. In a large organization, problems often occur that thwart creativity and innovation, particularly in activities not directly related to the organization's main mission. The growth and diversification that can result from flexibility and creativity are particularly critical since large, vertically integrated, diversified corporations are often more efficient in a competitive market than smaller firms. Internally administered coordination in a large corporation can often be more effective than the coordination achieved via market mechanisms.[4]

The resistance against flexibility, growth, and diversification can, in part, be overcome by developing a spirit of entrepreneurship within the existing organization, called *intrapreneurship*. An increase in intrapreneurship has been caused by an increase in social, cultural, and business pressures. Hypercompetition, both at home and abroad, has forced U.S. companies to have an increased interest in such areas as new product development, diversification, and increased productivity. The increased productivity has caused reductions in the company's labor force. During a recent five-year period, employment in Fortune 500 companies decreased by several million people. Yet these and new individuals are being absorbed into the workforce. Where has this employment occurred? Basically, in small businesses, particularly start-up efforts.

Intrapreneurship is most strongly reflected in entrepreneurial activities as well as in top management orientations in organizations. These entrepreneurial endeavors consist of the following four key elements: new business venturing, innovativeness, self-renewal, and proactiveness.[5]

New business venturing (sometimes called corporate venturing) refers to the creation of new business within an existing organization. These entrepreneurial activities consist of creating something new of value either by redefining the company's current products or services, by developing new markets, or by forming more formally autonomous or semiautonomous units or firms. Formations of new corporate ventures are the most salient manifestations of intrapreneurship. Organizational innovativeness refers to product and service innovation with an emphasis on development and innovation in technology. It includes new product development, product improvements, and new production methods and procedures. Self-renewal reflects the transformation of organizations through the renewal of the key ideas on which they are built. It has strategic and organizational change connotations and includes a redefinition of the business concept, reorganization, and the introduction of systemwide changes to increase innovation. Proactiveness includes initiative and risk taking, as well as competitive aggressiveness and boldness that are particularly reflected in the orientations and activities of top management. A proactive organization is inclined to take risks by conducting experiments; it also takes initiative and is bold and aggressive in pursuing opportunities. Organizations with such a proactive spirit attempt to lead rather than follow competitors in such key business areas as the introduction of new products or services, operating technologies, and administrative techniques.

CORPORATE VERSUS INTRAPRENEURIAL CULTURE

Business and sociological conditions have given rise to a new era in American business: the era of the entrepreneur. The positive media exposure and success of entrepreneurs are threatening to some established corporations as these smaller, aggressive, entrepreneurially driven firms are developing more new products and becoming major factors in certain markets. Recognizing the results that occur when employees of other large corporations catch the "entrepreneurial fever," many companies are now attempting to create the same spirit, culture, challenges, and rewards of entrepreneurship in their organizations. What are the differences between corporate and entrepreneurial cultures? Among managers, entrepreneurs, and intrapreneurs?

The typical *corporate culture* has a climate and reward system that favor conservative decision making. Emphasis is on gathering large amounts of data as the basis for a rational decision and then using the data to justify the decision should the intended results not occur. Risky decisions are often postponed until enough hard facts can be gathered or a consultant hired to "illuminate the unknown." Frequently, there are so many sign-offs and approvals required for a large-scale project that no individual feels personally responsible.[6]

corporate culture The environment of a particular organization

The traditional corporate culture differs significantly from an *intrapreneurial culture*. The guiding directives in a traditional corporate culture are as follows: Adhere to the instructions given, do not make any mistakes, do not fail, do not take the initiative but wait for instructions, and stay within your turf and protect your backside. This restrictive environment is, of course, not conducive to creativity, flexibility, independence, or risk taking—the guiding principles of intrapreneurs. The goals of an intrapreneurial culture are quite different: to develop visions, goals, and action plans; to be rewarded for actions taken; to suggest, try, and experiment; to create and develop regardless of the area; and to take responsibility and ownership.

intrapreneurial culture The environment of an entrepreneurial-oriented organization

There are also differences in the shared values and norms of the two cultures. The traditional corporation is hierarchical in nature with established procedures, reporting systems, lines of authority and responsibility, instructions, and control mechanisms. These support the present corporate culture and do not encourage new venture creation. The culture of an intrapreneurial firm is in stark contrast to this model. Instead of a hierarchical structure, an intrapreneurial climate has a flat organizational structure with networking, teamwork, sponsors, and mentors abounding. Close working relationships help establish an atmosphere of trust and counsel that facilitates the accomplishment of visions and objectives. Tasks are viewed as fun events, not chores, with participants gladly putting in the number of hours necessary to get the job done. Instead of building barriers to protect turfs, individuals make suggestions within and across functional areas and divisions, resulting in a cross-fertilization of ideas.

As would be expected, these two cultures produce different types of individuals and management styles. A comparison of traditional managers, entrepreneurs, and intrapreneurs reveals several differences (see Table 2.3). While *traditional managers* are

traditional managers Managers in a non-intrapreneurial-oriented organization

	Traditional Managers	Entrepreneurs	Intrapreneurs
Primary motives	Promotion and other traditional corporate rewards, such as office, staff and power	Independence, opportunity to create, and money	Independence and ability to advance in the corporate rewards
Time orientation	Short term—meeting quotas and budgets, weekly, monthly, quarterly, and the annual planning horizon	Survival and achieving 5- to 10-year growth of business	Between entrepreneurial and traditional managers, depending on urgency to meet self-imposed and corporate timetable
Activity	Delegates and supervises more than direct involvement	Direct involvement	Direct involvement more than delegation
Risk	Careful	Moderate risk taker	Moderate risk taker
Status	Concerned about status symbols	No concern about status symbols	Not concerned about traditional status symbols—desires independence
Failure and mistakes	Tries to avoid mistakes and surprises	Deals with mistakes and failures	Attempts to hide risky projects from view until ready
Decisions	Usually agrees with those in upper management positions	Follows dream with decisions	Able to get others to agree to help achieve dream
Who serves	Others	Self and customers	Self, customers, and sponsors
Family history	Family members worked for large organizations	Entrepreneurial small-business, professional, or farm background	Entrepreneurial small-business, professional, or farm background
Relationship with others	Hierarchy as basic relationship	Transactions and deal making as basic relationship	Transactions within hierarchy

TABLE 2.3   Comparison of Entrepreneurs, Intrapreneurs, and Traditional Managers

Source: An extensively modified version of table in G. Pinchot, *Intrapreneuring* (New York: Harper & Row, 1985), pp. 54–56.

motivated primarily by promotion and typical corporate rewards, entrepreneurs and intrapreneurs thrive on independence and the ability to create. The intrapreneurs expect their performance to be suitably rewarded.

There is a different time orientation in the three groups, with managers emphasizing the short run, entrepreneurs the long run, and intrapreneurs somewhere in between. Similarly, the primary mode of activity of intrapreneurs falls between the delegation activity of managers and the direct involvement of entrepreneurs. Whereas intrapreneurs and entrepreneurs are moderate risk takers, managers are much more cautious about taking any risks. Protecting one's backside and turf is a way of life for many traditional managers, and risky activities are avoided at almost any cost. On the other hand, most entrepreneurs usually fail at least once, and intrapreneurs learn to conceal risky projects from management until the last possible moment.

Whereas traditional managers tend to be most concerned about those at a higher level in the organization, entrepreneurs serve themselves and their customers, and in-

A majority of the books and articles dealing with business ethics are focused on individuals who work within an established organization. This has three basic assumptions: (1) there are people within the authority possessing greater authority than yourself; (2) there may be some form of guidelines, either in writing, in organizational culture, or in the form of an "ombudsman" (generally an older, wiser, respected individual within the organization who provides advice and counsel); and (3) many situations can be avoided if they are not "your business." For the entrepreneur, these assumptions are not valid. The entrepreneur is in authority, and everything that occurs within or connected to the business is the entrepreneur's responsibility. This focuses moral issues to individual and business survival. How does an entrepreneur decide if the resolution to a moral dilemma is worth the business? One method is to utilize basic moral reasoning, questioning the alternatives on each of the following six dimensions:

1. **Economic** (and responsibility to stakeholders): Is this action efficient? Will it produce more of the desired output? Will it require less input (which may be scarce) than the alternatives? What are the bottom-line consequences of the alternatives?

2. **Legal** (and responsibility to the community): Is this action in accordance with all applicable laws? Does this alternative meet the assumed minimal moral standards of a majority of the citizens?

3. **Beneficiency** (and responsibility to society): Who will benefit from this alternative? To what degree? Who will be adversely affected or hurt by this alternative? To what extent? Can the benefit be achieved without causing harm?

4. **Consistency** (and responsibility to society): How would I feel if I were the individual who would be adversely affected by this action? Would I allow another to take the same or a similar action?

5. **Justice** (and responsibility to society): Is this causing the greatest harm to those who are the least capable and able to influence the activity? Is this taking advantage of someone who cannot protect themselves and therefore must be protected by society?

6. **Liberty** (and responsibility to society): Does this action affect the ability and opportunity of anyone for a free, informed choice as to their own self-development and self-fulfillment?

trapreneurs add sponsors to these two entrepreneurial categories. This reflects the respective backgrounds of the three types of individuals. Instead of building strong relationships with those around them the way entrepreneurs and intrapreneurs do, managers tend to follow the relationships outlined in the organizational chart. Another aspect of culture that is of concern to businesspeople at all levels is ethics. Some aspects of these concerns are indicated in the Ethics box.

CLIMATE FOR INTRAPRENEURSHIP

How can the climate for intrapreneurship be established in an organization? In establishing an intrapreneurial environment, certain factors and leadership characteristics need to be operant.[7] The overall characteristics of a good intrapreneurial environment are summarized in Table 2.4. The first of these is that the organization operates on the frontiers of technology. Since research and development are key sources for successful new product ideas, the firm must operate on the cutting edge of the industry's technology, encouraging and supporting new ideas instead of discouraging them, as frequently occurs in firms that require a rapid return on investment and a high sales volume.

TABLE 2.4   Intrapreneurial Environment
• Organization operates on frontiers of technology.
• New ideas encouraged.
• Trial and error encouraged.
• Failures allowed.
• No opportunity parameters.
• Resources available and accessible.
• Multidiscipline teamwork approach.
• Long time horizon.
• Volunteer program.
• Appropriate reward system.
• Sponsors and champions available.
• Support of top management.

Second, experimentation—trial and error—is encouraged. Successful new products or services usually do not appear fully developed; instead, they evolve. It took time and some product failures before the first marketable computer appeared. A company wanting to establish an intrapreneurial spirit has to establish an environment that allows mistakes and failures in developing new innovative products. Although this is in direct opposition to the established career and promotion system of the traditional organization, without the opportunity to fail in an organization, few, if any, corporate intrapreneurial ventures will be developed. Almost every entrepreneur has experienced at least one failure in establishing a successful venture.

Third, an organization should make sure that there are no initial *opportunity parameters* inhibiting creativity in new product development. Frequently in an organization, various "turfs" are protected, frustrating attempts by potential intrapreneurs to establish new ventures. In one Fortune 500 company, an attempt to establish an intrapreneurial environment ran into problems and eventually failed when the potential intrapreneurs were informed that a proposed new product and venture was not possible because it was in the domain of another division.

opportunity parameters Barriers to new product creation and development

Fourth, the resources of the firm need to be available and easily accessible. As one intrapreneur stated, "If my company really wants me to take the time, effort, and career risks to establish a new venture, then it needs to put money and people resources on the line." Often, insufficient funds are allocated not to creating something new, but instead to solving problems that have an immediate effect on the bottom line. Some companies—like Xerox, 3M, and AT&T—have recognized this problem and have established separate venture-capital areas for funding new internal ventures. Even when resources are available, all too often the reporting requirements become obstacles to obtaining them, causing frustration and dissatisfaction.

Fifth, a multidisciplined team approach needs to be encouraged. This open approach, with participation by needed individuals regardless of area, is the antithesis of the typical corporate organizational structure. An evaluation of successful cases of intrapreneurship indicated that one key to success was the existence of "skunkworks" involving relevant people. Developing the needed teamwork for a new venture is further complicated by the fact that a team member's promotion and overall career within the corporation are related to his or her job performance in the current position, not to his or her contribution to the new venture being created.

Besides encouraging teamwork, the corporate environment must establish a long time horizon for evaluating the success of the overall program as well as the success of each individual venture. If a company is not willing to invest money without a guarantee of return for 5 to 10 years, it should not attempt to create an intrapreneurial environment. This patient attitude toward money in the corporate setting is no different from the investment/return line horizon used by venture capitalists and others in the risk-capital market when investing in an entrepreneurial effort.

Sixth, the spirit of intrapreneurship cannot be forced upon individuals; it must be on a volunteer basis. There is a difference between corporate thinking and intrapreneurial thinking, with certain individuals performing much better on one side of the continuum or the other. Most managers in a corporation are not capable of being successful intrapreneurs. Those who do emerge from this self-selection process must be allowed the latitude to carry a project through to completion. This is not consistent with most corporate procedures for new product development, where different departments and individuals are involved in each stage of the development process. An individual willing to spend the excess hours and effort to create a new venture needs the opportunity and the accompanying reward of completing the project. An intrapreneur falls in love with the newly created internal venture and will do almost anything to help ensure its success.

The seventh characteristic is a *reward system*. The intrapreneur needs to be appropriately rewarded for all the energy, effort, and risk taking expended in the creation of the new venture. These rewards should be based on the attainment of established performance goals. An equity position in the new venture is one of the best methods for motivating and eliciting the amount of activity and effort needed for success.

Eighth, a corporate environment favorable for intrapreneurship has sponsors and champions throughout the organization who not only support the creative activity and resulting failures but also have the planning flexibility to establish new objectives and directions as needed. As one intrapreneur stated, "For a new business venture to succeed, the intrapreneur needs to be able to alter plans at will and not be concerned about how close they come to achieving the previously stated objectives." Corporate structures frequently measure managers on their ability to come close to objectives, regardless of the quality of performance reflected in this accomplishment.

Finally, and perhaps most important, the intrapreneurial activity must be wholeheartedly supported and embraced by top management, both by their physical presence and by making sure that the personnel and the financial resources are readily and easily available. Without top management support, a successful intrapreneurial environment cannot be created.

INTRAPRENEURIAL LEADERSHIP CHARACTERISTICS

Within this overall corporate environment, certain individual characteristics have been identified that constitute a successful intrapreneur. As summarized in Table 2.5, these include understanding the environment, being visionary and flexible, creating management options, encouraging teamwork while employing a multidisciplined approach, encouraging open discussion, building a coalition of supporters, and persisting.

TABLE 2.5   Intrapreneurial Leadership Characteristics
• Understands the environment
• Visionary and flexible
• Creates management options
• Encourages teamwork
• Encourages open discussion
• Builds a coalition of supporters
• Persists

An entrepreneur needs to understand all aspects of the environment. Part of this ability is reflected in the individual's level of creativity. Creativity, perhaps at its lowest level in large organizations, generally tends to decrease with age and education in most individuals. To establish a successful intrapreneurial venture, the individual must be creative and have a broad understanding of the internal and external environments of the corporation.

The person who is going to establish a successful new intrapreneurial venture must also be a visionary leader—a person who dreams great dreams. Although there are many definitions of leadership, the one that best describes that needed for intrapreneurship is: "A leader is like a gardener. When you want a tomato, you take a seed, put it in fertile soil, and carefully water under tender care. You don't manufacture tomatoes; you grow them." Another good definition is that "leadership is the ability to dream great things and communicate these in such a way that people say yes to being a part of the dream." Martin Luther King, Jr., said "I have a dream" and articulated that dream in such a way that thousands followed him in his efforts, in spite of overwhelming obstacles. To establish a successful new venture, the intrapreneurial leader must have a dream and overcome all the obstacles in achieving it by selling the dream to others.

The third necessary characteristic is that the intrapreneur must be flexible and create management options. An intrapreneur does not "mind the store," but rather is open to and even encourages change. By challenging the beliefs and assumptions of the corporation, an intrapreneur has the opportunity to create something new in the organizational structure.

The intrapreneur must possess a fourth characteristic: the ability to encourage teamwork and use a multidisciplined approach. This also violates the organizational practices and structures taught in most business schools that are apparent in established corporate plans. Every new company formation requires a broad range of business skills, such as engineering, production, marketing, and finance. In forming a new venture, recruiting those in the organization usually requires crossing established departmental structure and reporting systems. To minimize the negative effect of any disruption caused, the intrapreneur must be a good diplomat.

Open discussion must be encouraged in order to develop a good team for creating something new. Many corporate managers have forgotten the frank, open discussions and disagreements that were a part of their educational process. Instead, they spend time building protective barriers and insulating themselves in their corporate empires. A successful new intrapreneurial venture can be formed only when the team involved feels the freedom to disagree and to critique an idea in an effort to reach the best solution. The degree of openness among the team depends on the degree of openness of the intrapreneur.

Openness leads also to the establishment of a strong coalition of supporters and encouragers. The intrapreneur must encourage and affirm each team member, particularly during difficult times. This encouragement is very important, as the usual motivators of career paths and job security are not operational in establishing a new intrapreneurial venture. A good intrapreneur makes everyone a hero.

Last, but not least, is persistence. Throughout the establishment of any new intrapreneurial venture, frustration and obstacles will occur. Only through the intrapreneur's persistence will a new venture be created and successful commercialization result.

ESTABLISHING INTRAPRENEURSHIP IN THE ORGANIZATION

An organization desiring to establish an intrapreneurial environment must implement a procedure for its creation. Although this can be done internally, frequently an organization finds it easier to use someone outside to facilitate the process. This is particularly true when the organization's environment is very traditional and has a record of little change and few new products being introduced.

The first step in this process is to secure a commitment to intrapreneurship in the organization by top, upper, and middle management levels. Without *top management commitment*, the organization will never be able to go through all the cultural

---
top management commitment   Managers in an
organization strongly supporting intrapreneurship
---

changes necessary for implementation. Once the top management of the organization has committed to intrapreneurship for a sufficient period of time (one to three years), the concept is introduced throughout the organization. This is accomplished most effectively through seminars, where the aspects of intrapreneurship are introduced and strategies are developed to transform the organizational culture into an intrapreneurial one. General guidelines need to be established for intrapreneurial venture development. Once the initial framework is established and the concept embraced, intrapreneurial leaders need to be identified, selected, and trained. This training needs to focus on obtaining resources within the organization, identifying viable opportunities and their markets, and developing the appropriate business plan.

Second, ideas and general areas that top management are interested in supporting should be identified, along with the amount of risk money that is available to develop the concept further. Overall program expectations and the target results of each intrapreneurial venture should be established. As much as possible, these should specify the time frame, volume, and profitability requirements for the new venture, and the impact of the organization. Along with the intrapreneurial training, a mentor/sponsor system needs to be established. Without sponsors or champions, there is little hope that the culture of the organization can be transformed into an intrapreneurial one.

Third, a company needs to use technology to make itself more flexible. Technology has been used successfully for the past decade by small companies that behave like big ones.[8] How else could a small firm like Value Quest Ltd. compete against very large money management firms, except through a state-of-the-art personal computer and access to large data banks? Similarly, large companies can use technology to make themselves responsive and flexible like smaller firms.

Fourth, the organization can firmly establish an intrapreneurial culture by using a group of interested managers to train employees as well as share their experiences.

The training sessions should be conducted one day per month for a specified period of time. Informational items about intrapreneurship in general, and about the specifics of the company's activities in developing ideas into marketable products or services that are the basis of new business venture units, should be well publicized. This will require the intrapreneurial team to develop a business plan, to obtain customer reaction and some initial intentions to buy, and to learn how to coexist within the organizational structure.

Fifth, the organization needs to develop ways to get closer to its customers.[9] This can be done by tapping the database, hiring from smaller rivals, and helping the retailer (see Table 2.6). PepsiCo., Inc., is spending about $20 million to create electronic profiles of about 9 million Pizza Hut customers. Dannon is sharing its research with retailers and tailoring much of its marketing effort to the individual chains.

Sixth, an organization that wants to become more entrepreneurial must learn to be more productive with fewer resources.[10] This has already occurred in many companies that have downsized. Top-heavy organizations are out-of-date in today's hypercompetitive environment. To accommodate the large cutbacks in middle management, much more control has to be given to subordinates at all levels in the organization. Not surprisingly, the span of control may become as high as 30 to 1 in divisions of such companies. The concept of "lean and mean" needs to exist if intrapreneurship is to prevail.

Seventh, the organization needs to establish a strong support structure for intrapreneurship. This is particularly important since intrapreneurship is usually a secondary activity in the organization. Since intrapreneurial activities do not immediately affect the bottom line, they can be easily overlooked and receive little funding and support. To be successful, these ventures require flexible, innovative behavior, with the intrapreneurs having total authority over expenditures and access to sufficient funds. When the intrapreneur has to justify expenses on a daily basis, it is really not a new internal venture but merely an operational extension of the funding source.[11]

TABLE 2.6	Methods for Getting Closer to the Customer
How Big Marketers Can Act as Deftly as Small Companies . . .	
Tap the database	Use purchase data to customize incentives and direct mail based on demographics, location, product preference, and price.
Hire from smaller rivals	They excel at "guerrilla marketing"—using local promotions to get closer to customers and break through advertising clutter.
Help your retailer	Create store-specific marketing programs—as Dannon does for retailers selling its yogurt—to win retailer loyalty, differentiate your product, and build local sales.
. . . and Small Marketers Can Outwit the Giants	
Find the missed opportunities	Small marketers can often focus on a relatively neglected product—such as duct tape, or dental floss—and take share from a bigger player or increase sales in a tired category.
Apply the personal touch	Smaller marketers can get a big payoff when top executives pay personal attention to customers' letters, retailers' queries, and the sales staff's suggestions.
Embrace technology	The cost of database technology is dropping, making direct-mail marketing a viable tactic for small marketers with tight budgets.

Source: Christopher Power, "How to Get Closer to Your Customers," *Business Week/Enterprise 1993*, p. 45.

Eighth, support must also involve tying the rewards to the performance of the intrapreneurial unit. This encourages the team members to work harder and compete more effectively since they will benefit directly from their efforts. Because the intrapreneurial venture is a part of the larger organization and not a totally independent unit, the equity portion of the compensation is particularly difficult to handle.

Finally, the organization needs to implement an evaluation system that allows successful intrapreneurial units to expand and unsuccessful ones to be eliminated. As is the case in an entrepreneurial firm, when a job is done well, an intrapreneurial unit should be allowed to expand to fill market demands as warranted. The organization can establish constraints to ensure that this expansion does not run contrary to the corporate mission statement. Similarly, inefficient intrapreneurial venture units should not be allowed to exist just because of vested interests. To have a successful intrapreneurial environment, the organization must allow some ventures to fail even as it allows more successful ones to expand.

PROBLEMS AND SUCCESSFUL EFFORTS

Intrapreneurship, or what is alternatively called corporate venturing, is not without its problems. One study found that new ventures started within a corporation performed worse than those started independently by entrepreneurs.[12] The reasons cited were the corporation's difficulty in maintaining a long-term commitment, a lack of freedom to make autonomous decisions, and a constrained environment. Generally, independent, venture-capital-based start-ups by entrepreneurs tend to outperform corporate start-ups significantly. On average, not only did the independents become profitable twice as fast, but they ended up twice as profitable.[13]

These findings should not deter organizations committed to intrapreneurship from starting the process. There are numerous examples of companies that, having understood the environmental and intrapreneurial characteristics necessary, have adopted their own version of the implementation process previously discussed to launch new ventures successfully. One of the best known of these firms is Minnesota Mining and Manufacturing (3M). Having had many successful intrapreneurial efforts, 3M, in effect, allows employees to devote 15 percent of their time to independent projects. This enables the divisions of the company to meet an important goal: to generate a significant percent of sales from new products introduced within the last five years. One of the most successful of these intrapreneurial activities was the development of Post-It Notes by entrepreneur Arthur Fry. This effort developed out of Fry's annoyance that pieces of paper marking his church hymnal constantly fell out while he was singing. As a 3M chemical engineer, Fry knew about the discovery by a scientist, Spencer Silver, of a very-low-sticking-power adhesive, which to the company was a poor product characteristic. However, this characteristic was perfect for Fry's problem; a marker with lightly sticking adhesive that is easy to remove provided a good solution. Obtaining approval to commercialize the idea proved to be a monumental task until the samples distributed to secretaries within 3M, as well as to other companies, created such a demand that the company eventually began selling the product under the name Post-It. Sales have reached more than $800 million.

Another firm committed to the concept of intrapreneurship is Hewlett-Packard (HP). After failing to recognize the potential of Steven Wozniak's proposal for a personal computer (which was the basis for Apple Computer Inc.), Hewlett-Packard has taken steps to ensure that it will be recognized as a leader in innovation and not miss future opportunities. However, the intrapreneurial road at HP is not an easy one. This

As Seen in Business Week:
Gold Clubs Online: A Better Idea?

There are 67 sites on Yahoo! selling golf clubs, but only one claims to have its own dot.com, made-to-order brand. Chipshot.com is betting on that innovation to help it stand out among the glut of e-biz golf merchandisers.

Amar Goel, the twentysomething chief executive who started chipshot.com in 1995 with $350, says it has since attracted $21 million in venture funds. Goel wants chipshot.com to be to golf clubs what Dell Computer is to PCs: the dominant direct seller. With custom clubs for sale on many sites, Goel says that chipshot.com needs more than just low prices to prosper, though it has those too. Its XT-55 Custom Iron with a graphite shaft, for ex-

ample, compares favorably, pricewise, with Cobra's $109 Gravity Back Iron. The company says it sells 5,000 clubs a week—though not all are its own.

So far, however, chipshot pulls in only 1 million page views a month versus 13 million at Sports Line.com, which has several big golf sites where purchases average $200 per customer. With an emphasis on sports news, SportsLine believes content drives sales, since almost all fans are players. Chipshot thinks its name is enough to lure buyers from bigger sites.

Source: "Gold Clubs Online: A Better Idea?" *Business Week*, October 25, 1999, p. 7.

was the case for Charles House, an engineer who went far beyond his intrapreneurial duty when he ignored an order from David Packard to stop working on a high-quality video monitor. The monitor, once developed, was used in NASA's manned moon landings and in heart transplants. Although projected to achieve sales of no more than 30 units, more than 17,000 of these large-screen displays (about $35 million in sales) have already been sold.

IBM also decided that intrapreneurship would help spur corporate growth. The company developed the independent business unit concept in which each unit is a separate organization with its own miniboard of directors and autonomous decision-making authority on many manufacturing and marketing issues. The more than 11 business units have developed such products as the automatic teller machine for banks, industrial robots, and the IBM personal computer. The latter business unit was given a blank check with a mandate to get IBM into the personal computer market. Intrapreneur Philip Estridge led his group to develop and market the PCs, through both IBM's sales force and the retail market, breaking some of the most binding operational rules of IBM at that time.

These and other success stories indicate that the problems of intrapreneurship are not insurmountable and that the concept of intrapreneurship can lead to new products, growth, and the development of an entirely new corporate environment and culture.

IN REVIEW

Summary

There is more to a successful business than a good idea; there must also be a good entrepreneur. Although the ideal entrepreneur cannot be profiled, there are certain characteristics of a potential entrepreneur and certain trends they may follow. This entrepreneur then goes through the entrepreneurial process, which involves finding, evaluating, and developing opportunities for creating a new venture. Each step is essential to the eventual success of the new firm and is closely related to the other steps. Before the opportunity identification stage can result in a meaningful search, the potential entrepreneur must have a general idea about the type of company desired.

There are both formal and informal mechanisms for identifying business opportunities. Although formal mechanisms are generally found within a more established company, most entrepreneurs use informal sources for their ideas, such as being sensitive to the complaints and chance comments of friends and associates.

Once the opportunity is identified, the evaluation process begins. Basic to the screening process is understanding the factors that create the opportunity: technology, market changes, competition, or changes in government regulations. From this base, the market size and time dimension associated with the idea can be estimated. It is important that the idea fit the personal skills and goals of the entrepreneur, and that the entrepreneur have a strong desire to see the opportunity brought to fruition. In the process of evaluating an opportunity, the required resources should be clearly defined and obtained at the lowest possible cost.

Managing a new venture differs in many ways from managing an existing operation, particularly along the five key dimensions of strategic orientation, commitment to opportunity, commitment of resources, control of resources, and management structure. The entrepreneurial venture presents the manager with a different set of circumstances from the one the corporate manager typically faces. A distinctly different set of skills often needs to be developed, either through the entrepreneurial experience or through education. This may include obtaining an MBA degree. Social and business pressures have caused an increase in new venture creation, both outside and inside existing corporate structures. Within existing corporate structures, this entrepreneurial spirit and effort is called *intrapreneurship.*

To develop successful innovation, a corporation should establish a conducive organizational climate. Traditional managers tend to adhere more strictly to established hierarchical structures, to be less risk oriented, and to emphasize short-term results, all of which inhibit the creativity, flexibility, and risk required for new ventures. Organizations desiring an intrapreneurial climate need to encourage new ideas and experimental efforts, eliminate opportunity parameters, make resources available, promote a teamwork approach and voluntary intrapreneurship, and enlist top management's support.

The intrapreneur must also have appropriate leadership characteristics. In addition to being creative, flexible, and visionary, the intrapreneur must be able to work within the corporate structure. Intrapreneurs need to encourage teamwork and work diplomatically across established structures. Open discussion and strong support of team members are also required. Finally, the intrapreneur must be persistent in order to overcome the inevitable obstacles.

The process of establishing intrapreneurship within an existing organization requires the commitment of management, particularly top management. The organization must carefully choose intrapreneurial leaders, develop general guidelines for ventures, and delineate expectations before the intrapreneurial program begins. Training sessions are an important part of the process. As role models and intrapreneurial ventures are introduced, the organization must establish a strong organizational support system, along with a system of incentives and rewards to encourage team members. Finally, it should establish a system to expand successful ventures and to eliminate unsuccessful ones.

Questions for Discussion

1. List five opportunities for a new business that have come to your attention recently. How were you made aware of these needs? List the sources of opportunities you have encountered in the last week or two. If your list is short, indicate how you could cultivate more sources.

2. List examples of new products or services that have resulted from the different sources of change discussed in this chapter.

3. As entrepreneurship becomes more popular and the education of entrepreneurs becomes more widespread, do you believe that a well-defined entrepreneurial career path will emerge? Support your answer.

4. Why do you think that some successful entrepreneurs have had difficulty in managing their companies beyond the start-up stage? How could entrepreneurial education help this problem?

5. Discuss business pressures that have led to intrapreneurship.

6. Explain why traditional corporate management has not been conducive to intrapreneurship.

7. Discuss the characteristics necessary for a successful intrapreneur. In what ways do these characteristics differ from those of an entrepreneur?

Key Terms

administrative domain

business plan

corporate culture

entrepreneurial domain

entrepreneurial process

intrapreneurial culture

intrapreneurship

opportunity identification

opportunity parameters

top management commitment

traditional managers

window of opportunity

More Information—Net Addresses in This Chapter

Allied Signal
   www.alliedsignal.com

Apple Computer, Inc.
   www.apple.com

AT&T
   www.att.com

AT&T Ventures
   www.attventures.com

Ewing Marion Kauffman Foundation
   www.emkf.com

Ford Motor Company
   www.ford.com/global

Hewlett-Packard (HP)
   www.hp.com

IBM
   www.ibm.com

Kmart
   www.kmart.com

Minnesota Mining and Manufacturing (3M)
   www.3m.com

National Aeronautics and Space Administration (NASA)
   www.nasa.gov

PepsiCo.
   pepsico.pcy.mci.net/web-pages/pepsicohome.htm

Pizza Hut
   www.pizzahut.com

Service Merchandise
   www.servicemerchandise.com

Small Business Administration
   www.sbaonline.sba.gov

Target
   www.targetstores.com

Xerox
   www.xerox.com

Xerox Technology Ventures (XTV)
   www.caprel.com/xtv/xtv.html

Selected Readings

Bartlett, Christopher A.; and Sumantra Goshal. (1996). Release the Entrepreneurial Hostages from Your Corporate Hierarchy. *Strategy & Leadership*, vol. 24, no. 4, pp. 36–42.

Companies that succeed in developing an effective entrepreneurial process at the core of their operations share three key organizational characteristics: (1) disaggregated performance units, (2) performance-driven systems, and (3) clear mission and standards. To build managerial entrepreneurship, it is necessary to reinforce the changes in the roles and responsibilities not only of front-line managers but also of those in middle and top-level positions.

Carrier, Camille. (1994). Intrapreneurship in Large Firms and SMEs: A Comparative Study. *International Small Business Journal*, vol. 12, no. 3, pp. 54–61.

Whereas in large businesses the structures and systems often constitute important barriers to intrapreneurship, in small and medium-sized enterprises the owner–managers themselves may become the main inhibitors or, conversely, the best catalysts in the process. The more personalized internal environment in SMEs creates a better partnership between the intrapreneurial actors involved, but also makes it more difficult for intrapreneurs to maintain their anonymity.

Carter, Nancy M.; William B. Gartner; and Paul D. Reynolds. (1996). Exploring Start-Up Event Sequences. *Journal of Business Venturing*, vol. 11, no. 3, pp. 151–66.

Research analyzing new venture start-up activities with three broad questions addressing the following areas: (1) what activities nascent entrepreneurs initiate in attempting to establish a new business, (2) the number of activities initiated during the gestation of the start-up, and (3) when particular activities are initiated and completed. Significant differences were found in these areas among entrepreneurs who were able to get a business up and running, those still working on putting a business in place, and those who had given up.

Chen, Chao C.; Patricia G. Greene; and Ann Crick. (1998). Does Entrepreneurial Self-Efficacy Distinguish Entrepreneurs from Managers? *Journal of Business Venturing*, vol. 13, pp. 295–316.

Entrepreneurial self-efficacy—which refers to the strength of a person's belief that he or she is capable of successfully performing various roles and tasks, and which includes five dimensions (marketing, innovation, management, risk taking, and financial control)—was proposed to be an individual characteristic that is distinctively entrepreneurial.

David, Byron L. (1994). How Internal Venture Groups Innovate. *Research-Technology Management*, vol. 37, no. 2, pp. 38–43.

A study based on a survey of 139 Fortune 500 companies identifies three modes of internal corporate venturing (ICV) that are differentiated by (1) the origin of the product concepts; (2) the roles of research and development (R&D), intrapreneurs, and venture managers; and (3) the degree of their products' commercial success, technical performance, radicalness, and marketing and technologic diversification.

Fulop, Liz. (1991). Middle Managers: Victims or Vanguards of the Entrepreneurial Movement? *Journal of Management Studies*, vol. 28, no. 1, pp. 25–44.

Three approaches to corporate entrepreneurship are identified: (1) the approach in which entrepreneurship is made synonymous with rationalizations in labor, technology, and management structures; (2) the innovation process model approach; and (3) the resource mobilization approach.

Ireland, R. Duane; Michael A. Hitt; Michael Camp; and Donald L. Sexton. (2001). Integrating Entrepreneurship and Strategic Management Actions to Create Firm Wealth. *Academy of Management Executive*, vol. 15, no. 1, pp. 49–63.

Creating wealth is at the heart of both entrepreneurship and strategic management. For general managers and entrepreneurs, a keen interest is to learn how to apply entrepreneurial and strategic tools, techniques, and concepts in ways that help the firm create increasing amounts of wealth. Many of the activities that the organizations engage in to create wealth take place within six domains: innovation, networks, internationalization, organization learning, top management teams and governance, and growth.

Knight, G. A. 1997. Cross-Cultural Reliability and Validity of a Scale to Measure Firm Entrepreneurial Orientation. *Journal of Business Venturing*, vol. 12, no. 3, pp. 213–25.

A popular scale for measuring entrepreneurship at the firm level (the ENTRESCALE), which includes eight measurement items reflecting the innovative and proactive disposition at a given firm, was found to be reliable across two cultures in Canada.

Lumpkin, G. T.; and G. G. Dess. (1996). Clarifying the Entrepreneurial Orientation Construct and Linking It to Performance. *Academy of Management Review*, vol. 12, no. 1, pp. 135–72.

The nature of the entrepreneurial orientation construct was clarified by identifying five distinctive dimensions (autonomy, innovativeness, risk taking, proactiveness, and competitive aggressiveness) of entrepreneurial processes, and by proposing a contingency framework for investigating the relationship between entrepreneurial orientation and firm performance.

Miner, J.; R. Norman; and J. S. Brecker. (1992). Defining the Inventor–Entrepreneur in the Context of Established Typologies. *Journal of Business Venturing*, vol. 7, no. 2, pp. 103–13.

What is really indicative of inventor–entrepreneurship is a strong commitment to a company strategy of product development, not a proclivity for taking out patents. These entrepreneurs develop an organization not as an end in itself, but as a vehicle for invention and production of various products.

Ostgaard, Tone A.; and Sue Birley. (1996). New Venture Growth and Personal Networks. *Journal of Business Research*, vol. 36, no. 1, pp. 37–50.

A survey of 159 owner-managed companies in England exploring the effectiveness of personal networks in terms of firm performance and growth. Multiple regression confirmed the importance of networks for company performance and development. The research establishes a link between the entrepreneur's networking behavior and the growth of the firm.

Pryor, Austin K.; and Michael E. Shays. (1993). Growing the Business with Intrapreneurs. *Business Quarterly*, vol. 57, no. 3, pp. 42–50.

An intrapreneurship program creates a different kind of environment that encourages people with ideas to step forward and provides special training for people with commitment to be successful in the intrapreneurial role. Four requirements for successful intrapreneurship are presented.

Stewart, Wayne H. Jr.; Warren E. Watson; Joann C. Carland; and James W. Carland. (1998). A Proclivity for Entrepreneurship: A Comparison of Entrepreneurs, Small Business Owners, and Corporate Managers. *Journal of Business Venturing*, vol. 14, pp. 189–214.

Entrepreneurs (i.e., small business owners who have goals of profit and growth for their ventures and use strategic planning) were compared to small business owners (i.e., small business owners who focus on providing family income and view the venture as an extension of their personality) and corporate managers on psychological characteristics. Entrepreneurs were found to be higher in achievement motivation, risk-taking propensity, and preference for innovation than both other groups. The small business owners were more comparable to managers than to entrepreneurs.

Stopford, John M.; and Charles W. F. Baden-Fuller. (1994). Creating Corporate Entrepreneurship. *Strategic Management Journal*, vol. 15, no. 7, pp. 521–36.

The various types of corporate entrepreneurship—individual managers, business renewal and Schumpeterian, or industry, leadership—share five bundles of attributes. Each type can exist in one firm, though at different times, as the common attributes change their role and relative importance.

Zahra, Shaker A. (1993). Environment, Corporate Entrepreneurship, and Financial Performance: A Taxonomic Approach. *Journal of Business Venturing,* vol. 8, no. 4, pp. 319–40.

Four environmental settings (dynamic growth, hostile and rivalrous but technologically rich, hospitable product-driven growth, and static environment) were used to examine the relationships among a firm's external environment, corporate entrepreneurship, and financial performance.

Endnotes

1. A developed version of this process can be found in Howard H. Stevenson, Michael J. Roberts, and H. Irving Grousbeck, *New Business Ventures and the Entrepreneur* (Burr Ridge, IL: Richard D. Irwin, 1985), pp. 16–23.
2. These differences are fully delineated in H. H. Stevenson and W. A. Sahlman, "Importance of Entrepreneurship in Economic Development." In *Entrepreneurship, Intrapreneurship, and Venture Capital,* ed. Robert D. Hisrich (Lexington, MA: Lexington Books, 1986), pp. 1–6.
3. For a discussion of XTV, see Larry Armstrong, "Nurturing an Employee's Brainchild," *Business Week/Enterprise 1993,* p. 196.
4. These concepts are developed in D. Chandler, *The Visible Hand: The Managerial Revolution in American Business* (Cambridge: Harvard University Press, 1977); and O. E. Williamson, *Markets and Hierarchies: Analysis and Antitrust Information* (New York: The Free Press, 1979).
5. For a discussion of intrapreneurship elements and their measures, see G. T. Lumpkin and G. G. Dess, "Clarifying the Entrepreneurial Orientation Construct and Linking It to Performance," *Academy of Management Review,* 12(1) (1996), pp. 135–72; and B. Antoncic and R. D. Hisrich, "Intrapreneurship: Construct Refinement and Cross-Cultural Validation," *Journal of Business Venturing,* forthcoming.
6. For a discussion of this aspect, see N. Fast, "A Visit to the New Venture Graveyard," *Research Management* 22 (March 1979), pp. 18–22.
7. For a thorough discussion of the factors important in intrapreneurship, see R. M. Kanter, *The Change Masters* (New York: Simon & Schuster, 1983); and G. Pinchot III, *Intrapreneuring* (New York: Harper & Row, 1985).
8. For a discussion of this aspect, see Peter Coy, "Start with Some High-Tech Magic . . . ," *Business Week/Enterprise 1993,* pp. 24–5, 28, and 32.
9. This is discussed in Christopher Power, "How to Get Closer to Your Customers," *Business Week/Enterprise 1993,* pp. 42, 44–45.
10. For a good discussion of this aspect, see John A. Byrne, "Tightening the Smart Way," *Business Week/Enterprise 1993,* pp. 34–35, 38.
11. For a discussion of this aspect, see R. Peterson and D. Berger, "Entrepreneurship in Organizations," *Administrative Science Quarterly* 16 (August 1971), pp. 97–106; and D. Miller and P. Friesen, "Innovation in Conservative and Entrepreneurial Firms: Two Models of Strategic Momentum," *Strategic Management Journal* 3 (May 1982), pp. 1–25.
12. N. Fast, "Pitfalls of Corporate Venturing," *Research Management* (March 1981), pp. 21–24.
13. For complete information on the relative performance, see R. Biggadike, "The Risky Business of Diversification," *Harvard Business Review* (May–June 1979), pp. 103–11; L. E. Weiss, "Start-Up Business: A Comparison of Performances," *Sloan Management Review* (Fall 1981), pp. 37–53; and N. D. Fast and S. E. Pratt, "Individual Entrepreneurship and the Large Corporation," *Proceedings,* Babson Research Conference (April 1984), pp. 443–50.

3

The Individual Entrepreneur

LEARNING OBJECTIVES

1. To identify some key entrepreneurial feelings and motivations.

2. To identify key elements in an entrepreneur's background.

3. To discuss the importance of role models and support systems.

4. To identify the similarities and differences between male and female entrepreneurs.

5. To explain the differences between inventors and entrepreneurs.

LILLIAN VERNON KATZ

Lillian Vernon was born in Leipzig, Germany, in 1927 to parents she characterizes as hardworking and scrupulously honest. The family moved to Holland, subsequently emigrating to the United States in 1937 to escape the Nazis and World War II, when Lillian was 10 years old. She found the freedom of her New York City home exhilarating. The dominant figure in her early life, her father, who was a leather goods manufacturer, instilled in Vernon the same characteristics of hard work and honesty that her mother possessed. He taught her that girls, no less than boys, could achieve any goal they wished in any field they chose. This paternal guidance gave his young daughter confidence in herself and her dreams.

In 1949, after majoring in psychology at New York University for two years, she married Sam Hochberg. Two years later, at 24, she was pregnant with her first child. They were living in a three-room apartment in Mount Vernon on Sam's $75 per week earnings. Feeling they would need an additional $50 per week to support the new baby, Vernon decided to open her own business. Her father's influence on her early life left her with no doubts about her ability to succeed. Since she did not want a 9-to-5 job, but rather something that could be run from her own home, Vernon chose mail order after considering several alternatives.

Using $2,000 of wedding gift money, she launched her venture—Vernon Specialties Company—which offered personalized leather handbags and belts designed by Vernon and made by her father. Her concept for the business was to offer by mail something personalized that could not be readily found at an affordable price. A $495 advertisement in the September 1951 issue of *Seventeen* magazine generated $32,000 in orders for the fledgling company. While mail ordering was not new, Lillian Vernon provided a unique service—personalization with the customer's initials free of charge, without the weeks of waiting generally associated with custom orders. Profits were used to purchase more ads and buy more handbags and belts, putting into practice what she considered part of the best investment advice she ever received. Her father taught her to never spend what she did not have, and to put earnings back into her company. Lillian worked during the day in a loft rented from her father and did the clerical work on her kitchen table at night. The line was soon expanded to include three colors of handbags and belts and personalized bookmarks costing $1. In 1956, Lillian published her first 16-page black and white catalog, mailing it to 125,000 customers who had responded to her ads, further expanding the product lines to include personalized combs, blazer buttons, collar pins, and cuff links. After the birth of her second son, David, she decided to include her own designs, and Vernon Products, the manufacturing division, was born.

Since the mid-1950s did not offer a positive environment for female entrepreneurs, Lillian confronted many obstacles. Some bankers would not even bother to talk to her, and neighbors felt she was not being a good mother because she left her sons with a nanny. However, Lillian overcame these problems, using her AT&T stock as collateral for bank loans and managing her business around her children's schedules. While the nanny did the cleaning, cooking, and laundry, Lillian did the shopping, ran the house, and joined in car pooling. There were times, however, when motherhood took second place, such as one Christmas when she sent her children to her mother's for the holidays due to a backlog of orders. While regretting this instance, Lillian accepts it as part of the cost of success: "I wasn't burdened with the guilt many working mothers have, because being a working mother seemed normal."

In 1956, Sam closed his retail store and turned it into a warehouse for the Vernon Specialties mail-order business. The manufacturing part of the business was worth around $1 million and the mail-order division around $1 million. While the business thrived, the marriage did not; Sam and Lillian were divorced after 20 years of marriage. Lillian chose to retain the mail-order business, a decision that later proved to have been an excellent one.

A year after her divorce, Lillian married Robbie Katz, a professional engineer and businessman who ran his own Lucite manufacturing business. With both her children in college, Lillian could begin to really devote herself to the company, which grew from $1 million in sales in 1970 to $137 million in sales by 1986—her 35th anniversary in business. In August 1987, just before the stock market crashed, Lillian Vernon went public, relinquishing 31 percent of the company to the public for $28 million. By 1989, sales had risen to $155 million; they climbed to $238 million in 1996 and reached $287.1 million in the year 2000. The past 15 years have seen sales advance nearly every year, while earnings suffered setbacks only twice. (In 1999, Vernon made less than in 1998.) During this period, revenues grew on an average of 9 percent annually, and operating profits grew 15 percent annually.

In developing the company from a million- to a multi-million-dollar business, Lillian found it necessary to hire professional managers, veterans of large corporate cultures, some of whom were unable to make the timely decisions required in the smaller company's fast-paced competitive situation. This opportunity allowed Lillian to identify both the entrepreneurial process through which the company began and grew and the management process necessary to help it continue to expand: "If I've learned anything over the past 35 years, it is the importance of drawing from the best qualities of both the entrepreneur and the professional manager. These are truly the left and right sides of the business brain, and they must harmonize in a healthy corporation."

With the day-to-day business operations in the hands of a competent manager, Lillian concentrates on finding the best products for her catalog. In this search, she and her 20 merchandising professionals travel approximately 16 weeks each year, with Lillian personally approving every item listed in the catalog. An item usually will not be carried unless someone she knows would like it or use it. Lillian was one of the first to handle goods from mainland China, after completing a visit there in the 1970s.

Even with the time required for selecting the items in the catalog, Lillian still is personally involved in every aspect of the company's operation. As she puts it,

"You pay attention to the details that really can't be fixed except by you—the ones that are going to kill you." She signs checks, reviews and helps write copy, and approves the catalog photos. The copy accompanying the catalog items is renowned in the industry.

Today, Lillian's son David is vice president and director of public affairs. The Lillian Vernon Corporation has grown from an initial investment of $2,000 to a publicly traded company with 2000 sales, as previously stated, of $287.1 million. Evolving from a $495 magazine ad for a personalized purse and belt, the company now introduces more than 3,000 new products each year. In 2000, the Lillian Vernon Corporation mailed 33 editions of its catalogs with a total circulation of over 178 million. In fiscal 2000, the company received 4.6 million orders averaging $55. The company now includes the New Company, Inc., a wholesale division that makes brass items; Lillian Vernon International in Italy and Hong Kong; Lillian Vernon; The Store in Rye, New York; and a state-of-the-art, fully automated 454,000-square-foot fulfillment center, including 123,552 square feet of warehouse space and a mainframe computer used for inventory control, as well as numerous outlet stores in New York, Delaware, South Carolina, Virginia, and the Washington, DC, suburbs. In addition to choosing the right items to showcase in each catalog, Lillian admits that due to intense competition, they must utilize technology to supplement their efforts. The firm relies totally on some form of technology to deal with the large volume of orders, complex offerings, and demographic modeling to track and predict customer behavior and buying patterns.

Lillian Katz adamantly supports other entrepreneurial efforts. Many of the companies that supply her catalog items are owned by fellow entrepreneurs. In one speech, she urged the financial community to take a risk on an entrepreneur: "You are investing in potential, which can pay tremendous dividends." She sits on the board of several charities and foundations, is a member of the Women's Forum and the Committee of 200 (both organizations of the brightest "fast-track" female executives in the country), is the chairperson of the White House National Business Women's Council, and is the first female member of the American Business Conference. Lillian was named to the Direct Marketing Association Hall of Fame in 1994 and was named one of Retailing's Entrepreneurs of the Year in 1992. The success of the Lillian Vernon Corporation lies primarily in the dedication and hard work of its founder, Lillian Katz: "Hard work, long hours, and personal sacrifice are just some of the disciplines necessary to achieve this [success], but the end rewards are worth it!" It also required a pioneering instinct. In addition to introducing personalized mail order in 1951, Lillian has indelibly influenced direct marketing by pioneering deferred billing and credit purchasing as well as being one of the first to offer online purchasing through the Internet. In 1999, Lillian Vernon continued to innovate, successfully launching *www.lillianvernon.com*, a state-of-the-art online catalog. Vernon also successfully introduced Lillian Vernon Gardening catalogs, another specialty offering that added to the Lilly's Kids, Personalized Gift, Neat Ideas for an Organized Life, Christmas Memories and Favorites catalogs already available. Lillian Vernon Katz's goals continue to be expansive; she stated that she would continue "striving to have a Lillian Vernon product in every household" in the new millennium.

Lillian Katz exhibits one profile of an entrepreneur, while others that appear in this book present different types. Is there an exact entrepreneurial profile in terms

of characteristics and background? This chapter addresses this question by looking at an individual's feelings about control, independence, and willingness to take
risks; one's family, education, and occupational backgrounds; motivation; skills;
male versus female entrepreneurs; entrepreneurs versus inventors; and general
entrepreneurial profiles.

ƒ◐

ENTREPRENEURIAL FEELINGS

Although Lillian Katz is indeed a very successful entrepreneur, she is not a typical
entrepreneur. Neither is anyone else. There is really no such thing as a "true entrepreneurial profile." Entrepreneurs come from a variety of educational backgrounds,
family situations, and work experiences. A potential entrepreneur may presently be
a nurse, secretary, assembly line worker, salesperson, mechanic, homemaker, manager, or engineer. A potential entrepreneur can be male or female and of any race or
nationality.

Locus of Control

One concern people have when they consider forming a new venture is whether
they will be able to sustain the drive and energy required not only to overcome the
inertia in forming something new but also to manage the new enterprise and make
it grow. Are you driven by an inner need to succeed and win? You can make an initial assessment by answering the 10 questions in Table 3.1. After answering these
questions, determine whether you are internally or externally driven by comparing
your answers with the responses below. Answering Yes to questions 4, 5, 8, 9, and
10 indicates that you possess the internal control aspect of being an entrepreneur.
Yes answers to questions 1, 2, 3, 6, and 7 indicate that you are more geared toward
external controls, which may inhibit your entrepreneurial tendencies and ability to
sustain drive.

In evaluating these results and your internal-external control dimension, keep
in mind that research is not conclusive about the role of *locus of control* in entrepreneurship. For example, only three of the nine research studies of Rotter's

locus of control   An attribute indicating the sense of
control that a person has over life

internality-externality (I-E) dimensions of entrepreneurs
depicted them as having a sense of control over their
lives, that is, being internals. One study indicated that entrepreneurial intentions were associated with internality, and another reported a
positive correlation between career success and internality.[1] Two studies of entrepreneurs under stress had mixed results. Some entrepreneurs under stress shifted
toward greater internality, while others shifted toward greater externality. Studies
of 31 entrepreneurs in St. Louis indicated that more successful entrepreneurs
were decidedly internal, and that entrepreneurs overall were more internal than
the general populace, but not more so than male managers.[2] Although internal beliefs appear to differentiate entrepreneurs from the general public, they do not
differentiate entrepreneurs from managers since both have a tendency toward internality.

TABLE 3.1	**Checklist for Feelings about Control**		
1.	Do you often feel "That's just the way things are and there's nothing I can do about it"?	____ Yes	____ No
2.	When things go right and are terrific for you, do you think, "It's mostly luck!"?	____ Yes	____ No
3.	Do you think you should go into business or do something with your time for pay because everything you read these days is urging you in that direction?	____ Yes	____ No
4.	Do you know that if you decide to do something, you'll do it and nothing can stop you?	____ Yes	____ No
5.	Even though it's scary to try something new, are you the kind who tries it?	____ Yes	____ No
6.	Your friends, spouse, and mother tell you that it's foolish of you to want a career. Have you listened to them and stayed home all these years?	____ Yes	____ No
7.	Do you think it's important for everyone to like you?	____ Yes	____ No
8.	When you do a good job, is your pleasure in a job well done satisfaction enough?	____ Yes	____ No
9.	If you want something, do you ask for it rather than wait for someone to notice you and "just give it to you"?	____ Yes	____ No
10.	Even though people tell you "it can't be done," do you have to find out for yourself?	____ Yes	____ No

Source: Reprinted with the permission of Lexington Books, an imprint of Macmillan Publishing Company, from *The Woman Entrepreneur,* by Robert D. Hisrich and Candida G. Brush. © 1985 by Lexington Books, p. 6.

Feelings about Independence and Need for Achievement

Closely related to this feeling of control is the *need for independence.* An entrepreneur is generally the type of person who needs to do things in his or her own way and has a difficult time working for someone else. To evaluate your feelings on independence, answer the questions in Table 3.2. After completing the questions, compare your answers with those below. Yes answers to questions 1, 4, 5, 8, 9, and 10 indicate that you do not have a strong need for independence.

need for independence Being one's own boss—one of the strongest needs of an entrepreneur

An even more controversial characteristic is the entrepreneur's *need for achievement.* McClelland's work regarding this desire identified psychological characteristics present in entrepreneurs.[3] He specified the three following attributes from his overall theory of the need for achievement (*n* Ach) as characteristics of entrepreneurs: (1) individual responsibility for solving problems, setting goals, and reaching these goals through their own efforts; (2) moderate risk taking as a function of skill, not chance; and (3) knowledge of results of decision/task accomplishment. McClelland's conclusion that a high *n* Ach leads individuals to engage in entrepreneurial behavior sparked several studies, the results of which are inconclusive; some studies report that there is a relationship between *n* Ach and entrepreneurs, while others do not. Perhaps a modification of McClelland's concept, complete with a different set of measurements, may result in a better understanding of the relationship between achievement and entrepreneurship.[4]

need for achievement An individual's need to be recognized

TABLE 3.2	Checklist for Feelings about Independence		
1. I hate to go shopping for clothes alone.		____ Yes	____ No
2. If my friends won't go to a movie I want to see, I'll go by myself.		____ Yes	____ No
3. I want to be financially independent.		____ Yes	____ No
4. I often need to ask other people's opinions before I decide on important things.		____ Yes	____ No
5. I'd rather have other people decide where to go on a social evening out.		____ Yes	____ No
6. When I know I'm in charge, I don't apologize; I just do what has to be done.		____ Yes	____ No
7. I'll speak up for an unpopular cause if I believe in it.		____ Yes	____ No
8. I'm afraid to be different.		____ Yes	____ No
9. I want the approval of others.		____ Yes	____ No
10. I usually wait for people to call me to go places, rather than intrude on them.		____ Yes	____ No

Source: Reprinted with the permission of Lexington Books, an imprint of Macmillan Publishing Company, from *The Woman Entrepreneur*, by Robert D. Hisrich and Candida G. Brush. © 1985 by Lexington Books, p. 7.

Risk Taking

Virtually all recent definitions of entrepreneurs mention a risk-taking component. Risk taking—whether financial, social, or psychological—is part of the entrepreneurial process. You can assess your risk-taking behavior by answering the questions in Table 3.3 and then comparing your responses with those below. If you answered Yes to questions 2, 5, and 9, you may need to develop a greater willingness to take risks. Many studies of risk taking in entrepreneurship have focused on the component of a general propensity for risk taking. Since no conclusive causal relationships have been determined, it has not yet been empirically established that a risk-taking propensity is a distinguishing characteristic of entrepreneurs. Although this may be a function of the research instrument (Kogan-Wallach CDQ is the research instrument predominantly used), little can yet be concluded from the results of the empirical research on the risk-taking propensities of entrepreneurs of either gender.

ENTREPRENEUR BACKGROUND AND CHARACTERISTICS

Although many aspects of an entrepreneur's background have been explored, only a few have differentiated the entrepreneur from the general populace of managers. The background areas explored include childhood family environment, education, personal values, age, and work history.

Childhood Family Environment

Specific research topics concerning the family environment of the entrepreneur include birth order, parents' occupation(s) and *social status*, and relationship with parents. The studies of birth order have had conflicting results since Henning and Jardim found that female executives tend to be the firstborn.[5] Being the firstborn or an only

social status   The level at which an individual is viewed by society

TABLE 3.3	**Checklist for Willingness to Take Risks**		
1.	Can you take risks with money, that is, invest, and not know the outcome?	____ Yes	____ No
2.	Do you taken an umbrella with you every time you travel? A hot water bottle? A thermometer?	____ Yes	____ No
3.	If you're frightened of something, will you try to conquer the fear?	____ Yes	____ No
4.	Do you like trying new foods, new places, and totally new experiences?	____ Yes	____ No
5.	Do you need to know the answer before you'll ask the question?	____ Yes	____ No
6.	Have you taken a risk in the last six months?	____ Yes	____ No
7.	Can you walk up to a total stranger and strike up a conversation?	____ Yes	____ No
8.	Have you ever intentionally traveled an unfamiliar route?	____ Yes	____ No
9.	Do you need to know that it's been done already before you're willing to try it?	____ Yes	____ No
10.	Have you ever gone out on a blind date?	____ Yes	____ No

Source: Reprinted with the permission of Lexington Books, an imprint of Macmillan Publishing Company, from *The Woman Entrepreneur*, by Robert D. Hisrich and Candida G. Brush. © 1985 by Lexington Books.

child is postulated to result in the child receiving special attention and thereby developing more self-confidence. For example, in a national sample of 408 female entrepreneurs, Hisrich and Brush found 50 percent to be firstborn.[6] Conversely, in many studies of male and female entrepreneurs, the firstborn effect has not been present. Since the relationship to entrepreneurship has not been established, further research on the firstborn effect is still needed to determine if it really does have an effect on an individual's becoming an entrepreneur.[7]

In terms of the occupation of the entrepreneurs' parents, there is strong evidence that entrepreneurs tend to have self-employed or entrepreneurial fathers. Female entrepreneurs are as likely to report self-employment or entrepreneurial fathers as male entrepreneurs. Having a father who is self-employed provides a strong inspiration for the entrepreneur. The independent nature and flexibility of self-employment exemplified by the father is ingrained at an early age. As one entrepreneur stated, "My father was so consumed by the venture he started and provided such a strong example, it never occurred to me to go to work for anyone else." This feeling of independence is often further enforced by an entrepreneurial mother.

The overall parental relationship to the child, regardless of whether they are entrepreneurs, is perhaps the most important aspect of the childhood family environment in establishing the desirability of entrepreneurial activity in an individual. Parents of entrepreneurs need to be supportive and encourage independence, achievement, and responsibility. This supportive relationship of the parents (particularly the father) appears to be the most important for female entrepreneurs. Female entrepreneurs tend to grow up in middle- to upper-class environments, where families are likely to be relatively child centered and tend to be similar to their fathers in personality.[8]

Education

The educational level of the entrepreneur has also received significant research attention. Although some may feel that entrepreneurs are less educated than the general population, research findings indicate that this is clearly not the case. Education was important in the upbringing of the entrepreneur. Its importance is reflected not only in the level of education obtained but in the fact that it continues to play a major role in helping to cope with problems entrepreneurs confront. Although a formal education is not necessary for starting a new business—as is reflected in the success of such high school dropouts as Andrew Carnegie, William Durant, Henry Ford, and William Lear—it does provide a good background, particularly when it is related to the field of the venture. In terms of type and quality of education, female entrepreneurs previously experienced some disadvantage. Although nearly 70 percent of all women entrepreneurs have a college degree, with many having graduate degrees, the most popular college majors are English, psychology, education, and sociology. Few have degrees in engineering, science, or math.[9] However, a mere count of the number of women in business and engineering schools indicates that the numbers have significantly increased. Both male and female entrepreneurs have cited an educational need in the areas of finance, strategic planning, marketing (particularly distribution), and management. The ability to deal with people and communicate clearly in the written and spoken word is also important in any entrepreneurial activity.

Personal Values

Although there have been many studies indicating that personal values are important for entrepreneurs, frequently these studies fail to indicate that entrepreneurs can be differentiated from managers, unsuccessful entrepreneurs, or even the general populace with regard to these values. For example, although entrepreneurs tend to be effective leaders, this does not distinguish them from successful managers. Although personal value scales for leadership—as well as those scales for support, aggression, benevolence, conformity, creativity, veracity, and resource seeking—are important for identifying entrepreneurs, they also identify successful individuals. Studies have shown that the entrepreneur has a different set of attitudes about the nature of the management process and business in general.[10] The nature of the enterprise, opportunism, institution, and individuality of the entrepreneur diverge significantly from the bureaucratic organization and the planning, rationality, and predictability of its managers. Perhaps all these traits, not individual ones, are encompassed in a winning image that allows the entrepreneur to create and enhance the new venture. In one study, winning emerged as the term best describing companies having an excellent reputation.[11] Five consensus characteristics found across consumer and leadership groups include superior product quality; quality service to customers; flexibility, or the ability to adapt to changes in the marketplace; high-caliber management; and honesty and ethics in business practices. A successful entrepreneur is frequently characterized as a winner; perhaps winning is a prerequisite for his or her actually becoming one.

Another aspect of personal values that is very important to entrepreneurs is ethics and ethical behavior on the part of the entrepreneur as well as stockholders. These concerns are reflected in the Ethics box.

When is it permissible to tell a lie? In the dictionary, a lie is a "false statement or piece of information deliberately presented as being true" (*American Heritage Dictionary of the English Language*, 1976). Knowledge and intention are both central to the concept of lying; there must be an intention to mislead others. For most of us to consider a statement as a "lie," we maintain that the person speaking must know the relative truth or falsehood of the statement and must intend to deceive the listeners. At the same time, however, some deliberately deceptive statements are considered acceptable by businesspersons. Is there a difference in the following two examples?

1. You have just been informed that some highly toxic by-products from your plant have been improperly stored in steel drums. Fortunately, your company responded quickly and remedied the situation before there was "too much" leakage. While you have been assured that this unfortunate incident poses no danger to public health, the local media have somehow heard of a potential toxic leak and have requested an interview. Your attorney has cautioned you that even though your people acted properly and quickly, there is little doubt that you will be sued, and under no circumstances should you admit to liability. What should you do? Is it all right to say that there was no leakage and consequently no danger?

2. Your company provides specialty steel prefabrication products for large construction projects. A $20 million order has just arrived, and you need final approval from a local government official. During a meeting in the official's office he verbally requests a $20,000 bribe. You are surprised because the official policy in the country was recently changed under a reformist regime, making bribes strictly forbidden. You comment that it is against U.S. law and your company rules to make any payments. The official shrugs slightly and says, "Fine, we will give the order to a competitor." It happens that the battery-powered tape recorder you generally use to dictate memos following meetings is in your briefcase. While it has not been turned on, of course, the official doesn't know this. Is it OK for you to take the tape recorder out of your briefcase, show it to the official, and say, "It is a policy of our company to record all conversations with government officials in Central and South America. Do you want this tape to be given to the minister in charge of your agency, or do you want to sign the necessary papers for our import permit?"

Sources: The second paragraph is adapted from Larue Hosmer, *The Ethics of Management* (Boston: Richard D. Irwin, 1996), p. 51. The third paragraph is adapted from Professor Joanne Ciulla of the

Age

The relationship of age to the entrepreneurial career process has also been carefully researched.[12] In evaluating these results, it is important to differentiate between entrepreneurial age (the age of the entrepreneur reflected in the experience) and chronological age. As discussed in the next section, entrepreneurial experience is one of the best predictors of success, particularly when the new venture is in the same field as the previous business experience.

In terms of chronological age, most entrepreneurs initiate their entrepreneurial careers between the ages of 22 and 45. Although a career can be initiated before or after these years, it is not as likely because an entrepreneur requires experience, financial support, and a high energy level in order to launch and manage a new venture successfully. Although an average age has little meaning, earlier starts in an entrepreneurial career are better than later ones. Also, there are milestone years every five years (25, 30, 35, 40, and 45) when an individual is more inclined to start an entrepreneurial career. As one entrepreneur succinctly stated, "I felt it was now or never in terms of starting a new venture when I approached 30." Generally, male entrepreneurs tend to start their first significant venture in the early 30s, while women entrepreneurs tend to do so in their middle 30s.

Work History

Work history not only can be a negative displacement in the decision to launch a new entrepreneurial venture but also plays a role in the growth and eventual success of the new venture. While dissatisfaction with various aspects of one's job—such as a lack of challenge or promotional opportunities, as well as frustration and boredom—often motivates the launching of a new venture, previous technical and industry experience is important once the decision to launch has been made. Experience in the following areas is particularly important: financing, product or service development, manufacturing, development of distribution channels, and preparation of a marketing plan.

work history   The past work experience of an individual

As the venture becomes established and starts growing, managerial experience and skills become increasingly important. Although most ventures start with managing one's own activities and those of a few part- or full-time employees, as the number of employees increases along with the size, complexity, and geographic diversity of the business, the entrepreneur's managerial skills come more and more into play. This is particularly true when other managers are added.

In addition to managerial experience, entrepreneurial experience becomes increasingly important as the complexity of the venture increases. Most entrepreneurs indicate that their most significant venture was not their first one. Throughout their entrepreneurial careers, they are exposed to more new venture opportunities than individuals in other career paths.

MOTIVATION

What motivates an entrepreneur to take all the risks and launch a new venture, pursuing an entrepreneurial career against the overwhelming odds of failure? Although many people are interested in starting a new venture and even have the background and financial resources to do so, few decide to actually start their own business. Individuals who are comfortable and secure in a job situation, have a family to support, and prefer their present lifestyle and reasonably predictable leisure time often do not want to take the risks associated with venturing out alone.

Although the *motivations* for venturing out alone vary greatly, the reason cited most frequently for becoming an entrepreneur is independence—not wanting to work for anyone else. This desire to be one's own boss is what drives both male and female entrepreneurs around the world to accept all the social, psychological, and financial risks and to work the large number of hours needed to create and develop a successful new venture. Nothing less than this motivation would be enough to inspire the entrepreneur to endure all the frustrations and hardships. Other motivating factors differ between male and female entrepreneurs and vary by country. Money is the second reason for starting a new venture for men, whereas job satisfaction, achievement, opportunity, and money are the reasons in rank order for women. These second-order motivations reflect, in part, the work and family situation as well as the role model of the entrepreneur.

motivations   What causes people to do something

ROLE MODELS AND SUPPORT SYSTEMS

One of the most important factors influencing entrepreneurs in their career path is their choice of a *role model*.[13] Role models can be parents, brothers or sisters, other relatives, or other entrepreneurs. Successful entrepreneurs are viewed frequently as catalysts by potential entrepreneurs. As one entrepreneur succinctly stated, "After evaluating Ted and his success as an entrepreneur, I knew I was much smarter and could do a better job. So I started my own business."

role models   Individuals influencing an entrepreneur's career choice and style

Role models can also serve in a supportive capacity as mentors during and after the launch of a new venture. An entrepreneur needs a strong support and advisory system in every phase of the new venture. This support system is perhaps most crucial during the start-up phase, as it provides information, advice, and guidance on such matters as organizational structure, obtaining needed financial resources, marketing, and market segments. Since entrepreneurship is a social role embedded in a social context, it is important that an entrepreneur establish connections to these support resources early in the new venture formation process.

As initial contacts and connections expand, they form a network with similar properties prevalent in a social network—density (the extensiveness of ties between the two individuals) and centrality (the total distance of the entrepreneur to all other individuals and the total number of individuals in the network). The strength of the ties between the entrepreneur and any individual in the network is dependent upon the frequency, level, and reciprocity of the relationship. The more frequent, in-depth, and mutually beneficial a relationship, the stronger and more durable the network between the entrepreneur and the individual.[14] Although most networks are not formally organized, an informal network for moral and professional support still greatly benefits the entrepreneur.

Moral-Support Network

It is important for each entrepreneur to establish a *moral-support network* of family and friends—a cheering squad. This cheering squad plays a critical role during the many difficult and lonely times that occur throughout the entrepreneurial process. Most entrepreneurs indicate that their spouses are their biggest supporters and allow them to devote the excessive amounts of time necessary to the new venture.

moral-support network   Individuals who give psychological support to an entrepreneur

Friends also play key roles in a moral-support network. Not only can friends provide advice that is often more honest than that received from other sources, but they also provide encouragement, understanding, and even assistance. Entrepreneurs can confide in friends without fear of criticism.

Finally, relatives (children, parents, grandparents, aunts, and uncles) can also be strong sources of moral support, particularly if they are also entrepreneurs. As one entrepreneur stated, "The total family support I received was the key to my success. Having an understanding cheering squad giving me encouragement allowed me to persist through the many difficulties and problems."

Professional-Support Network

In addition to moral encouragement, the entrepreneur needs advice and counsel throughout the establishment of the new venture. This advice can be obtained from *professional-support network*   Individuals who help the entrepreneur in business activities

a mentor, business associates, trade associations, or personal affiliations—all members of a *professional-support network*.

A mentor–protégé relationship is an excellent avenue for securing needed professional advice, as well as providing an additional source of moral support. Many entrepreneurs indicate that they have mentors. How does one find a mentor? This task sounds much more difficult than it really is. Since a mentor is a coach, a sounding board, and an advocate—someone with whom the entrepreneur can share both problems and successes—the individual selected needs to be an expert in the field. An entrepreneur can start the "mentor-finding process" by preparing a list of experts in various fields—such as in the fundamental business activities of finance, marketing, accounting, law, or management—who can provide the practical "how-to" advice needed. From this list, an individual who can offer the most assistance can be identified and contacted. If the selected individual is willing to act as a mentor, he or she should be periodically apprised of the progress of the business so that a relationship can gradually develop.

Another good source of advice can be cultivated by establishing a network of business associates. This group can be composed of self-employed individuals who have experienced starting a business; clients or buyers of the venture's product or service; experts such as consultants, lawyers, or accountants; and the venture's suppliers. Clients or buyers are a particularly important group to cultivate. This group represents the source of revenue to the venture and is the best provider of word-of-mouth advertising. There is nothing better than word-of-mouth advertising from satisfied customers to help establish a winning business reputation and promote goodwill. Customers, excited about the entrepreneur's concern with the product or service fulfilling their need, provide valuable feedback on the present product or service as well as on new products or services being developed.

Suppliers are another important component in a professional-support network since they help to establish credibility with creditors and customers. A new venture needs to establish a solid track record with suppliers in order to build a good relationship and to ensure the adequate availability of materials and other supplies. Suppliers can also provide good information on the nature and trends, as well as competition, in the industry.

In addition to mentors and business associates, trade associations can offer an excellent professional-support network. Trade association members can be developed into a regional or national network and can be carefully cultivated to keep the new venture competitive. Trade associations keep up with new developments and can provide overall industry data.

Finally, personal affiliations of the entrepreneur can also be a valuable part of a professional-support network. Affiliations developed with individuals through shared hobbies, participation in sporting events, clubs, civic involvements, and school alumni groups are excellent potential sources of referrals, advice, and information.

Each entrepreneur needs to establish both a moral- and a professional-support network. These contacts provide confidence, support, advice, and information. As one entrepreneur stated, "In your own business, you are all alone. There is a definite need to establish support groups to share problems with and gain overall support for the new venture."

MALE VERSUS FEMALE ENTREPRENEURS

There has been a significant growth in female self-employment, with women now starting new ventures at three times the rate of men. By forming over 70 percent of

As Seen in *Business Week* . . .

According to a recent *Business Week* story of the six top entrepreneurs mentioned, one was a woman—Kate Spade—and one was a minority—Robert Knowling, Jr.

Most women put their money in their handbags: that's where trendy designer Kate Spade is making hers. Spade's line of elegant and whimsical bags, which range from pink herringbone carryalls and velvet tiger-print shoppers to simple nylon totes, are among fashion's hottest must-haves. A former *Mademoiselle* magazine editor, Spade, 37, and her husband Andy, 37, started Kate Spade in 1993 with $35,000 of his 401(k) savings. Midwestern innocence meets European runways in Kansas City native "Katie," who favors hoop skirts and kitten heels. She has scored big by making handbags fashionable as well as functional. Last year, sales doubled to $50 million as Kate Spade branched out into stationery, shoes, and a line of men's bags from creative director Andy. In February, the company pocketed $33.6 million when Neiman Marcus Group Inc. bought a 56 percent stake.

As CEO of Covad Communications, Robert E. Knowling, Jr., has turned copper phone wires into gold. Knowling, 44, runs the most successful of a crop of new phone companies that sell speedy digital Internet connections. Surging demand has sent Covad's revenues skyrocketing, from $5.3 million in 1998 to an expected $60 million in 1999, though the company is still in the red. Covad's subscribers should grow to 290,000 this year, up from 55,000 in 1999. Knowling—a veteran of the Baby Bells who joined the three-year-old Covad in 1998—oversaw its IPO last January. The stock has since more than quintupled, to around 60, giving Covad a market cap of $5.6 billion. For Knowling, who grew up in poverty in rural Missouri, the sixth of 13 children, entrepreneurialism has brought sweet success indeed.

Source: "The Top Entrepreneurs," *Business Week*, January 10, 2000, pp. 80–81.

all new businesses, women now own over 8.5 million small businesses employing over 17 million people, an increase of over 45 percent since 1990. Much is known about the characteristics of entrepreneurs, their motivations, backgrounds, families, educational background, occupational experiences, and the problems of both female and male entrepreneurs.

Although the characteristics of both male and female entrepreneurs are generally very similar, female entrepreneurs differ in terms of motivation, business skills, and occupational backgrounds.[15] Factors in the start-up process of a business for male and female entrepreneurs are also different, especially in such areas as support systems, sources of funds, and problems.[16] The major differences between male and female entrepreneurs are summarized in Table 3.4. As indicated, men are often motivated by the drive to control their own destinies, to make things happen. This drive often stems from disagreements with their bosses or a feeling that they can run things better. In contrast, women tend to be more motivated by the need for achievement arising from job frustration in not being allowed to perform and grow in their previous situation.

Departure points and reasons for starting the business are similar for both men and women. Both generally have a strong interest and experience in the area of their venture. However, for men, the transition from a past occupation to the new venture is often facilitated when the new venture is an outgrowth of a present job, sideline, or hobby. Women, on the other hand, often leave a previous occupation with a high level of job frustration as well as enthusiasm for the new venture rather than practical ex-

departure points The activities occurring when the venture is started

75

TABLE 3.4	**Comparison between Male and Female Entrepreneurs**	
Characteristic	Male Entrepreneurs	Female Entrepreneurs
Motivation	Achievement—strive to make things happen Personal independence—self-image as it relates to status through their role in the corporation is unimportant Job satisfaction arising from the desire to be in control.	Achievement—accomplishment of a goal Independence—to do it alone
Departure point	Dissatisfaction with present job Sideline in college, sideline to present job, or outgrowth of present job Discharge or layoff Opportunity for acquisition	Job frustration Interest in and recognition of opportunity in the area Change in personal circumstances
Sources of funds	Personal assets and savings Bank financing Investors Loans from friends and family	Personal assets and savings Personal loans
Occupational background	Experience in line of work Recognized specialist or one who has gained a high level of achievement in the field Competent in a variety of business functions	Experience in area of business Middle-management or administrative-level experience in the field Service-related occupational background
Personality characteristics	Opinionated and persuasive Goal oriented Innovative and idealistic High level of self-confidence Enthusiastic and energetic Must be own boss	Flexible and tolerant Goal oriented Creative and realistic Medium level of self-confidence Enthusiastic and energetic Ability to deal with the social and economic environment
Background	Age when starting venture: 25–35 Father was self-employed College educated—degree in business or technical area (usually engineering) Firstborn child	Age when starting venture: 35–45 Father was self-employed College educated—degree in liberal arts Firstborn child
Support groups	Friends, professional acquaintances (lawyers, accountants) Business associates Spouse	Close friends Spouse Family Women's professional groups Trade associations
Type of business started	Manufacturing or construction	Service related—educational services, consulting, or public relations

perience, thereby making the transition somewhat more difficult. Sometimes what ends up as a business venture for women begins as a personal search. Such was the case for Kimberly Porrazzo, who planned to return to her previous job after her pregnancy. Frustrated in her search for a good nanny, she decided to create The Nanny Kit and also start the Southern California Nanny Center, a source of advice that houses an informational database maintained and updated by Porrazzo.

Start-up financing is another area where male and female entrepreneurs differ (see Table 3.4). Whereas men often list investors, bank loans, or personal loans in addition to personal funds as sources of start-up capital, women usually rely solely on personal assets or savings. This points out a major problem for many women entrepreneurs—obtaining financing and lines of credit.

Occupationally, there are also vast differences between men and women entrepreneurs. Although both groups tend to have experience in the field of their ventures, men more often have experience in manufacturing, finance, or technical areas. Most women, in contrast, usually have administrative experience that is limited to the middle-management level, often in service-related areas.

In terms of personality, there are strong similarities between men and women entrepreneurs. Both tend to be energetic, goal oriented, and independent. However, men are often more confident and less flexible and tolerant than women, which can result in very different management styles.

The backgrounds of men and women entrepreneurs tend to be similar, except that most women are a little older when they embark on their ventures (35 to 40 versus 25 to 35), and their educational backgrounds are different. Men often have studied in technical or business-related areas, whereas women frequently have a liberal arts education. Also, many women business owners are empty nesters or single and, as a result, need to be concerned about business insurance as well as personal life insurance.

Support groups also provide a point of contrast between the two. Men usually list outside advisors (lawyers, accountants) as their most important supporters, with the spouse being second. Women list their spouses first, close friends second, and business associates third. Moreover, women usually rely heavily on a variety of sources for support and information, such as trade associations and women's groups, whereas men are not as likely to have as many outside supporters.

Finally, businesses started by men and women entrepreneurs differ in terms of the nature of the venture. Whereas women are more likely to start a business in a service-related area such as retail, public relations, or educational services, men are likely to enter manufacturing, construction, or high-technology fields. The result is often smaller women-owned businesses with lower net earnings. However, opportunities for women are greater than ever, with women starting businesses at a faster rate than men in the fastest growing area of the economy—the service area.

MINORITY ENTREPRENEURSHIP

Research on entrepreneurs defined by ethnicity or race has been sporadic. The problem is understanding the differences in the behavior of various ethnic groups in the context of the environment and the economic opportunities (or lack thereof) available in the societal context.

Most of the sparse literature dealing with minority entrepreneurship has focused on the characteristics of the group under study. Several studies have looked at the ownership rates and trends among minority groups. In terms of ownership, one study found the lowest participation rate for African Americans, the second highest but fastest growing for Hispanics, and the highest rate of ownership participation for Asians.[17] One of the earliest studies comparing African American and white business owners found more similarities than differences and found that white owners were less likely to be separated or divorced, more likely to have graduated from college, and had been in business longer. They also base their business on a special idea.[18] A later study found that minority business owners tended to be younger or better educated but otherwise were from family backgrounds similar to those of white business owners.[19] A study of minority and nonminority women entrepreneurs found significant differences only on six of nine personality measures. Also, the typical minority woman was married, older, started her business at an older age, and was less likely to be a college graduate.[20] Exploring just minority business owners, one study found that the typical minority business owner was the oldest child in a blue-collar family, was married, had children, had a college degree and related business experience, and was primarily motivated by achievement, opportunity, and job satisfaction.[21]

A study of African American and white business owners in three urban areas found that African American business owners had fewer years of education and business experience. Even though African American businesses were smaller and less profitable, there were no differences in survival rates between African American–and white-owned businesses.[22] Another study comparing different minority entrepreneurs as well as business start-ups found that Asian business owners (84 percent) were much more likely to have a college education than African Americans (54 percent), Hispanics (51 percent), and Native Americans (33 percent).[23]

The study of ethnic entrepreneurship has revealed differences among ethnic groups and instances where some ethnic entrepreneurs have access to established community resources. In order to truly understand the nature and role of this aspect of entrepreneurship, future research needs to focus on the overall process of ethnic entrepreneurs developing and maintaining an enterprise. In spite of this lack of research, entrepreneurship has been significantly increasing among Asians, African Americans, Hispanics, and Native Americans. For example, in one time period the number of African American–owned businesses rose an impressive 46 percent compared with the total number of businesses, which increased by 26 percent. During this same time period, the sales of these African America–owned businesses increased 63 percent compared with a 50 percent increase for all firms. With an increase in the encouragement of entrepreneurship among minority groups, particularly in their formative high school years, and the increase in the number of role models, the result will most likely be that more minorities will select entrepreneurship as a viable career option. This is reflected in the increasing number of websites aimed squarely at minority entrepreneurs such as Latin Exchange, SBA Office of Minority Enterprise Development, National Black Business Trade Association, and the Minority Business Development Agency.

ENTREPRENEURS VERSUS INVENTORS

There is a great deal of confusion about the nature of an entrepreneur as opposed to an inventor and the similarities and differences between the two. An *inventor*, an individual who creates something for the first time, is a highly driven individual motivated by his or her own work and personal ideas. Besides being highly creative, an inventor tends to be well educated, with college or, most often, postgraduate degrees; has family, education, and occupational experiences that contribute to creative development and free thinking; is a problem solver able to reduce complex problems to simple ones; has a very high level of self-confidence; is willing to take risks; and has the ability to tolerate ambiguity and uncertainty.[24] A typical inventor places a high premium on being an achiever and measures achievement by the number of inventions developed and the number of patents granted. An inventor is not likely to view monetary benefits as a measure of success.

inventor   An individual who creates something new

As indicated in this profile, an inventor differs considerably from an entrepreneur. Whereas an entrepreneur falls in love with the organization (the new venture) and will do almost anything to ensure its survival and growth, an inventor falls in love with the invention and will only reluctantly modify the invention to make it more commercially feasible. The development of a new venture based on an inventor's work often requires the expertise of an entrepreneur and a team approach to new venture creation.

GENERAL NONENTREPRENEURIAL PROFILES

In addition to inventors, there are several other personality types that have a difficult time in successfully creating and managing a new venture. These personality types have characteristics that can lead even the brightest entrepreneur with the best idea into bankruptcy, a concern of resource providers such as venture capitalists, bankers, suppliers, and customers. Eight of these personality types are profiled in Table 3.5: Shotgun Sam, Simplicity Sue, Prima Donna Paul, Ralph the Rookie, Meticulous Mary, Underdog Ed, Hidden Agenda Harry, and Inventor Irving. Each has certain flaws, such as lacking follow-through (Shotgun Sam), making everything much simpler than it really is (Simplicity Sue), falling in love with the idea itself (Prima Donna

TABLE 3.5   Eight Entrepreneurial Profiles

Profile	Description
Shotgun Sam	An entrepreneurial type who quickly identifies new promising business opportunities but rarely, if ever, follows through on the opportunity to create a successful new venture.
Simplicity Sue	An entrepreneurial type who always thinks everything is a lot simpler and feels one can create a successful business through one or two easy solutions. Usually a great salesperson, this entrepreneur can make even the most improbable deal seem possible.
Prima Donna Paul	An entrepreneurial type so in love with his own idea that he feels everyone is out to take his idea and take advantage of him. This paranoia does not allow any trust to be established or help given.
Ralph the Rookie	An entrepreneurial type who is well grounded in theory but lacks real-world business experience.
Meticulous Mary	A perfectionist entrepreneurial type who is so used to having things under control that she cannot manage during a catastrophe and cannot handle periods of ambiguity and chaos.
Underdog Ed	An entrepreneurial type who is not comfortable with actually transforming the invention into a tangible business success. This entrepreneurial type likes to attend seminars and discuss problems but does not like putting things into action, so needs a strong managerial team.
Hidden Agenda Harry	An entrepreneur who does not have the right motives and objectives for developing and expediting a new enterprise.
Inventor Irving	An inventor more than an entrepreneur, who is more concerned with the invention itself rather creating and expediting a business.

Source: "8 Demons of Entrepreneurship," *Success* (March 1986), pp. 54–57.

Paul), lacking real-world experience (Ralph the Rookie), being a perfectionist (Meticulous Mary), lacking the ability to put things into concrete action (Underdog Ed), lacking the right motives (Hidden Agenda Harry), and loving creating more than doing (Inventor Irving). Although in moderation these tendencies pose no problems, an entrepreneur with an excess of any of these traits may need to modify them in order to have a higher probability of successfully launching a new venture.

IN REVIEW

Summary

Is there something that differentiates an entrepreneur from the rest of the population? This chapter outlines the current thinking and research related to identifying the unique characteristics of a person who successfully launches a new venture. Developing an understanding of the characteristics and background of individuals starting new ventures is an important step in encouraging potential entrepreneurs and improving their probability of success.

A typical entrepreneurial profile in terms of experience and family background has been more clearly defined. Adult encouragement, successful entrepreneurial parents who serve as role models, and a supportive relationship that encourages independence and achievement are factors strongly linked to later entrepreneurial behavior. Although there are personal characteristics and skills frequently present in successful entrepreneurs—such as leadership traits, creativity, opportunism, and intuition—so far no unique combination of traits, experiences, and acquired skills differentiates a successful entrepreneur from an unsuccessful one, or even from a manager.

The research clearly indicates that there are many variables involved in the decision to become an entrepreneur. There are many successful corporate business careers. Perhaps these individuals lack an appropriate role model or support system. Watching a peer face the challenges and overcome risks associated with a new venture start-up is frequently mentioned as a key influence in the entrepreneurial decision process. Although an individual can act as an inspiration to the new entrepreneur, a new venture is also in need of support from an individual or group providing information, advice, and guidance. There are many sources of support systems, starting with friends and family and moving into the wider circle of professional contacts, clients, and industry organizations.

Significant growth in the number of women employed outside the home has created a new field of research that is concerned with the question of whether female employees, managers, and entrepreneurs are different from their male counterparts. It is clear that male and female entrepreneurs have much in common. Although some of the background and personality characteristics are quite similar, there are striking differences between the sexes in terms of motivation, departure point, and business skills brought to the venture. The difference in the types of businesses started can be attributed in large part to differences in education and work history.

In developing a unique description of an entrepreneur, there are several personality types that appear to be only entrepreneurial. One of these is the inventor, who can take on the role of an entrepreneur if a business is started around the product invented. Care needs to be taken to ensure that the business is not second in importance to the invention itself. Other problem character traits include a lack of tenacity, perfectionism, the tendency to oversimplify, and paranoia.

Questions for Discussion

1. What is gained from analyzing the characteristics of an entrepreneur?
2. Recalling the definitions of entrepreneurship in Chapter 1, what characteristics would you expect to find in a "typical" entrepreneur? Compare these with the characteristics described in this chapter.
3. Discuss why the research work on entrepreneurs, using standardized tests, has not led to conclusive results.
4. What factors present in our society could account for the differences between male and female entrepreneurs today? How do you think men and women entrepreneurs will differ in 10 years?

Key Terms

departure points
inventor
locus of control
moral-support network
motivations
need for achievement

need for independence
professional-support network
role models
social status
work history

More Information—Net Addresses in This Chapter

Lillian Vernon
www.lillianvernon.com
IMPAC Medical Systems
www.impac.com
Southern California Nanny Source
www.sandcastleweb.com/nanny
Latin Exchange
www.latinexchange.com/resourcew.htm
Minority Business Development Agency
www.mbda.gov

National Center for American Indian
Enterprise Development
www.ncaied.org
SBA Office of Minority Enterprise
Development
www.sbaonline.sba.gov/MED
National Black Business Trade Association
http://homepages.infoseek.com

Selected Readings

Bates, Timothy. (1997). Financing Small Business Creation: The Case of Chinese and Korean Immigrant Entrepreneurs. *Journal of Business Venturing*, vol. 12, no. 2, pp. 109–24.

Supportive peer and community subgroups are not major sources of start-up capital for Korean and Chinese immigrants. The majority of all loan funds are raised by borrowing from financial institutions. The major single funding source is equity capital, which derives almost entirely from family wealth holdings. Controlling for firm and owner traits, nonminority and

Asian American nonimmigrant self-employed borrowers are shown to have greater access to loan sources than Korean and Chinese immigrants. High equity capital investment was proposed to offset this disadvantage.

Brush, Candida B. (1992). Research on Women Business Owners: Past Trends, a New Perspective, and Future Directions. *Entrepreneurship: Theory and Practice*, vol. 16, no. 4, pp. 5–30.

A review of 57 articles indicates that there are more differences than similarities between male- and female-owned businesses. Women perceive their businesses as cooperative networks of relationships rather than separate economic units, with the business being integrated into the women business owners' lives.

Ensley, Michael D; James W. Carland; Jo Ann C. Carland. (2000). Investigating the existence of the Lead Entrepreneur. *Journal of Small Business Management*, vol. 38, no. 4, pp. 59–77.

This research empirically confirmed the existence of lead entrepreneurs among macro-entrepreneurial firms and suggested that the strength of their strategic or entrepreneurial vision and their self-confidence set them apart from other entrepreneurial team members.

Fagenson, Ellen A.; and Eric C. Marcus. (1991). Perceptions of Sex Role Stereotypic Characteristics of Entrepreneurs: Women's Evaluations. *Entrepreneurship: Theory and Practice*, vol. 15, no. 4, pp. 33–47.

A survey found that women in female-headed companies gave greater weight to feminine attributes than women who worked in companies headed by men. Regardless of the sex of the head of the company, the women assigned more weight to masculine attributes in their profile of a successful entrepreneur.

Hisrich, Robert D. (1986). The Woman Entrepreneur: Characteristics, Skills, Problems, and Prescriptions for Success. In *The Art and Science of Entrepreneurship*. Cambridge, MA: Ballinger Publishing Co., pp. 61–84.

The findings of a nationwide survey indicate the characteristics of women entrepreneurs, their degree of management and other business skills, and the problems they encounter in starting and operating a business. Prescriptions for success set forth include establishing a track record, continuing education, previous experience, ability to set priorities in personal responsibilities, development of a support system, and determination.

Hisrich, Robert D.; and Candida G. Brush. (1985). Women and Minority Entrepreneurs: A Comparative Analysis. *Proceedings*, 1985 Conference on Entrepreneurship, pp. 566–87.

Based on surveys, women and minority entrepreneurs are profiled and compared based on demographic composition and background of the entrepreneurs, the nature of their business ventures, the skills and personalities, and the problems encountered in starting and operating the business.

Jackson, John E.; and Gretchen R. Rodkey. (1994). The Attitudinal Climate for Entrepreneurial Activity. *Public Opinion Quarterly*, vol. 58, no. 3, pp. 358–80.

A study examines the attitudes that, taken collectively within a region, may contribute to a climate that is conducive to and supportive of successful entrepreneurial activity. Four different components that characterize these attitudes are identified—the willingness to take risks and accept the possibility of failure, the perceived difficulty of starting new firms, the importance and respect accorded to new and small firms and their owners, and the socialization children are likely to receive from their parents. Pro-entrepreneurial attitudes are lower among individuals working in large organizations and among those who live in areas dominated by large organizations regardless of the size of the employer.

Kuratko, Donald F.; Jeffrey S. Hornsby, and Douglas W. Naffziger. (1997). An Examination of Owner's Goals in Sustaining Entrepreneurship. *Journal of Small Business Management*, vol. 35, no. 1, pp. 24–33.

The study investigated the existence of a set of goals that motivate entrepreneurs to sustain their business development efforts. A four-factor structure of goal statements was identified on the basis of the responses from 234 entrepreneurs. Motivating factors included extrinsic rewards, independence/autonomy, intrinsic rewards, and family security.

Langan-Fox, Janice; and Susanna Roth. (1995). Achievement Motivation and Female Entrepreneurs. *Journal of Occupational & Organizational Psychology,* vol. 68, no. 3, pp. 209–18.

A typology of the female entrepreneur was developed on the basis of psychological characteristics of 60 Australian founder businesswomen. A number of projective and self-report measures were used to assess multiple dimensions of personality. Analyses revealed three psychological types of female entrepreneurs: the need achiever entrepreneur, the pragmatic entrepreneur, and the managerial entrepreneur.

Lerner, Miri; Candida Brush; and Robert Hisrich. (1997). Israeli Women Entrepreneurs: An Examination of Factors Affecting Performance, *Journal of Business Venturing,* vol. 12, no. 4, pp. 315–39.

This study analyzes the relationship between individual factors and business performance of 220 Israeli women entrepreneurs. The applicability of five theoretical perspectives—motivations and goals, social learning, network affiliation, human capital, and environmental factors—is examined in terms of business performance. Findings indicate that network affiliation, human capital, and motivation theories have greater explanatory power than social learning or environmental perspectives.

Sanchez, Angel Martinez; and Olga Urbina Perez. (1998). Entrepreneurship Networks and High Technology Firms: The Case of Aragon. *Technovation,* vol. 18, no. 5, pp. 335–45.

This study examines characteristics of 50 high-tech entrepreneurs and their companies in Aragon, a region in northeast Spain. The characteristic entrepreneur has a self-employed father, a master's degree, and is in his or her mid-30s at the time the company is founded, with nine years of prior work experience. The number of cofounders, work development experience, and a need for achievement are factors influencing the company's success. The regional entrepreneurship network is also described.

Shaver, Kelly G. (1995). The Entrepreneurial Personality Myth. *Business & Economic Review,* vol. 41, no. 3, pp. 20–3.

In research comparing entrepreneurs to nonentrepreneurs on achievement motivation, locus of control, risk taking, and creativity, only achievement motivation shows a clear relationship to entrepreneurial activity. Attitudes, interpersonal skills, and processes of social cognition can be learned later in life. Thus, entrepreneurs may not be born, but they might be made. An inquiry into the psychology of new venture creation had two interesting implications: (1) a person's beliefs about entrepreneurial potential can be changed; and (2) education, training, and business counseling need to take seriously the possibility that the psychological contributors to entrepreneurial success may be quite different in women than in men.

Stuart, Toby E.; Ha Hoang; and Ralph C. Hybels. (1999). Interorganizational Endorsements and the Performance of Entrepreneurial Ventures. *Administrative Science Quarterly,* vol. 44, no. 2, pp. 315–49.

The study investigates how the interorganizational networks of young companies affect their ability to acquire the resources necessary for survival and growth. It is proposed that, faced with great uncertainty about the quality of young companies, third parties rely on the prominence of the affiliates of those companies to make judgments about their quality.

Endnotes

1. For a review of these nine studies, see D. E. Jennings and C. P. Zietham, "Locus of Control: A Review and Directions for Entrepreneurial Research," *Proceedings* of the 43rd Annual Meeting of the Academy of Management (April 1983), pp. 417–21. A discussion of the concept itself can be found in J. B. Rotter, "Generalized Expectancies for Internal versus External Control of Reinforcement," *Psychological Monographs* General and Applied Number 80 (1966).

2. See Robert H. Brockhaus, "Psychological and Environmental Factors Which Distinguish the Successful from the Unsuccessful Entrepreneur," *Proceedings* of the 40th Annual Meeting of the Academy of Management (August 1980), pp. 368–72; and Robert H. Brockhaus and W. R. Nord, "An Exploration of Factors Affecting the Entrepreneurial Decision: Personal Characteristics versus Environmental Conditions," *Proceedings* of the 40th Annual Meeting of the Academy of Management (August 1979), pp. 364–8.

3. This is developed in three works by David McClelland: *The Achieving Society* (Princeton, NJ: Van Norstrand Publishing Co., 1961); "Business Drive and National Achievement," *Harvard Business Review* 40 (July–August 1962), pp. 99–112; and "Achievement Motivation Can Be Developed," *Harvard Business Review* 43 (November–December 1965), pp. 6–24.

4. A good discussion of some alternative measurements is found in Alan L. Carsrud and Kenneth W. Olm, "The Success of Male and Female Entrepreneurs: A Comparative Analysis." In *Managing Take-Off in Fast Growth Firms*, eds. Ray M. Smilor and Robert L. Kuhn (New York: Praeger Publishers, 1986), pp. 147–62.

5. M. Henning and A. Jardim, *The Managerial Woman* (Garden City, NY: Anchor Press/Doubleday, 1977).

6. Robert D. Hisrich and Candida G. Brush, "The Woman Entrepreneur: Management Skills and Business Problems," *Small Business Management* 22 (January 1984), pp. 30–37.

7. For a review of some of this research, see C. J. Auster and D. Auster, "Factors Influencing Women's Choices of Nontraditional Careers," *Vocational Guidance Quarterly* (March 1981), pp. 253–63; J. H. Chusmin, "Characteristics and Predictive Dimensions of Women Who Make Nontraditional Vocational Choices," *Personnel and Guidance Journal* 62 (September 1983), pp. 43–47; and D. L. Sexton and C. A. Kent, "Female Executives and Entrepreneurs: A Preliminary Comparison," *Proceedings*, 1981 Conference on Entrepreneurship, April 1981, pp. 40–55.

8. See Robert D. Hisrich and Candida G. Brush, *The Woman Entrepreneur: Starting, Financing, and Managing a Successful New Business* (Lexington, MA: Lexington Books, 1986).

9. Ibid..

10. See, for example, Y. Gasse, *Entrepreneurial Characteristics and Practices* (Sherbrooke, Quebec: Rene Prumber Imprimeur, Inc., 1971).

11. For a summary of the results of this study, see "To the Winners Belong the Spoils," *Marketing News* 20 (October 10, 1986), pp. 1 and 13.

12. Much of this information is based on research findings in Robert C. Ronstadt, "Initial Venture Goals, Age, and the Decision to Start an Entrepreneurial Career," *Proceedings* of the 43rd Annual Meeting of the Academy of Management (August 1983), p. 472; and Robert C. Ronstadt, "The Decision Not to Become an Entrepreneur," *Proceedings*, 1983 Conference on Entrepreneurship (April 1983), pp. 192–212.

13. The influence of role models on career choice is discussed in E. Almquist and S. Angust, "Role Model Influences on College Women's Career Aspirations," *Merrill-Palmer Quarterly* 17 (July 1971), pp. 263–97; J. Strake and C. Granger, "Same-Sex and Opposite-Sex Teacher Model Influences on Science Career Commitment among High School Students," *Journal of Educational Psychology* 70 (April 1978), pp. 180–6; Alan L. Carsud, Connie Marie Gaglio, and Kenneth W. Olm, "Entrepreneurs-Mentors, Networks, and Successful New Venture Development: An Exploratory Study," *Proceedings*, 1986 Conference on Entrepreneurship (April 1986), pp. 29–35; and Howard Aldrich, Ben Rosen, and William Woodward, "The Impact of Social Networks on Business Foundings and Profit: A Longitudinal Study," *Proceedings*, 1987 Conference on Entrepreneurship (April 1987), pp. 154–68.

14. A thoughtful development of the network concept can be found in Howard Aldrich and Catherine Zimmer, "Entrepreneurship through Social Networks," in *The Art and Science of Entrepreneurship* (Cambridge, MA: Ballinger Publishing Co., 1986), pp. 3–24.

15. An interesting comparison is found in Alan L. Carsrud and Kenneth W. Olm, "The Success of Male and Female Entrepreneurs: A Comparative Analysis," in *Managing Take-Off*

in Fast Growth Firms, eds. Ray M. Smitor and Robert L. Kuhn (New York: Praeger Publishers, 1986), pp. 147–62. For a summary of information on female entrepreneurs, see Candida B. Brush, "Research on Women Business Owners: Past Trends, a New Perspective, and Future Directions," *Entrepreneurship: Theory and Practice* 16, no. 4, pp. 5–30.

16. This material is also discussed in Robert D. Hisrich and Candida G. Brush, *The Woman Entrepreneur: Starting, Financing, and Managing a Successful New Business* (Lexington, MA: Lexington Books, 1986).

17. See B. A. Kirchhoff, R. L. Stevens, and N. I. Hurwitz, "Factors Underlying Increases in Minority Entrepreneurship: 1972–1977." In *Frontiers of Entrepreneurship Research* ed. K. H. Vesper, (Wellesley, MA: Babson College Center for Entrepreneurial Studies, 1982).

18. See J. A. Hornaday and J. Aboud, "The Characteristics of Successful Entrepreneurs," *Personnel Psychology* 24 (1971), pp. 141–53.

19. See E. Gomolka, "Characteristics of Minority Entrepreneurs and Small Business Enterprises," *American Journal of Small Business* 2, no. 1 (1977), pp. 12–21.

20. See J. F. DeCarlo and P. R. Lyons, "A Comparison of Selected Personal Characteristics of Minority and Non-Minority Female Entrepreneurs," *Journal of Small Business Management* 17 (1979), pp. 222–29.

21. See R. D. Hisrich and C. Brush, "Characteristics of the Minority Entrepreneur," *Journal of Small Business Management* 24 (1986), pp. 1–8.

22. See E. R. Auster, "Owner and Organizational Characteristics of Black- and White-Owned Businesses," *American Journal of Economics and Sociology* 47, no. 3 (1988), pp. 331–44.

23. See H. D. Feldman, C. S. Koberg, and T. J. Dean, "Minority Small Business Owners and Their Paths to Ownership," *Journal of Small Business Management* 29, no. 4 (1991), pp. 12–27.

24. This and other information on inventors and the invention process can be found in Robert D. Hisrich, "The Inventor: A Potential Source for New Products," *The Mid-Atlantic Journal of Business* 24 (Winter 1985/86), pp. 67–80.

4

International Entrepreneurship Opportunities

LEARNING OBJECTIVES

1. To identify the aspects and importance of international entrepreneurship.

2. To identify the important strategic issues in international entrepreneurship.

3. To identify the available options for entering international markets.

4. To present the problems and barriers to international entrepreneurship.

A. MALACHI MIXON III

Creativity, risk taking, and innovation in entrepreneurship are essential not only to the inception of brand-new products and ventures but also to a firm's successful transition into global markets. The case of Mal Mixon's notable domestic revitalization of the once ailing Invacare, which eventually segued into Invacare's successful integration into the unpredictable world market, exemplifies this connection.

Invacare, the world's leading U.S. manufacturer and distributor of home medical products, traces its existence to the 1885 beginnings of the Worthington Company, a small Elyria, Ohio, firm that manufactured a line of vehicles especially designed for the physically challenged. Having undergone numerous changes due to mergers and acquisitions, the Worthington Company's core business of wheelchairs became a small and relatively obscure part of Johnson & Johnson in the 1970s and was put up for sale. On the basis of traditional business evaluation measures, there was not much to buy. Sales in 1979 were $19 million with 350 employees; the principal products were unwieldy, clunky steel manual wheelchairs, and no new products were on the drawing boards. The 1979 pro forma earning statement that followed a Mixon-led leveraged buyout (LBO) indicated net earnings of only $100,000 (2 of 1 percent profit). Everest & Jennings, a high-quality manufacturing competitor more than six times larger than Invacare, controlled 80 percent of the wheelchair market, while Invacare maintained less than a 10 percent market share.

Mal Mixon, then vice president of marketing for the CT scanner products division of Johnson & Johnson's Technicare subsidiary, saw beyond these drawbacks and focused instead on the potential for in-home health care products. Assembling a group of Cleveland area investors, he spearheaded a leveraged acquisition funded with $1.5 million of equity and $6.5 million in debt. The influence of Mixon's nurturing father, coupled with the effects of his upbringing in the small, supportive Oklahoma farming town of Spiro, instilled Mixon with confidence, a strong sense of purpose, and determination. Intellectually curious and a voracious reader, he learned to dream of the possibilities in life, to question everything, to take intelligent risks, to be persistent, and to become a fierce competitor. These traits were reinforced and supplemented with leadership skills acquired through four years of service in the Marine Corps, where he also learned how to deal with adversity. "You are taught to reach your objective no matter what . . . you are almost brainwashed to never have an excuse for failure." Along with that, however, came the knowledge of self-empowerment and a sense of pride in achieving excellence. Returning from the Marine Corps in

1966, Mal returned to Harvard University for his MBA, graduating with distinction near the top of his class. He initially worked as a salesman and later as director of marketing for the Cleveland-based Harris Corporation and then moved to Ohio Nuclear, a subsidiary of Technicare, where he rose to vice president of marketing of the CT scanner division. Mal was 39 years old when Johnson & Johnson divested Invacare.

Investing $10,000 of his own funds and $40,000 borrowed from friends, Mal took control of the company on January 2, 1980, retaining a 15 percent share. With a fierce tenacity reminiscent of the Marine Corps "bulldog" mascot, Mixon's restructuring of Invacare was immediate and total. He soon replaced 16 of the 18 direct sales staff—"they didn't have fire in their bellies, and they didn't have the necessary talent"—and, more important, began working with the company's engineers to produce new products, believing that without a good product, nothing else matters. Tactical genius was combined with entrepreneurial innovation. He initiated "one-stop shopping" by expanding the home health care line and cajoling, pleading, and offering volume discounts to skeptical customers in order to increase business. The three-pronged attack of revitalization, product/service development, and aggressive competitive orientation proved effective, and soon Invacare was capturing market share from Everest & Jennings. Invacare reduced the weight of its wheelchairs from 60 to 15 pounds, introduced microprocessor electronic control systems, and offered "30 different crazy colors," together with dramatically reducing lead times. Everest & Jennings watched their wheelchair market share erode from 80 to 18 percent.

Sales and earnings accelerated through the early 1980s, and by the end of 1983 Invacare had $70 million in sales and $2.8 million in net earnings. Although standard wheelchairs still represented a major portion of Invacare's business (50 percent of sales), the company had an increasingly broad product line of patient aids, home care beds, newly introduced prescription wheelchairs, and oxygen concentrators. Invacare prospered, but not without adversity. In 1984, the company went public to obtain operating capital and to pay down short-term debt that helped fund the company's growth during the 1980s. The initial public offering ($11.00 adjusted for two stock splits, or $2.75/share on NASDAQ) raised $15 million. The same year took a substantial charge against earnings due to poor quality in one of its products and start-up costs associated with a new factory. This was compounded by the government changing Medicare reimbursement rules, which affected many of the products sold by Invacare. The company regrouped to restore its financial health. Major cost reduction efforts were launched, and the company was reorganized into divisions. New product developments and enhancements were emphasized, rapidly exhibiting an impact on the market. By the fourth quarter of 1985, Invacare had returned to profitability, requiring less than one year for the turnaround.

The second major challenge presented itself in 1986 when a Taiwanese competitor began selling in the United States at 20 percent below prevailing prices. Aided by the facilities consolidations and plant reconfigurations that were launched in 1985, Invacare relocated some of its manufacturing to Mexico. This further improved its overall cost structure and competitive position. Invacare attacked the competition, meeting the imports head-on in price, with a superior product and a more extensive distribution and service capability. Due to Invacare's aggressive response, the Taiwanese imports failed to gain a foothold and ceased to be a major market factor by 1987. Sales, product lines, and earnings have increased steadily since. Invacare posted $100 million in sales in 1986, surpassed the $200 million mark in 1990, and achieved $619 million in 1996. The company has experienced 22.5 percent annual compounded average sales growth per year since 1979, accompanied by a 33 percent compounded annual growth in net income and a 37 percent compounded annual growth in share value in the past five years. Shares have undergone two splits and are currently trading in the $18 to $27 range, a 3,500 percent return on the original $2.75 public offering price. The original investors who backed Mal have about a 20-cent-per-share basis on their stock.

Product lines include, to name only a few, standard and prescription wheelchairs (manual and powered); home respiratory equipment; personal care items such as home care beds, walkers, and rollators; infusion therapy pumps; replacement parts; and electronic control systems. From a tenuous and ambitious beginning (with $19 million in sales and a 10 percent market share in standard wheelchairs), Invacare achieved $1 billion in sales in 2000 and is now the market share leader for home health care mobility products and medical equipment for people with disabilities. Based in Ohio, Invacare has 23 plants throughout the United States, Europe, Mexico, and Australia/New Zealand, all supported by a direct sales force working with 10,000 medical equipment providers throughout the world. Invacare has a unique organizational structure that combines the benefits of both centralized and decentralized operations. Its internal structure consists of an executive committee that manages four focused operating groups, worldwide. Each group consists of several dedicated business units, encouraging entrepreneurial attitudes and responsiveness to market demands. Externally, the company has one "face" to the customer, as products are sold through a single domestic sales and service organization with complete account responsibility.

Mal Mixon was able to successfully grow and manage an expanding company on a global level. Beyond being competitive, Mixon is recognized as a visionary leader. As stated by a friend and business acquaintance, "He's able to develop a vision faster than most people can pick up the telephone." The ability to develop and articulate a sound vision, plan and execute an appropriate strategy for the enterprise, and maintain sound values are three important elements of leadership according to Mixon. Frequently, however, it is difficult for an entrepreneur to bridge the gap, or to both manage and expand a venture, as evidenced by Steve Jobs and the turbulent growth of Apple Computer. As a new venture grows, there can be a need for more and more administration. It appears that this has been attended to in Invacare, as Mal has built a strong management team. Also, at times, a new infusion of the entrepreneurial spirit that formed the venture is needed. Balancing entrepreneurship with administration becomes the challenge. As Mal puts it, "Entrepreneurship is creating a business as opposed to administering a business and having extensive capital risk to create value as opposed to compensation for a job."

Unlike Mal Mixon, many entrepreneurs find it difficult to both manage and expand the venture they created, especially in terms of the global marketplace. In order to expand a venture, an entrepreneur needs to access his or her abilities in the management area to identify methods for domestic and even international expansion, as well as to determine when it may be necessary to turn the reins over to someone else. The latter is especially true in the case of international branches or plants that, by virtue of geography, limit the founding American entrepreneur's control over operations. As a new venture grows and matures, a need can develop for more administration as well as for a new infusion of entrepreneurial spirit (intrapreneurship), as discussed in Chapter 2. Some entrepreneurs tend to forget a basic axiom in business: the only constant is change. Entrepreneurs who understand this axiom, like Mal Mixon, will effectively manage change by continually adapting organizational culture, structure, procedures, strategic direction, and products in both a domestic and an international orientation. Entrepreneurs in developed countries like the United States, Japan, Great Britain, and Germany must sell their products in a variety of new and different market areas early on in the development of their firms or, as in the case of Mal Mixon's Invacare, determine how to expand into and prosper in international markets.

Never before in the history of the world have there been such interesting and exciting international business opportunities. The opening of the once-controlled economies of Eastern and Central Europe, the former U.S.S.R., and the People's Republic of China to market-oriented enterprise and the advancement of the Pacific Rim provide a myriad of possibilities for entrepreneurs wanting to start in a foreign market as well as for existing entrepreneurial firms desiring to expand their businesses.

As more and more countries become market oriented and developed, the distinction between foreign and domestic markets is becoming less pronounced. What was once only produced domestically is now produced internationally. For example, Yamaha pianos are now manufactured in the United States. Digital Equipment Company has plants in Puerto Rico. Nestle's chocolate is made in Europe. This blurring of national identities will continue to accelerate as more and more products are introduced outside domestic boundaries earlier in the life of entrepreneurial firms.[1]

ƒ◗

THE NATURE OF INTERNATIONAL ENTREPRENEURSHIP

Simply stated, *international entrepreneurship* is the process of an entrepreneur conducting business activities across national boundaries. It may consist of exporting, licensing, opening a sales office in another country, or something as simple as placing a classified advertisement in the Paris edition of the *Herald Tribune*. The activities necessary for ascertaining and satisfying the needs and wants of target consumers often take place in more than one country. When an entrepreneur executes his or her business in more than one country, international entrepreneurship is occurring.

international entrepreneurship   An entrepreneur doing business across his or her national boundary

With a commercial history of only 300 years, the United States is a relative newcomer to the international business arena. As soon as settlements were established in the New World, American businesses began an active international trade with Europe. Foreign investors helped build much of the early industrial trade with Europe as well as much of the early industrial base of the United States. The future commercial strength of the United States will similarly depend on the ability of U.S. entrepreneurs and established U.S. companies to take advantage of markets outside the country's borders.

THE IMPORTANCE OF INTERNATIONAL BUSINESSES TO THE FIRM

International business has become increasingly important to firms of all sizes, not only for the largest U.S. firms. Every firm is now competing in a hypercompetitive global economy.

There can be little doubt that today's entrepreneur must be able to move in the world of international business. The successful entrepreneur will be someone who fully understands how international business differs from purely domestic business and is able to respond accordingly. An entrepreneur entering the international market should be able to answer the following questions:

1. Is managing international business diferent from managing domestic business?
2. What are the strategic issues to be resolved in international business management?
3. What are the options available for engaging in international business?
4. How should one assess the decision to enter into an international market?

INTERNATIONAL VERSUS DOMESTIC ENTREPRENEURSHIP

Although international and domestic entrepreneurs alike are concerned with sales, costs, and profits, what differentiates domestic from international entrepreneurship is the variation in the relative importance of the factors involved in each decision. International entrepreneurial decisions are more complex due to such uncontrollable factors as economics, politics, culture, and technology.

Economics

When entrepreneurs design a domestic business strategy, a single country at a specified level of economic development is the focus of their efforts. The entire country is almost always organized under a single economic system and has the same currency. Creating a business strategy for a multicountry area means dealing with differences in the following areas: levels of economic development; currency valuations; government regulations; and banking, economic, marketing, and distribution systems. These differences manifest themselves in each aspect of the entrepreneur's international business plan and methods of doing business.

Stage of Economic Development

The United States is an industrially developed nation with regional variances of relative income. While needing to adjust the business plan according to regional differences, an entrepreneur doing business only in the United States does not have to worry about a significant lack of such fundamental infrastructures as roads, electricity, communication systems, banking facilities and systems, adequate educational systems, a well-developed legal system, and established business ethics and norms. These factors vary greatly in other countries, from those industrialized to those in the process of developing. The extent of the quality of these factors significantly impacts the ability to successfully engage in international business.

Balance of Payments

With the present system of flexible exchange rates, a country's *balance of payments* (the difference between the value of a country's imports and exports over time)

---

balance of payments   The trade status between
countries

---

affects the valuation of its currency. The valuation of one country's currency affects how businesses of that country do business in other countries. At one time, Italy's chronic balance of payments deficit led to a radical depreciation in the value of the lira, the currency of Italy. Fiat responded by offering significant rebates on cars sold in the United States. These rebates cost Fiat very little because fewer dollars purchased many more lira due to the decrease in the value of the lira.

Type of System

Pepsi-Cola began considering the possibility of marketing in the former U.S.S.R. as early as 1959, when then U.S. Vice President Richard Nixon visited there. When Premier Nikita Khrushchev expressed his approval of Pepsi's taste, the slow wheels of East-West trade began moving, with Pepsi entering the former U.S.S.R. 13 years later. Instead of using its traditional type of franchise bottler in this entry, Pepsi used a

---

barter   A method of payment using nonmoney items

---

third-party arrangements   Paying for goods
indirectly through another source

---

barter-type arrangement that satisfied both the Soviet socialized system of the former U.S.S.R. and the U.S. capitalist system. In return for receiving technology and syrup from Pepsi, the former U.S.S.R. provided the company with Soviet vodka and the right to distribute it in the United States. Many such *barter* or *third-party arrangements* have been used to increase the amount of business activity with the former U.S.S.R. and Eastern and Central European countries, as well as other countries in various stages of development and transition.

There are many difficulties in doing business in developing and transition economies. These problems reflect the gaps in the basic knowledge of the Western system regarding business plans, product promotion, marketing, and profits; widely variable rates of return; nonconvertibility of the ruble, which necessitates finding a countertrade item; differences in the accounting system; and nightmarish communications.

Political-Legal Environment

The multiplicity of political and legal environments in the international market creates vastly different business problems, opening some market opportunities for entrepreneurs and eliminating others. For example, U.S. environmental standards have eliminated the possibility of entrepreneurs establishing ventures to import several models of European cars. In addition, as part of a political agreement, Japanese entrepreneurs and companies have agreed to an established limited volume of their exports to the United States. Another significant event in the political-legal environment involves the price fluctuations in oil and other energy products.

Each element of the business strategy of an international entrepreneur has the potential to be affected by the multiplicity of legal environments. Pricing decisions in a country that has a value-added tax are different from those decisions made by the same entrepreneur in a country with no value-added tax. Advertising strategy is affected by the variations in what can be said in the copy or in the support needed for advertising claims in different countries. Product decisions are affected by legal requirements with respect to labeling, ingredients, and packaging. Types of ownership and organizational forms vary widely throughout the world. The laws governing business arrangements also vary greatly in the over 150 different legal systems and national laws.

As Seen in *Business Week . . .*
A Business-to-Business E-Boom

Aaeon Technology, a Taiwan maker of specialty computers, is typical of the thousands of small companies that make Asia the world's workshop. The hardworking managers who run Aaeon have watched every penny as they pushed sales to $20 million.

That thriftiness is what makes a recent purchase by Aaeon so exceptional. Its board, after contentious debate, has decided to shell out $500,000 for a system from software giant Oracle Corp. that will let Aaeon manage parts procurement, inventory, sales, and finances over the Web. It's a huge leap for Aaeon, but the company figures it has no choice. "If we want to stay competitive, we need to have e-commerce," says Jessica Chu, Aaeon's marketing manager.

Internet mania is sweeping through Asia, with venture capitalists rushing to buy stakes in portals that cater to consumers. Those portals may generate most of the sizzle. But it's business-to-business e-commerce that could have a profound impact on the way Asia's manufacturers operate.

Leapfrog. Already, the business-to-business segment is Asia's fastest growing area of e-commerce. By 2003, sales of business-to-business e-commerce software alone are expected to top $1.3 billion a year, says International Data Corp. Online e-commerce sales in Asia are expected to surge, from $2 billion this year to $32.6 billion in 2003.

The authorities are getting into the act. Taiwan wants 50,000 companies to be online by 2001. Thailand is requiring all export and import documents to go online. Governments "have recognized the Internet as the vehicle to leapfrog them into the new millennium," says Pete Hitchen, a Singapore-based Internet analyst at IDC.

Building this new model isn't going to be easy. Unlike in North America and Europe, the supply chains and distribution networks of East Asian companies often stretch from Taiwan to mainland China to the Philippines and other countries. Businesspeople also prefer dealing face to face and relying on relationships cultivated over years.

But plenty of entrepreneurs are betting that these attitudes will change. Wang Xiaolai is setting up an online service in Shanghai to integrate car manufacturers with parts suppliers around China. His China Automotive Rainbow Network hopes to have 1,000 members and charge them for transactions made on its system. "We can make a complete supply chain," says Wang.

Taiwan has been among the fastest to adapt to e-commerce. Zero One Technology Co., a $45 million maker of computer-network servers, now generates 10 percent of its sales through the Taiwan Computer Association's Computex Online Website. The embrace of e-commerce by Asia's largest companies is also helping drive this growth. Singapore-based Advanced Manufacturing Online—which boasts such giants as Motorola, Matsushita, and Taiwan Semiconductor Manufacturing as clients—runs a system that enables suppliers and customers to send orders and solicit price quotations over the Web.

New Mind-Set. One big obstacle to e-commerce is the reluctance of Asian companies to outsource important functions, such as accounting and billing, which is a key element of business-to-business e-commerce. Many supply-chain management programs require users to open their inventory and procurement processes to suppliers and customers.

That calls for a big change in mind-set. "People don't have the confidence to put sensitive information on the Internet," says Kevin Jiang, director of Computex Online, the Net marketplace for computer-hardware makers.

But here, too, there are signs of change. In Asia, IBM used to sell its e-commerce services almost entirely to huge conglomerates, but now there is strong growth from small and midsized companies. And these small companies are asking for more advice on redesigning management. "They used to say: 'Tell more what I should buy,' " observes Howie Lau, who heads IBM's e-commerce operations out of Singapore. "Now they are asking more sophisticated questions." They should keep asking. The faster Asian business gets Net-savvy, the better.

Source: Jonathan Moore and Bruce Einhorn, "A Business-to-Business E-Boom," *Business Week*, October 25, 1999, p. 62.

Cultural Environment

The impact of culture on entrepreneurs and strategies is also significant. Entrepreneurs must make sure that each element in the business plan has some degree of congruence with the local culture. For example, in some countries, point of purchase displays are not allowed in retail stores as they are in the United States. Some cultures provide a specific opportunity for new ventures, as in the case of Eric Hautemont, a Frenchman who founded Ray Dream Inc. in California.

Understanding the local culture is essential to the entrepreneur's development of worldwide strategies and plans. The degree of adaptation and the amount of standardization in worldwide plans center around the concept of culture and must be determined by each entrepreneur doing international business.

An increasingly important aspect of the cultural environment in some countries concerns bribes and corruption. How should an entrepreneur deal with these situations when it may mean losing the business? Several situations regarding ethics and ethical behavior are indicated in the Ethics box.

Technological Environment

Technology, like culture, varies significantly across countries. The variations and availability of technology are often surprising, particularly to an entrepreneur from a developed country like the United States. Many Americans, for example, have a difficult time understanding how a technologically advanced military economy like the former U.S.S.R. could have shortages of food and consumer goods and an almost Third World communication system. While U.S. firms produce mostly standardized, relatively uniform products that can be sorted to meet industry standards, this is not the case in many countries, making it more difficult to achieve a consistent level of quality.

New products in a country are created based on the conditions and infrastructure operant in that country. For example, U.S. car designers can assume wider roads and less expensive gasoline than European designers. When these same designers work on transportation vehicles for other parts of the world, their assumptions have to be significantly altered.[2]

Strategic Issues

Four strategic issues are of paramount importance to the international entrepreneur or an entrepreneur thinking about going international: (1) the allocation of responsibility between the U.S. and foreign operations; (2) the nature of the planning, reporting, and control systems to be used throughout the international operations; (3) the appropriate organizational structure for conducting international operations; and (4) the degree of standardization possible.

The problems of allocation of responsibility between headquarters and subsidiaries essentially concern the degree of decentralization. As entrepreneurs move through their experience with international operations, they tend to change their approach to the allocation of responsibility. This frequently occurs in the following progression:

- *Stage 1.* When making his or her first movements into international business, an entrepreneur typically follows a highly centralized decision-making process. Since the entrepreneur generally has access to a limited number of individuals with international experience, a centralized decision-making network is usually

Beyond balancing the benefits, costs, and risks associated with doing business in different countries, entrepreneurs must be aware of some ethical issues that emerge when the business environment is expanded internationally.

- *Human Rights.* Some totalitarian countries routinely violate the human rights of their citizens. Should an entrepreneur conduct business within this environment? Some will argue that investing in regions with totalitarian control provides support for repressive regimes. Without external investment, critics claim that many repressive regimes would collapse and be replaced by more democratically inclined governments. In recent years, firms investing in Chile, China, Iraq, and South Africa have been subject to criticism for supporting repressive regimes. Offering some support to this perspective is the 1994 collapse of the apartheid system in South Africa, credited by some to have been hastened by economic sanctions initiated by Western nations, which in turn reduced investment by Western firms. On the other hand, others feel that investment raises the level of economic development, encouraging the country to change from within, feeling that political freedom is related to economic well-being. This was the philosophy behind the trade sanctions against China following the 1989 government repression of pro-democracy demonstrations. President George Bush's argument was that U.S. firms should continue investing in mainland China, since economic growth would result in increased political freedom.

- *Safety.* Product safety, work safety, and environmental protection standards in the United States are among the most stringent in the world. When entrepreneurs enter a different country, should they adhere to the same standards as they do domestically even if not required by local laws? What if adhering to Western standards makes the internationalization unprofitable, thereby negating the investment initiative? Adhering to Western standards and not investing may result in denying local people much needed jobs, while relaxing standards to adhere to local requirements might provide jobs and income.

- *Bribes.* Is it appropriate to pay bribes to officials in order to gain access to a foreign country? While most Westerners consider bribery to be morally wrong and corrupt, in many parts of the world, the fact remains that payoffs to government officials are a part of the process of doing business in that country. Furthermore, assuming that an entrepreneur's investment will create jobs where none existed previously, withholding this investment in situations where bribes are expected ignores the benefits from increased income and job opportunities for the local population. While it is clearly unethical to offer bribes per se, given the complexity of the issue, what really is the appropriate action for the entrepreneur in the specific situation?

Source: Adapted from Charles W. L. Hill, *International Business*, 2nd ed. (Boston: Richard D. Irwin, Inc., 1997), pp. 60–61.

used. The attitude is often: "What do those people from another country know about our product and its needs? We'd better do it all from here."

- *Stage 2.* When the business is successful, the entrepreneur no longer finds it possible to use a completely centralized decision-making process. The multiplicity of environments becomes far too complex to handle from central headquarters. In response, an entrepreneur often decentralizes the entire international operation. The philosophy at this point can be summed up as follows: "There's no way I am ever going to be able to understand the differences between all of those markets. Let them make their own decisions."

- *Stage 3.*   The process of decentralization carried out in Stage 2 becomes intolerable once further success is attained. Business operations in the different countries end up in conflict with each other. The U.S. headquarters is often the last to receive information about problems. When this occurs, limited amounts of power, authority, and responsibility are pulled back to the U.S. base of operations. A balance is usually achieved, with the U.S. headquarters having reasonably tight control over major strategic marketing decisions and the in-country operating unit having the responsibility for the tactical implementation of corporate strategy. Planning, reporting, and control systems become very important aspects of international success at this stage.

To understand what is required for effective planning, reporting, and control in international operations, the entrepreneur should consider the following questions:

Environmental Analysis

1. What are the unique characteristics of each national market? What characteristics does each market have in common with other national markets?
2. Can any national markets be clustered together for operating and/or planning purposes? What dimensions of markets should be used to cluster markets?

Strategic Planning

3. Who should be involved in marketing decisions?
4. What are the major assumptions about target markets? Are these valid?
5. What needs are satisfied by the company's products in the target markets?
6. What customer benefits are provided by the product in the target markets?
7. What are the conditions under which the products are used in the target markets?
8. How great is the ability to buy our products in the target markets?
9. What are the company's major strengths and weaknesses relative to existing and potential competition in the target markets?
10. Should the company extend, adapt, or invent products, prices, advertising, and promotion programs for target markets?
11. What are the balance-of-payments and currency situations in the target markets? Will the company be able to remit earnings? Is the political climate acceptable?
12. What are the company's objectives, given the alternatives available and the assessment of opportunity, risk, and company capability?

Structure

13. How should the organization be structured to optimally achieve the established objectives, given the company's skills and resources? What is the responsibility of each organizational level?

Operational Planning

14. Given the objectives, structure, and assessment of the market environment, how can an effective operational marketing plan be implemented? What products should be marketed, at what prices, through what channels, with what communications, and to which target markets?

Controlling the Marketing Program

15. How does the company measure and monitor the plan's performance? What steps should be taken to ensure that marketing objectives are met?[3]

One key to successful strategic planning is an appreciation of the market. While questions 1 and 2 of the preceding list of 15 questions focus on this dimension of the planning process, the first step in identifying markets and clustering countries is to analyze data on each country in the following six areas:

1. Market Characteristics
   a) Size of market; rate of growth
   b) Stage of development
   c) Stage of product life cycle; saturation levels
   d) Buyer behavior characteristics
   e) Social/cultural factors
   f) Physical environment

2. Marketing Institutions
   a) Distribution systems
   b) Communication media
   c) Marketing services (advertising and research)

3. Industry Conditions
   a) Competitive size and practices
   b) Technical development

4. Legal Environment (laws, regulations, codes, tariffs, and taxes)

5. Resources
   a) Personnel (availability, skill, potential, and cost)
   b) Money (availability and cost)

6. Political Environment
   a) Current government policies and attitudes
   b) Long-range political environment

ENTREPRENEURIAL ENTRY INTO INTERNATIONAL BUSINESS

There are various ways an entrepreneur can become a player in international business and market products internationally. The method of entry into a market and the mode of operating overseas are dependent on the goals of the entrepreneur and the company's strengths and weaknesses. The modes of entering or engaging in international business can be divided into three categories: exporting, nonequity arrangements, and direct foreign investment.

Exporting

exporting Selling goods made in one country to another country

As a general rule, an entrepreneur starts doing international business through exporting. *Exporting* normally involves the sale and shipping of products manufactured in one country to a customer located in another country. There are two general classifications of exporting: direct and indirect.

Indirect Exporting   *Indirect exporting* involves having a foreign purchaser in the local market or using an export management firm. For certain commodities and manufactured goods, foreign buyers actively seek out sources of supply and have purchasing offices in markets throughout the world. An entrepreneur wanting to sell into one of these overseas markets can deal with one of these buyers. In this case, the entire transaction is handled as though it were a domestic transaction, even though the goods will be shipped out of the country. This method of exporting involves the least amount of knowledge and risk for the entrepreneur.

indirect exporting   Selling goods to another country through a person in the entrepreneur's home country

Export management firms, another method of indirect exporting, are located in most commercial centers. For a fee, these firms will provide representation in foreign markets. Typically, they represent a group of noncompeting manufacturers from the same country who have no interest in becoming directly involved in exporting. The export management firm handles all of the selling, marketing, and delivery, in addition to any technical problem involved in the export process.

Direct Exporting   If the entrepreneur wants more involvement without any financial commitment, *direct exporting* through independent distributors or the company's own overseas sales office is a way to get involved in international business. Independent foreign distributors usually handle products for firms seeking relatively rapid entry into a large number of foreign markets. This independent distributor directly contacts foreign customers and potential customers and takes care of all the technicalities of arranging for export documentation, financing, and delivery for an established rate of commission.

direct exporting   Selling goods to another country by taking care of the transaction

Entrepreneurs who do not wish to submit to the loss of control over their marketing efforts that occurs when using independent distributors can open their own overseas sales offices and hire their own salespeople to provide market representation. In starting out, the entrepreneur may send a U.S. or domestic salesperson to be a representative in the foreign market. As more business is done in the overseas sales in the foreign market, warehouses are usually opened, followed by a local assembly process when sales reach a level high enough to warrant the investment. The assembly operation can eventually evolve into the establishment of manufacturing operations in the foreign market. Entrepreneurs then export the output from these manufacturing operations to other international markets.

Nonequity Arrangements

When market and financial conditions warrant the change, an entrepreneur can enter into international business by one of three types of *nonequity arrangements:* licensing, turn-key projects, and management contracts. Each of these allows the entrepreneur to enter a market and obtain sales and profits without direct equity investment in the foreign market. Entrepreneurs who either cannot export or make direct investments or who simply choose not to engage in those activities still have the possibility of doing international business through nonequity arrangements.

nonequity arrangements   Doing international business through an arrangement that does not involve any investment

Licensing   *Licensing* involves an entrepreneur who is a manufacturer (licensee) giving a foreign manufacturer (licensor) the right to use a patent, trademark, technology, production process, or product in return for the payment of a royalty. The licensing arrangement is most appropriate when the entrepreneur has no intention of entering a particular market through exporting or direct investment. Since the process is low risk, yet provides a way to generate incremental income, a licensing arrangement can be a good method for the entrepreneur to engage in international business. Unfortunately, some entrepreneurs have entered into these arrangements without careful analysis and have later found that they have licensed their largest competitor into business or that they are investing large sums of time and money in helping the licensor to adopt the technology or know-how being licensed.

licensing   Allowing someone else to use something of the company's

Wolverine World Wide, Inc., opened a Hush Puppies store in Sofia, Bulgaria, through a licensing agreement with Pikin, a combine. Similar arrangements were made a year later in the former U.S.S.R. with Kirov, a shoe combine.[4] The stores have done well through these licensing arrangements.

Turn-Key Projects   Another method by which the entrepreneur can gain some international business experience without much risk is via *turn-key projects*. The underdeveloped or lesser-developed countries of the world have recognized their need for manufacturing technology and infrastructure and yet do not want to turn over substantial portions of their economy to foreign ownership. One solution to this dilemma has been to have a foreign entrepreneur build a factory or other facility, train the workers to operate the equipment, train the management to run the installation, and then turn it over to local owners once the operation is going, hence the name turn-key operation.

turn-key projects   Developing and operationalizing something in a foreign country

Entrepreneurs have found the turn-key project an attractive alternative. Initial profits can be made from this method, and follow-up export sales can result. Financing is often provided by the local company or the government with periodic payments being made over the life of the project.

Management Contracts   A final nonequity method the entrepreneur can use in international business is the *management contract*. Several entrepreneurs have successfully entered international business by contracting their management techniques and managerial skills. These contracts sometimes follow a turn-key project where the foreign owner wants to use the management of the turn-key supplier.

management contract   A method for doing a specific international task

The management contract allows the purchasing country to gain foreign expertise without giving ownership of its resources to a foreigner. For the entrepreneur, the management contract is another way of entering foreign markets that would otherwise be closed and of obtaining a profit without a large equity investment.

Direct Foreign Investment

The wholly owned foreign subsidiary has been the preferred mode of ownership for entrepreneurs using a direct foreign investment for doing business in international markets. Joint ventures and minority and majority equity positions are also methods for making direct foreign investments. The percentage of ownership obtained in the foreign venture by the entrepreneur is related to nationality, the amount of overseas experience, the nature of the industry, and the rules of the host government.

Minority Interests   Japanese companies have been frequent users of the minority equity position in direct foreign investment. A *minority interest* can provide a firm with a source of raw materials or a relatively captive market for its products. Entrepreneurs have used minority positions to gain a foothold or acquire experience in a market before making a major commitment. When the minority shareholder has something of strong value, the ability to influence the decision-making process is often far in excess of the shareholding.

minority interest   Having less than 50 percent ownership position

Joint Ventures   Another direct foreign investment method used by entrepreneurs to enter foreign markets is the *joint venture*. Although a joint venture can take on many forms, in its most traditional form, two firms (for example, one U.S. firm and one German firm) get together and form a third company in which they share the equity.

joint venture   Two companies forming a third company

Joint ventures have been used by entrepreneurs most often in two situations: (1) when the entrepreneur wants to purchase local knowledge as well as an already established marketing or manufacturing facility, and (2) when rapid entry into a market is needed. Sometimes joint ventures are dissolved and the entrepreneur takes 100 percent ownership.

Even though using a joint venture to enter a foreign market is a key strategic decision, the keys to its success have not been well understood, and the reasons for forming a joint venture today are different from those of the past. Previously, joint ventures were viewed as partnerships and often involved firms whose stock was owned by several other firms. Originally, joint ventures were used for trading purposes and were one of the oldest ways of transacting business. Merchants of ancient Babylon, Egypt, and Phoenicia used joint ventures to conduct large trading operations. This use continued through the 15th and 16th centuries when merchants in Great Britain used joint ventures to trade all over the world.

Joint ventures in the United States took a somewhat different form, being used by mining concerns and railroads as early as 1850. The use of joint ventures, mostly vertical joint ventures, started increasing significantly during the 1950s. Through the vertical joint venture, two firms could absorb the large volume of output when neither could afford the diseconomies associated with a smaller plant.

What has caused this significant increase in the use of joint ventures, particularly when many have not worked? The studies of success and failure of joint ventures have indicated many different motives for their formation.

One of the most frequent reasons an entrepreneur forms a joint venture is to share the costs and risks of a project. Projects where new, very costly technology is involved frequently need resource sharing. This can be particularly important when an entrepreneur does not have the financial resources necessary to engage in capital intensive activities.

Synergy between firms is another reason that an entrepreneur may form a joint venture. Synergy is the qualitative impact on the acquiring firm brought about by complementary factors inherent in the firm being acquired. Synergy in the form of people, customers, inventory, plant, or equipment provides leverage for the joint venture. The degree of the synergy determines how beneficial the joint venture will be for the companies involved.

synergy   Two parties having things in common

Another reason for forming a joint venture is to obtain a competitive advantage. A joint venture can preempt competitors, allowing an entrepreneur to access new customers and to expand the market base. It can also result in an entity that is more competitive than the original company since hybrids of companies tend to possess the strength of each of the joint venture partners.

Joint ventures are frequently used by entrepreneurs to enter markets and economies that pose entrance difficulties or to compensate for a company's lack of foreign experience. This has been the case for the transition economies of Eastern Europe and the former U.S.S.R. Since the rules of joint ventures in these countries vary greatly, it is not surprising that it is easier to establish a joint venture in Hungary because of fewer registration requirements. Having neither foreign experience nor a foreign distribution network, MicroPatent Inc. used a joint venture to enter the British market.

Majority Interest   Another equity method for the entrepreneur to enter international markets is by purchasing a majority interest in a foreign business. In a technical sense, anything over 50 percent of the equity in a firm is *majority interest*. The majority interest allows the entrepreneur to obtain managerial control while maintaining the acquired firm's local identity. When entering a volatile international market, some entrepreneurs take a smaller position, which they increase up to 100 percent as sales and profits occur. This practice, often enforced according to regulatory restrictions imposed by many countries out of concern for the rights of minority shareholders, is a means of reducing possible conflict with the local owner.

majority interest   Having more than 50 percent ownership position

100 Percent Ownership   An entrepreneur using 100 percent ownership to engage in international business ensures complete control. U.S. entrepreneurs have the tendency to desire complete ownership and control in cases of foreign investments. If the entrepreneur has the capital, technology, and marketing skills required for successful entry into a market, there may be no reason to share ownership.

Mergers and acquisitions have been used significantly in international business as well as within the United States. During periods of intense merger activity, entrepreneurs may spend significant time searching for a firm to acquire and then finalizing the transaction. The deal should reflect basic principles of any capital investment decision and make a net contribution to shareholders' wealth. The merits of a particular merger are often difficult to assess. Not only do the benefits and cost of a merger need to be determined, but special accounting, legal, and tax issues must be addressed. The entrepreneur therefore must have a general understanding of the benefits and problems of mergers as a strategic option as well as an understanding of the complexity of integrating an entire company into present operations.

horizontal merger   Combination of at least two firms doing similar businesses at the same market level

There are five basic types of mergers: horizontal, vertical, product extension, market extension, and diversified activity. A *horizontal merger* is the combination of two firms that produce one or more of the same or closely related products in the same geographic area. They are motivated by economies of scale in marketing, production, or sales, an example of which is the acquisition of convenient food store chain Southland Stores by 7-Eleven Convenience Stores.

vertical merger   Combination of at least two firms at different market levels

A *vertical merger* is the combination of two or more firms in successive stages of production that often involve a buyer-seller relationship. This form of merger stabilizes supply and production and offers more control of these critical areas. Examples are McDonald's acquiring its store franchises, and Phillips Petroleum acquiring its gas station franchises. In each case, these outlets became company-owned stores.

product extension merger   Combination of two firms with noncompeting products

A *product extension merger* occurs when acquiring and acquired companies have related production and/or distribution activities but do not have products that compete directly with each other. Examples are the acquisitions of Miller Brewing (beer) by Philip Morris (cigarettes), and Western Publishing (children's books) by Mattel (toys).

market extension merger   Combination of at least two firms with similar products in different geographic markets

A *market extension merger* is a combination of two firms producing the same products but selling them in different geographic markets. The motivation is that the acquiring firm can economically combine its management skills, production, and marketing with that of the acquired firm. An example of this type of merger is the acquisition of Diamond Chain (a West Coast retailer) by Dayton Hudson (a Minneapolis retailer).

diversified activity merger   Combination of at least two totally unrelated firms

The final type of merger is a *diversified activity merger.* This is a conglomerate merger involving the consolidation of two essentially unrelated firms. Usually, the acquiring firm is not interested in either using its cash resources to expand shareholder wealth or actively running and managing the acquired company. An example of a diversified activity merger is Hillenbrand Industries (a caskets and hospital furniture manufacturer) acquiring American Tourister (a luggage manufacturer).

Mergers are a sound strategic option for an entrepreneur when synergy is present. Several factors cause synergy to occur and make two firms worth more together than apart.

The first factor, economies of scale, is probably the most prevalent reason for mergers. Economies of scale can occur in production, coordination and administration, sharing central services such as office management and accounting, financial control, and upper-level management. Economies of scale increase operating, financial, and management efficiency, thereby resulting in better earnings.

The second factor is taxation or, more specifically, unused tax credits. Sometimes a firm has had a loss in previous years but not enough profits to take tax advantage of the loss. Corporate income tax regulations allow the net operating losses of one company to reduce the taxable income of another when they are combined. By combining a firm with a loss with a firm with a profit, the tax-loss carryover can be used.

The final important factor for mergers is the benefits received in combining complementary resources. Many entrepreneurs will merge with other firms to ensure a source of supply for key ingredients, to obtain a new technology, or to keep the other firm's product from being a competitive threat. It is often quicker and easier for a firm to merge with another that already has a new technology developed—combining the innovation with the acquiring firm's engineering and sales talent—than to develop the technology from scratch.

BARRIERS TO INTERNATIONAL TRADE

There are varying attitudes throughout the world concerning free trade. Generally, a positive attitude started around 1947 with the development of general trade agreements and the reduction of tariffs and other trade barriers.

General Agreement on Tariffs and Trade (GATT)

One of the longest-lasting agreements on trade is the General Agreement on Tariffs and Trade (GATT), which was established in 1947 under U.S. leadership. GATT is a multilateral agreement with the objective of liberalizing trade by eliminating or re-ducing tariffs, subsidies, and import quotas. GATT membership includes over 100 nations and has had eight rounds of tariffs reductions, the most recent being the Uruguay Round that lasted from 1986–1993. In each round, mutual tariff reductions are negotiated between member nations and monitored by a mutually agreed upon system. If a member country feels that a violation has occurred, it can ask for an in-vestigation by the Geneva-based administrators of GATT. If the investigation un-covers a violation, member countries can be asked to pressure the violating country to change its policy and conform to the agreed upon tariffs and agreements. Some-times this pressure has not been sufficient to get an offending country to change. While GATT has assisted in developing more unrestricted trade, its voluntary mem-bership gives it little authority to ensure that this type of trade will occur.

Increasing Protectionist Attitudes

The support of GATT goes up and down. Although down in the 1970s, the support increased in the 1980s due to the rise in protectionist pressures in many industrial-ized countries. The renewed support reflected three events. First, the world trading system was strained by the persistent trade deficit of the United States, the world's largest economy, a situation that caused adjustments in such industries as automo-biles, semiconductors, steel, and textiles. Second, the economic success of a country perceived as not playing by the rules (e.g., Japan) has also strained the world's trad-ing systems. Japan's success as the world's largest trader and the perception that its internal markets are, in effect, closed to imports and foreign investment have caused problems. Finally, in response to these pressures, many countries have established bi-lateral voluntary export restraints to circumvent GATT. The economic prosperity of the 1990s has lessened the interest in GATT.

Trade Blocs and Free Trade Areas

Around the world, groups of nations are banding together to increase trade and in-vestment between nations in the group and exclude those nations outside the group. One little-known agreement between the United States and Israel, signed in 1985, establishes a Free Trade Area (FTA) between the two nations. All tariffs and quotas except on certain agricultural products were phased out over a 10-year pe-riod. In 1989, an FTA went into effect between Canada and the United States that phased out tariffs and quotas between the two countries, which are each other's largest trading partners.

Many trading alliances have evolved in the Americas. In 1991, the United States signed a framework trade agreement with Argentina, Brazil, Paraguay, and Uruguay to support the development of more liberal trade relations. The United States has also signed bilateral trade agreements with Bolivia, Chile, Colombia, Costa Rica, Ecuador, El Salvador, Honduras, Peru, and Venezuela. The North American Free Trade Agreement (NAFTA) among the United States, Canada, and Mexico is a much publicized agreement to reduce trade barriers and quotas and encourage investment among the three countries. Similarly, the Americas, Argentina, Brazil, Paraguay, and Uruguay operate under the Treaty of Asuncion, which created the Mercosul trade zone, a free-trade zone among the countries.

Another important trading bloc has been developed by the European Commu-nity (EC). Unlike GATT or NAFTA, the EC is founded on the principle of supranationality, with member nations not being able to enter into trade agreements on their own that are inconsistent with EC regulations. As nations are added, this EC trading bloc becomes an increasingly important factor for entrepreneurs doing international business.

Entrepreneur's Strategy and Trade Barriers

Clearly, *trade barriers* pose problems for the entrepreneur who wants to become involved in international business. First, trade barriers increase an entrepreneur's costs of exporting products or semifinished products to a country. If the increased cost puts the entrepreneur at a competitive disadvantage with respect to indigenous competitive products, it may be more economical to establish production facilities in the country. Second, voluntary export restraints may limit an entrepreneur's ability to sell products in a country from production facilities outside the country, which may also warrant establishing production facilities in the country in order to compete. Finally, an entrepreneur may have to locate assembly or production facilities in a country to conform to the local content regulations of the country.

trade barriers   Hindrances to doing international business

ENTREPRENEURIAL PARTNERING

One of the best methods for an entrepreneur to enter an international market is to partner with an entrepreneur in that country. These foreign entrepreneurs know the country and culture and therefore can facilitate business transactions while keeping the entrepreneur current on business, economic, and political conditions. This partnering is facilitated by understanding the nature of entrepreneurship in the country. Three areas of particular interest to U.S. entrepreneurs are Europe, the Far East, and transition economies.

Europe

Europe has only recently become interested in the growth of entrepreneurship. Risk taking in general is discouraged by most European cultures since business failure is often considered a social disgrace. Several changes in the social and political climate have conspired to change this traditional, security-conscious culture. Successful entrepreneurs, some of whom have become cultural heroes, are breaking through the stigma associated with striking out on one's own. In spite of the overregulation, new tax laws are providing incentives to would-be entrepreneurs in some countries.

One group exemplifying this new thinking consists of academics, especially scientists and engineers. Previously, many European academic circles disliked the practical world of commerce. Even for scientists and engineers working in commercial enterprises, entrepreneurship was not very enticing, as private corporations and public research organizations where they were employed offered secure, well-paid, risk-free careers. Today, more individuals are emerging in both academic circles and large companies who are looking for a challenge and are finding it in entrepreneurship. New government policies are making it easier to raise money for starting up businesses. Whereas Britain and France have an abundance of venture capital, German and Italian entrepreneurs are faced with limited access to bank credit for financing growth.

In 1983, the government of the United Kingdom created the Business Expansion Scheme (BES) to provide external capital to new and small business ventures. Investors in the BES receive a tax break on their investments in "unquoted" enterprises.[5]

In France, there are several difficulties confronting aspiring entrepreneurs. French venture capital is managed by bankers who are risk averse and have little understanding of the needs of small businesses and little regard for new venture creation. A second major hurdle for entrepreneurs is the French contempt for both failure and success. Inherited fortunes are respected, but created wealth is generally considered of lesser value, regardless of the money's origin.

Research in Ireland has produced a general profile of Irish entrepreneurs. The typical entrepreneur is a 40-year-old man who was the firstborn in his middle-class family. He is married, with three children. Although his parents are not educated, he typically completed high school and has experience in the field in which he is operating. This individual tends to be independent, energetic, goal-oriented, competitive, and flexible.[6]

One study of Northern Ireland entrepreneurs has similar findings. Despite the United Kingdom's significant investment in the education and financial support of entrepreneurs in Northern Ireland as well as other efforts made by the Industrial Development Board and the Northern Ireland Economic Council, entrepreneurship has not taken root. Many people are hesitant to start new businesses because, in addition to a volatile political situation, they must contend with high taxes, the high cost of capital, and customs regulations.[7]

In Sweden, a national survey of 1,500 female entrepreneurs and 300 male entrepreneurs broke down the population of entrepreneurs into three subclasses: single women (16 percent), married women (37 percent), and co-entrepreneurs, or husband and wife teams (47 percent). Although female entrepreneurs, ranging in age from 19 to 65, were found in almost every line of business and in every geographic location, they tended to be more active than men in areas of retail, restaurants, and service, and were found less in the manufacturing, construction, and transportation industries.[8] Another research study of businesses with 2 to 20 employees in the same industries found that entrepreneurs' willingness to let their businesses grow is influenced by an anticipated loss of control over the enterprise (deterrent), increased independence as a result of growth (motivator), and financial gains (motivator).[9]

The Far East

Entrepreneurial success in some Asian countries has been significant because of the culture and the political and economic systems in place. For example, while Malaysia and Singapore are very close geographically, share some common history, and were once a part of the British Empire, both have evolved in very different ways.

The people of the Malaysia peninsula converted from Islam in the 15th century, not long before the advent of European rule that lasted more than 400 years. The natives traditionally lived in rural areas, leaving the cities to the dominant foreign powers, a situation that delayed industrialization and produced a lack of social mobility in the country. While the government established the Malaysian Industrial Development Authority to promote and coordinate efforts to eradicate poverty and to restructure the social environment through economic development and stability, the agency has not accomplished much.

The roots of entrepreneurship in Singapore reach as far back as the 14th century. In 1819, Sir Stamford Raffles bought the island and transformed it into a refuge for entrepreneurs, establishing a free port open to merchants of any ethnic background. When Singapore claimed its independence from Malaysia in 1965, the island became ethnically pluralistic, wrote secularism into its constitution, and gave tax incentives to entrepreneurs. In 1985, the Small Enterprise Bureau of Singapore was established to provide information and guidance to entrepreneurs in starting and expanding their enterprises. Social mobility is high, and entrepreneurial success is greatly esteemed.[10]

Japan is a country whose social structure does not encourage entrepreneurship. Large corporations have dominated the economy for some time, and most Japanese entrepreneurial activity is limited to service and information-technology industries. Even though these giant organizations encourage innovation and invention in their employees, research findings indicate that the five most important motivators for starting a high-technology firm in Japan were all centered on desires for self-actualization and creativity, a need not addressed by this consensus-oriented society.[11] Trailblazers like Wataru Ohashi and Kazuhiko Nishi are slowly breaking down the psychological barriers that block entrepreneurship. Ohashi began a parcel-delivery service in 1981 that has since evolved into an enterprise that directly markets luxury items. The company makes over half of its earnings from the sales of items like melons, fresh salmon, caviar, and furs.[12] Similarly, Nishi, at the age of 20, left the highly acclaimed Waseda University to start his own company. Eventually teaming up with Microsoft's Bill Gates, Nishi's company, ASCII, within years became the biggest PC software supplier in Japan.[13]

By contrast, Hong Kong is a hotbed of entrepreneurial activity. Many of the present entrepreneurs were previously managers of large companies before they broke away to start their own businesses. As a center for venture capital, Hong Kong has produced some of the wealthiest men in the world. For example, Sir Yu Pao, driven out by Chinese Communists in 1948, worked initially to establish his family in the import-export business. In the mid-1980s, he bought his first ship, a coal-burning steamer. Since that time, Pao has built his fleet to become the world's largest private independent shipowner and has amassed a personal fortune of over $1 billion. Kuang-Piu Chao is another refugee of Communist China who left in the 1950s. Chao runs one of Hong Kong's largest textile operations, which, in 1987, claimed a 4 percent share of Hong Kong's knitwear exports market. Li Ka-Shing arrived in Hong Kong with his parents at age 12. When his father died two years later, Li became the family breadwinner. By 20, Li was factory manager at the plastics factory where he first went to work, and several years later he had enough money to start his own plastic flower factory. With an estimated net worth of over $230 million, Li has a controlling interest in companies that are valued at over $1 billion.[14]

Controlled and Transition Economies

Although China's centralized, planned economy has not openly encouraged entrepreneurship, there still has been a great deal of entrepreneurial activity taking place under the Communist umbrella. Guau Guarymei, a worker from Benxi, is just one of many examples. Guarymei leased eight government-run shops in 1985 and rapidly changed them from businesses operating at a loss to profitable enterprises. How did she do it? Guarymei reduced the managerial staff by 50 percent, devised a method of pay that made wages a function of performance, and instituted a system of fines for those who broke discipline. Controversy occurred over the amount of Guarymei's income, as it was 20 times the wage of an average salesperson. This income level stands in opposition to the egalitarian socialist system in which every person enjoys equal benefits, regardless of the amount and quality of his or her contribution. These old values are slowly giving way to the idea of a society that rewards those making contributions.[15]

Guau Guarymei is an example of a rising number of women entrepreneurs in China. One study indicated that Chinese women entrepreneurs were mainly in the textile and clothing industries and have enterprises that have been operating for 10 or more years, mainly in the coastal area of the country. The majority of the women entrepreneurs were between the ages of 40 and 50, received secondary technical training or higher education, and were members of the Communist party.[16]

Although the educational level of women entrepreneurs in China is lower than their counterparts in other countries, the problems they encounter are much the same. Capital is lacking. There is a need for training and education in management, administration, and coordination of personnel. Finally, there is a need for supportive government policy and infrastructure.

In Poland, the transitional upheaval and lack of adequate reform have led to a thriving black market, particularly in hard currency. One man who saw an opportunity was Bogdan Chosna, a 36-year-old Polish manager and co-owner of Promotor, a trading company based in Warsaw. In the 1980s, Chosna made a fortune by using investors' stashes of hard Western currency to buy cheap personal computers from Taiwan and Singapore. He then sold them to businesses at a premium in zloty, the country's currency, and exchanged the vast profits in zlotys for dollars on the black market.

Another successful entrepreneur is Leonid Melamed from Riga, Latvia, in the former U.S.S.R. Melamed began his professional life as a military lawyer, but since the advent of perestroika, he has established 15 businesses—among them three newspapers, a stainless steel cutlery operation, and a women's lingerie business. When the government began allowing joint ventures, Melamed promptly reinvested 4 million rubles of his earnings in a joint venture with a Polish company and later found other partners in West Germany and the United States.

The economic reforms taking place in both once-controlled and less-developed economies have been supported by the Overseas Private Investment Corporation (OPIC) of the U.S. government. OPIC provides a number of services, such as (1) selling political risk insurance that covers currency inconvertibility, appropriation, and political violence (long-term policies, up to 20 years); (2) offering direct loans—up to $6 million to individuals with a total outlay of $20 million; (3) providing loan guarantees up to $200 million; (4) organizing overseas missions through which U.S. businesspeople can explore investment possibilities; and (5) providing investor information services.

One country becoming more entrepreneurial, due in part to OPIC, is Hungary. The reforms in this country have supported decentralization, private initiative, and market orientation of the economy. A survey of Hungarian entrepreneurs found that most of them were between the ages of 30 and 50 and equally divided among three educational levels: craftsman school, high school, and university. Most of the entrepreneurs are operating in the service sector, with firm size generally small, although the number of employees ranges from 1 to 300.[17]

IN REVIEW

Summary

International business is becoming increasingly important to more and more entrepreneurs and to their country's economy. International entrepreneurship—the conducting of business activities by an entrepreneur across national boundaries—is occurring much earlier in the growth of new ventures as opportunities open up in the hypercompetitive global arena. Several factors (economics, stage of economic development, balance of payments, type of system, political-legal environment, cultural environment, and technological environment) make decisions in international entrepreneurship more complex than those in domestic entrepreneurship.

The following four strategic issues are important for an entrepreneur to consider before going international: the allocation of responsibility between the U.S. and foreign operation; the type of planning, reporting, and control system to be used; the appropriate organizational structure; and the degree of standardization possible.

Once an entrepreneur decides to be involved in international business, three general modes of market entry need to be considered: exporting, nonequity arrangements, and equity arrangements. Each mode has several alternatives providing varying degrees of risk, control, and ownership.

Entrepreneurs in the United States can find their counterparts in a wide variety of economies. Entrepreneurship is thriving from Dublin to Hong Kong, providing new products and new jobs, and providing an opportunity for partnering.

Questions for Discussion

1. Why is international business so important to an entrepreneur and the United States specifically?
2. What are the similarities and differences between international and domestic business management?
3. Discuss the various options for entrepreneurs to enter into international business and the advantages and disadvantages of each.
4. Discuss the use of joint ventures as a method for entering such markets as Hungary, the former U.S.S.R., Thailand, and Iran.
5. What are the similarities and differences among entrepreneurs in the United States, Europe, and the Far East, and in areas with controlled economies?

Key Terms

balance of payments	indirect exporting
barter	international entrepreneurship
direct exporting	joint venture
diversified activity merger	licensing
exporting	majority interest
horizontal merger	management contract

market extension merger

minority interest

nonequity arrangements

product extension merger

synergy

third-party arrangements

trade barriers

turn-key projects

vertical merger

More Information—Net Addresses in This Chapter

Adobe Systems
www.adobe.com

American Tourister
www.vacations.com/American_Tourister

ASCII
www.ASCII.com

Invacare
www.invacare.com

Logitech
www.logitech.com

Malaysian Industrial Development
Authority
www.jaring.my/mida

McDonald's
www.mcdonalds.com

MicroPatent Inc.
www.micropat.com

Microsoft
www.microsoft.com

Miller Brewing
millerlite.com

Mouse Systems Corp.
www.mousesystems.com

Nestle
www.nestle.com

Olivetti
www.olivetti.it

Phillips Petroleum
www.phillips66.com

Ricoh Corporation
www.ricohpg.com

7-Eleven
www.7-11.com

Venrock Associates
www.venrock.com

Yamaha
www.yamaha.com

Selected Readings

Acs, Zoltan J.; Randall Morck; J. Myles Shaver; and Bernard Yeung. (1997). The Internationalization of Small and Medium-Sized Enterprises: A Policy Perspective. *Small Business Economics,* vol. 9, no. 1, pp. 7–20.

> *The international diffusion of innovations of small and medium-sized enterprises is discussed. These firms face two challenges in globalization: property rights protection and barriers to entry. It is suggested that these barriers can frequently be circumvented by using existing multinationals as international conduits for innovations of small and medium-sized firms. Policy guidelines to improve the overall rate of international diffusion of innovation by small and medium enterprises are proposed.*

Antoncic, Bostjan; and Robert D. Hisrich. (1999). An Integrative Conceptual Model. In Leo Paul Dana, ed., *International Entrepreneurship: An Anthology.* Singapore: NTU-Entrepreneurship Development Centre, pp. 15–32.

> *Two main streams in international entrepreneurship research (SME internationalization and international start-ups) are integrated into a conceptual model. Central to this model is the concept of internationalization that consists of internationalization properties (time and mode) and internationalization performance. Other elements of the model are internationalization antecedents (environmental conditions and organizational characteristics) and internationalization consequences (organizational performance).*

Chirinko, Robert S.; and C. Morris. (1994). Fiscal Policies Aimed at Spurring Capital Formation: A Framework for Analysis. *Economic Review*, vol. 79, no. 1, pp. 59–73.

The article is divided into four sections: (1) why capital formation is an important determinant of economic growth; (2) how the optimal amount of capital formation (therefore, economic growth) is determined; (3) nature of economic distortions and how they cause capital formation to be suboptimal; and (4) impact of various fiscal policies. Highlights interaction among markets and uncertainties of the responsiveness of investment and saving to interest rates and other factors. Conclusion is that policy should focus on distortions that disrupt the capital formation process.

Davis, Peter S. and Paula D. Harveston. (2000) Internationalization and Organizational Growth: The Impact of Internet Usage and Technology Involvement among Entrepreneur-Led Family Business. *Family Business Review*, vol. 13, no. 2, pp. 107–120.

Using data from a U.S. survey of entrepreneur-led family business, this paper examines the extent to which certain entrepreneurial characteristics, Internet usage, and investments in information technology influence internationalization and organizational growth among such firms.

Hisrich, Robert D.; and Gyula Fulop. (1993). Women Entrepreneurs in Controlled Economies—A Hungarian Perspective. *Proceedings*, 1993 Conference on Entrepreneurship, pp. 25–40.

The results of a survey of women entrepreneurs in Hungary indicate that they possess many attributes similar to their U.S. counterparts and are playing an important role in the market transformation occurring in the country.

Hisrich, Robert D.; and Mikhail Gratchev. (1993). The Russian Entrepreneur. *Journal of Business Venturing*, vol. 8, no. 6, pp. 487–97.

The historical background of entrepreneurship in Russia is discussed along with scenarios of three present-day entrepreneurial firms—a high-tech company, a Russian brokerage company, and an educational organization.

Hisrich, Robert D.; and Janos Vecsenyi. (1990). Entrepreneurship and the Hungarian Transformation. *Journal of Managerial Psychology*, vol. 5, no. 5, pp. 11–16.

Characteristics of entrepreneurs and their businesses are presented as well as the changes suggested to support new venture creation such as education, business, infrastructure, and government policy initiatives.

McDougall, Patricia Phillips; Scott Shane; and Benjamin M. Oviatt. (1994). Explaining the Formation of International New Ventures: The Limits of Theories from International Business Research. *Journal of Business Venturing*, vol. 9, pp. 469–87.

Analysis of 24 international new ventures reveals formation processes that are not explained by existing theories from international business. Beyond an opportunistic orientation, the founders of INVs create international business competencies from the time of venture formation, using hybrid structures for their international activities as a way to overcome the usual poverty of resources at the time of start-up.

McDougall, P. P.; and B. M. Oviatt. (1997). International Entrepreneurship Literature in the 1990s and Directions for Future Research. In D. L. Sexton and R. W. Smilor, eds., *Entrepreneurship 2000*. Chicago, IL: Upstart Publishing Company, pp. 291–320.

International entrepreneurship research is at the intersection of two growing areas of interest: entrepreneurship and international business. Seven major topics of international entrepreneurship research are identified: (1) cooperative alliances, (2) economic development initiatives, (3) entrepreneur characteristics and motivations, (4) exporting and other market entry modes, (5) new ventures and IPOs, (6) transitioning economies, and (7) venture financing.

Moini, A. H. (1998). Small Firms Exporting: How Effective Are Government Export Assistance Programs? *Journal of Small Business Management*, vol. 36, no. 1, pp. 1–15.

Small firms were segmented using an internationalization process model into four categories: (1) nonexporters, (2) partially interested exporters, (3) growing exporters, and (4) regular ex-

porters. The results suggest that awareness and effectiveness of government export assistance programs vary by the degree of internationalization of the firm, and that firm and decision-maker characteristics influence the effectiveness of these programs.

Oviatt, Benjamin M. (1995). Entrepreneurs on a Worldwide Stage. *Academy of Management Executive*, vol. 9, no. 2, pp. 30–43.

Most people expect new ventures to begin domestically and their internal operations to evolve slowly, but global start-ups are international at inception. The founders of 12 multinational start-ups are interviewed, demonstrating that the current and increasingly global nature of demand in many markets is one of the main forces encouraging the formation of global start-ups.

Reuber, A. Rebecca; and Eileen Fischer. (1997). The Influence of the Management Team's International Experience on the Internationalization Behaviors of SMEs. *Journal of International Business Studies*, vol. 28, no. 4, pp. 807–25.

The role of the international team's experience in small and medium-sized enterprises is examined for internationalization of Canadian software product firms. Findings suggest that internationally experienced management teams have a greater propensity to develop foreign strategic partners and to delay less in obtaining foreign sales after start-up. These behaviors are associated with a higher degree of internationalization.

Endnotes

1. Portions of this profile were adapted from Jolly and Bechler, "Logitech: The Mouse That Roared," *Strategy & Leadership* 20, no. 6 (1992), pp. 20–48.
2. J. A. Lee, "Cultural Analysis in Overseas Operations," *Harvard Business Review* (March–April 1966), pp. 106–14.
3. W. J. Keegan, "A Conceptual Framework for Multinational Marketing," *Journal of World Business* (November–December 1972), p. 75.
4. J. A. Cohen, "Footwear and the Jet Set," *Management Review* (March 1990), pp. 42–45.
5. R. T. Harrison and C. M. Mason, "Risk Finance, the Equity Gap, and New Venture Formation in the United Kingdom: The Impact of the Business Expansion Scheme," *Frontiers of Entrepreneurship Research* (1988), pp. 595–611.
6. R. D. Hisrich and B. O'Cinneide, "The Irish Entrepreneur: Characteristics, Problems, and Future Success," *Frontiers in Entrepreneurship Research* (1986), pp. 66–75.
7. R. D. Hisrich, "The Entrepreneur in North Ireland: Characteristics, Problems, and Recommendations for the Future," *Journal of Small Business Management*, pp. 32–39.
8. C. Holmquist and E. Sundin, "Women as Entrepreneurs in Sweden: Conclusions from a Survey," *Frontiers of Entrepreneurship Research* (1988), pp. 626–42.
9. P. Davidsson, "Entrepreneurship—and After? A Study of Growth Willingness in Small Firms," *Journal of Business Venturing* 4 (May 1989), pp. 211–26.
10. L. P. Dana, "Entrepreneurship and Venture Creation—An Entrepreneurial Comparison of Five Commonwealth Nations," *Frontiers of Entrepreneurship Research* (1987), pp. 573–89.
11. D. M. Ray, "Factors Influencing Entrepreneurial Events in Japanese High-Technology Venture Business," *Frontiers of Entrepreneurial Research* (1987), pp. 557–72.
12. T. Holden, "Deliverymen Who Always Ring Twice," *Business Week* (May 23, 1988), p. 135.
13. S. M. Dabrot, "Tensaiji: Whiz Kid Wins Business—Even in Japan," *Scientific American* (January 1990), p. 104.
14. "Hong Kong's Entrepreneurs on a Winning Streak," *Euromoney* (November 1987), pp. 44, 46, and 48.
15. L. Delysin, "The Case of an Entrepreneur," *World Press Review* (January 1988), pp. 23–24.
16. R. D. Hisrich and Zhang Fan, "Women Entrepreneurs in the People's Republic of China: An Exploratory Study," *Journal of Managerial Psychology* 6, no. 1 (March–April 1991).
17. J. Vecsenyi and R. D. Hisrich, "Entrepreneurship and the Hungarian Transformation: An Entrepreneurial Perspective," *Journal of Managerial Psychology* 5 (1990), pp. 11–16.

CASE Ia   Rock and Roll Bilge Pump

The Rock and Roll Bilge Pump. The name alone should attract some interest in the product, owners Craig Peters and Burt Larson thought when they decided to market a new bilge pump for boats. Their product was innovative. It was the only bilge pump that didn't need batteries or electricity. It worked solely on the natural rocking motion of the waves.

Peters, who had invented the product, took care of manufacturing. Larson, who had over 20 years of experience as an advertising salesman, took care of marketing. So far, he had written retailers, distributors, and individual boat owners telling them about the product. He had also placed ads for the product in the leading trade magazines.

Positive publicity about the product had been generated, and retailers had expressed interest in it. While sales had been slow in coming, Larson and Peters didn't think there was anything wrong with their current strategy. They just felt it was a matter of time before the Rock and Roll Bilge Pump would catch on.

THE BOATING INDUSTRY

Pleasure boating began in the United States as a pastime for the wealthy, whose yachts decorated the coastal waterways from Bar Harbor, Maine, to Palm Beach, Florida. After World War II and the development of fiberglass, boating was popularized around the country, especially in the freshwater areas.

No matter how successful boating became as an inland pastime, it was still primarily a coastal business. Boat ownership in the coastal states accounted for 52 percent of U.S. pleasure boat sales but more than 69 percent of marine dealer sales.

In addition, the bulk of money spent on boating was spent by people who owned larger boats. Sixty percent of the money was spent on boats ranging from 16 to 26 feet, even though these boats represented only 5 percent of the number of total boat sales.

Between 1975 and 1980, there was a 17.7 percent increase in the total number of pleasure boats in service. While boats under 16 feet in length represented the bulk of U.S. pleasure fleets, these smaller boats had increased only 11.5 percent from 1975 to 1980, well behind the 17.7 percent average rate of gain for all size segments.

Boats 16 to 26 feet, on the other hand, had experienced an incredible growth. There were 29 percent more new boats in this size range than in the smaller size group.

Growth in the 26- to 40-foot range had been a little under 15 percent. One reason for this was that boat owners experienced difficulty in finding mooring spots for large boats. In contrast, launching spots for the under-26-foot pleasure boat could be found almost anywhere in the United States.

Beyond the 40-foot market, the absolute numbers were small, but the growth rates were high—160 percent above average. These owners were not sensitive to inhibitors such as cost, inflation, and interest rates.

Surveys and sales analyses showed that powerboaters usually entered and left the market as the spirit moved them. They were not as interested in boating per se as sailors were. One reason cited was the cost of fuel. Sailboat builders had to cope with interest and inflation problems, but the fuel situation was much less relevant for them than it was for powerboaters.

ROCK AND ROLL BILGE PUMP

In October 1981, Craig Peters and Burt Larson formed a partnership to manufacture and market the bilge pump for boats.

Peters, 28, had grown up in Miami, Florida. As an only child, Peters began sailing with his marine biologist parents when he was five. He fell in love with the ocean and spent as much time as possible there when he was growing up. His peers called him a loner because he spent most of his free time reading on his parents' boat. He did well in school and eventually received a college degree in engineering at a local university. Largely at his parents' urging, he took a job with Honeywell as an engineer. However, Peters soon decided he could not sit at a desk for the rest of his life and found himself back at the ocean—this time as a professional skipper of large yachts. He eventually married and moved to Newport, Rhode Island, where he had been stationed for 15 years prior to this time.

In his spare time, Peters invented the Rock and Roll Bilge Pump. After acquiring the necessary financing to manufacture the product, he had quit the skipper business largely in response to his wife's disenchantment with his extended time away from home. For the last year, Peters had worked full time on the manufacturing aspect of the product.

Burt Larson, a man whom Peters had contacted about investing in the pump, had over 20 years of experience as an advertising salesman. He was originally from New York but had moved to the West Coast when he graduated from college. The urge to move closer to his family had brought Larson back to Newport, Rhode Island. His hobby was reading up on new inventions and investing in the ones he thought had a chance of becoming marketable products. To date, most of his investments had not been very successful. Even though he had no previous experience in the boating industry, he was sure the Rock and Roll Bilge Pump was a winner. He had initially been a silent investor in the project. However, as plans for the product progressed, Larson became more involved and more excited about it. Since he wasn't that happy with his present advertising job, he eventually decided to make marketing the Rock and Roll Bilge Pump his full-time job.

The Product

The product's mode of operation was very simple. It worked on the natural action of waves, which rock a boat back and forth. Operating in a fashion similar to a hand pump, a weighted pendulum provided the priming needed to drive the pump. The rougher the water, the more motion from the pendulum and the more pumping exerted. The bilge pump could flush out approximately 500 gallons of water per day.

The product's most distinctive feature was its ability to work automatically without a conventional power system. It was the only pump on the market that would work on an unattended boat that had no conventional power system. This feature allowed boat owners to feel at ease while their boats were collecting water from leaks, rain, or rough water wash. The pump could also act as a backup to automatic electric pumps when battery drain was a problem.

Price

The pump was midrange within the competition in both feature and price. At the high end were the higher-priced automatics and the industrial hand pumps. The lower end included the hand-operated mounted and portable pumps.

A suggested retail price of $49.50 was originally established. However, due to increased manufacturing costs, the price was recently raised to $60 per unit. This was still competitive with comparable automatic and hand pumps. The cost to marine retailers was originally set at $29.55 per unit, but due to the price increase it was now $35.50. The shipping price was $2.50 F.O.B. manufacturer. A discount of $22.50 per unit, plus shipping costs, was offered if 10 or more units were ordered.

Manufacturing

Peters and Larson had established a small manufacturing facility outside of Chicago. The cost involved to set up the plant was $20,000: $10,000 in machinery investment and $10,000 in inventory.

As one size was suitable for boats ranging in length from 10 to 40 feet, the production process was standardized. Peters did all the manufacturing, assembling, and packaging of the product himself. Capacity was limited to approximately 100 units per week. However, production had halted completely for two months when Peters' wife was in the hospital.

Promotion

Since the beginning of the operations six months before, ads had been placed in several trade magazines. Form letters had been sent to retailers, distributors, and boat owners. Professionally designed flyers were created to respond to requests for information generated by the mail-order program.

Good local exposure had been achieved through the company's participation in a local boat show. Reaction to the bilge pump was quite favorable from both boat owners and retailers.

Sail, a prestigious trade magazine, had recently written an editorial about the bilge pump that elaborated upon its distinctive features. Since the editorial amounted to an endorsement, Larson felt sure it would stimulate the reader's interest in the product.

So far, a total of $5,000 had been spent to promote the product. Larson had received approximately 50 requests for further product information and 30 sales from the mail-order campaign. Five sales were generated from the boat show. Although 12 units had been placed with various retailers as display models, there had been no sales from that source.

EXHIBIT 1   Pro Forma Income Statement

Sales	Year 1	Year 2	Year 3
Volumne	525	1,688	5,290
Selling price	$ 35.50	$ 39	$ 43
Variable expenses/unit	27	30	33
Dollar	18,638	65,832	227,470
Less variable expenses	14,175	50,640	174,570
Gross margin:	$ 4,463	$ 15,192	$ 52,900
Less fixed expenses	31,650	35,595	48,635
Income (loss) before taxes	$(27,187)	$(20,403)	$ 4,265

Distribution

Little progress had been made in terms of establishing a distribution channel for the product. Limited production capacity was cited as the main deterrent. The partners felt that establishing a distribution channel would create a demand that Peters could not handle at the plant himself.

Financial Information

Exhibit 1 is a pro forma income statement that Larson had prepared for the next three years. The projections assumed that distribution efforts would begin in Illinois and then move into the Great Lakes states by the end of year 2. The pro forma statement indicates that the bilge pump would lose $27,187 and $20,403 in years 1 and 2, but would show a fair profit of $4,265 in year 3.

Over the six months of operation, Larson had not concentrated on segmenting the boating industry. He had determined neither a clearly defined target market nor the appropriate distribution channels. Recently, he had broken down the categories of the boating population into the three segments and listed the pros and cons he felt were attached to each segment (see Exhibit 2). From this information, Larson had determined that the best market for the Rock and Roll Bilge Pump was weekend sailors who owned boats less than 30 feet in length. However, no analysis had been done of the potential market size and demand, the geographic location of that market, or the characteristics and buying habits of the end user.

Despite these problems, the partners felt they had made significant progress in achieving product awareness in the first year and felt optimistic about the future of the Rock and Roll Bilge Pump.

EXHIBIT 2   Alternative Markets

ALTERNATIVE MARKET 1—SAILBOATS

1–15 Feet

PRO
1. Usually do not come equipped with a pump
2. Large, growing market for day sailor
3. Appeal to energy-conscious consumer

CON
1. Some of these sailboats do not have an open cockpit or have no cockpit
2. These smaller boats are trailered or pulled from water when not in use
3. Rock and Roll Pump is too expensive for buyer

16–26 Feet

PRO
1. Usually do not come equipped with a pump
2. Large use in ocean(s) where wave action is best
3. Large growing market
4. These boats stay moored
5. Owned by middle- to upper-income-level people with disposable income
6. Energy-conscious consumer

CON
1. Sailboats in the upper end of this category tend to have an onboard electrical system and built-in bilge pump

27 Feet and Above

PRO
1. High disposable income; may want to try gadget

CON
1. All boats in this class come equipped with automatic electric bilge pump
2. The larger boats may not feel the effect of wave motion sufficiently to operate pump

ALTERNATIVE MARKET 2—MOTORBOATS

0-15 Feet

PRO
1. Pump works better in smaller boat
2. Expensive motors need protection from submersion
3. Large population of older, leaky wooden boats

CON
1. Usually are trailered
2. Cyclical market
3. Declining market
4. Price-sensitive market due to gas prices
5. Consumer not concerned with natural energy
6. Pump is too expensive for typical buyer

16 Feet and Above

PRO
1. Owner typically has more disposable income
2. Relatively stable market
3. Stays moored

CON
1. These boats come equipped with electrical system and bilge pump
2. Consumer not concerned with natural energy

ALTERNATIVE MARKET 3—MANUAL POWERED BOATS

All Lengths

PRO
1. May be used for the boat left moored while the boat is being used for the day or weekend

CON
1. Owner is not interested in gadgets
2. Too expensive for buyers
3. These boats are trailered or pulled out of water

CASE Ib   A. Monroe Lock and Security Systems

Ray Monroe was sitting back in his chair in his home office trying to understand why the new venture had not made him the rich man he thought he would be. A. Monroe Lock and Security Systems (AMLSS) had been established about two years ago and offered locksmithing services to residential and commercial customers as well as automobile owners in the greater Boston area. These services included lock rekeying, lock and deadbolt installation and repair, master key systems, emergency residential lockouts, foreign and domestic automobile lockouts, and window security locks. In addition, AMLSS was certified by the Commonwealth of Massachusetts to perform alarm installation and offered a full range of alarm products.

Financial results have been relatively poor, with losses of $6,500 in the first year and a profit of only about $3,500 in year 2. Currently, AMLSS's target market is three local communities in the Boston area with similar demographics (see Exhibit 1).

EXHIBIT 1 Demographic Profile of Present Market			
Demographics	Newton	Needham	Wellesley
Total population	83,704	29,890	28,288
Total # households	31,378	11,139	9,229
Percent family	67.4	74.5	75.6
Percent nonfamily	32.6	25.5	24.4
Total # families	19,952	7,675	6,492
# married-couple families	16,662	6,633	5,607
# female-householder families	2,536	818	700
Average household income	$98,487	92,214	121,919
Education			
Percent high school educated	91.7	94.4	95.4
Percent college or higher educated	57.2	53.7	68.5
Labor force			
Percent of total population employed	70.1	67.1	63.9
Percent of female population employed	62.7	57.2	54.9
Disability			
Percent w/mobility or self-care dis. (16−64)	5	4.6	3.9
Percent w/mobility or self-care dis. (65+)	24.7	28.2	21.1
Total # housing units	30,497	10,405	8,764
Median # of rooms	6.4	6.7	7.2
Total # of owner-occupied housing units	20,297	8,097	6,847
Total # of renter-occupied housing units	9,158	2,063	1,625
Total # of housing units authorized in permit issuing places (1991)	31	34	36
Retail industry— # of establishments (1987)	609	175	196
Service industry—# of establishments (1987)	1,106	343	490
Total # of lodging places	9	3	3

BACKGROUND

Ray Monroe is the only child of parents who were both successful entrepreneurs. His parents are now deceased, and Monroe received a substantial inheritance that would satisfy any of his financial needs for the rest of his life. Ray had been educated at a local private high school and then at a small liberal arts college in Vermont. He was not a great student but always seemed to get by. His summers were usually spent at the college, taking summer courses.

Upon graduation, his father had helped him get a job with a friend who owned a security and alarm manufacturing business in the western part of the state. Ray worked in various areas of the business learning a great deal about alarms and locks. After two years there, Ray decided that he'd prefer to be his own boss and, using some of his inheritance, entered a special program to learn more about the locksmith business. His intent upon completion of the program was to start his own lock and security business. He felt from his experience and education that this market offered tremendous opportunities. Increased crime and residential house sales that often required new locks offered many opportunities to succeed in this business.

Ray did not want to offer alarm installations as part of his new venture since he felt that they were bothersome to install. He also knew that there were many large competitors already in the alarm market that would be able to offer products and service at much lower prices.

INDUSTRY STRUCTURE/COMPETITION

The locksmith industry was dominated by small operators, 60 percent of which consisted of an owner and one employee. Only about 20 percent of these firms had five or more employees.

Because of the low entry barriers, the number of small operators had grown dramatically in the past few years. These businesses were often operated out of the home with no storefront and concentrated mainly on the residential market. There were also a large number of family-owned businesses that usually had a retail store serving their communities for several generations of family members. The larger operators were the most sophisticated in terms of service and products and relied primarily on commercial accounts.

The Boston area was densely populated, with 160 locksmiths all advertising in the local yellow pages. In the three communities on which AMLSS concentrated, there were 37 other locksmiths.

PRESENT STRATEGY

Excluding alarms, Ray offered just about every locksmith service. His company van was used to store these products and any necessary tools for servicing his clients. This company van was 10 years old with a few minor dents, but it ran quite well.

Ray had a beeper system and a cellular phone in order to respond to customer requests. After 5 P.M., however, Ray turned off the system and refused to take calls. During his operating hours he was able to respond to all requests fairly quickly even if he was not in the office, primarily because of the beeper and cellular phone. He had tried using an answering machine, but it did not allow him to respond to a customer fast enough, especially if he was at a job that kept him out of the office for a number of hours. He also knew that many job requests were emergencies and required a quick response.

EXHIBIT 2   A. Monroe Monthly Billings for Year Two

January	$ 900.01
February	1,960.85
March	2,477.26
April	1,448.62
May	622.20
June	1,114.12
July	1,295.18
August	1,352.37
September	1,964.64
October	2,102.19
November	3,447.37
December	1,605.80
Total	$20,260.61

EXHIBIT 3   Year Two Expenses

Business expenses	
Selling expenses	$ 7,574
Memberships (Chambers of Commerce and Associated Locksmiths of America)	1,190
Answering service	720
Telephone	900
Office expenses (materials/supplies)	1,575
Yellow pages	4,200
Other promotional expenses	600
Total expenses	$16,759

During the past year, Ray had decided to advertise in the yellow pages. He felt that with all the locksmiths listed in the yellow pages he needed to be at the top of the list, so he decided to use his middle name initial (for Arthur) to form A. Monroe Locksmith and Security Systems. The yellow pages ad seemed to help business and contributed to the $2,500 profit (see Exhibits 2 and 3 for billing and expenses).

Ray spent a lot of his time in the office thinking of ways to increase his business, yet to this point nothing had been very successful. His understanding was that many of his competitors had found that the yellow pages were the most likely place for customers to find a locksmith. His ad identified the three communities, the services he offered, and a telephone number. In addition, he included that he was bonded and insured and a member of the Massachusetts Locksmith Association. Competitors typically stressed products and services, 24-hour emergency service, follow-up guarantee service, being bonded and insured, and membership in the locksmith association.

Time was running out for Ray, and he was trying to think of other businesses that he could start up. He would often question his decision to enter the locksmith business, but then he would quickly decide that since he didn't really need the money, it wasn't a big deal. However, at some point he felt he should try to establish himself so he could settle down to a more routine life.

CASE Ic   Display Products Technology Limited

INTRODUCTION

David Wares had a problem. He had decided to leave IBM when his current contract expired to start his own business, Display Products Technology, but was then offered a permanent position with a very attractive package. His dilemma was compounded by the conflicting views of his potential partners and his family. Should he stay or should he go?

BACKGROUND

David Wares, a 26-year-old test engineer with IBM, developed the idea for Display Products Technology (DPT) after a series of events had left him wondering where his career within IBM was going. As a contract employee, David was concerned about the uncertainty of his position. This was most evident in early 1993: His four-year contract was running out in October of that year, and he had not had a satisfactory meeting with his manager to discuss his future.

David had developed a significant specialty in liquid crystal display (LCD) technology and regarded himself as something of a guru in this field. He enjoyed the challenge of this new technology and was concerned that, with the market failure of IBM's new LCD monitor and the loss of local control over the development of the IBM notebook computer, he would be unable to continue to work in this area at IBM. All indicators pointed to LCDs as the display products of the future, and Wares wanted to capitalize on his expertise.

In February 1993, Wares decided to seek some advice on setting up his own business. He approached Glasgow Opportunities, an advisory service for start-up and small businesses, to discuss his ideas for a consulting business. He was advised to carry out some market testing of his idea and approached a number of companies using LCD panels in their products, including Compaq and Apple. It quickly became apparent that there was a need for a service but not simply for consulting. All LCD panels were manufactured in the Far East, and when there was a problem in manufacturing or with a warranty claim by a user, it was necessary to ship the panel overseas for testing and repair, an expensive process.

During his conversations with the computer manufacturers and LCD panel manufacturers, he realized that in many cases the LCDs need not have been dispatched to the Far East at considerable cost because either the units were beyond repair and should simply have been scrapped locally, or the fault lay not in the LCD panel but in the computer itself. No one in Europe had the skills to test the panels, so all faulty LCDs had to be shipped.

The opportunity David was looking for had materialized. He decided to set up a screening service for testing faulty LCDs. Along with two friends, Bill and Ted, David

This case study forms part of a series of case studies developed on behalf of Scottish Enterprise to highlight the role of the entrepreneur in the creation and development of a business.
It was prepared by John Anderson of Price Waterhouse under the supervision of Frank Martin, University of Stirling. www.dpt.ltd.co.uk/

produced a business plan (Exhibit 2) and set up DPT. David would leave IBM when his contract expired and would be joined in the future by Bill and Ted at a time when the business could afford them.

THE HORNS OF A DILEMMA

David was now very excited by these plans and was counting the days until the end of October. However, one morning in July his boss threw a monkey wrench in the works. He called David into his office saying that he had some very good news for him:

Boss: David—great news. I have managed to persuade the guys upstairs that we should give you a permanent position with the company. That work that you did on the LCD monitor project was noticed up the line. Like me, they believe you have a great future with us. Here is an offer letter, just a formality really. I have managed to get you a big increase, too. Isn't that great?

David: Eh . . . yes. Great.

That evening:

David: What on earth do we do now? This offer is really good. I'm confused.

Bill: I don't think this changes anything. You have already decided to leave, and you shouldn't let this change your mind.

Ted: Yes. The opportunities for DPT are too good. We have to go for it.

David: What do you mean we! I'm the one who's leaving my job, not you. You two still have the security of employment and a salary. This offer would give me that, too.

Ted: David, we both have families and a mortgage—you don't.

Bill: Look, David. Before today there was only one way forward. You were going into the business full time, and we were working with you in the evenings and on weekends. We are not suggesting that this changes anything at all. We are just as committed to DPT as you. Have you spoken to your mother about this?

David: Yes. She hasn't said much, but I think that she would be happier if I accepted and "had a proper job"!

Bill: So what are you going to do?

David: I don't know. I'll sleep on it and talk to you tomorrow.

EXHIBIT 1   Background Information on David Wares

SCIENCE-BASED EDUCATION

David Wares' fascination with science and how things worked began at school, and when it came to choosing a university course, he settled on a program of practical science that focused on a new area of study. He chose laser physics and optoelectronics at Strathclyde University in Glasgow, England and graduated in 1989 with a BSc Honors degree. His frequent comments to his friends that one day he would be a millionaire seemed increasingly unrealistic as, along with the rest of the new graduates, he started the arduous task of applying for a job through the graduate recruitment "milkround."

He quickly found out that the only potential employers in his discipline were the major defense contractors. As David puts it:

> I was naive. I had not thought about where my course would lead me and I found myself staring at offers of employment from companies that made things that were designed to kill people. Even though I needed a job I felt that there was no way I could work in such an industry.

A CAREER IN IBM DEVELOPMENT

David's brother was by this time working for IBM and clearly enjoying it. He suggested to David that he approach IBM, which he did, and he secured a four-year contract at the IBM development laboratory in Hampshire.

Although the work was predominantly in electronics, David quickly picked up the relevant knowledge and was put on a development project looking at the analog design of color monitors. With the backing and encouragement of his manager he was awarded a patent in 1990 that related to the automated adjustment of user controls (brightness and contrast).

He was selected for an IBM Graduate Experience Module and returned to Scotland on a grant to be a part of the manufacturing development team working at Greenock. Here he was involved in designing test processes for both monochrome and color liquid crystal display (LCD) monitors. In view of the specialist nature of the LCD, which represented a major new step for IBM, the test engineer's role was combined with that of procurement engineer, which involved frequent visits and liaison with the Japanese manufacturers of LCD panels. In particular he gained access to DTI in Japan, which was a manufacturing joint venture between IBM and Toshiba, where he was able to more fully understand the manufacture of LCD panels.

A MOVE INTO MANUFACTURING

Structural changes at Greenock meant that responsibility for LCDs was transferred from David's area into mainstream laptop PC manufacturing. David decided formally to move from development into manufacturing as a test engineer, a decision that was regarded by some of his development colleagues as a backward move. However, it gave David the opportunity to pursue his dream of becoming an "LCD guru" by remaining with the product.

At one point, faced with a tight deadline, David and some of his new colleagues formed a project team to resolve a problem unrelated to LCDs. This was a radical step within IBM, where functional boundaries were strictly observed, and the team took responsibility for planning, budgeting, capital expenditure requisition, business process development, and reporting on the project. As David explained:

It was like having your own business. We now had to consider what the financial effect of working overtime would be on the outcome of the project instead of simply authorizing it. It was not easy but we all learned a great deal.

The project was an outstanding success, and the team attracted attention from the senior management, who were anxious to learn how the original problem was solved in such a beneficial way.

FRUSTRATION SETS IN

In early 1993, David's enjoyment of his job started to wane when his former colleagues from the development team in Portsmouth were relocated to Greenock with substantial relocating packages. His sense of inequity was compounded with the discovery that these individuals were all on permanent contracts, whereas he was still on a four-year contract that was due to expire in October of that year. No one at IBM had even talked to him about the options that were open to him in spite of the profile that he now enjoyed. He felt extremely let down and made up his mind to leave IBM when his contract expired and set up his own business. He did not want to be at the behest of an employer again.

EVALUATING THE OPTIONS FOR SELF-EMPLOYMENT

His first thoughts were to act as a consultant to original equipment manufacturers (OEM) that used LCD panels. While still at IBM he approached his local Enterprise Trust and was persuaded to undertake some market research. During this process he established that there was potential for a screening and repair facility. Because of the high cost of the LCD panel, when a defective panel was discovered during the manufacturing and testing process, the OEMs had to ship them back to Japan for rework, which was an expensive exercise. The companies that David spoke to seemed enthusiastic about a service that would allow them to establish which panels were not capable of being repaired and therefore would not be sent back to Japan, a differentiation that would result in a savings of time and costs.

David prepared a business plan with the help of the Enterprise Trust and two friends in the industry who were attracted to the idea of partnering with him in this venture. The plan was that they would continue to work at their employer's company, a vendor to IBM based near IBM's Greenock site, until the new business was of a sufficient size to justify their employment in DPT on a full-time basis.

DECISION TIME

An off-the-shelf company was purchased in July 1993, and David started to plan for the day he could leave IBM in October. He began to approach several possible sources of finance. Things were going according to plan until David's manager called him in one day to make him an offer of a permanent contract. Little did he know that David had other plans. The package offer was very attractive, and David now had a tough decision to make.

EXHIBIT 2   Original Business Plan

DISPLAY PRODUCTS TECHNOLOGY LIMITED BUSINESS PLAN

Section 1—Introduction

This Business Plan has been prepared on behalf of the persons specified in Section 2 to demonstrate the viability of the proposed business and to assist in the securing of appropriate financial assistance.

It seeks to demonstrate the proposed business's ability to generate sufficient income to fund repayment of amounts borrowed and provide a reasonable rate of return.

In addition to the financial aspect, the Business Plan also seeks to highlight the employment potential and the innovative nature of the proposed business.

The Business Plan has been prepared using information available at this time, and certain assumptions have been necessarily made (see Appendix D).

Section 2—The People

NAME:	David Wares
ADDRESS:	94 Hyndland Road
	Glasgow G12 9ZP
TELEPHONE:	339 4963
AGE:	26

Career Information:

1990–1993

Transferred to IBM manufacturing in Greenock. Involved in designing test processes for both monochrome and color STN notebook LCDs and more recently TFT desktops. This was combined with the role of procurement engineer, which involved liaising with LCD vendors in Japan.

During this period, has published four papers relating to his work on LCDs.

1989–1990

Graduated from Strathclyde University with a BSc (Honors) in laser physics and optoelectronics. Commenced working for IBM in their Monitor Development

EXHIBIT 2   Original Business Plan (*continued*)

Laboratory in Hampshire. Was involved in analog design of color monitors and was awarded a patent in 1990 relating to the automated adjustment of user controls.

NAME:	William Graham
ADDRESS:	31 Old Mill Road
	Johnstone PA3
TELEPHONE:	01505 363886
AGE:	32

Career Information:

1988–To date

Joined an IBM vendor company as senior associate engineer in the area of display manufacturing engineering. Responsible for coordinating the establishment of third-party-vendor manufacturing processes for computer display assembly under contract to IBM.

1985–1988

Design engineer with a major IT company in the Packaging and Material Handling Department. Responsible for the design and procurement of recyclable packaging to suit an automated manufacturing facility. This involved technical and contractual negotiations with suppliers and contractors. During this period successfully completed a postgraduate diploma in management studies at Glasgow College of Technology.

1978–1985

Employed by Polaroid UK Limited as one of their first technical trainees. This involved a joint academic and practical training program in the form of a four-year apprenticeship while studying for an HND in mechanical engineering. On successful completion of this course, moved into the drawing office with responsibility for the design and implementation of production tooling and specialist fixtures, thereafter, progressing into industrial engineering with responsibility for the preparation and presentation of methods, layout, and planning targets to allow optimum use of resource.

NAME:	Edward Morrison
ADDRESS:	23 Margaret Street
	Greenock PA6
TELEPHONE:	0475 635159
AGE:	30

Career Information:

1989–1993

Currently a senior associate test engineer with an IBM vendor company with responsibility for leading project teams in the development of test processes for new display technologies. During the past three years has held the lead role in the commissioning of test processes for liquid crystal displays.

EXHIBIT 2   Original Business Plan (*continued*)

1987–1989

Worked for a major IT company involved in the test and manufacture of cathode ray tube computer displays and gained acknowledgment in this field through the publishing of a number of papers on the subject and the filing of an invention relating to the setup of color displays. Before moving into LCD technology, was solely responsible for the development and installation of the image setup process for the company's first automatically controlled digital adjustment display.

1985–1987

Graduated from Strathclyde University with a BSc (Honors) in electrical and electronic engineering. Joined a major IT company upon graduating and was assigned to the team developing the in-circuit and functional testers for the company's first color VGA display.

Section 3—The Business

The proposed business aims to offer the manufacturers, importers, and dealers in visual products within the electronic consumer industry an expert technical service with specialty skills and expertise in LCD technology. Initially the service will involve the following facets:

- Screening/quality inspection
- Repair/reutilization
- Failure analysis and reporting
- Consulting

In the second stage of development the company intends to offer a rework service based on the premise that new product releases invariably involve a certain percentage of recalls on which certain remedial action has to be taken.

The third stage of development and a longer-term aim would move the company into the areas of product development and prototype manufacture.

The majority of larger companies in the visual products industry have established subcontract repair vendors for their conventional display products (i.e., non-LCD). Few choose to repair at site of manufacture due to the logistics, inventory, and cost implications.

In the LCD market, however, the manufacturing capability in high-volume LCD products lies exclusively in Japan (there is no LCD manufacture in the U.K.). LCDs are imported into the U.K. as subassemblies but are subject to process warranty and out-of-warranty failures. Due to the lack of appropriate screening and repair facilities in the U.K., Japanese manufacturers with U.K. interests such as Toshiba, Hitachi, Sharp, and NEC must return defective screens to Japan, where the repair capability exists. This obviously has cost implications and is also known to be disruptive to normal production rotations.

In addition to the Japanese companies, over 30 other companies in the U.K. with LCD products use Japanese LCD technology, including:

Compaq

Elonex

EXHIBIT 2   Original Business Plan (*continued*)

> Ambra
>
> AST
>
> Dell
>
> NCR
>
> Panasonic
>
> Texas Instruments

These companies also return faulty LCD panels to Japan, and it is clear that many panels are scrapped due to the cost and time factors involved in such a process.

The company will offer a service to all of the above companies and will be capable of dealing with the full range of defects arising on LCD products (e.g., contamination, backlighting problems, drive card failure, damaged polarizers, tab delamination, and miscellaneous hardware defects). The services to be offered can be divided into three distinct aspects, each offering a variety of advantages.

# Screening	"no defect found" notification thereby saving costs in shipping and time
	fast process feedback
	accurate fault verification and measurement
	symptom/cause/remedy analysis
# Replace	reduce inventory holding of companies as replacement available at a faster rate giving quick turnover and cost-effective solution
# Repair	offering quick turnaround and cost-effective repair together with local expertise, eliminating the impact that returning faulty units has on the ongoing manufacturing process in Japan

LCDs are the visual display products of the future. The demand for LCDs is now in excess of supply particularly with respect to TFT panels. The increase in usage will cause an increasing level of returns to Japan as manufacturers attempt to increase production to meet demand.

It is estimated that the TFT market will triple over the next two years, increasing from 1.7 billion U.S. dollars this year to 4.5 billion U.S. dollars in 1995 and 6.4 billion U.S. dollars by 1997. It is this section of the LCD market that offers the greatest potential due to the high unit cost. Currently a notebook TFT LCD costs in excess of £1,000 with little likelihood of a reduction due to the supply constraints that exist.

There are a number of relatively new products that use LCD technology, including the following:

- Notebook/palmtop computers
- Viewcam video cameras
- Mini TVs

EXHIBIT 2   Original Business Plan (*continued*)

- Video phones
- Airline personal video units
- Virtual reality equipment
- Overhead projectors
- Car instrumentation
- Game Boy
- Projection TV

It is clear that the market for LCD technology is an increasing one and that a market exists for a local repair facility.

In order to be able to offer this service the company must locate and customize a facility with a "clean air" environment (enclosed area where air is circulated through filters to remove dust particles and the like, and there are temperature and humidity controls).

There will also be a major commitment to specialized equipment, and it is envisaged that the following types of items will be acquired:

- PC equipment
- Microscopes
- ESD benches
- Vacuum handling fixtures
- Test fixtures
- Miniature camera systems

A specific element of the repair service offered will be to replace LCD panel polarizers. The LCD panel consists of a variety of layers of glass and film. The outermost film is known as the front polarizer. It is secured in place by an adhesive bond in a controlled clean air environment. A significant percentage of LCD fallout is a result of damage to the front polarizer. The repair process is complex and requires special equipment. The business intends to purchase and develop such equipment after the initial screen, replace, and repair service has settled in. In the projection this is indicated as arising at the six-month stage.

The provision of this U.K. service will create seven full-time jobs within year 1 with further expansion envisaged in the short term due to the increasing size of the LCD market.

Section 4—Financial Summary

The business is one in which a high element of initial capital expenditure is required. It is envisaged that £90,000 will be expended in year 1 as follows:

£25,000	General equipment
£40,000	Polarizer
£25,000	Polarizer development costs
£90,000	

EXHIBIT 2   Original Business Plan (*continued*)

This will be followed by further polarizer development costs of around £40,000 in year 2 in addition to ongoing additional general equipment costs.

The project will initially employ five people (three technical and two administrative), and this will have increased to seven by the end of year 1. The principals intend to inject £20,000 in share capital into the business, and the cash flow projections in Appendix A suggest that further funding of around £110,000 will be required. It has been anticipated for the purpose of the exercise that it will be a combination of grant, loan, and bank overdraft funding. It has been anticipated that due to the innovative nature of the project, some form of grant aid will be available.

The profit and loss projections indicate a modest profit in year 1 followed by a significant profit (circa £75,000) in year 2 (see Appendix B).

Appendix D Key Assumptions

1. Sales will start from a low base and build consistently to a peak of £30,000 per month.
2. Sales invoices will be paid in the 60- to 90-day time scale.
3. All costs will be met on a monthly basis.
4. Employees at the end of year 1 will number seven from an initial setup figure of five. Additional employees will be taken on in year 2.
5. The project will attract grant aid and conventional loan funding.

Appendix A Cash Flow Projection, Year 1

	Month 1	Month 2	Month 3	Month 4	Month 5	Month 6	Month 7	Month 8	Month 9	Month 10	Month 11	Month 12	Total
Sales	0	0	1469	5875	10281	11750	11750	14588	17625	23500	23500	23500	143938
Direct/Capital Costs:													
Capital	8613	8813	1175	1175	1175	48175	15863	1175	1175	1175	1175	1175	105750
Salaries	1855	1855	1855	1855	1855	1855	1855	1855	1855	2355	2355	2355	23760
Paye & Nic	0	876	876	876	876	876	876	876	876	876	1112	1112	10103
Gross	−10668	−11543	−2437	1969	6376	−39156	−6843	−3906	13719	19094	18858	18858	4324
Inflow/(Outflow)													
Other Income:													
Share Capital	20000												20000
Grants/Loans		36000				32000		12000					80000
Total Inflow/(Outflow)	9333	24457	−2437	1969	6376	−7156	−6843	8094	13719	19094	18858	18858	104324
Expenditure:													
Salaries	1188	1188	1188	1188	1188	1188	1188	1188	1188	1938	1938	1938	16500
Wages	875	875	875	875	875	875	875	875	875	875	875	875	10500
Paye & Nic	0	974	974	974	974	974	974	974	974	974	1328	1328	11417
Rent & Rates	862	862	862	862	862	862	862	862	862	862	862	862	10340
Power	411	411	411	411	411	411	411	411	411	411	411	411	4935
Heat & Light	353	353	353	353	353	353	353	353	353	353	353	353	4230
Insurance	416	416	416	416	416	416	516	516	516	516	516	516	5592
Vehicle Lease	353	353	353	353	353	353	940	940	940	940	940	940	7755
Full	176	176	176	235	235	235	588	588	588	588	588	588	4759
Maintenance	212	212	212	212	212	212	212	212	212	212	212	212	2538
Stationery	470	470	470	235	235	235	235	235	235	235	235	235	3525
Rentals/Supplies	705	705	705	470	470	470	353	353	353	353	353	353	4935
Professional Fees	705	705	705	705	705	705	705	705	705	705	705	705	8460
Telephone & Postage	294	294	294	353	353	353	470	470	470	470	470	470	4641
Advertising	294	294	294	294	294	294	294	294	294	294	294	294	3525
Travel	588	588	588	588	588	588	588	588	588	588	2938	588	9400
Bad Debts	13	50	88	100	100	125	150	200	200	200	200	200	1625
Vat Due/(Repaid)				−2492			−4102			2058			−4536
Total Expenditure	7912	8688	8490	6128	8620	8645	5491	9760	9760	12568	13214	10864	110140
Net Cast Flow	1421	15769	−10927	−4159	−2244	−15801	−12334	−1666	3959	6526	5644	7994	(5816)
Bank:													
Opening Balance	0	1421	17190	6263	2104	−141	−16048	−28571	−30438	−26655	−20263	−14717	
Net Cash Flow	1421	15769	−10927	−4159	−2244	−15801	−12334	−1666	3959	6526	5644	7994	
	1421	17190	6263	2104	−140	−15942	−28382	−30237	−26479	−20129	−14619	−6722	
Overdraft Charge	0	0	0	0	1	106	189	202	177	134	97	45	
Closing Balance	1421	17190	6263	2104	−141	−16048	−28571	−30438	−26655	−20263	−14717	−6767	

Appendix A Cash Flow Projection, Year 2

	Month 1	Month 2	Month 3	Month 4	Month 5	Month 6	Month 7	Month 8	Month 9	Month 10	Month 11	Month 12	Total
Sales	23500	23500	23500	23500	23500	29375	29375	29375	29375	35250	35250	35250	340750
Direct/Capital Costs:													
Capital	1763	1763	48763	5875	3525	1763	1763	1763	1763	1763	1763	1763	74025
Salaries	2826	2826	2826	2826	2826	2826	2826	2826	2826	2826	2826	2826	33912
Paye & Nic	1112	1334	1334	1334	1334	1334	1334	1334	1334	1334	1334	1334	15784
Gross Inflow/(Outflow)	17800	17578	−29422	13465	15815	23453	23453	23453	23453	29328	29328	29328	217029
Other Income:													
Share Capital													
Grants/Loans			16000										16000
Total Inflow/(Outflow)	17800	17578	−13422	13465	15815	23453	23453	23453	23453	29328	29328	29328	233029
Expenditure:													
Salaries	2438	2438	2438	2438	2438	2438	2438	2438	2438	2438	2438	2438	29256
Wages	1050	1050	1050	1050	1050	1050	1050	1050	1050	1050	1050	1050	12600
Paye & Nic	1328	1646	1646	1646	1646	1646	1646	1646	1646	1646	1646	1646	19438
Rent & Rates	948	948	948	948	948	948	948	948	948	948	948	948	11374
Power	452	452	452	452	452	452	452	452	452	452	452	452	5429
Heat & Light	388	388	388	388	388	388	388	388	388	388	388	388	4653
Insurance	568	568	568	733	733	733	733	733	733	733	733	733	8300
Vehicle Lease	987	987	987	1540	1540	1540	1540	1540	1540	1540	1540	1540	16821
Full	676	676	676	906	906	906	906	906	906	906	906	906	10181
Maintenance	243	243	243	317	317	317	317	317	317	317	317	317	3583
Stationery	259	259	259	259	259	259	259	259	259	259	259	259	3108
Rentals/Supplies	388	388	388	388	388	388	388	388	388	388	388	388	4656
Professional Fees	740	740	740	740	740	740	740	740	740	740	740	740	8883
Telephone & Postage	540	540	540	540	540	540	540	540	540	540	540	540	6480
Advertising	308	308	308	308	308	308	308	308	308	308	308	308	3701
Travel	617	617	617	617	617	617	617	617	617	617	3084	617	9870
Bad Debts	200	200	200	250	250	250	250	300	300	300	300	300	3100
Vat Due/(Repaid)	6941			−212			8155			10780			25662
Total Expenditure	19070	12448	12448	13308	13521	13521	21675	13571	13571	24350	16038	13571	187094
Net Cash Inflow/(Outflow)	−1271	5129	−25871	157	2294	9932	1777	9882	9882	4977	13289	15757	45935
Bank:													
Opening Balance	−6767	−8091	−2982	−29045	−23081	−26965	−17147	−15472	−5627	4254	9232	22521	
Net Cash Flow	−1271	5129	−25871	157	2294	9932	1777	9882	9882	4977	13289	15757	
	−8038	−2962	−28852	−28888	−26786	−17033	−15369	−5590	4254	9232	22521	38278	
Overdraft Charges	54	20	192	193	179	114	102	37	0	0	0	0	
Closing Balance	−8091	−2982	−29045	−29081	−26965	−17147	−15472	−5627	4254	9232	22521	38278	

Appendix B Profit and Loss Account, Year 1

	Month 1	Month 2	Month 3	Month 4	Month 5	Month 6	Month 7	Month 8	Month 9	Month 10	Month 11	Month 12	Total
Sales	1250	5000	8750	10000	10000	12500	15000	20000	20000	20000	20000	20000	162500
Cost of Sales:													
Salaries	1855	1855	1855	1855	1855	1855	1855	1855	1855	2355	2355	2355	23760
Paye & Nic	876	876	876	876	876	876	876	876	876	1112	1112	1112	11215
Gross Profit	−1481	2269	6019	7269	7269	9769	12269	17269	17269	16533	16533	16533	127525
Expenditure:													
Salaries	1188	1188	1188	1188	1188	1188	1188	1188	1188	1938	1938	1938	16500
Wages	875	875	875	875	875	875	875	875	875	875	875	875	10500
Paye & Nic	974	974	974	974	974	974	974	974	974	1328	1328	1328	12745
Rent & Rates	733	733	733	733	733	733	733	733	733	733	733	733	8800
Power	350	350	350	350	350	350	350	350	350	350	350	350	4200
Heat & Light	300	300	300	300	300	300	300	300	300	300	300	300	3600
Insurance	150	150	150	200	200	200	500	500	500	500	500	500	5592
Vehicle Lease	300	300	300	300	300	300	800	800	800	800	800	800	6600
Fuel	150	150	150	200	200	200	500	500	500	500	500	500	4050
Maintenance	180	180	180	180	180	180	180	180	180	180	180	180	2160
Stationery	600	400	200	200	200	200	200	200	200	200	200	200	3000
Rentals/Supplies	400	400	400	400	400	400	300	300	300	300	300	300	4200
Professional Fees	600	600	600	600	600	600	600	600	600	600	600	600	7200
Telephone and Postage	250	250	250	300	300	300	300	400	400	400	400	400	3950
Advertising	250	250	250	250	250	250	250	250	250	250	250	250	3000
Travel	500	500	500	500	500	500	500	500	500	500	2500	500	8000
Bad Debts	13	50	88	100	100	125	150	200	200	200	200	200	1625
Depreciation	156	313	333	354	375	1229	1510	1792	1813	1833	1854	1875	13438
Bank O/D Charge	0	0	0	0	1	106	189	202	177	134	97	45	951
Total Expenditure	8734	8228	8086	8719	8241	9226	10415	10859	10854	11937	13921	11890	120110
Net Profit/(Loss)	−9715	−5958	−2067	−950	−972	544	1854	6411	6415	4597	2612	4643	7415

Appendix B Profit and Loss Account, Year 2

	Month 1	Month 2	Month 3	Month 4	Month 5	Month 6	Month 7	Month 8	Month 9	Month 10	Month 11	Month 12	Total
Sales	20000	20000	20000	25000	25000	25000	25000	30000	30000	30000	30000	30000	310000
Cost of Sales:													
Salaries	2826	2826	2826	2826	2826	2826	2826	2826	2826	2826	2826	2826	33912
Paye & Nic	1334	1334	1334	1334	1334	1334	1334	1334	1334	1334	1334	1334	16007
Gross Profit	15840	15840	15840	20840	20840	20840	25840	25840	25840	25840	25840	25840	260081
Expenditure:													
Salaries	2438	2438	2438	2438	2438	2438	2438	2438	2438	2438	2438	2438	29256
Wages	1050	1050	1050	1050	1050	1050	1050	1050	1050	1050	1050	1050	12600
Paye & Nic	1646	1646	1646	1646	1646	1646	1646	1646	1646	1646	1646	1646	19756
Rent & Rates	807	807	807	807	807	807	807	807	807	807	807	807	9680
Power	385	385	385	385	385	385	385	385	385	385	385	385	4620
Heat & Light	330	330	330	330	330	330	330	330	330	330	330	330	3960
Insurance	568	568	568	733	733	733	733	733	733	733	733	733	8300
Vehicle Lease	840	840	840	1311	1311	1311	1311	1311	1311	1311	1311	1311	14316
Fuel	575	575	575	771	771	771	771	771	771	771	771	771	8665
Maintenance	207	207	207	270	270	270	270	270	270	270	270	270	3049
Stationery	220	220	220	220	220	220	220	220	220	220	220	220	2645
Rentals/Supplies	330	330	330	330	330	330	330	330	330	330	330	330	3963
Professional Fees	630	630	630	630	630	630	630	630	630	630	630	630	7560
Telephone and Postage	460	460	460	460	460	460	460	460	460	460	460	460	5515
Advertising	263	263	263	263	263	263	263	263	263	263	263	263	3150
Travel	525	525	525	525	525	525	525	525	525	525	2625	525	8400
Bad Debts	200	200	200	250	250	250	250	300	300	300	300	300	3100
Depreciation	1906	1938	2802	2906	2969	3000	3031	3063	3094	3125	3156	3188	34177
Bank O/D Charge	54	20	192	193	179	114	102	37	0	0	0	0	890
Total Expenditure	13433	13431	14468	15517	15566	15532	15552	15568	15562	15593	17724	15655	183601
Net Profit/(Loss)	7407	2410	1372	5373	5275	5308	5288	10272	10278	10247	8116	10185	76481

Appendix C Balance Sheet, Year 1

	Month 1	Month 2	Month 3	Month 4	Month 5	Month 6	Month 7	Month 8	Month 9	Month 10	Month 11	Month 12	Total
Fixed Assets:													
Cost	7500	15000	16000	17000	18000	59000	72500	86000	87000	88000	89000	90000	90000
Agg Depreciation	156	469	802	1156	1531	2760	4271	6063	7865	9708	11563	13438	13438
	7344	14531	15198	15844	16469	56240	68229	79938	79125	79125	77438	76563	76563
Trade Debtors	1469	7344	16156	22031	23500	26438	32313	41125	47000	47000	47000	47000	47000
Bank Balance	1421	17190	6263	2104	−141	−16048	−28571	−30438	−26655	−20263	−14717	−6767	−6767
Paye & Nic	−1849	−1849	−1849	−1849	−1849	−1849	−1849	−1849	−1849	−2439	−2439	−2439	−2439
Vat	1901	3111	2492	−820	−1640	4120	615	372	−2058	−2430	−4510	−6941	−6941
	10285	40327	38260	37310	36338	68882	70737	89147	95562	100159	102772	107416	107416
Represented by:													
Profit & Loss Account	−9715	−15673	−17740	−18690	−19667	−19118	−17263	−10853	−4438	159	2772	7416	7416
Share Capital	20000	20000	20000	20000	20000	20000	20000	20000	20000	20000	20000	20000	20000
Grant/Loan Reserve	0	36000	36000	36000	36000	68000	68000	80000	80000	80000	80000	80000	80000
	10285	40327	38760	37310	36338	68882	70737	89147	95562	100159	102772	107416	107416

Year 2

	Month 1	Month 2	Month 3	Month 4	Month 5	Month 6	Month 7	Month 8	Month 9	Month 10	Month 11	Month 12
Fixed Assets:												
Opening Balance	90000	90000	90000	90000	90000	90000	90000	90000	90000	90000	90000	90000
Additions	1500	3000	44500	49500	52500	54000	55500	57000	58500	60000	61500	63000
Agg Depreciation	15344	17281	20083	22990	25958	28958	31990	35052	38146	41271	44427	47615
	76156	75719	114417	116510	116542	115042	113510	111948	110354	108729	107073	105385
Trade Debtors	47000	47000	47000	52875	58750	58750	58750	65625	70500	70500	70500	70500
Bank Balance	−8091	−2982	−29045	−29081	−26965	−17147	−15472	−5627	4254	9232	22521	38278
Paye & Nic	−2980	−2980	−2980	−2980	−2980	−2980	−2980	−2980	−2980	−2980	−2980	−2980
Vat	−2263	−4525	212	−2397	−5145	−8155	−3010	−6895	−10780	−3885	−7402	−11287
	109822	112232	129604	134927	140202	145510	150799	161071	171349	181596	189711	199896
Represented by:												
Profit & Loss Account	9822	12237	13604	18927	24202	29510	34799	45071	55349	65596	73711	83896
Share Capital	20000	20000	20000	20000	20000	20000	20000	20000	20000	20000	20000	20000
Grant/Loan Reserve	80000	80000	96000	96000	96000	96000	96000	96000	96000	96000	96000	96000
	109822	112232	129604	134927	140202	145510	150799	161071	171349	181596	189711	199896

CASE Id   Michael Flatley, Lord of the Dance?

Michael Flatley, lead male dancer and main choreographer of www.riverdance.ie/ *Riverdance—The Show*, was dismissed from the widely acclaimed dance musical just 48 hours before the opening of an extended second London run of the show in Labatt's Apollo Theatre, Hammersmith, in October 1995.

Following the phenomenal success of the *Riverdance* interlude piece during Ireland's hosting of the Eurovision Song Contest in Dublin, April 1994, Flatley had been lauded for his highly personalized dance style and choreographic expertise that contributed so significantly to the follow-up theatrical production, *Riverdance—The Show*, which premiered at The Point Theatre, Dublin, in February 1995.

> **Note:** For further information on the background of the development of *Riverdance*, readers are referred to the current author's case study, *Riverdance*, available from the ECCH, European Case Clearing House, Cranfield, Berks, U.K. and Babson College, Babson Park, MA, U.S. (ref 395 - 039 - 1); and also to the commercially available video, *Riverdance—The Journey*, Abhann Productions, Dublin.

With unprecedented box-office successes in London (May to July 1995), and a rerun in Dublin (August to September 1995), protracted negotiations were undertaken to firm up Flatley's contract for the autumn season in Hammersmith. Although Flatley's fees for the Dublin appearances at The Point Theatre were close to £50,000, it was considered necessary to halve his salary at Labatt's due to the huge cost of staging *Riverdance* in London (see "Demands for Control Left Show Reeling," *Irish Independent*, April 19, 1996).

The demands that the Irish-American star sent to the *Riverdance* management before negotiations broke down are reported to have included the following (according to the above article in the *Irish Independent* and other media sources):

- That Flatley be billed as the star in all advertising, with two pages of the program devoted to him.
- A percentage of royalties from his contracts as performer, choreographer, and coauthor/creator.
- Freedom to use his work in a film or otherwise.
- Complete autonomy in auditioning new talent.
- A personal assistant.

Inevitably, considerable debate and counterdebate arose between the promoters of *Riverdance*—Abhann Productions—and Flatley. The main breaking point from the promoters' perspective was the alleged excessive control demanded by Flatley, whereas he or his manager pointed out his claimed right to creativity (or "intellectual property") rights associated with his contribution to the development of *The Show*.

It is difficult to establish the rights (and the wrongs) of the issues. Indeed, it is likely that the situation will only be clarified when the legal proceedings that are reported to have been initiated by Flatley's lawyers are finally resolved. The following commentary on the spat between the two parties is instructive:

> Riverdance's management claim he was too headstrong, too autocratic, and that the real stars of the show are the music and the dances. Flatley insists that those are his dances and the copyright should be his, but they wanted him to sign away his rights. He also claims that he was blocked from doing interviews—while he wanted to build

This case study was prepared by Dr. Barra O'Cinneide, College of Business, University of Limerick, Ireland, with the intention of providing a basis for class discussion rather than illustrating either good or bad management practices © 1996.

his name and profile for the future, he was gagged from talking to the media. The show's publicists say there was little interest in him. The root of the problem is a contract they wanted him to sign.

According to Flatley:

We had a very simple one [contract] on a couple of sheets of paper. It was more of an agreement between friends. But they wanted complete artistic control as well as everything else. I wasn't going to sign that. (Simon Kinnersley, "Riskiest Step Even for the 'Lord of the Dance,' " *The Mail*, July 21, 1996)

When asked if he was hurt that he ultimately left *Riverdance* amid controversy, Flatley said:

It was a fall all the way down from that moment, that's for sure. And it did hurt.

He denied reports at the time of the break with *Riverdance* that his ego "ran riot":

There is a huge difference between being egotistical and being self-confident. I'm confident about what I do, that's the bottom line. And as for the question of my fee, I didn't even choose my fee, they did. (Tony O'Brien, "Flatley Steps Up Show Claim," *Irish Independent*, April 18, 1996)

According to the same media source, Flatley's lawyers were seeking a 2 percent choreographer's royalty fee from all future productions of *Riverdance*. Following his dramatic firing from the show, Flatley admits to being "devastated" and "close to tears." He recounts how his father phoned him from Chicago to console him. He said: "Mike, you created *Riverdance:* you can create another one. What goes around comes around."

Following his father's advice, Flatley spent a minimal amount of time considering his options and decided instead to devise a new Irish dance show that would tour the world. In developing his new production, he was conscious of the need to capitalize as quickly as possible on the success enjoyed by *Riverdance—The Show*, which in just over eight months had gained theatrical acclaim, record box-office revenues, and chart-topping audio/video sales.

In formulating the new show's content, Flatley was insistent that it would add extra dimensions to existing formats of Irish dancing and that it would not be merely a "me too" *Riverdance*. One of the first decisions he made was to appoint a new personal manager, John Reid, who manages the well-known entertainer Elton John. John Reid replaced Deke Arlon, who had unsuccessfully negotiated on behalf of Flatley in the abortive discussions with the *Riverdance* management. He also attracted Harvey Goldsmith, a well-established theatrical personality, as the promoter of the new show, which, it was announced, would be called *Lord of the Dance*. Other appointments included Arlene Philips as director and Jonathan Park as designer.

Flatley quickly augmented his management team, including the appointment of PR consultants and legal advisors. The latter were instructed to pursue as vigorously as possible his entitlement to personal revenues from his former Riverdance associations (including his disputed claim for royalties, reportedly valued at 2 percent of gross Riverdance revenues).

With alacrity he began negotiations with one of Ireland's most celebrated composers, Eurovision award winner Phil Coulter, to write the score for *Lord of the Dance*. In parallel with this, it was reported that Van Morrison, another distinguished composer/performer, promised to write five musical pieces for the show. After several weeks, it was announced that Phil Coulter would not be contributing and a new composer, Ronan Hardiman, was appointed.

Michael Flatley says of Ronan Hardiman, "What he's been able to do for me is absolutely priceless." Hardiman realized the enormity of the challenge; that is, he understood that composing what would be seen as a follow-up to *Riverdance* could easily prove to be an impossible task. He admits:

> In the beginning it was a bit intimidating. *Riverdance* is a fantastic success and an institution at this stage, and our show was going to be launched in Dublin at the shrine of *Riverdance*, so it was a bit daunting. (Eamonn Carr, "Maestro Keyed Up for the *Lord of the Dance*," *Evening Herald*, July 23, 1996)

For 10 weeks, the composer locked himself away against the clock:

> It wasn't just a case of composing the music and that's it. There was quite a bit of re-adapting and tailoring it to the dancers'/musicians' needs. (See above reference.)

Hardiman had trained as a classical pianist for 12 years. At the age of 17, he caught the rock' n' roll bug and worked with a succession of bands and in search of a lucky break. He had a promising "day job" with a bank, but when he was 28, he knew he wanted to make a career of music. Eventually, he got his first assignment as composer, scoring six half-hour programs for the TV series *My Riviera*. Hardiman met Flatley for the first time in March 1996 and was involved with him in a TV special presentation featuring Flatley in a prestigious Prince's Trust production at the Albert Hall, London.

When working on the score for *Lord of the Dance*, Michael Flatley recounts Hardiman's creativity in relation to one dance sequence, "Hell's Kitchen":

> Within two days, working on just rhythm patterns I had suggested he produced the most fantastic music I ever heard, down to the last beat. Perfect! He's out on his own, and he's so darned easy to work with. (See above reference.)

Ronan Hardiman scotches suggestions that Flatley is a prima donna figure and adds:

> Michael is a genius as anyone who has seen him on stage will agree.

Despite Flatley's insistence that he is self-confident, not egocentric, several media commentators chided him on his alleged self-importance, as illustrated by a disparaging cartoon in the Irish edition of a British tabloid newspaper (see Appendix 1).

How does Hardiman feel about some of the more negative criticisms of his *Lord of the Dance* music?

> We set out to achieve something and the fact that the show is getting standing ovations every night, both in Ireland and Britain, speaks for itself. (See, again, the *Evening Herald* article.)

One of Flatley's primary concerns was the formation of a high-calibre dance troupe (see Appendix 2). Although *Riverdance* had already recruited many of the best-known performers, the talent within the amateur Irish traditional dancing sector was extensive, with literally hundreds of young dancers vying, competitively, to demonstrate their skills at regional, national, and international levels. As a result, Flatley attracted many enthusiastic contenders to his hastily convened auditions. His previous experience as a talent scout when assembling the *Riverdance* troupe proved particularly helpful in this exercise. In particular, he succeeded in attracting several prominent dancers from *Riverdance* itself—including Arlene Ni Bhaoill, who had been understudy to the main female dancer, Jean Butler. It is of interest that Arlene had played the lead role at Labatt's Apollo for the first couple of weeks of *Riverdance* in October 1995, that is, from the opening of the show's fateful second run in London, when Jean Butler could not go on stage due to a serious ankle injury. As theatrical tradition dictates that "the show must go on," Arlene Ni Bhaoill assumed the lead part at a few hours' notice and, in so doing, became an overnight star.

For several months before its launch, a high level of publicity was generated about Flatley's upcoming show. Media commentators began to speculate how it might compare with *Riverdance*. Would it be a direct competitor, attempting to appeal to similar audiences? How quickly would it attempt to go international? Simultaneously, Abhann Productions, the promoters of *Riverdance*, were publicizing the continuing success of their show. Intense speculation was being created within the entertainment sector and in the media in advance of details of Flatley's new offering.

Before its world premiere at The Point Theatre, Dublin, on July 2, 1996, Michael Flatley indicated his show would cost over £1 million to stage and would have a cast of 32 performers. It would have "different steps and different shapes and patterns to *Riverdance*. It will be good, hard, fast, in your face hard shoe dancing. That's what I'm made of . . . that's what I do best, flying around the stage a lot, as a soloist and doing what I do best" (Eddie Rowley, "I'm No Dirty Dancer, Says Angry Flatley," *Sunday World*, June 2, 1996).

Following its successful launch in Dublin, the show quickly transferred to Britain. During its tour of the U.K., Flatley was forced to withdraw from a number of performances of the show in Manchester and in the debut in London. This caused concern by both the fans and the show's management team. His injuries were ascribed to severely torn leg muscles, and it transpired that, two months previously, Flatley's legs had been insured to the tune of £25 million. A spokesperson explained that this sum applied only if the star could never dance again. Although his understudy, John Carey, was called on to perform for three performances (gaining standing ovations), Flatley quickly recovered his fitness through intensive physiotherapy, assuaging fears that the show's U.K. tour could suffer irreparable damage through the nonappearance of its star.

In London, Flatley undertook a comparative analysis of *Lord of the Dance* with *Riverdance* and, as might be expected, claimed his show was superior.

> Our show has a storyline. The dance numbers are much bigger, more intricate and in-your-face. It is a lot cleaner and much more attacking. I have the greatest team of dancers in the world today. (Bernard Purcell, "Flatley: The Agony and the Ecstasy," *Irish Independent*, July 24, 1996)

During the show's debut at the Coliseum, London, a wrangle was featured in the media between promoters of *Riverdance* and *Lord of the Dance* concerning the imposition of "barring clauses" in relation to theatre bookings by the latter. *Riverdance* had negotiated conditions within their agreements for performances in a number of U.K. theatres, "excluding shows of a similar nature" appearing in the venue for six months either side of *Riverdance*. In announcing plans for extensive overseas touring of *Lord of the Dance*, John Reid, Flatley's manager, claimed he had tried to reserve the Sydney Entertainment Centre for a brief run in October 1996, but the booking had been blocked by *Riverdance*, due to an appearance in Australia in March 1997. "It's just not fair and we're not going to take it lying down," said John Reid (Dermot Hayes, "War of the Dance," *Evening Herald*, July 24, 1996).

Flatley himself expressed his annoyance with the restrictions imposed on theatre bookings, appealing to the principle of free trade:

> The world is big enough for Coke and Pepsi, so it's big enough for both of us. (Decca Aitkenhead, "*Lord of the Dance* Hit by Jinx," *Independent*, July 21, 1996)

Inevitably, comparisons were made with *Riverdance* with most commentators indicating that the two shows were very different entities, although they shared the common characteristic of traditional Irish dance and music. Theatre critics in both Ireland and Britain expressed a wide range of opinions on the show. Many praised Flatley's personal performance and the originality of his choreography; others were highly critical of what might be considered Flatley's avant-garde approach to the presentation of Irish dance. Several critics referred to the "Celtic dance rock fusion" aspects of the show, regretting its orientation to the Broadway stage *pzazz* formula.

From an early date, it was clear that, like Moya Doherty and John McColgan, both principals in Abhann Productions, Michael Flatley was investing his life's fortune (and, of course, his professional reputation) in the new show. He had negotiated an indeterminate level of funding from other promoters, but he, personally, "had all to lose" if the venture should prove unsuccessful.

It was apparent, also, that in the initial sequence of presentations, Michael Flatley and promoters had purposely concentrated on Dublin and London in order to obtain high-profile media exposure. After the initial series in the two capital cities, it soon emerged that *Lord of the Dance* was being promoted for a sequence of short runs in a range of cities encompassing a wide geographic spread of the U.K. (see Appendix 3). This was in stark contrast with *Riverdance's* concentration on the Apollo Theatre, London. It emerged, also, that Flatley had commenced negotiations to bring the show to as wide an international audience as possible in Australia, New Zealand, South Africa, and, in 1997, the United States. In addition, Flatley soon announced that both a video and CD of *Lord of the Dance* would be produced and launched in October 1996.

Several months after the Dublin and London debuts of the Flatley show, the media revealed that Abhann Productions was forming a second theatrical company. This "cloning" of *Riverdance—The Show* had been widely forecast as soon as the box-office success of the production's second run in London was maintained despite Flatley's absence and Jean Butler's indisposition for the first two weeks in October 1995. A spokesperson for Abhann Productions said that the continued success showed that "the show was bigger than any of the individual performers." The formation of the second theatrical company was completed by the autumn of 1996, enabling simultaneous productions of *Riverdance* in Radio City Music Hall, New York, and at Hammersmith, London. With the opening of its second run in New York in October 1996, Abhann Productions announced an extended tour in the United States, including appearances at the Rosemount Theatre, Chicago; Pantages, Los Angeles; the Masonic Auditorium, Detroit; the Orpheum, Minneapolis; and the Wang Centre, Boston. Additionally, it was formally revealed that *Riverdance* would travel to Australia in 1997, with appearances in Sydney, Melbourne, Perth, Adelaide, and Brisbane.

In September 1996, Flatley acknowledged he had faced heartache in the previous months following the break-up of his marriage of 11 years to Polish-born Beata. He rebuked those sections of the media that had encroached on his personal life. Notwithstanding this, he revealed to the media his plans "for conquering the world," as one commentator put it; he indicated that he had offers "on the table" from Disney and Polygram in relation to a film, "an updated musical," in which he would take a starring role.

Ironically, it was suggested by an Irish columnist that the proposed film might signal the end of Flatley's dancing career if "insider" information was to be believed:

> He has reached the pinnacle of his profession as a dancer, one source told me. The film will put a seal on his achievement. (Dermott Hayes, "Lord of the Movies," *Evening Herald*, September 17, 1996)

Before the launch of the *Lord of the Dance* video/CD (see Appendix 4), it was claimed that three British television stations—BBC, ITV, and Sky TV—were vying to secure the rights to screen the show. It was reported that the bidding price could be £3 million. At the same time, it was revealed that a new recording of the "best-selling music video of all time," *Riverdance—The Show*, was planned, in which Michael Flatley would be replaced by Colin Dunne, who took over the lead male role in *Riverdance*. This event did in fact occur with the re-recording of the show taking place during Riverdance's return season at Radio City Music Hall, New York, in October 1996. This has again provoked questions on Michael Flatley's standing in the dance world, particularly in terms of his stature in Irish dance vis-à-vis performers such as Colin Dunne.

It is interesting, therefore, to note the comments of Jean Butler, Flatley's erstwhile dance partner. She admits to having been stunned when her partnership with Flatley was abruptly ended:

> Michael leaving the show affected me enormously. I felt I was losing my right hand. However, Colin Dunne is the best Irish dancer on the face of the earth. His dancing is completely different to that of Michael, who is far more showy. Colin is far more rhythmic and dramatic. It's a different kind of buzz with Colin. (Davis Rowe, "Dance Star Jean Turns Flatley Down Flat," *Sunday Mirror*, August 25, 1996)

So the question remains, is Michael Flatley "Lord of the Dance"?

APPENDIX 1: LORD OF THE DANCE

"This is the only venue big enough to accommodate Michael Flatley's ego."

APPENDIX 2: *LORD OF THE DANCE*

Cast/Credits

"Lord of the Dance"	Michael Flatley
"Sadirse"	Bernadette Flynn
"Temptress"	Gillian Norris
"Erin the Goddess"	Anne Buckley
"Don Dorcha"	Daire Nolan
Producer	Michael Flatley
Creator & Choreographer	Michael Flatley
Composer	Ronan Hardiman
Director	Arlene Philips
Designer	Jonathan Park
Management	John Reid
Promotion	Harvey Goldsmith

APPENDIX 3: *LORD OF THE DANCE*: SCHEDULE OF PERFORMANCES

Note: All dates are 1996, unless otherwise stated.

July 2–5	The Point Theatre, Dublin
July 11–13	Liverpool Empire
July 17–20	Manchester Apollo
July 23–August 17	London Coliseum
August 27–September 1	Academy at the NIA, Birmingham
September 6–7	Glasgow SECC
September 11–13	Cardiff International Arena
September 18–21	The Point Theatre, Dublin
	Sheffield
September 30–October 4	Brighton Centre
October–December	Australia (6-city tour) including Sydney, Melbourne, Perth, Adelaide, and Brisbane
December 29–31	Newcastle Arena
January 3–4, 1997	Nynex Arena, Manchester
January 7–10, 1997	Wembley Arena, London
February 1997	New York (plus other U.S. cities)
Summer 1997	Croke Park GAA Stadium, Dublin

APPENDIX 4: *LORD OF THE DANCE* VIDEO

Copy of Advertisement

Launch of Video/CD (Source: *Daily Mail*, October 23, 1996)
Michael Flatley, *Lord of the Dance*

Out now in video, *available on CD and cassette.*
"There's only one Michael Flatley"

Quotes:
> "Flatley is the fantastic Lord of the Dance" (Jack Tinker—*Daily Mail*).
> "Genius on Tap" (*Sunday Times*).
> "The Show of the Nineties" (*The Sun*).

Note: VVL, a subsidiary of the giant multinational corporation Polygram, is reported to have invested £1.2 million in production and marketing of the *Lord of the Dance* video (see Siobhan O'Connell, "Polygram Backs Flatley," *Sunday Business Post*, April 21, 1996).

CASE Ie   Heartware International Corporation

A MEDICAL EQUIPMENT COMPANY "BORN INTERNATIONAL" (A)

In May 1990, Mr. Gerald Seery, chief executive and founder of Heartware International Corporation (Heartware), a two-year-old multinational venture headquartered in Atlanta, was looking toward the future. He had recently sent a fax that captured his thoughts to Dr. Pedro Cortez,* in Aalst, Belgium. Dr. Cortez was one of the two developers of the medical equipment that inspired Heartware's formation. That fax read:

> Date: May 30, 1990
>
> To: Pedro Cortez
>
> From: Gerald Seery
>
> Without repeating myself too much, this past year has been both challenging and greatly frustrating. I believe we all anticipated making further advances than we have.
>
> Certainly, I am able to report several positive developments . . . FDA approval, some early sales, and establishing Heartware as an organization. But as every businessman knows, every business needs cash, cash, cash. For Heartware, that cash has been tough to come by.
>
> I remain a believer, however. I have spoken with my wife, Tricia, and our investors about refocusing the attention of Heartware onto the European market. They have a number of questions. In general, they feel that we should capitalize on the opportunity where it makes the most sense. Obviously, the United States offers a very large market for our products. However, we should exploit the position of leadership we currently enjoy in the international markets.
>
> The key to building upon our early success will be the availability of money. Having expended all that I can afford (and then some), Heartware will be able to expand quickly only with an additional capital infusion. This can come from several sources: sales, private investors, venture capital, and a partner. Pedro, I am committed to making this happen. If we can get through these early months, I know we can build Heartware into a company with great products and a sound future.

*Names that are disguised are marked with an asterisk the first time they appear.
Source: This case was written by Benjamin M. Oviatt, associate professor of management, Georgia State University (USA); Patricia Phillips McDougall, associate professor of strategic management, Georgia Institute of Technology (USA); Mark Simon, Oakland University (USA); and Rodney C. Shrader (University of Alberta, Canada). Copyright 1994 by authors. This case is intended as a basis for class discussion rather than to illustrate either effective or ineffective handling of an administrative situation.

Heartware entered into the international arena at start-up. Its headquarters and investors were located in the United States, while human resources were in the United States and The Netherlands. Product development and technical support originated in The Netherlands. Early sales came from the United States, United Kingdom, Italy, Spain, and Brazil. The company set up distributorships in the United States, United Kingdom, Saudi Arabia, South Africa, and Turkey. Multinational start-ups headquartered in the United States (sometimes called "global start-ups") are unusual. However, Mr. Seery's dedication to international business was evident when in the summer of 1990 he said:

> If all of a sudden someone said, "Here's a chunk of money for your company and for all you've done," and asked, "Now what will you do?" I would definitely do something international. It's in my blood. Atlanta has the Olympics coming up in 1996, so I'd get involved in that. I would love to help smaller and mid-size companies expand overseas, because I think it's a great opportunity and because I could help them overcome that fear factor. It opens up a world that they don't know about.

THE FOUNDER'S BACKGROUND

Acquaintances described Heartware's founder as a friendly, humorous, and personable man. He was born in 1956, raised on Long Island, New York, and traced his international interest to childhood. He had been fascinated by stories about the uncle he was named after who worked overseas. During the summer between his junior and senior years in high school, Mr. Seery traveled to Spain on a student exchange program and studied Spanish with students from England, France, Ireland, and Italy. His international interests were expanded at the Catholic University of America in Washington, DC, where he earned a BA in international economics. He went on in 1980 to earn an MBA degree with a specialty in marketing from Columbia University.

Mr. Seery's international exposure continued after completing his undergraduate degree. Six months after taking his first job, he completed the management development program in a large chemical company in Philadelphia and was transferred to the international sales department. There he learned the nuts and bolts of international business, including letters of credit, financing, and shipping. In just one year with the chemical company, Mr. Seery generated $7 million in sales.

In 1982, Mr. Seery changed jobs but continued in international sales as product manager for a New Jersey medical supply company. In this job he gained familiarity with medical devices through managing a product line that produced $5 million in revenue annually. Mr. Seery also developed a program to bring doctors from other nations to the United States to introduce them to the company and its products. In 1984, he assumed a position as senior product manager for a dental supply company in New York. For the next two years he managed the worldwide marketing of a dental product line that produced $10 million in revenue annually.

During the five years prior to founding his own company in 1988, Mr. Seery was the director of international marketing and sales for Hospicath* Corporation, a small medical device company in New Jersey. Under his leadership, annual domestic sales increased from $5.6 million in 1986 to $9.3 million in 1988, and international sales increased by more than 40 percent. Mr. Seery managed a network of exclusive distributors in Europe, Canada, and Japan; and during his tenure with Hospicath, he traveled to Western Europe five or six times a year for two to three weeks at a time. On these trips he met with salespeople and distributors, called on hospitals, and met cardiologists in several European countries. On one of these trips Mr. Seery was introduced to the technology on which he founded Heartware.

ELECTROPHYSIOLOGY LAB AND MAPPING SYSTEM

During a September 1987 trip to Europe, Hospicath's Dutch distributor introduced Mr. Seery to Dr. Pedro Cortez. Dr. Cortez was a Spanish cardiologist who held both an MD and a PhD degree. He was employed as a director of the Hospital of Maastricht, located in Maastricht, The Netherlands. The Netherlands was well regarded in the medical community for its pioneering role in cardiology. At the time of Mr. Seery's trip, Dr. Cortez and Mr. Jan van der Swoort,* chairman of the Engineering Department at the University of Limburg in Maastricht, were actively seeking a commercial outlet for the electrophysiology lab and mapping system they had jointly developed.

Electrophysiology (EP) is the study of the electrical signals of the heart, and Dr. Cortez's equipment was used for the diagnosis and treatment of irregular heartbeats (i.e., cardiac arrhythmias). General[1] EP studies were used to diagnose the type of arrhythmia. The standard approach involved the insertion of a catheter, a thin plastic tube, into the blood vessel at the groin, which fed into the heart. Wires were fed through the catheter so that 12 electrode leads at the end of the wires touched the heart. A cardiologist then used a cardiac stimulator to deliver a series of electrical signals to the heart. This procedure was known as pacing the heart. The cardiologist studied the resulting pattern of the heartbeat in order to better understand the nature of the arrhythmia.

Mapping studies were special EP procedures performed in a hospital operating room because the studies required that the chest cavity be surgically opened so electrodes could be moved to various positions on the heart's surface. This procedure generated a detailed map of the electrical activity on the heart's surface and inner wall. A general EP study often preceded mapping.

Growing use of EP led Dr. Cortez and Mr. van der Swoort to invest roughly four years of the mid-1980s in the development of their EP system. By 1987, when Mr. Seery was introduced to the system, it was already in use at the Hospital of Maastricht. The only computerized system in the world, it was owned and managed by the University of Limburg's Instrumentation and Engineering Department. The full $125,000 EP lab and mapping system (i.e., EP system) is described in Exhibit 1. It could be sold in its entirety to perform both types of studies or it could be sold in subsystems—the EP lab subsystem to perform general EP studies and the mapping subsystem to perform mapping studies. Separate components could be sold for incorporation into a hospital's existing system.

HEARTWARE FOUNDED

Mr. Seery was especially interested in the University of Limburg's EP products because he had already directed the launch of an EP product line for Hospicath. That product line produced $1.1 million in sales over a two-year period. Upon returning from Europe to the United States, Mr. Seery proposed that Hospicath acquire all the university's products. Hospicath's president began immediately to work with Dr. Cortez and Mr. van der Swoort to further develop the catheter and to incorporate it into Hospicath's product line. The president decided to further investigate the university's EP system.

In February 1988, Hospicath sent an engineer to Maastricht with Mr. Seery to examine the EP system. Seery and the engineer recommended acquisition and further development of the system. However, the president of Hospicath decided not to pursue capital equipment product lines and to concentrate instead on disposable products like the cardiac catheter.

EXHIBIT 1   Components of the EP Lab and Mapping System

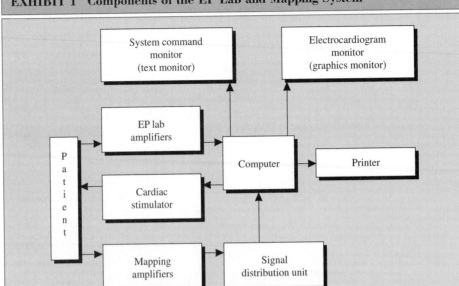

Computer: All the modular parts of the EP lab and mapping system were connected to the personal computer, which served as the heart of the system.

Cardiac Stimulator: The programmable cardiac stimulator (price: $25,000) delivered electrical signals to the heart.

Amplifiers and Signal Distribution Unit: The amplifiers and the signal distribution unit transformed electrical signals received from the heart into a form that could be interpreted by the computer and output to the printer or monitor. Although other components were used for both EP studies and mapping studies, the amplifiers were specially designed for one or the other type study. Each amplifier was priced at $25,000.

Output Devices: One color monitor displayed a menu of command options for running the system, while the other displayed output about the patient's heart. The printer produced hard copy of this output.

EP Lab Subsystem and Mapping Subsystem: The EP lab subsystem (price: $100,000) contained all system components except the mapping amplifiers (EP lab amplifiers were included) and was only used to perform general EP studies. Similarly, the mapping subsystem (price: $100,000) contained all components except the EP lab amplifiers (mapping amplifiers were included).

Supplementary Products Developed by Dr. Cortez:

Belt Electrode: The belt electrode (price: $2,500) used for the mapping procedure contained 21 electrodes and was wrapped around the surface of the heart, enabling information from 21 locations on the heart to be simultaneously replayed to the mapping system.

Cardiac Catheter: The cardiac catheter (price: $100) could be used with the EP lab in general EP studies or in conjunction with other cardiac car products on the market.

Frustrated by the president's response, Mr. Seery began to explore the possibility of forming his own company to acquire and market the EP system. During 1988, while still working at Hospicath, Mr. Seery took steps to form Heartware. He solicited funds, prepared a submission for the Food and Drug Administration (FDA), and negotiated with the University of Limburg.

Because FDA approval was of such vital importance in the U.S. medical products market, Mr. Seery began to seek approval in April 1988, several months before he acquired the product rights. Medical products without FDA approval could not be marketed in the United States, and investors and potential partners were usually not interested in a company whose product was months or even years away from market. The FDA required that medical devices be proved safe and effective. If the product was comparable to others already on the market, it had to be proved equivalent to or better than the others. On September 10, 1988, Heartware contracted the services of Medsys, Inc., a consulting firm that specialized in submitting medical equipment proposals to the FDA. For a fee of $5,000, over the next seven months Medsys prepared Heartware's submission with help from Mr. Seery. This submission included a product instruction book, sample advertisements, quality control procedures, results from general EP and mapping studies, manufacturing procedures, and charts comparing Heartware's product to similar products already sold in the United States.

Heartware International Corporation was incorporated in the state of New Jersey on October 28, 1988. The following week, the founder opened a corporate suite for the new company in New York City. Six months later Mr. Seery resigned from Hospicath to devote his full attention to Heartware.

During the spring of 1989, Mr. Seery's wife, Ms. Patricia Browne, developed Heartware's business plan as an MBA class assignment. By midsummer, Ms. Browne became Heartware's chief financial officer. The position was a part-time one with a deferred salary. Before joining Heartware, Ms. Browne ran her own financial consulting firm for three years. Altogether she had nearly 10 years' experience as corporate controller and accountant. Ms. Browne held a BA degree in economics/accounting from Catholic University and an MBA in finance from New York University.

Initial funding for Heartware came from Mr. Seery and his wife. They provided $185,000 from savings, personal debt, and loans against their home equity. In May 1989, Heartware's founder sent a summary of the company's five-year plan to more than a dozen private individuals. Within five weeks, four close relatives invested a total of $85,000.

HEARTWARE'S CONTRACT WITH THE UNIVERSITY

Heartware acquired exclusive worldwide rights to market the EP system and belt electrodes on May 4, 1989. Under the agreement with the University of Limburg, Heartware would be credited with all sales of the EP system regardless of whether Heartware or the university generated the sales lead. All price quotations outstanding at the time of the agreement were included. The university would provide assembly, inspection, and testing of all systems ordered for about 50 percent of the list price of the system. Mr. Seery expected that this percentage would decrease dramatically when the sales level made mass production possible.

In exchange for the above services, Heartware was to make an initial payment of 50,000 Dutch guilders[2](DGfl) followed by 10 quarterly payments of 50,000 DGfl. Rights to the product would revert to the University of Limburg if Heartware failed to meet its obligations.

Mr. van der Swoort was to be Mr. Seery's point of contact at the University. Separate agreements were drawn up for Mr. van der Swoort and Dr. Cortez. They would receive royalties from Heartware on units sold in exchange for providing assistance with sales demonstrations, installations, and service calls. Heartware's founder counted on Mr. van der Swoort to service and support all European customers. In addition to the royalties received, Mr. van der Swoort received about $400 a month for providing general support, such as answering inquiries. To Mr. Seery, the spirit of the contract implied that the University of Limburg would provide technical support to further the development and sales of the EP system to the mutual benefit of both Heartware and the university.

Mr. Seery counted on Dr. Cortez's international reputation as a leader in the field of electrophysiology to help sell the system. Because product and company credibility were crucial in the medical equipment industry, Dr. Cortez was retained in a consultant capacity as medical advisor to the company.

PRODUCTS LAUNCHED

From May 4–6, 1989, Mr. Seery set up a display in Toronto, Canada, at the annual meeting of the North American Society of Pacing and Electrophysiology (NASPE), the professional association for electrophysiologists. Approximately 1,500 doctors, nurses, technicians, and engineers attended the meeting that year, and nearly 75 percent of the 800 cardiologists in attendance had a specialty in electrophysiology. Heartware's products generated significant interest among NASPE members, and Mr. Seery made several important contacts at the meeting.

Heartware's founder felt that launching the company at this NASPE meeting was crucial due to the very broad exposure the meeting would bring. Mr. Seery acknowledged that the product needed aesthetic improvements, design alterations to facilitate mass production, and FDA approval for the U.S. market. However, he did not want to wait a full year for the 1990 NASPE meeting.

THE EP MARKET

In the late 1980s, EP was still a relatively new field. EP techniques were used in clinical diagnosis beginning about 1980. However, EP was not widely used in the medical community until about 1986. In 1989, there were 1,300 U.S. coronary care units. These units treated 390,000 patients. Approximately 10 percent of those patients required pacing to return the heart to a normal rhythm. Use of EP was closely tied to the amount of government reimbursement for EP procedures. On October 1, 1989, the reimbursement rate to coronary care units rose from $2,700 to $8,100.

Mr. Seery anticipated that Heartware could take advantage of expansion in the EP market.[3] Growth in the market was expected to come from several sources. An EP study was the preferred diagnostic test in candidates for sudden cardiac death. However, in the late 1980s, less than 10 percent of patients who were at significant risk actually underwent the test. One of the major reasons for this low usage was a shortage of cardiologists trained in EP. However, EP represented an attractive specialty, and the number of physicians in this area was growing rapidly.

The EP market was segmented into two primary areas: systems designed to perform general EP studies in EP laboratories within hospitals, and systems for performing mapping studies in operating rooms. EP labs offered the best growth potential. The bulk of this growth was expected to be generated by the expansion of cardiology departments into EP technology. By the end of 1989, 400 U.S. EP labs had an installed base of EP equipment. These labs were not expected to purchase replacement systems in the near future. However, these labs were potential customers for add-on components such as Heartware's cardiac stimulator. It was expected that 400 additional hospitals would add EP programs to their cardiology departments between 1990 and 1994. Equipment sales during that time period were expected to be about $45 million.

Heartware's mapping system would be sold in the surgical market. At the end of 1989, 80 U.S. hospitals performed arrhythmia surgery and another 80 were expected to expand into such surgery by 1994.

Heartware's initial product line consisted of the EP lab and mapping system and belt electrodes. Mr. Seery planned to add cardiac catheters later. The company expected to subcontract catheter production until 1992 or 1993, at which point Heartware would build its own production facilities. The market for cardiac catheters was growing. Hospitals were expected to purchase new catheters at an increasing rate because the resterilization and reuse of catheters increased infection-control problems and hospital liability for malfunctioning products. In 1989, EP catheter sales totaled about $6.5 million. Had hospitals used new catheters for each procedure rather than sterilizing and reusing some, the 1989 market would have been about $15 million. The expected market in 1994 was $35 million.

The number of hospitals using EP was expected to increase most quickly in the United States, as health care delivery abroad had greater financial limitations. In the international market, about 80 hospitals in Western Europe, South America, Canada, and Japan used EP. Although smaller, the international market presented several advantages over the U.S. market. First, with the notable exception of Japan, governmental regulations abroad tended to be less stringent than FDA regulations in the United States. Second, the smaller market size and slower growth resulted in less competition. Third, appearance and design features that did not enhance the performance of medical products were not as important outside the United States.

HEARTWARE'S MARKET POSITION

In 1989 several companies competed in the EP market. Exhibit 2 profiles Heartware's major competitors. Heartware's EP system offered several advantages over the noncomputerized systems that dominated the market in the late 1980s. These advantages are summarized in Exhibit 3.

EXPLORING STRATEGIC PARTNERSHIPS

Mr. Seery spent much of his time seeking strategic partnerships with established medical device companies that might want to add Heartware's products to their current product lines. He envisioned an agreement in which another company would receive an equity interest in Heartware in return for that company's financial, marketing, and technical support. Mr. Seery hoped such an agreement might later lead the partner to buy Heartware and provide Heartware's investors a significant return on their investment. With basically only one product, he expected that Heartware would exhaust its market in five years. Thus, his goal was to ally with a company that offered multiple products.

Heartware's CEO contacted dozens of companies of all sizes throughout the United States, Australia, and Japan; sent them a condensed version of Heartware's business plan; and followed up by phone. The contacts led to extensive dialogue in some cases. However, most companies were only casually interested in Heartware's products.

EXHIBIT 2   Heartware's Major Competitors

Most competitors were headquartered in the United States, and less than 20 percent of their sales were generated overseas.

	Bard Electrophysiology
Parent:	C. R. Bard, Inc. (a medical supply company with $100 M annual revenue).
Annual sales:	Approximately $11 M.
Main product:	Cardiac catheters.
EP product:	$100,000 cardiac mapping system.
Product advantages:	Bard's system excelled Heartware's in graphics capability by producing a picture of the heart with shading to indicate the intensity of electrical activity.
Product drawbacks:	Bard's system was not portable, and its components could not be used for general EP studies. Foreign doctors were unwilling to pay for added graphics capability.
Competitive advantages:	Bard dominated the catheter market, offered a full product line and extensive service, and had a large distribution system and established training programs. Bard derived a significant competitive advantage from the fact that many cardiologists received their initial EP training on Bard equipment. Later, when these cardiologists were in the position of ordering equipment for their own practices or of giving advice about such a purchase, they were inclined to order the familiar brand.
Research and development:	Developing a general EP lab system.

Biomedical Business Instrumentation (BBI)

EP product:	EP system that needed FDA approval.
Drawbacks:	Product had not been commercially marketed or produced.
Other:	Founded in 1986 by two Canadian engineers. In 1989, BBI was considering signing a joint venture agreement with another more-established Canadian medical firm.

Bloom Associates

Annual sales:	Approximately $3 M.
EP product:	Noncomputerized general EP system and mapping system.
Product advantages:	Lower cost than Heartware's systems.
Product drawbacks:	Bloom's systems were slower and stored information on paper rather than disk.
Other:	The firm was for sale for $10 million.

(Continued)

Negotiations progressed furthest with Electrophysiology Company (EPCO),* a U.S. company that specialized in equipment associated with arrhythmia detection and treatment. At the 1989 NASPE meeting, Mr. Seery had discussed Heartware and its products with a cardiologist who recommended he contact EPCO. That cardiologist also told EPCO's officers about Heartware. The day after Mr. Seery returned to New York from Toronto, EPCO's president called Mr. Seery to express interest in Heartware.

EXHIBIT 2   Heartware's Major Competitors (continued)

Digital Cardiovascular Incorporated (DCI)	
EP product:	$20,000 computer-controlled stimulator for use in EP studies.
Product drawbacks:	Stimulator could not store or record output. DCI marketed its stimulator through Medtronic Inc., the leading manufacturer of cardiac pacemakers. As of 1989, Medtronic was emphasizing pacemaker products, not DCI's stimulator.
Electrophysiology Company (EPCO)	
Annual sales:	Approximately $5 M.
Research and development:	EPCO's mapping system prototype needed FDA approval, and the firm was developing a general EP system.

EXHIBIT 3   Heartware's Product Advantages

- Computerization of the EP system allowed electrical signals from the heart to be displayed or saved in a variety of ways. Certain time segments (e.g., critical episodes) could be marked for later analysis, the scale of output could be changed, or readings from different parts of the heart could be emphasized or deemphasized. This clarified relevant information, led to easier analysis, decreased the chance of error, and decreased the amount of time needed after the study to diagnose the arrhythmia.

- Heartware's computerized cardiac stimulator was the only one that could constantly monitor the patient's condition by measuring and reporting beat-to-beat time intervals.

- Computerization allowed preprogrammed pacing protocols (ordered series of electrical signals sent to the heart by the stimulator) to be used instead of manually delivering individual signals. Pacing protocols could be stored on disk for quick retrieval, thus drastically reducing the time required to deliver protocols and potential errors.

- Computerization allowed the hospital to permanently store output on disk instead of paper, significantly simplifying storage. A single general EP study could last up to four hours, generating a stack of printed output between four and six inches tall.

- Heartware's mapping system could simultaneously obtain and display information about a heart's electrical patterns, reducing the time required in surgery by approximately 30 to 40 minutes.

- In about 60 percent of the mapping studies, even more time could be saved when the belt electrodes were used. The conventional method of obtaining signals to map the heart involved the use of only two to four electrodes that were moved from one small area of the heart to another, taking between 20 and 30 minutes to locate the problem site. Because the belt electrode contained 21 leads that were in direct contact with the heart, the time needed to locate a problem site could be reduced to under a minute.

Over the next several months, Heartware's founder and EPCO representatives met three times and communicated frequently via telephone and fax. They discussed the possibility of EPCO investing in Heartware in return for equity in the company. Mr. Seery anticipated EPCO would eventually buy out Heartware and hire him as a consultant or manager. Negotiations with EPCO, consultations with lawyers, flights to EPCO's home office, and product demonstrations for EPCO consumed much of Mr. Seery's time and resources. During this period he concentrated on these negotiations and greatly curtailed efforts with other companies.

In July 1989, Mr. Seery sent EPCO a two-page summary of the general terms that they had agreed upon to date. A few days later, EPCO sent Mr. Seery a letter of intent, but did not mention his letter regarding terms of agreement. On July 20, 1989, Mr. Seery sent a letter to Heartware's stockholders with the following details:

> We have negotiated with several firms over the past several months. Our efforts have focused most recently on concluding an agreement with EPCO. EPCO has a proven technology in the field of electrophysiology. They are seeking to expand their product line. Heartware's EP system is an attractive opportunity for EPCO.
>
> Consequently, we have concluded an agreement under which EPCO would invest up to $350,000 in Heartware, in exchange for an equity position of up to 35 percent. At the thirty-month point, EPCO could exercise its option to purchase the remaining equity of Heartware for $750,000.
>
> While a final agreement has not been concluded, we are confident of the respective commitment each party has to closing the deal. We believe that the current shareholders of Heartware are well served by this agreement.

In addition to the compensation described above, Mr. Seery also negotiated with EPCO to receive an "earnout"[4] over four years.

FDA ASKS FOR CLARIFICATION

Mr. Seery's negotiations to obtain strategic partners, investments, and sales continued to be blocked by the EP system's lack of FDA approval. After having reviewed Heartware's submission, the FDA responded on July 8, 1989, by asking for further clarification of a few issues. With the help of Medsys' consulting services, Mr. Seery responded to these questions. The issues that needed to be clarified were all relatively minor, and all indications were that FDA approval would be forthcoming. However, the FDA would have another 90 days before it was required to respond to Heartware's clarifications.

FURTHER NEGOTIATIONS WITH EPCO

In August 1989, negotiations with EPCO intensified. Mr. Seery shipped equipment from The Netherlands at Heartware's expense to conduct a demonstration in Atlanta for EPCO's chairman. An engineer from the University of Limburg flew to Atlanta to make the presentation and Mr. Seery flew in from New York.

During the demonstration, Mr. Seery stood in the hallway of the hospital. On one pay phone he spoke to his attorney in Boston; on another he spoke simultaneously to EPCO's president. Mr. Seery recalled the incident as follows:

> The president of EPCO said that the final hitch was FDA approval. I said, "We agreed to this back in June. This agreement is not subject to FDA approval." He agreed. Right then and there he agreed with me that the deal was not subject to FDA approval. I said, "Do we have a deal?" He said, "Yes, we have a deal." I hung up the phone and walked back into the clinical lab where the chairman was. I said, "I just got off the phone and we've got a deal." He shook my hand and said, "Ah, that's great. And of course it's subject to FDA approval." I said, "No. We just agreed that it's not." He said, "Yes it is." I blew up.
>
> Because the chairman knew cash was tight, he said, "I'll tell you what we'll do. We'll give you a working capital loan for $50,000 to carry you until the FDA approval." We expected FDA approval to come in September or October, so we weren't that far away, and I had every expectation we would get it. With $50,000 working capital, that could work.

He told me to call him later to solidify this $50,000 commitment. By then of course the deal was subject to this and that and some other things. A few days later the $50,000 working capital loan was for one year at some percent interest rate, and the collateral was the technology, and they weren't required to sign the deal even if the FDA approved. They had about 10 days after approval to decide whether they wanted it or not.

After consulting with his attorney about the deal, Mr. Seery decided not to go through with it.

ANOTHER MAJOR PUSH FOR FUNDING

When negotiations with EPCO broke down, Mr. Seery responded with what he called "a frantic effort to make new contacts."

I probably sent out letters to and called everybody who was anybody who knew somebody who may have once invested, and I wrote off letters and made phone calls to just about every major medical company that might have an interest. I felt that it was only a matter of time before competitors would develop EP technology as sophisticated as the EP lab.

In addition to reinitiating contacts with possible strategic partners and private investors, Mr. Seery began to actively pursue the venture capital market.

FDA APPROVAL

On October 2, 1989, less than six months after Heartware's initial submission, Mr. Seery received a letter from the FDA stating that Heartware's EP system was approved for the U.S. market. Within days of receiving the FDA's letter, Mr. Seery called EPCO once again to tell them Heartware had received FDA approval and to ask if a new deal was possible. He recalled that phone conversation as follows:

They said, "Same terms?" And I said, "No, we now have FDA approval." That was the last I talked to them for a while. They had no interest in revisiting it because they were now advancing their own system. Not that they didn't have it to start with. I don't want you to think they just took what we had, but they saw our technology and possibly benefited from it. In my heart of hearts, I don't think they wanted to deal. They wanted the information.

SALES

Just as Mr. Seery's efforts to strike an agreement with EPCO seemed to come to a dead end, Heartware began to generate orders. When Mr. Seery acquired rights to the EP system, he also acquired rights to all outstanding quotations made by the University of Limburg. One quote was to Dr. Jacob Atie, a Brazilian doctor, who had worked on the EP system as a graduate student at the University of Maastricht. Dr. Atie later decided to buy amplifiers for a mapping system. On October 30, 1989, Heartware's CEP received the following fax from Jan van der Swoort in Holland.

Date: 30 October 1989

To: Gerry Seery

From: Jan van der Swoort

Subject: Orders and safety regulations

Congratulations! You got your first order. Today I got a visit from Dr. Atie and Dr. Cruz. They will finance the system with their personal means. They asked me to inform you about the order. I put it on the fax. I informed them that I needed a deposit of 25 percent for the University in order to start working on the system. Then I have to ask the Financial Department to send them an invoice for this deposit. Now in order not to confuse the Financial Department it makes sense that you order the University to prepare this system and that the invoice should be sent directly to these doctors. The difference between the invoice and the agreed compensation for the University will be credited to the installments or otherwise.

Heartware's second sale occurred the following day and also stemmed from an outstanding quotation to a former Brazilian graduate student at the university. During 1989, three hospitals, the two in Brazil and one in Spain, ordered amplifiers to add to existing EP systems. The sales totaled $66,000. Because these orders were not shipped until May 1990, however, Heartware received no cash in 1989 and the sales appeared on the 1990 income statement. Heartware's only revenue in 1989 was $6,900 from the sale of three belt electrodes. In most cases, customers paid the university directly in Dutch guilders and the university credited the amount Heartware owed for the technology.

MOVE TO ATLANTA, GEORGIA

In December 1989, Mr. Seery relocated Heartware's headquarters to Atlanta, Georgia. He knew that Heartware would be operating on a tight budget and felt that Atlanta's lower cost of living would increase the business's chance for success. Atlanta offered several additional advantages. Mr. Seery had already established a relationship with a cardiology group there. He also planned to apply for entry into the Advanced Technology Development Center (ATDC) headquartered at and administered by the Georgia Institute of Technology.

The ATDC was an incubator, a technology business development center that acted to promote high-technology start-ups. The center was created in 1980 by the state of Georgia to help high-technology entrepreneurs by providing technical and business assistance. The Technology Business Center, an arm of ATDC, offered office space, shared secretarial services, and shared office equipment with its tenants. The sharing of services and assets gave young firms access to resources that might otherwise have been prohibitively expensive.

The technological benefits were as important to Mr. Seery as the other services provided because Heartware had not yet been able to employ an in-house engineering staff. ATDC members had access to the resources of all public universities within Georgia. Most important, Heartware also benefited from its proximity to other high-tech firms. For example, a firm located at ATDC that specialized in engineering development work was helpful to Heartware by suggesting minor product improvements on a limited, informal basis at no charge.

After arrival in Atlanta, Patricia Browne accepted the position of controller at Turner Broadcasting System. She continued to serve as Heartware's CFO.

HEARTWARE'S RELATIONSHIP WITH THE UNIVERSITY OF LIMBURG

Although ATDC offered some technical assistance, most technological support and product improvement came from the University of Limburg. The system was sound in terms of performance. However, it was not particularly attractive in terms of design and aesthetics. Further product design work was also needed before the system could be manufactured efficiently.

Demonstrations for potential customers and distributors were often held at the University of Limburg, while Mr. van der Swoort attended shows like NASPE with Mr. Seery. Mr. Seery, customers, and potential customers contacted Mr. van der Swoort when they had questions about the system's capabilities, service, or installation.

Heartware's founder felt his relationship with the two co-developers was quite favorable, although not problem free. In addition to contractual issues that needed clarifying, confusion about sales or payments often arose. The following fax sent by Mr. Seery to Mr. van der Swoort is an example of some of the confusion that arose as a result of what Heartware's CEO called a "3,000-mile umbilical cord":

> Based upon your first phone call, I thought the doctors were ready to place an immediate order during their visit to you. Now it appears that a great deal of time will go by before they either place an order or accept delivery of the systems.
>
> Because of my initial impression, I compromised significantly on the price, recognizing the potential value of an immediate order and the fact that the University had already provided quotations to these doctors. Now the quotations from Heartware are being interpreted by others as applying to their situation.
>
> I am in a very difficult situation. We cannot increase the quotations that are outstanding despite the longer delivery date. And how am I to modify the quotation to the new doctor to more accurately reflect the value of the product? Heartware cannot survive unless we price our products at a rate that yields a reasonable return.

Mr. Seery also felt that differences in cultural perceptions may have caused difficulty. Mr. van der Swoort seemed to believe that Americans and their firms were wealthy and could therefore afford to pay higher fees and royalties to him. Mr. Seery tried to correct that impression, especially as it pertained to start-up ventures, but the issue was a constant thorn in their relationship. According to the founder,

> When Heartware *could not* afford to do something, the developer interpreted this to mean that we *did not* want to do something.

Nevertheless, Mr. van der Swoort continually upgraded the software for the EP system. Even though Heartware had the most technologically advanced system on the market, Mr. Seery feared that competitors could easily catch up. No other company had FDA approval on a computer-based EP system, but both Bard and EPCO had functioning prototypes. For competitors, the stimulator represented the primary hurdle in obtaining FDA approval. Mr. Seery felt that "if you're a decent engineer, you can put a stimulator together." Time was the main issue. He anticipated that a competitor would need six months to develop a stimulator compatible with a computerized EP system and another year or more to obtain FDA approval.

To lessen dependence on the University of Limburg, Heartware's founder wanted in-house ability to continuously improve products. He felt confident, given his contacts in the industry, that he would have no difficulty finding qualified candidates to fill the position of technical director. However, poor cash flow delayed his plans.

In February 1990, another problem developed, and Heartware's relationship with the university and the hospital changed. Dr. Cortez announced his intention to leave the hospital in May and to move into private practice in Belgium. His future role in Heartware was unclear.

EXHIBIT 4   Heartware International Income Statement for Period Ended 6/30/90

	6 Months	Ratio
Sales Revenue		
Amplifiers and signal distribution unit	$53,263.30	69.9%
Electrodes	21,919.05	28.8
Miscellaneous income	1,000.00	1.3
Total sales revenue	$76,182.35	100.00
Distribution Commissions		
Distributor commissions	405.00	.5
Royalties	2,889.50	3.8
Net sales revenue	$72,887.85	95.7
Cost of Sales		
Amplifiers and signal distribution unit	39,728.80	52.1
Electrodes	12,030.75	15.8
Other cost of sales	5.00	0.0
Gross profit	$21,123.30	27.7
Operating Expenses		
Employment	2,617.12	3.4
Marketing and sales	3,955.12	5.2
Travel and entertainment	5,490.35	7.2
Professional fees	2,045.00	2.7
General and administrative	6,032.97	7.9
Depreciation	802.26	1.1
Amortization expense	15,000.00	19.7
Total operating expenses	$35,942.82	47.2
Income before interest and tax	(14,819.52)	(19.5)
Interest	(8,521.41)	(30.6)
Net income before tax	(23,340.93)	(30.6)
Income tax	25.00	0.0
Income after tax	$(23,365.93)	(30.7)%

EXPANDING SALES

Heartware's ability to hire additional staff depended heavily on securing more capital and increasing sales. In total, during Heartware's first 19 months of business, the company had sold $83,000 worth of products and had another $60,000 in orders. Exhibits 4 and 5 provide the financial statements as of June 1990.

EXHIBIT 5   Heartware International, General Ledger, Balance Sheet as of 6/30/90

Assets		
Current Assets		
Cash and marketable securities	$2,919.41	
Accounts receivable	5,025.00	
Total current assets		$7,944.41
Fixed Assets		
Furniture and equipment	8,022.66	
Accumulated depreciation	(1,604.53)	
Total fixed assets		6,418.13
Noncurrent Assets		
System license	150,000.00	
Accumulated amortization	(30,000.00)	
System license, net	120,000.00	
Deposits	604.45	
Total noncurrent assets		120,604.45
Total assets		$134,966.99

Liabilities and Shareholder's Equity Liabilities		
Current Liabilities		
Accounts payable	$1,758.84	
Payable to officers	33,364.20	
Interest payable	4,529.05	
Total current liabilities		$39,652.09
Long-Term Liabilities		
License payable	88,042.69	
Total long-term liabilities		88,042.69
Total liabilities		$127,694.78

Shareholder's Equity		
Common stock	2,000.00	
Paid-in capital	$103,000.00	
Retained earnings	(74,361.86)	
Current earnings	(23,365.93)	
Total shareholder's equity		7,272.21
Total liability and shareholder's equity		$134,966.99

All sales had been a function of Mr. Seery's personal efforts or contact made by the university. While no one pattern was evident in the way sales evolved, many of the orders came through the university from former students. To prepare for the future, Heartware's founder also began to develop a network of distributors. Most of these distributorships arose from contacts Mr. Seery had made in previous business deals. To date, all associations with distributors were informal.

CONTINUED PURSUIT OF FUNDING AND PARTNERSHIPS

During the spring of 1990, fund-raising proceeded much more slowly than Heartware's founder anticipated. He was unable to raise funds beyond the $270,000 invested by family members. Most of those funds had been spent to acquire the technology, travel to Europe, display and demonstrate the product, and seek FDA approval. Mr. Seery anticipated that further development and sales of the EP system would require an additional $1 million.

When Mr. Seery contacted venture capitalists, some told him their companies did not invest in ventures that required less than about $3 million. Others expressed reluctance because Heartware had no track record, was too dependent on one product, was too high-tech, or did not have a well-rounded management team.

Negotiations with potential strategic partners progressed further than negotiations with venture capitalists. However, none had yet come to fruition. Companies approached about partnerships gave various reasons for not forming an alliance. Some were not interested because the EP system required too large a capital investment for too small a market niche. Others indicated that the EP system was not a good fit with their current product lines. Negotiations with several companies continued.

ESOPHAGEAL EP TECHNOLOGY

During this period, Mr. Seery also began to explore an opportunity to extend Heartware's product line into esophageal EP technology. This technology took advantage of the fact that the heart and part of the esophagus are very close together. Thus, a specially designed catheter could be placed down the esophagus along with leads from a cardiac stimulator for sending electrical signals to the atria of the heart. The distance from the esophagus to the ventricles was significantly greater; such a system could therefore be used only to diagnose and treat atrial arrhythmias.

Atrial arrhythmias were relatively less life threatening than ventricular arrhythmias and could be treated fairly quickly without a hospital stay. Once an atrial arrhythmia was diagnosed, an esophageal EP system could often be used to pace the heart out of the arrhythmia. Thus, esophageal pacing was less invasive to the body and could be performed in an increased number of locations, without a cardiologist, and in a decreased amount of time.

The procedure's speed and mobility often made esophageal treatment an ideal method for stimulating the heart in emergency situations, such as in coronary care units. In contrast to a general EP study, a patient did not need to be disconnected from all other support systems and moved to another location.

Before 1988, esophageal diagnosis and treatment had primarily been used on a clinical basis with the results recorded in scientific journals. Medical equipment could be sold on a "clinical-use basis" prior to FDA approval. Clinical-use sales allowed for a system to be evaluated to obtain FDA acceptance. However, no marketing was allowed, only a limited quantity could be sold, and the product could only be sold at or below cost. Although esophageal technology became more routinely used in coronary care units and emergency rooms after 1988, it was still considered a fairly recent development in 1990.

While Mr. Seery was employed by Hospicath, the company had been approached about the possibility of acquiring an esophageal EP product developed at an American university. But Hospicath deferred its decision, never telling the developer yes or no. Mr. Seery's interest in the technology had been keen, however, and this interest continued after he founded Heartware.

Mr. Seery projected that each of the 1,300 U.S. coronary care units would install a minimum of two esophageal systems between 1990 and 1995, generating a market of $10 million for the period. In 1990, over 5,300 emergency rooms were providing care in the United States. Mr. Seery estimated this segment of the market would generate sales of $35 million in esophageal products between 1990 and 1995. Other possible market segments included field response teams (ambulances and paramedics) and general practitioners. Hospitals with EP systems could also use an esophageal system to screen a patient. If the arrhythmia was located in the atria, a general EP study might not be needed.

Acquisition of the esophageal stimulator would also potentially lead to the sale of esophageal catheters. Each stimulator sold would generate sales of 15 to 20 catheters per year. The esophageal catheter market was expected to total $40 million between 1990 and 2000. Few companies marketed esophageal products, however. Mr. Seery knew of only one Italian company marketing an esophageal system in Europe and one small U.S.-based medical device company marketing a system in the United States.

HEARTWARE ACQUIRES ESOPHAGEAL TECHNOLOGY

In March 1990, knowing that negotiations were not progressing between Hospicath and the developer of the esophageal stimulator, Mr. Seery decided to approach the developer about acquiring the rights for Heartware. The two agreed that Heartware would make no fixed payments. Rather, Heartware would pay 10 to 15 percent in royalties to the developer on any units sold in exchange for the product rights. The company gave the schematics to Mr. Seery. However, no formal agreement was signed because Heartware did not have funding available to develop and promote the product.

Before this agreement, the developer had already sold two dozen stimulators on a clinical-use basis. However, Mr. Seery realized that he would need assistance to further develop the product. He believed that until he could hire in-house technical expertise, the system's developer would provide support. The system still required FDA approval, clinical evaluations, and a new casing. Additionally, the system had to be redesigned to simplify manufacture. The founder estimated that $250,000 would be needed to complete the development process and to cover management expenses. Another year and a half would be needed before the product was ready to be marketed commercially in the United States. Initially, to limit expenses, Mr. Seery planned to concentrate sales efforts for the esophageal product in the U.S. market. He felt that this was feasible since the United States contained many outlets and almost no competition.

Heartware's CEO planned to target the domestic distributors of cardiology products as sources of capital. Ideally, he hoped to raise the needed $250,000 in lots of $25,000. Mr. Seery believed that if distributors invested in the product, they would also actively promote it. Distributors would be offered 15 to 20 percent commission to generate sales, collect receivables, and maintain inventory. The product was expected to sell for about $7,000. Mr. Seery anticipated exhibiting the esophageal system at the next NASPE meeting in 1990.

In addition, Mr. Seery planned to sell esophageal catheters and started to investigate manufacturers that would make catheters under Heartware's label. He anticipated that the selling price per esophageal catheter would be $100. Hospicath was one of the only companies selling esophageal catheters.

NEWS FROM THE UNIVERSITY OF LIMBURG

On Mr. Seery's way to work on May 1, 1990, he contemplated the strategic direction his company should take. When he arrived at the office, the following fax from an attorney at the University of Limburg awaited him:

From: Ben van Werscht

To: Mr. Gerry Seery

Dear Mr. Seery,

I have a painful message for you. The Head of the Instrumental Department, Mr. Jan van der Swoort, has been suspended from duty. I will take duty from him, and in this capacity I would like to settle some things with you.

As we both know there is a contract between Heartware Corporation and the University of Limburg for the Cortez Electrophysiology System. So far Mr. van der Swoort settled this business, but I have no sound judgment on the administration yet.

It is important for me to get answers on the following questions: What is the general rule of conduct when a new system is ordered? Who fixes the price? Who is taking care of product liability, and so forth?

News of Mr. van der Swoort's suspension from the university, coming from an attorney and accompanied by a question about product liability, led Mr. Seery to wonder if the system had failed and a patient had died. However, a letter soon arrived from Mr. van der Swoort explaining that his suspension was due to budget problems and internal politics. Mr. Seery promptly arranged a trip to Holland to meet Mr. van Werscht, get an explanation of events, and reevaluate Heartware's relationship with the University of Limburg.

Mr. van Werscht became the main contact between Heartware and the university, but Mr. Seery felt the attorney was more concerned with enforcing the strict letter of their contract than abiding by the spirit of the agreement worked out between Mr. Seery and the product's developers. University support and interest in further development of the EP system's hardware and software waned.

HEARTWARE'S OPTIONS

With technical support no longer coming from the university, Mr. Seery began to explore alternatives. He continued to contact U.S. companies with technical infrastructures already in place who might be interested in a partnership. Mr. Seery identified several small U.S. firms that had the ability to upgrade the technology and the willingness to do so on a contract basis, but Heartware lacked the operating cash to pay for their services. Another alternative was to add a full-time technical expert to Heartware's payroll, but Mr. Seery did not feel comfortable bringing someone on board until Heartware had a solid capital base.

On several occasions the founder had examined the possibility of moving his home and Heartware's headquarters to Europe, where he could better manage relations with the university, Dr. Cortez, and Mr. van der Swoort. Both The Netherlands and Belgium were considered possible locations. Heartware's products were receiving recognition and sales in Europe, and competition was hardly an issue there. Investors in Europe consistently presented the warmest responses to Heartware's business plan. By spring 1990, Mr. Seery was spending approximately one-fourth of his time overseas. The main obstacle to making the move was the need for a steady cash flow for personal support while the company got off the ground. A major disadvantage to a European headquarters would be that less attention would be given to the larger U.S. market, where Heartware had the most advanced system with FDA approval.

If the company did not move to Europe, another option Heartware's CEO considered was to begin concentrating exclusively on marketing the esophageal technology in the United States. If Mr. Seery focused on the esophageal technology, he would have to essentially abandon Heartware's relationship with the University of Limburg, since the start-up did not have enough resources to invest in both directions.

A final alternative was simply to go out of business. Resources were already stretched, and the other options would risk additional capital. To Mr. Seery, no option was clearly superior.

Endnotes

1. Often the prefix "general" is dropped.
2. On May 4, 1989, the date the contract was signed, 2.132 Dfl were the equivalent of $1 U.S.
3. The statistics and market estimates in this section are from Heartware's business plan.
4. An earnout is a series of payments, usually made over several years, based upon some measure of the company's performance such as profits or sales.

5

Creativity and the Business Idea

❧

LEARNING OBJECTIVES

1. To identify various sources of ideas for new ventures.

2. To discuss methods available for generating new venture ideas.

3. To discuss creativity and the techniques for creative problem solving.

4. To discuss the aspects of the product planning and development process.

5. To discuss aspects of e-commerce and starting an e-commerce business.

FREDERICK W. SMITH

Who would think that an entrepreneur with a $10 million inheritance would need more capital to get his company off the ground? The business world is filled with stories of companies, large and small, that started in a garage with an initial investment of a few hundred dollars. But none of those companies needed a nationwide distribution system in place, complete with a fleet of airplanes and trucks, before accepting its first order. And none of those garage start-ups grew to be Federal Express.

www.fedex.com

Frederick W. Smith, a Memphis native whose father made his fortune in founding a bus company, conceived of the idea for his air-cargo company while studying economics at Yale University in the 1960s. The professor of one of Smith's classes was a staunch supporter of the current system of air freight handling in which a cargo package literally hitched a ride in any unused space on a passenger flight. Fred Smith saw things differently and, in a paper, described the concept of a freight-only airline that would fly all packages to one central point, where they would then be distributed and flown out again to their destinations. This operation could take place at night when the airports were less crowded, and, with proper logistics control, the packages could be delivered the next day. Whether it was the novelty of the idea, the fact that it went against the professor's theories, or the fact that it was written in one night and was turned in late, the first public display of Smith's grand idea earned him a C.

Smith's idea constituted far more than a concept for a creative term paper, however. He had seen how the technological base of the country was changing. More companies were becoming involved in the production and use of small, expensive items such as computers, and Smith was convinced that businesses could use his air-cargo idea to control their inventory costs. Overnight delivery from a single distribution center to anywhere in the country could satisfy customers' needs without a company needing a duplicate investment in inventory to be stored in regional warehouses. Smith even thought of the Federal Reserve Banks as a potential customer with the vast quantities of checks that had to be delivered to all parts of the country every day. But the Vietnam War and a family history of patriotic service intervened. Smith joined the Marine Corps and was sent to Vietnam, first as a platoon leader and then as a pilot.

After nearly four years of service and 200 ground support missions as a pilot, he left Vietnam, ready to start building something. He went to work with his stepfather, first managing and subsequently purchasing a controlling interest in Arkansas Aviation Sales, a struggling aircraft modification and overhaul shop. Difficulty in

165

getting parts to the shop in Little Rock, Arkansas, revived his interest in the air-cargo concept. He commissioned two feasibility studies, both of which returned favorable results based on a high initial investment. The key to this company would be its ability to serve a large segment of the business community from the very beginning, and the key to the required level of service was cash. Full of optimism, Smith went to Chicago and New York, confident that he would be returning with basket loads of investment checks. Progress turned out to be slower than Smith had anticipated, but through his boundless energy, belief in his idea, and technical knowledge of the air freight field, he was finally able to get enthusiastic backing (around $5 million in capital) from New Court Securities, a Manhattan-based, Rothschild-backed venture-capital investment bank. This commitment from New Court spurred substantial additional financing. Five other institutions, including General Dynamics and Citicorp Venture Capital, Ltd., got involved, and Smith went back to Memphis with $72 million. This was the largest venture-capital start-up deal in the history of American business.

Federal Express took to the skies on March 12, 1973, to test its service. Servicing an 11-city network (extending from Dallas to Cincinnati), it initially shipped only six packages. On the night of April 17, the official start-up of Federal Express, the network had been expanded to include 25 cities (from Rochester, New York, to Miami, Florida, shipping a total of 186 packages. Volume picked up rapidly and service was expanded; it looked as though Federal Express was a true overnight success. Smith's understanding of a market need had been accurate, but he had not counted on OPEC causing a massive inflation of fuel costs just as his company was getting started. By mid-1974, the company was losing more than $1 million a month. His investors were not willing to keep the company going, and his relatives were suing him for mismanaging the family fortune (nearly $10 million of Smith money was invested). But Smith never lost faith in his idea and finally won enough converts in the investment community to keep the doors open long enough to straighten out the pricing problems caused by OPEC. After losing $27 million in the first two years, Federal Express turned a profit of $3.6 million in 1976. The development and growth of Federal Express were tightly regulated. Due to old laws designed to protect the early pioneers of the passenger airline industry, Smith was required to obtain approval for operating any aircraft with a payload in excess of 7,500 pounds. Since the major airlines—at the time, the giants of the industry—were not ready to share the cargo market, he was not able to obtain this needed approval and had to operate a fleet of small Falcon jets instead. While this situation worked well at start-up, by 1977 his operation had reached the capacity of these smaller planes. Since they were already flying several planes on the most active routes, it did not make sense to buy more Falcons. Smith took his salesmanship to Washington and, with the help of a grassroots Federal Express employee effort, was able to obtain legislation creating a new class of all-cargo carriers. This gave Smith the operating latitude he needed.

Although Smith had the approval to operate large jets, he needed to find a way to purchase them. The corporate balance sheet of the company was still a mess from early losses, and the long-suffering early investors needed some reward. Smith took his company public on April 12, 1978, raising enough money to purchase used Boeing 727s from ailing passenger airlines. The investors were indeed richly rewarded, with General Dynamics watching its $5 million grow to more than $40 million by the time Federal Express was first traded on the New

York Stock Exchange in December 1978. The company has continued to perform well since its public offering, combining technical innovation and an obsession with customer orientation (Federal Express was the first company to win the Malcolm Baldrige National Quality Award in the service category, and in 1994 it became the first global express transportation company to receive simultaneous worldwide ISO 9001 certification) to ensure exceptional growth. Today, Federal Express, the world's largest express transportation company, boasts the following: 215,000 employees worldwide; 43,500 vehicles in its ground fleet; 643 total aircraft in its air fleet; and daily delivery of 3.3 million packages worldwide. From a 1974 operating budget of $150,000, sales have steadily increased (excepting for 1992), reaching $5.5 million in 1978, $14 billion in 1999, and $18 billion in 2000. Similarly, the earnings per share and stock price, and therefore return to shareholders, have continued to rise, with earnings per share climbing to $6.22 in 2000 and with the stock trading around 40 in 2001.

At the heart of Frederick Smith's success story is the concept that becoming an entrepreneur and developing a new venture is the initial and most integral step to offering a product or service. This part of the new venture creation process is perhaps the most difficult to actualize. What are the specific features of the new product or service? A basic prototype or conceptual model is usually internally generated through research and development, other sources of new ideas, or creative problem solving. A wide variety of techniques can be used to obtain the new product idea. Smith expressed his original idea in a paper he wrote to complete a college course. For others—such as Bob Reis of Final Technology, Inc., and Frank Perdue of Perdue Chickens—the idea came from work experience. No matter how it occurs, a sound idea for a new product (or service), properly evaluated, is essential to successfully launching a new venture.

SOURCES OF NEW IDEAS

Some of the more frequently used sources of ideas for new entrepreneurs include consumers, existing companies, distribution channels, the federal government, and research and development.

Consumers

Potential entrepreneurs should pay close attention to the final focal point of the idea for a new product or service—the potential consumer. This attention can take the form of informally monitoring potential ideas and needs or formally arranging for consumers to have an opportunity to express their opinions. Care needs to be taken to ensure that the idea or need represents a large enough market to support a new venture.

Existing Companies

Potential entrepreneurs and intrapreneurs should also establish a formal method for monitoring and evaluating competitive products and services on the market. Frequently, this analysis uncovers ways to improve on these offerings that may result in a new product that has more market appeal.

Distribution Channels

Members of the distribution channels are also excellent sources for new ideas because of their familiarity with the needs of the market. Not only do channel members frequently have suggestions for completely new products, but they can also help in marketing the entrepreneur's newly developed products. One entrepreneur found out from the salesclerks that the reason his hosiery was not selling was due to its color. By heeding the suggestion and making the appropriate color changes, his company became the leading supplier of nonbrand hosiery in that region of the United States.

Federal Government

The federal government can be a source of new product ideas in two ways. First, the files of the Patent Office contain numerous new product possibilities. Although the patents themselves may not be feasible new product introductions, they can frequently suggest other more marketable product ideas. Several government agencies and publications are helpful in monitoring patent applications. The *Official Gazette*, published weekly by the U.S. Patent Office, summarizes each patent granted and lists all patents available for license or sale. Also, the Government Patents Board publishes lists of abstracts of thousands of government-owned patents; a good resource of such information is the *Government-Owned Inventories Available for License*. Other government agencies, such as the Office of Technical Services, assist entrepreneurs in obtaining specific product information.

Second, new product ideas can come in response to government regulations. For example, the Occupational Safety and Health Act (OSHA), aimed at eliminating unsafe working conditions in industry, mandated that first-aid kits be made available in business establishments employing more than three people. The kit had to contain specific items that varied according to the company and the industry. The weatherproofed first-aid kit needed for a construction company had to be different from the one needed by a company manufacturing facial cream or a company in retail trade. In response to OSHA, both established and newly formed ventures marketed a wide variety of first-aid kits. One newly formed company, R&H Safety Sales Company, was successful in developing and selling first-aid kits that allowed companies to comply with the act.

Research and Development

The largest source of new ideas is the entrepreneur's own "research and development," efforts that may be a formal endeavor connected with one's current employment or an informal lab in the basement or garage. A more formal research and development department is often better equipped and enables the entrepreneur to conceptualize and develop successful new product ideas. One research scientist in a Fortune 500 company developed a new plastic resin that became the basis of a new product, a plastic molded modular cup pallet, as well as a new venture—the Arnolite Pallet Company, Inc.—when the Fortune 500 company was not interested in developing the idea.

METHODS OF GENERATING IDEAS

Even with a wide variety of sources available, coming up with an idea to serve as the basis for a new venture can still be a difficult problem. The entrepreneur can use several methods to help generate and test new ideas, including focus groups, brainstorming, and problem inventory analysis.

Focus Groups

Focus groups have been used for a variety of purposes since the 1950s. A moderator leads a group of people through an open, in-depth discussion rather than simply asking questions to solicit participant response. For a new product area, the moderator focuses the discussion of the group in either a directive or a nondirective manner.

focus groups Groups of individuals providing information in a structured format

The group of 8 to 14 participants is stimulated by comments from other group members in creatively conceptualizing and developing a new product idea to fulfill a market need. One company interested in the women's slipper market received its new product concept for a "warm and comfortable slipper that fits like an old shoe" from a focus group of 12 women from various socioeconomic backgrounds in the Boston area. The concept was developed into a new product that was a market success. The basis of the advertising message was formed by comments of focus group members.

In addition to generating new ideas, the focus group is an excellent method for initially screening ideas and concepts. Using one of several procedures available, the results can be analyzed more quantitatively, making the focus group a useful method for generating new product ideas.[1]

Brainstorming

The *brainstorming* method for generating new product ideas is based on the fact that people can be stimulated to greater creativity by meeting with others and participating in organized group experiences. Although most of the

brainstorming A group method for obtaining new ideas and solutions

ideas generated from the group have no basis for further development, often a good idea emerges. This has a greater frequency of occurrence when the brainstorming effort focuses on a specific product or market area. When using this method, the following four rules should be followed:

1. No criticism is allowed by anyone in the group—no negative comments.
2. Freewheeling is encouraged—the wilder the idea the better.
3. Quantity of ideas is desired—the greater the number of ideas, the greater the likelihood of the emergence of useful ideas.
4. Combinations and improvements of ideas are encouraged; ideas of others can be used to produce still another new idea.

The brainstorming session should be fun, with no one dominating or inhibiting the discussion.

A large commercial bank successfully used brainstorming to develop a journal that would provide quality information to its industrial clients. The brainstorming among executives focused on the characteristics of the market, the information content, the frequency of issue, and the promotional value of the journal for the bank. Once a general format and issue frequency were determined, focus groups of vice presidents of finance of Fortune 1000 companies formed in three cities—Boston, Chicago, and Dallas—and discussed the new journal format and its relevancy and value to them.

Problem Inventory Analysis

Problem inventory analysis uses individuals in a manner that is analogous to focus groups to generate new product ideas. However, instead of generating new ideas themselves, consumers are provided with a list of problems in a general product

problem inventory analysis   A method for obtaining
new ideas and solutions by focusing on problems

category. They are then asked to identify and discuss products in this category that have the particular problem. This method is often effective since it is easier to relate known products to suggested problems and arrive at a new product idea than to generate an entirely new product idea by itself. Problem inventory analysis can also be used to test a new product idea.

An example of this approach in the food industry is illustrated in Table 5.1. One of the most difficult problems in this example was in developing an exhaustive list of problems, such as weight, taste, appearance, and cost. Once a complete list of problems is developed, individuals can usually associate products with the problem.

Results from product inventory analysis must be carefully evaluated as they may not actually reflect a new business opportunity. For example, General Foods' introduction of a compact cereal box in response to the problem that the available boxes did not fit well on the shelf was not successful. The perceived problem of package size had little effect on actual purchasing behavior. To ensure the best results, problem inventory analysis should be used primarily to identify product ideas for further evaluation.

TABLE 5.1   Problem Inventory Analysis

Psychological	Sensory	Activities	Buying Usage	Psychological/ Social
A. Weight • Fattening • Empty calories B. Hunger • Filling • Still hungry after eating C. Thirst • Does not quench • Makes one thirsty D. Health • Indigestion • Bad for teeth • Keeps one awake • Acidity	A. Taste • Bitter • Bland • Salty B. Appearance • Color • Unappetizing • Shape C. Consistency/ texture • Tough • Dry • Greasy	A. Meal planning • Forget • Get tired of it B. Storage • Run out • Package would not fit C. Preparation • Too much trouble • Too many pots and pans • Never turns out D. Cooking • Burns • Sticks E. Cleaning • Makes a mess in oven • Smells in refrigerator	A. Portability • Eat away from home • Take lunch B. Portions • Not enough in package • Creates leftovers C. Availability • Out of season • Not in supermarket D. Spoilage • Gets moldy • Goes sour E. Cost • Expensive • Takes expensive ingredients	A. Serve to company • Would not serve to guests • Too much last-minute preparation B. Eating alone • Too much effort to cook for oneself • Depressing when prepared for just one C. Self-image • Made by a lazy cook • Not served by a good mother

Source: Edward M. Tauber, "Discovering New Product Opportunities with Problem Inventory Analysis," *Journal of Marketing* (January 1975). Reprinted from *Journal of Marketing*, published by the American Marketing Association.

CREATIVE PROBLEM SOLVING

Creativity is an important attribute of a successful entrepreneur. Unfortunately, creativity tends to decline with age, education, and lack of use. Creativity declines in stages, beginning when a person starts school. It continues to deteriorate through the teens and continues to progressively lessen through ages 30, 40, and 50. Also, the latent creative potential of an individual can be stifled by perceptual, cultural, emotional, and organizational factors. Creativity can be unlocked and creative ideas and innovations generated by using any of the creative problem-solving techniques such as those in Table 5.2.[2]

creative problem solving A method for obtaining new ideas focusing on the parameters

Brainstorming

The first technique, brainstorming, is probably the most well known and widely used for both creative problem solving and idea generation. It is an unstructured process for generating all possible ideas about a problem within a limited time frame through the spontaneous contributions of participants. A good brainstorming session starts with a problem statement that is neither too broad (which would diversify ideas too greatly so that nothing specific would emerge) nor too narrow (which would tend to confine responses).[3] Once the problem statement is prepared, 6 to 12 individuals are selected to participate to ensure the representation of a wide range of knowledge. To avoid inhibiting responses, no group member should be a recognized expert in the field of the problem. All ideas, no matter how illogical, must be recorded, with participants prohibited from criticizing or evaluating during the brainstorming session.

TABLE 5.2   Creativity and Problem-Solving Techniques

- Brainstorming
- Reverse brainstorming
- Synectics
- Gordon method
- Checklist method
- Free association
- Forced relationships
- Collective notebook method
- Heuristics
- Scientific method
- Kepner-Tregoe method
- Value analysis
- Attribute listing method
- Morphological analysis
- Matrix charting
- Sequence-attribute/modification matrix
- Inspired (big-dream) approach
- Parameter analysis

Reverse Brainstorming

Reverse brainstorming is similar to brainstorming, except that criticism is allowed. In fact, the technique is based on finding fault by asking the question, "In how many ways can this idea fail?" Since the focus is on the negative, care must be taken to maintain the group's morale. Reverse brainstorming can be effectively used before other creative techniques to stimulate innovative thinking.[4] The process most often involves the identification of everything wrong with an idea, followed by a discussion of ways to overcome these problems.

reverse brainstorming   A group method for obtaining new ideas focusing on the negative

Synectics

Synectics is a creative process that forces individuals to solve problems through one of four analogy mechanisms: personal, direct, symbolic, and fantasy.[5] A group works through a two-step process, as indicated in Figure 5.1. The first step is to make the strange familiar. This involves, through generalizations or models, consciously reversing the order of things and putting the problem into a readily acceptable or familiar perspective, thereby eliminating the strangeness. Once the strangeness is eliminated, participants engage in the second step, making the familiar strange through personal, direct, or symbolic analogy, which ideally results in a unique solution being developed.

synectics   A method for individuals to solve problems through one of four mechanisms

Gordon Method

The *Gordon method*, unlike many other creative problem-solving techniques, begins with group members not knowing the exact nature of the problem. This ensures that the solution is not clouded by preconceived ideas and behavioral patterns.[6] The entrepreneur starts by mentioning a general concept associated with the problem. The group responds by expressing a number of ideas. Then a concept is developed, followed by related concepts, through guidance by the entrepreneur. The actual problem is then revealed, enabling the group to make suggestions for implementation or refinement of the final solution.

Gordon method   Method for developing new ideas when the individuals are unaware of the problem

Checklist Method

In the *checklist method*, a new idea is developed through a list of related issues or suggestions. The entrepreneur can use the list of questions or statements to guide the direction of developing entirely new ideas or concentrating on specific "idea" areas. The checklist may take any form and be of any length. One general checklist is as follows:[7]

checklist method   Developing a new idea through a list of related issues

- Put to other uses? New ways to use as is? Other uses if modified?
- Adapt? What else is like this? What other ideas does this suggest? Does past offer parallel? What could I copy? Whom could I emulate?
- Modify? New twist? Change meaning, color, motion, odor, form, shape? Other changes?
- Magnify? What to add? More time? Greater frequency? Stronger? Larger? Thicker? Extra value? Plus ingredient? Duplicate? Multiply? Exaggerate?

FIGURE 5.1   Example of Synectics Process

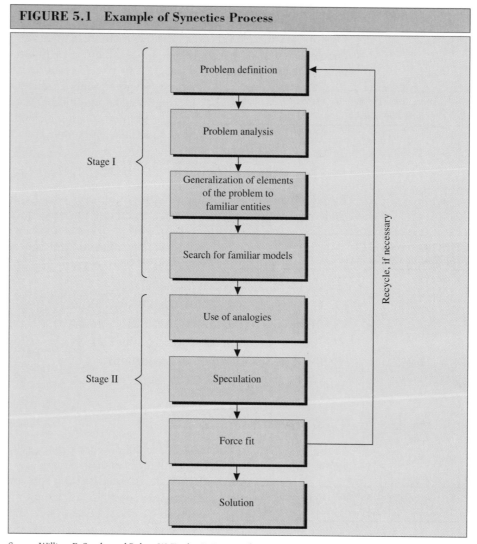

Source: William E. Souder and Robert W. Ziegler, "A Review of Creativity and Problem Solving Techniques," *Research Management* (July 1975), p. 35.

- Minify? What substitute? Smaller? Condensed? Miniature? Lower? Shorter? Lighter? Omit? Streamline? Split up? Understated?
- Substitute? Who else instead? What else instead? Other ingredient? Other material? Other process? Other power? Other place? Other approach? Other tone of voice?
- Rearrange? Interchange components? Other pattern? Other layout? Other sequence? Transpose cause and effect? Change pact? Change schedule?
- Reverse? Transpose positive and negative? How about opposites? Turn it backward? Turn it upside down? Reverse roles? Change shoes? Turn tables? Turn other cheek?
- Combine? How about a blend, an alloy, an assortment, an ensemble? Combine units? Combine purposes? Combine appeals? Combine ideas?

Free Association

One of the simplest yet most effective methods that entrepreneurs can use to generate new ideas is *free association*. This technique is helpful in developing an entirely new slant to a problem. First, a word or phrase related to the problem is written down, then another and another, with each new word attempting to add something new to the ongoing thought processes, thereby creating a chain of ideas ending with a new product idea emerging.

free association   Developing a new idea through a chain of word associations

Forced Relationships

Forced relationships, as the name implies, is the process of forcing relationships among some product combinations. It is a technique that asks questions about objects or ideas in an effort to develop a new idea. The new combination and eventual concept is developed through a five-step process:[8]

forced relationships   Developing a new idea by looking at product combinations

1. Isolate the elements of the problem.
2. Find the relationships between these elements.
3. Record the relationships in an orderly form.
4. Analyze the resulting relationships to find ideas or patterns.
5. Develop new ideas from these patterns.

Table 5.3 illustrates the use of this technique with paper and soap.

Collective Notebook Method

In the *collective notebook method*, a small notebook that easily fits in a pocket—containing a statement of the problem, blank pages, and any pertinent background data—is distributed. Participants consider the problem and its possible solutions, recording ideas at least once, but preferably three times, a day. At the end of a month, a list

collective notebook method   Developing a new idea by group members regularly recording ideas

TABLE 5.3 Illustration of Forced Relationship Technique		
Elements: Paper and Soap		
Forms	Relationship/Combination	Idea/Pattern
Adjective	Papery soap	Flakes
	Soapy paper	Wash and dry travel aid
Noun	Paper soaps	Tough paper impregnated with soap and usable for washing surfaces
Verb-correlates	Soaped papers	Booklets of soap leaves
	Soap "wets" paper	In coating and impregnation processes
	Soap "cleans" paper	Suggests wallpaper cleaner

Source: William E. Souder and Robert W. Ziegler, "A Review of Creativity and Problem Solving Techniques," *Research Management* (July 1975), p. 37.

of the best ideas is developed, along with any suggestions.[9] This technique can also be used with a group of individuals who record their ideas, giving their notebooks to a central coordinator who summarizes all the material. The summary becomes the topic of a final creative focus group discussion by the group participants.

Heuristics

Heuristics relies on the entrepreneur's ability to discover through a progression of thoughts, insights, and learning. The technique is probably used more than imagined, because entrepreneurs frequently must settle for an estimated outcome of a decision rather than a certainty. One specific heuristic approach is called the heuristic ideation technique (HIT).[10] The technique involves locating all relevant concepts that could be associated with a given product area and generating a set of all possible combinations of ideas.

heuristics   Developing a new idea through a thought process progression

Scientific Method

The *scientific method*, widely used in various fields of inquiry, consists of principles and processes, conducting observations and experiments, and validating the hypothesis. The approach involves the entrepreneur defining the problem, analyzing the problem, gathering and analyzing data, developing and testing potential solutions, and choosing the best solution.

scientific method   Developing a new idea through inquiry and testing

Value Analysis

The *value analysis* technique develops methods for maximizing value to the entrepreneur and the new venture.[11] To maximize value, the entrepreneur asks such questions as, "Can this part be of lesser quality, since it isn't a critical area for problems?" In a value analysis procedure, regularly scheduled times are established to develop, evaluate, and refine ideas.

value analysis   Developing a new idea by evaluating the worth of aspects of ideas

Attribute Listing

Attribute listing is an idea-finding technique that requires the entrepreneur to list the attributes of an item or problem and then look at each from a variety of viewpoints. Through this process, originally unrelated objects can be brought together to form a new combination and possible new uses that better satisfy a need.[12]

attribute listing   Developing a new idea by looking at the positives and negatives

Matrix Charting

Matrix charting is a systematic method of searching for new opportunities by listing important elements for the product area along two axes of a chart and then asking questions regarding each of these elements. The answers are recorded in the relevant boxes of the matrix. Example questions that can elicit creative new product ideas include: What can it be used for? Where can it be used? Who can use it? When can it be used? How can it be used?

matrix charting   Developing a new idea by listing important elements on two axes of a chart

---

FIGURE 5.2   Illustration of Parameter Analysis

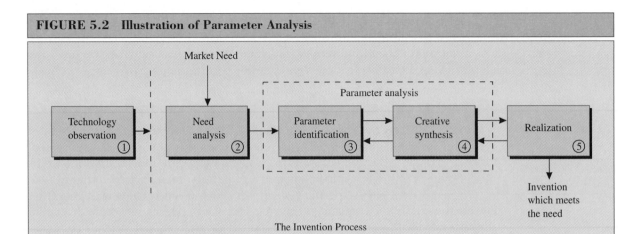

Big-Dream Approach

The *big-dream approach* to coming up with a new idea requires that the entrepreneur dream about the problem and its solution, in other words, thinking big. Every possibility should be recorded and investigated without regard to all the negatives involved or the resources required. Ideas should be conceptualized without any constraints until an idea is developed into a workable form.[13]

big-dream approach   Developing a new idea by thinking about constraints

Parameter Analysis

A final method for developing a new idea—*parameter analysis*—involves two aspects: parameter identification and creative synthesis.[14] As indicated in Figure 5.2, step one (parameter identification) involves analyzing variables in the situation to determine their relative importance. These variables become the focus of the investigation, with other variables being set aside. After the primary issues have been identified, the relationships between parameters that describe the underlying issues are examined.

parameter analysis   Developing a new idea by focusing on parameter identification and creative synthesis

Through an evaluation of the parameters and relationships, a solution(s) is developed; this solution development is called *creative synthesis*.

PRODUCT PLANNING AND DEVELOPMENT PROCESS

Once ideas emerge from idea sources or creative problem solving, they need further development and refinement into the final product or service to be offered. This refining process—the product planning and development process—is divided into five major stages: idea stage, concept stage, product development stage, test marketing stage, and commercialization; it results in the start of the *product life cycle* (see Figure 5.3).[15]

product life cycle   The stages each product goes through from introduction to decline

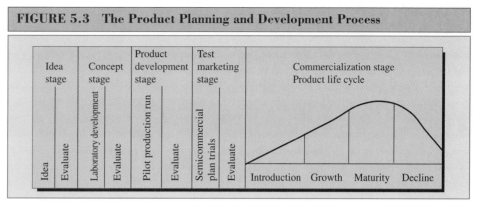

FIGURE 5.3   The Product Planning and Development Process

Source: Reprinted with permission of Macmillan College Publishing Company from *Marketing Decisions for New and Mature Products*, 2/e, by Robert D. Hisrich and Michael P. Peters, © 1991 by Macmillan College Publishing Company, Inc., p. 165.

Establishing Evaluation Criteria

At each stage of the *product planning and development process*, criteria for evaluation need to be established. These criteria should be broad, yet quantitative enough to screen the product carefully in the particular stage of development. Criteria should be developed to evaluate the new product in terms of market opportunity, competition, the marketing system, financial factors, and production factors.

product planning and development process   The stages in developing a new product

A market opportunity in the form of a new or current need for the product idea must exist. The determination of market demand is by far the most important criterion of a proposed new product idea. Assessment of the market opportunity and size needs to include consideration of the following: the characteristics and attitudes of consumers or industries that may buy the product, the size of this potential market in dollars and units, the nature of the market with respect to its stage in the life cycle (growing or declining), and the share of the market the product could reasonably capture.

Current competing producers, prices, and marketing policies should also be evaluated, particularly in terms of their impact on the market share of the proposed product. The new product should be able to compete successfully with products already on the market by having features that will meet or overcome current and anticipated competition. The new product should have some unique differential advantage based on an evaluation of all competitive products filling the same consumer needs.

The new product should be compatible with existing management capabilities and marketing strategies. The firm should be able to use its marketing experience and other expertise in this new product effort. For example, General Electric would have a far less difficult time adding a new kitchen appliance to its line than Procter & Gamble. Several factors should be considered in evaluating the degree of fit: the degree to which the ability and time of the present sales force can be transferred to the new product; the ability to sell the new product through the company's established channels of distribution; and the ability to "piggyback" the advertising and promotion required to introduce the new product.

The proposed product should be able to be supported by and contribute to the company's financial structure. This should be evaluated by estimating manufacturing

Young upstart entrepreneurs dream the dreams of competition, but, most of the time, competition isn't the spur to action; rather, it is just one of the possible obstacles to be faced. Many times competition is not a significant obstacle at all, because the most insightful entrepreneurs, such as Jobs and Wozniak at Apple, don't enter a market that is already crowded with competitors. Instead, they identify or invent an entirely new one. They are moved by the excitement of their ideas, by the challenge of the project, by the promise of success, but not, particularly, by competition. Some societies think capitalism and business competition destroy age-old structures. There is "healthy" competition, and there is sick, debilitating, and depraved competition. There is fair competition and there is underhanded competition. There is constructive, positive, even inspiring competition; and there is mutually destructive, negative, inhibiting competition. War and jungle metaphors give us the latter, along with all zero-sum games, where the objective is to eliminate the opponent, debilitate the competition, and win at all costs. Justice Arthur Goldberg once argued, "Our devotion to freewheeling industrial competition must not force us into accepting the law of the jungle as the standard of morality expected in our commercial relations."

Competition consists in trying to do things better than someone else, that is, making or selling a better article at a lesser cost or otherwise giving better service. It is not competition to resort to methods of the prize ring and simply "knock the other man out." This is killing a competitor.

A client invites you to a coffee shop to discuss the written proposal for a major project that you submitted to him last week. He indicates that your proposal is excellent, but that he has some difficulties with the price you quote for the project. He leaves to go to the washroom, and you are alone for a short while. Next to your proposal on top of the counter are the written proposals from your two main competitors. You know that it would take only a few seconds to open the rival proposals to see what prices they quote. Should you look at your competitors' written proposals? Would it make a difference if you were sitting in the customer's office and he had them in front of him on the desk, requiring you to read them "upside down"? What if it were your proposal and your competitor was the client?

Sources: The first paragraph is adapted from Robert C. Solomon, *Ethics and Excellence* (New York: Oxford University Press), 1993, p. 66. The second paragraph is from Justice Louis Brandeis, "Competition," in Robert C. Solomon, p. 65. The third paragraph is from E. Solymossy and R. D. Hisrich, "Entrepreneurial Ethics: The Impact of Accountability and Independence," Babson Research Conference, March 1996 (Boston: Babson College).

cost per unit, sales and advertising expense per unit, and amount of capital and inventory required. The break-even point and the long-term profit outlook for the product need to be determined.

Along with financial criteria, the compatibility of the new product's production requirements with existing plant, machinery, and personnel should be determined. If the new product idea cannot be integrated into existing manufacturing processes, not only is the new idea less positive, but new plant and production costs as well as amount of plant space must be determined if the new product is to be manufactured efficiently. All required materials needed in the production of the product should be available and accessible in sufficient quantity.

When dealing with competition and competitive situations, concerns regarding ethics and ethical behavior frequently arise, as indicated in the Ethics box.

Entrepreneurs need to be concerned with formally evaluating an idea throughout its evolution. Care must be taken to be sure the product can be the basis for a new venture (see the *Business Week* boxes). From the marketing perspective, three pretest marketing stages can be delineated in the product's evolutionary process: the idea stage, the concept stage, and the product development stage.

As Seen in Business Week
The Top Technological Blunders of the (Just Past) Century

Remember Murphy's Law ("Whatever can go wrong will go wrong")? The 20th century gave birth to that chestnut, along with such classic screwups as the *Titanic*, the *Hindenburg*, and the Union Carbide chemical disaster at Bhopal. Following is a small sampling of other catastrophes:

1940 A design flaw causes the Tacoma (Washington) Narrows Bridge to collapse in high winds.

1952 The DeHavilland Comet, a commercial jet aircraft, debuts. Seven of twenty-one copies promptly crash, owing to faulty design.

1959 The Malpasset Dam on the French Riviera, built too close to unstable ground, bursts, killing hundreds.

1958–62 "The Great Leap Forward," China's botched technological revolution, causes widespread famine; 30 million die.

1970s The glass-clad John Hancock Tower in Boston sheds its 500-lb windows, a major construction embarrassment.

1986 The space shuttle *Challenger* explodes just after liftoff.

1986 In the former Soviet Union, the Chernobyl nuclear power plant suffers a partial meltdown.

1994 Juan Pablo Davila, trading commodities via computer in Chile, accidentally types "buy" instead of "sell." To rectify his mistake, he starts a frenzy of buying and selling, losing .5 percent of his country's GNP. His name becomes a verb, *davilar*, meaning "to screw up royally."

Source: "The Top Technological Blunders of the (Just Past) Century," Annals of Improbable Research, *Business Week* (January 17, 2000), p. 8.

Idea Stage

Promising new product ideas should be identified and impractical ones eliminated in the *idea stage*, allowing maximum use of the company's resources. One evaluation method successfully used in this stage is the systematic market evaluation checklist, where each new product idea is expressed in terms of its chief values, merits, and benefits.[16] Consumers are presented with clusters of new product values to determine which, if any, new product alternatives should be pursued and which should be discarded. A company can test many new product idea alternatives with this evaluation method; promising ideas can be further developed and resources not wasted on ideas that are incompatible with the market's values.

---

idea stage   First stage in product development process

It is also important to determine the need for the new product as well as its value to the company. If there is no need for the suggested product, its development should not be continued. Similarly, the new product idea should not be developed if it does not have any benefit or value to the firm. In order to accurately determine the need for a new product, it is helpful to define the potential needs of the market in terms of timing, satisfaction, alternatives, benefits and risks, future expectations, price-versus-product performance features, market structure and size, and economic conditions. A form for helping in this need determination is indicated in Table 5.4. The factors indicated in this table should be evaluated not only in terms of the characteristics of the potential new product but also in terms of the new product's competitive strength relative to each factor. This comparison with competitive products will indicate the proposed product's strengths and weaknesses.

The need determination should focus on the type of need, its timing, the users involved with trying the product, the importance of controllable marketing variables, the overall market structure, and the characteristics of the market. Each of these factors should be evaluated in terms of the characteristics of the new idea being considered

179

As Seen in Business Week
The Cat's Meow for Old Pets

The guests at the Golden Years Retirement Home lead an ideal life. For a fee of $10,000 they live out their remaining years scratching the furniture and sleeping in the sun. No, they're not at a frisky adults-only community in Arizona. Based in West-hampton, New York, Golden Years is for cats and dogs. It's part of a relatively new trend: pet retirement homes.

Maybe it's a sign that some people just have too many stock options. But the owners of animal retirement homes say they provide a valuable service for those who can no longer care for Fluffy or Fido. Jeanne Toomey, director of Last Post in Falls Village, Connecticut, says she often gets calls from attorneys: "They're trying to make provisions for pets in their clients' wills."

These businesses are usually registered nonprofits, founded out of compassion for owners and pets. Cat Nap Estates in Houston sends out letters "signed" by the pets, who are fed gourmet food. Says owner Donna Rice, "If you're doing this right, you don't make money." Maybe not. But you do have to buy a lot of extra slipcovers.

Source: Stacey Higginbotham, "The Cat's Meow for Old Pets," *Business Week* (January 24, 2000), p. 10.

---

and the aspects and capabilities of present methods for satisfying the particular need. This analysis will indicate the extent of the opportunity available.

In determining the value of the new product to the firm, financial scheduling—such as cash outflow, cash inflow, contribution to profit, and return on investment—needs to be evaluated in terms of other product ideas as well as investment alternatives. Using the form indicated in Table 5.5, the dollar amount of each of the considerations important to the new product idea should be determined as accurately as possible so that a quantitative evaluation can be made. These figures can then be revised as better information becomes available and the product continues to be developed.

Concept Stage

After a new product idea has been identified in the idea stage as viable, it should be further developed and refined through interaction with consumers. In the *concept stage*, the refined product idea is tested to determine consumer acceptance without necessarily incurring the costs of manufacturing the physical product. Initial reactions to the concept are obtained from potential customers or members of the distribution channel when appropriate. One method of measuring consumer acceptance is the conversational interview in which selected respondents are exposed to statements that reflect the physical characteristics and attributes of the product idea. Where competing products exist, these statements can also compare the primary features of existing products. Favorable as well as unfavorable product features can be discovered by analyzing consumers' responses, with favorable features then being incorporated into the product.

concept stage Second stage in product development process

Features, price, and promotion should be evaluated for both the concept being studied and any major competing products. By identifying any major problems in the product concept, research and development can be directed to develop a more marketable product, or the concept can be dropped and not receive further attention.

TABLE 5.4 Determining the Need for a New Product Idea

Factor	Aspects	Competitive Capabilities	New Product Idea Capability
Type of need			
Continuing need			
Declining need			
Emerging need			
Future need			
Timing of need			
Duration of need			
Frequency of need			
Demand cycle			
Position in life cycle			
Competing ways to satisfy need			
Doing without			
Using present way			
Modifying present way			
Perceived benefits/risks			
Utility to customer			
Appeal characteristics			
Customer tastes and preferences			
Buying motives			
Consumption habits			
Price versus performance features			
Price-quantity relationship			
Demand elasticity			
Stability of price			
Stability of market			
Market size and potential			
Market growth			
Market trends			
Market development requirements			
Threats to market			
Availability to customer funds			
General economic conditions			
Economic trends			
Customer income			
Financing opportunities			

Source: Reprinted with permission of Macmillan College Publishing Company, from *Marketing Decisions for New and Mature Products*, 2/e, by Robert D. Hisrich and Michael P. Peters, © 1991 by Macmillan College Publishing Company, Inc., p. 190.

TABLE 5.5 Determining the Value of a New Product Idea	
Value Consideration	**Cost (in $)**
Cash outflow	
R&D costs	
Marketing costs	
Capital equipment costs	
Other costs	
Cash inflow	
Sales of new product	
Effect on additional sales of existing products	
Salvageable value	
Net cash flow	
Maximum exposure	
Time to maximum exposure	
Duration of exposure	
Total investment	
Maximum net cash in a single year	
Profit	
Profit from new product	
Profit affecting additional sales of existing products	
Fraction of total company profit	
Relative return	
Return on shareholder's equity (ROE)	
Return on investment (ROI)	
Cost of capital	
Present value (PV)	
Discounted cash flow (DCF)	
Return on assets employed (ROA)	
Return on sales	
Compared to other investments	
Compared to other product opportunities	
Compared to other investment opportunities	

Source: Reprinted with permission of Macmillan College Publishing Company from *Marketing Decisions for New and Mature Products*, 2/e, by Robert D. Hisrich and Michael P. Peters, © 1991 by Macmillan College Publishing Company, Inc., p. 196.

The relative advantages of the new product versus competitive products can be determined through the following questions. How does the new concept compare with competitive products in terms of quality and reliability? Is the concept superior or deficient compared with products currently available in the market? Is this a good market opportunity for the firm? Similar evaluations should be done for each of the remaining aspects of the product—price, promotion, and distribution.

Product Development Stage

In the *product development stage*, consumer reaction to the physical product is determined. One tool frequently used in this stage is the consumer panel, in which a group of potential consumers are given product samples. Participants keep a record of their use of the product and comment on its virtues and deficiencies.

product development stage   Third stage in product development process

The panel of potential customers can also be given a sample of the product and one or more competitive products simultaneously. One test product may already be on the market, whereas the other test product is new. Both products may also be new, with some significant variation between them. Then one of several methods—such as multiple brand comparisons, risk analysis, level of repeat purchases, or intensity of preference analysis—can be used to determine consumer preference.

Test Marketing Stage

Although the results of the product development stage provide the basis of the final marketing plan, a market test can be done to increase the certainty of successful commercialization. This last step in the evaluation process, the *test marketing stage*, provides actual sales results, which indicate the acceptance level of consumers. Positive test results indicate the degree of probability of a successful product launch and company formation.

test marketing stage   Final stage before commercialization in product development process

E-COMMERCE AND BUSINESS START-UP AND GROWTH

The development of what is now known as the Internet started in the 1970s, when the U.S. Defense Department program named ARPA started to develop a network that would not be vulnerable and could still operate even if parts were missing. In the early 1990s, the concept of World Wide Web pages was developed simplifying connections between many academic documents. This established the technological base for Internet commerce, which gained momentum after 1994 in the United States. The Internet can be viewed as a channel that provides opportunities for the creation of profitable companies and for an entire industry. The Internet can also be regarded as having a revolutionary role in the democratization of communication through advanced technologies and as a force that represents a major shift in technological, organizational, and cultural paradigms.

Electronic business (e-business) is any process that a business organization conducts over a computer-mediated network. Electronic business processes can be conducted among businesses (business-to-business), between businesses and consumers (business-to-consumer), and within a business (intranets). Examples are numerous: automated stock replenishment, procurement, electronic selling, processing of customers orders and payments, and within company training, information sharing, and video conferencing. Electronic commerce (e-commerce) is any transaction completed over a computer-mediated network that involves the transfer of ownership or rights to use goods or services.[17] The consumer market will grow from $9.2 billion in 1999 to over $120 billion by 2003, while annual business-to-business e-commerce is projected to soar from $90 billion to over $1 trillion in the same time period. New, ambitious companies that look for inefficiencies in an industry and introduce new business models and markets to overcome them will contribute to much of this growth. Factors that facilitated the high growth of electronic commerce are the widespread use of personal computers, the adoption of intranets in companies, and the acceptance of the Internet as a business communications platform. Numerous benefits—such as access to a broader customer base, lower information dissemination costs, lower transaction costs, and the interactive nature of the Internet—will continue to expand the volume of e-commerce.

Starting an E-Commerce Company

Electronic commerce is increasingly used by existing corporations to extend their marketing and sales channels, as well as being the basis for a large number of start-ups. The Internet is especially important for small and medium-sized companies, as it enables them to minimize marketing costs while reaching broader markets. An entrepreneur starting an Internet commerce venture needs to address the same strategic and tactical questions as any other entrepreneur. Additionally, some specific issues of doing business online need to be addressed due to the new and perpetually evolving technology used in Internet commerce. An entrepreneur has to decide whether he or she will run the Internet operations within the company or outsource these operations to Internet specialists. In the case of in-house operations, computer servers, routers, and other hardware have to be maintained and at least one phone line has to be dedicated to the Internet connection, though more expensive optical fiber connections are rapidly becoming standard. Other parts of e-commerce infrastructure include software, support services such as website development and electronic payment, and human resources. Alternatively, there are numerous possibilities for outsourcing the Internet business. The entrepreneur can hire Web developers to design the company's Web pages and then upload them on the server maintained by the Internet service provider. In this case, the entrepreneur's main task is to regularly update the information on the Web pages. Another option is to use the packages for e-commerce available from different software companies. The decision for in-house operations or outsourcing depends on the size of the Internet-related business, whether Internet operations are the company's primary business, and the availability of resources, especially Web professionals.

The two major components of Internet commerce are front-end and back-end operations. Front-end operations are encompassed in the website's functionality. Search capabilities, shopping cart, and secure payment are only a few examples. The biggest mistake of many companies on the Internet is believing that an attractive, interactive website will secure success; this leads to underestimating the importance of back-end operations. Seamless integration of customer orders with distribution channels and manufacturing capabilities should be developed that are flexible enough to handle any specific customer's desire. The integration of front-end and back-end operations represents the greatest challenge for Internet companies and at the same time provides the opportunity for developing a sustained competitive advantage.

Website

A website is an online connection between the company and its customers. A professional design is critical to its success, because it is one indicator of the legitimacy of the online company. While Microsoft Front Page 2000 provides a very user friendly application for website design, the entrepreneur should also consider the use of professional Web designers. Other sources of organizational legitimacy for young

Internet companies are endorsements by prominent Internet organizations and certification authorities like VeriSign (www.verisign.com), GTE CyberTrust, and IBM VaultRegistry, which provide authentication, validation, and payment for e-commerce companies. Certification authorities use registered credentials and commercial databases to verify the company's identity, which is then used to ensure the identity of participating companies.

One of the most important features of every website is search capability. It should be easy to find information about the products and services that a company offers over the Internet. This function can be accomplished through an advanced search tool, site map, or subject browsing. Other functions that should be available on every e-commerce website are shopping cart, secure server connection, credit card payment, and customer feedback feature. Shopping cart is software that accepts product orders and automatically calculates and totals customers' orders based on the product availability information. Orders and other sensitive customer information should be transferred only through secure servers identified by URL "https://", where "s" stands for secure. Secure servers encrypt confidential data for customer protection. An Internet company should obtain a merchant account, which will allow the acceptance of major credit cards (http://www.ezmerchantaccounts.com, http://www.mastercard.com). Many banks have rigid requirements and regulations regarding the issuing of a merchant account. When choosing a merchant account provider, the entrepreneur should watch out for hidden fees or high setup costs. Another important feature of the website is an e-mail response system that allows customers to send their feedback to the company.

There are three characteristics of successful websites: speed, speed, and speed. While Internet technology allows for rich audio and video graphics, audio, and video, the majority of Internet users still connect through slow phone dial-up connections. The important question is whether the potential customer will have the patience to wait for a Web page with a long download time; the answer is almost always no. In time, this will no longer be an issue, since broadband communications are being developed to be used throughout the general population; presently, short download time should be the primary concern of website developers. Additionally, a website should be easy to use, customized for specific market target groups, compatible with different browsers, and take into consideration the international nature of the Internet. Ease of use goes hand in hand with speed; if visitors find Web pages easy to navigate, then they will be able to quickly find the products, services, or information. One of the greatest advantages of the Internet is the simplicity of customization of the website content for different market segments. An entrepreneur should also keep in mind any nontargeted segments. For example, if a company is not planning to sell products beyond the U.S. border, then it should clearly indicate on its website that it is shipping its products only within the United States. If, on the other hand, the company is targeting international markets as well, then issues of translation and cultural adaptation need to be considered. As for the technical aspects, the designer should ensure that the website works properly in different browsers and platforms that are used by Internet visitors. An entrepreneur can analyze Web pages for compatibility with various browsers with a free Internet tool called Bobby (http://www.cast.org/bobby/advanced.html). A checklist for successful website design is found in Table 5.6.

The next aspect of setting up an online business, and probably the most difficult one, is advertising and promoting the company's Web pages. Online advertising yields many of the benefits important for doing business on the Web: favorable

TABLE 5.6   Checklist for Website Design
• Professional outlook
• Credibility
• Functionality: search capability, shopping cart, secure server connection, credit card payment, customer feedback
• Characteristics: speed, ease of use, customization, international orientation, browser compatibility

demographics, cost-effective market reach, the ability to target customers, and quick response time. An entrepreneurial company can advertise its website through search engines, banner ads, e-mail, and classifieds. There are over 400 search engines, which assist customers in finding different online businesses (http://www.altavista.com, http://www.yahoo.com, to name a few). Banner ads are a more expensive but usually more efficient way of advertising. Price is usually set on the basis of the number of advertising impressions; on pages like Yahoo, this can be several million impressions per day. This advertising can also be targeted to the exact audience of the firm. Whenever possible, the entrepreneur should collect e-mail addresses from customers, because effective e-mail campaigns can significantly increase the number of recipients who become repeat customers. Classifieds are another inexpensive and sometimes even a free option for promoting the e-business. A company can place several ads in the appropriate categories of Web classifieds, which are often published on high traffic sites (http://www.yahoo.com, http://www.classifieds2000.com/). A number of Internet service companies offer these promotions for a reasonable price (http://www.bcentral.com/), but there is of course no guarantee that customers will actually buy from the website.

The Internet offers a myriad of low-cost or free services for small businesses. Free services include Internet access (www.netzero.com, www.altavista.com), unlimited e-mail accounts (www.hotmail.com, www.yahoo.com), online calendar and file sharing services (www.visto.com), communication services such as instant messaging (www.icq.com, MSN Messenger, AOL messenger), and online conference rooms for electronic meetings (www.icq.com). Some websites offer a unified system of these services, which is in the company's name instead of the name of the free e-mail or the free Internet service provider, giving the entrepreneurial business a very professional look (www.bcentral.com, www.vjungle.com, www.makeyour.com). These websites also offer a number of premium services such as e-commerce tools, human resources and accounting applications, financing, marketing, purchasing, and computing services.

Tracking Customer Information

Electronic databases support the strategy of personalized one-to-one marketing. The database can not only track activity of the industry, segment, and company but also support personal marketing targeted at individual clients. An entrepreneurial company can capture customers' information in many ways: through membership in communities of interest; by offering free services or products (free software, free e-mail, or free website hosting), for which users have to provide information; and by tracking all the sites that users visit. AOL's acquisition strategy was to buy the most frequently visited sites. The motivation for tracking customer information is to capture customer attention with customized one-to-one marketing. While the U.S. government has generally maintained the position of noninvolvement in the regulation of the Internet, the Federal Trade Commission has criticized the online industry for its failure to protect privacy rights. In 1998, the agency successfully pressed for a new law that prohibits websites from collecting personal information from children without parental permission. It is expected that similar laws will be extended to cover the adult population as well.

Relationships and Endorsements by Other Companies

Depending on the company's position in the supply chain (for example, manufacturer, vendor, distributor, service provider), it has to establish strong connections with other companies to create an end-to-end value stream that allows every customer's need to be satisfied efficiently. The necessary condition for success of Internet companies is that they begin with the customer need and efficiently integrate the entire supply chain in order to achieve flexibility for customizing products and services. However, customer orientation and process integration are not sufficient conditions for a company's success. The entrepreneur should always strive to bring unique knowledge into the process and, whenever possible, protect the innovations (patents, trademarks) and relationships with other companies (exclusive contracts, joint ventures).

Another type of relationship is endorsements by prominent Internet companies and associations. Legitimization is a critical problem for young organizations. This liability of newness is particularly problematic in the emerging industries, where operations are technically problematic and organizational forms are fluid. As young organizations develop stronger exchange relationships with other organizations and become endorsed by prominent institutions, the likelihood of their survival and success increases. Participation in merchant networks (www.mysimon.com) or equity acquisition by well-known players (for example, Amazon.com's investments in Drugstore.com, Pets.com, HomeGrocer.com, NextCard.com) can bring needed credibility to young Internet companies.

Doing E-Commerce as an Entrepreneurial Company

Existing entrepreneurs face a somewhat different situation when they decide to start an Internet business. The fact that they already run a business increases their threshold for expected profitability of new opportunities, and the insider knowledge and previous experience increase the probability of success of the new venture. The decision to go online should be made on a case-by-case basis and should be based on several factors. First, the products should be able to be delivered economically and conveniently. Fresh fruits and vegetables for individual consumers are not very appropriate for online sales and long-distance deliveries. Second, the product has to be interesting for a large number of people and the company must be ready to ship the product outside its own geographical location. Third, online operations have to bring significant cost reductions compared with the present brick-and-mortar operations. The fourth factor reflects the company's ability to economically draw customers to its website.

TABLE 5.7   E-Commerce Examples

Egghead.com Inc. would agree that the Internet is a great place to do business. An early leader in storefront software retailing, Egghead hit tough times in the mid-1990s as it faced competitors, such as Best Buy and CompUSA and many new Web-based software retailers, from Beyond.com (www.beyond.com) to Buy.com (www.buy.com). Facing decreasing sales and the mounting costs of running traditional retail stores, Egghead threw in the towel and closed its real-world shops in early 1998 to concentrate exclusively on online retailing at www.egghead.com, where it now has over 1 million customers.

Wine Country Inc. (www.winecountryonline.com) has wine stores as well as its Internet counterpart. Based on the proposition that all the wines sell for $19 or less and are rated 85 or higher by a prestige publication (such as *Wine Spectator*), both the brick-and-mortar operations that opened in November 1998 and the online store launched a month later are profitable. The owner feels that store and website are working together to build his business. The online operation needs some real-world warehousing for merchandise. The website provides convenience for customers outside the area, as well as an additional source of information for customers that visit the real-world store.

Levi Strauss launched its online stores (www.levi.com and www.dockers.com) with a proviso: its key retail partners were not allowed to sell its merchandise over the Web. By opting to control all of its online sales, Levi Strauss created channel conflict, the competition that can arise between a manufacturer and its retailers. Disgruntled by the decision, retail partners simply turned their attention to pushing private brand offerings. Levi Strauss had to tackle the overwhelming task of single unit deliveries and customer support. Only a year later, Levi Strauss retracted its initial decision and allowed JC Penney to sell its products online.

Sources: Robert McGarvey, "Connect the Dots," *Entrepreneur*, March 2000, pp. 80–81; Cindy Waxer, "501 Blues," *Business2.0*, January 2000, pp. 53–56.

Conflict between traditional and online marketing channels (channel conflict) arises because of disagreements between manufacturers and retailers, which eventually lead into a hostile, competing position of once partnering companies. Partners in supply chains have to focus on their core competencies and outsource the noncore activities. When introducing the competing distribution channels, companies have to weigh costs and benefits of that decision while taking into account the loss of existing business. Table 5.7 provides three different examples of e-commerce: a brick-and-mortar company going completely online, a synergistic combination of both, and a channel conflict.

IN REVIEW

Summary

The starting point for any successful new venture is the basic product or service to be offered. This idea can be generated internally or externally through various techniques.

The possible sources of new ideas range from the comments of consumers to changes in government regulations. Monitoring the comments of acquaintances, evaluating the new products offered by competitors, becoming familiar with the ideas contained in previously granted patents, and becoming actively involved in research and development are techniques for coming up with a good product idea. In addition, there are specific techniques entrepreneurs can use to generate ideas. For example, a better understanding of the consumer's true opinions can be gained from using a focus group. Another consumer-oriented approach is problem inventory analysis, through which consumers associate particular problems with specific products and then develop a new product that does not contain the identified faults.

Brainstorming, a technique useful in both idea generation and problem solving, stimulates creativity by allowing a small group of people to work together in an open, nonstructured environment. Other techniques useful in enhancing the creative process are checklists of related questions, free association, idea notebooks, and the "big-dream" approach. Some techniques are very structured, while others are designed to be more free form. Each entrepreneur should know the techniques available.

Once the idea or group of ideas is generated, the planning and developing process begins. If a large number of potential ideas have been uncovered, they must be screened and evaluated to determine their appropriateness for further development. Ideas showing the most potential are then moved through the concept stage, the product development stage, the test marketing stage, and finally into commercialization. The entrepreneur should constantly evaluate the idea throughout this process in order to be able to successfully launch the venture.

Questions for Discussion

1. How would you go about monitoring and evaluating the new products being offered by existing companies? Is this a viable technique for generating new ideas? Why or why not?
2. Prepare a list of problems associated with the fast-food industry that could be used for a problem inventory analysis. How would the results generated by the analysis be of use to a potential fast-food entrepreneur?
3. Choose three problem-solving techniques and explain how each functions to overcome mental blocks.

Key Terms

attribute listing	idea stage
big-dream approach	matrix charting
brainstorming	parameter analysis
checklist method	problem inventory analysis
collective notebook method	product development stage
concept stage	product life cycle
creative problem solving	product planning and development process
focus groups	reverse brainstorming
forced relationships	scientific method
free association	synectics
Gordon method	test marketing stage
heuristics	value analysis

More Information—Net Addresses in This Chapter

Kodak
    www.kodak.com

MCI
    www.mci.com

Oracle
    www.oracle.com

Procter & Gamble (P&G)
    www.pg.com

U.S. Steel
    www.ussteel.com/uss.html

Selected Readings

Amabile, Teresa M. (1998). How to Kill Creativity. *Harvard Business Review*, September–October, pp. 77–87.

This article explains what kinds of management practices foster creativity and which practices inhibit creativity in organizations. Creativity needs to be understood in light of its three individual-level components: creative thinking skills, expertise, and motivation. Managerial practices that affect creativity are in six general categories: challenge, freedom, resources, workgroup features, supervisory encouragement, and organizational support.

Barrett, Frank J. (1998). Creativity and Improvisation in Jazz and Organizations: Implications for Organizational Learning. *Organization Science*, vol. 9, no. 5, pp. 605–22.

Jazz improvisation is explored as an example of an organization designed for maximizing learning and innovation. The paper outlines seven characteristics that allow jazz bands to improvise coherently and maximize social innovation in coordination, and discusses their implications for organizational contexts. The seven characteristics are (1) deliberate efforts to interrupt habit patterns (provocative competence), (2) embracing errors as a source of learning, (3) shared orientation toward minimal structures that allow maximum flexibility, (4) continual negotiation and dialogue toward dynamic synchronization (distributed task), (5) reliance on retrospective sense-making, (6) membership in a community or practice ("hanging out"), and (7) taking turns soloing and supporting.

Barrier, Michael. (1994). Innovation as a Way of Life. *Nation's Business*, vol. 82, no. 7, pp. 18–27.

It is not a single innovation that matters but a climate of innovation that leads to one small triumph after another and makes possible the real breakthrough. For many small businesses, creating such a climate can be especially difficult. Innovation's value is the continuing vitality it can give to a business by helping that business service its customers better.

Brouwer, Maria. Entrepreneurship and Uncertainty: Innovation and Competition among the Many. *Small Business Economics*, vol. 15, no. 2, pp. 149-60.

Schumpeter stressed innovation and Knight stressed uncertainty as preconditions for entrepreneurship and productivity growth. This paper analyzes the effects of entry, market structures, and uncertainty on the incidence and diffusion of innovation.

Farnham, Alan. (1994). How to Nurture Creative Sparks. *Fortune*, vol. 129, no. 1, Asian, pp. 62–6.

Creativity is the source of all intellectual property. Though techniques to encourage innovative ways of thinking can be taught, few creative people apply them consciously. Champion creatives are self-motivated, love risk, thrive on ambiguity, and delight in novelty, twists, and reversals.

Ford, Cameron M. (1996). A Theory of Individual Creative Action in Multiple Social Domains. *Academy of Management Review*, vol. 21, no. 4, pp. 1112–42.

This article integrates psychological and sociological descriptions of creativity and conformity to present a theory of individual creative action within organizational settings composed of intertwined group, organizational, institutional, and market domains. The theory illustrates how intentional action and evolutionary processes that legitimize action interact to facilitate creativity and innovation.

Glynn, Mary Ann. (1996). Innovative Genius: A Framework for Relating Individual and Organizational Intelligences to Innovation. *Academy of Management Review,* vol. 21, no. 4, pp. 1081–111.

This article views organizational innovation as fundamentally cognitive, and the concept of organizational intelligence is developed and related to innovation. A conceptual framework is proposed that relates types and levels of intelligence, moderated by contextual factors, to the two stages of the organizational innovation process: initiation and implementation.

Higgins, Lexis F. (1999). Applying Principles of Creativity Management to Marketing Research Efforts in High-Technology Markets. *Industrial Marketing Management,* vol. 28, no. 3, pp. 305–17.

The paper discusses the measurement and meaning of creativity and how creativity techniques can be used in marketing research. Exploratory on-site studies at two Fortune 500 companies examined if creativity techniques could improve their marketing research efforts in the design and development of a marketing information system.

Kessler, Eric H.; and Alok K. Chakrabarti. (1996). Innovation Speed: A Conceptual Model of Context, Antecedents, and Outcomes. *Academy of Management Review,* vol. 21, no. 4, pp. 1143–91.

This article organizes and integrates the innovation speed literature and develops a conceptual framework of innovation speed. It argues that innovation speed (1) is most appropriate in environments characterized by competitive intensity, technology and market dynamism, and low regulatory restrictiveness; (2) can be positively or negatively affected by strategic orientation and organizational-capability factors; and (3) has an influence on development costs, product quality, and, ultimately, project success.

Klein, Katherine J.; and Joann Speer Sorra. (1996). The Challenge of Innovation Implementation. *Academy of Management Review,* vol. 21, no. 4, pp. 1055–80.

The consistency and quality of targeted organizational members' use of innovation are a function of the strength of an organization's climate for the implementation of that innovation and the fit of that innovation to targeted users' values.

Krueger, Norris F. Jr. (2000). The Cognitive Infrastructure of Opportunity Emergence. *Entrepreneurship Theory & Practice,* vol. 24, no. 3, pp. 5-23.

Understanding what promotes or inhibits entrepreneurial activity requires understanding how we construct perceived opportunities. This paper proposes an intentions-based model of the cognitive infrastructure that supports or inhibits how we perceive opportunities.

Oldham, Greg R.; and Anne Cummings. (1996). Employee Creativity: Personal and Contextual Factors at Work. *Academy of Management Journal,* vol. 39, no. 3, pp. 607–34.

This study examines the independent and joint contributions of employees' creativity-relevant personal characteristics and three characteristics of the organizational context—job complexity, supportive supervision, and controlling supervision—and relates them to three indicators of employees' creative performance—patent disclosures written, contributions to an organization suggestion program, and supervisor ratings of creativity. Participants produced the most creative work when they had appropriate creativity-relevant characteristics, worked on complex, challenging jobs, and were supervised in a supportive, noncontrolling fashion.

Peters, Michael P. (1996). Market Information Scanning Activities and Growth in New Ventures: A Comparison of Service and Manufacturing Businesses. *Journal of Business Research,* vol. 36, no. 1, pp. 81–89.

A study investigating market information scanning practices in a sample of 120 new ventures. Types, methods, and sources of market information are compared in service and manufacturing ventures, and relationships between these practices and growth are assessed.

Sternberg, Robert J., ed. (1994). *Thinking and Problem Solving.* San Diego, CA: Academic Press, Inc.

This book represents a review of psychological literature on thinking and problem solving. Various topics from this area are discussed, such as history of thinking research, models in cognitive psychology, classifications of people's thinking, cognitive deductions, inductive reasoning, problem solving, intelligence, and creativity.

Endnotes

1. For an in-depth presentation on focus group interviews in general and quantitative applications, see "Conference Focuses on Focus Groups: Guidelines, Reports, and 'the Magic Plaque,'" *Marketing News* (May 21, 1976), p. 8; Keith K. Cox, James B. Higginbotham, and John Burton, "Application of Focus Group Interviews in Marketing," *Journal of Marketing* 40, no. 1 (January 1976), pp. 77–80; and Robert D. Hisrich and Michael P. Peters, "Focus Groups: An Innovative Marketing Research Technique," *Hospital and Health Service Administration* 27, no. 4 (July–August 1982), pp. 8–21.

2. A discussion of each of these techniques can be found in Robert D. Hisrich and Michael P. Peters, *Marketing Decisions for New and Mature Products* (Columbus, OH: Charles E. Merrill, 1984), pp. 131–46; and Robert D. Hisrich, "Entrepreneurship and Intrapreneurship: Methods for Creating New Companies That Have an Impact on the Economic Renaissance of an Area," in *Entrepreneurship, Intrapreneurship, and Venture Capital* (Lexington, MA: Lexington Books, 1986), pp. 77–104.

3. For a discussion of this aspect, see Charles H. Clark, *Idea Management: How to Motivate Creativity and Innovation* (New York: ANA Com., 1980), p. 47.

4. For a discussion of this technique, see J. Geoffrey Rawlinson, *Creative Thinking and Brainstorming* (New York: John Wiley & Sons, 1981), pp. 124 and 126; and W. E. Souder and R. W. Ziegler, "A Review of Creativity and Problem-Solving Techniques," *Research Management* 20 (July 1977), p. 35.

5. For a thorough discussion and application of this method, see W. J. Gordon, *Synectics: The Development of Creative Capacity* (New York: Harper & Row, 1961), pp. 37–53.

6. This method is discussed in J. W. Haefele, *Creativity and Innovation* (New York: Van Nostrand Reinhold, 1962), pp. 145–7; Sidney J. Parnes and Harold F. Harding, *A Source Book for Creative Thinking* (New York: Charles Scribner's Sons, 1962), pp. 307–23; and Souder and Ziegler, "Review of Techniques," pp. 34–42.

7. Alex F. Osborn, *Applied Imagination* (New York: The Scribner Book Companies, Inc., 1957), p. 318.

8. Rawlinson, *Creative Thinking*, pp. 52–59.

9. For a thorough discussion of the collective notebook method, see J. W. Haefele, *Creativity and Innovation*, p. 152.

10. See Edward M. Tauber, "HIT: Heuristic Ideation Technique," *Journal of Marketing* (January 1972), pp. 58–70.

11. For a discussion of value analysis and its application at General Electric, see "A Study on Applied Value Analysis," *Purchasing* 46 (June 8, 1959), pp. 66–67.

12. S. J. Parnes and H. F. Harding, eds., *A Source Book for Creative Thinking* (New York: Charles Scribner's Sons, 1962), p. 308.

13. For a discussion of this approach, see M. O. Edwards, "Solving Problems Creatively," *Journal of Systems Management* 17, no. 1 (January–February 1966), pp. 16–24.

14. The procedure for parameter analysis is thoroughly discussed in Yao Tzu Li, David G. Jansson, and Ernest G. Cravalho, *Technological Innovation in Education and Industry* (New York: Reinhold Publishing Company, 1980), pp. 26–49, 277–86.

15. For a detailed description of this process, see Robert D. Hisrich and Michael P. Peters, *Marketing Decisions for New and Mature Products* (Columbus, OH: Charles E. Merrill Publishing, 1991), pp. 157–78.

16. An example of the use and importance of this process is given in Louis Gedimen, "How to Screen New Product Ideas More Effectively," *Printer's Ink* 291, no. 4 (August 27, 1965), pp. 63–4.

17. Definitions are adopted from Thomas L. Mesenbourg, "Measuring Electronic Business: Definitions, Underlying Concepts, and Measurement Plans," Bureau of the Census, 2000. http://www.census.gov/epcd/www/ebusines.htm, 2/1/2000

6

Legal Issues for the Entrepreneur

ℱ

LEARNING OBJECTIVES

1. To identify and distinguish intellectual property assets of a new venture including software and websites.

2. To understand the nature of patents, the rights they provide, and the process for filing one.

3. To understand the purpose of a trademark and the procedure for filing.

4. To learn the purpose of a copyright and how to file for one.

5. To identify procedures that can protect a venture's trade secrets.

6. To understand the value of licensing to either expand a business or start a new venture.

7. To illustrate some of the fundamental issues related to contracts.

8. To understand important issues related to insurance and product safety and liability.

DANIEL SCHREIBER

While employed as an attorney for a large Tel Aviv–based law firm, Daniel Schreiber's client responsibility was primarily high-tech mergers and acquisitions. At the same time that he was employed by this law firm, he was also pursuing a master's degree in copyright law. He often dreamed about starting his own company, and one day while commiserating with one of his friends, Andrew Goldman, a software engineer, he revealed this strong desire. Andrew told him to come up with a good idea and he would design it. Then one day while traveling home the idea hit him that the Internet had no real safeguard to protect material once it left the server. With the tremendous growth of the Internet (from 142 million people in 1998 to forecasts of 320 million by 2002) it was likely that the issue of intellectual property protection would become an even more serious problem that could inevitably inhibit its use, especially by anyone who wanted to display valuable images on their website. For example, organizations such as movie or television studios, museums, and photographers, to name a few, that want to promote their protected images and merchandise are vulnerable to illegal duplication and use. In fact anything that is made available on the Internet can be downloaded and then copied, distributed, or sold illegally. What was needed was some way to prevent Web surfers from actually downloading any information, graphics, or images that were sensitive to illegal use.

www.alchemedia.com

Research indicated that there were products that marked copywritten material so that anyone trying to sell it could be caught and prosecuted. However, if these instances of violation were large in number, it was unlikely that many of these individuals would be found and prosecuted. Daniel's conclusion was that a product that could actually prevent anyone from downloading protected material would be much more desirable to firms that share valuable images or information on their websites.

With the assistance of Andrew Goldman they each contributed their own savings totaling $200,000 and officially started their new venture, cSafe, in March 1998. Armed with a business plan the two entrepreneurs then received an additional $1.5 million from Israel Seed Partners, a venture-capital fund, to develop a product that would meet their prescribed goals. The result of their efforts was PixSafe—a product that provided protection to any image that a user deemed proprietary. Thus, if a Web surfer tried to download an image, say from a Hollywood studio, he or she would get a message in a dialogue box indicating that the material the user was trying to copy was protected. The Web surfer would thus be able to view images on the screen but not be able to reproduce them. With this product, there was immediate interest from many segments of the market, particularly the movie and television studios.

In October 1999 cSafe raised an additional $8.5 million and changed the name of its company to Alchemedia and its product from PixSafe to Clever Content Server. It also moved its headquarters from Beit Shemesh, Israel, to San Francisco, California. The large second round of financing was to be used for marketing and further research and development of solutions to image protection problems. The venture now employs 40 people including additional high-level management such as Steven Miller, who is a former vice president of Oracle Corporation.

Daniel Schreiber and Andrew Goldman are good examples of entrepreneurs who are finding solutions to the myriad of problems that now exist in protecting one's intellectual property. Growth in the Internet and and the development of computer software has raised many new questions regarding intellectual property. Entrepreneurs need to be aware of not only the problems but also what they can do to prevent potential problems with their products or services. This chapter provides insight for the entrepreneur to identify what solutions might exist and how they can implement them.[1]

WHAT IS INTELLECTUAL PROPERTY?

Intellectual property—which includes patents, trademarks, copyrights, and trade secrets—represents important assets to the entrepreneur and should be understood even before engaging the services of an attorney. Too often entrepreneurs, because of their lack of understanding of intellectual property, ignore important steps that they should have taken to protect these assets. This chapter will describe all the important types of intellectual property, including software and websites, that have become unique problems to the Patent and Trademark Office.[2]

---

intellectual property   Any patents, trademarks, copyrights, or trade secrets held by the entrepreneur

---

NEED FOR A LAWYER

Since all business is regulated by law, the entrepreneur needs to be aware of any regulations that may affect his or her new venture. At different stages of the start-up, the entrepreneur will need legal advice. It is also likely that the legal expertise required will vary based on such factors as whether the new venture is a franchise, an independent start-up, or a buyout; whether it produces a consumer versus industrial product; whether it is nonprofit; and whether it involves some aspect of computer software, exporting, or importing.

The chapter begins with a discussion of how to select a lawyer. Since most lawyers have developed special expertise, the entrepreneur should carefully evaluate his or her needs before hiring one. By being aware of when and what legal advice is required, the entrepreneur can save much time and money. Many of the areas in which the entrepreneur will need legal assistance are discussed in this chapter.

HOW TO SELECT A LAWYER

Lawyers, like many other professionals, are specialists not just in the law but in specific areas of the law. The entrepreneur does not usually have the expertise or know-how to handle possible risks associated with the many difficult laws and regulations. A competent attorney is in a better position to understand all possible circumstances and outcomes related to any legal action.

In today's environment, lawyers are much more up-front about their fees. In fact, in some cases these fees, if for standard services, may even be advertised. In general, the lawyer may work on a retainer basis (stated amount per month or year) by which he or she provides office and consulting time. This does not include court time or other legal fees related to the action. This gives the entrepreneur the opportunity to call an attorney as the need arises without incurring high hourly visit fees.

In some instances the lawyer may be hired for a one-time fee. For example, a patent attorney may be hired as a specialist to help the entrepreneur obtain a patent. Once the patent is obtained, this lawyer would not be needed, except perhaps if there was any litigation regarding the patent. Other specialists for setting up the organization or for purchase of real estate may also be paid on a service-performed basis. Whatever the fee basis, the entrepreneur should confront the cost issue initially so that no questions arise in the future.

Choosing a lawyer is like hiring an employee. The lawyer with whom you work should be someone you can relate to personally. In a large law firm, it is possible that an associate or junior partner would be assigned to the new venture. The entrepreneur should ask to meet with this person to ensure that there is compatibility.

A good working relationship with a lawyer will ease some of the risk in starting a new business and will give the entrepreneur necessary confidence. When resources are very limited, the entrepreneur may consider offering the lawyer stock in exchange for his or her services. The lawyer then will have a vested interest in the business and will likely provide more personalized services. However, in making such a major decision, the entrepreneur must consider any possible loss of control of the business.

LEGAL ISSUES IN SETTING UP THE ORGANIZATION

The form of organization as well as franchise agreements are discussed in Chapters 10 and 15 and will not be addressed in detail here. Since there are many options that an entrepreneur can choose in setting up an organization (see Chapter 10), it will be necessary to understand all of the advantages and disadvantages of each regarding such issues as liability, taxes, continuity, transferability of interest, costs of setting up, and attractiveness for raising capital. Legal advice for these agreements is necessary to ensure that the most appropriate decisions have been made.

PATENTS

A *patent* is a contract between the government and an inventor. In exchange for disclosure of the invention, the government grants the inventor exclusivity regarding the invention for a specified amount of time. At the end of this time, the government publishes the invention and it becomes part of the public domain. As part of the public domain, however, there is the assumption that the disclosure will stimulate ideas and perhaps even the development of an even better product that could replace the original.[3]

patent Grants holder protection from others making, using, or selling similar idea

Basically, the patent gives the owners a negative right because it prevents anyone else from making, using, or selling the defined invention. Moreover, even if an inventor has been granted a patent, in the process of producing or marketing the invention he or she may find that it infringes on the patent rights of others. The inventor should recognize the distinction between utility and design patents and some of the differences in international patents that are discussed later in this chapter.

- *Utility Patents.* When speaking about patents, most people are referring to utility patents. A utility patent has a term of 17 years, beginning on the date the Patent and Trademark Office (PTO) issues it. NAFTA (North American Free Trade Agreement) establishes a minimum period of exclusivity of 20 years from the date of filing or 17 years from the date of the grant. Any invention requiring FDA approval has also been amended to extend the term of the patent by the amount of time it takes the FDA to review the invention.

    A utility patent basically grants the owner protection from anyone else making, using, and/or selling the identified invention and generally reflects protection of new, useful, and unobvious processes such as film developing, machines such as photocopiers, compositions of matter such as chemical compounds or mixtures of ingredients, and articles of manufacture such as the toothpaste pump.

- *Design Patents.* Covering new, original, ornamental, and unobvious designs for articles of manufacture, a design patent reflects the appearance of an object. These patents are granted for a 14-year term and, like the utility patent, provide the inventor with a negative right excluding others from making, using, or selling an article having the ornamental appearance given in the drawings included in the patent. Filing fees for these types of patents range from $150 to $300 depending on the size of the firm. There are also issuance fees, which can exceed $400 depending on the size of the item. These fees are much lower than for a utility patent discussed above.

    Traditionally, design patents were thought to be useless because it was so easy to design around the patent. However, there is renewed interest in these patents. Examples are shoe companies such as Reebok and Nike that have become more interested in obtaining design patents as a means of protecting their ornamental designs. These types of patents are also valuable for businesses that need to protect molded plastic parts, extrusions, and product and container configurations.

- *Plant Patents.* These are issued for 17 years on new varieties of plants. These patents represent a limited area of interest, and thus very few of these types of patents are issued.

Patents are issued by the Patent and Trademark Office (PTO). In addition to patents, this office administers other programs. One of these is the Disclosure Document Program, whereby the inventor files disclosure of the invention, giving recognition that he or she was the first to develop or invent the idea. In most cases, the inventor will subsequently patent the idea. A second program is the Defensive Publication Program. This gives the inventor the opportunity to protect an idea for which he or she does not wish to obtain a patent. It prevents anyone else from patenting this idea, but gives the public access to the invention.

International Patents

With the GATT (General Agreement on Tariffs and Trade) that took effect on January 1, 1996, any application by a foreign company will be treated the same as one by an American firm. In the past, if there was a filing by a foreign company and a

U.S. company at the same time, the American firm would always win as long as it could prove that it had begun work on an idea before the date the foreign firm filed for a U.S. patent. Now the decision is based totally on when the filing companies (including the foreign firm) began work on the idea. Because of this change it will be even more important for the entrepreneur to prepare a disclosure document, discussed below, as early as possible.[4] The new pact will mandate stronger protection for entrepreneurs and new ventures in the international market since it commits all signatory countries to 7 years of protection for trademarks, 20 years for patents, and 50 years for films, music, and software. There are still some problems with China and other Southeast Asian countries where "knock-offs" have been produced and thus affected sales of U.S. manufacturers. Recently, however, attitudes toward Taiwan and China by U.S. investors have changed, particularly for Internet ventures. For example, China.com Corp., the Hong Kong portal company, was the first to go public in the United States and successfully listed on Nasdaq. Sina.com, a Taiwanese venture, moved its headquarters to Silicon Valley and hired U.S. management talent to help secure its efforts to go public. However, this venture has incurred serious problems recently, with much of its powerful executive team leaving amidst a serious rift with the founders, Daniel Chiang and Wang Zhidong. As more of the Chinese firms begin to realize the opportunity to meet all of the international requirements of intellectual property, the government will likely be more willing to live up to its responsibilities.[5]

The Disclosure Document

It is recommended that the entrepreneur first file a *disclosure document* to establish a date of conception of the invention. This document can be important when two entrepreneurs are filing for patents on similar inventions. This filing date is now also relevant when there is a foreign company involved. In that instance, the entrepreneur who can show that he or she was the first one to conceive of the invention will be given the rights to the patent.

disclosure document   Statement to U.S. Patent and Trademark Office by inventor disclosing intent to patent idea

To file a disclosure document, the entrepreneur must prepare a clear and concise description of the invention. In addition to the written material, photographs may be included. A cover letter and a duplicate are included with the description of the invention. Upon receipt of the information, the PTO will stamp and return the duplicate copy of the letter to the entrepreneur, thus establishing evidence of conception. There is also a fee for this filing, which can be determined by contacting the PTO.

The disclosure document is not a patent application. Before actually applying for the patent it is advisable to retain a patent attorney to conduct a patent search. After the attorney completes the search, a decision can be made as to the patentability of the invention.

The Patent Application

The patent application must contain a complete history and description of the invention as well as claims for its usefulness. The actual form can be downloaded from the Patent and Trademark Office website listed at the conclusion of this chapter. In general, the application will be divided into the following sections:

- *Introduction.* This section should contain the background and advantages of the invention and the nature of problems that it overcomes. It should clearly state how the invention differs from existing offerings.

- *Description of Invention.* Next the application should contain a brief description of the drawings that accompany it. These drawings must comply with PTO requirements. Following this would be a detailed description of the invention, which may include engineering specifications, materials, components, and so on, that are vital to the actual making of the invention.
- *Claims.* This is probably the most difficult section of the application to prepare since claims are the criteria by which any infringements will be determined. They serve to specify what the entrepreneur is trying to patent. Essential parts of the invention should be described in broad terms so as to prevent others from getting around the patent. At the same time, the claims must not be so general that they hide the invention's uniqueness and advantages. This balance is difficult and should be discussed and debated with the patent attorney.

In addition to the above sections, the application should contain a declaration or oath that is signed by the inventor or inventors. This form will be supplied by an attorney. The completed application is then ready to be sent to the PTO, at which time the status of the invention becomes patent pending. This status is important to the entrepreneur because it now provides complete confidential protection until the application is approved. At that time, the patent is published and thus becomes accessible to the public for review.

A carefully written patent should provide protection and prevent competitors from working around it. However, once granted, it is also an invitation to sue or be sued if there is any infringement.

The fees for filing an application will vary, depending on the patent search and on claims made in the application. Attorney fees are also a factor in completing the patent application. The initial average cost of a patent seems to be about $1,500 to $2,000. There are, however, three maintenance fees that must be paid at intervals during the life of a patent.

Patent Infringement

To this point, we have discussed the importance and the procedure of filing for a patent. It is also important for the entrepreneur to be sensitive about whether he or she is infringing on someone else's patent. The fact that someone else already has a patent does not mean the end of any illusions of starting a business. Many businesses, inventions, or innovations are the result of improvements on, or modifications of, existing products. Copying and improving on a product may be perfectly legal (no patent infringement) and actually good business strategy. If it is impossible to copy and improve the product to avoid patent infringement, the entrepreneur may try to license the product from the patent holder. Figure 6.1 illustrates the steps that an entrepreneur should follow as he or she considers marketing a product that may infringe on an existing patent. To ascertain the existence of a patent the entrepreneur can now make use of the Internet. Websites listed at the end of the chapter can assist in determining whether a patent even exists. If there is an existing patent that might involve infringement by the entrepreneur, licensing may be considered. If there is any doubt as to this issue, the entrepreneur should hire a patent attorney to ensure that there will not be any possibility of patent infringement. Table 6.1 provides a simple checklist that should be followed by an entrepreneur to minimize any patent risks.

FIGURE 6.1 Options to Avoid Infringement

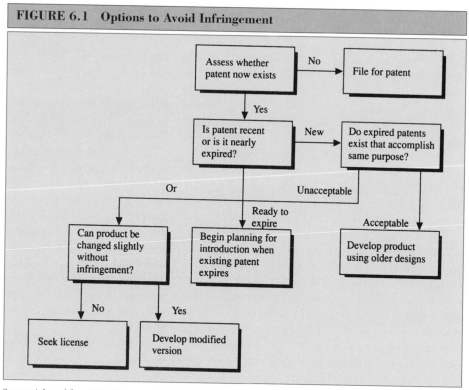

Source: Adapted from H. D. Coleman and J. D. Vandenberg, "How to Follow the Leader," *Inc.* (July 1988), pp. 81–82.

TABLE 6.1 Checklist for Minimizing Patent Risks

- Seek a patent attorney who has expertise in your product line.
- The entrepreneur should consider a design patent to protect the product design or product look.
- Before making an external disclosure of an invention at a conference or to the media, or before setting up a beta site, the entrepreneur should seek legal counsel since this external disclosure may negate a subsequent patent application.
- Evaluate competitor patents to gain insight as to what they may be developing.
- If you think your product infringes on the patent of another firm, seek legal counsel.
- Verify that all employment contracts with individuals who may contribute new products have clauses assigning those inventions or new products to the venture.
- Be sure to properly mark all products granted a patent. Not having products marked could result in loss or damages in a patent suit.
- Consider licensing your patents. This can enhance the investment in a patent by creating new market opportunities and can increase long-term revenues.

As Seen in *Business Week:*
Why We Don't Need Patent Reform—Yet

Every few years, it seems, the U.S. Patent & Trademark Office throws the business community into a complete panic. In 1993, for example, the PTO granted a sweeping multimedia software patent to Compton's NewMedia Inc., which immediately sought hefty licensing fees from competitors. There were dire warnings that the patent would retard the development of multimedia technology and the CD-ROM industry. The PTO "could decimate the very industry it seeks to protect," complained one software executive.

Just a couple of years before, a similar outcry arose when the PTO gave an Arizona ophthalmologist a patent on a new technique for stitchless cataract surgery. Critics worried that other doctors would start patenting their own innovations—and new medical techniques would no longer be freely shared. Before that, there were similar protests about the first patent awards in software, gene therapy, and biotechnology.

This time, the scare is about patenting business processes. And the focal point for the outcry is Amazon.com Inc.'s September patent on a one-click system for online orders. The worry: Amazon will block other sites from using this seemingly obvious innovation and thereby render e-commerce less efficient.

Over the past three years, applications for business-process patents have tripled. "It tends to happen every time there is a significant advance in technology," says PTO Commissioner Q. Todd Dickinson. Think Internet: Some of the hottest e-commerce stocks are propelled, at least in part, by the value of their patented business processes. Priceline.com Inc., for example, has a patent on so-called reverse auctions on the Internet and has sued Microsoft Corp. for adding a similar type of name-your-price bidding to the company's Expedia site. This suit and a similar one brought by Amazon.com against barnesandnoble.com have various patent experts calling for a sweeping reevaluation of how intellectual-property law applies to the Internet.

The issue deserves to be taken seriously. But it's useful to keep in mind how other patent scares have played out. They tend to follow a pattern: First, an inventor lays claim to a broad swath of promising new technology. Because the PTO is unfamiliar with the area, it grants the patent, at least initially. Wild predictions of doom and gloom—usually from rivals—follow.

But ultimately, the legal system finds a way to manage the new technology, and the dire predictions never come true. Consider the Compton's patent. Bowing to industry concerns, the PTO reexamined the patent and revoked it. The problem of medical-technique patents was solved by a 1996 law making it nearly impossible for doctors to block other physicians from using their innovations. And despite early fears, owners of some key biotechnology and gene-therapy patents have been willing to license them freely, and innovation in both areas is thriving.

At this point, there's still ample reason to believe that the PTO and the courts will be able to cope with the problem of Internet business-method patents in the same way. Yes, the Web is unique. It tends to give first movers big rewards and therefore provides companies with a disproportionate incentive to patent everything in sight.

Still, traditional patent law provides adequate tools for weeding out bogus claims. For example, there's a basic requirement that patents can only be granted for innovations that aren't obvious. If patent examiners and courts apply this test stringently, they should be able to block applicants who are importing simple ideas from the outside world into the Net. This requirement, many experts believe, will eventually doom the disputed Amazon.com and priceline.com patents.

It's possible that in spite of the best efforts of the PTO and the courts, business-process patents will wind up jeopardizing innovation on the Net. In that case, a fundamental revision of patent law may well be necessary. But it's early yet, and history gives plenty of reasons to be skeptical of the Chicken Littles.

Source: M. France, "Why We Don't Need Patent Reform—Yet," *Business Week* (December 20, 1999), p. 54.

ONLINE PATENT ISSUES

A new era for patents is evolving. Recently Pitney Bowes Inc. sued a start-up company, stamp.com, for patent violation. Several days later stamp.com returned the favor, and its founder Jim McDermott and CEO John Payne announced that it was cooperating with the Justice Department in an investigation that Pitney Bowes had violated antitrust laws because of its patent claims. As a provider of stamps through the Internet, stamps.com has raised an important question of whether patents are applicable to e-commerce. Pitney Bowes' action has also become commonplace for large corporations that spend millions on research and development and are stockpiling patents in order to protect themselves from the new wave of start-ups. Large corporations are then suing the start-ups in order to get compensation for their intellectual property. Thus, patents that were exclusively used to protect inventions have become increasingly important as weapons to intimidate entrepreneurs or discourage investors to enter their marketing territory. Compensation can often be a licensing fee or lump sum payment that satisfies the cash flow of the large corporation.[6]

TRADEMARKS

A *trademark* may be a word, symbol, design, or some combination of such, or it could be a slogan or even a particular sound that identifies the source or sponsorship of certain goods or services. Unlike the patent, a trademark can last indefinitely, as long as the mark continues to perform its indicated function. The trademark is given an initial 20-year registration with 20-year renewable terms. In the fifth to sixth year, the registrant is required to file an affidavit with the PTO indicating that the mark is currently in commercial use. If no affidavit is filed, the registration is canceled.

trademark   A distinguishing word, name, or symbol used to identify a product

Trademark law allows the filing of a trademark solely on the intent to use the trademark in interstate or foreign commerce. The filing date then becomes the first date use of the mark. This does not imply that the entrepreneur cannot file after the mark has already been in use. In fact, there are benefits to registering a mark that has already been in use. For example, if the business is not yet national in scope, the filing for a mark already in use on a regional basis will provide freedom to expand nationally under the same name.[7]

The protection awarded is dependent on the character of the mark itself. There are four categories of trademarks: (1) coined marks denote no relationship between the mark and the goods or services (e.g., Polaroid, Kodak) and afford the possibility of expansion to a wide range of products; (2) an arbitrary mark is one that has another meaning in our language (e.g., Apple) and is applied to a product or service; (3) a suggestive mark is used to suggest certain features, qualities, ingredients, or characteristics of a product or service (i.e., Halo shampoo). It differs from an arbitrary mark in that it tends to suggest some describable attribute of the product or services. Finally, (4) a descriptive mark must have become distinctive over a significant period of time and gained consumer recognition before it can be registered. The mark then is considered to have secondary meaning; that is, it is descriptive of a particular product or service (e.g., Rubberoid as applied to roofing materials that contain rubber).[8]

Registering a trademark can offer significant advantages or benefits to the entrepreneur. Table 6.2 summarizes some of these benefits.

TABLE 6.2 Benefits of a Registered Trademark
• It provides notice to everyone that you have exclusive rights to the use of the mark throughout the territorial limits of the United States.
• It entitles you to sue in federal court for trademark infringement, which can result in recovery of profits, damages, and costs.
• It establishes incontestable rights regarding the commercial use of the mark.
• It establishes the right to deposit registration with customs to prevent importation of goods with a similar mark.
• It entitles you to use the notice of registration®.
• It provides a basis for filing trademark application in foreign countries.

Registering the Trademark

As indicated earlier, the PTO is responsible for the federal registration of trademarks. To file an application, the entrepreneur must complete a simple form that can be downloaded from the PTO website identified at the conclusion of this chapter.

Filing of the trademark registration must meet four requirements: (1) completion of the written form, (2) a drawing of the mark, (3) five specimens showing actual use of the mark, and (4) the fee. Each trademark must be applied for separately. Upon receipt of this information, the PTO assigns a serial number to the application and sends a filing receipt to the applicant.

The next step in the registering process is a determination by the examining attorney at the PTO as to whether the mark is suitable for registration. Within about three months, an initial determination is made as to its suitability. Any objections by the entrepreneur must be raised within six months, or the application is considered abandoned. If the trademark is refused, the entrepreneur still has the right to appeal to the PTO.

Once accepted, the trademark is published in the *Trademark Official Gazette* to allow any party 30 days to oppose or request an extension to oppose. If no opposition is filed, the registration is issued. This entire procedure usually takes about 13 months from the initial filing.

COPYRIGHTS

A *copyright* protects original works of authorship. The protection in a copyright does not protect the idea itself, and thus it allows someone else to use the idea or concept in a different manner.

copyright Right given to prevent others from printing, copying, or publishing any original works of authorship

The copyright law has become especially relevant to computer software companies. In 1980, The Computer Software Copyright Act was added to the Federal Code of Copyright Laws. It provided explanation of the nature of software protection under the copyright laws. Authors or publishers of software are protected similarly to creators of artistic works. The idea of the software (e.g., spreadsheets) is not eligible for protection, but the actual program to produce the spreadsheet is eligible. The Copyright Office now regularly issues registrations for source code programs (English words or signs) and object code programs (machine language).

Protection of material on the Internet has become an important issue in Congress. A number of firms are locked in legal battles regarding the rights over data that they publish and that may have required significant resources to obtain. For example, the *New York Times* has recently claimed that Amazon.com cannot use its best-seller list without its permission. Amazon.com had been not only publishing the list but offering large discounts on any of the listed books. *The Times* has an exclusive arrangement with barnesandnoble.com and feels that it owns the rights to the list and it therefore should not be copied by anyone else. Ownership of stock quotes, judicial decisions, and real estate postings is also being questioned. New legislation regarding ownership of Internet information is inevitable given the rapid growth of this new technology and as more and more legal battles occur.[9]

Copyrights are registered with the Library of Congress and will not usually require an attorney. All that is necessary is that the form—which can be downloaded from the PTO website identified at the end of this chapter—two copies of the work, and the appropriate fee be sent to the Register of Copyrights. The term of copyright is the life of the author plus 50 years. If the author is an institution, the term of the copyright is 75 years from publication.

Besides computer software, copyrights are desirable for such things as books, scripts, articles, poems, songs, sculptures, models, maps, blueprints, collages, printed material on board games, data, and music. In some instances, several forms of protection may be available. For example, the name of a board game may be protected by trademark, the game itself protected by a utility patent, the printed matter or the board protected by a copyright, and the playing pieces covered by a design patent.[10]

TRADE SECRETS

In certain instances, the entrepreneur may prefer to maintain an idea or process as confidential and sell or license it as a *trade secret*. The trade secret will have a life as long as the idea or process remains a secret.

trade secret   Protection against others revealing or disclosing information that could be damaging to business

A trade secret is not covered by any federal law but is recognized under a governing body of common laws in each state. Employees involved in working with an idea or process may be asked to first sign a confidential information agreement that will protect against their giving out the trade secret either while an employee or after leaving the organization. A simple example of a trade secret nondisclosure agreement is illustrated in Figure 6.2. The entrepreneur should hire an attorney to help draw up any such agreement. The holder of the trade secret has the right to sue any signee who breaches such an agreement.

What or how much information to give to employees is difficult to judge and is often determined by the entrepreneur's judgment. Historically, entrepreneurs tended to protect sensitive or confidential company information from anyone else by simply not making them privy to this information. Today, there is a tendency to take the opposite view, that the more information entrusted to employees, the more effective and creative employees can be. The argument is that employees cannot be creative unless they have a complete understanding of what is going on in the business.[11]

Most entrepreneurs have limited resources, so they choose not to find means to protect their ideas, products, or services. This could become a serious problem in the future, since extolling competitive information legally is so easy to accomplish,

FIGURE 6.2   A Simple Trade Secret Nondisclosure Agreement

WHEREAS, New Venture Corporation (NVC), Anywhere Street, Anyplace, U.S.A., is the Owner of information relating to; and

WHEREAS, NVC is desirous of disclosing said information to the undersigned (hereinafter referred to as "Recipient") for the purposes of using, evaluating, or entering into further agreements using such trade secrets as an employee, consultant, or agent of NVC; and

WHEREAS, NVC wishes to maintain in confidence said information as trade secret; and

WHEREAS, the undersigned Recipient recognizes the necessity of maintaining the stricter confidence with respect to any trade secrets of NVC.

Recipient hereby agrees as follows:

1. Recipient shall observe the strictest secrecy with respect to all information presented by NVC and Recipient's evaluation thereof and shall disclose such information only to persons authorized to receive same by NVC. Recipient shall be responsible for any damage resulting from any breach of this Agreement by Recipient.

2. Recipient shall neither make use of nor disclose to any third party during the period of this Agreement and thereafter any such trade secrets or evaluation thereof unless prior consent in writing is given by NVC.

3. Restriction on disclosure does not apply to information previously known to Recipient or otherwise in the public domain. Any prior knowledge of trade secrets by the Recipient shall be disclosed in writing within (30) days.

4. At the completion of the services performed by the Recipient, Recipient shall within (30) days return all original materials provided by NVC and any copies, notes, or other documents that are in the Recipient's possession pertaining thereto.

5. Any trade secrets made public through publication or product announcements are excluded from this agreement.

6. This agreement is executed and delivered within the State of ____ and it shall be construed, interpreted, and applied in accordance with the laws of that State.

7. This agreement, including the provision hereof, shall not be modified or changed in any manner except only in writing signed by all parties hereto.

Effective this _____ day of _____ 19 _____

RECIPIENT: _____

NEW VENTURE CORPORATION:

By: _____

Title: _____

Date: _____

unless the entrepreneur takes the proper precautions. For example, it is often easy to learn competitive information through such means as trade shows, transient employees, or media interviews or announcements. In all three instances, overzealous employees are the problem. To try to control this problem, entrepreneurs should consider some of the ideas listed below.

- Train employees to refer sensitive questions to one person.
- Provide escorts for all office visitors.
- Avoid discussing business in public places.

Protection of Trade Secrets for a New Venture

We are continually hearing of the problems that big business has in trying to protect its trade secrets. In 1993 Roger Farah left Federated Department Stores Inc. for an executive position at R. H. Macy & Co. His former employer, however, was concerned that his new position would make all of their plans and other proprietary information vulnerable to a major competitor. Thus, Federated slapped him with a lawsuit to protect any of their trade secrets. A similar lawsuit was filed by Procter & Gamble against Clorox Co. when a top global planner left P&G to become a group vice president for Clorox.

The issue faced by these large companies is no different for new ventures. For example, an entrepreneur started a new venture whose major innovation was a grill-cleaning chemical product that could effectively clean a grill at operating temperatures. A CEO was hired with the agreement that he would be given equity in the business once it became profitable. Within 18 months the company became profitable, but the founders, who were also running another business, chose to maintain this new venture's size at its existing level with no new investment to grow the business. The CEO, who was expecting an equity position of a potentially fast-growing company, now had to make a decision as to whether he should honor the handshake agreement. His feeling was that the original founders were reneging on their agreement, and therefore he had the right to leave and start his own grill-cleaning company using some of the knowledge as well as new product ideas that he had learned while CEO. Determining who is wrong and who is right in this case could conceivably take a lot of time and money. What is important is that the problems of protecting trade secrets are just as important to a new venture as they are to big business.

Even though you may have a good legal case against an employee, it may take money and time to resolve. To minimize the likelihood of these events happening it is recommended that entrepreneurs protect their investment by:

- **Restricting access to sensitive documents.**
- **Defining in an employee contract what belongs to the venture and what belongs to the employee.**
- **Using specific nondisclosure agreements and noncompete clauses to protect against scenarios described above.**
- **Preparing to file a lawsuit, if all else fails.**

Source: Linda Himelstein, Laura Zinn, and Zachary Schiller, "Are Trade-Secret Police Patrolling Your Company?" *Business Week* (August 23, 1993), p. 23.

- Keep important travel plans secret.
- Control information that might be presented by employees at conferences or published in journals.
- Use simple security such as locked file cabinets, passwords on computers, and shredders where necessary.
- Have employees and consultants sign nondisclosure agreements.
- Debrief departing employees on any confidential information.
- Avoid faxing any sensitive information.
- Mark documents confidential when needed.

Unfortunately, protection against the leaking of trade secrets is difficult to enforce. More important, legal action can be taken only after the secret has been revealed. It is not necessary for the entrepreneur to worry extensively about every document or piece of information. As long as minimal precautions are taken, most problems can be avoided, primarily because leaks usually occur inadvertently.

LICENSING

Licensing may be defined as an arrangement between two parties, where one party has proprietary rights over some information, process, or technology protected by a patent, trademark, or copyright. This arrangement, specified in a contract (discussed later in this chapter), requires the licensee to pay a royalty or some other specified sum to the holder of the proprietary rights (licensor) in return for permission to copy the patent, trademark, or copyright.

---

licensing   Contractual agreement giving rights to others to use intellectual property in return for a royalty or fee

---

Thus, licensing has significant value as a marketing strategy to holders of patents, trademarks, or copyrights to grow their business in new markets when they lack resources or experience in those markets. It is also an important marketing strategy for entrepreneurs who wish to start a new venture but need permission to copy or incorporate the patent, trademark, or copyright with their ideas.

A patent license agreement specifies how the licensee would have access to the patent. For example, the licensor may still manufacture the product but give the licensee the rights to market it under their label in a noncompetitive market (i.e., foreign market). In other instances, the licensee may actually manufacture and market the patented product under its own label. This agreement must be carefully worded and should involve a lawyer, to ensure the protection of all parties.

Licensing a trademark generally involves a franchising agreement. The entrepreneur operates a business using the trademark and agrees to pay a fixed sum for use of the trademark, pay a royalty based on sales volume, buy supplies from the franchisor (examples would be Shell, Exxon, Dunkin Donuts, Pepsi Cola or Coca Cola bottlers, or Midas Muffler shops), or some combination of these. Chapter 15 discusses franchising as an option for the entrepreneur to start a new business or as a means of financing growth.

Copyrights are another popular licensed property. They involve rights to use or copy books, software, music, photographs, and plays, to name a few. In the late 1970s, computer games were designed using licenses from arcade games and movies. Television shows have also licensed their names for board games or computer games. Celebrities will often license the right to use their name, likeness, or image in a product (i.e., Andre Agassi tennis clothing, Elvis Presley memorabilia, or Mickey Mouse lunch boxes). This is actually analogous to a trademark license. A good example of this occurred in 1990 when Eagle Eyewear was granted a license by Yoko Ono to affix John Lennon's signature to a line of eyewear that reflected the John Lennon look. In addition, the license gave Eagle Eyewear the right to use John Lennon's likeness in promotional materials.[12]

Walt Disney Co., which is one of the most significant players in licensing agreements, is also one of the most selective. The company has been actively engaged in licensing for 65 years with more than 600 U.S. licensees. Disney's share of the $65 billion business is over $2 billion at retail.[13] The Star Wars Movies have also been a huge influence in the licensing business, particularly for toys, video games, clothing, and food-related products.[14] Pokemon was the 1999 hot item with collectible characters, games, a movie, and most recently trading cards. Burger King held one of the largest licensing agreements by developing a $20 million tie-in to the Pokemon movie by offering 152 collectible characters released at the rate of one per day. Unfortunately, this program came to an end after a 13-month-old infant suffocated from one of the plastic balls in which the Pokemon characters were contained.[15]

Licensing is also popular around special sporting events, such as the Olympics, marathons, bowl games, and tournaments. Licenses to sell T-shirts, clothing, and other accessories require written permission in the form of a license agreement before sales are allowed.

Although licensing opportunities are often plentiful, they must be carefully considered as part of the venture's planning process. A perfect example was Rose Evangelista's toy company, Just Toys, a start-up venture that had experienced both favorable and unfavorable results from licensing of toys and dolls. In 1990, she manufactured 50,000 Little Mermaid Ariel dolls in anticipation of the video release of the movie. However, the market was soft, and she almost was ready to give up her effort when suddenly the demand for the rubber figurines began to soar. By the time the demand had peaked, her firm had sold two million dolls. In 1993 this venture had achieved $42 million in sales, mostly from licensed figurines and indoor sports equipment. By 1994, however, all the successful growth took a wrong turn. The company had taken some extensive risk in a few new products that failed. This all resulted in a $16 million loss in 1994, which led the board of directors to fire Rose and her husband Allan Rigberg in 1995. They subsequently filed a lawsuit against the board, which was settled in late 1995. With sales last year of about $18 million the company has licenses with Spalding, Louisville Slugger, The Adventures of Rocky & Bullwinkle and Friends, the World Wrestling Federation, and Rollerjam.[16]

One of the most successful examples of licensing of figurines was the Teenage Mutant Ninja Turtles, which has accounted for over $2 billion in licensing revenues. Most of the firms that made Turtles products were small entrepreneurial ventures.[17]

Licensing can be particularly valuable for a high-technology firm lacking the resources to conduct R&D to develop a product. Technology licensing usually entails a contractual agreement by which a firm (licensee) acquires the rights to a product, process, and/or management technology from another firm (licensor) for a lump sum payment and/or royalties. According to recent research, technology licensing is becoming extremely popular among small ventures as a means to develop new products. This research indicated that the two most important reasons for licensing were to gain competitive advantage and to improve the venture's technical skills. Firms participating in the study found that licensing technology reduced their R&D costs, lowered marketing and legislative risks, and enhanced the speed of market entry.[18]

Before embarking in a license agreement, the entrepreneur should ask the following questions:

- Will the customer recognize the licensed property?
- How well does the licensed property complement my products or services?
- How much experience do I have with the licensed property?
- What is the long-term outlook for the licensed property? (For example, the loss of popularity of a celebrity can also result in an end to a business involving that celebrity's name.)
- What kind of protection does the licensing agreement provide?
- What commitment do I have in payment of royalties, sales quotas, and so on?
- Are renewal options possible and under what terms?

Licensing is an excellent option for the entrepreneur to increase revenues, without the risk and costly start-up investment. To be able to license requires the entrepreneur to have something to license, which is why it is so important to seek protection for any product, information, name, and so on, with a patent, trademark, or copyright. On the other hand, licensing can also be a way to start a new venture when the idea may infringe on someone else's patent, trademark, or copyright. In this instance, the entrepreneur has nothing to lose by trying to seek a license agreement from the holder of the property.

Licensing continues to be a powerful marketing tool. With the advice of a lawyer, entrepreneurs may find that licensing opportunities are a way to minimize risk, expand a business, or complement an existing product line.

PRODUCT SAFETY AND LIABILITY

It is very important for the entrepreneur to assess whether any product that is to be marketed in the new venture is subject to any regulations under the Consumer Product Safety Act. The act, which was passed in 1972, created a five-member commission that has the power to prescribe safety standards for more than 10,000 products.

product safety and liability   Responsibility of company to meet any legal specifications regarding a new product covered by the Consumer Product Safety Act

In addition to setting standards for products, the commission also has a great deal of responsibility and power to identify what it considers to be substantial hazards and bar products it considers unsafe. It is especially active in recognizing whether possible product defects may be hazardous to consumers. When this is the case, the commission will request the manufacturer, in writing, to take corrective action.

The act was amended and signed into law in 1990. The amended law establishes stricter guidelines for reporting product defects and any injury or death resulting from such defects. Manufacturers could be subject to fines of $1.25 million for failing to report product liability settlements or court awards. Manufacturers have presented their concerns to the Consumer Product Safety Commission about information in these reports becoming public prematurely. This information could prove damaging even when the commission may subsequently find that the firm was not negligent.[19]

Any new product that is responsible for the entrepreneur's entry into a business should be assessed to ascertain whether it falls under the Consumer Product Safety Act. If it does, the entrepreneur will have to follow the appropriate procedures to ensure that he or she has met all the necessary requirements.

Product liability problems are complex and continue to be an important consideration for entrepreneurs. Recent attempts to reform the legislation were successful in Congress but were quickly vetoed by President Bill Clinton. Changes in the legislation were felt to be necessary to address many longtime concerns of businesses such as the amount of punitive damages allowed in certain cases and the application of the product liability laws to durable goods that have been in use for more than 15 years. Changes in the global market have also contributed to the need for reform. Risk managers claim that without new reform legislation start-up companies that do not have a product liability track record may have difficulty finding this type of coverage.[20]

Claims regarding product liability usually fall under one of the following categories:

1. *Negligence.* Extends to all parts of the production and marketing process. It involves being negligent in the way a product is presented to a client, such as using deficient labels, false advertising, and so on.

2. *Warranty.* Consumers may sue if advertising or information overstate the benefits of a product, or if the product does not perform as stated.

3. *Strict Liability.* In this action, a consumer is suing because the product in question was defective before its receipt.

4. *Misrepresentation.* This occurs when advertising, labels, or other information misrepresent material facts concerning the character or quality of the product.

The best protection against product liability is to produce safe products and to warn consumers of any potential hazards. It is impossible to expect zero defects, so entrepreneurs should be sensitive to what kinds of product liability problems may occur.

INSURANCE

Some of the problems relating to product liability were discussed in the previous section. Besides being cautious, it is also in the best interests of the entrepreneur to purchase insurance in the event that problems do occur. Service-related businesses such as day-care centers, amusement parks, shopping centers, and so on, have had significant increases in the number of lawsuits.

In general, most firms should consider coverage for those situations described in Table 6.3. Each of these types of insurance provides a means of managing risk in the new business. The main problem is that the entrepreneur usually has limited resources in the beginning. Thus, it is important to first determine if any of these types

TABLE 6.3	**Types of Insurance and Possible Coverage**
Type of Insurance	**Coverage Possible**
Property	• Fire insurance to cover losses to goods and premises resulting from fire and lightning. Can extend coverage to include risks associated with explosion, riot, vehicle damage, windstorm, hail, and smoke.
	• Burglary and robbery to cover small losses for stolen property in cases of forced entry (burglary) or if force or threat of violence was involved (robbery).
	• Business interruption will pay net profits and expenses when a business is shut down because of fire or other insured cause.
Casualty	• General liability covers the costs of defense and judgments obtained against the company resulting from bodily injury or property damage. This coverage can also be extended to cover product liability.
	• Automobile liability is needed when employees use their own cars for company business.
Life	• Life insurance protects the continuity of the business (especially a partnership). It can also provide financial protection for survivors of a sole proprietorship or for loss of a key corporate executive.
Workers' compensation	• May be mandatory in some states. Provides benefits to employees in case of work-related injury.
Bonding	• This shifts responsibility for employee or performance of a job. It protects company in case of employee theft of funds or protects contractor if subcontractor fails to complete a job within agreed-upon time.

of insurance are needed. Note that some insurance, such as disability and vehicle coverage, is required by law and cannot be avoided. Other insurance such as life insurance of key employees is not required but may be necessary to protect the financial net worth of the venture. Once the entrepreneur determines what types of insurance are needed, then a decision can be made on how much insurance and from what company. It is wise to get quotes from more than one insurance firm since rates and options can also vary. The total insurance cost represents an important financial planning factor, and the entrepreneur needs to consider increasing premiums in cost projections.

Skyrocketing medical costs have probably had the most significant impact on insurance premiums. This is especially true for workers' compensation premiums, which for some entrepreneurs have doubled or tripled in the last few years. Insurance companies calculate the premium for workers' compensation as a percentage of payroll, the type of business, and the number of prior claims. Given the problems with fraudulent or suspicious claims, some states are beginning to undertake reforms in the coverage. Even before reforms are enacted, the entrepreneur can take some action to control the premiums by paying attention to details, such as promoting safety through comprehensive guidelines that are communicated to every staff member. Being personally involved with safety can, in the long run, significantly control workers' compensation premiums.

Entrepreneurs also have to consider health care coverage. This is an important benefit to employees and will require the venture to cover a significant portion of this expense for the employee. Rates to the company will vary significantly depending on the plan and its various options. Health insurance premiums are less expensive if there is a large group of insured participants. This is, of course, difficult for a start-up venture but can be resolved by joining a group such as a professional association that offers such coverage.

However, if you are a self-employed entrepreneur, the options are limited. If you are leaving a corporate position, consider extending your health care benefits with a COBRA. This usually allows you to continue on the same health policy you were on for about three years. However, you will have to now pay the entire premium on the policy. If your COBRA has expired or one is not available, you can consider contacting your state insurance department, which can supply a list of insurance companies that provide individual health care insurance. Policies that have higher deductibles can also be considered because of their lower premiums. For additional assistance in these matters it is recommended that the entrepreneur contact the Association of Health Insurance Agents, the Health Insurance Association of America, or the U.S. Labor Department, all located in Washington, DC.

Officers' or directors' liability insurance has now become a serious financial consideration for start-up ventures. To enlist high-level professionals for the board of directors, the entrepreneur may be required to provide liability protection. If the potential for liability is high, the amount of coverage will need to be significant to protect each director. In some states it is also possible to obtain director liability coverage as an extension of one's home owner policy. The other option, of course, is for the entrepreneur to set up a board of advisors instead of an extended board of directors. Advisors would not be subject to liability since they do not formulate final policy for the venture but only provide recommendations to the actual board of directors, which in this case could consist of the management of the start-up venture. If a venture capitalist or even an angel investor were involved, they would require a board seat, in which case the use of a board of advisors would not likely be acceptable and liability protection would be necessary.

Most recently there has been some controversy regarding safety for employees in home-based businesses. The government's response has been that the company is responsible for the safety or health violations in home-based offices. The best protection for entrepreneurs operating home-based businesses is to write handbooks with stated policies on home office safety.

Seeking advice from an insurance agent is often difficult because the agent is trying to sell insurance. However, there are specialists at universities or the Small Business Administration who can provide this advice at little or no cost.

CONTRACTS

The entrepreneur, in starting a new venture, will be involved in a number of negotiations and *contracts* with vendors, landlords, and clients. A contract is a legally enforceable agreement between two or more parties as long as certain conditions are met. Table 6.4 identifies these conditions and the outcomes (breaches of contract) should one party not live up to the terms of the contract. It is very important for the entrepreneur to understand the fundamental issues related to contracts while also recognizing the need for a lawyer in many of these negotiations.

contract   A legally binding agreement between two parties

Often business deals are concluded with a handshake. Ordering supplies, lining up financing, reaching an agreement with a partner, and so on, are common situations in which a handshake consummates the deal. Usually, when things are operating smoothly, this procedure is sufficient. However, if there are disagreements, the entrepreneur may find that there is no deal and that he or she may be liable for something never intended. The courts generally provide some guidelines based on precedence of cases. One rule is to never rely on a handshake if the deal cannot be completed within one year. For example, a company that trains salespeople asked

---

TABLE 6.4   Contract Conditions and Results of a Breach of Contract

Contract Conditions

- An offer is made. It can be oral or written but is not binding until voluntary acceptance of offer is given.
- Voluntary acceptance of offer.
- Consideration (something of value) is given by both parties.
- Both parties are competent and/or have the right to negotiate for their firms.
- Contract must be legal. Any illegal activities under a contract are not binding. An example might be gambling.
- Any sales of $500 or more must be in writing.

Results of a Contract Breach

- The party in violation of a contract may be required to live up to the agreement or pay damages.
- If one party fails to live up to its end of a contract, the second party may also agree to drop the matter and thus not live up to the agreement as well. This is referred to as contract restitution.

another firm to produce videotapes used in the training. The training firm was asked to promise to use the tapes only for its own sales force and not to sell the tapes to others. Some time after the tapes were produced, this firm began to produce and sell the tapes under a newly formed company. The original developer of the tapes brought suit, and the courts ruled that an oral agreement for more than one year is not enforceable. The only way that this could have been prevented was if the copying firm had signed a contract.

In addition to the one-year rule of thumb, the courts insist that a written contract exist for all transactions over $500. Even a quote on a specified number of parts from a manufacturer may not be considered a legal contract. For example, if an entrepreneur asked for and received a quote for 10 items and then ordered only one item, the seller would not have to sell that item at the original quoted price unless a written contract existed. If the items totaled over $500, even the quoted price could be changed without a written contract.

Most sellers would not want to try to avoid their obligations in the above example. However, unusual circumstances may arise that force the seller to change his or her mind. Thus, the safest way to conduct business deals is with a written contract, especially if the amount of the deal is over $500 and is likely to extend beyond one year.

Any deal involving real estate must be in writing to be valid. Leases, rentals, and purchases all necessitate some type of written agreement.

Although a lawyer might be necessary in very complicated or large transactions, the entrepreneur cannot always afford one. Therefore, it is helpful for the entrepreneur to understand the four essential items in an agreement to provide the best legal protection.[21]

1. All of the parties involved should be named and their specific roles in the transaction specified (e.g., buyer, seller, consultant, client).
2. The transaction should be described in detail (e.g., exact location of land, dates, units, place of delivery, payor for transportation).
3. The exact value of the transaction should be specified (e.g., installment payment with finance charges).
4. Obtain signature(s) of the person(s) involved in the deal.

IN REVIEW

Summary

This chapter explores some of the major legal concerns regarding intellectual property of the entrepreneur. The problems with intellectual property have become more complicated with the growth of the Internet. It is important for the entrepreneur to seek legal advice in making any intellectual property legal decisions such as patents, trademarks, copyrights, and trade secrets. Lawyers have specialties that can provide the entrepreneur with the most appropriate advice under the circumstances. There are also resources identified in the chapter that should be considered before hiring an attorney. Some of this information can save time and money for the entrepreneur.

A patent requires a patent attorney, who assists the entrepreneur in completing an application to the Patent and Trademark Office with the history and description of the invention, as well as claims for its usefulness. Patent fees will vary but in general will cost about $2,000. An assessment of the existing patent(s) will help to ascertain whether infringement is likely and to evaluate the possibilities of modifying the patented product or licensing the rights from the holder of the patent.

A trademark may be a word, symbol, design, or some combination, or a slogan or sound that identifies the source of certain goods or services. Trademarks give the entrepreneur certain benefits as long as the following four requirements are met: (1) completion of the written application form, (2) submission of a drawing of the mark, (3) submission of five specimens showing actual use of the mark, and (4) payment of the required fee.

Copyrights protect original works of authorship. Copyrights are registered with the Library of Congress and do not usually require an attorney. Copyrights have become especially relevant to computer software firms and to firms using the Internet. With the rapid growth in technology legal protection has lagged and only more recently has been recognized as an important issue among legislators.

Licensing is a viable means of starting a business using someone else's product, name, information, and so on. It is also an important strategy that the entrepreneur can use to expand the business without extensive risk or large investments.

The entrepreneur should also be sensitive to possible product safety and liability requirements. Careful scrutiny of possible product problems, as well as insurance, can reduce the risk. Other risks relating to property insurance, life insurance, health insurance, workers' compensation, and bonding should be evaluated to ascertain the most cost-effective program for the entrepreneur.

Contracts are an important part of the transactions that the entrepreneur will make. As a rule of thumb, oral agreements are invalid for deals over one year and over $500. In addition, all real estate transactions must be in writing to be valid. It is important in a written agreement to identify all the parties and their respective roles, to describe the transaction in detail, to specify the value of the deal, and to obtain the signatures of the persons with whom you are doing business.

Questions for Discussion

1. What is intellectual property and why is it considered an asset to a company?
2. Patents are often imitated, thus raising a much-debated issue as to their relevance. What can an entrepreneur do to protect his or her product? What procedures must be followed to file for a patent?
3. Discuss the appropriateness of a disclosure document.
4. Using examples, discuss the differences among the four categories of trademarks. What are the benefits of a trademark to an entrepreneur?
5. Discuss the pros and cons of legislation that would protect information published on the Web.
6. What are the advantages and disadvantages of starting a business as a licensee?
7. What are the essential ingredients of an acceptable written contract?

Key Terms

contract

copyright

disclosure document

intellectual property

licensing

patent

product safety and liability

trade secret

trademark

More Information—Net Addresses in This Chapter

Biz Women
www.bizwomen.com

Biz Starters Online
www.bizstarters.com/

Business Resource Center
www.morebusiness.com

Domain Name Search
www.domainsarefree.com/

Dunn & Bradstreet Information Service
www.dnb.com

Entrepreneur's Electronic Resource Center
www.enterprise.org/enet/index.html

Entrepreneurs on the Web
www.entrepreneur-web.com/

IBM Intellectual Property Network (free search site)
www.patent.net/index.html

Idea Cafe
www.ideacafe.com

Inventor Information
www.patentcafe.com/smallbiz/café/index.html

Small Business Administration
www.sbaonline.sba.gov/

Small Business Advisor
www.openmarket.com/

Small Business Resource Center
www.smallbusinessresources.com/

U.S. Patent and Trademark Office
www.uspto.gov patents world.std.com

World Wide Yellow Pages
www.yellow.com

Selected Readings

Adams, P. (1996). *155 Legal Do's (and Don'ts) for the Small Business.* New York: John Wiley and Sons.

This book discusses a long list of legal issues that require the entrepreneur's attention. Although many of these are unlikely to affect many start-ups and small businesses, it is valuable to be aware of what to do and what to avoid.

Battersby, G. J.; and C. W. Grimes. (1996). *A Primer on Technology Licensing.* Stamford CT: Kent Press.

The licensing of technologic intellectual property is a big business today. Large and small companies may use licensing to generate revenue or to start a new venture. This book provides the basics involved in technology licensing.

Bauman, A. (October 1992). Strictly Confidential. *Entrepreneur,* pp. 126–31.

The decision of whether or not to share sensitive information with employees can be difficult for an entrepreneur. Letting employees in on sensitive information can be a boon to the venture, yet opens the door to possible problems. Safeguards that can minimize these problems are presented and discussed.

Carey, J. (November 22, 1999). Patent Reform Pending. *Business Week*, pp. 74–77.

Congress is considering reforms to patent laws primarily based on the changes taking place with technology products and services. Many independent inventors are concerned over this legislation because they believe the new reforms will give more power to the big companies.

Dorr, R. C.; and C. H. Munch. (1995). *Protecting Trade Secrets, Patents, Copyrights, and Trademarks*, 2nd ed. New York: John Wiley & Sons.

This is a comprehensive source on key intellectual property assets. It takes the reader through a step-by-step procedure to register for any of the above items and indicates what to look out for in case of a lawsuit. There is also some discussion of unfair competition, personal liability, and advertising legal risks.

France, M.; and S. Siwolop. (October 21, 1996). How to Skin a Copycat. *Business Week*, pp. 4–7.

Small businesses are particularly vulnerable to knock-offs because of their limited resources. A number of examples with effective strategies that can be used to fight knock-offs are presented.

Henry, T. (October 16, 1996). Protecting the Corporate Jewels. *The Indiana Lawyer*, p. 23.

Entrepreneurs and small business owners often ignore intellectual property rights that they should have or that belong to others. A simple explanation and review of trade secrets, patents, trademarks, and copyrights are provided.

Manley, M. (June 1986). Let's Shake on That. *Inc.*, pp. 131–2.

Courts are usually unwilling to enforce oral agreements. Thus, as the article points out, it is important to get something in writing even if it is a note, telegram, letter, or receipt. The written item should include the names of the parties, a description of the transaction, the value of the deal, and signatures.

Mergenhagen, P. (June 1995). Product Liability: Who Sues? *American Demographics*, pp. 48–54.

The number of people who are suing businesses because of injury from products is increasing. Any firm that is marketing a product subject to these laws should take care in new product development and in making any unsubstantiated advertising claims.

Oz, E. (July–August 1995). Software Intellectual Property Protection Alternatives. *Journal of Systems Management*, pp. 50–58.

The protection of software as intellectual property is the focus of this article. Unlike other creations, the law allows developers to protect software as a patent, trade secret, or copyright. The advantages and disadvantages of these alternatives with regard to software protection are discussed.

Patent and Trademark Office, U.S. Department of Commerce. (May 1992). *General Information Concerning Patents*. Washington, DC: U.S. Government Printing Office.

Provides a general overview of the operations of the Patent and Trademark Office and the process required to file for a patent. Useful to inventors, students, and others who may be interested in learning how the system functions.

Steingold, F. S. (1998). *Legal Guide for Starting and Running a Small Business (Vol 1)*. Berkeley, CA: Nolo Press.

This is a practitioner-oriented guidebook that covers various legal issues important for small business formation and operation.

Endnotes

1. See *The Jerusalem Post* (April 11, 1999), Economics Section, p. 10; and *Strategy Week.Com* (December 1, 1999), online interview with Daniel Schreiber, CEO cSafe Ltd.
2. K. Millonzi and W. G. Passannante, "Beware of the Pirates: How to Protect Intellectual Property," *Risk Management* (August 1996), pp. 39–42.

3. See U.S. Department of Commerce, Patent and Trademark Office, *Patents* (Washington, DC: U.S. Government Printing Office, 1992); and M. Mann and P. Canary, "Protecting Innovation through Patents," *Business and Economic Review* (January–March 1993), pp. 25–27.

4. "Memo to U.S. Inventors: File Early," *Business Week* (January 29, 1996), p. 73.

5. B. Einhorn and L. Himelstein, "Is This Any Way to Dress Up for an IPO?" *Business Week* (October 11, 1999), p. 58.

6. S. Herhold, "Patents Emerge as Online Battleground," *San Jose Mercury News* (July 18, 1999), pp. B1, B3.

7. A. Baum, "Overlooking the Basics Causes Disaster for Clients: How to Choose, Search for and Register a Trademark," *New York Law Journal* (April 12, 1993), p. 4.

8. D. A. Burge, *Patent and Trademark Tactics and Practice*, 2nd ed. (New York: John Wiley & Sons, 1984), pp. 124–5.

9. S. Garland, "Whose Info Is It, Anyway?" *Business Week* (September 13, 1999), pp. 114, 118.

10. T. Husch, "Protecting Your Ideas," *Nation's Business* (September 1991), p. 62

11. A. Bauman, "Strictly Confidential," *Entrepreneur* (October 1992), pp. 126–31.

12. T. Owens, "A Contractual Approach to Partnering," *Small Business Reports* (July 1991), pp. 29–40.

13. "Disney Sets the Gold Standard," *Nations' Business* (August 1995), p. 21.

14. "A Disturbance in the Force?" *Discount Store News* (August 1999), p. A6.

15. T. Howard, "B.K.Emon Strikes," *Brandweek* (July 12, 1999), p. 3; and E. Walker, "How Pokemon Blitz Became Nightmare for Burger King," *The Miami Herald* (January 9, 2000), pp. 1E, 4E.

16. P. Furman, "Microwave Flop Singes Hot Toy Firm," *Crain's New York Business* (April 17, 1995), pp. 17–19; and "Just Toys Named Licensee for Rollerjam," *Dow Jones Interactive Publications Library* (October 14, 1999), p. 1.

17. A. Hornaday, "Cashing In on the Little Green Turtles," *Working Woman* (February 1992), pp. 48–53.

18. K. Atuahene-Gima, "Buying Technology for Product Development in Smaller Firms," *Industrial Marketing Management* (August 1993), pp. 223–32.

19. C. Johnson, "Product Liability Payouts to Be Told to Federal Agency," *Business Insurance* (January 14, 1991), pp. 3, 47.

20. D. Lenckus, "Managing New Product Liability Exposures," *Business Insurance* (May 6, 1996), pp. 32–33.

21. M. Manley, "Let's Shake on That," *Inc.* (June 1986), pp. 131–2.

7

The Business Plan: Creating and Starting the Venture

LEARNING OBJECTIVES

1. To define what the business plan is, who prepares it, who reads it, and how it is evaluated.

2. To understand the scope and value of the business plan to investors, lenders, employees, suppliers, and customers.

3. To identify information needs and sources for business planning.

4. To enhance awareness of the ability of the Internet as an information resource and marketing tool.

5. To present examples and a step-by-step explanation of the business plan.

6. To present helpful questions for the entrepreneur at each stage of the planning process.

7. To understand how to monitor the business plan.

MARTHA STEWART

The business plan, although often criticized for being "dreams of glory," is probably the single most important document to the entrepreneur at the start-up stage. Potential investors are not likely to consider investing in a new venture until the business plan has been completed. In addition, the business plan helps maintain a perspective for the entrepreneur of what needs to be accomplished. No one knows this better than Martha Stewart, who has achieved great success through careful business planning and strategy that required integrating business objectives across a multitude of businesses.[1]

www.marthastewart.com

Martha Stewart—born Martha Kostyra in Jersey City and raised in Nutley, New Jersey—has been an entrepreneur for most of her adult life. Although she actively modeled during her college years at Barnard College, she became a stockbroker upon graduation. There she gained important knowledge about the stock market that proved invaluable later in her career when she decided to take her venture public. Even as a stockbroker her passion for finding new and creative ways to cook, decorate, garden, and entertain consumed most of her free time. Not able to find existing sources for many of her questions on these topics, she believed that many others would benefit from her newfound knowledge. Thus, in 1982 she published her first how-to book, *Entertaining*, with the publishing company Clarkson Potter. This book has sold more than 500,000 copies in its now 30 printings. Following the success of this first book she published a number of other titles, all by Clarkson Potter, on such topics as cooking, gardening, wedding planning, and Christmas decorating.

Each new idea added to the multitude of existing income-generating products and services, which made the need for professional management and control more and more evident. Martha also saw the opportunity to leverage her success in publishing how-to books in other mediums such as magazines, radio, and television. She was also ready to publish her own magazine, which would highlight many of the topics that had consumed her earlier success in book publishing. At that point a business plan was needed to provide direction and integration of all the existing business products and services as well as some direction for the future of these efforts, especially with the addition of a new magazine, which would need some external funding.

In 1991, armed with a business plan, she created a multimedia company, Martha Stewart Living Omnimedia, which linked all of the various products and services under one roof with Martha as its leader and inspiration. This plan was also the basis for the introduction of her monthly magazine, *Martha Stewart Living*. The lifestyle magazine was partially funded and published by Time Publishing Ventures, Inc. (a subsidiary of Time Warner, Inc.). Following this success her business expanded into a television program, a syndicated "ask Martha" weekly newspaper column, a radio program, a website, marthastewart.com, and guest appearances.

The business plan was based on two primary objectives. First, it was to disseminate how-to information to as many people as possible. Second, it was to turn its customers into doers by offering the merchandise they would need to complete these do-it-yourself projects. Much of this merchandise was to be exclusively distributed through Kmart stores in the United States and Zellers stores in Canada. There has also been other merchandise distributed through such partners as Sears, Jo-Ann Fabrics, and Crafts and Calico Corners stores. Year-end revenue (12/31/00) reached $285.8 million and net income of $21.3 million.

On October 19, 1999, Martha Stewart Living Omnimedia Inc. went public and quickly dispelled any doubts about being a single celebrity corporation. The stock opened with an IPO of $18 per share and closed over $35 on the first day. The funds raised in the IPO were to be used to develop new opportunities and revenue sources in its main business areas: publishing, television, direct merchandising, and the Internet. About $45 million of the funds raised were also to be used to buy back stock held by Time Publishing Ventures, which had financed the launch of her magazine in 1991.

Although there remain concerns about the future of a company that is primarily owned by one person, Martha Stewart is certainly recognized as one of the most successful entrepreneurs in the 1990s. Her passion and creativity, as well as understanding of the importance of good planning, should continue to lead her to growth and success in the new millennium.

PLANNING AS PART OF THE BUSINESS OPERATION

Before beginning a discussion of the *business plan*, it is important for the reader to understand the different types of plans that may be part of any business operation. Planning is a process that never ends for a business. It is extremely important in the early stages of any new venture when the entrepreneur will need to prepare a preliminary business plan. The plan will become finalized as the entrepreneur has a better sense of the market, the product or services to be marketed, the management team, and the financial needs of the venture. As the venture evolves from an early start-up to a mature business, planning will continue as management seeks to meet its short-term or long-term business goals.

business plan   Written document describing all relevant internal and external elements and strategies for starting a new venture

For any given organization, it is possible to find financial plans, marketing plans, human resource plans, production plans, and sales plans, to name a few. Plans may be short-term or long-term, or they may be strategic or operational. Plans will also differ in scope depending on the type of business or the anticipated size of the start-up operation. Even though they may serve different functions, all of these plans have one important purpose: to provide guidance and structure to management in a rapidly changing market environment.

WHAT IS THE BUSINESS PLAN?

The business plan is a written document prepared by the entrepreneur that describes all the relevant external and internal elements involved in starting a new venture. It is often an integration of functional plans such as marketing, finance, manufacturing, and human resources. As in the case of Martha Stewart it addresses the integration and coordination of effective business objectives and strategies when the venture contains a variety of products and services. It also addresses both short-term and long-term decision making for the first three years of operation. Thus, the business plan—or, as it is sometimes referred to, the game plan or road map—answers the questions, Where am I now? Where am I going? How will I get there? Potential investors, suppliers, and even customers will request or require a business plan.

If we think of the business plan as a road map, we might better understand its significance. Let's suppose you were trying to decide whether to drive from Boston to Los Angeles (mission or goal) in a motor home. There are a number of possible routes, each requiring different time frames and costs. Like the entrepreneur, the traveler must make some important decisions and gather information before preparing the plan.

The travel plan would consider external factors such as emergency car repair, weather conditions, road conditions, sights to see, available campgrounds, and so on. These factors are basically uncontrollable by the traveler but must be considered in the plan, just as the entrepreneur would consider external factors such as new regulations, competition, social changes, changes in consumer needs, or new technology.

On the other hand, the traveler does have some idea of how much money is available, how much time he or she has, and the choices of highways, roads, campgrounds, sights, and so forth. Similarly, the entrepreneur has some control over manufacturing, marketing, and personnel in the new venture.

The traveler should consider all these factors in determining what roads to take, what campgrounds to stay in, how much time to spend in selected locations, how much time and money to allow for vehicle maintenance, who will drive, and so on. Thus, the travel plan responds to three questions: Where am I now? Where am I going? How do I get there? Then the traveler in our example—or the entrepreneur, the subject of our book—will be able to determine how much money will be needed from existing sources or new sources to achieve the plan.

We saw in the opening example of this chapter how Martha Stewart used the business plan to address these questions across a multitude of products and services. The functional elements of the business plan are discussed here but are also represented as separate chapters in this book.

WHO SHOULD WRITE THE PLAN?

The business plan should be prepared by the entrepreneur; however, he or she may consult with many other sources in its preparation. Lawyers, accountants, marketing consultants, and engineers are useful in the preparation of the plan. Some of the above sources can be found through services offered by the Small Business Administration (SBA), Service Core of Retired Executives (SCORE), Small Business Development Centers (SBDC), universities, and friends or relatives. The Internet also provides a wealth of information as well as actual sample templates or outlines for business planning. Most of these sources are free of charge or have minimal fees for workshop attendance or to purchase or download any information. In many instances entrepreneurs

FIGURE 7.1	Skills Assessment			
Skills	Excellent	Good	Fair	Poor
Accounting/taxes				
Planning				
Forecasting				
Marketing research				
Sales				
People management				
Product design				
Legal issues				
Organizing				

will actually hire or offer equity (partnership) to another person who might provide the appropriate expertise in preparing the business plan as well as become an important member of the management team.

To help determine whether to hire a consultant or to make use of other resources, the entrepreneur can make an objective assessment of his or her own skills. Figure 7.1 is an illustration of a rating to determine what skills are lacking and by how much. For example, a sales engineer recently designed a new machine that allows a user to send a 10-second personalized message in a greeting card. A primary concern was how best to market the machine: as a promotional tool a firm could use for its distributors, suppliers, shareholders, or employees; or as a retail product for end users. This entrepreneur, in assessing his skills, rated himself as excellent in product design and sales, good in organizing, and only fair or poor in the remaining skills. To supplement the defined weaknesses the entrepreneur found a partner who could contribute those skills that were lacking or weak. Through such an assessment, the entrepreneur can identify what skills are needed and where to obtain them.

SCOPE AND VALUE OF THE BUSINESS PLAN—WHO READS THE PLAN?

The business plan may be read by employees, investors, bankers, venture capitalists, suppliers, customers, advisors, and consultants. Whoever is expected to read the plan can often affect its actual content and focus. Since each of these groups reads the plan for different purposes, the entrepreneur must be prepared to address all their issues and concerns. In some ways, the business plan must try to satisfy the needs of everyone; whereas in the actual marketplace the entrepreneur's product will be trying to meet the needs of selected groups of customers.

However, there are probably three perspectives that should be considered when preparing the plan. First is the perspective of the entrepreneur, who understands better than anyone else the creativity and technology involved in the new venture. The entrepreneur must be able to clearly articulate what the venture is all about. Second is the marketing perspective. Too often, an entrepreneur will consider only the product or technology and not whether someone would buy it. Entrepreneurs must try to view their business through the eyes of their customer. This customer orientation is discussed further in Chapter 8. Third, the entrepreneur should try to view his or her business through the eyes of the investor. Sound financial projections are required; if the entrepreneur does not have the skills to prepare this information, then outside sources can be of assistance.[2]

The depth and detail in the business plan depend on the size and scope of the proposed new venture. An entrepreneur planning to market a new portable computer will need a comprehensive business plan, largely because of the nature of the product and market. An entrepreneur who plans to open a retail video store will not need the comprehensive coverage required by a new computer manufacturer. A new e-commerce business however may require a very different focus, particularly on how to market the website that will offer the goods and services. Thus, differences in the scope of the business plan may depend on whether the new venture is a service, involves manufacturing, or is a consumer good or industrial product. The size of the market, competition, and potential growth may also affect the scope of the business plan.

The business plan is valuable to the entrepreneur, potential investors, or even new personnel, who are trying to familiarize themselves with the venture, its goals, and objectives. The business plan is important to these people because:

- It helps determine the viability of the venture in a designated market.
- It provides guidance to the entrepreneur in organizing his or her planning activities.
- It serves as an important tool in helping to obtain financing.

Potential investors are very particular about what should be included in the business plan. Even if some of the information is based on assumptions, the thinking process required to complete the plan is a valuable experience for the entrepreneur since it forces him or her to assess such things as cash flow and cash requirements. In addition, the thinking process takes the entrepreneur into the future, leading him or her to consider important issues that could impede the road to success.

The process also provides a self-assessment by the entrepreneur. Usually, he or she feels that the new venture is assured of success. However, the planning process forces the entrepreneur to bring objectivity to the idea and reflect on such questions as: "Does the idea make sense? Will it work? Who is my customer? Does it satisfy customer needs? What kind of protection can I get against imitation by competitors? Can I manage such a business? Whom will I compete with?" This self-evaluation is similar to role playing, requiring the entrepreneur to think through various scenarios and consider obstacles that might prevent the venture from succeeding. The process allows the entrepreneur to plan ways to avoid such obstacles. It may even be possible that, after preparing the business plan, the entrepreneur will realize the obstacles cannot be avoided or overcome. Hence, the venture may be terminated while still on paper. Although this certainly is not the most desirable conclusion, it would be much better to terminate the business endeavor before investing further time and money.

HOW DO POTENTIAL LENDERS AND INVESTORS EVALUATE THE PLAN?

As stated earlier there are a number of cookbook or computer-generated software packages or samples on the Internet that are available to assist the entrepreneur in preparing a business plan. Some of these Internet websites can be found listed at the end of the chapter. These sources, however, should be used only to assist in its preparation, since the business plan should address the needs of all the potential readers or evaluators. As stated above, these needs may vary considerably and, thus, could result in rejection of the entrepreneur's request if not addressed accordingly in the business plan.

It is conceivable that the entrepreneur will prepare a preliminary business plan from his or her own personal viewpoint without consideration of the constituencies that will ultimately read and evaluate the plan's feasibility. As the entrepreneur becomes aware of who will read the plan, appropriate changes will be necessary. For example, one constituency may be suppliers, who may want to see a business plan before signing a contract to either produce components or finished products or even supply large quantities of materials on consignment. Customers may also want to review the plan before buying a product that may require significant long-term commitment, such as a high-technology telecommunications system. In both cases the business plan should consider the needs of these constituencies, who may pay more attention to the experience of the entrepreneur(s) and their projection of the marketplace.

Another group that may evaluate the plan are the potential suppliers of capital. These lenders or investors will likely vary in terms of their needs and requirements in the business plan. For example, lenders are primarily interested in the ability of the new venture to pay back the debt including interest within a designated period of time. Banks want facts with an objective analysis of the business opportunity and all the potential risks inherent in the new venture. Gilda and Amir Salmon found this important in their business plan for a hair salon. In fact, their objectivity and longer-term projections (five years) led to the bank loaning them an additional $5,000. Because of this venture's ability to meet its short-term goals with a strong likelihood of substantially increasing profits in the future, the bank was favorably impressed and willingly loaned them the funds.[3] Typically, lenders focus on the four Cs of credit: character, cash flow, collateral, and equity contribution. Basically, what this means is that lenders want the business plan to reflect the entrepreneur's credit history, the ability of the entrepreneur to meet debt and interest payments (cash flow), the collateral or tangible assets being secured for the loan, and the amount of personal equity that the entrepreneur has invested.

Investors, particularly venture capitalists, have different needs since they are providing large sums of capital for ownership (equity) and the expected cashing out within five to seven years. Investors often place more emphasis on the entrepreneur's character than lenders and often spend much time conducting background checks. This is important not only from a financial perspective but also because the venture capitalist will play an important role in the actual management of the business. Hence, they want to make sure that the entrepreneur(s) is compliant and willing to accept this involvement. These investors will also demand high rates of return and will thus focus on the market and financial projections during this critical five- to seven-year period.

In preparing the business plan, it is important for entrepreneurs to consider the needs of these external sources and not merely provide their own perspective. This will keep the plan from being an internalized document that emphasizes only the technical advantages of a product or market advantages of a service, without consideration of the feasibility of meeting market goals and long-term financial projections.

Entrepreneurs, in sharing their business plan with others, often become paranoid that their idea will be stolen by one of the external readers. Most external advisors and potential investors are bound by a professional code of ethics, and the entrepreneur should not be deterred from seeking external advice (see Ethics box).

PRESENTING THE PLAN

It is often necessary for an entrepreneur to orally present the business plan before an audience of potential investors. In this typical forum the entrepreneur would be expected

PROTECTING YOUR BUSINESS IDEA

One of the serious concerns that entrepreneurs voice relates to how to protect their business ideas, when they are also advised to share their business plans with many friends and associates. Since these plans provide comprehensive discussion of the new venture, the concern is understandable. Most individuals who are asked to comment and review a business plan would act in an ethical and professional manner in providing any advice to entrepreneurs. However, there are also many examples of situations where a family member, friend, or business associate has been accused of "stealing" an idea.

The best strategy for an entrepreneur, outside of seeking the advice of an attorney, is to ask all readers who are not representing a professional firm (such as a venture capitalist) to sign a non-compete or nondisclosure agreement. An example of such an agreement can be found in Chapter 6. Those representing a professional organization (such as a bank or venture capitalist) need not be asked to complete a nondisclosure form since they would be insulted and would be inclined to reject the venture before they have even read the plan.

to provide a short (perhaps 20 minutes or half-hour) presentation of the business plan. For example, the MIT forum is held monthly with entrepreneurs selected (based on review of business plans) to give a short 30-minute presentation of their business plans before an audience, mostly of venture capitalists and private investors. The entrepreneurs are expected to "sell" their business concept in this short time period with the audience given the opportunity to ask difficult and penetrating questions. However, the benefit is that they are presenting in one place, to a number of firms or individuals who could immediately decide they like the plan and request further negotiation, leading to a final investment decision. Some investors describe these plans as the elevator plan. It's analogous to a situation where an entrepreneur would get on an elevator with an investor and try to persuade that he or she is a good investment before the elevator reaches its final destination.

It is also likely that a venture capitalist or angel group would ask the entrepreneur to present to their partners before making a final decision on whether to invest. In all of these instances the entrepreneur must decide what to say in this short time frame. Typically the focus is on why this is a good opportunity, an overview of the marketing program (addresses how the opportunity will convert to reality), and the results of this effort (sales and profits). Concluding remarks might reflect the recognized risks and how the entrepreneur plans to address them. Remember, this effort is really designed to sell the investors on why this would be a good investment for them.

INFORMATION NEEDS

Before committing time and energy to preparing a business plan, the entrepreneur should do a quick feasibility study of the business concept to see if there are any possible barriers to success. The information, obtainable from many sources, should focus on marketing, finance, and production. The Internet, discussed below, can be a valuable resource for the entrepreneur. Before beginning the feasibility study, the entrepreneur should clearly define the goals and objectives of the venture. These goals help define what needs to be done and how it will be accomplished. These goals and objectives also provide a framework for the business plan, marketing plan, and financial plan.

Goals and objectives that are too general or that are not feasible make the business plan difficult to control and implement. An example illustrates this point.

Jim McCurry and Gary Kusin had a great concept: a retail store that would sell computer software and video games to the home market rather than the business market. At the time of their brainstorm they discovered that there were no retailers trying to meet the needs of this target market. Thus, their idea was a virtually untapped market niche.[4]

The plan they prepared was weak and overly optimistic in terms of reaching any of their goals. Fortunately for them, Gary was able to turn to an old family friend, Ross Perot, for advice on their business plan. Ross shot holes in their sloppily written business plan but imparted new learning for these entrepreneurs as to what was a good plan. For example, they had planned to open 12 stores in the first month, with many other openings scheduled throughout the year and across the country. They had no idea how or where these stores would be opened. With their newfound supporter and partner Ross Perot, who liked the business concept and was willing to guarantee their $3 million line of credit with a bank for one-third equity, the two entrepreneurs restructured their plan and began pursuit of more reasonable goals. Their first store was opened in Dallas in 1983. They christened their company Babbage's, after the 19th century mathematician Charles Babbage, who was credited with designing the first computing machine. The company, which achieved sales of over $250 million, was acquired by Barnes and Noble in 1998.

The preceding example illustrates the lack of feasible business goals and an understanding of how these goals would be achieved. These two entrepreneurs were lucky to have a connection with someone who could provide them with direction. Not all entrepreneurs are as fortunate. The important lesson is that the business plan cannot be taken lightly and that it must reflect reasonable goals.

Market Information

One of the initial important elements of information needed by the entrepreneur is the market potential for the product or service. In order to ascertain the size of the market, it is first necessary for the entrepreneur to define the market. For example, is the product most likely to be purchased by men or women? people of high income or low income? rural or urban dwellers? highly educated or less educated people? A well-defined target market will make it easier to project market size and subsequent market goals for the new venture. For example, an entrepreneur has developed a unique training aid for golfers. This product allows the user to practice in the basement or garage during the off-season. The product will determine distance, slice, or hook of a drive. The product would thus appeal to a well-defined market: avid golfers who are interested in improving their score.

To assess the total market potential, the entrepreneur should consider trade associations, government reports, the Internet, and published studies. In some instances, this information is readily available.[5] In our golfing example, the entrepreneur should be able to estimate the size of the market from secondary data. Golf magazines and associations would provide information on the golf market by geographic area. Other demographic information about this market is also likely to be available. Information from golf stores or from pro shops regarding training aids would also be helpful. Contacting a few of these stores to discuss training aids could provide valuable insights for the business plan. From this, the entrepreneur would be able to determine an approximate size of the market.

Operations Information Needs

The relevance of a feasibility study of the manufacturing operations depends on the nature of the business. Most of the information needed can be obtained through direct contact with the appropriate source. The entrepreneur may need information on the following:

- *Location.* The company's location and its accessibility to customers, suppliers, and distributors need to be determined.
- *Manufacturing Operations.* Basic machine and assembly operations need to be identified, as well as whether any of these operations would be subcontracted and by whom.
- *Raw Materials.* The raw materials needed and suppliers' names, addresses, and costs should be determined.
- *Equipment.* The equipment needed should be listed and whether it will be purchased or leased.
- *Labor Skills.* Each unique skill needed, the number of personnel in each skill, pay rate, and an assessment of where and how these skills will be obtained should be determined.
- *Space.* The total amount of space needed should be determined, including whether the space will be owned or leased.
- *Overhead.* Each item needed to support manufacturing—such as tools, supplies, utilities, and salaries—should be determined.

Most of the above information should be incorporated directly into the business plan. Each item may require some research, but each is necessary to those who will assess the business plan and consider funding the proposal.

Financial Information Needs

Before preparing the business plan, the entrepreneur must have a complete evaluation of the profitability of the venture. The assessment will primarily tell potential investors if the business will be profitable, how much money will be needed to launch the business and meet short-term financial needs, and how this money will be obtained (e.g., stock and debt).

There are traditionally three areas of financial information that will be needed to ascertain the feasibility of the new venture: (1) expected sales and expense figures for at least the first three years, (2) cash flow figures for the first three years, and (3) current balance sheet figures and pro forma balance sheets for the first three years.

Determination of the expected sales and expense figures for each of the first 12 months and each subsequent year is based on the market information discussed earlier. Each expense item should be identified and given on a monthly basis for the year. Estimates of cash flow consider the ability of the new venture to meet expenses at designated times of the year. The cash flow forecast should identify the beginning cash, expected accounts receivable and other receipts, and all disbursements on a monthly basis for the entire year.

Current balance sheet figures provide the financial conditions of the business at any particular time. They identify the assets of the business, the liabilities (what is owed), and the investment made by the owner or other partners.

USING THE INTERNET AS A RESOURCE TOOL

The changing world of technology offers new opportunities for entrepreneurs to be able to access information for many business activities efficiently, expediently, and at very little cost. The *Internet* can serve as an important source of information in the preparation of the business plan for such segments as the industry analysis, competitor analysis, and measurement of market potential, to name a few. Entrepreneurs will also find the Internet a valuable resource in later-stage planning and decision making. Besides being a business intelligence resource, the Internet also provides opportunities for actually marketing the new venture's products and services through the preparation of a home page or website. Some of these opportunities will be discussed below. However, it is advised that entrepreneurs consult a library or some of the sources at the end of this chapter to gain the necessary knowledge to maximize their use of the Internet.

Internet   Computer online service providing important sources of information for starting a new venture

A website or home page typically describes a firm's history, existing products or services, background of the founders or management team, and any other information that might create a favorable image for any Internet viewer. Thus, the website can be a vehicle for advertising or for the direct marketing of the venture's products and services. Incoming orders can actually be processed through e-mail or the online service. Telephone numbers and addresses can also be provided for those interested in a sales call or more information. Many new ventures are using the website to increase sales contacts and to enhance their opportunities to reach potential customers.[6]

An entrepreneur should access competitors' websites to gain more knowledge about their strategy in the marketplace. Internet services are not costly and would be an important vehicle for the entrepreneur to gather information about the market, competition, and customers as well as to distribute, advertise, and sell company products and services.

In addition to websites, the entrepreneur can also investigate newsgroups to gather information anonymously from experts and customers on competitors and market needs. There are thousands of newsgroups online that cover a wide range of topics. These newsgroups represent online customers having the same interest in a topic (for example, gourmet food). Using the Usenet, which represents the newsgroups on the Internet, the entrepreneur can use key words to identify the most appropriate newsgroups. These newsgroups represent potential customers who can be asked specific questions on their needs, competitive products, and potential interest in the new venture's products and services. Individuals who are members of the newsgroups will then respond to these questions, providing valuable information to the entrepreneur.

Compared with alternative sources the entrepreneur need only make a small investment in hardware and software to be ready to use these online services. With the continuous improvements and modifications in the Internet, the opportunities for the entrepreneur in planning the start-up or the growth of a venture will be invaluable.

WRITING THE BUSINESS PLAN

The business plan could take more than 200 hours to prepare, depending on the experience and knowledge of the entrepreneur as well as the purpose it is intended to serve. It should be comprehensive enough to give any potential investor a complete picture and understanding of the new venture and will help the entrepreneur clarify his or her thinking about the business.

Many entrepreneurs incorrectly estimate the length of time that an effective plan will take to prepare. Once the process has begun, however, the entrepreneur will realize that it is invaluable in sorting out the business functions of a new venture.

The outline for a business plan is illustrated in Figure 7.2. Each of the items in the outline is detailed in the following paragraphs of this chapter. Key questions in each section are also appropriately detailed.[7]

Introductory Page

This is the title or cover page that provides a brief summary of the business plan's contents. The introductory page should contain the following:

The name and address of the company.

The name of the entrepreneur(s), telephone number, fax number, e-mail address, and website address if available.

A paragraph describing the company and the nature of the business.

The amount of financing needed. The entrepreneur may offer a package, that is, stock, debt, and so on. However, many venture capitalists prefer to structure this package in their own way.

A statement of the confidentiality of the report. This is for security purposes and is important for the entrepreneur.

This title page sets out the basic concept that the entrepreneur is attempting to develop. Investors consider it important because they can determine the amount of investment needed without having to read through the entire plan. An illustration of this page can be found in Figure 7.3.

Executive Summary

This section of the business plan is prepared after the total plan is written. About two to three pages in length, the executive summary should stimulate the interest of the potential investor. This is a very important section of the business plan and should not be taken lightly by the entrepreneur since the investor uses the summary to determine if the entire business plan is worth reading. Thus, it would highlight in a concise and convincing manner the key points in the business plan.

Although determining what is important in any executive summary would be difficult since every business plan is different, there are a number of significant issues that should be addressed. First, the entrepreneur should briefly describe the business concept. Second, any data that support the opportunity for this venture should be briefly stated. For example, trends and potential growth in the industry should be mentioned. If this were an Internet business, the entrepreneur should state such facts as growth in the number of Internet users, growth in the average amount of time spent on the Internet, and growth in sales dollars generated on the Internet, to name a few. After establishing the reality of the opportunity the executive summary should then state how this opportunity will be pursued. What is the marketing strategy that will be implemented, and how does it differ from others in the market? Next the executive summary should highlight some of the key financial results that can be achieved from the implemented marketing strategy. Important experience of the entrepreneur(s), any important contracts or other legal documents that are in place, and any other information that is felt can assist in selling the business venture to a

FIGURE 7.2 Outline of a Business Plan

I. Introductory Page
   A. Name and address of business
   B. Name(s) and address(es) of principals
   C. Nature of business
   D. Statement of financing needed
   E. Statement of confidentiality of report

II. Executive Summary—Three to four pages summarizing the complete business plan

III. Industry Analysis
   A. Future outlook and trends
   B. Analysis of competitors
   C. Market segmentation
   D. Industry forecasts

IV. Description of Venture
   A. Product(s)
   B. Service(s)
   C. Size of business
   D. Office equipment and personnel
   E. Background of entrepreneurs

V. Production Plan
   A. Manufacturing process (amount subcontracted)
   B. Physical plant
   C. Machinery and equipment
   D. Names of suppliers of raw materials

VI. Marketing Plan
   A. Pricing
   B. Distribution
   C. Promotion
   D. Product forecasts
   E. Controls

VII. Organizational Plan
   A. Form of ownership
   B. Identification of partners or principal shareholders
   C. Authority of principals
   D. Management-team background
   E. Roles and responsibilities of members of organization

VIII. Assessment of Risk
   A. Evaluate weakness of business
   B. New technologies
   C. Contingency plans

IX. Financial Plan
   A. Pro forma income statement
   B. Cash flow projections
   C. Pro forma balance sheet
   D. Break-even analysis
   E. Sources and applications of funds

X. Appendix (contains backup material)
   A. Letters
   B. Market research data
   C. Leases or contracts
   D. Price lists from suppliers

FIGURE 7.3   Sample Introductory Page

KC CLEANING SERVICE

OAK KNOLL ROAD

BOSTON, MA 02167

(617) 96900100

www.cleening.com

Co-owners: Kimberly Peters, Christa Peters

Description of Business:

This business will provide cleaning service on a contract basis to small and medium-sized businesses. Services include cleaning of floors, carpets, draperies, and windows, and regular sweeping, dusting and washing. Contracts will be for one year and will specify the specific services and scheduling for completion of services.

Financing:

Initial financing requested is a $100,000 loan to be paid off over 6 years. This debt will cover office space, office equipment and supplies, two leased vans, advertising, and selling costs.

This report is confidential and is the property of the co-owners listed above. It is intended only for use by the persons to whom it is transmitted, and any reproduction or divulgence of any of its contents without the prior written consent of the company is prohibited.

---

potential investor should also be mentioned. Because the executive summary is limited to two to three pages, it is important for the entrepreneur to ascertain what is important to the audience to whom this plan is directed.

Environmental and Industry Analysis

It is important to put the new venture in a proper context by first conducting an *environmental analysis* to identify trends and changes occurring on a national and international level that may impact the new venture. A fast and effective means of gathering some of these data is through the Internet using websites listed at the end of this chapter. Examples of these environmental factors are:

environmental analysis   Assessment of external uncontrollable variables that may impact the business plan

Economy. The entrepreneur should consider trends in the GNP, unemployment by geographic area, disposable income, and so on.

Culture. An evaluation of cultural changes may consider shifts in the population by demographics, for example, the impact of the baby boomers or the growing elderly population. Shifts in attitudes, such as "Buy American," or trends in safety, health, and nutrition, as well as concern for the environment, may all have an impact on the entrepreneur's business plan.

Technology. Advances in technology are difficult to predict. However, the entrepreneur should consider potential technologic developments determined from resources committed by major industries or the U.S. government. Being in a market that is rapidly changing due to technologic development will require the entrepreneur to make careful short-term marketing decisions as well as to be prepared with contingency plans given any new technologic developments that may affect his or her product or service.

Legal Concerns. There are many important legal issues in starting a new venture; they are discussed in Chapter 6. The entrepreneur should be prepared for any future legislation that may affect the product or service, channel of distribution, price, or promotion strategy. The deregulation of prices, restrictions on media advertising (e.g., ban on cigarette ads or requirements for advertising to children), and safety regulations affecting the product or packaging are examples of legal restrictions that can affect any marketing program.

All the above external factors are generally uncontrollable. However, as indicated, an awareness and assessment of these factors using some of the sources identified can provide strong support for the opportunity and can be invaluable in developing the appropriate marketing strategy.

industry analysis   Reviews industry trends and competitive strategies

Once an assessment of the environment is complete, the entrepreneur should conduct an *industry analysis* that will focus on specific industry trends. Some examples of these factors are:

Industry Demand. Demand as it relates to the industry is often available from published sources. Knowledge of whether the market is growing or declining, the number of new competitors, and possible changes in consumer needs are all important issues in trying to ascertain the potential business that might be achieved by the new venture. The demand for the entrepreneur's product or service will require some additional marketing research that will be discussed in Chapter 8.

Competition. Most entrepreneurs generally face potential threats from larger corporations. The entrepreneur must be prepared for these threats and should be aware of who the competitors are and what their strengths and weaknesses are so that an effective marketing plan can be implemented. Most competitors can be easily identified from experience, trade journal articles, advertisements, websites, or even the yellow pages.

The last part of this section should focus on the specific market, which would include such information as who the customer is and what the business environment is like in the specific market segment and geographic area where the venture will compete. Thus, any differences in any of the above variables that reflect the specific market area in which the new venture will operate must be considered. This information is particularly significant to the preparation of the marketing plan section of the business plan, which is discussed in Chapter 8.

A list of some key questions the entrepreneur should consider for this section of the business plan is described in Figure 7.4.

Description of Venture

The *description of the venture* should be detailed in this section of the business plan. This will enable the investor to ascertain the size and scope of the business. This section should begin with the mission statement or *company mission* of the new venture. This statement basically describes the nature of the business and what the entrepreneur hopes to accomplish with that business. This mission statement or business definition will guide the firm through long-term decision-making. After the mission statement a number of important factors that provide a clear description and understanding of the business venture should be discussed. Key elements are the

description of the venture   Provides complete overview of product(s), services, and operations of new venture

FIGURE 7.4   Critical Issues for Environmental and Industry Analysis

1. What are the major economic, technological, legal, and political trends on a national and international level?
2. What are total industry sales over the past five years?
3. What is anticipated growth in this industry?
4. How many new firms have entered this industry in the past three years?
5. What new products have been recently introduced in this industry?
6. Who are the nearest competitors?
7. How will your business operation be better than this?
8. Are the sales of each of your major competitors growing, declining, or steady?
9. What are the strengths and weaknesses of each of your competitors?
10. What trends are occurring in your specific market area?
11. What is the profile of your customers?
12. How does your customer profile differ from that of your competition?

FIGURE 7.5   Describing the Venture

1. What is the mission of the new venture?
2. What are your reasons for going into business?
3. Why will you be successful in this venture?
4. What development work has been completed to date?
5. What are your product(s) and/or service(s)?
6. Describe the product(s) and/or service(s), including patent, copyright, or trademark status.
7. Where will the business be located?
8. Is your building new? old? in need of renovations? (If renovation needed, state costs.)
9. Is the building leased or owned? (State the terms.)
10. Why is this building and location right for your business?
11. What office equipment will be needed?
12. Will equipment be purchased or leased?
13. What experience do you have and/or will you need to successfully implement the business plan?

product(s) or service(s), the location and size of the business, the personnel and office equipment that will be needed, the background of the entrepreneur(s), and the history of the venture. Figure 7.5 summarizes some of the important questions the entrepreneur needs to answer when preparing this section of the business plan.

Location of any business may be vital to its success, particularly if the business is retail or involves a service. Thus, the emphasis on location in the business plan is a function of the type of business. In assessing the building or space the business will occupy, the entrepreneur may need to evaluate such factors as parking, access from roadways to facility, and access to customers, suppliers, distributors, delivery rates, and town regulations or zoning laws. An enlarged local map may help give the location some perspective with regard to roads, highways, access, and so forth.

Recently an entrepreneur considered opening a new doughnut shop at a location diagonally across from a small shopping mall on a heavily traveled road. Traffic counts indicated a large potential customer base if people would stop for coffee, and so on, on their way to work. After enlarging a local map, the entrepreneur noted that the morning flow of traffic required drivers to make a left turn into the doughnut shop, crossing the outbound lane. Unfortunately, the roadway was divided by a concrete center strip with no break to allow for a left-hand turn. The only possibility for entry into the shop required the customer to drive down about 400 yards and make a U-turn. It would also be difficult for the customer to get back on the roadway traveling in the right direction. Since the town was unwilling to open the road, the entrepreneur eliminated this site from any further consideration.

This simple assessment of the location, market, and so on, saved the entrepreneur from a potential disaster. Maps that locate customers, competitors, and even alternative locations for a building or site can be helpful in this evaluation. Some of the important questions that might be asked by an entrepreneur are as follows:

How much space is needed?

Should I buy or lease the building?

What is the cost per square foot?

Is the site zoned for commercial use?

What town restrictions exist for signs, parking, and so forth?

Is renovation of the building necessary?

Is the facility accessible to traffic?

Is there adequate parking?

Will the existing facility have room for expansion?

What is the economic and demographic profile of the area?

Is there an adequate labor pool available?

What are local taxes?

Are sewage, electricity, and plumbing adequate?

If the building or site decision involves legal issues, such as a lease, or requires town variances, the entrepreneur should hire a lawyer. Problems relating to regulations and leases can be avoided easily, but under no circumstances should the entrepreneur try to negotiate with the town or a landlord without good legal advice.

Production Plan or Operational Plan

If the new venture is a manufacturing operation, a *production plan* is necessary. This plan should describe the complete manufacturing process. If some or all of the manufacturing process is to be subcontracted, the plan should describe the subcontractor(s), including location, reasons for selection, costs, and any contracts that have been completed. If the manufacturing is to be carried out in whole or in part by the entrepreneur, he or she will need to describe the physical plant layout; the machinery and

---

production plan   Details how product(s) will be manufactured

equipment needed to perform the manufacturing operations; raw materials and suppliers' names, addresses, and terms; costs of manufacturing; and any future capital equipment needs. In a manufacturing operation, the discussion of these items will be important to any potential investor in assessing financial needs.

If the venture is not a manufacturing operation but a retail store, service, or some other type of nonmanufacturing business, this section would be titled *operational plan* and the entrepreneur would then need to describe the chronological steps in completing a business transaction. For example, a retail store would need to describe the process of purchasing merchandise, how the merchandise will be stored and presented for sale, as well as the control system to be used for inventory control. For a service such as a retail Internet business the entrepreneur would need to describe the complete transaction process from the actual development of the website, how it functions, the procedure for ordering, and the final steps involved in completing a transaction. Figure 7.6 summarizes some of the key questions needed for this section of the business plan.

Marketing Plan

The *marketing plan* (discussed in detail in Chapter 8) is an important part of the business plan since it describes how the product(s) or service(s) will be distributed, priced, and promoted. Marketing research evidence to support any of the critical marketing decision strategies as well as for forecasting sales should be described in this section. Specific forecasts for product(s) or service(s) are indicated in order to project profitability of the venture. The budget and appropriate controls needed

---

marketing plan   Describes market conditions and strategy related to how products and services will be distributed, priced, and promoted

---

FIGURE 7.6   **Production Plan**

1. Will you be responsible for all or part of the manufacturing operation?
2. If some manufacturing is subcontracted, who will be the subcontractor(s)? (Give names and addresses.)
3. Why were these subcontractors selected?
4. What are the costs of the subcontracted manufacturing? (Include copies of any written contracts.)
5. What will be the layout of the production process? (Illustrate steps if possible.)
6. What equipment will be needed immediately for manufacturing?
7. What raw materials will be needed for manufacturing?
8. Who are the suppliers of new materials and what are the appropriate costs?
9. What are the costs of manufacturing the product?
10. What are the future capital equipment needs of the venture?

If a Retail Operation or Service:

1. From whom will merchandise be purchased?
2. How will the inventory control system operate?
3. What are the storage needs of the venture and how will they be promoted?
4. Chronologically, what are the steps involved in a business transaction?

for marketing strategy decisions are also discussed in detail in Chapter 8. Potential investors regard the marketing plan as critical to the success of the new venture. Thus, the entrepreneur should make every effort to prepare as comprehensive and detailed a plan as possible so that investors can be clear as to what the goals of the venture are and what strategies are to be implemented to effectively achieve these goals. Marketing planning will be an annual requirement (with careful monitoring and changes made on a weekly or monthly basis) for the entrepreneur and should be regarded as the road map for short-term decision making.

Organizational Plan

The *organizational plan* is the part of the business plan that describes the venture's form of ownership—that is, proprietorship, partnership, or corporation. If the venture is a partnership, the terms of the partnership should be included. If the venture is a corporation, it is important to detail the shares of stock authorized, share options, as well as names and addresses and resumes of the directors and officers of the corporation. It is also helpful to provide an organization chart indicating the line of authority and the responsibilities of the members of the organization. Alternative forms of organization and discussion of the various layouts of an organization are included in Chapter 8. Figure 7.7 summarizes some of the key questions the entrepreneur needs to answer in preparing this section of the business plan. This information provides the potential investor with a clear understanding of who controls the organization and how other members will interact in performing their management functions.

organizational plan   Describes form of ownership and lines of authority and responsibility of members of new venture

Assessment of Risk

Every new venture will be faced with some potential hazards, given the particular industry and competitive environment. It is important that the entrepreneur make an *assessment of risk* in the following manner. First, the entrepreneur should indicate the potential risks to the new venture. Next should be a discussion of what might happen if these risks become reality. Finally, the entrepreneur should discuss

assessment of risk   Identifies potential hazards and alternative strategies to meet business plan goals and objectives

---

FIGURE 7.7   Organization Structure

1. What is the form of ownership of the organization?
2. If a partnership, who are the partners and what are the terms of agreement?
3. If incorporated, who are the principal shareholders and how much stock do they own?
4. How many shares of voting or nonvoting stock have been issued, and what type?
5. Who are the members of the board of directors? (Give names, addresses, and resumes.)
6. Who has check-signing authority or control?
7. Who are the members of the management team and what are their backgrounds?
8. What are the roles and responsibilities of each member of the management team?
9. What are the salaries, bonuses, or other forms of payment for each member of the management team?

the strategy that will be employed to either prevent, minimize, or respond to the risks should they occur. Major risks for a new venture could result from a competitor's reaction; weaknesses in the marketing, production, or management team; and new advances in technology that might render the new product obsolete. Even if these factors present no risks to the new venture, the business plan should discuss why that is the case.

Financial Plan

The *financial plan* is discussed further in Chapter 9. Like the marketing, production, and organization plans, this is an important part of the business plan. It determines the potential investment commitment needed for the new venture and indicates whether the business plan is economically feasible.

financial plan Projections of key financial data that determine economic feasibility and necessary financial investment commitment

Generally, three financial areas are discussed in this section of the business plan. First, the entrepreneur should summarize the forecasted sales and the appropriate expenses for at least the first three years, with the first year's projections provided monthly. The form for displaying this information is illustrated in Chapter 9. It includes the forecasted sales, cost of goods sold, and the general and administrative expenses. Net profit after taxes can then be projected by estimating income taxes.

The second major area of financial information needed is cash flow figures for three years, with the first year's projections provided monthly. Since bills have to be paid at different times of the year, it is important to determine the demands on cash on a monthly basis, especially in the first year. Remember that sales may be irregular, and receipts from customers may also be spread out, thus necessitating the borrowing of short-term capital to meet fixed expenses such as salaries and utilities. A form for projecting the cash flow needs for a 12-month period can be found in Chapter 9. The last financial item needed in this section of the business plan is the projected balance sheet. This shows the financial condition of the business at a specific time. It summarizes the assets of a business, its liabilities (what is owed), the investment of the entrepreneur and any partners, and retained earnings (or cumulative losses). A form for the balance sheet is included in Chapter 9, along with more detailed explanations of the items included. Any assumptions considered for the balance sheet or any other item in the financial plan should be listed for the benefit of the potential investor.

Appendix

The appendix of the business plan generally contains any backup material that is not necessary in the text of the document. Reference to any of the documents in the appendix should be made in the plan itself.

Letters from customers, distributors, or subcontractors are examples of information that should be included in the appendix. Any documentation of information—that is, secondary data or primary research data used to support plan decisions—should also be included. Leases, contracts, or any other types of agreements that have been initiated may also be included in the appendix. Finally, price lists from suppliers and competitors may be added.

USING AND IMPLEMENTING THE BUSINESS PLAN

The business plan is designed to guide the entrepreneur through the first year of operations. It is important that the implementation of the strategy contain control

FIGURE 7.8   Sources of Information

Small Business Administration

Department of Commerce

Federal information centers

Bureau of Census

State and municipal governments

Banks

Chambers of commerce

Trade associations

Trade journals

Libraries

Universities and community colleges

Source: R. Siklos, "Oxygen Gets Airborne," *Business Week* (September 28, 1998), p. 52. (See p. 241)

points to ascertain progress and to initiate contingency plans if necessary. Some of the controls necessary in manufacturing, marketing, financing, and the organization are discussed in subsequent chapters. Most important to the entrepreneur is that the business plan not end up in a drawer somewhere once the financing has been attained and the business launched.

There has been a tendency among many entrepreneurs to avoid planning. The reason often given is that planning is dull or boring and is something used only by large companies. This may be an excuse; perhaps the real truth is that some entrepreneurs are afraid to plan.[8] Planning is an important part of any business operation. Without good planning, the entrepreneur is likely to pay an enormous price. All one has to do is consider the planning done by suppliers, customers, competitors, and banks to realize that it is important for the entrepreneur. It is also important to realize that without good planning the employees will not understand the company's goals and how they are expected to perform in their jobs.

Bankers are the first to admit that few business failures result from a lack of cash but, instead, fail because of the entrepreneur's inability to plan effectively. Intelligent planning is not a difficult or impossible exercise for the inexperienced entrepreneur. With the proper commitment and support from many outside resources, such as those shown in Figure 7.8, the entrepreneur can prepare an effective business plan.

In addition, the entrepreneur can enhance effective implementation of the business plan by developing a schedule to measure progress and to institute contingency plans. These frequent readings or control procedures will be discussed further below.

Measuring Plan Progress

During the introductory phases of the start-up, the entrepreneur should determine the points at which decisions should be made as to whether the goals or objectives are on schedule. Typically, the business plan projections will be made on a 12-month schedule. However, the entrepreneur cannot wait 12 months to see if the plan has been successfully achieved. Instead, on a frequent basis (i.e., the beginning of each month) the entrepreneur should check the profit and loss statement, cash flow projections, and information on inventory, production, quality, sales, collection of accounts receivable, and disbursements for the previous month. This feedback should be simple but should provide key members of the organization with current information in time to correct any major deviations from the goals and objectives outlined. A brief description of each of these control elements is given below:

- *Inventory Control.* By controlling inventory, the firm can ensure maximum service to the customer. The faster the firm gets back its investment in raw materials and finished goods, the faster that capital can be reinvested to meet additional customer needs.

- *Production Control.* Compare the cost figures estimated in the business plan with day-to-day operation costs. This will help to control machine time, worker hours, process time, delay time, and downtime cost.

- *Quality Control.* This will depend on the type of production system but is designed to make sure that the product performs satisfactorily.

- *Sales Control.* Information on units, dollars, specific products sold, price of sales, meeting of delivery dates, and credit terms is useful to get a good perspective of the sales of the new venture. In addition, an effective collection system for accounts receivable should be set up to avoid aging of accounts and bad debts.

- *Disbursements.* The new venture should also control the amount of money paid out. All bills should be reviewed to determine how much is being disbursed and for what purpose.

Updating the Plan

The most effective business plan can become out-of-date if conditions change. Environmental factors such as the economy, customers, new technology, or competition—and internal factors such as the loss or addition of key employees—can all change the direction of the business plan. Thus, it is important to be sensitive to changes in the company, industry, and market. If these changes are likely to affect the business plan, the entrepreneur should determine what revisions are needed. In this manner, the entrepreneur can maintain reasonable targets and goals and keep the new venture on a course that will increase its probability of success.

WHY SOME BUSINESS PLANS FAIL

Generally a poorly prepared business plan can be blamed on one or more of the following factors:

- Goals set by the entrepreneur are unreasonable.
- Goals are not measurable.
- The entrepreneur has not made a total commitment to the business or to the family.
- The entrepreneur has no experience in the planned business.
- The entrepreneur has no sense of potential threats or weaknesses to the business.
- No customer need was established for the proposed product or service.

Setting goals requires the entrepreneur to be well informed about the type of business and the competitive environment. Goals should be specific and not so mundane as to lack any basis of control. For example, the entrepreneur may target a specific market share, units sold, or revenue. These goals are measurable and can be monitored over time.

In addition, the entrepreneur and his or her family must make a total commitment to the business in order to be able to meet the demands of a new venture. For example, it is difficult to operate a new venture on a part-time basis while still holding onto a full-time position. And it is also difficult to operate a business without an understanding from family members as to the time and resources that will be needed. Lenders or investors will not be favorably inclined toward a venture that does not have full-time commitment. Moreover, lenders or investors may expect the entrepreneur to make a significant financial commitment to the business even if it means a second mortgage or a depletion of savings.

Generally, a lack of experience will result in failure unless the entrepreneur can either attain the necessary knowledge or team up with someone who already has it. For example, an entrepreneur trying to start a new restaurant without any experience or knowledge of the restaurant business would be a disastrous situation.

The entrepreneur should also document customer needs before preparing the plan. Customer needs can be identified from direct experience, letters from customers, or marketing research. A clear understanding of these needs and how the entrepreneur's business will effectively meet them is vital to the success of the new venture.

IN REVIEW

Summary

This chapter has established the scope and value of the business plan and has outlined the steps in its preparation. The business plan may be read by employees, investors, lenders, suppliers, customers, and consultants. The scope of the plan will depend on who reads it, the size of the venture, and the specific industry for which the venture is intended.

The business plan is essential in launching a new venture. The results of many hours of preparation will represent a comprehensive, well-written, and well-organized document that will serve as a guide to the entrepreneur and as an instrument to raise necessary capital and financing.

Before beginning the business plan, the entrepreneur will need information on the market, manufacturing operations, and financial estimations. The Internet represents a low-cost service that can provide valuable information on the market, customers and their needs, and competitors. This information should be evaluated based on the goals and objectives of the new venture. These goals and objectives also provide a framework for setting up controls for the business plan.

The chapter presents a comprehensive discussion and outline of a typical business plan. Each key element in the plan is discussed, and examples are provided. Control decisions are presented to ensure the effective implementation of the business plan. In addition, some insights as to why business plans fail are discussed.

Questions for Discussion

1. Why is a business plan so important to the entrepreneur? To the investor? To the customer? To suppliers?
2. How can the Internet be used to gather market data for the business plan?
3. What kind of information should be provided in the industry analysis of the business plan? Identify any industry (i.e., golf) and make a list of the various sources that might be used to provide industry information and data. Which sources will be more likely to provide statistics on size of market and industry sales growth?
4. What are some examples of potential hazards that should be evaluated in the risk assessment section of the business plan? How would they differ for a service, manufacturer, or retailer?
5. Discuss the purpose and value of the financial plan to the potential investor. To the potential lender. To the entrepreneur. Are there likely to be any differences in the financial information needed by each? Why?
6. Why is it necessary to update the business plan? What specific factors can enhance the need to update it?
7. Why do some business plans fail?

Key Terms

assessment of risk	industry analysis
business plan	Internet
description of the venture	marketing plan
financial plan	organizational plan
environmental analysis	production plan

More Information—Net Addresses in This Chapter

Biz Women
www.bizwomen.com

Business Decision Resources
www.bdrproduct.com

The Business Planning Resource Center
www.bplans.com

Business Resource Center
www.morebusiness.com

The Business Start Page
www.bspage.com

The Census Bureau
www.census.gov/

CNN Financial News
www.cnnfn.com

Dunn & Bradstreet Information Service
www.dnb.com

Entrepreneurs' Association
www.grow-biz.com

Entrepreneurs on the Web
www.entrepreneur-web.com/

Idea Cafe
www.ideacafe.com

Small Business Administration
www.sbaonline.sba.gov/

Small Business Advancement National Center
www.sbanet.uca.edu/

Small Business Resource Center
www.webcom.com/seaquest/sbrc

Statistical Abstracts
www.census.gov/stat_abstract/

World and Local economies
www.stat-usa.gov

Women Entrepreneurs Online Network
www.weon.com

World Wide Yellow Pages
www.yellow.com

Young Americas Business Network
www.ybiz.com

Selected Readings

Abrams, Rhonda M. (March–April 1996). Business Plan Stumbling Blocks. *Working Woman*, pp. 45–48.

The 10 typical mistakes that are made in the preparation of a business plan are presented. The article, in addition to discussing these 10 mistakes, also provides some insight as to how to avoid them.

Brokaw, Leslie. (March–April 1996). The Business Plan: Dream vs. Reality. *Executive Female*, pp. 60–71.

Elaine Salazar, the founder of Ampersand Art Supply, describes how it took 12 weeks to write the perfect plan. The process started as a class project that won a business plan competition. With refinement, other competitions were won until Ms. Salazar and her partner were given incubator space at a university and were awarded $290,000 in seed capital from a local investor.

Cronin, Mary J. (1995). *Doing More Business on the Internet*, 2nd ed. New York: Van Nostrand Reinhold.

This is a good resource for anyone who wants to use the Internet to conduct business. It offers the reader opportunities to understand the advantage of matching Internet capabilities with key opportunities in marketing, sales, customer relations, and information management.

Ernst & Young LLP. (1997). *Outline for a Business Plan.*

This generalized outline for a business plan is simple to follow and provides additional understanding of the information that should be included in a quality business plan.

Morrow, J. (January 1999). Ten Year Plan. *Success*, pp. 54–66.

Finding the answers to critical business questions in the next decade is going to be extremely difficult. This article interviews some of the leading economists, marketers, and futurists to determine what the most likely issues will be and how an entrepreneur can plan for them.

Poon, Simpson; and Paula M. C. Swatman. (1999). *Information and Management*, vol. 35, pp. 9–18.

The small business Internet commerce phenomenon is still in its infancy. Small businesses are finding e-mail useful for business communication and document transfer. The perception of long-term benefits and potential business opportunities is driving this market sector. Current Internet-based transaction engagement is still slow, and almost no integration exists between the Internet and internal applications. Small business Internet commerce is likely to continue to expand if small firms actually experience tangible effects in the future.

Prince, C. J. (January 2000). The Ultimate Business Plan. *Success*, pp. 44–49.

Provides a simplified approach to business plan preparation. There is also a review of three business plan software products.

Sahlman, William A. (1997). How to Write a Great Business Plan. *Harvard Business Review*, vol. 75, no. 4, pp. 98–108.

The paper proposes that a great business plan is one that focuses on a series of questions relating to four factors critical to the success of every new venture. These factors are the people, the opportunity, the context, and the possibilities for both risk and reward. The questions about these three factors are discussed.

West, E. J. W. (1997). Using the Internet for Business—Web Oriented Routes to Market and Existing IT Infrastructures. *Computer Networks and ISDN Systems*, vol. 29, pp. 1769–76.

The rapid expansion of the Internet is opening up new opportunities. Companies can better exploit these opportunities if they make better use of their existing information technology and integrate their Internet-oriented routes to market with those systems that support traditional routes.

Endnotes

1. For more information on this venture, see http://www.marthastewart.com; J. Schoolman, "Martha Stewart the High Priestess of Hausfraus Says Sharing 'Is A Good Thing,'" *New York Daily News* (October 18, 1999), p. 35; and M. Summers, "USA: Martha Stewart IPO Cleans Up on Wall Street," *Reuters English News Service* (October 19, 1999).
2. Donald F. Kuratko and Arnold Cirtin, "Developing a Business Plan for Your Clients," *The National Public Accountant* (January 1990), pp. 24–27.
3. Carolyn M. Brown, "The Do's and Don'ts of Writing a Winning Business Plan," *Black Enterprise* (April 1996), pp. 114–22.
4. Bob Weinstein, "Soft Sell," *Entrepreneur* (July 1993), pp. 143–27.
5. For more information on issues and questions relating to market information needs, see Michael P. Peters, "The Role of Planning in the Marketing of New Products," *Planning Review* (November 1980), pp. 24–28.
6. For developing a website, see Robert McGarvey, "Ready Set Net!" *Entrepreneur* (June 1996), pp. 143–9.
7. For additional material, see *Business Plan for Small Manufacturers*, 2nd ed. (Lexington, MA: Haley Publications, 1985); and Eric S. Siegel, Brian R. Ford, and Jay M. Bornstein, *The Ernst & Young Business Plan Guide*, 2nd ed. (New York: John Wiley & Sons, 1993).
8. Bruce G. Posner, "Real Entrepreneurs Don't Plan," *Inc.* (November 1985), pp. 129–35.

APPENDIX   A Sample Business Plan—Gopher It

The following business plan has been condensed and edited somewhat because of space requirements. However, the areas where editing has taken place are clearly identified and do not in any way detract from the meaningfulness of this example.

An average business plan will vary in length depending on the industry, size of the appendix, and the number of illustrations. The actual text of a business plan would conservatively range between 15 and 25 pages.

Venture Description

Gopher It is a personal shopping service located in the downtown business district of Boston, Massachusetts. It is based on the belief that people's schedules today are more demanding; thus the value of personal leisure time has increased. In the 1990s with more and more dual-career families, personal convenience services are a high-growth market opportunity. The professional white-collar employee in the downtown district, who has high disposable income and a strong motive to increase leisure time, represents the main focus of the venture's marketing efforts.

Running errands before work, during lunch breaks, or after work takes time and is often irritating. People often have to wait in line for services, fight traffic, and skip lunch or an opportunity for a quiet time away from the pressures of the office. Gopher It has established an errand service for professionals in the heart of the downtown business district of Boston. The company will be located at _____ Street, on the first floor, where employees will have direct access to public transportation and customers will be able to stop by and conveniently request any service. Employees will typically be college students, who will perform services on foot, use public transportation, or ride a bicycle to efficiently meet customer needs. The office will contain storage space for pickup and delivery items as well as refrigeration for any specific food products. The entry area where customers will place their service order will be professionally decorated and staffed with trained individuals to answer questions and attend to customer needs. The number of staff will vary, depending on when the office is most busy (early morning, lunchtimes, and at close of business day).

The diverse services that will be offered are categorized as standard or custom. Standard services include dropping and/or picking up laundry, dry cleaning, mail, tickets such as airline or theater, prescriptions; shopping for groceries or gifts; and making bank deposits. Customized or special services, not specifically listed or identified, may also be offered based on the amount of time it takes to complete the errand. An example of a special service would be picking up an automobile that was being repaired. These special services would be priced on an hourly basis and, in the case of an automobile, may also include the expense of parking.

Industry Analysis

The service sector in the United States continues to grow. Entrepreneurs have initiated many new ventures in the service sector in response to greater demand for leisure time, the increasing number of dual-career families, and more disposable income.

Demographic Trends   [*This section of the business plan would provide statistical data and discussion of some of the significant demographic trends that would support the needs being addressed by this proposed venture.*]

Competitor Analysis   Although there are many indirect competitors to Gopher It, there are none in the Boston market that offer such a broad range of services. Courier services have existed for many years, but other service businesses have been slow in their response to customer needs by offering only pickup and delivery services. Today it is more common to find supermarkets, dry cleaners, restaurants, video stores, and auto repair shops offering pickup and/or delivery for their customers. Typically this service tends to be ad hoc, with little effort made to organize it based on customer needs.

Although there are a number of small businesses in other states that offer pickup and delivery services, none compares with Gopher It in terms of the extent of services offered. Shopping services for professional clients exist in almost every major market. However, Gopher It will not offer this service since it requires a distinctive trained and knowledgeable staff. There are also businesses that will pickup and deliver laundry, and others that will provide grocery shopping services. Most of these businesses are in the specific retail business for which they are providing the service; hence their purpose is to offer pickup and delivery as an incentive to buy their retail goods. Some of the companies that offer pickup and delivery services that would indirectly compete with Gopher It are as follows:

[Direct and indirect competitors would be listed here with a description of their businesses and the services they provide.]

Marketing Plan

The marketing strategy was designed on the basis of personal interviews conducted with employers and business professionals in the downtown Boston market, which represents our target market. These interviews indicated that the individuals preferred to have someone else perform many of the time-consuming errands that they were required to do on a weekly or regular basis. The majority of these individuals commented that they had less leisure time than in the past and, as a result, valued this free time more than ever before. They indicated a need for the types of services offered by Gopher It and a willingness to pay for these services.

The errand market is untapped and has a large customer base. The target market for our services would be white-collar, highly educated baby boomers, working in professional jobs and likely members of two-career professional households. The office is located in the downtown business district and near a major transit station where there are many individuals who fit our target market. Recent traffic statistics indicated that more than 13,000 individuals would pass our office to and from their office to their transit stop. This high traffic location lends itself to the convenience services that we can provide for our target market.

Marketing Goals

- To meet the growing needs of a target market defined on the basis of geography, demographics, lifestyle, and buyer intentions.
- To evaluate the competitive environment and continue to establish a differential advantage.
- To establish an effective and profitable marketing mix of service, place, price, and promotion.

Marketing Objectives

- To establish a customer base of 10 percent of the defined target market in the first year.
- To generate $150,000 in sales for the first year.

- To increase sales by 10 percent annually for the first three years.
- To expand to at least two new locations by the end of the first three years.

Size of Market   According to our research, there are about 250,000 people in the central business district of the city of Boston. There are approximately 10,300 to 13,200 people (represents the primary market) who pass our office every business day. On the basis of our research and on demographic studies conducted in the city of Boston, about 75 percent of these individuals match our target market. This would consist of individuals between the ages of 28 and 65, male or female, with high disposable income, employed as professional businesspersons or office staff.

There is also the potential to reach an additional 10,000 customers who work on the fringe of this area and may not directly pass our office on a regular basis. This secondary market may be penetrated through advertising, word of mouth, and the distribution of marketing literature.

On the basis of the above information, it is estimated that the potential market is between 17,000 and 20,000 people. Our objective is to reach 10 percent of the primary market and 5 percent of the secondary market. Thus, in our first year the market would consist of about 1,275 customers.

Service   The services that will be provided by Gopher It are designed to provide customers with the benefits of convenience and the saving of time. Although the services vary widely, there are standard services offered to the customer. Standard services include lunch delivery, dry cleaning pickup and drop-off, grocery shopping (maximum of 10 items), and gift shopping in the downtown area. Customized services of almost any kind will also be offered on a fee-for-time basis. Examples of these customized services are auto pickup and/or drop-off, pickup of theater tickets, supply pickup, post office visits, and bank deposits. Delivery and pickup will typically involve walking, riding a bicycle, or using the transit. The most efficient and economic solution will be chosen for each situation.

Price   Pricing strategy is based on a fee per errand. This strategy was determined from an evaluation of Errands Unlimited, a similar business located in Milwaukee, Wisconsin, as well as a marketing research study of the target market. For the customized services the price will be based on the amount of time necessary to perform the errand, including time in transit. The lowest fee would be $5 for a quick errand that took less than five minutes. Prices for errands taking longer than five minutes would increase accordingly and are indicated below.

Miscellaneous Personal Services

Pick up tickets for theater district shows

Pick up tickets for sporting events

Wait in line for a book autograph

Pick up automobile at repair shop

Post office visits

Office supply shopping

Bank deposits

Any other personal errands

Time Spent (in Minutes)	Price
0–5	$5
6–10	$10
11–15	$15
16–20	$20
21–25	$25
26 +	$30

Regular or Standard Services	Price
Express lunch delivery	$5
Dry cleaning drop-off	$5
Dry cleaning pickup	$5
Grocery shopping (maximum of 10 items)	$10
Gift shopping in downtown area	$15

Promotion   Gopher It will rely extensively on word-of-mouth advertising. How-ever, it will be important to create an awareness of our services to the target market. To attract attention and to create awareness, signs will display our name and describe our services to the many individuals who actually pass by the office. Pamphlets will also be distributed to office buildings in the target market.

Facilities Plan

The location of Gopher It will be in the lobby at _____ Street in the downtown district of Boston. This location is ideal because it provides access to a large base of potential customers who pass the office going to and from work to the transit station or garage as well as those who stroll around the area during lunchtime. Estimates of the daily traffic are between 4,000 and 5,000 individuals passing through the lobby at each rush hour, which projects to between 8,000 and 10,000 passes per day. There are also about 1,000 people who work in this building and another 1,300 to 2,200 individuals who pass through the lobby at non-rush-hour time. Thus, in a typical day there are between 10,300 and 13,200 potential consumers who are likely to pass by our business location. If we also include the Bank of Boston and Shawmut building, both on a connecting street, we have effectively extended our potential market to over 20,000 people. This large base of potential consumers is an excellent target mar-ket for our services. Even with limited resources, our store front and location will be an important asset in promoting an awareness of Gopher It's services.

The initial location will be leased. Rent will be based on a $40 per square foot price. With electricity and other charges the rental cost will be $50 per square foot or $10,000 per month.

Certain equipment will also be necessary to operate the business effectively—a multiline phone system, computer and printer, fax machine, storage for hot and cold foods, and storage for garments, gifts, and groceries. Counters will be set up in a small area at the front of the office for conducting business with clients. Little space is needed for the attendant, whose main function will be to take orders from walk-in clients and to answer the phone for call-in orders. The storage space would have food storage on one side, and garment and gift storage on the other wall.

Organizational Plan

Gopher It will be established as a partnership. There will be three partners: Chris Bentley, Shane Welch, and Laura Shanley. Each will assume an equal ownership in the business. Background and roles of each of the three partners are described below. A partnership agreement is summarized in the Appendix.

Management Team Background   Chris Bentley was born in San Diego, California, and graduated from Swarthmore College with an accounting degree. Past employers include numerous restaurants, a specialty retailer, and a large bank (mutual funds). He has significant experience in managing and training people as well as financial management.

Shane Welch was born in Baltimore, Maryland, and has a food science degree from the University of Maryland and an MBA degree from Boston College. He has had extensive experience in food retailing and more recently in sales and marketing with a large consumer food producer.

Laura Shanley was born in Jamaica Plain, Massachusetts, and has a bachelor of science degree in marketing from Boston College. She has extensive experience in a family business, a chain of small retail gift shops. This gift shop experience involved expansion to new locations, buying, promotion, and customer relations. The business has since been sold, and Laura is seeking new endeavors in a start-up venture.

Duties and Responsibilities of the Partners

Laura Shanley—General Administrator and Manager

Laura will oversee the daily operations of the business. This includes the hiring and firing of employees as well as training and supervising. Periodic employee evaluations will be completed by the general administrator and manager. She will also handle all purchasing for the office and will be responsible for opening and closing the office each day.

Shane Welch—Marketing and Sales Manager

Shane will be responsible for creating promotional activities, monitoring sales, and establishing effective strategies for creating awareness of the business. He will be responsible for the design and distribution of all direct marketing materials.

Chris Bentley—Financial Manager

Chris will be responsible for finance, accounting, payroll, billing, taxes, and any other matters related to sales and revenue budgets.

The Financial Plan

Financial statements are presented in the following pages. Explanations of all financial information are also provided. The business is expected to break even in the early part of the second year with the first positive profit achieved in the month of August. Total start-up expenditures will be about $20,000. We are seeking a $40,000 loan that will be paid back over five years at 12 percent.

Risk Assessment

The proposed errand service offered by Gopher It, although free from any direct competition, has a very low barrier to entry. Setup costs and high liquidity will be a significant attraction to competitors, who could subsequently penetrate some of Gopher It's market. Gopher It will need to rely on its quality of service and being first in the market to protect its market share. Our convenient location and flexibility in providing a wide range of services should support the long-term success of Gopher It in this market.

Appendix*

Resumes of Partners

Partnership Agreement

Lease Agreement

Facility Layout

Market Research Survey Results

Marketing Brochure with Price List

*The actual information in the Appendix has not been included because of space. However, the student should be able to infer from the example provided here the scope and content of a complete business plan.

8

The Marketing Plan

LEARNING OBJECTIVES

1. To understand the differences among business planning, strategic planning, and market planning.

2. To describe the role of marketing research in determining marketing strategy for the marketing plan.

3. To illustrate an effective and feasible procedure for the entrepreneur to follow in engaging in a market research study.

4. To define the steps in preparing the marketing plan.

5. To explain the marketing system and its key components.

6. To illustrate different creative strategies that may be used to differentiate or position the new venture's products or services.

MICHAEL S. DELL

Some experts might argue that organizing and launching a business is the easiest part of getting started but that sustaining the business is the most difficult and challenging. As we've seen in earlier chapters, businesses fail at an alarming rate, yet too often we blame lack of finances or poor management for the demise. A closer look will often reveal that the real problems relate to marketing issues such as identifying the customer, defining the right product and service to meet customer needs, pricing, distribution, and promotion.

www.dell.com

Because the entrepreneur must anticipate these issues in both the short run and the long run, it is important for him or her to develop and prepare a marketing plan. Planning, as discussed in the previous chapter, spans a wide range of activities and is intended to formally detail the business activities, strategies, responsibilities, budgets, and controls to meet specific, designated goals.

No one knows this better than Michael S. Dell. Now in his thirties, Michael Dell is the upstart in the very competitive microcomputer market, where many of the more established firms have had difficulties or failed. He has been described as the most innovative and creative person in marketing computers in the last decade, and he has been able to achieve success in a market that others have thought impossible.[1]

Michael always had entrepreneurial tendencies. At age 12, he started a nationwide mail-order stamp auction, which netted him his first $2,000. Even though his parents wanted him to be a doctor, Michael always knew, especially after extending his knowledge of computers at the University of Texas at Austin, that he would some day own his own computer business.

Fed up with salespeople in electronics stores who lacked knowledge, Dell dropped out of school in 1984 at age 19 and took $1,000 of savings to launch PCs Limited, soon renamed Dell Computer Corporation. His business idea was to use innovative mail-order marketing to reach his customers. It was here that Dell faced his first hurdle: where to find a source of machines. Initially, he decided to buy IBM computers on the gray market because IBM would not allow its dealers to sell PCs to anyone intending to resell them. However, this was not sufficient to meet his customers' needs, so Dell again resorted to his creativity, realizing that many dealers often carried a large inventory of hardware, much of which they could not sell. Dell knocked on the doors of these retailers and offered to buy their surplus at cost. He then modified the PCs with graphics cards and hard disks and sold them by direct marketing.

By 1985, the company, with the help of 40 employees, was assembling its own PCs by buying off-the-shelf components. In 1986, he hired E. Lee Walker and made him president and chief operating officer. Whereas Michael Dell was basically a shy person, Walker was an aggressive venture capitalist who had excellent financial and managerial experience. Walker became Dell's mentor and helped him gain the confidence he needed to run the business. This experience was also supplemented with the hiring of Morton H. Meyerson, former president of Electronic Data Systems Corporation, who helped Dell make the jump from a fast-growing, medium-sized firm to a mature large one.

In 1988, Dell Computer went public and raised $31.1 million of much needed capital. Dell, however, still retained more than 75 percent ownership of the company. In 1991, his company received the number one ranking by J. D. Power & Associates for customer satisfaction. Although Dell faced some problems in a second public offering that was withdrawn, his firm grew by 126 percent in 1993 with sales of $2 billion, making Dell Computer the fourth largest PC maker in the United States behind IBM, Apple, and Compaq.

In 1996 the company began selling computers over the Internet, and by 1999 Internet sales had reached about $35 million per day, which now represents about 50 percent of its total $23.6 billion in sales over the past four quarters. Dell is now number two among computer systems companies worldwide. In the United States it is the number one supplier of PCs to business customers, government agencies, educational institutions, and consumers. It is ranked as number 78 among the Fortune 500 companies and number 210 in the Fortune Global 500. Recently Dell opened an application and solutions center in China, which is expected to become one of Dell's top 10 markets in the world. In 2001, the company had year-end sales of $31.89 billion and net income of $2.24 billion and was ranked number one in global market share. With an increased worldwide presence and with double-digit growth in Internet sales the company is expecting to maintain its rapid ascent to be the number one provider of computer systems in the world.

The above story reveals an intriguing yet simple marketing approach: Eliminate dealers and distributors and work hard to meet customer needs through quality service. Dell's marketing plan was simple yet aggressive in trying to position the company as a lower-priced, assemble-to-order, direct-response business. This aggressiveness was demonstrated by Dell's use of comparative ads that tossed barbs at Compaq, one of the firm's major competitors. Compaq's subsequent lawsuit that claimed these comparisons were not between similar models led to a settlement in 1991. We can also see how the company has continued to develop new marketing plans to reach new market segments such as the business-to-business and international markets. Recently Michael has agreed to appear in television and print advertising as the company spokesperson. He feels that this effort will put a human face on the company and enhance recognition among business customers, particularly for Internet sales.

Dell's future will continue to involve one marketing challenge after another as other firms begin to imitate its success with similar direct-marketing and Internet strategies. Price competition, as well as the challenge of facing more international competition, will necessitate aggressive countermarketing strategies to maintain the firm's successful growth. Michael Dell insists that the competitors are now playing the game in his ballpark and that with his direct marketing experience and Internet success the company will continue to grow.

As can be seen from the Dell Computer example, there are many creative alternatives to marketing a product or service. The entrepreneur must assess the needs of the target market, estimate the size of the market, and then implement a strategy that effectively positions the product or service in a competitive environment. The positioning strategy, as described in the marketing section of the business plan, is critical in determining the resources needed to launch the business.

꽃

PURPOSE AND TIMING OF THE MARKETING PLAN

The marketing plan represents a significant element in the business plan for a new venture. It serves a number of important functions or purposes. Primarily the marketing plan establishes how the entrepreneur will effectively compete and operate in the marketplace and thus meet the business goals and objectives of the new venture. Once the strategies of how the business will operate have been established, the entrepreneur can then assign costs to these strategies, which then serves the important purpose of establishing budgets and making financial projections.

Marketing planning should be an annual activity that focuses on implementing decisions related to the marketing mix variables (product, price, distribution, and promotion). Like the annual budgeting cycle, market planning has also become an annual activity and should be incorporated by all entrepreneurs, regardless of the size or type of the business. These marketing plans must be monitored frequently, especially in the early stages of start-up, in order to determine if the business is "on plan." If not "on plan," changes in the marketing mix or even in the goals and objectives may be warranted.

As part of the business plan, the marketing plan section should focus on strategies for the first three years of the new venture. The first year's goals and strategies will be the most comprehensive, with monthly projections. For years 2 and 3, the entrepreneur will need to project market results based on longer-term strategic goals of the new venture. Each year the entrepreneur should prepare an annual marketing plan before any decisions are made regarding production/manufacturing, personnel changes, or financial resources needed. This annual plan becomes the basis for planning other aspects of the business and for developing budgets for the year. Table 8.1

TABLE 8.1   Outline for a Marketing Plan
Situation analysis
Background of venture
Market opportunities and threats
Competitor analysis
Strengths and weaknesses of venture
Marketing objectives and goals
Marketing strategy and action programs
Budgets
Controls

provides a suggested outline for the marketing plan. Variations of this outline will depend on the market and nature of the product, as well as the general company mission. This chapter focuses on the short-term aspects of the marketing plan, while not ignoring the fact that the entrepreneur will also need to provide market projections for years 2 and 3 as part of the business plan.

MARKETING RESEARCH FOR THE NEW VENTURE

Information for developing the marketing plan may necessitate conducting some marketing research. Marketing research involves the gathering of data in order to determine such information as who will buy the product or service, what is the size of the potential market, what price should be charged, what is the most appropriate distribution channel, and what is the most effective promotion strategy to inform and reach potential customers. Since marketing research costs vary significantly, the entrepreneur will need to assess available resources and the information needed. There are also some research techniques that are not costly and can provide, at least initially, significant evidence to support the market potential for the new venture. One of these techniques is the focus group, which is discussed later in this section.

Marketing research may be conducted by the entrepreneur or by an external supplier or consultant. There are also opportunities for entrepreneurs to contact their local colleges or universities to identify faculty who teach marketing and are willing to have external clients for student research projects. Suggestions on how to conduct market research are discussed below.

Market research begins with a definition of objectives or purpose. This is often the most difficult step since many entrepreneurs lack knowledge or experience in marketing and often don't even know what they want to accomplish from a research study. This, however, is the very reason for which marketing research can be so meaningful to the entrepreneur.[2]

Step One: Defining the Purpose or Objectives

The most effective way to begin is for the entrepreneur to sit down and make a list of the information that will be needed to prepare the marketing plan. For example, the entrepreneur may think there is a market for his or her product but is not sure who the customer will be or even if the product is appropriate in its present form. Thus, one objective would be to ask people what they think of the product or service and if they would buy it, and to collect some background demographics and attitudes of these individuals. This would satisfy the objective or problem that the entrepreneur defined above. Other objectives may be to determine the following:

- How much potential customers would be willing to pay for the product or service.
- Where potential customers would prefer to purchase the product or service.
- Where the customer would expect to hear about or learn about such a product or service.

Step Two: Gathering Data from Secondary Sources

The most obvious source of information for the entrepreneur is data that already exist, or secondary data. This is usually found in trade magazines, libraries, government agencies, universities, and the Internet. A search in a library will often reveal published information on the industry, competitors, trends in consumer tastes and preferences, innovations in the market, and even specific information about strategies now being employed by competitors already in the market. An Internet search can also provide extensive information on competitors, the industry, and even insightful primary information directly from potential consumers who respond to chat groups. Commercial data may also be available, but the cost may be prohibitive to the entrepreneur. However, business libraries may subscribe to some of these commercial services such as Nielsen Indexes, Audits and Survey's National Market Indexes, Selling Areas Marketing Inc. (SAMI), and Information Resources, Inc.

Before considering either primary sources or commercial sources of information, the entrepreneur should exhaust all free secondary sources. At the federal level, the U.S. Bureau of Census publishes a wide range of census reports, as does the Department of Commerce. Other excellent sources at the state and local levels are the State Department of Commerce, Chambers of Commerce, local banks, state departments of labor and industry, and local media. Private sources of data, some of which can be found in a good business library, are Predicasts, Simmons Reports, Dun and Bradstreet's Million Dollar Directory, Gale's Encyclopedia of Small Business Opportunities, the Business Index, and the SBA's Directory of Business Development Publications, to name a few.

It is also recommended that the entrepreneur spend time in a local business library scanning online catalogs and reference sources to locate articles that have been written about competitors or the industry. These articles, although defined as secondary data, should be scanned to identify the names of individuals who were interviewed, referenced, or even mentioned in the article. These individuals can then represent sources to be contacted directly. If their affiliation, telephone number, or address is not given in the article, then the entrepreneur should contact the author(s) of the article to see if they have these affiliations or could even provide their personal insights to some of the important market issues. The entrepreneur should exhaust all possible secondary data sources, observation, and networking before beginning any more costly primary data research.

Step Three: Gathering Information from Primary Sources

Information that is new is primary data. Gathering primary data involves a data collection procedure—such as observation, networking, interviewing, focus groups, or experimentation—and usually a data collection instrument, such as a questionnaire.

Observation is the simplest approach. The entrepreneur might observe potential customers and record some aspect of their buying behavior. Networking, which is more of an informal method to gather primary data from experts in the field, can also be a valuable low-cost method to learn about the marketplace. One study of new ventures found that the most successful ventures (based on growth rate) were focused on information about competitors, the customer, and the industry, using networking, trade associations, and recent publications. Less successful ventures were more focused on gathering information on general economic and demographic trends and hence had less of a sense of what was happening in their specific target market.[3]

Interviewing or surveying is the most common approach used to gather market information. It is more expensive than observation but is more likely to generate more meaningful information. Interviews would be conducted in person, by telephone, or

TABLE 8.2   A Comparison of Survey Methods

Method	Characteristics of Methods				
	Costs	Flexibility	Response Rate	Speed	Depth
Telephone	Can be inexpensive, depending on telephone distance and length of interview. For local research, probably the least expensive.	Some flexibility possible to clarify or explain questions.	Good response rate possible (possible 80%) depending on not-at-homes or refusals.	Fastest method of obtaining information. Can contact many respondents in a short period.	Least detail possible because of 8- to 10-minute time limitation. Also limited open-ended questions.
Mail	Can be very inexpensive, depending on number of units mailed and weight of mailing.	No flexibility since questionnaire self-administered. Instrument needs to be self-explanatory, or data will be invalid.	Poorest response rate since respondent has choice of whether to complete questionnaire.	Slowest method because of time required to mail and wait for respondents to complete questionnaire and then return to researcher.	Some depth possible since respondent completes questionnaire at his or her leisure.
Personal	Most expensive of these techniques. Requires face-to-face contact, which is time consuming per interview.	Most flexible of all methods because of face-to-face contact. Can also record facial expressions or emotion.	The most effective response rate because of face-to-face contact.	Somewhat slow because of dead time needed for travel between interviews.	Most detail possible because of extensive use of open-ended questions.

through the mail. Each of these methods offers advantages and disadvantages to the entrepreneur and should be evaluated accordingly.[4] Table 8.2 provides comparisons of each of these three methods of data collection.

The questionnaire, or data collection instrument, used by the entrepreneur should include questions specifically designed to fulfill one or more of the objectives the entrepreneur listed earlier. Questions should be designed so they are clear and concise, do not bias the respondent, and are easy to answer. Table 8.3 illustrates a sample questionnaire employed by an entrepreneur trying to assess the need for a personal errand service, such as the venture Gopher It, whose business plan is used as an example in Chapter 7. The questions are designed to satisfy the objectives of the entrepreneur, which are to ascertain the need, location, and determination of the most important services to offer and price. Support in the design of questionnaires can often be attained through Small Business Development Centers, members of SCORE, or students in marketing research classes at a local college or university. Since the instrument is important in the research process, it is recommended that entrepreneurs seek assistance if they have no experience in designing questionnaires.

Focus groups are a more informal method for gathering in-depth information. A focus group is a sample of 10 to 12 potential customers who are invited to participate in a discussion relating to the entrepreneur's research objectives. The focus

TABLE 8.3   Sample Questionnaire for Personal Errand Service

1. Of the following, please check the three most frequent errands that you are likely to carry out during the workweek.

_____ Dry cleaners	_____ Post office
_____ Drugstore	_____ Bank
_____ Shopping for clothing items	_____ Shopping for nonclothing and nongrocery items
_____ Buying a gift	_____ Automotive service or repair
_____ Other _____	_____ Other _____
Please specify	Please specify

2. Of the following, please indicate which items you would be willing to pay for someone to carry out for you.

_____ Dry cleaners	_____ Post office
_____ Drugstore	_____ Bank
_____ Shopping for clothing items	_____ Shopping for nonclothing and nongrocery items
_____ Buying a gift	_____ Automotive service or repair
_____ Other _____	_____ Other _____
Please specify	Please specify

3. What do you consider the two most important reasons for having someone else complete an errand? (Check only two).

    _____ Waiting in lines
    _____ Inconvenient location
    _____ Imposes on my relaxation time
    _____ Difficult work schedule
    _____ Traffic
    _____ Other _____
          Please specify
    _____ Other _____
          Please specify

4. If an errand service was conveniently available to you, how much would you be willing to pay for a standard errand such as delivering or picking up dry cleaning, going to the post office, or picking up a prescription?

_____ $3.00	_____ $4.00	_____ $5.00
_____ $6.00	_____ $7.00	_____ $8.00
_____ $9.00	_____ $10.00	_____ More than $10.00

5. Please indicate by rank ordering (1 being highest rank, 2 second highest rank, and so on) your preference for the most convenient location for a personal errand service.

    _____ In my building
    _____ Near my office
    _____ Near the train station
    _____ Prefer to have item(s) delivered to my office

6. The following information is needed for categorizing the results of the survey. Please check the appropriate box.

Sex: _____ Male _____ Female

Marital/household status:
        _____ Bachelor
        _____ Single parent
        _____ Married, both spouses working
        _____ Married, one spouse working

Age:
        _____ Under 25
        _____ 25–34
        _____ 35–44
        _____ 45–54
        _____ 55 and over

Household income:
        _____ Under $40,000
        _____ $40,000–$54,000
        _____ $55,000–$69,000
        _____ $70,000–$84,000
        _____ $85,000–$99,000
        _____ $100,000 and above

group discusses issues in an informal, open format, enabling the entrepreneur to ascertain certain information. For example, an entrepreneur was recently interested in whether consumers would be willing to sit in front of a computer at a kiosk in a shopping mall and design their own greeting cards. A focus group of a cross section of people was formed so the entrepreneur could learn about card buying, pricing, and the public's interest in designing their own cards, including the message. It was found from the focus group that individuals felt uncomfortable sitting in front of a computer in a mall and would not be willing to pay a premium price for such a benefit. This information became important in the marketing plan for this new venture. Focus groups should be led by an experienced monitor or someone other than the entrepreneur. Often this is a good project for students at a college or university in a marketing research class.[5]

Experimentation involves control over specific variables in the research process. Typically, this process would require a laboratory setting where the experimenter could control and investigate the effects of defined variables. But given the needs of most new ventures, this method would not be very appropriate at this point.

Step Four: Analyzing and Interpreting the Results

Depending on the size of the sample, the entrepreneur can hand-tabulate the results or enter them on a computer. In either case, the results should be evaluated and interpreted in response to the research objectives that were specified in the first step of the research process. Often, summarizing the answers to questions will give some preliminary insights. Then data can be cross-tabulated in order to provide more focused results. For example, the entrepreneur may want to compare the results to questions by different age groups, sex, occupation, location, and so on. Continuing this fine-tuning can provide valuable insights particularly regarding the segmentation of the market, which is discussed later in this chapter.

UNDERSTANDING THE MARKETING PLAN

Once the entrepreneur has gathered all the necessary information, he or she can sit down to prepare the marketing plan. The marketing plan, like any other type of plan, may be compared to a road map used to guide a traveler. It is designed to provide answers to three basic questions:[6]

1. Where have we been? When used as a stand-alone document (operational plan), this would imply some background on the company, its strengths and weaknesses, some background on the competition, and a discussion of the opportunities and threats in the marketplace. When the marketing plan is integrated as part of the business plan, this segment would focus on some history of the marketplace, marketing strengths and weaknesses of the firm, and market opportunities and threats.

2. Where do we want to go (in the short term)? This question primarily addresses the marketing objectives and goals of the new venture in the next 12 months. In the initial business plan, the objectives and goals often go beyond the first year because of the need to project profits and cash needs for the first three years.

3. How do we get there? This question discusses the specific marketing strategy that will be implemented, when it will occur, and who will be responsible for

TABLE 8.4	What Market Planning Can and Cannot Do	
Can Do		**Cannot Do**
• It will enhance the firm's ability to integrate all marketing activities so as to maximize efforts toward achieving the corporate goals and objectives.		• It will not provide a crystal ball that will enable management to predict the future with extreme precision.
• It will minimize the effects of surprise from sudden changes in the environment.		• It will not prevent management from making mistakes.
• It establishes a benchmark for all levels of the organization.		• It will not provide guidelines for every major decision. Judgment by management at the appropriate time will still be critical.
• It can enhance management's ability to manage since guidelines and expectations are clearly designated and agreed to by many members of the marketing organization.		• It will not go through the year without some modification as the environment changes.

the monitoring of activities. The answers to these questions are generally determined from the marketing research carried out before the planning process is begun. Budgets will also be determined and used in the income and cash flow projections.

Management should understand that the marketing plan is a guide for implementing marketing decision making and not a generalized, superficial document. When entrepreneurs do not take the appropriate time to develop a marketing plan, they usually have misunderstood the meaning of the marketing plan and what it can and cannot accomplish. Table 8.4 illustrates some of the things that the marketing plan can and cannot do.

The mere organization of the thinking process involved in preparing a marketing plan can be helpful to the entrepreneur because in order to develop the plan, it is necessary to formally document and describe as many marketing details as possible that will be part of the decision process during the next year. This process will enable the entrepreneur not only to understand and recognize the critical issues but also to be prepared in the event that any change in the environment occurs.

CHARACTERISTICS OF A MARKETING PLAN

The marketing plan should be designed to meet certain criteria. Some important characteristics that must be incorporated in an effective marketing plan are as follows:

• It should provide a strategy for accomplishing the company mission or goal.
• It should be based on facts and valid assumptions. Some of the facts needed are illustrated in Table 8.5. It must provide for the use of existing resources. Allocation of all equipment, financial resources, and human resources must be described.
• An appropriate organization must be described to implement the marketing plan.

TABLE 8.5   Facts Needed for Market Planning

- Who are the users, where are they located, how much do they buy, from whom do they buy, and why?
- How have promotion and advertising been employed and which approach has been most effective?
- What are the pricing changes in the market, who has initiated theses changes, and why?
- What are the market's attitudes concerning competitive products?
- What channels of distribution supply consumers, and how do they function?
- Who are the competitors, where are they located, and what advantages/disadvantages do they have?
- What marketing techniques are used by the most successful competitors? By the least successful?
- What are the overall objectives of the company for the next year and five years hence?
- What are the company's strengths? Weaknesses?
- What are one's production capabilities by product?

- It should provide for continuity so that each annual marketing plan can build on it, successfully meeting longer-term goals and objectives.
- It should be simple and short. A voluminous plan will be placed in a desk drawer and likely never used. However, the plan should not be so short that details on how to accomplish a goal are excluded.
- The success of the plan may depend on its flexibility. Changes, if necessary, should be incorporated by including "what if" scenarios and appropriate responding strategies.
- It should specify performance criteria that will be monitored and controlled. For example, the entrepreneur may establish an annual performance criterion of 10 percent of market share in a designated geographic area. To attain this goal, certain expectations should be made at given time periods (e.g., at the end of three months we should have a 5 percent share of market). If not attained, then new strategy or performance standards may be established.

It is clear from the preceding discussion that the market plan is not intended to be written and then put aside. It is intended to be a valuable document, referred to often, and a guideline for the entrepreneur during the next time period.

marketing plan Written statement of marketing objectives, strategies, and activities to be followed in business plan

marketing system Interacting internal and external factors that affect venture's ability to provide goods and services to meet customer needs

Since the term *marketing plan* denotes the significance of marketing, it is important to understand the *marketing system*. The marketing system identifies the major interacting components, both internal and external to the firm, that enable the firm to successfully provide products and/or services to the marketplace. Figure 8.1 provides a summary of the components that constitute the marketing system.[7]

As can be seen from Figure 8.1, the environment (external and internal) plays a very important role in developing the market plan. These factors should be identified and discussed in the Environmental and Industry Analysis section of the business plan (see Chapter 7). It should also be noted that these factors are typically uncontrollable but need to be recognized as part of the marketing plan.

FIGURE 8.1   The Marketing System

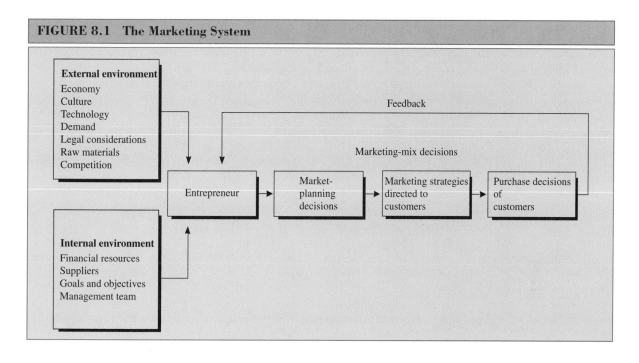

In addition to the external environmental factors, there are internal environmental factors that are more controllable by the entrepreneur but can also affect the preparation of the marketing plan and implementation of an effective marketing strategy. Some of the major internal variables are as follows:

- *Financial Resources.* The financial plan, discussed in the next chapter, should outline the financial needs for the new venture. Any marketing plan or strategy should consider the availability of financial resources as well as the amount of funds needed to meet the goals and objectives stated in the plan.

- *Management Team.* It is extremely important in any organization to make appropriate assignments of responsibility for the implementation of the marketing plan. In some cases the availability of a certain expertise may be uncontrollable (e.g., a shortage of certain types of technical managers). In any event, the entrepreneur must build an effective management team and assign the responsibilities to implement the marketing plan.

- *Suppliers.* The suppliers used are generally based on a number of factors such as price, delivery time, quality, and management assistance. In some cases, where raw materials are scarce or there are only a few suppliers of a particular raw material or part, the entrepreneur has little control over the decision. Since the price of supplies, delivery time, and so on, are likely to impact many marketing decisions, it is important to incorporate these factors into the marketing plan.

- *Company Mission.* As indicated in Chapter 5, every new venture should define the nature of its business. This statement that helps to define the company's mission basically describes the nature of the business and what the entrepreneur hopes to accomplish with that business. This mission statement or business definition will guide the firm through long-term decision making.

TABLE 8.6	Critical Decisions for Marketing Mix
Marketing Mix Variable	**Critical Decisions**
Product	Quality of components or materials, style, features, options, brand name, packaging, sizes, service availability, and warranties
Price	Quality image, list price, quantity, discounts, allowances for quick payment, credit terms, and payment period
Channels of distribution	Use of wholesalers and/or retailers, type of wholesalers or retailers, how many, length of channel, geographic coverage, inventory, and transportation
Promotion	Media alternatives, message, media budget, role of personal selling, sales promotion (displays, coupons, etc.), and media interest in publicity

THE MARKETING MIX

The above environmental variables will provide much important information in deciding what will be the most effective marketing strategy to be outlined in the marketing plan. The actual short-term marketing decisions in the marketing plan will consist of four important marketing variables: product or service, pricing, distribution, and promotion. These four factors are referred to as the *marketing mix*. Each variable will be described in detail in the strategy or action plan section of the marketing plan discussed later in this chapter. Although flexibility may be an important consideration, the entrepreneur needs a strong base to provide direction for the day-to-day marketing decisions. Some of the critical decisions in each area are described in Table 8.6.

marketing mix   Combination of product, price, promotion, and distribution and other marketing activities needed to meet marketing objectives

STEPS IN PREPARING THE MARKETING PLAN

Figure 8.2 illustrates the various stages involved in preparing the marketing plan. Each of these stages, when followed, will complete the necessary information to formally prepare the marketing plan. Each of the steps is outlined and discussed, using examples to assist the reader in fully understanding the necessary information and procedure for preparing the marketing plan.[8]

Defining the Business Situation

The *situation analysis* is a review of where we have been. It responds to the first of the three questions mentioned earlier in this chapter. It also considers many of the factors that were defined in the environmental analysis section of the business plan (see Chapter 7).

To fully respond to this question, the entrepreneur should provide a review of past performance of the product and the company. If this is a new venture, the background will be more personal, describing how the product or service was developed and why it was developed (e.g., to satisfy consumer needs). If the plan is being written after the new venture has started up, it

situation analysis   Describes past and present business achievements of new venture

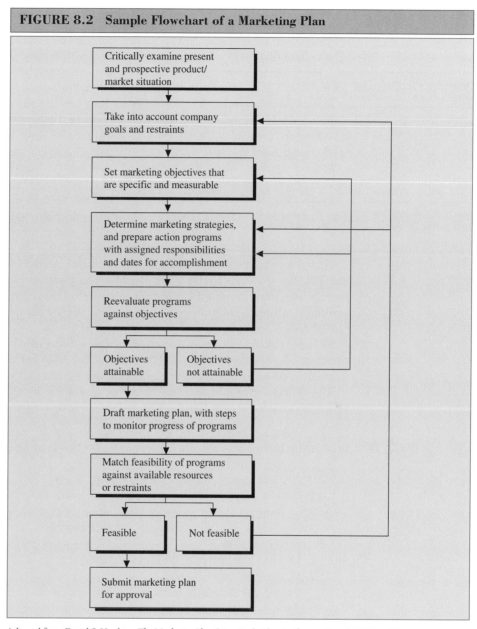

FIGURE 8.2 Sample Flowchart of a Marketing Plan

Adapted from David S. Hopkins, *The Marketing Plan* (New York: The Conference Board, 1981), p. 17.

would contain information on present market conditions and performance of the company's goods and services. Any future opportunities or prospects should also be included in this section of the plan.

The industry and competitive environment have already been discussed in an earlier section of the business plan. Thus, at this point the entrepreneur should simply review some of the key elements of this section to help provide a context for the marketing segmentation and actions that will be stated in this section of the business plan.

Defining the Target Market/Opportunities and Threats

From the marketing research done earlier, the entrepreneur should have a good idea of who the customer or *target market* will be. Knowledge of the target market provides a basis for determining the appropriate marketing action strategy that will effectively meet its needs. The defined target market will usually represent one or more segments of the entire market. Thus, it is important even before beginning the research to understand what market segmentation is before determining the appropriate target market.

target market   Specific group of potential customers toward which venture aims its marketing plan

Market segmentation is the process of dividing the market into small homogeneous groups. Market segmentation allows the entrepreneur to more effectively respond to the needs of more homogeneous consumers. Otherwise the entrepreneur would have to identify a product or service that would meet the needs of everyone in the marketplace.

market segmentation   Process of dividing a market into definable and measurable groups for purposes of targeting marketing strategy

Henry Ford's vision was to manufacture a single product (one color, one style, one size, etc.) for the mass market. His Model T was produced in large numbers on assembly lines, enabling the firm to reduce costs through specialization of labor and materials. Although his strategy was unique, any successful mass-market strategy employed today would be unlikely.

In 1986, Paul Firestone of Reebok discovered that many consumers who bought running shoes were not athletes. They bought the shoe for comfort and style. Firestone then developed a marketing plan that was targeted directly to this segment.

The process of segmenting and targeting customers by the entrepreneur should proceed as follows:[9]

I.   Decide what general market or industry you wish to pursue.
II. Divide the market into smaller groups based on characteristics of the customer or buying situations.
    A. Characteristics of the customer
        1. Geographic (e.g., state, country, city, region)
        2. Demographic (e.g., age, sex, occupation, education, income, and race)
        3. Psychographic (e.g., personality and lifestyles)
    B. Buying situation
        1. Desired benefits (e.g., product features)
        2. Usage (e.g., rate of use)
        3. Buying conditions (e.g., time available and product purpose)
        4. Awareness of buying intention (e.g., familiarity of product and willingness to buy)
III. Select segment or segments to target.
IV. Develop a marketing plan integrating product, price, distribution, and promotion.

Let's assume that an entrepreneur has developed a unique liquid cleaner that could clean a restaurant grill at operating temperatures; remove grease from household appliances; clean whitewall tires, bumpers, upholstery, and engines; and clean boats. At least four markets could be identified from its uses: restaurants, households, automobiles, and boats. Each of the markets is then segmented on the basis of the variables discussed above. The entrepreneur finds that in the restaurant market there is little competition, the product's advantages are most evident, and massive marketing resources are not necessary for entry. On this basis, the entrepreneur chooses

As Seen in *Business Week:* To The Victors Belong the Ads
Yahoo! and Just a Few Other Sites Rake in the Big Bucks

One question plaguing Internet stocks lately has been whether companies that charge nothing for using their websites could succeed simply by selling advertising. The good news: Yes, the companies can thrive on advertising alone. The bad news: The number of those that can do this seems to be shrinking, as marketers spend more and more with just a handful of big sites. According to the most recent survey by the Internet Advertising Bureau (IAB), the share of ad revenues among the top 10 sites continued to expand, from 64 percent a year ago, to 75 percent in the first quarter of this year.

The most important sign of this phenomenon is the growing clout of the top site, Yahoo!, which confirms that it will raise ad rates next year. It's not giving out the details, but analysts peg the hike as high as 20 percent. And with its 80 million users, Yahoo! should be able to make the rates stick, analysts say. That mass audience is the closest thing in cyberspace to network TV—making it a must-buy for many advertisers. "We have a brand that commands a premium," says Anil Singh, the Yahoo! senior vice-president for business operations.

This isn't TV, however, and numbers alone won't work for many advertisers who want to take advantage of the new medium's ability to identify exactly who is in the audience. For these advertisers, it doesn't matter how many eyeballs a portal can deliver: They want only motivated buyers. "We were disappointed with the portals. They didn't even reach our low expectations," says Peter M. Neupert, CEO of drugstore.com Inc.

What are some of the strategies not working on the Web these days? Banner ads is a top example. They're still the staple of online advertising, accounting for 58 percent of Net ad sales in the first quarter. But advertisers are beginning to see that such vaguely targeted ads bring little response. In an August survey, researcher Strategis Group found that 52 percent of the people polled hadn't clicked on an ad within the past week, and 40 percent couldn't recall the ads that induced them to click.

So ad rates for banners are on the decline. According to Forrester Research Inc., the cost for banner ads has dropped from $20 last year for every 1,000 times an ad was displayed, to about $10 this year. "The standard ad buy is not effective for most advertisers," says Scott Heiferman, CEO of i-traffic, a New York online ad agency whose clients include Staples Inc. and Walt Disney Co. Instead, websites are modifying or even dumping banner ads in favor of specialized programs, such as targeted e-mail or sponsorship agreements where a company is the permanent advertiser on a site. For instance, women's site iVillage.com has created an area on its site for Ford that asks visitors to design their dream car.

But new ideas are still needed. While Forrester estimates that U.S. online ad revenue will zoom from $2.8 billion this year to $22.2 billion by 2004, Heiferman says that companies need more basic testing and creativity to hit those estimates. Yahoo! Inc., for example, will start charging extra for finely targeted ads. Other sites that understand their audiences are expected to mimic Yahoo! in raising rates. Meanwhile, at least for the big sites getting the most bucks, Yahoo! will spread some New Year's cheer with its rate hike. "It will give other companies the leeway to follow Yahoo!'s lead," says IAB Chairman Rich LeFurgy.

Source: Heather Green and Linda Himelstein, "To the Victors Belong the Ads," *Business Week* (October 4, 1999), p. 39.

the restaurant market. This market is then segmented by state, type of restaurant (e.g., fast-food, family), and whether the restaurant is part of a hospital, school, company, and so forth. Each of these segments is evaluated, and the entrepreneur chooses to initially target independent family restaurants in a four-state region.

This market offers the greatest opportunity because no other product exists that can perform grill cleaning at operating temperature and without damage to the grill. The threats in this market include ease of entry and potential imitation by major competitors: in fact, a number of large firms such as Colgate-Palmolive and Procter & Gamble may be interested in the market. However, regardless of the threats, the greatest opportunity is presented in the restaurant grill cleaning segment. This becomes the target market.

Considering Strengths and Weaknesses

It is important for the entrepreneur to consider strengths and weaknesses in the target market. For example, referring to the liquid grill cleaner, the primary strength in its market is clearly its unique application: It can be used on a hot operating grill with no discernible odor. Other strengths might relate to the fact that the company has experience in the restaurant business and understands the customer.

Weaknesses could relate to the production capacity limited by space and equipment. In addition, the company lacks a strong distribution system for the product and would have to depend on manufacturers' representatives. Lack of cash to support a heavy promotional effort could also be identified as a weakness.

Establishing Goals and Objectives

Before any marketing strategy decisions can be outlined, the entrepreneur must establish realistic and specific goals and objectives. These *marketing goals and objectives* respond to the question: "Where do we want to go?" and should specify such things as market share, profits, sales (by territory and region), market penetration, number of distributors, awareness level, new product launching, pricing policy, sales promotion, and advertising support.

marketing goals and objectives Statements of level of performance desired by new venture

For example, the entrepreneur of a new frozen diet product may determine the following objectives for the first year: 10 percent market penetration, 60 percent of market sampled, distribution in 75 percent of the market. All these goals must be considered reasonable and feasible given the business situation described earlier.

All the above goals were quantifiable and could be measured for control purposes. However, not all goals and objectives must be quantified. It is possible for a firm to establish such goals or objectives as, research customer attitudes toward a product, set up a sales training program, improve packaging, change name of product, or find new distributor. It is a good idea to limit the number of goals or objectives to between six and eight. Too many goals make control and monitoring difficult. Obviously, these goals should represent key areas to ensure marketing success.

Defining Marketing Strategy and Action Programs

Once the marketing goals and objectives are established, the entrepreneur can begin to develop the *marketing strategy and action plan* to achieve them. These strategy and action decisions respond to the question "How do we get there?" As indicated earlier, these decisions reflect on the marketing mix variables. Some possible decisions that would be made for each variable are discussed below.

marketing strategy and action plan Specific activities outlined to meet the venture's business plan goals and objectives

Product or Service   This element of the marketing mix indicates a description of the product or service to be marketed in the new venture. This product or service definition may consider more than the physical characteristics. For example, Dell Computer's product is computers, which is not distinctive from many other existing competitors. What makes the products distinctive is the fact that they are assembled from off-the-shelf components and are marketed with direct-marketing and Internet techniques promising quick delivery and low prices. Dell also provides extensive customer service with e-mail and telephone available to the customer to ask technical or nontechnical questions. Thus, the product is more than its physical components. It involves packaging, the brand name, price, warranty, image, service, delivery time, features, style, and even the website that will be seen by most customers. When considering market strategy, the entrepreneur will need to consider all or some of these issues, keeping in mind the goal of satisfying customer needs. Since it is sometimes difficult to separate the product from the service, such as in the case of Dell Computer Corporation, it is important for the entrepreneur to understand the role of an effective customer service program.

Customer Service   Meeting customer needs and creating loyalty should be primary goals of any new venture. If customer service is poor or mediocre, the customer may choose to buy from a competitor. There are a number of low-cost simple steps that an entrepreneur can take to ensure customer satisfaction. These steps are as follows:

1. In writing develop a statement of customer service principles. Employees should be made aware of what these principles are and their importance to sales and profits.
2. Train those employees who have direct contact with customers. Consistency in service can be enhanced with a good training program.
3. Establish a process for evaluating customer service. Follow-up registration cards or a telephone call from an employee are two simple methods that can provide feedback. One car dealership had a very unique way of following up a sale by having the salesperson send a handwritten personal note thanking the customer for buying the vehicle from them.
4. Reward employees who are most effective in providing quality customer service.
5. Make regular contact with customers with a newsletter, telephone call, e-mail, or fax. These contacts could provide important industry data or trends or be used to inform customers of new developments in the new venture. A quality website can also be used to provide this kind of information to the customer. These regular contacts keep the name of the company fresh in the minds of the customers.
6. Invest in quality telephone equipment that can provide quick and easy transmission of requests from customers. There is nothing worse than a nonresponse or late response to a customer's problem.
7. The ultimate in quality service is meeting customer expectations. This requires the venture to be a good listener, to ask questions, and to make a commitment to meeting the customer's expectations.

E-commerce businesses have recently discovered the importance of customer service even though online they are in direct one-to-one contact with the customer. The fact is that the customer can easily move to another site, which supports the necessity of customer service. Furniture.com, a start-up in Worcester, Massachusetts, offers a unique website where the customer, upon clicking on style preferences, will have a live salesperson available in five seconds to discuss options via web chatting

The Practice of Deception

Marketing as a discipline and marketing managers more specifically are being increasingly scrutinized and criticized by society. They are being questioned as to such issues as making false claims about products, manufacturing inferior products, charging the consumer more than the product is worth, using deceptive advertising practices, and using irresponsible sales techniques. Unfortunately, like most other ethical issues, one or two examples that are highly publicized seem to become the norm for behavior when in fact they are clearly the exceptions rather than the rule. Ethics in marketing is a very complex area that involves some very tough questions about what is right or wrong as evidenced by the following example.

Chin-Ning Chu, a native of China (where she was born and educated), promotes books and seminars to entrepreneurs on the science of deception. In these books and seminars Chu presents tools of deception that entrepreneurs can use to gain competitive advantages. She uses the example of a salesperson who knows the customer needs the product but needs further convincing before closing the sale. Deception, according to Chu, would be for the salesperson to lead the customer to the result that is right for them in order to close the sale. Chu argues that

this is not deceitful. She also feels that the word *deception* is regarded as offensive when in fact it has been practiced by the military for legitimate good.

Customers of Chu's books and seminars argue that the knowledge of deception helps them to be prepared, if used by their rivals. Does this make these principles of deception acceptable if they are used to protect oneself from evil?

Matthew Goldworm indicated how he used deception to keep his competitors away from his market niche. He portrayed his company as a small entity with only a single product and very little interest in growth, when the truth was the opposite. This strategy of deception gave Goldworm's company, TerraLogics Inc., about five years without any interference from competitors, so that by then he had been able to build a strong customer base and good revenue system. He was then able to sell the company to one of the firms he had actually duped with his strategy.

Was this unethical behavior? The debate still continues since there are no laws broken and entrepreneurs will probably always be in disagreement as to whether such practices are right or wrong.

Source: M. Henricks, "On the Sly," *Entrepreneur* (November 1994), pp. 44–47. Reprinted with permission.

---

or on netphone. Customer service does not end here, since each customer is assigned a representative who will follow up on all transactions and keep the customer informed about new products, styles, sales, and the like.[10]

Pricing   One of the more difficult decisions in this section of the marketing plan is determining the appropriate price for the product or service. A product with quality and expensive components will require a high price to maintain the proper image. The entrepreneur will also have to consider many other factors such as costs, discounts, freight, and markups. The problem in estimating price is often associated with the difficult task of estimating costs, since they are often reflected in demand, which in itself is difficult to project. Knowledge of competitors' prices can be useful in positioning the entrepreneur's products or services. Marketing research can also assist the entrepreneur in determining a reasonable price that consumers would be willing to pay.

Distribution   This factor provides utility to the consumer; that is, it makes a product convenient to purchase when it is needed. This variable must also be consistent with other marketing mix variables. For example, a high-quality product not only will carry a high price but also should be distributed in outlets that have a quality image.

There are many options for the entrepreneur to consider in distributing the product. Issues such as type of channel, number of intermediaries, and location of channel members should be described in this section of the marketing plan. In a new venture, it may be appropriate, because of the costs in starting the venture, to consider the Internet, direct mail, or telemarketing as a means of distributing the product or service. Regardless of the type of business it is usually necessary for the new venture to have a website. Many retailers and manufacturers are finding that the percentage of sales conducted over the Internet is growing. Dell Computer Corporation's success in Internet sales is strong evidence of the role that Internet marketing can have on product sales and profits.

Projections are that the Internet will becoming an increasingly important medium for information and distribution of products and services. In 1999 more than $43 billion in goods and services were bought and sold over the Internet. Forrester Research Inc. predicts that by the year 2003 this figure will reach $1.3 trillion, which would represent more than 9 percent of all business and trade conducted in the United States.[11]

In addition to the Internet, direct-mail marketing can be one of the simplest low-cost means for an entrepreneur to launch a new business.[12] All you need is a good mailing list, a catalog or brochure with products described, and a toll-free number for customers. With the growth and expansion in computer technology, mailing lists not only are inexpensive but can be directed to a very narrowly defined target market. Mailing lists can be easily purchased at very reasonable costs from mailing list brokers, who are listed in the yellow pages.

Direct-marketing or Internet strategies are not a guarantee for success. The entrepreneur should evaluate all possible options for distribution before making a decision in the marketing plan. Marketing research as well as networking among business associates and friends can often provide helpful insights.

Promotion   It is usually necessary for the entrepreneur to inform potential consumers about the product's availability or to educate the consumer, using advertising media such as print, radio, or television. Usually television is too expensive unless the entrepreneur considers cable television a viable outlet. A local service or retail company such as a pet store may find that using community cable stations is the most cost effective method to reach customers. Larger markets can be reached using the Internet, direct mail, trade magazines, or newspapers. The entrepreneur should carefully evaluate each alternative medium, considering not just costs but the effectiveness of the medium in meeting the market objectives mentioned earlier in the marketing plan. As stated earlier a website may also be valuable to create awareness and to promote the products and services of the new venture.

It is also possible to make use of publicity as a means of introduction to the market. Unique or creative marketing ideas are often of special interest to the media. Local newspapers or trade magazines will often write articles about new start-ups. A public relations strategy that sends news releases to these media can often result in free advertising.[13] Entrepreneurs should consider these outlets in conjunction with any other promotional methods.

All of these marketing mix variables will be described in detail in the marketing strategy or action plan section of the marketing plan. As indicated earlier, it is important that the marketing strategy and action programs be specific and detailed enough to guide the entrepreneur through the next year. Examples of a poor and a good marketing strategy are as follows:

- Poor strategy—We will increase sales for our product by lowering the price.
- Good strategy—We will increase sales for our product by 6 to 8 percent by (1) lowering the price 10 percent, (2) attending an important trade show in New York, and (3) conducting a mailing to 5,000 potential customers throughout the United States.

Coordination of the Planning Process

For a new venture, the management team must coordinate the planning process. Since many of the members of the team may lack expertise in market planning, this presents problems in its effective completion. In many cases, the entrepreneur may be the only person involved in preparing the market plan, especially if it is a new venture. In this case, coordination may not be an issue. However, the entrepreneur may still lack the understanding and experience for preparing a market plan. In this instance, the entrepreneur should seek help from available sources such as the Small Business Administration, Small Business Development Centers, universities, marketing consultants, and even textbooks.

Designating Responsibility for Implementation

Writing the marketing plan is only the beginning of the marketing process. The plan must be implemented effectively in order to meet all the desired goals and objectives. Someone must take the responsibility for implementing each of the strategy and action decisions made in the marketing plan. Typically, the entrepreneur will assume this responsibility since he or she will be interested in the control and monitoring of the venture.

Budgeting the Marketing Strategy

Effective planning decisions must also consider the costs involved in the implementation of these decisions. If the entrepreneur has followed the procedure of detailing the strategy and action programs to meet the desired goals and objectives, costs should be reasonably clear. If assumptions are necessary, they should be clearly stated so that anyone else who reviews the written marketing plan (e.g., a venture-capital firm) will understand these implications.

   This budgeting of marketing action and strategy decisions will also be useful in preparing the financial plan. Details of how to develop a financial plan are discussed in Chapter 9.

Implementation of the Market Plan

The marketing plan is meant to be a commitment by the entrepreneur to a specific strategy. It is not a formality that serves as a superficial document to outside financial supporters or suppliers. It is meant to be a formal vehicle for answering the three questions posed earlier in this chapter and a commitment to make adjustments as needed or dictated by market conditions.

Monitoring Progress of Marketing Actions

Generally, monitoring of the plan involves tracking specific results of the marketing effort. Sales data by product, territory, sales rep, and outlet are a few of the specific results that should be monitored. What is monitored is dependent on the specific goals and objectives outlined earlier in the marketing plan. Any "weak" signals from the monitoring process will provide the entrepreneur with the opportunity to redirect or modify the existing marketing effort to allow the firm to achieve its initial goals and objectives.

CONTINGENCY PLANNING

Generally, the entrepreneur does not have the time to consider many alternative plans of action should the initial plan fail. However, as stated earlier, it is important for the entrepreneur to be flexible and prepared to make adjustments where necessary. It is unlikely that any marketing plan will succeed exactly as expected.

WHY SOME PLANS FAIL

Marketing plans are ineffective or fail in meeting marketing goals for different reasons. In fact, failure may also be considered a matter of degree since some goals may be met and others missed completely. The overall failure of the plan will be judged by management and may depend on the mere solvency of the organization. Some of the reasons for failure can be avoided if the entrepreneur is careful in preparing the marketing plan. Some of the more common reasons for failure that can be controlled are as follows:

- Lack of a real plan—The marketing plan is superficial and lacks detail and substance, especially regarding goals and objectives.
- Lack of an adequate situation analysis—It is invaluable to know where you are and where you have been, before deciding where you want to go. Careful analysis of the environment can result in reasonable goals and objectives.
- Unrealistic goals—This generally results because of a lack of understanding of the situation.
- Unanticipated competitive moves, product deficiencies, and acts of God—With a good situation analysis, as well as an effective monitoring process, competitive decisions can be assessed and predicted with some degree of accuracy. Deficiencies in the product often result from rushing the product to the market. For an act of God—such as an oil spill, flood, hurricane, or war—the entrepreneur has no control.

IN REVIEW

Summary

Marketing planning is a critical element in ensuring the long-term success of any entrepreneurial effort. The marketing plan designates the response to three questions: Where have we been? Where are we going? How do we get there?

To be able to respond effectively to these questions, it is generally necessary for the entrepreneur to conduct some marketing research. This research may involve secondary sources or a primary data collection process. Information from the research will be very important in determining the marketing mix factors or the marketing strategy to be implemented in the marketing plan.

The marketing plan entails a number of major steps. First, it is important to conduct a situation analysis to assess the question, "Where have we been?" Market segments must be defined and opportunities identified. This will help the entrepreneur determine a profile of the customer. Goals and objectives must be established. These goals and objectives must be realistic and detailed (quantified if possible). Next, the marketing strategy and action programs must be defined. Again, these should be detailed so that the entrepreneur clearly understands how the venture is going to get where it wants to go.

The marketing strategy section or action plan describes how to achieve the goals and objectives already defined. There may be alternative marketing approaches that could be used to achieve these defined goals. The use of creative strategies such as direct marketing may give the entrepreneur a more effective entry into the market.

The action programs should also be assigned to someone to ensure their implementation. If the plan has been detailed, the entrepreneur should be able to assign some costs and budgets for implementing the marketing plan. During the year, the marketing plan will be monitored in order to discern the success of the action programs. Any "weak" signals will provide the entrepreneur with the opportunity to modify the plan and/or develop a contingency plan.

Careful scrutiny of the marketing plan can enhance its success. However, many plans fail, not because of poor management or a poor product but because the plan was not specific or had an inadequate situation analysis, unrealistic goals, or did not anticipate competitive moves, product deficiencies, and acts of God.

Questions for Discussion

1. The following statistics have been identified in your market: (a) the number of dual-income earners is 50 percent of the total, (b) the average household income is 20 percent higher than the U.S. average, and (c) the majority of the households in this market have teenage children. What impact would each of these statistics have on the marketing of clothing, travel, toys, and furniture?

2. Marketing research data may be collected from either secondary or primary sources. Discuss the differences in these sources, using specific examples.

3. What are the major characteristics of an effective marketing plan?

4. One of the important elements of the marketing plan is the goals and objectives. Assume that you are launching a new e-commerce retail business. Give some examples of goals and objectives that might be in a marketing plan for such a business. How would you monitor these goals?

5. Why do some marketing plans fail?

Key Terms

market segmentation

marketing goals and objectives

marketing mix

marketing plan

marketing strategy and action plan

marketing system

situation analysis

target market

More Information—Net Addresses in This Chapter

Advertising Age Magazine
www.adage.com

Advertising Research Foundation
www.arfsite.org

Biz Women
www.bizwomen.com

Business Resource Center
www.morebusiness.com

The Census Bureau
www.census.gov/

CNN Financial News
www.cnnfn.com

Dun & Bradstreet Information Service
www.dnb.com

Entrepreneurial Edge
www.edge.lowe.org

Entrepreneur on the Web
www.entrepreneur-web.com/

Free Marketing for Entrepreneurs
www.freeway101.com

Idea Cafe
www.ideacafe.com

Marketing Direct
http://mardirect.com

Money Methods
www.money-methods.com

Small Business Administration
www.sbaonline.sba.gov/

Small Business Advancement National Center
www.sbanet.uca.edu/

Statistical Abstracts
www.census.gov/stat_abstract/

World Wide Yellow Pages
www.yellow.com

Selected Readings

Auger, P.; and J. M. Gallaugher. (1997). Factors Affecting the Adoption of an Internet-Based Sales Presence for Small Businesses. *The Information Society*, vol. 13, pp. 55–74.

This paper examines critical issues surrounding the use of the Internet in emerging enterprises. These issues are (1) development and use of the online sales presence, (2) motivating factors for investing in electronic commerce, (3) the importance of the expected benefits of the online sales presence for the decision to go online; and (4) barriers preventing small businesses from further development of their online presence.

Bennett, S. (March 1999). The ABCs of E-Commerce. *Small Business Computing & Communications*, pp. 62–68.

Conducting business online does not suggest that you must be a large established company. This is a simplified guide for entrepreneurs interested in offering products and services online.

Emerick, D.; and K. Round. (2000). *Exploring Web Marketing and Project Management.* Upper Saddle River, NJ: Prentice Hall Inc.

This paperback book provides the entrepreneur with the core skills needed to develop a website and to utilize the Web to market goods and services. The first section, which focuses on marketing and communications, is the most beneficial to those considering online marketing.

Hester, E. (April 1996). Successful Marketing Research: Know Your Market and Your Competition. *Potentials in Marketing*, pp. 10–13.

The investment in marketing research to save the entrepreneur time and money in the long run is emphasized in this article. It stresses setting goals and identifies many important issues that entrepreneurs will need to research before preparing their plans.

Hiebing, R. G.; and S. W. Cooper. (1997). *The Successful Marketing Plan*, 2nd ed. Upper Saddle River, NJ: Prentice Hall Inc.

Provides a 10-step method to writing a marketing plan. It details the information you need with work sheets, flowcharts, and outlines to show how the information is applied to the preparation of the plan.

Pelham, Alfred M. (2000). Market Orientation and Other Potential Influences on Performance in Small and Medium-Sized Manufacturing Firms. *Journal of Small Business Management*, vol. 38, no. 1, pp. 48–67.

Author argues that, compared to strategy selection, firm size, or industry characteristics, market orientation has the strongest positive relationship with measures of performance.

Pitt, Leyland F.; and Kannemeyer, Rushieda. (2000). The role of Adaptation in Microenterprise Development: A Marketing Perspective. *Journal of Developmental Entrepeneurship*, vol. 5, no. 2, pp. 137–155.

The entrepreneur's willingness to adapt key marketing mix variables impacts the performance of the venture. The concept of adaptation is explored as it applies to marketing efforts of the start-up entreprenuer, in order to determine whether traits commonly associated with the entrepreneurial personality are associated with successful adaptation of one's business.

Prior, T. L. (February 1995). Channel Surfers. *Inc.*, pp. 65–68.

Provides some interesting and creative ways to distribute products, and gives examples of creative approaches used by entrepreneurs that allowed them to effectively reach more customers in their markets.

Strauss, J.; and R. Frost. (1999). *Marketing on the Internet.* Upper Saddle River, NJ: Prentice Hall, Inc.

This book is organized similarly to a typical principles text using the Internet as the focal point. Thus, it presents the Internet as a tool for product development, pricing, promotion, and distribution. Many interesting websites are also identified.

Endnotes

1. See the following for a comprehensive history of Michael S. Dell: S. A. Forest and C. Arnst, "The Education of Michael Dell," *Business Week* (March 22, 1993), pp. 82–88; A. Alper, "Dell Withdraws $200M Stock Offering," *Computerworld* (March 1, 1993), p. 20; G. McWilliams, "Dell's CEO Bets His Own Cash on the Web," *Wall Street Journal* (August 26, 1999), p. B6; and Dell's website www.dell.com.
2. A. C. Burns and R. Bush, *Marketing Research*, 3rd ed. (Upper Saddle River, NJ: Prentice Hall Inc., 2000), pp. 7–12.
3. M. Peters and C. Brush, "Market Information Scanning Activities and Growth in New Ventures: A Comparison of Service and Manufacturing Businesses," *Journal of Business Research* (May 1996), pp. 81–89.
4. Burns and Bush, *Marketing Research*, pp. 262–96.
5. Burns and Bush, *Marketing Research*, pp. 237–50.
6. R. D. Hisrich and M. P. Peters, *Marketing Decisions for New and Mature Products*, 2nd ed. (New York: Macmillan Publishing, 1991), pp. 63–78.
7. E. Berkowitz, R. Kerin, S. Hartley, and W. Rudelius, *Marketing*, 6th ed. (Burr Ridge, IL: Irwin McGraw-Hill, 2000) pp. 5–25.

8. D. R. Lehmann and R. S. Winer, *Analysis for Marketing Planning*, 4th ed. (Burr Ridge, IL: Richard D. Irwin, Inc., 1997), p. 8.
9. Berkowitz, *Marketing*, pp. 255–73.
10. M. Stepanek, "You'll Wanna Hold Their Hands," *Business Week E.Biz* (March 22, 1999), p. 30.
11. R. Hof, "What Every CEO Needs to Know about Electronic Business," *Business Week E.Biz* (March 22, 1999), pp. 10–11.
12. J. Chun, "Going the Distance," *Entrepreneur* (February 1996), pp. 114–27.
13. B. Solomon, "Tricks of the Trade," *Entrepreneur* (November 1993), pp. 144–9.

APPENDIX   Marketing Plan Outlines

1. Marketing Plan for a Consumer Products Company
2. Marketing Plan for a Business-to-Business Company
3. Marketing Plan for a Service Company

EXHIBIT 1   **Marketing Plan for a Consumer Products Company**

I. ANALYZE AND DEFINE THE BUSINESS SITUATION—past, present, and future
An analysis of where we are, perhaps how we got there. Data and trend lines should go back three to five years.

Suggested items to cover:
A. The scope of the market (class of trade)
B. Sales history by products, by class of trade, by regions
C. Market potential, major trends anticipated
D. Distribution channels
   1. Identification of principal channels (dealer or class of trade), sales history through each type
   2. Buying habits and attitudes of these channels
   3. Our selling policies and practices
E. The customer or end user
   1. Identification of customers making the buying decision, classified by age, income level, occupation, geographical location, etc.
   2. Customer attitudes on product or services, quality, price, etc. Purchase or use habits that contribute to attitudes.
   3. Advertising history: expenditures, media and copy strategy, measurements of effectiveness
   4. Publicity and other educational influences
F. The product or services
   1. Story of the product line, quality development, delivery and service
   2. Comparison with other approaches to serve the customers' needs
   3. Product research; product improvements planned

II. IDENTIFY PROBLEMS AND OPPORTUNITIES

A. In view of the facts cited in (I) above, what are the major problems that are restricting or impeding our growth?

B. What opportunities do we have for

—Overcoming the above problems?

—Modifying or improving the product line or adding new products?

—Serving the needs of more customers in our market or developing new markets?

—Improving the efficiency of our operation?

III. DEFINE SPECIFIC AND REALISTIC BUSINESS OBJECTIVES

A. Assumptions re future conditions

—Level of economic activity

—Level of industry activity

—Changes in customer needs

—Changes in distribution channels

—Changes beyond our control, increased costs, etc.

B. Primary marketing objectives (the establishment of aim points and goals). Consider where you are going and how you will get there. Objectives are the necessary base of any plan since a plan must have precise direction.

C. Overall strategy for achievement of primary objectives. The division's overall strategy to accomplish its primary objective—sample: shifting of sales emphasis, products, or classes of trade; changes for improvement of sales coverage, etc.

D. Functional (departmental) objectives. (In this section "explode" your primary objectives into subobjectives, or goals, for each department. Show the interrelation vertically, by marketing project. Show time schedule on objectives below.)

1. Advertising and promotion objectives
2. Customer service objectives
3. Product modification objectives
4. New product objectives
5. Expense control objectives
6. Workforce objectives
7. Personnel training objectives
8. Market research objectives

IV. DEFINE MARKETING STRATEGY AND ACTION PROGRAMS— to accomplish the objectives

A. Here, *detail the action steps*, priorities, and schedules relating to each of the functional objectives above. If, for example, one of your estimates was "an increase in sales of product X from 10,000 to 20,000 units," now is the time to pinpoint specific customers. In order to explain who must do what, and when, you can show the interaction of the departments listed above (III-D) and how their objectives serve to meet this increased demand.

B. If one of your objectives was to introduce a new product by "x" date, now show the details and deadlines, production schedule, market introduction plans, advertising and merchandising support, sales and service training needed, etc. Define responsibility and dates for each step.

    C. Alternatives—In the event of a delay in a project or program, what alternative plans are available?

V. CONTROL AND REVIEW PROCEDURES

How will the execution of the plan be monitored?

    A. What kinds of "feedback" information will be needed?

    B. When and how will reviews be scheduled (departments, regions, etc.)?

    C. Date for full-scale review of progress vs. plan.

Source: David S. Hopkins, *The Marketing Plan* (New York: The Conference Board, 1981), pp. 50–51.

EXHIBIT 2   Marketing Plan for a Business-to-Business Company

MARKETING PLAN OUTLINE

For each major product/product category: Time Period—One, Three, and Five Plus Years

I. MANAGEMENT SUMMARY

What is our marketing plan for this product in brief?

This is a one-page summary of the basic factors involving the marketing of the product in the plan period, along with the results expected from implementing the plan. It is intended as a brief guide for management.

II. ECONOMIC OUTLOOK

What factors in the overall economy and industry will affect the marketing of the product in the plan period, and how?

This section will contain a summary of the specific economic and industry factors that will affect the marketing of this product during the plan period.

III. THE MARKET—qualitative

Who or what kinds of market segments constitute the major prospects for this product?

This section will define the qualitative nature of our market segments. It will include definitive descriptions and profiles of major distributors, specifiers, users, and/or consumers of the product.

IV. THE MARKET—quantitative

What is the potential market for this product?

This section will apply specific quantitative measures to this product. Here we want to include numbers of potential customers, dollar volume of business, our current share of the market—any specific measures that will outline our total target for the product and where we stand competitively now.

V. TREND ANALYSIS

Based on the history of this product, where do we appear to be headed?

This section is a review of the past history of this product. Ideally, we should include annual figures for the last five years showing dollar volume, accounts opened, accounts closed, share of market, and all other applicable historical data.

VI. COMPETITION

Who are our competitors for this product, and how do we stand competitively?

This section should define our current competition. It should be a thoughtful analysis outlining who our competitors are, how successful they are, and what actions they might be expected to take regarding this product during the coming year.

VII. PROBLEMS AND OPPORTUNITIES

Internally and externally, are there problems inhibiting the marketing of this product, or are there opportunities we have not taken advantage of?

This section will include a frank commentary on both inhibiting problems and unrealized opportunities. It should include a discussion of the internal and external problems we can control, for example, by changes in policies or operational programs. It should also point to areas of opportunity regarding this product that we are not now exploring.

VIII. OBJECTIVES AND GOALS

Where do we want to go with this product?

This section will outline the immediate short- and long-range objectives for this product. Short-range goals should be specific and will apply to next year. Intermediate to long-range goals will necessarily be less specific and should project for the next three to five years and beyond. Objectives should be stated in two forms.

(1) qualitative—reasoning behind the offering of this product and what modification or other changes we expect to make.

(2) quantitative—number of accounts, dollar volume, share of market, and profit goals.

IX. ACTION PROGRAMS

Given past history, the economy, the market, competition, etc., what must we do to reach the goals we have set for this product or service?

This section will be a description of the specific actions we plan to take during the coming plan period to ensure reaching the objectives we have set for the product in VIII. These would include the full range of factors comprising our marketing mix. The discussion should cover what is to be done, schedules for completion, methods of evaluation, and assignment of accountability for executing the program and measuring results.

Source: David S. Hopkins, *The Marketing Plan* (New York: The Conference Board, 1981), pp. 65–66.

EXHIBIT 3   Marketing Plan for a Service Company

MARKETING PLAN OUTLINE

For each major bank service:

I. MANAGEMENT SUMMARY

What is our marketing plan for this service in brief?

This is a one-page summary of the basic factors involving the marketing of the service next year along with the results expected from implementing the plan. It is intended as a brief guide for management.

II. ECONOMIC PROJECTIONS

What factors in the overall economy will affect the marketing of this service next year, and how?

This section will include a summary of the specific economic factors that will affect the marketing of this service during the coming year. These might include employment, personal income, business expectations, inflationary (or deflationary) pressures, etc.

III. THE MARKET—quantitative

Who or what kinds of organization could conceivably be considered prospects for this service?

This section will define the qualitative nature of our market. It will include demographic information, industrial profiles, business profiles, and so on, for all people or organizations that could be customers for this service.

IV. THE MARKET—quantitative

What is the potential market for this service?

This section will apply specific quantitative measures to this bank service. Here we want to include numbers of potential customers, dollar volume of business, our current share of the market—any specific measures that will outline our total target for the service and where we stand competitively now.

V. TREND ANALYSIS

Based on the history of this service, where do we appear to be headed?

This section is a review of the past history of this service. Ideally, we should include quarterly figures for the last five years showing dollar volume, accounts opened, accounts closed, share of market, and all other applicable historical data.

VI. COMPETITION

Who are our competitors for this service, and how do we stand competitively?

This section should define our current competition, both bank and nonbank. It should be a thoughtful analysis outlining who our competitors are, how successful they are, why they have (or have not) been successful, and what actions they might be expected to take regarding this service during the coming year.

VII. PROBLEMS AND OPPORTUNITIES

Internally and externally, are there problems inhibiting the marketing of this service, or are there opportunities we have not taken advantage of?

This section will contain a frank commentary on both inhibiting problems and unrealized opportunities. It should include a discussion of the internal and external problems we can control, for example, changes in policies or operational procedures. It should also point to areas of opportunity regarding this service that we are not now exploiting.

VIII. OBJECTIVES AND GOALS

Where do we want to go with this service?

This section will outline the immediate short- and long-range objectives for this service. Short-range goals should be specific and will apply to next year. Long-range goals will necessarily be less specific and should project for the next five years. Objectives should be stated in two forms:

(1) qualitative—reasoning behind the offering of this service and what modifications or other changes we expect to make.

(2) quantitative—number of accounts, dollar volume, share of market, profit goals.

IX. ACTION PROGRAMS

Given past history, the economy, the market, competition, and so on, what must we do to reach the goals we have set for this service?

This section will be a description of the specific actions we plan to take during the coming year to ensure reaching the objectives we have set for the service in VIII. These would include advertising and promotion, direct mail, and brochure development. It would also include programs to be designed and implemented by line officers. The discussion should cover what is to be done, schedules for completion, methods of evaluation, and officers in charge of executing the program and measuring results.

Source: David S. Hopkins, *The Marketing Plan* (New York: The Conference Board, 1981), pp. 64–65.

9

The Financial Plan

LEARNING OBJECTIVES

1. To understand why positive profits can still result in a negative cash flow.

2. To understand the role of budgets in preparing pro forma statements.

3. To learn how to prepare monthly pro forma cash flow, income, balance sheet, and sources and uses of funds statements for the first year of operation.

4. To explain the application and calculation of the break-even point for the new venture.

5. To illustrate the alternative software packages that can be used for preparing financial statements.

E*TRADE

Although the Internet has only recently changed the lives of many consumers, one entrepreneur in 1982 recognized its future relevance as to how an individual could digitally trade securities. Bill Porter, now 70 years old, identified an opportunity that has had a significant impact on the brokerage industry. As an individual investor he had been curious as to why it was necessary to pay a broker hundreds of dollars for stock transactions. His vision was that eventually everyone would own a computer and thus would be able to invest online. In 1982 he founded Trade Plus, which provided online quotes and trading services for Fidelity, Charles Schwab, and Quick & Reilly. His first online trade took place on July 11, 1983. Porter soon realized that this would be the wave of the future. However, it would take years before the marketplace would recognize the significance of computer technology, but his persistence paid off.[1]

Bill Porter had been an entrepreneur all his life, although he admits that he really did not understand what entrepreneurship was all about. His early years as president of Treton Shoes, as a management consultant, as founder of Commercial Electronics Inc., as director of research and planning at Textron, and as research manager at General Electric's Electronic Center had given him many opportunities to see the future in online business. During this period he had also developed more than 20 products and obtained 14 patents.

While providing the online services for other brokerage houses Trade Plus began to develop its own in-house systems to accommodate traders. Trade Plus was thus competing with its own clients for trader services. So in 1992, Porter created E*TRADE Securities Inc. as a subsidiary of Trade Plus that became Compuserve's and later America Online's online trading service. The demand for these services exploded. In 1996 he created www.etrade.com, one of the original Internet stock trading companies offering consumers stock transactions for $14.95 on Dow Jones stocks and $19.95 on NASDAQ stocks. That summer the company went public, and the revolution had begun.

The financial issues in launching E*TRADE, as is the case with most Internet ventures, are unique. The process is as follows: You launch a new innovative company using futuristic technology, you raise substantial amounts of capital, you go public with dramatic gains in stock price, and after more than four years you still have not earned a profit. This is the history of E*TRADE, which is repeated often with regard to Internet companies. However, the future of E*TRADE remains bright as evidenced by the favorable assessment the company receives from financial analysts. At the fiscal year-end 1999 the company reported revenues of more than $660 million, an increase of 130 percent over the prior year—yet still resulting in a $54.4 million loss. Services were now being offered to all 50 states and 119 countries. The successful growth continued into the first quarter of 2000 with record increases in revenue, the number of new accounts, and average transactions per day compared with the fourth fiscal quarter of 1999. During this quarter the company acquired 330,000 new accounts bringing the total number of active accounts to 1.9 million. In addition, the average transactions per day increased to 133,000, an increase of 208 percent from the 43,000 in the prior year and an increase of 65 percent from the 80,000 transactions per day in the prior quarter. Being affected by the significant turbulence in the entire .com market and online transactions, E*trade achieved transaction revenues of $754.5 million in 2000 and $131 million in 2001. However, total accounts grew 41% from 2.6 million in 2000 to 3.7 million in 2001.

You would expect Bill Porter to be basking in his success. However, Bill felt that he needed someone else to manage the successful growth of the company and, right after the IPO, hired Christos Cotsakos to take over the reins as chairman and CEO while he assumed the role of chairman emeritus. However, Bill has not quit being an entrepreneur even at age 70 and recently announced that he is launching a new venture called International Securities Exchange, which will offer online options trading.

The financial plan provides the entrepreneur with a complete picture of how much and when funds are coming into the organization, where funds are going, how much cash is available, and the projected financial position of the firm. It provides the short-term basis for budgeting control and helps prevent one of the most common problems for new ventures—lack of cash. We can see from the above example how important it is to understand the role of the financial plan. Without careful financial planning in the early stages E*TRADE could have suffered serious cash flow problems, especially since like many Internet firms it had not yet achieved a profit. The financial plan must explain to any potential investor how the entrepreneur plans to meet all financial obligations and maintain its liquidity in order to either pay off debt or provide a good return on investment. In general, the financial plan will need three years of projected financial data to satisfy any outside investors. The first year should reflect monthly data.

This chapter discusses each of the major financial items that should be included in the financial plan: pro forma income statements, pro forma cash flow, pro forma balance sheets, and break-even analysis. As we saw in the E*TRADE example above Internet start-ups have some unique financial characteristics, which are included in the discussion below. Decisions about how to manage and control assets, cash, inventory, and so on, are discussed as part of Chapter 13 on managing the venture in its early stages of existence.

꽃

OPERATING AND CAPITAL BUDGETS

Before developing the pro forma income statement, the entrepreneur should prepare operating and capital budgets. If the entrepreneur is a sole proprietor, then he or she would be responsible for the budgeting decisions. In the case of a partnership, or

FIGURE 9.1   A Sample Manufacturing Budget for First Three Months ($000s)

	Jan	Feb	Mar
Projected sales (units)	50	60	70
Desired ending inventory	3	2	6
Available for sale	53	62	76
Less: beginning inventory	0	3	2
Total production required	53	59	74

where employees exist, the initial budgeting process may begin with one of these individuals, depending on his or her role in the venture. For example, a sales budget may be prepared by a sales manager, a manufacturing budget by the production manager, and so on. Final determination of these budgets will ultimately rest with the owners or entrepreneurs.

As can be seen below, in the preparation of the pro forma income statement, the entrepreneur must first develop a sales budget that is an estimate of the expected volume of sales by month. Methods of projecting sales are discussed below. From the sales forecasts the entrepreneur will then determine the cost of these sales. In a manufacturing venture the entrepreneur could compare the costs of producing these internally or subcontracting them to another manufacturer. Included will also be the estimated ending inventory needed as a buffer against possible fluctuations in demand and the costs of direct labor and materials.

Figure 9.1 illustrates a simple format for a production or manufacturing budget for the first three months of operation. This provides an important basis for projecting cash flows for the cost of goods produced, which includes units in inventory. The important information from this budget is the actual production required each month and the inventory that is necessary to allow for sudden changes in demand. As can be seen, the production required in the month of January is greater than the projected sales because of the need to retain three units in inventory. In the second month, the actual production required is less than projected sales because the inventory needs are less than in the first month. Thus, this budget reflects seasonal demand or marketing programs that can increase demand and inventory. The pro forma income statement will only reflect the actual costs of goods sold as a direct expense. Thus, in those ventures in which high levels of inventory are necessary or where demand fluctuates significantly because of seasonality, this budget can be a very valuable tool to assess cash needs.

After completing the sales budget, the entrepreneur can then focus on operating costs. First a list of fixed expenses (incurred regardless of sales volume) such as rent, utilities, salaries, interest, depreciation, and insurance should be completed. Anticipating when new employees will be hired or new storage space added can also be reflected in the fixed expense budget. Then the entrepreneur will need to ascertain variable expenses, which may change from month to month depending on sales volume, seasonality, or opportunities for new business. Examples of these operating expenses would be advertising and selling expenses. By breaking down these expenses item by item, and with input from the appropriate employees, the entrepreneur can more effectively develop the pro forma statements discussed in this chapter.

Capital budgets are intended to provide a basis for evaluating expenditures that will impact the business for more than one year. For example, a capital budget may project expenditures for new equipment, vehicles, computers, or even a new facility. It may also consider evaluating the costs of make or buy decisions in manufacturing or a comparison of leasing, buying used, or buying new equipment. Because of the complexity of these decisions, which can include the computation of the cost of capital and the anticipated return on the investment using present value methods, it is recommended that the entrepreneur enlist the assistance of an accountant.

PRO FORMA INCOME STATEMENTS

The marketing plan discussed in the previous chapter provides an estimate of sales for the next 12 months. Since sales are the major source of revenue and since other operational activities and expenses relate to sales volume, it is usually the first item that must be defined.

Figure 9.2 summarizes all the profit data during the first year of operations for MPP Plastics. This company makes plastic moldings for such customers as hard goods manufacturers, toy manufacturers, and appliance manufacturers. As can be seen from the *pro forma income* statement in Figure 9.2, the company begins to earn a profit in the fourth month. Cost of goods sold fluctuates because of the higher costs incurred for materials and labor in order to meet the sales demands in a particular month.

pro forma income   Projected net profit calculated from projected revenues minus projected costs and expenses

In preparing the pro forma income statement, sales by month must be calculated first. Marketing research, industry sales, and some trial experience might provide the basis for these figures. Forecasting techniques such as survey of buyers' intentions, composite of sales force opinions, expert opinions, or time series may be used to project sales.[2] As would be expected, it will take a while for any new venture to build up sales. The costs for achieving these increases can be disproportionately higher in some months, depending on the given situation in any particular period.

Sales revenues for an Internet start-up are often more difficult to project since extensive advertising will be necessary to attract customers to the website. For example, a giftware Internet company could anticipate no sales in the first few months until awareness of the website has been created. Heavy advertising expenditures discussed below will also be incurred to create this awareness. There is some data now available on the number of "hits" by type of website. Thus, a giftware Internet start-up could project the number of average hits expected per day or month based on industry data. From the number of "hits" it is possible to project the number of consumers who will actually buy products from the website and the average dollar amount per transaction. Using a reasonable percentage of these "hits" times the average transaction will provide an estimate of sales revenue for the Internet start-up.

The pro forma income statements also provide projections of all operating expenses for each of the months during the first year. Each of the expenses should be listed and carefully assessed to make sure that any increases in expenses are added in the appropriate month.[3] For example, selling expenses such as travel, commissions, entertainment, and so on, should be expected to increase somewhat as territories are expanded and as new salespeople or representatives are hired by the firm. Selling expenses as a percentage of sales may also be expected to be higher initially since more sales calls will have to be made to generate each sale, particularly when the firm is

FIGURE 9.2   MPP Plastics, Inc., Pro Forma Income Statement, First Year by Month ($000s)

	July	Aug	Sept	Oct	Nov	Dec	Jan	Feb	Mar	Apr	May	June
Sales	40.0	50.0	60.0	80.0	80.0	80.0	90.0	95.0	95.0	100.0	110.0	115.0
Less: cost of												
goods sold	26.0	34.0	40.0	54.0	50.0	50.0	58.0	61.0	60.0	64.0	72.0	76.0
Gross profit	14.0	16.0	20.0	26.0	30.0	30.0	32.0	34.0	35.0	36.0	38.0	39.0
Operating expenses												
Selling expenses	3.0	4.1	4.6	6.0	6.0	6.0	7.5	7.8	7.8	8.3	9.0	9.5
Advertising	1.5	1.8	1.9	2.5	2.5	2.5	3.0	7.0*	3.0	3.5	4.0	4.5
Salaries and wages	6.5	6.5	6.8	6.8	6.8	6.8	8.0	8.0	8.0	8.3	9.5	10.0
Office supplies	0.6	0.6	0.7	0.8	0.8	0.8	0.9	1.0	1.0	1.2	1.4	1.5
Rent	2.0	2.0	2.0	2.0	2.0	2.0	2.0	2.0	2.0	2.0	3.0	3.0
Utilities	0.3	0.3	0.4	0.4	0.6	0.6	0.7	0.7	0.7	0.8	0.9	1.1
Insurance	0.2	0.2	0.2	0.2	0.3	0.3	0.3	0.3	0.3	0.3	0.6	0.6
Taxes	1.1	1.1	1.2	1.2	1.2	1.2	1.6	1.6	1.6	1.7	1.9	2.0
Interest	1.2	1.2	1.2	1.2	1.2	1.2	1.2	1.5	1.5	1.5	1.5	1.5
Depreciation	3.3	3.3	3.3	3.3	3.3	3.3	3.3	3.3	3.3	3.3	3.3	3.3
Miscellaneous	0.1	0.1	0.1	0.1	0.1	0.1	0.1	0.2	0.2	0.2	0.2	0.2
Total operating expenses	19.8	21.1	22.4	24.5	24.8	24.8	28.6	33.4	29.4	31.1	35.3	37.2
Profit (loss) before	(5.8)	(5.2)	(2.4)	1.5	5.2	5.2	3.4	0.6	5.6	4.9	2.7	1.8
taxes												
Taxes	0.0	0.0	0.0	0.75	2.6	2.6	1.7	0.3	2.8	2.45	1.35	0.9
Net profit (loss)	(5.8)	(5.2)	(2.4)	0.75	2.6	2.6	1.7	0.3	2.8	2.45	1.35	0.9

*Trade show

an unknown. The cost of goods sold expense can be determined either by directly computing the variable cost of producing a unit times the number of units sold or by using an industry standard percentage of sales. For example, for a restaurant the National Restaurant Association or Food Marketing Institution publishes standard cost of goods percentages of sales. These percentages are determined from members and studies completed on the restaurant industry.

Salaries and wages for the company should reflect the number of personnel employed as well as their role in the organization (see the organization plan in the next chapter). As new personnel are hired to support the increased business, the costs will need to be included in the pro forma statement. In January, for example, a new secretary is added to the staff. Other increases in salaries and wages may also reflect raises in salary.

The entrepreneur should also consider the need to increase insurance, attend special trade shows, or add space for warehousing. All of these are reflected in the pro forma statement in Figure 9.2. Insurance for liability, medical, and so on, is increased in November and again in May. These charges can be determined easily from an insurance company and reflect the status of the operations at that time. In February, an important trade show increases the advertising budget significantly. Any unusual expenses such as the trade show should be flagged and explained at the bottom of the pro forma statement.

In February of the first year, the company incurs additional debt to finance inventory and additional space, which is added in May. Although no charges are reflected in this statement, any additional equipment that will be needed (e.g., new machinery, cars, and trucks) should also be reflected by additional depreciation expenses in the month incurred.

In addition to the monthly pro forma income statement for the first year, projections should be made for years 2 and 3. Generally, investors prefer to see three years of income projections. Year 1 totals have already been calculated in Figure 9.2. Figure 9.3 illustrates the yearly totals of income statement items for each of the three years. For the first year, the percent of sales is calculated. This percentage can then be used as a guide in determining the projected expenses for years 2 and 3. In year 3, the firm expects to significantly increase its profits as compared with the first year. In some instances, the entrepreneur may find that the new venture does not begin to earn a profit until sometime in year 2 or 3. This often depends on the nature of the business and start-up costs. For example, a service-oriented business may take less time to reach a profitable stage than a high-technology company or one that requires a large investment in capital goods and equipment, which will take longer to recover.

FIGURE 9.3   MPP Plastics, Inc., Pro Forma Income Statement, Three-Year Summary

		Year 1	Year 2	Year 3
Sales	100%	995.0	1450.0	2250.0
Less: COGS	64.8%	645.0	942.5	1460.0
Gross profit	35.2%	350.0	507.5	790.0
Operation expenses				
Selling expenses	8.0%	79.6	116.0	180.0
Advertising	3.8%	37.7	72.5	90.0
Saleries, wages	9.2%	92.0	134.0	208.0
Supplies	1.1%	11.3	16.5	25.6
Rent	2.6%	26.0	37.9	58.8
Utilities	0.8%	7.5	11.5	16.5
Insurance	0.4%	3.8	4.5	9.5
Taxes	1.8%	17.4	25.4	39.4
Interest	1.6%	15.9	15.5	14.9
Depreciation		39.6	39.6	39.6
Miscellaneous	0.2%	1.7	2.2	2.7
Total operating expenses	33.4%	332.5	475.6	685.0
Profit (loss) before taxes	1.8%	17.5	31.9	105.0
Taxes	0.9%	8.75	15.95	52.5
Net profit (loss)	0.9%	8.75	15.95	52.5

In projecting the operating expenses for years 2 and 3, it is helpful to first look at those expenses that will likely remain stable over time. Items like depreciation, utilities, rent, insurance, and interest can be more easily determined if you know the forecasted sales for years 2 and 3. Some utility expenses such as heat and power can be computed by using industry standard costs per square foot of space that is utilized by the new venture. Selling expenses, advertising, salaries and wages, and taxes may be represented as a percentage of the projected net sales. When calculating the projected operating expenses, it is most important to be conservative for initial planning purposes. A reasonable profit that is earned with conservative estimates lends credibility to the potential success of the new venture.

For the Internet start-up, capital budgeting and operating expenses will tend to be consumed by equipment purchasing or leasing, inventory, and advertising expenses. For example, the giftware Internet company introduced earlier would need to purchase or lease an extensive amount of computer equipment to accommodate the potential buyers from the website. Inventory costs would be based on the projected sales revenue just as would be the case for any retail store. Advertising costs, however, will need to be extensive to create the awareness for the giftware website. These expenses will typically involve a selection of search engines such as Yahoo and Lycos, links from other websites such as Martha Stewart online (discussed in Chapter 7) and Better Homes and Garden, and extensive media advertising in magazines, television, radio, and print, all selected because of their link to the target market.

Many of the recent Internet start-ups have not earned a profit in their first few years of operation. In spite of the lengthy time period to earn a profit these firms have attracted a significant amount of interest from the investment community.[4]

PRO FORMA CASH FLOW

Cash flow is not the same as profit. Profit is the result of subtracting expenses from sales, whereas cash flow results from the difference between actual cash receipts and cash payments. Cash flows only when actual payments are received or made. Sales may not be regarded as cash because a sale may be incurred but payment may not be made for 30 days. In addition, not all bills are paid immediately. On the other hand, cash payments to reduce the principal on a loan do not constitute a business expense but do constitute a reduction of cash. Also, depreciation on capital assets is an expense, which reduces profits, not a cash outlay.

For an Internet start-up such as our giftware company discussed above, the sales transaction would involve the use of a credit card in which a percentage of the sale would be paid as a fee to the credit card company. This is usually between 1 and 3 percent depending on the credit card. Thus, for each sale only 97 to 99 percent of the revenue would be net revenue because of this fee.

As stated earlier, one of the major problems that new ventures face is cash flow. On many occasions, profitable firms fail because of lack of cash. Thus, using profit as a measure of success for a new venture may be deceiving if there is a significant negative cash flow.

For strict accounting purposes there are two standard methods used to project cash flow, the indirect and the direct method. The most popular of these is the indirect method, which is illustrated in Figure 9.4. In this method the objective is to not repeat what is in the income statement but to understand there are some adjustments that need to be made to the net income based on the fact that actual cash may or may not have actually been received or disbursed. For example, a sale transaction

As Seen in *Business Week:* The Case for Losing Money
Sure, High-Flying Dot.coms Are Dropping a Bundle—but Profits Are on the Horizon

It's a running joke among Net entrepreneurs. Venture capitalists won't fund you unless you can prove your company will lose $50 million in the first six months—otherwise they figure you're not ambitious enough. Profits? Oh, please. Tell them your business model is so extensible that you'll scale up first and monetize later. Don't laugh, it works. But maybe not for long. Now, investors and analysts who advise them are suddenly changing their minds about e-commerce company losses. In early January, for instance, dot.coms became dog.coms almost overnight when Web superstore Amazon.com Inc. announced that—despite beating fourth-quarter revenue estimates handily—it would still show significant losses. Moméntum investors bailed out, and perennial naysayers crowed that e-tailers would never make money.

I think they're wrong—and those investors are wimps. Sure, there are way too many start-ups vying to become one of the two or three surviving online drugstores or toy emporiums. And I certainly can't devise a convincing defense of current stock premiums. But at least for now, the e-commerce leaders are right to keep spending—even if that means more losses.

For one thing, e-commerce is still in its infancy, showing little sign of slowing down. Companies that move first into a market, and spend enough to build it, capture the most customers at the lowest cost and tend to keep them. Just look at auctioneer eBay Inc. Despite site crashes, it continues to dominate person-to-person auctions.

Besides, it takes time to build real businesses online. For more than a decade, people thought America Online Inc. chief executive Stephen M. Case was nuts. From the time AOL started in 1985 until 1996, it didn't make a dime. Now, AOL is about to own the world's largest media company, Time Warner Inc. It's understandable why investors blanch when they see Amazon, eToys, and others spend millions on warehouses and customer service centers. But the recent holidays proved them right. They ended up pleasing customers—and that's the key to e-tailers ultimately turning profitable.

The big question is how long e-commerce companies should invest in expansion before producing profits. Answer: as long as opportunities keep popping up. "We think it would be a big mistake not to invest during this critical time," says Amazon CEO Jeffrey P. Bezos. Of course he'd say that, but others, such as Greg Kyle, president of Net market watcher Pegasus Research, agree: "There's so much opportunity that they shouldn't be managing for profits yet." That's even more true in emerging areas such as business-to-business e-commerce. Despite escalating net losses, for instance, investors value materials-procurement software maker Ariba Inc. at $16 billion. That's because its sales are more than tripling and it's expanding its market reach by creating online exchanges for buyers and sellers. Fact is, valuations such as Ariba's, or even Amazon's downsized $22 billion, prove most investors' thumbs are still way up.

Now, this can't go on forever. Already, Beyond.com Corp. and Egghead.com Inc. have lost their premiums by disappointing investors one too many times. Amazon and others may be in for the same unless they can show how and when they will turn the corner.

Still, the bottom line is this: Does anyone really think that only traditional companies will ever make money online? Some upstarts will prevail. They will be the very few who ignore the whiners, spend the bucks when it matters the most, and stay the course. Whom would you rather be: Steve Case or . . . uh, who's that guy who runs Prodigy Communications?

Source: Robert D. Hof, "The Case for Losing Money," *Business Week E.Biz* (February 7, 2000), p. EB102.

of $1,000 may be included in net income, but the amount has not yet been paid so no cash was received. Thus, for cash flow purposes there is no cash available from the sales transaction. For simplification and internal monitoring of cash flow purposes, many entrepreneurs prefer a simple determination of cash in less cash out. This method provides a fast indication of the cash position of the new venture at a point in time and is sometimes easier to understand.

FIGURE 9.4   Statement of Cash Flows: The Indirect Method

Cash Flow from Operating Activities: (+ or − Reflects Addition or Subtraction from Net Income)	
Net income	XXX
Adjustments to net income:	
Noncash nonoperating items:	
+ depreciation and amortization	XXX
Cash provided by changes in current assets or liabilities:	
Increase(+) or decrease(−) in accounts receivables	XXX
Increase(+) or decrease(−) in inventory	XXX
Increase(+) or decrease(−) in prepaid expenses	XXX
Increase(+) or decrease(−) in accounts payable	XXX
Net cash provided by operating activities	XX,XXX
Cash Flow from Other Activities	
Capital expenditures (−)	(XXX)
Payments of debt (−)	(XXX)
Dividends paid (−)	(XXX)
Sale of stock (+)	XXX
Net cash provided by other activities	(XXX)
Increase (Decrease) in Cash	XXX

It is important for the entrepreneur to make monthly projections of cash like the monthly projections made for profits. The numbers in the cash flow projections are constituted from the pro forma income statement with modifications made to account for the expected timing of the changes in cash. If disbursements are greater than receipts in any time period, the entrepreneur must either borrow funds or have cash in a bank account to cover the higher disbursements. Large positive cash flows in any time period may need to be invested in short-term sources or deposited in a bank in order to cover future time periods when disbursements are greater than receipts. Usually the first few months of the start-up will require external cash (debt) in order to cover the cash outlays. As the business succeeds and cash receipts accumulate, the entrepreneur can support negative cash periods.

Figure 9.5 illustrates the *pro forma cash flow* over the first 12 months for MPP Plastics. As can be seen, there is a negative cash flow based on receipts less disbursements for the first four months of operation. The likelihood of incurring negative cash flows is very high for any new venture, but the amounts and length of time before cash flows become positive will vary, depending on the nature of the business. Chapter 12 discusses how the entrepreneur can manage cash flow in the early years of a new venture. For this chapter, we will focus on how to project cash flow before the venture is launched.

pro forma cash flow   Projected cash available calculated from projected cash accumulations minus projected cash disbursements

The most difficult problem with projecting cash flows is determining the exact monthly receipts and disbursements. Some assumptions are necessary and should be conservative so that enough funds can be maintained to cover the negative cash months. In this firm, it is anticipated that 60 percent of each month's sales will be received in cash with the remaining 40 percent paid in the subsequent month. Thus,

FIGURE 9.5   MPP Plastics, Inc., Pro Forma Cash Flow, First Year by Month ($000s)

	July	Aug	Sept	Oct	Nov	Dec	Jan	Feb	Mar	Apr	May	June
Receipts												
Sales	24.0	46.0	56.0	72.0	80.0	80.0	86.0	93.0	95.0	98.0	106.0	113.0
Disbursements												
Equipment	100.0	100.0	40.0	0.0	0.0	0.0	0.0	0.0	0.0	0.0	0.0	0.0
Cost of goods	20.8	32.4	40.8	51.2	50.8	50.0	55.4	61.4	60.2	63.2	70.4	75.2
Selling expenses	1.5	3.55	5.35	5.3	6.0	6.0	6.75	7.65	7.8	8.05	8.55	9.25
Salaries	6.5	6.5	6.8	6.8	6.8	6.8	8.0	8.0	8.0	8.3	9.5	10.0
Advertising	1.5	1.8	1.9	2.5	2.5	2.5	3.0	7.0	3.0	3.5	4.0	4.5
Office supplies	0.3	0.6	0.65	0.75	0.8	0.8	0.85	0.95	1.0	1.1	1.3	1.45
Rent	2.0	2.0	2.0	2.0	2.0	2.0	2.0	2.0	2.0	2.0	3.0	3.0
Utilities	0.3	0.3	0.4	0.4	0.6	0.6	0.7	0.7	0.7	0.8	0.9	1.1
Insurance	0.8	0.8	0.8	0.0	0.4	0.0	0.0	0.5	0.0	0.0	0.0	0.0
Taxes	0.8	0.8	0.9	1.8	0.9	0.9	2.2	1.3	1.3	2.3	1.5	1.6
Loan principal and interest	2.6	2.6	2.6	2.6	2.6	2.6	2.6	2.9	2.9	2.9	2.9	2.9
Total disbursements	137.1	151.35	112.2	73.35	73.4	72.2	81.5	92.4	86.9	92.15	102.05	109.0
Cash flow	(113.1)	(105.35)	(46.2)	(1.35)	6.6	7.8	4.5	0.6	8.1	5.85	3.95	4.0
Beginning balance	275.0	161.9	56.55	10.35	9.0	15.6	23.4	27.9	28.5	36.6	42.45	46.4
Ending balance	161.9	56.55	10.35	9.0	15.6	23.4	27.9	28.5	36.6	42.45	46.4	50.5

in August, 60 percent of the August sales are received in cash, as are 40 percent of the July sales, giving a total of $46,000. Similar assumptions can be made for other disbursements. For example, from experience it is expected that 80 percent of the cost of goods will be a cash outlay in the month incurred. The remaining 20 percent is paid in the next month. Additional outlays will be made for materials to maintain an inventory.

Using conservative estimates, cash flows can be determined for each month. These cash flows will also assist the entrepreneur in determining how much money he or she will need to borrow. For this firm, $225,000 was borrowed from a bank and $50,000 from the personal savings of the two entrepreneurs. By the end of the year, the cash balance will reach $50,400 as sales build up and cash receipts exceed cash disbursements. This cash surplus can be used to repay any debt, can be invested in highly liquid assets as a buffer in case of negative cash months, or can be used to purchase any new capital equipment.

It is most important for the entrepreneur to remember that the pro forma cash flow, like the income statement, is based on best estimates. As the venture begins, it may be necessary to revise cash flow projections to ensure that their accuracy will protect the firm from any impending disaster. The estimates or projections should include any assumptions so that potential investors will understand how and from where the numbers were generated.[5]

In the case of both the pro forma income statement and the pro forma cash flow, it is sometimes useful to provide several scenarios, each based on different levels of success of the business. These scenarios and projections not only serve the purpose of generating pro forma income and cash flow statements but, more important, familiarize the entrepreneur with the factors affecting the operations.

PRO FORMA BALANCE SHEET

The entrepreneur should also prepare a projected balance sheet depicting the condition of the business at the end of the first year. The balance sheet will require the use of the pro forma income and cash flow statements to help justify some of the figures.[6]

---
pro forma balance sheet   Summarizes the projected assets, liabilities, and net worth of the new venture

---

The *pro forma balance sheet* reflects the position of the business at the end of the first year. It summarizes the assets, liabilities, and net worth of the entrepreneurs.

Every business transaction affects the balance sheet, but because of the time and expense, as well as need, it is common to prepare balance sheets at periodic intervals (i.e., quarterly or annually). Thus, the balance sheet is a picture of the business at a certain moment in time and does not cover a period of time.

Figure 9.6 depicts the balance sheet for MPP Plastics. As can be seen, the total assets equal the sum of the liabilities and owners' equity. Each of the categories is explained below:

- *Assets.* These represent everything of value that is owned by the business. Value is not necessarily meant to imply the cost of replacement or what its market value would be but is the actual cost or amount expended for the asset. The as-

---
assets   Represents items that are owned or available to be used in the venture operations

---

sets are categorized as current or fixed. Current assets include cash and anything else that is expected to be converted into cash or consumed in the operation of the business during a period of one year or less. Fixed assets are those that are tangible and will be used over a long period of time. These current assets are often dominated by receivables or money that is owed to the new venture from customers. Management of these receivables is important to the cash flow of the business since the longer it takes for customers to pay their bills, the more stress is placed on the cash needs of the venture. A more detailed discussion of management of the receivables is presented in Chapter 13.

- *Liabilities.* These accounts represent everything owed to creditors. Some of these amounts may be due within a year (current liabilities), and others may be long-term debts, such as the loan taken by MPP Plastics to purchase equipment and support cash flow. Although prompt payment of what is owed

---
liabilities   Represents money that is owed to creditors

(payables) establishes good credit ratings and a good relationship with suppliers, it is often necessary to delay payments of bills in order to more effectively manage cash flow. Ideally, any business owner wants bills to be paid on time by suppliers so that he or she can pay any bills owed on time. Unfortunately, during recessions, many firms hold back payment of their bills in order to better manage cash flow. The problem with this strategy is that while the entrepreneur may think that slower payment of bills will generate better cash flow, he or she may also find that their customers are thinking the same thing, with the result that no one gains any cash advantage. More discussion of these issues is in Chapter 12.

- *Owner Equity.* This amount represents the excess of all assets over all liabilities. It represents the net worth of the business. The $50,000 that was invested into

FIGURE 9.6   MPP Plastics, Inc., Pro Forma Balance Sheet, End of First Year

Assets		
Current assets		
Cash	$50,400	
Accounts receivable	46,000	
Merchandise inventory	10,450	
Supplies	1,200	
Total current assets		$108,050
Fixed assets		
Equipment	240,000	
Less depreciation	39,600	
Total fixed assets		200,400
Total assets		$308.450
Liabilities and Owners' Equity		
Current liabilities		
Accounts payable	$23,700	
Current portion of long-term debt	16,800	
Total current liabilities		$40,500
Long-term liabilities		
Notes payable		209,200
Total liabilities		249,700
Owners' equity		
C. Peters, capital	25,000	
K. Peters, capital	25,000	
Retained earnings	8,750	
Total owners' equity		58,750
Total liabilities and owners' equity		$308,450

the business by the two entrepreneurs is included in the owner equity or net worth section of the balance sheet. Any profit from the business will also be included in the net worth as retained earnings. Thus, all revenue increases assets and owner equity, and all expenses decrease owner equity and either increase liabilities or decrease assets.

owner equity   Represents the amount owners have invested and/or retained from the venture operations

BREAK-EVEN ANALYSIS

In the initial stages of the new venture, it is helpful for the entrepreneur to know when a profit may be achieved. This will provide further insight into the financial potential for the start-up business. Break-even analysis is a useful technique for determining how many units must be sold or how much sales volume must be achieved in order to break even.

FIGURE 9.7   Determining the Break-Even Formula

By definition, breakeven is where Total Revenue (TR)	= Total Costs (TC)
(TR)	= Selling Price (SP) × Quantity (Q)
and (TC)	= Total Fixed Costs (TFC)* + Total Variable Costs (TVC)†
Thus: SP × Q = TFC + TVC	
Where TVC	= Variable Costs/Unit (VC/Unit)‡ × Quantity (Q)
Thus SP × Q = TFC + (VC/Unit	= TFC × Q
(SP × Q) − (VC/Unit × Q)	
Q (SP − VC/Unit)	= TFC
Q	$= \dfrac{TFC}{SP - VC/Unit}$

---

*Fixed costs are those costs that, without change in present productive capacity, are not affected by changes in volume of output.

†Variable costs are those that are affected in total by changes in volume of output.

‡The variable cost per unit is all those costs attributable to producing one unit. This cost is constant within defined ranges of production.

We already know from the projections in Figure 9.2 that MPP Plastics will begin to earn a profit in the fourth month. However, this is not the break-even point since the firm has obligations for the remainder of the year that must be met, regardless of the number of units sold. These obligations, or fixed costs, must be covered by sales volume in order for a company to break even. Thus, *breakeven* is that volume of sales at which the business will neither make a profit nor incur a loss.

breakeven   Volume of sales where the venture neither makes a profit nor incurs a loss

The break-even sales point indicates to the entrepreneur the volume of sales needed to cover total variable and fixed expenses. Sales in excess of the break-even point will result in a profit as long as the selling price remains above the costs necessary to produce each unit (variable cost).[7]

The break-even formula is derived in Figure 9.7 and is given as:

$$\text{B/E(Q)} = \frac{TFC}{SP - VC/\text{unit (marginal contribution)}}$$

As long as the selling price is greater than the variable costs per unit, some contribution can be made to cover fixed costs. Eventually, these contributions will be sufficient to pay all fixed costs, at which point the firm has reached breakeven.

The major weakness in calculating the breakeven lies in determining whether a cost is fixed or variable. For new ventures these determinations will require some judgment. However, it is reasonable to expect such costs as depreciation, salaries and wages, rent, and insurance to be fixed. Materials, selling expenses such as commissions, and direct labor are most likely to be variable costs. The variable costs per unit can usually be determined by allocating the direct labor, materials, and other expenses that are incurred with the production of a single unit.

Thus, if we determine that the firm has fixed costs of $250,000, variable costs per unit of $4.50, and a selling price of $10.00, the breakeven will be as follows:

$$B/E = \frac{TFC}{SP - VC/unit}$$

$$= \frac{\$250,000}{\$10.00 - \$4.50}$$

$$= \frac{250,000}{5.550}$$

$$= 45,454 \text{ units}$$

Any units beyond 45,454 that are sold by the above firm will result in a profit of $5.50 per unit. Sales below 45,454 units will result in a loss to the firm. In those instances where the firm produces more than one product, breakeven may be calculated for each product. Fixed costs would have to be allocated to each product or determined by weighting the costs as a function of the sales projections. Thus, it might be assumed that 40 percent of the sales are for product X; hence 40 percent of total fixed costs would be allocated to that product. If the entrepreneur feels that a product requires more advertising, overhead, or other fixed costs, this should be included in the calculations.

One of the unique aspects of breakeven is that it can be graphically displayed, as in Figure 9.8. In addition, the entrepreneur can try different states of nature (e.g., different selling prices, different fixed costs and/or variable costs) to ascertain the impact on breakeven and subsequent profits.

PRO FORMA SOURCES AND USES OF FUNDS

pro forma sources and applications of funds
Summarizes all the projected sources of funds available to the venture and how these funds will be disbursed

The *pro forma sources and applications of funds* statement illustrates the disposition of earnings from operations and from other financing. Its purpose is to show how net income and financing were used to increase assets or to pay off debt.

It is often difficult for the entrepreneur to understand how the net income for the year was disposed of and the effect of the movement of cash through the business. Questions often asked are, Where did the cash come from? How was the cash used? What happened to asset items during the period?

Figure 9.9 shows the pro forma sources and applications of funds for MPP Plastics, Inc., after the first year of operation. Many of the funds were obtained from personal funds or loans. Since at the end of the first year a profit was earned, it too would be added to the sources of funds. Depreciation is added back because it does not represent an out-of-pocket expense. Thus, typical sources of funds are from operations, new investments, long-term borrowing, and sale of assets. The major uses or applications of funds are to increase assets, retire long-term liabilities, reduce owner or stockholders' equity, and pay dividends. The sources and applications of funds statement emphasizes the interrelationship of these items to working capital. The statement helps the entrepreneur as well as investors to better understand the financial well-being of the company as well as the effectiveness of the financial management policies of the company.

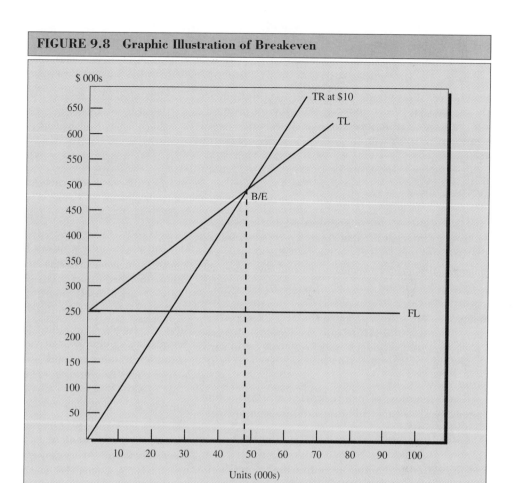

FIGURE 9.8   Graphic Illustration of Breakeven

$ 000s

650 —

600 —

550 —

500 —

450 —

400 —

350 —

300 —

250 —

200 —

150 —

100 —

50 —

TR at $10

TL

B/E

FL

10   20   30   40   50   60   70   80   90   100

Units (000s)

FIGURE 9.9   MPP Plastics, Inc., Pro Forma Sources and Applications of Funds, End of First Year

Sources of funds		
Mortgage loan	150,000	
Term loan	75,000	
Personal funds	50,000	
Net income from operations	8,750	
Add depreciation	39,600	
Total funds provided		$323,350
Applications of funds		
Purchase of equipment	240,000	
Inventory	10,450	
Loan repayment	16,800	
Total funds expended		267,250
Net increase in working capital		56,100
		$323,350

RESOURCE Discouraging the Inside Job

Since employees can manipulate the innards of computers more dexterously than most bosses, today's office workers are as likely to steal thousand-dollar data as 10-cent pencils. And the more modest the organization, the more likely it is that such white-collar theft will go undetected, warns theft-protection expert Edwin C. Bliss in *Are Your Employees Stealing You Blind?* (written with Isamu S. Aoki: Pfeiffer & Co., 619-578-5900, 1993, $12.95).

The author attributes one-third of small-business failures to internal theft of money, property, information, and time. Small entities lack the checks and balances that larger organizations take for granted. An individual given singular control over financial records holds "a license to steal," the cynical Bliss maintains. He cites as typical the case of an office manager who, assigned to pay her employer's business-related charge-card bills, pilfered $90,000 over a three-year period by throwing her own bills into the pot.

Bliss's catalog of crime portrays white-collar ingenuity at its most villainous. Some samples:

- *False Data Entry.* Known as data diddling, this ancient fraud is harder to trace when committed by computer rather than pen, since no one's handwriting is involved.
- *The Salami.* By slicing small amounts off, say, entries in a payroll, a dishonest manager can siphon significant sums into a personal account.

- *Superzapping.* A system with security controls must have a fail-safe program that can bypass those controls. If that protocol falls into the wrong hands, data become vulnerable.
- *Scanning.* A high-speed computer can be used to test a series of entries until it hits on one that does the nefarious trick.

Internal controls aren't enough to combat such deviousness because over time people regard them as mere guidelines. A check-writing system that requires two people to sign checks is fine on paper, but it doesn't work when one signs a bunch of blank checks in advance and entrusts them to the other. The book's tough-minded tenet: Trust *nobody*.

Even the most fastidious owner should undertake a semiannual audit of procedures. Samplings from Bliss's "checklist of vulnerability": Are bank statements opened and examined by someone other than the bookkeeper? Are all employees who handle financial transactions or records required to take annual vacations, and are their records and responsibilities handled by someone else in their absence? Are voided checks kept and accounted for? Are computer passwords changed regularly? Are surprise audits occasionally made?

Source: "Discouraging the Inside Job," *Inc.* (April 1994), p. 122.

SOFTWARE PACKAGES

There are a number of financial software packages available for the entrepreneur that can track financial data and generate any important financial statement. For purposes of completing the pro forma statements, at least in the business planning stage, it is probably easiest to use a spreadsheet program since numbers may change often as the entrepreneur begins to develop budgets for the pro forma statements. Microsoft Excel is the most widely used spreadsheet software and is available in Macintosh and PC formats.

The value of using a spreadsheet in the start-up phase for financial projections is simply being able to present different scenarios and to assess their impact on the pro forma statements. It helps answer such questions as, What would be the effect of a price decrease of 10 percent on my pro forma income statement? What would be the impact of an increase of 10 percent in operating expenses? How would the lease versus purchase of equipment affect my cash flow? This type of analysis, using the computer spreadsheet software, will provide a quick assessment of the likely financial projections given different scenarios.

It is recommended in the start-up stage, where the venture is very small and limited in time and resources, that the software selected be very simple and easy to use. The entrepreneur will need software to maintain the books and to generate financial statements. Most of these software packages allow for check writing, payroll, invoicing, inventory management, bill paying, credit management, and taxes.

The most popular software packages are QuickBooks (Intuit Inc.), Peachtree First Accounting (Peachtree Software, Inc.), MS Financial Manager for Excel (Microsoft Corp.), and Managing Your Money (Meca Software Co.). All of these packages are available for PCs or Macs at any local computer store, and all provide all or most of the features mentioned in the paragraph above. Before deciding on a purchase, the entrepreneur may want to discuss the options with a friend or business associate who has some knowledge of the entrepreneur's needs and the benefits of each of these software packages.

IN REVIEW

Summary

Several financial projection techniques were discussed in this chapter. Each of the planning tools is designed to provide the entrepreneur with a clear picture of where funds come from, how they are disbursed, the amount of cash available, and the general financial well-being of the new venture.

The pro forma income statement provides a sales estimate in the first year (monthly basis) and projects operating expenses each month. These estimates will be determined from the appropriate budgets that would be based on marketing plan projections and objectives.

Cash flow is not the same as profit. It reflects the difference between cash actually received and cash disbursements. Some cash disbursements are not operating expenses (e.g., repayment of loan principal); likewise, some operating expenses are not a cash disbursement (e.g., depreciation expense). Many new ventures have failed because of a lack of cash, even when the venture is profitable.

The pro forma balance sheet reflects the condition of the business at the end of a particular period. It summarizes the assets, liabilities, and net worth of the firm.

The break-even point can be determined from projected income. This measures the point where total revenue equals total cost.

The pro forma sources and applications of funds statement helps the entrepreneur to understand how the net income for the year was disposed of and the effect of the movement of cash through the business. It emphasizes the interrelationship of assets, liabilities, and stockholders' equity to working capital.

Although Internet start-ups have unique characteristics, the process of computing the pro forma statements is the same as for any other company. The uniqueness of these types of start-ups is reflected in the difficulty of projecting sales and the heavy cash investment made in capital equipment and for advertising.

Questions for Discussion

1. What are the major differences between the pro forma income statement and the pro forma cash flow? List and explain all of the reasons why $100,000 in sales may not equate to $100,000 in cash received that month.
2. Experience indicates that many new profitable ventures fail. Explain.
3. What is breakeven? What assumptions are made in break-even analysis? What is the effect of an increase in selling price on breakeven?
4. Explain the purpose of the pro forma balance sheet. How does the balance sheet reflect each transaction made by the business?
5. When should the sources and applications of funds statement be completed? What is the net increase in working capital?

Key Terms

assets

breakeven

liabilities

owner equity

pro forma balance sheet

pro forma cash flow

pro forma income

pro forma sources and applications of funds

More Information—Net Addresses in This Chapter

Biz Women
www.bizwomen.com

Business Planware—online financial services
www.planware.org/cashflow.htm

Business Resource Center
www.morebusiness.com

CNN Financial News
www.cnnfn.com

Datamerge—financial resources/ cashflow guide
www.datamerge.com/resources/ cashflow.html

Dun & Bradstreet Information Service
www.dnb.com

Entrepreneurs on the Web
www.entrepreneur-web.com

Idea Cafe
www.ideacafe.com

Small Business Administration
www.sbaonline.sba.gov/

Small Business Advancement National Center
www.sbanet.uca.edu/

Small Business Resource Center
www.webcom.com/seaquest/sbrc

World Wide Yellow Pages
www.yellow.com

Selected Readings

Brodsky, Norm. (2001). The Right Price. *Inc.*, April 2001.

Too many new entrepreneurs harm their own prospects by underpricing their goods and services. Author argues that if those company owners just take the time to think, they can set their prices closer to fair market value.

Comiskey, Eugene E.; and Charles W. Mulford. (1998). Analyzing Small-Company Financial Statements: Some Guidance for Lenders. *Commercial Lending Review*, vol. 13, no. 3, pp. 30–42.

The following aspects of small-company financial statements are identified as the most significant for lenders: inventories, income taxes and tax returns, depreciation and missing fixed assets, interest capitalization, rent expense and off-balance-sheet commitments, revenue recognition and matching policies, and other income and expense.

Fraser, J. (January 1995). The Tax Wise Cash Monitor. *Inc.*, pp. 75–77.

After experiencing a close call to bankruptcy because of poor management of cash, Tom Buschman developed a simple two-page cash flow report that he can prepare every week.

Fraser, L. M. (1998). *Understanding Financial Statements*, 5th ed. Upper Saddle River, NJ: Prentice Hall, Inc.

This paperback is a good overview of all the financial statements that will be needed to operate a new venture. The information is presented in a simple format with many examples.

Greco, S. (July 1996). Are We Making Money Yet? *Inc.*, pp. 52–56.

This article features Claudia Post, an entrepreneur, who in 1994 received an award from the SBA. She found that her sales were increasing but she was losing money. When she analyzed her situation with the assistance of an accountant (described in detail in the article), she found that her margins were a lot less than she had anticipated.

Mason, L.; and J. Fadley. (March 1996). Hanging Dollars on Dreams: How to Give Savvy Advice to Small Business Clients. *Outlook*, pp. 18–24.

This is a valuable assessment of how an accountant would analyze a new venture's financial picture. It identifies key areas that an entrepreneur should be aware of to ensure a favorable financial situation.

Endnotes

1. See "E*TRADE Founder Gives $25 Million to MIT's Sloan School," *Boston Herald* (October 29, 1999), p. 33; L. Lee, "Tricks of E*TRADE," *Business Week E.Biz* (February 7, 2000), pp. 18–31; and E*TRADE website, *www.etrade.com.*
2. E. Berkowitz, R. Kerin, S. Hartley, and W. Rudelius, *Marketing*, 5th ed. (Burr Ridge, IL: Irwin McGraw-Hill, 2000), pp. 246–49.
3. See E. A. Helfert, *Techniques of Financial Analysis*, 10th ed. (Burr Ridge, IL: Irwin McGraw-Hill, 2000), pp. 149–75.
4. D. Sparks, "Who Will Survive the Internet Wars?" *Business Week* (December 27, 1999), pp. 98–100.
5. J. Hertenstein and S. McKinnon, "Solving the Puzzle of the Cash Flow Statement," *Business Horizons* (January/February, 1997), pp. 69–76.
6. See Clyde P. Stickney, *Financial Statement Analysis: A Strategic Perspective* (Fort Worth TX: The Dryden Press: 1996), pp. 562–73.
7. E. Berkowitz et al., *Marketing*, pp. 378–80.

10

The Organizational Plan

LEARNING OBJECTIVES

1. To understand the importance of the management team in launching a new venture.

2. To understand the advantages and disadvantages of the alternative legal forms for organizing a new venture.

3. To explain the S Corporation and limited liability company as alternative forms of incorporation.

4. To learn how to prepare a job analysis, job description, and job specification.

5. To illustrate how the board of directors or board of advisors can be used to support the management of a new venture.

STARBUCKS

Building a strong, lasting organization requires careful planning and strategy. No one knows this better than Howard Schultz. In 1987, he purchased a floundering company, Starbucks, for $250,000 that sold whole coffee beans at retail. In order to transform this business, Schultz initiated an organization plan that focused on a quality workforce. His intent at the time of purchase was to build a local business into a national retail company, and to do so he needed loyal employees who took pride in their work and would carry this positive attitude to the customer.[1]

At the core of Schultz's vision was a very generous and comprehensive employee benefits package that included health care, stock options, training, career counseling, and product discounts for all employees full- or part-time. He also offers the highest entry-level pay of $7 to $8 per hour. Since most retailers experience high turnover, Schultz focused his plan on low turnover and loyalty. His unique plan was based on the concept that employees would work harder and more intelligently if they had a stake in their success. From 1987 to 1993, Starbucks expanded to 156 stores with about 2,000 employees, averaging $700,000 a week in sales.

From the beginning, Schultz saw the importance between Starbucks' growth and his ambitious organizational employee benefits plan. With more than half the employees working 20 hours per week, designing the plan was difficult because of higher insurance and training costs, especially since it was rare for any organization to support its part-time staff to this extent. However, in spite of the extensive range of benefits, the costs represented only one-quarter of the company's labor costs and have achieved a lower turnover and higher loyalty.

The plan initially led to a doubling of the company's losses to $1.2 million. By 1991, however, sales increased 84 percent, and the company earned its first profits. In 1992 the company went public at $17 per share. Within five months the stock had doubled. By the end of 1996 there were more than 1,000 Starbucks stores with annual profits of about $35 million. Sales reached $1 billion by the end of 1997. Schultz's worth in the company has reached about $70 million even though he has also cashed out more than $20 million in the last two years.

Employee training continues to be an important part of the consistency in product and service that this large organization has been able to maintain. Employees are referred to as partners and are all required to complete five classes totaling about 25 hours within the first six weeks of employment. During the orientation new employees are introduced to Star Skills, which are three guidelines for on-the-job interpersonal relations: (1) maintain and enhance self-esteem,

(2) listen and acknowledge, and (3) ask for help. In addition, the organization maintains ongoing refresher training courses for about 300 to 400 people each month. Partners are encouraged to share their feelings about selling, coffee, or their jobs. All of this growth and organization consistency has been accomplished without franchising.

The organization that Schultz has put into place has also enhanced marketing creativity, with new promotions and products and ways to save money for the company. From 1998 to 1999 revenues increased from $1.3 billion to $1.7 billion and profits reached $107 million primarily because of store expansion. The total number of stores at the close of 1999 was 2,498. Of this total there were 2,135 company-owned stores and 363 licensed stores that covered 34 states, Washington DC, five Canadian provinces, and the United Kingdom. There has been some cannibalization of store revenues as Schultz is not opposed to opening a new store near another. In 1999 there was continued expansion of product lines and acquisitions of such companies as Tazo L.L.C., a West Coast tea company. In 2000 Starbucks reported that not only was expansion proceeding as planned, but revenues had increased by 38 percent. Revenues in 2000 were $2.2 billion and profits were $94 million, and the total number of stores were 3,501, of which 2,619 were company-owned sales stores and 882 licensed stores.

As Schultz describes it, the unique organization plan with all the employee benefits acts as a glue that binds workers to the company, enhancing loyalty and, more important, encouraging effective customer service, which over time has contributed to high growth and profits.

DEVELOPING THE MANAGEMENT TEAM

We can see from the Starbucks example the importance of employees and their loyalty and commitment to the organization. Also significant to potential investors is the management team and its ability and commitment to the new venture. It is clear from the Starbucks example that without the creativity and vision of Schultz, the venture would have likely continued its demise, as was the case under the previous owners.

Investors will usually demand that the management team not attempt to operate the business as a sideline or part-time venture while employed full-time elsewhere. It is expected that the management team be prepared to operate the business full time and at a modest salary. It is unacceptable for the entrepreneurs to try to draw a large salary out of the new venture, and investors may perceive any attempt to do so as a lack of psychological commitment to the business. Later in this chapter the roles of various team members are discussed, particularly as the firm evolves to a legitimate ongoing concern. In addition the entrepreneur should consider the role of the board of directors and/or a board of advisors in supporting the management of the new venture. At this point, however, the entrepreneur needs to consider the alternatives regarding the legal form of the organization. Each of these forms has important implications on taxes, liability, continuity, and financing the new venture.

LEGAL FORMS OF BUSINESS

There are three basic legal forms of business formation and one new form that is gaining acceptance. The three basic legal forms are (1) proprietorship, (2) partnership, and (3) corporation, with variations particularly in partnerships and corporations. The newest form of business formation is the limited liability company, which is now possible in all 50 states and the District of Columbia. The typical corporation form is known as a C *Corporation*. Figure 10.1 describes the legal factors involved in each of these forms with the differences in the limited partnership and S Corporation noted where appropriate. These three basic legal forms are compared with regard to ownership, liability, start-up costs, continuity, transferability of interest, capital requirements, management control, distribution of profits, and attractiveness for raising capital. The limited liability company (LLC) is discussed separately after the comparisons of the three basic legal forms of business.

C Corporation   Most common form of corporation, regulated by statute and treated as a separate legal entity for liability and tax purposes

It is very important that the entrepreneur carefully evaluate the pros and cons of the various legal forms of organizing the new venture. This decision must be made before the submission of a business plan and request for venture capital.

The evaluation process requires the entrepreneur to determine the priority of each of the factors mentioned in Figure 10.1 as well as tax factors discussed later in this chapter. These factors will vary in importance, depending on the type of new business.

In addition to these factors, it is also necessary to consider some intangibles. Various types of organizational structures reflect an image to suppliers, existing clients, and prospective customers. For example, suppliers may prefer to deal with profit-making organizations rather than nonprofit companies. This attitude may be reflected in the perceived impressions that nonprofit firms are slow in paying their bills. Customers may sometimes prefer to do business with a corporation. Because of their continuity and ownership advantages, they are sometimes viewed as a more stable type of business. As a customer, it may be desirable to have assurance that the firm will be in business for a long time.

The variations of organizational structure as well as the advantages and disadvantages are numerous and can be quite confusing to the entrepreneur. In the next section of this chapter, some of the confusion is clarified and will assist the entrepreneur in making these important decisions.

Ownership

In the *proprietorship*, the owner is the individual who starts the business. He or she has full responsibility for the operations. In a *partnership*, there may be some general partnership owners and some limited partnership owners. In the *corporation*, ownership is reflected by ownership of shares of stock. Other than the S Corporations, where the maximum number of shareholders is 70, there is no limit as to the number of shareholders who may own stock.

proprietorship   Form of business with single owner who has unlimited liability, controls all decisions, and receives all profits

partnership   Two or more individuals having unlimited liablity who have pooled resource to own a business.

corporation   Separate legal entity that is run by stockholders having limited liability.

Liability of Owners

Liability is one of the most critical reasons for establishing a corporation rather than any other form of business. The proprietor and general partners are liable for all aspects of

FIGURE 10.1 Factors in Three Forms of Business Formation

Factors	Proprietorship	Partnership	Corporation
Ownership	Individual.	No limitation on number of partners.	No limitation on number of stockholders.
Liability of owners	Individual liable for business liabilities.	In general partnership, individuals all liable for business liabilities. In limited partnership, partners are liable for amount of capital contribution.	Amount of capital contribution is limit of shareholder liability.
Costs of starting business	None other than filing fees for trade name.	Partnership agreement, legal costs, and minor filing fees for trade name. Limited partnership requires more comprehensive agreement, hence higher costs.	Created only by statute. Articles of incorporation, filing fees, taxes, and fees for states in which corporation registers to do business.
Continuity of business	Death dissolves the business.	Death or withdrawal of one partner terminates partnership unless partnership agreement stipulates otherwise. In limited partnership, death or withdrawal of one of limited partners has no effect on continuity. Limited partner can withdraw capital after six months after notice is provided.	Greatest form of continuity. Death or withdrawal of owner(s) will not affect legal existence of business.
Transferability of interest	Complete freedom to sell or transfer any part of business.	General partner can transfer his/her interest only with consent of all other general partners. Limited partner can sell interest without consent of general partners.	Most flexible. Stockholders can sell or buy stock at will. Some stock transfers may be restricted by agreement. In S Corporation, stock may be transferred only to an individual.
Capital requirements	Capital raised only by loan or increased contribution by proprietor.	Loans or new contributions by partners require a change in partnership agreement.	New capital raised by sale of stock or bonds or by borrowing (debt) in name of corporation. In S Corporation, only one class of stock and limited to 35 shareholders.
Management control	Proprietor makes all decisions and can act immediately.	All partners have equal control and majority rules. In limited partnership, only the general partners have control of the business.	Majority stockholder(s) have most control from legal point of view. Day-to-day control in hands of management who may or may not be major stockholders.
Distribution of profits and losses	Proprietor responsible and receives all profits and losses.	Depends on partnership agreement and investment by partners.	Shareholders can share in profits by receipt of dividends.
Attractiveness for raising capital	Depends on capability of proprietor and success of business.	Depends on capability of partners and success of business.	With limited liability for owners, more attractive as an investment opportunity.

the business. Since the corporation is an entity or legal "person," which is taxable and absorbs liability, the owners are liable only for the amount of their investment. In the case of a proprietorship or regular partnership, no distinction is made between the business entity and the owner(s). Then, to satisfy any outstanding debts of the business, creditors may seize any assets the owners have outside the business.

In a partnership, the general partners usually share the amount of personal liability equally, regardless of their capital contributions, unless there is a specific agreement to the contrary. The only protection for the partners is insurance against liability suits and each partner putting his or her assets in someone else's name. The government may disallow the latter action if it feels this was done to defraud creditors.

In a limited partnership, the limited partners are liable only for the amount of their capital contributions. This amount, by law, must be registered at a local courthouse, thus making this information public.

Costs of Starting a Business

The more complex the organization, the more expensive it is to start. The least expensive is the proprietorship, where the only costs incurred may be for filing for a business or trade name. In a partnership, in addition to filing a trade name, a partnership agreement is needed. This agreement requires legal advice and should explicitly convey all the responsibilities, rights, and duties of the parties involved. A limited partnership may be somewhat more complex than a general partnership because it must comply strictly with statutory requirements.

The corporation can be created only by statute. This generally means that before the corporation may be legally formed, the owners are required to (1) register the name and articles of incorporation and (2) meet the state statutory requirements (some states are more lenient than others). In complying with these requirements, the corporation will likely incur filing fees, an organization tax, and fees for doing business in each state. Legal advice is necessary to meet all the statutory requirements.

Continuity of Business

One of the main concerns of a new venture is what happens if one of the entrepreneurs (or the only entrepreneur) dies or withdraws from the business. Continuity differs significantly for each of the forms of business. In a sole proprietorship, the death of the owner results in the termination of the business. Sole proprietorships are thus not perpetual, and there is no time limit on how long they may exist.

The partnership varies, depending on whether it is a limited or a general partnership and on the partnership agreement. In a limited partnership, the death or withdrawal of a limited partner (who can withdraw capital six months after giving notice to other partners) has no effect on the existence of the partnership. A limited partner may be replaced, depending on the partnership agreement. If a general partner in a limited partnership dies or withdraws, the limited partnership is terminated unless the partnership agreement specifies otherwise or all partners agree to continue.

In a partnership, the death or withdrawal of one of the partners results in termination of the partnership. However, this rule can be overcome by the partnership agreement. Usually the partnership will buy out the deceased or withdrawn partner's share at a predetermined price based on some appraised value. Another option is that a member of the deceased's family may take over as a partner and share in profits accordingly. Life insurance owned by the partnership is a good solution for protecting the interests of the partnership, along with carefully outlining contingencies in the partnership agreement.

The corporation has the most continuity of all the forms of business. Death or withdrawal has no impact on the continuation of the business. Only in a closely held corporation, where all the shares are held by a few people, may there be some problems trying to find a market for the shares. Usually, the corporate charter requires that the corporation or the remaining shareholders purchase the shares. In a public corporation this, of course, would not be an issue.

Transferability of Interest

There can be mixed feelings as to whether the transfer of interest in a business is desirable. In some cases the entrepreneur(s) may prefer to evaluate and assess any new owners before giving them a share of the business. On the other hand, it is also desirable to be able to sell one's interest whenever one wishes. Each of the forms of business offers different advantages as to the transferability of interest.

In the sole proprietorship, the entrepreneur has the right to sell or transfer any assets in the business. The limited partnership provides for more flexibility than the partnership regarding transfer of interest. In the limited partnership, the limited partners can sell their interests at any time without consent of the general partners. The person to whom the limited partner sells, however, can have only the same rights as the previous owner. A general partner in either a limited partnership or partnership cannot sell any interest in the business unless there is some provision for doing so in the partnership agreement. Usually the remaining partners will have the right of refusal of any new partner, even if the partnership agreement allows for transfer of interest.

The corporation has the most freedom in terms of selling one's interest in the business. Shareholders may transfer their shares at any time without consent from the other shareholders. The disadvantage of the right is that it can affect the ownership control of a corporation through election of a board of directors. Shareholders' agreements may provide some limitations on the ease of transferring interest, usually by giving the existing shareholders or corporation the option of purchasing the stock at a specific price or at the agreed-on price. Thus, they sometimes can have the right of first refusal. In the S Corporation, the transfer of interest can occur only as long as the buyer is an individual.

Capital Requirements

The need for capital during the early months of the new venture can become one of the most critical factors in keeping a new venture alive. In Chapter 9, we discussed how the lack of cash flow and need for pro formas emphasize the likely need for capital in the early stages of a new venture. The opportunities and ability of the new venture to raise capital will vary, depending on the form of business.

For a proprietorship, any new capital can come only from loans by any number of sources or by additional personal contributions by the entrepreneur. In borrowing money from a bank, the entrepreneur in this form of business may need collateral to support the loan. Often, an entrepreneur will take a second mortgage on his or her home as a source of capital. Any borrowing from an outside investor may require giving up some of the equity in the proprietorship. Whatever the source, the responsibility for payment is in the hands of the entrepreneur, and failure to make payments can result in foreclosure and liquidation of the business. However, even with these risks the proprietorship is not likely to need large sums of money, as might be the case for a partnership or corporation.

In the partnership, loans may be obtained from banks but will likely require a change in the partnership agreement. Additional funds contributed by each of the partners will also require a new partnership agreement. As in the proprietorship, the entrepreneurs are liable for payment of any new bank loans.

In the corporation, new capital can be raised in a number of ways. The alternatives are greater than in any of the other legal forms of business. Stock may be sold as either voting or nonvoting. Nonvoting stock will of course protect the power of the existing major stockholders. Bonds may also be sold by the corporation. This alternative would be more difficult for the new venture since a high bond rating will likely occur only after the business has been successful over time. Money may also be borrowed in the name of the corporation. As stated earlier, this protects the personal liability of the entrepreneurs.

Management Control

In any new venture, the entrepreneur(s) will want to retain as much control as possible over the business. Each of the forms of business offers different opportunities and problems as to control and responsibility for making business decisions.

In the proprietorship, the entrepreneur has the most control and flexibility in making business decisions. Since the entrepreneur is the single owner of the venture, he or she will be responsible for and have sole authority over all business decisions.

The partnership can present problems over control of business decisions if the partnership agreement is not concise regarding this issue. Usually in a partnership, the majority rules unless the partnership agreement states otherwise. It is most important that the partners are friendly toward one another and that delicate or sensitive decision areas of the business are spelled out in the partnership agreement.

The limited partnership offers a compromise between the partnership and the corporation. In this type of organization, we can see some of the separation of ownership and control. The limited partners in the venture have no control over business decisions. As soon as the limited partner is given some control over business decisions, he or she then assumes personal liability and can no longer be considered a limited partner.

Control of day-to-day business in a corporation is in the hands of management, who may or may not be major stockholders. Control over major long-term decisions, however, may require a vote of the major stockholders. Thus, control is separated based on the types of business decisions. In a new venture, there is a strong likelihood that the entrepreneurs who are major stockholders will be managing the day-to-day activities of the business. As the corporation increases in size, the separation of management and control becomes more probable.

Stockholders in the corporation can indirectly affect the operation of the business by electing someone to the board of directors who reflects their personal business philosophies. These board members, through appointment of top management, then affect the operation and control of the day-to-day management of the business.

Distribution of Profits and Losses

Proprietors receive all distributions of profits from the business. As discussed earlier, they are also personally responsible for all losses. Some of the profits may be used to pay back the entrepreneur for any personal capital contributions that are made to keep the business operating.

In the partnership, the distribution of profits and losses depends on the partnership agreement. It is likely that the sharing of profits and losses will be a function of the partners' investments. However, this can vary depending on the agreement. As in the proprietorship, the partners may assume liability. The limited partnership provides an alternative that protects against personal liability but may reduce shares of any profits.

Corporations distribute profits through dividends to stockholders. These distributions are not likely to absorb all the profits that may be retained by the corporation for future investment or capital needs of the business. Losses by the corporation will often result in no dividends. These losses will then be covered by retained earnings or through other financial means discussed earlier.

Attractiveness for Raising Capital

In both the proprietorship and the partnership, the ability of the entrepreneurs to raise capital depends on the success of the business and the personal capability of the entrepreneur. These two forms are the least attractive for raising capital, primarily because of the problem of personal liability. Any large amounts of capital needed in these forms of business should be given serious consideration.

The corporation, because of its advantages regarding personal liability, is the most attractive form of business for raising capital. Shares of stock, bonds, and/or debt are all opportunities for raising capital with limited liability. The more attractive the corporation, the easier it will be to raise capital.

TAX ATTRIBUTES OF FORMS OF BUSINESS

The tax advantages and disadvantages of each of the forms of business differ significantly. Some of the major differences are discussed below. There are many minor differences that, in total, can be important to the entrepreneur. If the entrepreneur has any doubt about these advantages, he or she should get outside advice. Figure 10.2 provides a summary of the major tax advantages of these forms of business, discussed below.

Tax Issues for Proprietorship

For the proprietorship, the IRS treats the business as the individual owner. All income appears on the owner's return as personal income. Thus, the proprietorship is not regarded by the IRS as a separate tax entity. As can be seen in Figure 10.2, this treatment of taxes affects the taxable year, distribution of profits to owners, organization costs, capital gains, capital losses, and medical benefits. Each of these is treated as if it is incurred by the individual owner and not the business.

The proprietorship has some tax advantages when compared with the corporation. First, there is no double tax when profits are distributed to the owner.

Implementing Employee Ethical Guidelines

Inevitably, entrepreneurs will need to confront employee unethical behavior. In the early stages of a new venture when there are relatively few employees, when the organization is flat, and when control is easier, these ethical behavior issues may be less likely to occur. However, it is important for the entrepreneur to consider these issues, especially as new employees are added and the organization grows. To minimize problems it is recommended that entrepreneurs develop employee ethical guidelines.

Examples of employee unethical behavior are wideranging and often depend on the industry as well as the specific roles of employees in the organization. One example was a new venture involved in importing and exporting food products. One employee who was given the responsibility of buying goods in Europe for import to the United States found a serious shortage of a specific product, making his job very difficult. With the assistance of a relative in Europe, he found a source of the product, which he suspected may have been obtained illegally. However, considering his job more important than questioning the legality of the source of goods, he continued to buy from them.

This type of employee behavior is difficult to control unless guidelines are in place. Good sources for establishing guidelines can be obtained from industry or trade associations and professional organizations such as the American Marketing Association and the American Management Association. Employee guidelines should be implemented in the early stages of a new venture by:

- Communicating the guidelines in writing to all employees.
- Incorporating these guidelines in employee manuals, if in existence, and any new-hire materials.
- Posting guidelines in an appropriate location.
- Stating guidelines in job descriptions.

No set of guidelines is going to eliminate the problem of employee unethical behavior. However, what it does do is define unethical behaviors as well as clarify outcomes if violations occur.

Source: K. W. Tyson, "The Problem of Ethics: Implementation," *Competitive Intelligence Review* (1996), pp. 515–7.

Another advantage is that there is no capital stock tax or penalty for retained earnings in the business. Again, these advantages exist because the proprietorship is not recognized as a separate tax entity; all profits and losses are part of the entrepreneur's tax return.

Tax Issues for Partnership

The partnership's tax advantages and disadvantages are similar to those of the proprietorship, especially regarding income distributions, dividends, and capital gains and losses. Limited partnerships can provide some unique tax advantages since the limited partner can share in the profits without being responsible for any liability beyond his or her investment.

Both the partnership and proprietorship are organizational forms that serve as nontaxable conduits of income and deductions. These forms of business do have a legal identity distinct from the partners or owners, but this identity is only for accounting reporting.

It is especially important for partnerships to report income since this serves as the basis for determining the share of each partner. The income is distributed based on the partnership agreement. The owners then report their share as personal income and pay taxes based on this amount.

FIGURE 10.2 Tax Attributes of Various Legal Forms of Business

Attributes	Proprietorship	Partnership	Corporation
Taxable year	Usually a calendar year.	Usually calendar year, but other dates may be used.	Any year-end can be used at beginning. Any changes require changes in incorporation.
Distribution of profits to owners	All income appears on owner's return.	Partnership agreement may have special allocation of income. Partners pay tax on their pro rata shares of income on individual return even if income not immediately distributed.	No income is allocated to stockholders.
Organization costs	Not amortizable.	Amortizable over 60 months.	Amortizable over 60 months.
Dividends received	$100 dividend exclusion for single return and $200 on joint return.	Dividend exclusion of partnership passes to partner (conduit).	80% or more of dividend received may be deducted (after 12/31/86).
Capital gains	Taxed at individual level. A deduction is allowed for long-term capital gains.	Capital gain to partnership will be taxed as a capital gain to the partner (conduit).	Taxed at corporate level. After July 1, 1987, the maximum rate will be 34%.
Capital losses	Carried forward indefinitely.	Capital losses can be used to offset other income. Carried forward indefinitely (conduit).	Carry back three years and carry over five years as short-term capital loss offsetting only capital gains.
Initial organization	Commencement of business results in no additional tax for individual.	Contributions of property to a partnership not taxed.	Acquisition of stock for cash entails no immediate taxes. Transfer of property in exchange for stock may be taxable if stock value greater than contributed property.
Limitations on losses deductible by owners	Amount at risk may be deducted except for real estate activities.	Partnership investment plus share of recourse liability if any. At-risk rules may apply except for real estate partnership.	No losses allowed except on sale of stock or liquidation of corporation. In S Corporation, shareholder's investment to corporation is deductible.
Medical benefits	Itemized deductions for medical expenses in excess of percentage of adjusted gross income on individual's return. No deduction for insurance premium.	Cost of partner's benefits not deductible to business as an expense. Possible deduction at partner level.	Cost of employee-shareholder coverage deductible as business expense if designed for benefit of employee.
Retirement benefits	Limitations and restrictions basically same as regular corporation.	Same as for corporations.	Limitations on benefits from defined benefit plans—lesser of $90,000 or 100% of compensation. Limitations on contributions to defined contribution plans—lesser of $30,000 or 25% of compensation (15% of aggregate for profit-sharing plans).

Tax Issues for Corporation

Since the corporation is recognized by the IRS as a separate tax entity, it has the advantage of being able to take many deductions and expenses that are not available to the proprietorship or partnership. The disadvantage is that the distribution of dividends is taxed twice, as income of the corporation and as income of the stockholder. This double taxation can be avoided if the income is distributed to the entrepreneur(s) in the form of salary. Bonuses, incentives, profit sharing, and so on, are thus allowable ways to distribute income of the corporation as long as the compensation is reasonable in amount and payment was for services rendered.

The corporate tax may be lower than the individual rate. The entrepreneur is best advised to consider the tax pros and cons and decide on that basis. Projected earnings may be used to calculate the actual taxes under each form of business in order to identify the one that provides the best tax advantage. Remember, tax advantages should be balanced by liability responsibility in the respective form of business.

S CORPORATION

The *S Corporation* combines the tax advantages of the partnership and the corporation. It is designed so that venture income is declared as personal income on a pro rata basis by the shareholders. In fact, the shareholders benefit from all the income and the deductions of the business. Before the passing of the Small Business Protection Act of 1996 the rules governing the S Corporation were considered too rigid. The passage of this law in 1996 provided more flexibility with regard to the number of shareholders who can be allowed to own shares, the role of trusts as stockholders, the ability of S Corporations to own more than 80 percent of stock of another corporation, distribution of profits, issuance of different classes of stock, and rules affecting the tax basis of incurred losses. With the new regulations S Corporations were also more easily able to raise capital.[2]

S Corporation   Special type of corporation where profits are distributed to stockholders and taxed as personal income

S Corporations have been a very popular business entity for entrepreneurs and represent almost half of all corporate filings. Even though limited liability companies (LLCs) are still more flexible than the S Corporation, there is a significant cost to convert to an LLC. To switch to an LLC the venture would have to be liquidated and then reorganized as an LLC. This switch could be complex if there are any appreciable assets. It should also be noted that more than half of all S Corporations have only one shareholder, which would not be possible as an LLC in all states.[3] The LLC as an alternative business entity is discussed in more detail below. The S Corporation also has some distinct advantages over the C Corporation, discussed below.

Advantages of an S Corporation

The S Corporation offers the entrepreneur some distinct advantages over the typical corporation, or C Corporation. However, there are also disadvantages. In those instances when the disadvantages are great, the entrepreneur should elect the C Corporation form. Some of the advantages of the S Corporation are as follows:

- Capital gains or losses from the corporation are treated as personal income or losses by the shareholders on a pro rata basis (determined by number of shares of stock held). The corporation is thus not taxed.

- Shareholders retain limited liability protection of C Corporation.
- S Corporation is not subject to a minimum tax, as is the C Corporation.
- Stock may be transferred to low-income-bracket family members (children must be 14 years or older).
- Stock may be voting or nonvoting.
- This form of business may use the cash method of accounting.
- Corporate long-term capital gains and losses are deductible directly by the shareholders to offset other personal capital gains or losses.

Disadvantages of an S Corporation

Although the advantages appear to be favorable for the entrepreneur, this form of business is not appropriate for everyone. The disadvantages of the S Corporation are as follows:

- Even with the regulations passed in 1996, there are still some restrictions regarding qualification for this form of business.
- If the corporation earns less than $100,000, then the C Corporation would have a lower tax.
- The S Corporation may not deduct most fringe benefits for shareholders.
- The S Corporation must adopt a calendar year for tax purposes.
- Only one class of stock (common stock) is permitted for this form of business.
- The net loss of the S Corporation is limited to the shareholder's stock plus loans to the business.

THE LIMITED LIABILITY COMPANY

Until recently, the recognized forms of business organization were proprietorships, partnerships (general or limited), and corporations (C or S). A new popular entity is the *limited liability company* (LLC), which can offer similar advantages to the S Corporation but with more liberal tax rules under Subchapter K.[4] This business form is a partnership-corporation hybrid that has the following distinctive characteristics:

limited liability company   Special type of partnership where liability is limited and continuity options are more flexible

- Whereas the corporation has shareholders and partnerships have partners, the LLC has members.
- No shares of stock are issued, and each member owns an interest in the business as designated by the articles of organization, which is similar to the articles of incorporation or certificates of partnership.
- Liability does not extend beyond the member's capital contribution to the business. Thus, there is no unlimited liability, which can be detrimental in a proprietorship or general partnership.
- Members may transfer their interest only with the unanimous written consent of the remaining members.
- The Internal Revenue Service now treats LLCs as partnerships for tax purposes.

- The standard acceptable term of an LLC is 30 years. Dissolution is also likely when one of the members dies, the business goes bankrupt, or all members choose to dissolve the business. Some states allow continuity with majority or unanimous consent of the members. One of the important characteristics of the LLC is that the laws governing its formation differ from state to state. Thus, a firm that is operating in more than one state may be subject to different treatment. An analysis of these differences should be considered before choosing this form of organization.

On the basis of the above characteristics, it appears that the LLC is similar to an S Corporation but is more flexible. The one major concern with LLCs is in international business where the context of unlimited liability is still unclear. Entrepreneurs should consult an attorney before making a final decision. Differences with the limited partnership are mainly a result of the fact that the limited partnership must have at least one general partner who has unlimited liability for partnership debts. In the LLC, every member has limited liability.

The acceptability of the LLC should grow as state statutes are clarified and international rules established. However, as stated earlier, the number of S Corporations is still quite extensive; and because of the restrictions on switching, any growth in the LLC business entity will likely be a function of new business formations.

Entrepreneurs should compare all of the alternative forms of organization before election. This should be done with the advice of a tax attorney, since once a decision is made, it is difficult to change again.

DESIGNING THE ORGANIZATION

Generally, the design of the initial organization will be simple. In fact, the entrepreneur may find that he or she performs all the functions of the organization alone. This is a common problem and a significant reason for many failures. The entrepreneur sometimes thinks that he or she can do everything and is unwilling to give up responsibility to others or even include others in the management team. In most cases when this occurs, the entrepreneur will have difficulty making the transition from a start-up to a growing, well-managed business that maintains its success over a long period of time.[5] Regardless of whether there is one or more individuals involved in the start-up, as the workload increases, the organizational structure will need to expand to include additional employees with defined roles in the organization. Effective interviewing and hiring procedures will need to be implemented to ensure that new employees will effectively grow and mature with the new venture. Personnel issues such as these are discussed in more detail in Chapter 13, which addresses some of the important management decisions in the early stages of an organization's life. A job analysis that may be included in the initial business plan submitted to investors is discussed below.

For many new ventures, predominantly part-time employees may be hired, raising important issues of commitment and loyalty that Schultz was able to successfully overcome with some creativity in his organization. However, regardless of the number of actual personnel involved in running the venture, the organization must identify the major activities required to operate it effectively.

The design of the organization will be the entrepreneur's formal and explicit indication to the members of the organization as to what is expected of them. Typically these expectations can be grouped into the following five areas:[6]

- *Organization Structure.* This defines members' jobs and the communication and relationship these jobs have with each other. These relationships are depicted in an organization chart.

- *Planning, Measurement, and Evaluation Schemes.* All organization activities should reflect the goals and objectives that underlie the venture's existence. The entrepreneur must spell out how these goals will be achieved (plans), how they will be measured, and how they will be evaluated.

- *Rewards.* Members of an organization will require rewards in the form of promotions, bonuses, praise, and so on. The entrepreneur or other key managers will need to be responsible for these rewards.

- *Selection Criteria.* The entrepreneur will need to determine a set of guidelines for selecting individuals for each position.

- *Training.* Training, on or off the job, must be specified. This training may be in the form of formal education or learning skills.

The organization's design can be very simple—that is, one in which the entrepreneur performs all the tasks (usually indicative of a start-up)—or more complex, in which other employees are hired to perform specific tasks. As the organization becomes larger and more complex, the preceding areas of expectation become more relevant and necessary.

Figure 10.3 illustrates two stages of development in an organization. In Stage 1, the new venture is operated by basically one person, the entrepreneur. This organizational chart reflects the activities of the firm in production, marketing/sales, and administration. Initially, the entrepreneur may manage all these functions. At this

FIGURE 10.3   Stages in Organizational Design

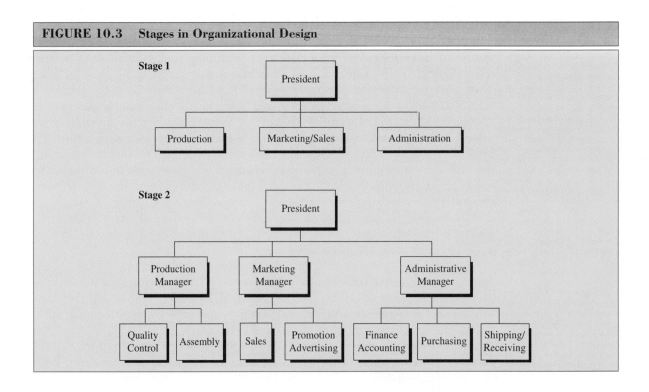

stage, there is no need for submanagers; the owner deals with everyone involved in the business and all aspects of the operation. In this example, the president manages production, which may be subcontracted; marketing and sales (possible use of agents or reps); and all administrative tasks such as bookkeeping, purchasing, and shipping. Planning, measurement and evaluation, rewards selection criteria, and training would not yet be critical in the organization.

As the business expands, the organization may be more appropriately described by Stage 2. Here, submanagers are hired to coordinate, organize, and control various aspects of the business. In the example in Figure 10.3, the production manager is responsible for quality control and assembly of the finished product by the subcontractor. The marketing manager develops promotion and advertising strategy and coordinates the efforts of the expanding rep organization. The administrative manager then assumes the responsibility for all administrative tasks in the business operation. Here the elements of measurement, evaluation, rewards, selection, and training become apparent.

A third stage may exist when the firm achieves a much larger size (i.e., 1,000 employees). The activities below each manager in Stage 2 would then be represented by a third level of managers (i.e., quality control manager).

As the organization evolves, the manager or entrepreneur's decision roles also become critical for an effective organization. As an entrepreneur, the manager's primary concern is to adapt to changes in the environment and seek new ideas. When a new idea is found, the entrepreneur will need to initiate development either under his or her own supervision (Stage 1 in Figure 10.3) or by delegating the responsibility to someone else in the organization (Stage 2 in Figure 10.3). In addition to the role of adaptor, the manager will also need to respond to pressures such as an unsatisfied customer, a supplier reneging on a contract, or a key employee threatening to quit. Much of the entrepreneur's time in the start-up will be spent "putting out fires."

Another role for the entrepreneur is that of allocator of resources. The manager must decide who gets what. This involves the delegation of budgets and responsibilities. The allocation of resources can be a very complex and difficult process for the entrepreneur since one decision can significantly affect other decisions. The final decision role is that of negotiator. Negotiations of contracts, salaries, prices of raw materials, and so on, are an integral part of the manager's job, and since he or she can be the only person with the appropriate authority, it is a necessary area of decision making.

BUILDING THE SUCCESSFUL ORGANIZATION

Once the legal form of organization is determined, and the roles necessary to perform all the important functions of the organization are identified, the entrepreneur will need to prepare job descriptions and a job analysis. The job analysis will serve as a guide in determining hiring procedures, training, performance appraisals, compensation programs, and job descriptions and specifications. In a very small venture this process would be simple, but as the size and complexity of the venture change, the process becomes more complex.

The best place to begin the job analysis is with the tasks or jobs that need to be performed to make the venture viable. The entrepreneur should prepare a list of necessary tasks and skills. Once a list is completed, the entrepreneur should determine how many positions will be necessary to accomplish these needs and what type of person or persons would be ideal. Decisions on where to advertise for employees, how they will be trained, who will train them, how they will be evaluated, and how they will be compensated are important in the early organizational planning for the new venture.[7]

Searching for more senior talent for the new venture requires a different strategy than for other positions. Usually networking using the external advisors, family, friends, and business associates provides the best source of candidates. Some recruiting firms are also specializing in placing senior people in start-ups. Tony Mazlish, CEO of the Healthy Back Store, which last year achieved $6.5 million in sales, has indicated that finding senior talent was easier than finding other types of employees. Barbara Todd, founder of the $25 million Good Catalog Company, has reported that the number of resumes received for senior positions averages two or three per week.[8] Compensation for these types of positions will also more likely include stock or stock options. The recent success of dot com IPOs has heightened the interest of a significant number of senior executives to seek start-up companies for employment.

Perhaps the most important issues in the business plan are the job descriptions and specifications, discussed in detail below. Many of the other decisions such as hiring procedures, training, performance appraisals, benefits, and so on, can be summarized in a personnel manual that does not need to be part of the business plan. However, the entrepreneur should consider these issues and may at some point find it necessary to hire a consultant to assist him or her in the preparation of such a manual.[9] These topics are discussed in more detail in Chapter 13 regarding the management of a growing organization.

JOB DESCRIPTIONS

The entrepreneur should clarify the roles of employees by preparing *job descriptions*. These job descriptions should specify the details of the work that is to be performed and any special conditions or skills involved in performing the job. The decision as to whether these job descriptions should be very detailed or generic has often been debated, especially for a new venture where it is sometimes necessary for individuals to assume more than one role as the need arises.[10] Regardless of which option is chosen by the entrepreneur, the job description should contain a job summary, skills or experience required, a summary of the responsibilities and duties, the authority of the individual, and standards of performance.[11] A job description communicates to candidates for employment what will be expected of them. It should be written in clear, direct, simple language. Figure 10.4 is an example of a job description for a sales manager.

job descriptions   Specify details of work to be performed by an employee

---

FIGURE 10.4   Example of a Job Description

Sales manager: Requires a BS degree and a minimum of five years of experience in sales and sales management. Responsible for hiring, training, coordinating, and supervising all sales representatives, internal and external to the firm. Monitors sales by territory in the four-state market area. Evaluates marketing programs in the defined territory and provides recommendations with objective to grow sales. Calls on key accounts in market area once every two weeks to provide sales promotion and merchandising support. Prepares annual sales plan for firm, including sales forecasts and goals by territory. Reports to the vice president of marketing and sales.

An entrepreneur may also need to list behavioral traits in a job description. Dave Weignand, president and founder of Advanced Network Design, a telecommunications firm, begins the job description with the activities needed in the job, but then itemizes the behaviors necessary to execute those activities. These behaviors can then be incorporated as questions in the interviewing process. For example, a sales manager's position may require him or her to build confidence in others who face rejection from potential clients and have difficulty making appointments. The only way to determine whether someone fits this requirement will be through careful questioning in an interview.[12]

The entrepreneur with no experience may find it difficult writing job descriptions. As stated earlier, the most effective method when no direct experience exists is to first outline the needs and objectives of the new venture and then work backward to determine the specific activities that will be needed to achieve these goals and objectives. These activities can then be categorized into areas of responsibility—that is, marketing, production, administration, and so on—and job descriptions may then be prepared. As the venture grows, these job descriptions may be upgraded or modified to meet the goals and objectives of the firm.

JOB SPECIFICATIONS

Job specifications should also be clear to the potential employee. The skills and abilities needed to perform the job must be outlined, including prior experience and education requirements. For example, the sales manager position in Figure 10.4 may require a minimum of five years of sales experience, a bachelor's degree in business, experience in sales training, management experience, writing skills, and communication skills. These skills may or may not be mentioned in the job description.

job specifications   The skills and abilities needed to perform a specific job within an organization

It is also important for the entrepreneur to stipulate how much travel will be necessary and how much effort will be devoted to developing new business. Reporting responsibilities should also be outlined. Will the sales manager report to the vice president, CEO, or some other designated individual in the new venture? This information will help prevent conflicts, misunderstandings, and communication breakdowns in the organization. Time spent deciding on these specifications and requirements before hiring will save the entrepreneur from personnel problems in the long run.

Outlining the job specifications for a trained employee is usually much easier than for untrained people who will be trained on the job. In this instance the entrepreneur should focus on specific qualities that will be required, such as personality, physical traits, interests, or sensory skills. Thus, a person who is needed to perform a function on an assembly line may require good hand and eye coordination.

With low unemployment, a growing Internet-driven economy, and changing work environment attitudes such as the liberalizing of dress codes, there has been more acceptance of flexible work schedules. This may include four-day workweeks, later or earlier start times, or some evenings rather than the traditional 9 to 5 workday. Some employees are also allowed to work at home, especially since the growth and acceptance of the Internet, which can provide easy access to company databases. Figure 10.5 illustrates the increasing trend toward more flextime workers. Entrepreneurs may need to offer this option for selected positions in order to attract the best quality employees.

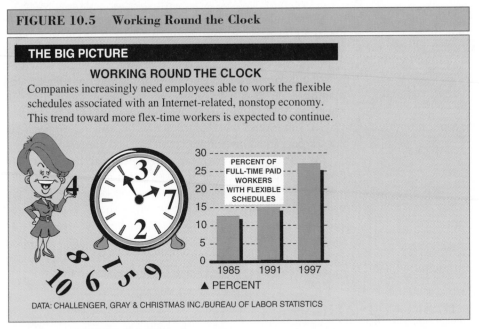

FIGURE 10.5   Working Round the Clock

Source: *Business Week* (February 7, 2000), p. 8.

THE ROLE OF A BOARD OF DIRECTORS

An entrepreneur may find it necessary in his or her organization plan to establish a board of directors or board of advisors. The board of advisors is discussed below. The board of directors may serve a number of functions: (1) reviewing operating and capital budgets, (2) developing longer-term strategic plans for growth and expansion, (3) supporting day-to-day activities, (4) resolving conflicts among owners or shareholders, (5) ensuring the proper use of assets, or (6) developing a network of information sources for the entrepreneurs. These functions may be a formal part of the organization, with assigned responsibility to the directors depending on the needs of the new venture.

Although it is most common to see a board of directors appointed after a venture has been launched, there may be provisions to include a board as part of the initial business plan. In this case, the board would represent an important part of the management team and the organization plan when the entrepreneur seeks funding for the new venture. Typically, this board would assist the entrepreneur in day-to-day decision making either for financial remuneration or, more likely, for stock or ownership in the business. As the venture grows, the role of the board may change to reflect more big-picture issues, with the day-to-day decision making determined by the staff. Since a board's involvement has been shown to be positively related to financial performance, the entrepreneurs can only benefit from its existence.[13]

The external board of directors can not only provide important expertise but also add prestige to the venture, which can be valuable in obtaining investors, establishing supply relationships, or identifying strong potential customers. The members of the board should be carefully selected considering the following criteria:[14]

• Select individuals who can work with a diverse group and will commit to the venture's mission.

As Seen in *Business Week*
Thomas Rogers: A Webmaster for Old Media

Back to the future? On Sept. 27, NBC Cable President Thomas Rogers was named chairman and CEO of Primedia, the publishing group backed by buy-out firm Kohlberg Kravis Roberts. At NBC Rogers was known for creating MSNBC and CNBC and pushing the network onto the Web. So what is he doing heading into Old Media at a time when most executives are stampeding to New Media and Internet start-ups? "I like traditional media assets," Rogers says. "I believe in using their brands to build new assets."

At Primedia, Rogers inherits a diverse roster of publishing titles assembled by departed Chairman Wilham Reilly, ranging from apartment-hunting guides to *New York* and *Seventeen* magazines. It's easy to see why KKR'S Henry Kravis sought out a CEO who could give Primedia a little Web magic. Recently its stock was trading barely above its 1995 IPO price. To juice it up, Rogers has to figure out how to extend it online. It may not be the next Yahoo!, but the company has nowhere to go but up.

Source: Richard Siklos, "A Webmaster for Old Media," *Business Week* (October 11, 1999), p. 50.

- Select candidates who understand the market environment or can contribute important skills to the new venture's achievement of planning goals.
- Select candidates who will show good judgment in business decision making.

Candidates should be identified using referrals of business associates or from any of the external advisors such as banks, investors, lawyers, accountants, or consultants. Ideally, the board should consist of 7 to 12 members with limited terms to allow for continuous infusion of new ideas from different people.

Board of director performance needs to be regularly evaluated by the entrepreneurs. It is the chair's responsibility to provide an appraisal of each board member. In order to provide this appraisal, the chairperson (and/or founders) should have a written description of the responsibilities and expectations of each member.

Compensation for board members can be shares of stock, stock options, or dollar payment. Often the new venture will tie compensation to the performance of the new venture. Compensation is important since it reinforces the obligation of board members. If board members were only volunteers, they would tend to take the role lightly and not provide any value to the entrepreneur.

In 1992, Wemco, Inc., a family-owned company, sold an estimated $85 million of neckties, thanks in part to its board of directors. Conflicts and bickering between two brothers had led to loss of business from two of their biggest customers, May Department Stores and Rich's Department Stores. The two brothers agreed on one thing and that was to appoint a board of directors to help govern the business as well as resolve disputes within the family. The 12 directors, of which 8 are not family members, have led to a revamping of the organization for specific management functions, with the overall board helping in long-term strategy issues.[15]

Many of the successful Internet and high-tech new ventures have deviated somewhat from the traditional board size by maintaining a smaller number of members. For example, Yahoo and Microsoft both have six directors and ebay has a five-person board. Supporters of these smaller boards argue that more gets done and individuals tend to become more involved in business activities. Detractors argue that boards should be diverse and small numbers of directors hinder diversity and good governance.[16]

THE BOARD OF ADVISORS

A board of advisors would be more loosely tied to the organization and would serve the venture only in an advisory capacity for some of the functions or activities mentioned above. It has no legal status, unlike the board of directors, and hence is not subject to the pressures of litigation with which many directors must be concerned. These boards are likely to meet less frequently or depending on the need to discuss important venture decisions. A board of advisors is very useful in a family business where the board of directors may consist entirely of family members.

The selection process for advisors can be similar to the process for selecting a board of directors, including determining desired skills and interviewing potential candidates. Advisors may be compensated on a per meeting basis or with stock or stock options. Just as in the case of the board of directors, the members should be evaluated as to their contribution to meeting the mission of the new venture.

A good example of a successful family business that makes good use of an outside board of advisors is Legal Seafoods. At the advice of an attorney, the family formed a five-member diverse board of advisors that included a dean of a business school, a lawyer, a chemical engineer, a venture capitalist, and the owner of a chain of supermarkets. The board of advisors meets every few months or whenever they are needed. The family board of directors finds that the board of advisors often provides a very different perspective since they are not so tied in with everyday business activities. For example, the family was debating the issue of whether to expand into the New Jersey market. The board of advisors recommended that the family not expand, which solidified the existing doubts that some of the family members had at that time.[17]

THE ORGANIZATION AND USE OF ADVISORS

The entrepreneur will usually use outside advisors such as accountants, bankers, lawyers, advertising agencies, and market researchers on an as needed basis. These advisors, who are separate from the more formal board of advisors mentioned above, can also become an important part of the organization and thus will need to be managed just like any other permanent part of the new venture.

The relationship of the entrepreneur and outside advisors can be enhanced by seeking out the best advisors and involving them thoroughly and at an early stage. Advisors should be assessed or interviewed just as if they were being hired for a permanent position. References should be checked and questions asked to ascertain the quality of service as well as compatibility with the management team.[18]

Hiring and managing outside experts can be effectively accomplished by considering these advisors as advice suppliers. Just as no manager would buy raw materials or supplies without knowledge of their cost and quality, the same approval can apply for advisors. Entrepreneurs should ask these advisors about fees, credentials, references, and so on, before hiring them.

Even after the advisors have been hired, the entrepreneur should question their advice. Why is the advice being given? Make sure you understand the decision and its potential implications. There are many good sources of advisors, such as the Small Business Administration, other small businesses, chambers of commerce, universities, friends, and relatives. Careful evaluation of the entrepreneur's needs and the competency of the advisor can make advisors a valuable asset to the organization of a new venture.

IN REVIEW

Summary

One of the most important decisions the entrepreneur(s) must make in the business plan is the legal form of business. The three major legal forms of business are the proprietorship, partnership, and corporation. Each differs significantly and should be evaluated carefully before a decision is made. This chapter provides considerable insight and comparisons regarding these forms of business to assist the entrepreneur in this decision.

The S Corporation and the limited liability company are alternative forms of business that are gaining popularity. Each of these allows the entrepreneur to retain the protection from personal liability provided by a corporation but retain the tax advantages of a partnership. There are important advantages as well as disadvantages of these forms of business, and entrepreneurs should carefully weigh both before deciding.

The organization plan for the entrepreneur also requires some major decisions that could affect long-term effectiveness and profitability. It is important to begin the new venture with a strong management team that is committed to the goals of the new venture. The management team must be able to work together effectively toward these ends. With pressures from competition, it is important to have an effective organization with clearly defined roles and job descriptions. Decisions are needed on hiring procedures, training, supervising, compensation, evaluation of performance, and so on.

A board of directors or board of advisors can provide important management support for the entrepreneurs in starting and managing the new venture. It may be appropriate to include a board in the initial business plan in order to enhance the credibility of the entrepreneurs as well as provide valuable expertise. Selecting the board should be done carefully, with the intent to select members who will take their roles seriously and provide the kind of support welcomed and necessary during the critical start-up and early stages of the new venture.

Advisors will also be necessary in the new venture. Outside advisors should be evaluated as if they were being hired as permanent members of the organization. Information on their fees and referrals can help determine the best choices.

Questions for Discussion

1. What role does the management team play in the assessment and evaluation of the new venture by potential investors? What criteria are used by the investors to evaluate the new venture?

2. The new venture is likely, over time, to develop into a larger organization that will require major changes in the organizational structure. Describe these changes.

3. What are some of the key advantages of the limited partnership over the partnership form of organization?

4. What effect does death or sale of one's interest by an entrepreneur have on each of the three major forms of business?

5. What is meant by the statement that the proprietorship and partnership are nontaxable conduits of income and deductions? How does this differ from the corporation?

6. What is an S Corporation and how does it differ from a regular corporation?

7. Contrast and compare the LLC and S Corporation as possible business entities for a new venture.

Key Terms

C Corporation

corporation

job descriptions

job specifications

limited liability company

partnership

proprietorship

S Corporation

More Information—Net Addresses in This Chapter

Biz Women
www.bizwomen.com

Business Resource Center
www.morebusiness.com

The Business Start Page
www.bspage.com

Dun & Bradstreet Information Service
www.dnb.com

Entrepreneurs on the Web
www.grow-biz.com

Equal Opportunity Commission—Legal Issues on Hiring and Firing
www.cflech.com

Foundation for Enterprise Development
www.fed.org

Idea Cafe
www.ideacafe.com

Small Business Administration
www.sbaonline.sba.gov/

Small Business Advancement National Center
www.sbanet.uca.edu/

Small Business Resource Center
www.webcom.com/seaquest/sbrc

U. S. Department of Employment and Training
www.doleta.com

U. S. Department of Labor
www.dol.com

Women Entrepreneurs Online Network
www.weon.com

World Wide Yellow Pages
www.yellow.com

Selected Readings

Bernard, B. W. (1997). *Selecting the Right Form of Business.* Burr Ridge, IL: Richard D. Irwin, Inc.

The objective of this book is to describe all the factors and situations that should be considered in selecting the most appropriate entity. It is written from a businessperson's perspective in easy-to-understand language.

Calderon, J. (January–February 1996). *Financial Executive,* pp. 49–51.

Recent legislation has made it easier to form limited liability companies and partnerships (LLCs and LLPs). This article describes some of the advantages of these popular forms of business.

Chandler, Gaylen N.; and Glenn M. McEvoy. (2000). Human Resource Management, TQM, and Firm Performance in Small and Medium-Sized Enterprises. *Entrepreneurship Theory & Practice,* vol. 25, no. 1, pp. 43–57.

The paper analyzes the moderating effect of 2 key human resource practices on the relationship between organizational strategy and firm performance.

Fiegener, Mark K.; Bonnie M. Brown; Dirk R. Derux IV; and William J. Dennis, Jr. (2000). CEO Stakes and Board Composition in Small Private Firms. *Entrepreneurship Theory & Practice*, vol. 24, no. 4, pp. 5–24.

This study investigates whether CEO ownership, family, and generational "stakes" in the business are related to board composition. The results indicate that CEOs with greater ownership and family stakes have less-independent board compositions.

Fried, Vance H.; Garry D. Bruton; and Robert D. Hisrich. (1998). Strategy and the Board of Directors in Venture Capital–Backed Firms. *Journal of Business Venturing*, vol. 13, no. 6, pp. 493–503.

This study demonstrates that boards of venture capital–backed firms are much more active than traditional boards. Prior research does not provide an adequate explanation for this difference. Outsider representation, small board size, and low diversification are factors that have been found conducive to an active board. However, they are not the primary drivers toward the high levels of involvement displayed by venture capital boards. Instead, agency theory and/or institutional theory may have more predictive validity.

Hohn, H. G. (June 1996). Solving the Board Puzzle: How to Select the Right Directors. *Chief Executive*, pp. 58–62.

One of the most important decisions for an executive to make is the selection of a board of directors. This article provides insight as to some qualities, both personal and professional, that should be considered.

Klaas, Brian S.; John McClendon; and Thomas W. Gainey. (2000). Managing HR in the Small and Medium Enterprise: The Impact of Professional Employer Organizations. *Entrepreneurship Theory & Practice*, vol. 25, no. 1, pp. 107–124.

Due to their limited size, many small and medium enterprises (SMEs) cannot justify full-time HR professionals in their organizations. Professional employer organizations (PEOs), however, offer SMEs and alternative for handling their workforce by providing compensation programs, regulatory compliance, and other HR-related services.

Mosakowski, Elaine. (1998). Entrepreneurial Resources, Organizational Choices, and Competitive Outcomes. *Organization Science*, vol. 9, no. 6, pp. 625–43.

The link between a firm's entrepreneurial resources and its efficient organization form is examined. It is assumed that entrepreneurial resources can be distributed in two ways throughout the firm: They can be held by one or a few individuals (individual entrepreneurial resources), or they can be dispersed among a team of individuals (team entrepreneurial resources). Agency theory is used to consider how various organizational characteristics will differ between these two forms.

Weinzimmer, Laurence G. (1997). Top Management Team Correlates of Organizational Growth in a Small Business Context: A Comparative Study. *Journal of Small Business Management*, vol. 35, no. 3, pp. 1–9.

This study examines whether relationships between top-management team (TMT) variables and growth behavior were consistent with large-firm studies in a small-firm context. Findings suggest that some large-firm TMT theory is also applicable to small-firm growth. However, relationships between certain TMT variables and organizational growth are moderated by firm size.

Endnotes

1. See M. Rothman, "Into the Black," *Inc.* (January 1993), pp. 59–65; J. Reese, "Starbucks," *Fortune* (December 9, 1996), pp. 190–5; and Starbucks Annual Report (1999).

2. J. D. August, "Stringent Rules for S Corporations Eased by New Law," *Estate Planning* (December 1996), pp. 466–72.

3. M. Stevens, "Artful S Corp Planning," *The Practical Accountant* (January 2000), pp. 35–38.

4. R. Kleinman, "The LLC: New Kid on the Block," *Inc.* (January 2000), pp. 90–93.

5. J. C. Collins, "Building Companies to Last," *Inc.* (May 16, 1995), pp. 83–88.

6. J. W. Lorsch, "Organization Design: A Situational Perspective," in *Perspectives on Behavior in Organizations*, 2nd ed., eds. J. R. Hackman, E. E. Lawler III, and L. W. Porter (New York: McGraw-Hill, 1983), pp. 439–47.

7. M. Messmer, "The Politics of Hiring," *Journal of Accountancy* (April 1996), pp. 59–61.

8. S. Greco, "Hire the Best," *Inc.* (June 1999), pp. 32–52.

9. E. S. Ellman, "How to Write a Personnel Manual," *Inc. Special Reports*, Stacey Lewis, ed. (1989), pp. 66–68.

10. B. P. Sunoo, "Generic or Non-Generic Job Descriptions," *Personnel Journal* (February 1996), p. 102.

11. G. Dessler, *Human Resource Management*, 8th ed. (Upper Saddle River, NJ: Prentice Hall, Inc., 2000), pp. 98–102.

12. E. E. Spragins, "Hiring without the Guesswork," *Inc.* (February 1992), pp. 80–87.

13. W. Q. Judge, Jr., and C. P. Zeithaml, "Institutional and Strategic Choice Perspectives on Board Involvement in the Strategic Decision Process," *Academy of Management Journal* (October 1992), pp. 766–94.

14. G. Faulkner, "Selecting a Board of Directors for the Emerging Company," *Governing Entrepreneurial Companies* (Fall 1998), pp. 6–7.

15. C. Poole, "Family Ties," *Forbes* (April 26, 1993), pp. 124–6.

16. J. Reingold, "Dot.Com Boards Are Flouting the Rules," *Business Week* (December 20, 1999), pp. 130–4.

17. E. Shein, "How External Boards Can Help Your Business," *New England Business* (April 1994), pp. 39–41.

18. H. H. Stevenson and W. A. Sahlman, "How Small Companies Should Handle Advisors," *Harvard Business Review* (March–April 1988), pp. 28–34.

II

CASE IIa   Voice Concepts

DESCRIPTION OF COMPANY

Voice Concepts is a new company that has been formed to market and sell the "talking chip," or message maker. The organization is a partnership consisting of two businesspeople from Washington, DC (Tom and Christa Tonis) and two from New Hampshire (Paul and Kim Russo). All parties believe that their knowledge of and experience in the retail market will pave the way for the message maker to be successful and profitable in the United States.

Omega Products of America is a subsidiary of a Japanese manufacturer. The talking chip was their second attempt at the U.S. market. The first product was a chip that was used in music cards and books. This product met with great price resistance among distributors and was eventually dropped. But with new technology and a strategy of finding an exclusive marketing and distribution partner, Omega was set to embark on its second entry into the market.

Omega's objective was to sell the machine and the chips to a company like Voice Concepts that would take the marketing responsibility for the product. In turn, Voice Concepts was interested in exclusive rights to the U.S. market. Both, of course, also needed to consider potential profits and risks. The founders of Voice Concepts all felt that a lease arrangement for the machines, with a purchase option, would be the strategy most acceptable to the retailer. The Russos had in fact conducted some preliminary research and found that for similarly priced products, a lease for $500 per year would be acceptable. After the first year, the retailer would have the option of purchasing the machine for $800, and after the second year, for $350. They believed that Omega might even be willing to drop its prices on the machines by another 20 percent if the Tonises and Russos could convince them that there existed a good market opportunity, especially for the chips, which were the most important element in the business operation.

PRODUCT

The product is a combination of a machine and a computer chip that records an individual's voice message. Once the message is recorded on the chip, it can be inserted into a blank greeting card. When the chip is pressed by the receiver of the card, it is activated to play back the recorded message a number of times. There is an enhanced value to the "talking chip" over prerecorded or written messages because it can be personalized. It is believed that people will pay more for the card because it is an extension of themselves; it contains their voice and the emotion expressed in their language. A Polaroid photo option is going to be combined with the "talking chip" to further personalize the card if the customer desires. Retail prices are set at $10 for the "talking chip" card and $15 for the "talking chip" photo card.

After exploring many different applications and uses for its "talking chip," the company believes that the retail market will be the most successful venue for the product introduction. Although Voice Concepts feels it should target the souvenir and novelty item segments of the retail market initially, it also believes there are many other possible applications for this product. This market, which includes all age groups, will be reached via the use of kiosks in tourist areas such as Faneuil Hall in Boston, theme parks such as Walt Disney World in Orlando, and large shopping malls.

SOUVENIR/NOVELTY INDUSTRY

The souvenir and novelty industry is a highly fragmented market that is experiencing rapid growth. The exact size of this market is difficult to assess since anything that has the name of a location on it could be construed as a souvenir, and the definition of a "novelty item" is also quite ambiguous. An annual survey conducted in 1992 by *Souvenirs and Novelties*, a bimonthly trade publication, estimates annual sales volume at $1.4 billion. This figure represents a consolidation of information collected from many sources including press releases, published surveys, phone contacts, trade shows, and reader service card information. Although 439 businesses were included in the survey, many attractions and outlets were not.

It has been determined that the theme park per capita spending is higher than spending at zoos, museums, and other educational attractions. Additionally, consumers are becoming more price sensitive and are increasingly looking to spend less than $10 for a souvenir.

GREETING CARD INDUSTRY

The greeting card industry is a $3.7 billion market that is dominated by three major players. Hallmark, American Greetings, and Gibson Greetings are all well-established greeting card companies with extensive distribution channels. These three companies command a combined market share of 85 percent. The remaining 15 percent market share is fragmented among an estimated 500 players.

The greeting card industry has begun to refocus its efforts away from traditional holiday cards to concentrate more on alternative products that are purchased and sent for no specific occasion or are personalized by the sender to reflect some specific occasion. Greeting card companies have found tremendous growth in this segment and have responded to consumer needs with many types of cards.

OPPORTUNITIES

The fastest-growing type of greeting card is the alternative or nonoccasion card. American Greetings' research found that alternative cards appeal to the baby boomers, ages 25 to 44. The card from Voice Concepts falls into this category and would suggest an opportunity to enter this nontraditional segment. The souvenir/novelty industry has very low capital requirement barriers, thus offering easy market entry.

THREATS

Since Voice Concepts' product is not a technologic innovation, once the product is introduced, it is very likely that competitors will be able to reproduce the technology and enter the marketplace. To counter this situation, Voice Concepts must capture a significant market share immediately when the product enters the market. Because the product will have a relatively low repeat purchase rate, continued expansion into new markets or changes in the use of the product must be planned.

PRODUCT POSITIONING AND STRATEGY

Voice Concepts' "talking chip" product will be initially positioned as a "souvenir" item from a tourist location. The "talking chip" can be purchased alone or combined with a Polaroid picture. The product can be kept as a souvenir for oneself or sent to a friend or loved one as a greeting.

The product will be distributed primarily through independent retail outlets located at resort and tourist areas. The "talking chip" can use a name that better fits this positioning and will inform consumers of what the product does. Possible names include "Sight and Sound Souvenirs" or "The Memory Maker."

DISTRIBUTION

Specialty leasing, such as kiosks, is a relatively new practice that is emerging in the retail industry. It involves the use of freestanding kiosks or pushcarts as supplemental tenants in a mall or retail area. This leasing allows retail merchants to capture increased traffic and achieve their own goals for maximum profit. It also gives the developer an added profit, usually based on the level of sales achieved by the merchant. Presentation of the kiosk must be in line with the specifications provided by the developer, and every aspect of the kiosk and the product must be approved.

TARGET MARKET

Using the number of annual visitors as a criterion for selecting markets, Voice Concepts has chosen three locations for the initial product introduction: Faneuil Hall Marketplace in Boston (14 million annual visitors), the Mall area in Washington, DC (19 million annual visitors), and Walt Disney World in Orlando (25 million annual visitors). Larger New England shopping malls will also be targeted for potential locations on a per kiosk basis. Voice Concepts' sales forecast is based on the assumption that the kiosk operators will generate sales from 0.2 percent of the visitors to the tourist location. Exhibit 1 shows the number of tourists to each destination and an estimated sales forecast.

EXHIBIT 1   Sales Forecast

Location	Visitors	Sales (.2%)
Faneuil Hall, Boston	14 million	28,000
The Mall, DC	19 million	38,000
Disney World, Orlando	25 million	50,000
Estimated annual sales		116,000

PRICING

The current suggested retail price of $10 for the "talking chip" and $15 for the chip and a Polaroid may cause a problem for Voice Concepts. Cards are generally in the range of $1 to $5. To combat this initial "price shock," the company will have to differentiate its product from a basic card. Additionally, profit margin analysis has shown that the margins are significantly below the norm (50 percent) for kiosk retailers, making decreases in the price structure from Omega integral to the success of the product.

The current price structure of the chip/card is as follows:

Price to Voice Concepts from Omega	$6.50
Price to retailers	$9.12
Price to end consumers	$9.95

The following profit margin analysis, based on Faneuil Hall kiosk rental information, illustrates that this price structure does not provide the retailers with enough of a margin to operate profitably. To simply increase the retailers' margin by decreasing Voice Concepts' margin would result in negative earnings for Voice Concepts. Combining this data with the fact that the retail price cannot be increased, based on findings from research and the focus group, makes it clear that Omega must reduce the price to Voice Concepts and either lower its profits or reduce its costs of manufacturing.

Given the total price to the kiosk operators of $9.12 ($8.12 for each chip and $1.00 for each card) and a suggested selling price of $9.95, the margin is only $.83 per sale. To cover estimated rental costs of $320 per month and salary expenses of $700 per week, the kiosk operator will have to sell 1,229 units per week to merely break even.

As part of their lease agreement, the kiosk operators will have to pay 10 percent on all additional sales over $1,500 per week, making the break-even point even higher. More units will have to be sold to cover the extra 10 percent variable cost. This point illustrates a fundamental problem in the cost structure: The kiosk operator makes a profit of $.83 per unit and yet will have to pay 10 percent of the sales price ($.995) to Faneuil Hall, resulting in a $.17 loss per unit sold on all sales over $1,500 per week.

Research has indicated that consumers will not be willing to spend more than the $10/$15 suggested retail price. Working with this $10 ceiling and allowing the kiosk operators to make a 50 percent profit, the cost per unit (card and chip) should be $6.67. However, reducing the cost to the kiosks to $6.67 will reduce Voice Concepts' profit margin to $.17 per unit or 3 percent, based on a card plus chip cost from Omega of $6.50. Voice Concepts must negotiate a lower price from Omega to achieve a 40 percent margin for the company and allow for a 50 percent margin to the kiosk operators (see Exhibit 2). Omega's cost for the chip was estimated by the Tonises and Russos to be below $2.00; therefore, a price of $4.76 to Voice Concepts would seem to be a reasonable solution. In the past, Omega has been open to these kinds of changes when given strong market evidence.

EXHIBIT 2 Price Structure		
	Chip	Chip and Photo
Price to end consumer	$10.00	$15.00
Cost to retailer	$6.67	$10.00
Cost to Voice Concepts	$4.76	$7.14

FINANCING

The Russos will work out of their home for the first year in order to reduce overhead expenses. Omega also agreed that, for the first year, Voice Concepts would not have to pay for machines or chips until they were sold to a retailer. Thus, Voice Concepts would not have to obtain business loans or venture capital to finance the start-up. Additional inventories will be maintained by Omega at its West Coast warehouse after being imported from Japan. Orders will be delivered to the retailer. Retailers will need to make an initial investment of $1,100 for the machine to record the messages on the "talking chip." Voice Concepts hopefully will be able to offer, as described earlier, the leasing program with the option to purchase in order to reduce the start-up costs and make the venture more attractive to retailers.

CASE IIb   The Beach Carrier

Mary Ricci has a new product concept, The Beach Carrier, that she is ready to bring to market. Ricci is creative, optimistic, enthusiastic, flexible, and motivated. She is willing to put substantial time into developing and bringing The Beach Carrier to market. Although she lacks capital, Ricci is unwilling to license or sell the pattern to a manufacturer; she is determined to maintain control and ownership of the product throughout the introduction and market penetration phases. Ricci believes there is a significant amount of money to be made and refuses to sell her product concept for a flat fee.

THE PRODUCT

The Beach Carrier is a bag large enough to carry everything needed for a day at the beach, including a chair. When empty, the bag can be folded down to a 12-by-12 square for easy storage. The bag's 36-inch by 36-inch size, adjustable padded shoulder strap, and various-sized pockets make it ideal for use in carrying chairs and other items to the beach or other outdoor activities, such as concerts, picnics, and barbecues. The bag can also be used to transport items, such as ski boots, that are difficult to carry. Manufactured in a lightweight, tear-resistant, fade-proof fabric that dries quickly, the bag will be available in a variety of fluorescent as well as conservative colors.

COMPETITION

There are currently no manufacturers producing a novelty bag similar to The Beach Carrier, but the product is easily duplicated. Ricci's success could bring new entrants with substantial manufacturing and distribution capabilities into the market.

MARKETING RESEARCH

Ricci commissioned a consulting company to perform a feasibility study for the product, which included a demographic profile, cost estimates, packaging recommendations, and a patent search. The patent search revealed two products that Ricci's product would infringe on. Both products, however, were chairs that could be disassembled into tote bags; Ricci's product is not a chair, nor would a chair be sold in conjunction with the product.

A focus group was used to determine potential consumer response. Results of the focus group indicated that several features of the product should be modified. For example, the material was perceived as durable; however, the fluorescent color was see-through and considered "trendy," lessening the perceived quality of the bag. The size also represented an issue, as the bag was perceived as much larger than necessary.

MARKET POTENTIAL

People who use suntan and sunscreen products have been identified as the primary target market for The Beach Carrier. Research indicates that 43.9 percent of the adult U.S. population, or 77,293,000 people, use suntan and sunscreen products. Of these, 57.8 percent are female. Assuming that women are the primary purchasers of beach bags, the potential market is estimated at 44,675,000. Beach bags are replaced every three years. The primary market for suntan and sunscreen products is described in Exhibit 1. The marketing share objectives for the first year of The Beach Carrier's sales have been determined based on the following assumptions:

- People who use suntan and sunscreen products represent the market for The Beach Carrier.
- Most men do not buy beach bags; consider women only (57.8 percent of population).
- Women buy new beach bags every three years on average; that is, one-third will buy a new bag this year.

Based on these assumptions, the unit sales needed to achieve market share objectives of 1 percent, 2 percent, and 5 percent of the total market during the first year of The Beach Carrier's sales are shown in Exhibit 2. Ricci is targeting 1 percent of this potential market. Regional market share objectives can be developed from the same data as seen in Exhibit 3A and 3B.

STRATEGY

Ricci investigated several methods of marketing The Beach Carrier, including selling it in upscale (i.e., Bloomingdale's) or discount (i.e., Wal-Mart) stores, licensing the product concept to a manufacturer, selling the idea for a flat fee, selling the bag to corporations for use as a promotional item, and setting up a mail-order operation. Ricci believes that the mail-order option, while requiring the most effort, will provide higher margins, lower risk, and the overall best fit with Ricci's strengths and weaknesses, her market penetration objectives, and her limited financial resources.

EXHIBIT 1	
Segment	Percentage of Total Users of Suntan/Sunscreen Products
Ages 18–44	66.9%
High school graduate	40.2%
Employed full time	60.5%
No child in household	54.5%
Household income of $30,000+	55.3%

EXHIBIT 2

	Population	Sunscreen Users	Replace Bag This Year
Total adults	176,250,000	77,293,000	25,764,333
Females	92,184,000	44,671,000	14,890,333
		Market Share	
	1%	2%	5%
Total adults	257,643	515,287	1,288,217
Females	148,903	297,807	744,517

EXHIBIT 3A

	Population	Sunscreen Users	Women	Replace Bag This Year
Northeast	37,366,000	17,165,000	9,921,370	3,307,123
Midwest	43,426,000	19,630,000	11,346,140	3,782,047
South	60,402,000	23,980,000	13,860,440	4,620,147
West	35,057,000	16,518,000	9,547,404	3,182,468
Total	176,251,000	77,293,000	44,675,354	14,891,785

EXHIBIT 3B

	Market Share		
	1%	2%	5%
Northeast	33,071	66,142	165,356
Midwest	37,820	75,641	189,102
South	46,201	92,403	231,007
West	31,825	63,649	159,123
Total	148,917	297,835	744,588

The mail-order sales strategy will be implemented nationally using a regional roll-out and following a seasonal demand pattern. With three-month intervals between rollout phases, national market exposure will be achieved within 12 months.

PROMOTION

The product will be promoted in novelty and general interest mail-order catalogs and special interest magazines that appeal to beachgoers and boat owners.

PRICING

The costs of manufacturing have been estimated at $6.50 per unit for material, zippers, Velcro, and so on. The costs for assembly and packaging have been estimated at $3.50 per unit, bringing the total manufacturing cost to $10.00. After analyzing competitive products and focus-group results, a mail-order price in the $12.99 to $14.99 range has been established.

DISTRIBUTION

The product will be manufactured at a local New England factory, drop-shipped to a storage facility, and shipped via UPS to the consumer. Initially, inventory can be carried at no cost in Ricci's house or garage.

FINANCING

A $30,000 small business loan is the minimum amount Ricci needs to fund her fixed costs for the first phase of the rollout for the mail-order program. Marketing the product through traditional retail channels would require approximately $250,000 for advertising and other selling costs associated with a new product introduction.

BREAK-EVEN ANALYSIS

Break-even analysis was performed at three mail-order prices, as seen in Exhibit 4. Based on this analysis, Ricci must meet only one-fourth of her target sales goal, or one-quarter of 1 percent of the total market, in order to break even in the first year.

EXHIBIT 4

	Unit Variable	Cost Unit	Price Contribution
Materials	$6.50	$12.99	$2.99
Assembly	3.00	$13.99	$3.99
Packaging	0.50	$14.99	$4.99
Total unit VC	$10.00		

Fixed Costs

	Northeast	Midwest	South	West	Total
Advertising	$25,000	$25,000	$25,000	$25,000	$100,000
Warehousing	266	305	372	256	1,199
General S&A	2,500	2,500	2,500	2,500	10,000
Total fixed costs	$27,766	$27,805	$27,872	$27,756	$111,199

Break-Even Units

	Northeast	Midwest	South	West	Total
$12.99	9,286	9,299	9,322	9,283	37,190
% of total market	0.28%	0.25%	0.20%	0.29%	0.25%
$13.99	6,959	6,969	6,985	6,956	27,869
% of total market	0.21%	0.18%	0.15%	0.22%	0.19%
$14.99	5,564	5,572	5,586	5,562	22,284
% of total market	0.17%	0.15%	0.12%	0.17%	0.15%

CASE IIc   Gooey Industries

EXECUTIVE SUMMARY

Grant Cleveland, Daniel Martin, and Laura Todd Cleveland founded the conceptual framework for Gooey Industries; the enterprise was officially opened in September 1996. These budding entrepreneurs were attending a university at the time, and amidst their search for entry into the career world, they were exposed to the inefficiencies of the college graduate placement process. The three founders put their heads together and spent 2 1/2 years conducting extensive research into the online Internet recruiting industry, planning and developing the organizational goals and objectives for the new company and actively beta testing the products into the market. This preparation resulted in detailed documentation of their findings and a succinct management model—the necessary tools required in launching a successful business. Subsequently, they agreed to start up an organization to facilitate the process of aiding college students, career offices, and businesses in the career placement field. Gooey Industries, named for its accessibility through 10 separate graphic user interfaces (GUI), formally established its offices in April 1999, and within a 10-month period it had expanded in size to over 35 employees and 17 advisory board members.

A Progressive Management Model and Operations Structure

In addition to Grant Cleveland (CEO), Dan Martin (CFO), and Laura Cleveland (COO), the executive management team has grown to include Aidan Kilker (CIO), Robert Sigman (EVP business development), Alin Armega (EVP technological development), and Anita Vokic (director of special projects). Each executive manager has his or her own advisory board, consisting of renowned academics, business executives, and entrepreneurs who participate in the guidance process for future growth and development in the company. This management structure includes the sales and marketing group, customer service, research and development, human resources, legal, and programming divisions. The entire team contributes toward the intellectual capital, which is the primary investment at Gooey Industries. Each member is valued highly for his or her combined experiences, knowledge, and commitment to growing the business, located in a 9,000-square-foot office space in Chagrin Falls, Ohio.

Establishment of Gooey Industries

The online recruiting industry is projected to grow between $18 billion and $41 billion by 2003. In 1998, job postings on the Internet grew by 60 percent, and in January 1999, 45 percent of the Fortune 500 companies were actively recruiting on the Web. Current trends show that over 66 percent of human resource managers use the Internet to hire potential candidates, and this number is expected to grow exponentially in the next decade.

Although competition is growing in the industry, the challenge remains to provide a solution responsive to the increased demands for products and services that reduce or eliminate hiring inefficiencies. Specifically, the focus is on reducing pre-screening waste, which represents significant economic savings to businesses. Gooey

Prepared by Ms. Alka Srivastva, Case Western Reserve University, Cleveland, Ohio, February 2000.

Industries has designed and completed construction of a Web-based hiring solution for employers, university career centers, and college students. The products are designed for management and ease, to aid professionals in their careers from entry through retirement. The unique feature pioneered at Gooey is a powerful management tool, which enables the capturing of data matching jobs and qualified candidates. The philosophy behind the products and services is to build superior resources to empower career center officials and human resource departments to effectively place students with prospective employers. The website offers an array of recruiting applications, Internet tools, integrated content, and entertainment.

In a climate of revolutionary technological advances, Gooey Industries is setting new standards for innovation and quality. The result is the most powerful, comprehensive, and easy-to-use recruiting tool on the market.

Investment Capital

In April 1999, the Gooey Industries offices were opened for business. The intent of the founders was to raise $700,000 by year's end to be comfortable and financially stable. They began development of their website with an accumulated amount of $150,000 of invested capital at 12½ cents per share. In June 1999, another $250,000 was raised, and the share price increased to $.50/share. The third round of investor offerings began in September 1999 and closed on December 1, 1999. Whereas Gooey hoped to raise approximately $700,000 on the share price offering at $2.00/share, on advice of several advisory board members, the founders increased the amount in the hope of raising $3 million. The result? Gooey raised over $3.5 million in this round, which well exceeded their expectations; the total amount invested as of February 2000 was $4.0 million raised among over 100 investors, including venture-capital firms, brokerage houses, businesses, and various strategic entrepreneurs. As a result of this successful round, the founders decided to open another round. This next round of investment contributions began in January 2000 and is expected to generate up to $3 million, selling at $3.00/share. In May 2000, an institutional round will be offered, with the expectation to raise between $15 million and $20 million, with the share price projected to value somewhere between $6 and $8/share. The strategy is to bring Gooey to the public market in third or fourth quarter 2000.

The key financial element as it relates to an Internet enterprise is the concept of valuation stepping. There are neither conventional nor traditional means of valuing an Internet venture, as the revenue stream is based on forward projections several years ahead and discounted back to create a present value. This value stepping approach is the means by which Gooey has founded its current success, even before breaking ground into actual and present sales. The major ingredients of the company include an innovative entrepreneurial management team, highly motivated employees, state-of-the-art technologies, and expert consultants and advisors—in sum, the value of the organization and its assets. In February 2000, the current valuation of Gooey Industries was over $60 million, and by mid-2000, it was expected to reach above and beyond the $100 million mark (see Exhibit 1).

THE BUSINESS

Successful Internet recruiting systems are beginning to form a tangible threat to the two most entrenched recruiting channels: print employment classifieds and employment search agencies. In 1997 the employment classifieds business in the United

EXHIBIT 1

Valuation Summary

	Round 1 April 1999	Round 2 June 1999	Round 3 September 1999	Projected Round 4 January 2000	Projected Round 5 May 2000
Actual $ amount raised	150,000	250,000	3.5 million	3.0 million	15–20 million
Actual valuation	3 million	12 million	40 million	60+ million	100 million
Price per share	12½ cents	$0.50	$2.00	$3.00	$6.00–$8.00
Assets to date (prior to sales)	*Business plan approval	*Office established	*Product and technology completed	*68+ universities participating	*Revenue stream generated
		*Employees hired	*25+ employees	*302,000+ students registered	*Strategic alliances confirmed
		*Technology under development	*Infrastructure formulated	*Launch of product to market	

339

States generated approximately $8 billion in revenues, with the costs for placing print "help wanted" ads ranging from $75 to $10,000. Meanwhile, the global search agency industry, totaling over 4,300 firms, generated over $22 billion in the same year. If successfully placed, fees for searches typically range from 25 to 33 percent of the candidates' first-year salary.

Online Recruiting

Because of their interactivity, electronic job boards are rapidly replacing the static print ads as the starting point for both employers and job seekers. Posting resumes and job openings online allows greater access and reviewing capabilities to a wider audience of job seekers and employers than ever before. Search capabilities, instant reference sources for background checks, and an overall reduction in communication, processing time, and cost add value to the recruiting process beyond the increased number of users who have access to postings. As job boards evolve and mature, they will also incorporate many features that mimic the experience of headhunters and agencies, such as industry specialization, privacy and control, counseling and advice, and management of extended communication between applicant and job seeker.

Over 70 percent of active job seekers prefer the Internet to other methods of job seeking, such as contacting agencies, attending job fairs, or relying on word of mouth.[1] More than half of the general public planned to use the Internet to look for a job sometime in the future, and over 70 percent of companies in the United States are actively using the Internet to advertise jobs and recruit employees, up from 51 percent in 1997.[2]

THE COMPANY

Gooey Industries is founded on the principle of employee-based leadership. The unique corporate culture permits each member of the organization to take an active role in furthering the visions of the company. Alongside the founders' initiative in establishing and promoting their ideas, the employees, advisors, and investors bring new perspectives and insight, fueling the energies driving their success.

A Model for Growth

The online recruiting industry has not yet found a way to capture hiring data on the majority of the job-seeking population or to connect employers with this demographic in any meaningful way. Gooey has developed the solution by going directly to the source—the existing institutions that currently place students. Currently there are over 12 million college students and over 14 million high school students. Gooey has determined that by working with the college career centers, high school counselors, students, and employers, it will maximize its database, affording the opportunity to link the great number of qualified candidates with the great number of job positions made available by the employers.

Currently, very few online recruiting companies focus on the 1.2 million college graduates entering the job market each year. Of those few, none have a true career management center for the students, nor do they provide a useful management tool for career centers; in essence, they operate as a simple resume exchange. Gooey has a unique approach in that it puts students in touch with opportunities in a much wider variety of industries and companies not recruiting on campus. Simultaneously, Gooey provides employers with a service to target hard-to-reach qualified candidates, a feature unknown to its competitors, which differentiates Gooey from the rest.

Organizational Business Development

The main emphasis for Gooey Industries has been the development of strategic alliances and relationships with individuals, educational institutions, businesses, government, associations, and organizations. With respect to individual involvement, Gooey has sought out investors in raising capital; has developed a referral network to engage in strategic connections in the fields of education, politics, and technology; and has immersed itself in building personal affiliations with major corporate contacts.

Gooey has focused its efforts on targeting businesses, an arena that will generate a revenue stream from the onset. These businesses vary in their involvement and range from companies that are purchasing the online services to those that are linking with other sites servicing a similar demographic base. Other relationships include investment in the company, development of alliances to enhance the corporate image, and possible partnerships to join the advisory board council.

The primary involvement with the government is to seek grants, low-interest loans, tax credits for Gooey, assistance in business development, and various degrees of accreditation. A grant program has recently been established for career center officials interested in furthering the academic study of the discipline. The Gooey Industries Grants for the Advancement of Career Center Studies program consists of three grants in the amount of $10,000 plus a laptop for each recipient. The purpose of the grant is to identify leaders in the collegiate career center field and continue the development of the science of career placement. Of note is a potential contract for distribution through the government to public universities in the United States. Because Gooey is offering its services free of charge to the career centers and the students, this philanthropic gesture has raised the issue that the government mandate the use of Gooey's Recruiting Plus in all state-sponsored universities to be eligible for funding. Time and bureaucracy will tell.

Gooey's association with targeted trade associations and business-to-business organizations is the vehicle to reach a large number of businesses and individuals. Further connections have been made with charitable organizations, which not only aid in the development of young students but result in further ways to enhance the system network at Gooey Industries.

PRODUCT DESCRIPTION

Recruiting Plus

Gooey Industries offers its Recruiting Plus on the Internet. The software and services are 100 percent Web-based and are powered by a Sequel 7.0 database, accessible through 10 different graphic user interfaces:

- High school, college, and postgraduate student
- Alumni

- Collegiate career center, high school counselor, and professor
- Employer and Fortune 500
- Gooey Information Central

Gooey's products have superior functionality, design, distribution, and resources as well as a serious destination site potential. Traffic is driven to the site initially through career centers and counselors to the recruiting and business tools that reside on it. Once on the site, users experience a rich variety of powerful career management tools: a host of accompanying resources including videoconferencing, chat rooms, free e-mail, and a number of demographically targeted resources to use on the site. These resources include local weather, news, horoscopes, Rolling Stone News, interactive surveys, and links to major libraries and research institutions around the world.

Gooey Entertainment

The Gooey Entertainment site will serve to spark and maintain student interest in the Gooey site, ultimately serving as a secondary revenue source. Every Recruiting Plus page will have a direct link to Gooey Entertainment, thus channeling thousands of college students to the site daily. Therefore, the features on the Gooey Entertainment page will be principally focused on the interests of college students. These features include a music site and downloadable music, a page displaying different forms of visual art, a prose/poetry page, a running novel, and a self-authored e-zine. Many of the features will be offered free to registered student users, providing them the incentive to visit the site.

MARKETING

The core product, Recruiting Plus, serves three distinct markets: university career centers, students, and small- to medium-sized employers. The immediate goals in the start-up phase are to sign up schools and increase name recognition in targeted U.S. markets, with the ultimate aim of canvassing the entire nation. Efforts will be directed at promoting the product through various means: attendance at national and regional conferences of colleges and employers will gain further recognition. Likewise, direct contact with universities, direct mailings, press releases, promotion, and advertising in school and trade publications and a national advertising campaign will be administered.

Gooey's multifaceted sales initiative includes an international component. The first phase of international expansion is focusing on English-speaking countries in Europe. Gooey is in the process of putting together an international advisory board of professors in 14 European universities. This advisory board will serve as a gateway into colleges and career centers in their respective regions.

Sales Projections

Gooey Industries will be "open for business" beginning March 2000, as employers will become part of the network generating revenue stream. To date, there have been over 68 universities registered in the system, which exposes Gooey to a student population of over 372,000 persons. A projected income statement (Exhibit 2) will illustrate sales projections for 2000 and 2001. A projected balance sheet (Exhibit 3)

EXHIBIT 2

	1999	2000	2001
Projected Income Statement: 1999–2001 (U.S. $)			
Total sales	$ —	$ 5,360,823.00	$76,054,842.00
Cost of goods sold			
	95,087	285,525	650,460
Hardware development	646,024	678,000	1,158,000
Gross profit	$ (741,111.00)	$4,397,298.00	$74,246,382.00
Marketing	134,366	2,236,769	6,863,351
Operational	217,062	1,421,760	1,618,284
Staffing	554,244	2,126,168	5,254,262
EBITDA	$(1,646,783.00)	$(1,387,399.00)	$60,510,485.00
Depreciation	12,985		
Amortization	1,196		
EBIT	$(1,660,964.00)	$(1,387,399.00)	$60,510,485.00
Interest expense	3,197	53,838	12,576,051
Income before taxes	$(1,664,161.00)	$(1,441,237.00)	$47,934,434.00
Income taxes			(18,597,279)
Net income	$(1,664,161.00)	$(1,441,237.00)	$29,337,155.00
Total sales growth			1419.00%
Gross margin		82%	97.60%
SG&A/sales		108%	18.10%
EBITDA margin		-25.90%	79.60%
EBIT margin		-25.90%	79.60%
Net income margin		-26.90%	38.60%
Tax rate			38%
EPS outstanding	$ (0.08)	$ (0.03)	$ 0.61

will show the intended assets and liabilities statement by quarter for the years 2000 and 2001, and the projected cash flow (Exhibit 4) will exemplify the proposed cash value structure for fiscal years 2000 and 2001.

Strategy

Career Centers   Career centers are an important asset to Gooey Industries as they are a gateway to job candidates. Gooey will partner with career centers to collect data on their students and graduates. Through this partnership, Gooey will provide career centers with a high-quality career center interface to allow them to collect, manage, and retrieve data on their students, free of charge. This effectively provides the career center with administrative and job placement tools.

EXHIBIT 3

Projected Balance Sheet: 2000–2001

	2000				2001			
	Q1	Q2	Q3	Q4	Q1	Q2	Q3	Q4
Assets								
Current assets								
Cash & equivalents	$4,517,527	$18,830,043	$18,605,210	$60,240,401	$17,093,064	$5,707,075	$14,715,936	$31,372,615
Available for sale securities	$34,670	$37,692	$1,577,630	$2,903,685	$4,289,329	$6,579,894	$10,483,008	$18,557,169
Other Current Assets	$429,165	$493,540	$3,155,424	$6,045,140	$4,876,375	$11,119,480	$22,489,393	$34,077,454
Total current assets	$4,981,362	$19,361,274	$23,338,266	$69,189,225	$26,258,768	$23,406,448	$47,688,337	$84,007,239
Property & equipment								
Real property								
Investments & acquisitions				$20,000,000	$70,000,000	$90,000,000	$90,000,000	$90,000,000
Total assets	$4,981,362	$19,361,274	$23,338,266	$89,189,225	$96,258,768	$113,406,448	$137,688,337	$174,007,239
Liabilities and stockholders' equity								
Current liabilities:								
Notes payable	$856,109	$486,577	$1,200,000	$2,000,000	$3,500,000	$5,000,000	$7,390,678	$16,530,000
Long-term debt	$1,251,488	$650,676	$3,043,646	$4,562,972	$6,344,186	$10,431,300	$16,996,814	$22,007,508
Accounts payable	$917,285	$2,116,902	$3,533,354	$6,130,463	$7,802,775	$12,239,760	$17,086,646	$16,660,637
Accrued income taxes	$—				$276,650	$3,155,865	$7,376,510	$16,425,884
Total current liabilities	$3,024,881	$3,254,155	$7,777,000	$12,693,435	$17,923,611	$30,826,925	$48,850,648	$71,624,029
Stockholders' equity								
Common stock (including additional paid-in capital)	$3,000,000	$18,000,000	$18,000,000	$78,000,000	$78,000,000	$78,000,000	$78,000,000	$78,000,000
Retained earnings	$(1,043,519)	$(1,892,881)	$(2,438,734)	$(1,504,209)	$335,157	$4,579,523	$10,837,689	$24,383,210
Total stockholders' equity	$1,956,481	$16,107,119	$15,561,266	$76,495,791	$78,335,157	$82,579,523	$88,837,689	$102,383,210
Total liabilities & stockholders' equity	$4,981,362	$19,361,274	$23,338,266	$89,189,226	$96,258,768	$113,406,448	$137,688,337	$174,007,239

EXHIBIT 4

	Projected Cash Flow: Fiscal 2000–2001	
	2000	2001
Net income	$(1,441,237.00)	$25,285,735.00
Adjustments for income to cash flow:	—	—
Changes in op. assets and liabilities	—	—
Prepaid expenses	—	—
AP & accrued expenses	4,086,975	23,680,754
Refundable & accrued income tax	—	821,294
Net cash (used) for operations	$2,645,738.00	$49,787,783.00
Cash flows from investments:		
Purchase of private companies		
Purchase of public companies		
Net provided by (used for) investments		
Cash flows from financing activities		
Notes payable	14,218	318,723
Cash from public issuance of stock		
Cash from private issuance of stock		
Repayment of notes payable	(3,269,580)	(9,803,328)
Net provided by (used for) financing	$(3,255,362.00)	$(9,484,605.00)
Increase (decrease) in cash & equity		
Cash & equity at beginning of period		
Cash & equity at end of period		

Gooey strives to empower these career centers to help them place their students in jobs and make their departments more cost effective and efficient. In return, the universities generally use Gooey as their exclusive career services center placement tool. They encourage other career centers, their students, employers, and alumni to use the system through a direct-mail effort.

College Students   Initially, Gooey will focus on recent four-year bachelor's degree graduates. Because the students who populate Gooey's database are initially those at registered universities, a large part of the marketing effort is school campus related. Approximately 1.2 million college graduates enter the job market each year from 2244 four-year institutions,[3] making them a concentrated and organized segment of the job candidate pool. This submarket represents approximately 10 percent of the total job candidate market. A retention factor plays a primary role in the marketing strategy for Gooey Industries, as the market size is continuously replenishing itself. Thus, the field of candidates posted on the site increases exponentially year after year.

Employers   Employers are expected to provide the majority of the revenues for Gooey, and thus the marketing campaign will be a mass-market strategy. National advertisements will be placed in human resource publications and general business journals. These ads will be geared toward educating potential customers and gaining new memberships.

Gooey Industries will also be utilizing existing relationships with career centers to gain employer memberships. Through the university, Gooey will receive employer contact information from companies traditionally recruiting from these schools. Gooey will then target these employers through direct contact and mailings.

The process involved for those employers recruiting on campus can be costly and time consuming, and even then only a fraction of the universities are covered. With Recruiting Plus, Gooey can offer opportunities in diverse career fields and locations that would otherwise go unrecognized.

Market Size

The initial target market will be small- and medium-sized businesses, as they are the most affected by a shortage of qualified job candidates and the upwardly spiraling cost of hiring new employees. The average cost per hire rose from $5672 in 1992 to $8090 in 1996. A great majority of the small- and mid-sized companies do not have the financial resources to invest in a customized hiring solution.

There are presently 546,000 businesses, each employing 20 to 500 employees and accounting for approximately 10 percent of the overall employer market. These small- to medium-sized firms provide jobs to over 1 million of the 1.2 million graduates and currently employ 60.3 percent of the workforce. They are expected to account for 70 percent of new jobs between 2000 and 2005.

Projected User Base	1999	2000	2001
College students	150,000	1,000,000	2,200,000
Employers	————	25,000	100,000

Targeting large businesses will be of critical value—and the next step for Gooey in terms of strategic growth. At present, the Fortune 500 companies that actively recruit via the Internet have risen from 17 percent in January 1998 to 45 percent in January 1999. About 71 percent of these companies will be spending more each year on Internet recruiting, allocating 20 percent of their recruiting budget on the Internet. This trend in the online recruiting industry is predicted to top $1.7 billion by the year 2003—an almost 700 percent increase from the 1999 figures.[4]

Pricing

Employers will be able to access all services on the site beginning March 2000. Once employers become part of the network, the charge will be $60/month for 35 job postings, 80 detailed searches, and unlimited use of all other online resources. Currently the average online posting retails at $160 per listing/month, and the only search costs $3000 per 10 candidates. Gooey's favorable price point is designed to maximize the number of employer users, as they are a viable, immediate revenue stream for other human resources products and services.

Recruiting Plus eliminates search time for both job seekers and employers. It provides a solution at a fraction of the price of any competitor, averaging $1.71 a job posting, including free features never offered before from any competitor. An important aspect critical to the targeted market is that the service is provided at no charge to the students.

Competition

Gooey Industries faces a variety of competitors on a number of different levels (Exhibit 5). Currently, Gooey has a narrow focus and is not in direct competition with the majority of these sites, products, and services. However, there are two major groups that Gooey has identified as its competition. They are companies generating their revenue from employers and those deriving their revenue from career centers.

An average of 67,000 new "netizens" are joining the Internet daily. With the growth of the online recruiting industry, current sites are spending vast amounts of money increasing their site awareness, trying to draw fresh new resumes. Others are merging with big name companies and other sites to create a more fluid brand awareness. The effects of these mergers are temporarily driving traffic to the site, but few are returning to use them as a career management tool.

Employers are enjoying the benefits of lower costs to post job openings, but still lack the efficiency and productivity of receiving qualified candidates. While there are

EXHIBIT 5

Competition Product Comparison*

	Job Trak	JobDirect	Crimson Solutions	Monster. com	Career Connections	Academic Software
Price to career centers	$2,500/yr	No charge	$1,500 setup, $3,000/yr.	$225/job posting	$5,000 to $10,000/yr	$2,500 to $6,500/yr
Implementation period	6 weeks	N/A	6–8 weeks	N/A	N/A	N/A
Job seeker features (8 possible services)	3 offered	2 offered	7 offered	5 offered	4 offered	2 offered
Career center features (9 possible services)	2 offered	4 offered	7 offered	2 offered	3 offered	5 offered
Employer Features (6 possible services)	———	3 offered	2 offered	3 offered	2 offered	———

*Note: Other competitors include the following companies:

Career Mosaic
Web Hire
Career-Central
Career Builder
HeadHunter
Future Step
Hot Jobs
1-Jobs
TopJobs
NationJob

many advantages to Internet recruiting—including lower costs, reduced time, real-time monitoring, and editing—there are still complaints about too many resumes, poor matching capabilities, and not enough qualified candidates. For the first half of 1999, on a total of seven sites, over $50 million was spent to advertise job openings, of which only a total of 49 hires resulted from the postings.

Competitive Advantage

Concerning functionality, Gooey Industries has no competition. In sum, their products and services offer:

- The only legitimate resume builder
- The only system to integrate a resume search, job posting, interview scheduling, note taking, automatic tracking with a host of other applications and entertainment sites
- The only comprehensive help system
- An extensive career-building information system
- All the features of the competitors, and more
- A tool offered to students and universities at no charge
- New product lines forthcoming

---

1. Study conducted by J. Walter Thompson's Specialized Communications Group.
2. The American Management Association.
3. Chronicle of Higher Education, August 1998.
4. Association of Internet Recruiting.

CASE IId   Gourmet to Go

INTRODUCTION

Today, many households have two incomes. At the end of the day the questions arise, "Who will cook?" or "What do I cook?" Time is limited. After a long day at work, few people want to face the lines at the grocery store. Often the choice is to eat out. But the expense of dining out or the boredom of fast food soon becomes unappealing. Pizza or fast-food delivery solves the problem of going out but does not always satisfy the need for nutritious, high-quality meals. Some people prefer a home-cooked meal, especially without the hassle of grocery shopping, menu planning, and time-consuming preparation.

Jan Jones is one of those people. She is a hard-working professional who would like to come home to a home-cooked meal. She would not mind fixing it herself but, once at home, making an extra trip to the store is a major hassle. Jones thought it would be great to have the meal planned and all the ingredients at her fingertips. She thought of other people in her situation and realized there might be a market need for this kind of service. After thinking about the types of meals that could be marketed, Jones discussed the plan with her colleagues at work. The enthusiastic response led her to believe she had a good idea. After months of marketing research, menu planning, and financial projections, Jones was ready to launch her new business. The following is the business plan for Gourmet to Go.

EXECUTIVE SUMMARY

Gourmet to Go is a new concept in grocery marketing. The product is a combination of menu planning and grocery delivery; a complete package of groceries and recipes for a week's meals are delivered to a customer's door. The target market consists of young urban professionals living in two-income households in which individuals have limited leisure time, high disposable income, and a willingness to pay for services.

The objective is to develop a customer base of 400 households by the end of the third year after start-up. This level of operation will produce a new income of about $100,000 per year and provide a solid base for market penetration in the future.

The objective will be achieved by creating an awareness of the product through an intense promotional campaign at start-up and by providing customers first-class service and premium-quality goods.

The capital required to achieve objectives is $199,800. Jones will invest $143,000 and will manage and own the business. The remainder of the capital will be financed through bank loans.

PRODUCT

The product consists of meal-planning and grocery-shopping services. It offers a limited selection of preplanned five-dinner packages delivered directly to the customer.

The criteria for the meal packages will be balanced nutrition, easy preparation, and premium quality. To ensure the nutritional requirements, Gourmet to Go will hire a nutritionist as a consultant. Nutritional information will be included with each order. The most efficient method for preparing the overall meal will be presented. Meals will be limited to recipes requiring no more than 20 minutes to prepare. Premium-quality ingredients will be a selling feature. The customer should feel that he or she is getting better-quality ingredients than could be obtained from the grocery store.

MANUFACTURING AND PACKAGING

Since the customer will not be shopping on the premises, Gourmet to Go will require only a warehouse-type space for the groceries. The store location or decor will be unimportant in attracting business. There will be fewer inventory expenses since the customer will not be choosing among various brands. Only premium brands will be offered.

It will be important to establish a reliable connection with a distributor for high-quality produce and to maintain freshness for delivery to the customer.

As orders are processed, the dinners will be assembled. Meats will be wrapped and ready for the home freezer. All ingredients will be labeled according to the dinner to which they belong. The groceries will be sorted and bagged according to storage requirements: freezer, refrigerator, and shelf. Everything possible will be done to minimize the customer's task. Included in the packaging will be the nutritional information and preparation instructions.

Customers will be given the option of selecting their own meals from the monthly menu list or opting for a weekly selection from the company.

FUTURE GROWTH

Various options will be explored in order to expand the business. Some customers may prefer a three- or four-meal plan if they eat out more often or travel frequently. Another possibility might be the "last-minute gourmet"; that is, they can call any evening for one meal only.

Increasing the customer base will increase future sales. Expansion of Gourmet to Go can include branches in other locations or even future franchising in other cities. With expansion and success, Gourmet to Go might be a prime target for a larger food company to buy out.

INDUSTRY

The Gourmet to Go concept is a new idea with its own market niche. The closest competitors would be grocery stores and restaurants with delivery services.

Of the 660 grocery stores in the Tulsa/Tulsa County region, only two offer a delivery service. It is a higher-priced store and will deliver for $4, regardless of order size. However, it offers no assistance in meal planning.

A number of pizza chains will deliver pizza as well as fried chicken. There is also a new service that will pick up and deliver orders from various restaurants. However, Gourmet to Go would not be in direct competition with these services because the meals available from them are either of a fast-food type or far more expensive than a Gourmet to Go meal.

SALES PREDICTION

The market segment will be households with an income of at least $50,000 per year. In Tulsa/Tulsa County, this will cover an area including over 16,600 households that meet the target requirements of income with an age range of 24 to 50 years. By the end of the third year, a customer base of 400 households will be developed (2.3 percent of the target market). At a growth rate of 2.73 percent a year, the target market of households should increase over three years to 18,000.

MARKETING

Distribution

The product will be delivered directly to the customer.

Sales Strategy

Advertising will include newspaper ads, radio spots, an Internet Web page, and direct-mail brochures. All four will be used during normal operations, but an intense campaign will precede start-up. A series of "teaser" newspaper ads will be run prior to start-up, announcing a revolution in grocery shopping. At start-up, the newspaper ads will have evolved into actually introducing the product, and radio spots will begin as well. A heavy advertising schedule will be used during the first four weeks of business. After start-up, a direct mailing will detail the description of the service and a menu plan.

Newspaper ads aimed at the target markets will be placed in entertainment and business sections. Radio spots will be geared to stations most appealing to the target market. Since the product is new, it may be possible to do interviews with newspapers and obtain free publicity.

Sales promotions will offer large discounts to first-time customers. These promotions will continue for the first six months of operations.

The service will be priced at $10 per week for delivery and planning, with the groceries priced at full retail level. According to the phone survey, most people who were interested in the service would be willing to pay the weekly service charge.

FINANCIAL

Various financial statements are included in Exhibits 1 through 8.

MANAGEMENT

The management will consist of the owner/manager. Other employees will be delivery clerks and order clerks. It is anticipated that after the business grows, an operations manager might be added to supervise the employees.

EXHIBIT 1 Start-Up Expenses		
Ad campaign		
Ad agency*	$2,000	
Brochures†	5,000	
Radio spots‡	5,600	
Newspaper ads§	5,000	
Total		$17,600
Prestart-up salaries**		14,300
Nutritionist consulting		5,000
Miscellaneous consulting (legal, etc.)		1,000
Prestart-up rent and deposits		3,000
Prestart-up utilities and miscellaneous supplies		1,000
		$41,900

*40 hrs. @ $50/hr
†20,000 brochures; printing, development, etc. @ $0.25/ea
‡4 weeks intense campaign: 20 spots/week (30 seconds); $70/spot
§50 ads at an average of $100/ad
**Jan Jones @ 3 months; clerks, two @ 2 weeks

EXHIBIT 2 Capital Equipment List		
Computers:		
Apple, MacIntosh Office System		
3 workstations	$7,500	
Laser printer	7,000	
Hard disk	2,400	
Networking	1,800	
Software	2,000	
Total		$20,700
Delivery vans, Chevrolet Astro		36,000
Food lockers and freezers		10,000
Phone system (AT&T)		1,000
Furniture and fixtures		3,000
		$70,700

EXHIBIT 3 Pro Forma Income Statement

	Mo. 1	Mo. 2	Mo. 3	Mo. 4	Mo. 5	Mo. 6	Mo. 7	Mo. 8	Mo. 9	Mo. 10	Mo. 11	Mo. 12
						Year 1						
Sales[1]	2,150	3,225	5,375	10,750	16,125	19,320	21,500	23,650	25,800	27,950	30,100	32,250
Less: Cost of Goods sold[2]	1,376	2,064	3,440	6,880	10,320	12,384	13,760	15,136	16,512	17,888	19,264	20,640
Gross profit	774	1,161	1,935	3,870	5,805	6,936	7,740	8,514	9,288	10,062	10,836	11,610
Less: Operating expenses												
Salaries and wages[3]	6,400	6,400	6,400	6,400	6,400	6,400	8,300	8,300	8,300	8,300	8,300	8,300
Operating supplies	300	300	300	300	300	300	300	300	300	300	300	300
Repairs and maintenance	200	200	200	200	200	200	200	200	200	200	200	200
Advertising and promotion[4]	110	160	270	540	810	970	1,080	1,180	1,290	1,400	1,500	1,610
Bad debts	50	50	50	50	50	50	50	50	50	50	50	50
Rent[5]	1,330	1,330	1,330	1,330	1,330	1,330	1,330	1,330	1,330	1,330	1,330	1,330
Utilities	1,000	1,000	1,000	1,000	1,000	1,000	1,000	1,000	1,000	1,000	1,000	1,000
Insurance	400	400	400	400	400	400	400	400	400	400	400	400
General office	100	100	100	100	100	100	100	100	100	100	100	100
Licenses	100	0	0	0	0	0	0	0	0	0	0	0
Interest[6]	340	340	340	340	340	340	465	465	465	465	465	465
Depreciation[7]	790	790	790	790	790	790	790	790	790	790	790	790
Total operating expenses	11,120	11,070	11,180	11,450	11,720	11,880	14,015	14,115	14,225	14,335	14,435	14,545
Profit (loss) before taxes	(10,346)	(9,909)	(9,245)	(7,580)	(5,915)	(4,944)	(6,275)	(5,601)	(4,937)	(4,273)	(3,599)	(2,935)
Less: Taxes	0	0	0	0	0	0	0	0	0	0	0	0
Net profit (loss)	(10,346)	(9,909)	(9,245)	(7,580)	(5,915)	(4,944)	(6,275)	(5,601)	(4,937)	(4,273)	(3,599)	(2,935)

[1]Sales—per Action Plan; see Exhibit 8 for detail. Average unit sale is $40.00 for groceries plus $10.00 per week for delivery (Exhibit 1), making the monthly unit sales per household (2 people) $215.00.

[2]Cost of goods sold—80% of retail grocery price, or $32.00 per household per week ($138.00/month household). (80% an average margin on groceries—*Progressive Grocer;* April 1984; p. 94.)

[3]Salaries and wages—Ms. Jones's salary will be $4500/month. Order clerks will be paid $1000/month, and delivery clerks will be paid $900/month. One additional order clerk and delivery clerk each will be added once sales reach 100 households, and again at 200 households. Salaries will escalate at 6%/year.

[4]Advertising and promotion—The grocery industry standard is 1% of sales. However, Gourmet to Go being a new business will require more than that level; 5% of sales is used in this plan. (Special prestart-up advertising is covered with other start-up expenses.)

[5]Rent—2000/ft.^{2} @ $8.00/ft.^{2}; 1333 $1/month; escalate at 6%/year.

[6]Interest-Loans on computer ($10,000) and delivery vehicles ($12,000 ea.) at 12.5%/year. (Delivery vehicles will be added with delivery clerks.) (Debt service—based on three-year amortization of loans with payments of 1/3 at the end of each of three years.)

[7]Depreciation—All equipment will be depreciated per ACRS Schedules: vehicles and computers—3 years; furniture and fixtures–10 years.

EXHIBIT 4 Pro Forma Income Statement

	Year 2				Year 3			
	Q1	Q2	Q3	Q4	Q1	Q2	Q3	Q4
Sales[1]	112,875	129,000	161,000	193,500	209,625	225,750	241,875	258,000
Less: Cost of goods sold[2]	72,240	82,560	103,200	123,840	134,160	144,800	154,800	165,120
Gross profit	40,635	46,440	57,800	69,660	75,465	80,950	87,075	92,880
Less: Operating expenses								
Salaries and wages[3]	24,900	32,700	32,700	38,400	40,800	40,800	40,800	40,800
Operating supplies	900	900	900	900	900	900	900	900
Repairs and maintenance	600	600	600	600	600	600	600	600
Advertising and promotion[4]	5,640	6,540	8,060	9,680	10,480	11,290	12,090	12,900
Bad debts	150	150	150	150	150	150	150	150
Rent[5]	4,230	4,230	4,230	4,230	4,480	4,480	4,480	4,480
Utilities	3,000	3,000	3,000	3,000	3,000	3,000	3,000	3,000
Insurance	1,200	1,200	1,200	1,200	1,200	1,200	1,200	1,200
General office	300	300	300	300	300	300	300	300
Licenses	0	0	0	0	0	0	0	0
Interest[6]	1,431	1,431	1,306	1,306	965	840	715	715
Depreciation[7]	3,900	3,900	3,900	3,900	4,230	4,230	4,230	4,230
Total operating expenses	46,251	54,951	56,346	63,666	67,105	67,790	68,465	69,275
Profit (loss) before taxes	(5,616)	(8,511)	1,454	5,994	8,360	13,160	18,610	23,605
Less: Taxes	0	0	0	0	0			
Net profit (loss)	(5,616)	(8,511)	1,454	5,994	8,360	13,160	18,610	23,605

[1]Sales—per Action Plan; see Exhibit 8 for detail. Average unit sale is $40.00 for groceries plus $10.00 per week for delivery (Exhibit 1), making the monthly unit sales per household (2 people) $215.00.

[2]Cost of goods sold—80% of retail grocery price, or $32.00 per household per week ($138.00/month household). (80% an average margin on groceries—*Progressive Grocer*; April 1984; p. 94.)

[3]Salaries and wages—Ms. Jones's salary will be $4500/month. Order clerks will be paid $1000/month, and delivery clerks will be paid $900/month. One additional order clerk and delivery clerk each will be added once sales reach 100 households, and again at 200 households. Salaries will escalate at 6%/year.

[4]Advertising and promotion—The grocery industry standard is 1% of sales. However, Gourmet to Go being a new business will require more than that level; 5% of sales is used in this plan. (Special prestart-up advertising is covered with other start-up expenses.)

[5]Rent—2000/ft.² @ $8.00/ft.²; 1333 $1/month; escalate at 6%/year.

[6]Interest—Loans on computer ($10,000) and delivery vehicles ($12,000 ea.) at 12.5% year. (Delivery vehicles will be added with delivery clerks.) (Debt service-based on three-year amortization of loans with payments of 1/3 at the end of each of three years.)

[7]Depreciation—All equipment will be depreciated per ACRS Schedules: vehicles and computers—3 years; furniture and fixtures–10 years.

EXHIBIT 5 Pro Forma Cash Flow Statement

							Year 1						
	Mo. 1	Mo. 2	Mo. 3	Mo. 4	Mo. 5	Mo. 6	Mo. 7	Mo. 8	Mo. 9	Mo. 10	Mo. 11	Mo. 12	Total
Cash receipts													
Sales	2,150	3,225	5,375	10,750	16,125	19,320	21,500	23,650	25,800	27,950	30,100	32,250	218,225
Other													
Total cash receipts	2,150	3,225	5,375	10,750	16,125	19,320	21,500	23,650	25,800	27,950	30,100	32,250	218,225
Cash disbursements													
Cost of goods sold	1,376	2,064	3,440	6,880	10,320	12,384	13,760	15,136	16,512	17,888	19,264	20,640	139,664
Salaries and wages	6,400	6,400	6,400	6,400	6,400	6,400	8,300	8,300	8,300	8,300	8,300	8,300	88,200
Operating supplies	300	300	300	300	300	300	300	300	300	300	300	300	3,600
Repairs and maintenance	200	200	200	200	200	200	200	200	200	200	200	200	2,400
Advertising and promotion	110	160	270	540	810	970	1,080	1,180	1,290	1,400	1,500	1,610	10,920
Bad debts	50	50	50	50	50	50	50	50	50	50	50	50	600
Rent	1,330	1,330	1,330	1,330	1,330	1,330	1,330	1,330	1,330	1,330	1,330	1,330	15,960
Utilities	1,000	1,000	1,000	1,000	1,000	1,000	1,000	1,000	1,000	1,000	1,000	1,000	12,000
Insurance	400	400	400	400	400	400	400	400	400	400	400	400	4,600
General office	100	100	100	100	100	100	100	100	100	100	100	100	1,200
Licenses	100	0	0	0	0	0	0	0	0	0	0	0	100
Interest	340	340	340	340	340	340	465	465	465	465	465	465	4,830
Debt service (principle)	0	0	0	0	0	0	0	0	0	0	0	10,900	10,900
Total cash disbursements	11,706	12,344	13,830	17,540	21,250	23,474	26,985	28,461	29,947	31,433	32,909	45,295	295,174
Net cash flow	(9,556)	(9,119)	(8,455)	(6,790)	(5,125)	(4,124)	(5,485)	(4,811)	(4,147)	(3,483)	(2,809)	(13,045)	(76,969)

EXHIBIT 6 Pro Forma Cash Flow Statement

	Year 2				Year 3			
	Q1	Q2	Q3	Q4	Q1	Q2	Q3	Q4
Cash receipts								
Sales	112,875	129,000	161,000	193,500	209,625	225,750	241,875	258,000
Other								
Total cash receipts	112,875	129,000	161,000	193,500	209,625	225,750	241,875	258,000
Cash disbursements								
Cost of goods sold	72,240	82,560	103,200	123,840	134,160	144,800	154,800	165,120
Salaries and wages	24,900	32,700	32,700	38,400	40,800	40,800	40,800	40,800
Operating supplies	900	900	900	900	900	900	900	900
Repairs and maintenance	600	600	600	600	600	600	600	600
Advertising and promotion	5,640	6,450	8,060	9,680	10,480	11,290	12,090	12,900
Bad debts	150	150	150	150	150	150	150	150
Rent	4,230	4,230	4,230	4,230	4,480	4,480	4,480	4,480
Utilities	3,000	3,000	3,000	3,000	3,000	3,000	3,000	3,000
Insurance	1,200	1,200	1,200	1,200	1,200	1,200	1,200	1,200
General office	300	300	300	300	300	300	300	300
Licenses	0	0	0	0	0	0	0	0
Interest	1,431	1,431	1,306	1,306	965	840	715	715
Debt service (principle)	0	4,000	0	10,900	4,000	4,000	0	10,900
Total cash disbursements	114,591	137,521	155,646	194,506	201,035	212,040	219,035	241,065
Net cash flow	(1,716)	(8,521)	5,354	(1,006)	8,590	13,710	22,840	16,935

EXHIBIT 7 Pro Forma Balance Sheets

End of:	Yr 1	Yr 2	Yr 3		Yr 1	Yr 2	Yr 3
	Assets				**Liabilities**		
Current assets				Accounts payable	10,320	17,200	25,800
Cash	2,000	3,000	4,000	Notes payable	0	0	0
Accounts receivable	16,125	26,833	40,313	Total current liabilities	10,320	17,200	25,800
Inventory	10,320	17,200	25,800	Long-term liabilities			
Supplies	300	300	300	Bank loans payable	33,800	30,900	12,000
Prepaid expenses	1,330	1,330	1,300	Personal loans payable	0	0	0
Total current assets	30,075	48,663	71,743	Total long-term liabilities	33,800	30,900	12,000
Fixed assets				Total liabiliites	44,120	48,100	37,800
Furniture and fixtures	12,600	11,200	9,800	Owner's equity			
Vehicles	18,000	17,880	4,440	Paid-in capital	110,744	52,882	0
Equipment	18,630	16,560	14,490	Retained earnings	(75,559)	(6,679)	63,735
Total fixed assets	49,230	45,640	28,730	Total owner's equity	35,185	46,203	63,735
Total assets	79,305	94,303	100,473	Total liabilities and equity	79,305	94,303	101,535

EXHIBIT 8 Sources and Uses of Funds

Sources of Funds	
Jan Jones (personal funds)	$143,086
Bank loans for computer and vehicles*	56,700
Total sources	$199,786
Uses of Funds	
Computer, peripherals, and software	$20,700
Food lockers and freezers	10,000
Delivery vehicles	36,000
Phone system	1,000
Miscellaneous furniture and fixtures	3,000
Start-up expenses†	41,900
Working capital‡	87,186
Total uses	$199,786

*Total for initial 3-year period. Computer and one delivery van will be acquired prior to start-up, one delivery van will be added 6 months after start-up, and another will be added 18 months after start-up. Financing will be handled simultaneously with procurement.
†To cover negative cash flow over first 1½ years of operation. (See pro forma cash flow statements.)
‡See detail, following.

CASE IIe   Academy Computers Limited

That advice had suddenly come back to haunt him! The advice had come from a critical judge when Academy Computers reached the semifinal of "The Business Game" on Scottish Television. He remembered his thoughts clearly: "Rubbish, they don't know what they are talking about!" Gordon Barraclough was not happy because he now knew what the judge had meant. He was even less happy because by rejecting that advice, he had put Academy Computers, the company he and two partners had started six years before, in serious trouble.

THE BIRTH

It had all seemed so rosy just a short time earlier. Barraclough and George Bissett were working as sales representatives for a Glasgow computer dealer. As he carried out his duties, Bissett observed the growing potential for computer-aided design (CAD) in architects' offices. The late 1980s were an exciting time in the office computing world. Powerful personal computers (PCs) were becoming readily available at affordable prices, and tasks that had previously required bulky and expensive computers were now possible with a desk-top PC. At this time, an emerging market leader in CAD was a software package called AutoCAD. Although it was engineers who mainly used the software, Barraclough and Bissett felt that there was real potential in selling it to architectural practices if some customization of the software could be carried out. They would also need to provide substantial ongoing technical support to back up the inexperienced architectural users.

Source: This case study forms part of a series of case studies developed on behalf of Scottish Enterprise to highlight the role of the entrepreneur in the creation and development of a business. It was written by Gordon Brown of Scottish Enterprise and Frank Martin, University of Stirling. Copyright: Scottish Enterprise 1996.

Professor Alec James, a CAD lecturer in the Mackintosh School of Architecture, supported their conviction that this was a real opportunity. Barraclough and Bissett, helped by James, worked overtime to assess the size of the business opportunity in the CAD architectural market. They also tried to persuade their computer dealer employer to invest in a specialist division to advance the business opportunity. "We begged him to let us set it up," recalls Barraclough. "But he just was not interested. George, Alec, and I were chatting it over, and we thought, OK, we'll do it ourselves."

Over many a sipped beer in the local hotel, Barraclough, Bissett, and James decided to go for the opportunity themselves and started work to develop a first business plan. However, after all their planning, they had their request for a $60,000 overdraft rejected by all four of the bank managers they approached. The reason given was that computer software businesses were too risky. Casually, and a little unwillingly (because this was mixing business and family), Barraclough mentioned this difficulty to his father-in-law, a very successful businessman. After seeking some independent advice, Barraclough's father-in-law agreed to back the plan by guaranteeing the required overdraft.

Confident of their chances for success, Barraclough and Bissett resigned their jobs with the computer dealer and set up Academy Computers Ltd. in January 1988. All three founders and their backer were equal directors, with 25 percent of the equity each. James, however, kept his job with the university and acted in a part-time capacity only. Initial financing was $1000 equity from each of the three founders and their investor, plus the guaranteed bank overdraft.

GETTING STARTED

Continuing the spirit of equal partnership, the three founders decided that they should have no managing director, but rather that Barraclough, because of his strength in sales, should act as sales and marketing director. James, because of his strong technical background, should be technical director; and because they knew someone ought to look after finance, Bissett agreed, albeit a little reluctantly, to act as finance and administration director.

Academy acted as a value-added reseller specializing in the provision of CAD systems and associated services for the architectural market. It added value to off-the-shelf CAD systems by customizing them to make them suitable for use by their architect customers. In mid-1989, recognizing that the company's architectural market was limited, Academy took on an important new recruit, Dave McLeod. McLeod had a background with computers in the engineering industry and rapidly expanded Academy's client list into the engineering design sector. He was so successful that he was offered an equity stake in the company and became an Academy director.

GROWTH

From start-up in 1988 to 1992, expansion of both turnover and profits was rapid. During this period, many "blue-chip" customers in the private and public sectors were added to Academy's client portfolio. Life was good for the company. The directors worked hard. Looking after customers and the drive for sales dominated their lives. They enjoyed it and were good at it. As Barraclough recalled:

Those days were totally electric. We were so pumped up, and the adrenaline was really flowing; we felt that we could do no wrong. We had a big portfolio of customers, and arguably a similar level of arrogance. . . . I think we felt we were bullet-proof.

Margins were high, and it was easy to take on new staff to meet customer needs without having to think much about justifying the increase in overhead. The management structure and style that had served Academy since its founding in 1988 seemed to be working well. Board meetings took place infrequently, and Bissett monitored the financial situation. Occasionally he complained that being responsible for finance was not very rewarding, and he did not always seem comfortable in his role. The overdraft guarantee was still the main source of finance and had been much increased.

Public acclaim also followed, with Academy reaching the semifinal stage of Scottish Television's "The Business Game" in 1993. This television program aimed to look at ambitious new companies and award prizes to the best. Although not eventual winners, Barraclough recalls well some of the questioning from the panel of judges. "They were impressed with our growth," Barraclough remembers, "and they asked a lot of questions about management systems and financial controls."

THE NEW STRATEGY

Then the recession began to bite; the flow of orders began to decrease. Academy's directors now had to consider how to counter this threat. After some discussion, they agreed to tackle the increasing competition and decreasing market size by pursuing a new strategy that involved Academy moving to become a high-volume, low-margin supplier to its existing markets. In addition, the board agreed to permit Barraclough to pursue a diversification that he saw as having opportunities, a move into a CAD mail-order catalog venture.

As part of the new strategy, the company opened a 5,000-square-foot purpose-built office in Manchester to target the market in the northwest of England. This first branch office was set up under the control of an existing engineering salesman, with a strong track record in CAD sales. This manager was set the task of building sales turnover in the north of England.

Academy also adopted a new tactic and, instead of relying largely on word of mouth and personal recommendation to build new business, committed itself to a heavy expenditure on advertising in order to generate sales. Control of this campaign was in the hands of senior sales and PR staff in the company, who decided where, when, and in what volume to use advertising and promotion.

By early 1994, Academy was employing about 50 people and was forecasting a turnover of more than $4 million. Clients varied in size from small businesses to large corporations such as United Distillers and British Telecommunications. Local government, health service, and educational bodies also featured prominently on the client list. Academy's Head Office consisted of 10,000 square feet of office space in Glasgow and included a comprehensive air-conditioned training suite.

TROUBLE

Then in December 1994, the crunch came. Barraclough, who had been happily concentrating on his catalog business, received a phone call from Bissett. "This board meeting at the hotel this afternoon . . . it's going to be difficult!"

When he arrived at the meeting, there was an air of resignation. Without a word, Bissett handed him a sheet of paper—belated management accounts for the nine months to October 1994. Academy was just not achieving its sales targets. They were in trouble. The television judge's words came flooding back. With a groan, Barraclough and his fellow directors sat down and thought, what do we have to do to get out of this?

TABLE 1   Summary of Turnover and Profits, 1989 to 1994

	1989	1990	1991	1992	1993	1994
Turnover	£1,029,000	£2,332,000	£4,290,000	£3,449,000	£3,155,000	£3,288,000
Cost of sales	773,000	1,703,000	2,842,000	1,918,000	1,819,000	1,835,000
Other operating income	——	19,000	68,000	39,000	24,000	4,000
Administrative expenses	168,000	477,000	953,000	1,180,000	1,301,000	1,331,000
Interest payable	4,000	23,000	48,000	19,000	31,000	38,000
Profit before tax	84,000	148,000	516,000	370,000	29,000	89,000
(Figures for year ending January 31)						

TABLE 2   Abbreviated Management Accounts for Nine Months—February 1994 to October 1994

	Actual	Forecast
Turnover	£2,630,289	£3,266,000
Cost of sales	1,920,483	2,679,000
Gross profit	709,806	587,000
Administrative expenses	955,837	520,000
Profit (loss) for the period	(246,031)	67,000

FINANCING THE NEW VENTURE

11

Sources of Capital

ฦ

LEARNING OBJECTIVES

1. To identify the types of financing available.

2. To understand the role of commercial banks in financing new ventures, the types of loans available, and bank lending decisions.

3. To discuss Small Business Administration (SBA) loans.

4. To understand the aspects of research and development limited partnerships.

5. To discuss government grants, particularly small business innovation research grants.

6. To understand the role of private placement as a source of funds.

WALT DISNEY

Where does an entrepreneur get the funds to turn his or her dreams into reality? Funds come from a variety of sources, but in the case of Walt Disney, it all started with a clandestine paper route.

Born in Chicago and raised on a small farm in Missouri, Walt Disney moved to Kansas City with his family when he was 10 years old. He and his brother worked without pay delivering newspapers for their father's circulation franchise. Whenever Walt found a new customer, he bypassed his father and bought the additional papers directly from the newspaper office, thereby establishing his own route. With the profits from his private venture, he was able to satisfy his sweet tooth without the knowledge of his parents, who forbade candy in their home.

From this beginning, Disney's entrepreneurial career branched out. As a teenager, he lied about his age and joined the Red Cross to serve in World War I in order to follow his revered older brother, Roy. After he arrived in France with the last of the volunteers, his age quickly became a detriment. When Walt was duped by his comrades into picking up a bar bill larger than his first paycheck (which he had yet to receive), he was forced to sell his boots on the black market. He swore that he would never be conned again. He learned to play a good game of poker and started a con game of his own—"doctoring" German steel helmets he collected from the battlefield to look as though the previous owner had been shot in the head. He sold them as "genuine war souvenirs" to soldiers passing through the Red Cross station. Walt amassed what he considered to be a small fortune and sent the money home to his mother for safekeeping.

Upon his return home at the end of the war, Walt tried to fulfill his childhood dream of being a newspaper cartoonist. Although he displayed artistic talent, Walt could not create the edgy, satirical cartoons the papers desired. Discouraged by the cold reception in Chicago, Walt moved to Kansas City with his brother Roy, who found him a job illustrating advertisements and catalogs.

The job was short term, and after the Christmas rush Walt Disney was again unemployed and bothering his brother. Teaming up with a skilled artist he had met on his first job, Walt Disney convinced a local publisher that the publisher's low-budget throwaway paper would be greatly improved by the addition of illustrated advertisements. The publisher was won over by Walt's charm, so he allowed the two artists to use a spare room (actually, a bathroom) as their studio. Walt used $250 from his wartime earnings to purchase enough equipment and supplies to start the business.

Always on the alert for more business opportunities, Walt contracted the service to other printers in town. Before long, "Iwerks & Disney" moved into a real office, and the two had enough money to attend the local movie house, where they were fascinated with the cartoon features. Eventually, Walt responded to an advertisement for a cartoonist for the Kansas City Film Ad Company and tried to sell the services of the partnership. When he was informed that the job was offered to him alone, he gave his half of the partnership to Iwerks and walked away from the illustration business.

Walt Disney quickly became the star of the artistic staff, but stayed with the Film Ad Company for only a short time before founding his own production company, Laugh-O-Gram Films, Inc. In an attempt to raise the capital needed to branch out from advertising, Disney sold shares in his company to a number of local citizens. With the $15,000 in capital, he created two cartoon shorts based on fairy tales that were distributed nationally. Even though they were extremely popular, Disney did not receive any payments for his work and was soon broke. However, he managed to save a camera and a copy of his most original work, *Alice's Wonderland*, from the creditors. After raising some money by taking news photographs for the local papers, Disney headed west to Hollywood to start anew.

Walt used his copy of *Alice's Wonderland* and the two fairy tale shorts to demonstrate his talent and relied on charm, old contacts, and family for financial support. For instance, a Laugh-O-Gram client agreed to finance the production of several short "Alice" adventures, his brother Roy assisted with business deals, and some of his old Kansas City supporters renewed their contributions. Disney Productions went through cycles of feast and famine that could be attributed to the founder's drive for perfection. When Disney got his way, the products were outstanding but expensive, and the two Disney brothers found themselves over their heads in dealing with the motion picture industry. Just when they thought they had a hit, ideas were stolen, profits were not accounted for, and their whole world seemed to be on the verge of collapse. Then, miraculously, a new idea would appear and the studio would flourish again. It was during this time that Disney Productions added sound and color to their increasingly popular short cartoons, which increased both their artistic impact and their cost. Although its name was known worldwide, Disney Productions found it difficult to turn a profit.

The turning point in terms of profit was the production of a full-length cartoon feature: *Snow White and the Seven Dwarfs*. It appeared in 1937 and was a costly box office success. With a production budget of nearly 10 times that of a "live" feature, the cartoon would have ruined the company had it been a failure. Fortunately, it became one of the most successful motion pictures in history. From the profits, Walt Disney started working on three new features and expanded the plan and facilities. The new movies—*Pinocchio, Bambi*, and *Fantasia*—were each completed well over budget and were not initially successful in the American market. To make matters worse, the outbreak of World War II occurred just as these films were being released, thus destroying the profitable European market. With construction debts increasing, the only financing alternative appeared to be going public—selling stock. In April 1940, 755,000 units of common stock and preferred shares were sold, raising nearly $8 million in capital, once again saving the company.

However, becoming a public corporation was not the ultimate salvation for Disney Productions. Walt Disney, like many typical entrepreneurs, was used to running the company with complete control over every detail and did not like relegating any responsibilities and duties to the shareholders. Walt was growing weary of cartooning and movies, so he turned his attention to another dream—creating an amusement park. Roy, however, did not see this as a moneymaker and convinced the board of directors and several bankers to turn down Walt's request for money. Desperate for the cash to fulfill his fantasy, Walt Disney turned to a different source of capital: television. Although television was the world's newest and most popular means of entertainment, Disney Productions had avoided it, viewing it as too demeaning. Since all other sources of revenue were blocked, Disney agreed to a joint venture with ABC, the newest and smallest of the broadcasting companies. In return for $5 million in financing for the park, Disney agreed to put Mickey Mouse on TV. Things were never the same again for ABC, Disney Productions, or the American public.

As in the case of Walt Disney's entrepreneurial career, one of the most critical problems each entrepreneur faces is securing financing for the venture. Although this is a problem throughout the life of any enterprise, it is particularly acute at start-up. From the entrepreneur's perspective, the longer the venture can operate without outside capital, the lower the cost of the capital in terms of interest rates or equity loss in the company. If an amount of money were invested in a company after three years following a track record of sales and profit, a stated security position would obtain perhaps about 10 percent. In contrast, the same amount of capital invested earlier in the history of the company might obtain a 30 percent equity position. From the perspective of the provider of the funds, a potential investment opportunity needs to have an appropriate risk/return ratio. A higher return is expected when there is a greater risk involved. An investor will seek to maximize return for a given level of risk or minimize risk for a given level of return. This chapter describes some common (as well as some not-so-common) sources of capital and the conditions under which the money was obtained. As was the case with Walt Disney, different sources of capital are generally used at different times in the life of the venture.

ϟ

AN OVERVIEW

One of the most difficult problems in the new venture creation process is obtaining financing. For the entrepreneur, available financing needs to be considered from the perspective of debt versus equity and using internal versus external funds as the funding source.

Debt or Equity Financing

Two types of financing need to be considered: debt financing and equity financing. *Debt financing* is a financing method involving an interest-bearing instrument,

debt financing Obtaining borrowed funds for the company

usually a loan, the payment of which is only indirectly related to the sales and profits of the venture. Typically, debt financing (also called asset-based financing) requires that some asset (such as a car, house, plant, machine, or land) be used as collateral.

Debt financing requires the entrepreneur to pay back the amount of funds borrowed as well as a fee expressed in terms of the interest rate. There can also be an additional fee, sometimes referred to as points, for using or being able to borrow the money. If the financing is short term (less than one year), the money is usually used to provide working capital to finance inventory, accounts receivable, or the operation of the business. The funds are typically repaid from the resulting sales and profits during the year. Long-term debt (lasting more than one year) is frequently used to purchase some asset such as a piece of machinery, land, or a building, with part of the value of the asset (usually from 50 to 80 percent of the total value) being used as collateral for the long-term loan. Particularly when interest rates are low, debt (as opposed to equity) financing allows the entrepreneur to retain a larger ownership portion in the venture and have a greater return on the equity. The entrepreneur needs to be careful that the debt is not so large that regular interest payments become difficult if not impossible to make, a situation that may inhibit growth and development and possibly end in bankruptcy.

Equity financing does not require collateral and offers the investor some form of ownership position in the venture. The investor shares in the profits of the venture, as well as any disposition of its assets on a pro rata basis. Key factors favoring the use of one type of financing over another are the availability of funds, the assets of the venture, and the prevailing interest rates. Usually, an entrepreneur meets financial needs by employing a combination of debt and equity financing.

equity financing   Obtaining funds for the company in exchange for ownership

All ventures will have some equity, as all ventures are owned by someone in a market economy. Although the owner may sometimes not be directly involved in the day-to-day management of the venture, there is always equity funding involved that is provided by the owner. The amount of equity involved will of course vary by the nature and size of the venture. In some cases, the equity may be entirely provided by the owner, such as in a small ice cream stand or pushcart in the mall or at a sporting event. Larger ventures may require multiple owners, including private investors and/or venture capitalists. This equity funding provides the basis for debt funding, which makes up the capital structure of the venture.

Internal or External Funds

Financing is also available from internal or external funds. The type of funds most frequently employed is internally generated funds. Internally generated funds can come from several sources within the company: profits, sale of assets, reduction in working capital, extended payment terms, and accounts receivable. In every new venture, the start-up years involve putting all the profits back into the venture; even outside equity investors do not expect payback in these early years. The needed funds can sometimes be obtained by selling little-used assets. Assets, whenever possible, should be on a rental basis (preferably on a lease with an option to buy), not an ownership basis, as long as there is not a high level of inflation and the rental terms are favorable. This will help the entrepreneur conserve cash, a practice that is particularly critical during the start-up phase of the company's operation.

A short-term, internal source of funds can be obtained by reducing short-term assets: inventory, cash, and other working-capital items. Sometimes an entrepreneur can generate the needed cash for a period of 30 to 60 days through extended payment terms from suppliers. Although care must be taken to ensure good supplier relations and continuous sources of supply, taking a few extra days in paying can

If the profit-seeking paradox is to be avoided, the businessperson must see herself as a professional and the service motive must dominate. Business can only really do well if it seeks to do good.

A client offers you a contract for a very large order if you guarantee delivery within two weeks. There is no possible way to deliver within two weeks. You know that a one-week delay will not cause your client any real harm, although he will complain a lot. Should you guarantee shipment to obtain the contract?

Your main product has been redesigned and requires modified raw minerals in the production process. Your main supplier reveals that he will be unable to meet the deadline for the launch of your redesigned product. There will be a delay of two months before he can ship the modified raw materials. Another supplier offers you an immediate supply of the raw material, but only if you sign a three-year exclusive supply contract with him. Your old and trusted supplier probably would go out of business if you change suppliers. Should you change suppliers?

Sources: The quote is from Norman Bowie, *The Profit-Seeking Paradox*, as cited in Robert C. Solomon, *Ethics and Excellence* (Boston: Richard D. Irwin, 1993), p. 136. The vignettes are from M. Nyaw and I. Ng, "A Comparative Analysis of Ethical Beliefs: A Four Country Study," *Journal of Business Ethics*, vol. 13, pp. 543–55.

generate needed short-term funds. A final method of internally generating funds is collecting bills (accounts receivable) more quickly. Key account holders should not be irritated by implementation of this practice, as certain customers have established payment practices. Mass merchandisers, for example, pay their bills to supplying companies in 60 to 90 days, regardless of a supplying company's accounts receivable policy, the size of the company, or the discount offered for prompt payment. If a company wants this mass merchandiser to carry its product, it will have to abide by this payment schedule.

The other general source of funds is external to the venture. Alternative sources of external financing need to be evaluated on three bases: the length of time the funds are available, the costs involved, and the amount of company control lost. In selecting the best source of funds, each of the sources indicated in Table 11.1 needs to be evaluated along these three dimensions. The more frequently used sources of funds (self, family and friends, commercial banks, Small Business Administration loans, R&D limited partnerships, government grants, and private placement) indicated in the table are discussed at length below.

Whenever an entrepreneur deals with items external to the firm, particularly with people and institutions that could become stakeholders, ethical dilemmas can sometimes occur. Some ethical situations in this regard are indicated in the Ethics box.

PERSONAL FUNDS

Few, if any, new ventures are started without the personal funds of the entrepreneur. Not only are these the least expensive funds in terms of cost and control, but they are absolutely essential in attracting outside funding, particularly from banks, private investors, and venture capitalists. These outside providers of capital feel that the entrepreneur may not be sufficiently committed to the venture if he or she does not have money invested. As one venture capitalist succinctly said, "I want the entrepreneurs so financially committed that when the going gets tough, they will work through the problems and not throw the keys to the company on my desk."

TABLE 11.1   Alternative Sources of Financing

Source of Financing	Length of Time		Cost				Control	
	Short Term	Long Term	Fixed Rate Debt	Floating Rate Debt	Percent of Profits	Equity	Covenants	Voting Rights
Self		X				X	X	X
Family and friends	X	X	X	X		X	X	X
Suppliers and trade credit	X				X			
Commercial banks	X		X	X			X	
Asset-based lenders		X	X	X			X	
Institutions and insurance companies		X	X	X	X		X	
Pension funds		X			X	X	X	
Venture capital		X				X	X	X
Private equity placements						X	X	X
Public equity offerings					X	X		X
Government programs		X						

This level of commitment is reflected in the percentage of total assets available that the entrepreneur has committed, not necessarily in the amount of money committed. An outside investor wants an entrepreneur to have committed all available assets, an indication that he or she truly believes in the venture and will work all the hours necessary to ensure success. Whether this is $1,000, $100,000, or $250,000 depends on the assets available. The entrepreneur should always remember that it is not the amount but rather the fact that all monies available are committed that makes outside investors feel comfortable with their commitment level and therefore more willing to invest.

FAMILY AND FRIENDS

After the entrepreneur, family and friends are the next most common source of capital for a new venture. They are most likely to invest due to their relationship with the entrepreneur. This helps overcome one portion of uncertainty felt by impersonal investors—knowledge of the entrepreneur. Family and friends provide a small amount of equity funding for new ventures, reflecting in part the small amount of capital needed for most new ventures. Even though it is relatively easy to obtain money from family and friends, like all sources of capital, there are positive and negative aspects. Even though the amount of money provided may be small, if it is in the form of equity financing, the family member or friend then has an ownership position in the venture and all rights and privileges of that position. This may make them feel they have a direct input into the operations of the venture, which may have a negative effect on employees, facilities, or sales and profits. Although this possibility must be guarded against as much as possible, frequently family and friends are not problem investors and in fact are more patient than other investors in desiring a return on their investment.

In order to avoid problems in the future, the entrepreneur must present the positive and negative aspects and the nature of the risks of the investment opportunity to try to minimize the negative impact on the relationships with family and friends should problems occur. One thing that helps to minimize possible difficulties is to keep the business arrangements strictly business. Any loans or investments from family or friends should be treated in the same businesslike manner as if the financing were from an impersonal investor. Any loan should specify the rate of interest and the proposed repayment schedule of interest and principal. The timing of any future dividends must be disowned in terms of an equity investment. If the family or friend is treated the same as any investor, potential future conflicts can be avoided. It is also beneficial to the entrepreneur to settle everything up front and in writing. It is amazing how short memories become when money is involved. All the details of the financing must be agreed upon before the money is put into the venture. Such things as the amount of money involved, the terms of the money, the rights and responsibilities of the investor, and what happens if the business fails must all be agreed upon and written down. A formal agreement with all these items helps avoid future problems.

Finally, the entrepreneur should carefully consider the impact of the investment on the family member or friend before it is accepted. Particular concern should be paid to any hardships that might result should the business fail. Each family member or friend should be investing in the venture because they think it is a good investment, not because they feel obligated.

COMMERCIAL BANKS

Commercial banks are by far the source of short-term funds most frequently used by the entrepreneur when collateral is available. The funds provided are in the form of debt financing and, as such, require some tangible guaranty or collateral—some asset with value. This collateral can be in the form of business assets (land, equipment, or the building of the venture), personal assets (the entrepreneur's house, car, land, stock, or bonds), or the assets of the cosigner of the note.

Types of Bank Loans

asset base for loans Tangible collateral valued at more than the amount of money borrowed

There are several types of bank loans available. To ensure repayment, these loans are based on the assets or the cash flow of the venture. The *asset base for loans* is usually accounts receivable, inventory, equipment, or real estate.

Accounts Receivable Loans Accounts receivable provide a good basis for a loan, especially if the customer base is well known and creditworthy. For those creditworthy customers, a bank may finance up to 80 percent of the value of their accounts receivable. When customers such as the government are involved, an entrepreneur can develop a factoring arrangement whereby the factor (the bank) actually "buys" the accounts receivable at a value below the face value of the sale and collects the money directly from the account. In this case, if any of the receivables is not collectible, the factor (the bank) sustains the loss, not the business. The cost of factoring the accounts receivable is of course higher than the cost of securing a loan against the accounts receivable without factoring being involved, since the bank has more risk when factoring. The costs of factoring involve the interest charge on the amount of money advanced until the time the accounts receivable are collected, the commission covering the actual collection, and protection against possible uncollectible accounts.

Inventory Loans   Inventory is another of the firm's assets that is often a basis for a loan, particularly when the inventory is liquid and can be easily sold. Usually, the finished goods inventory can be financed for up to 50 percent of its value. Trust receipts are a unique type of inventory loan used to finance floor plans of retailers, such as automobile and appliance dealers. In trust receipts, the bank advances a large percentage of the invoice price of the goods and is paid on a pro rata basis as the inventory is sold.

Equipment Loans   Equipment can be used to secure longer-term financing, usually on a 3- to 10-year basis. Equipment financing can fall into several categories: financing the purchase of new equipment, financing used equipment already owned by the company, sale-leaseback financing, or lease financing. When new equipment is being purchased or presently owned equipment is used as collateral, usually 50 to 80 percent of the value of the equipment can be financed depending on its salability. Given the entrepreneur's tendency to rent rather than own, sale-leaseback or lease financing of equipment is widely used. In the sale-leaseback arrangement, the entrepreneur "sells" the equipment to a lender and then leases it back for the life of the equipment to ensure its continued use. In lease financing, the company acquires the use of the equipment through a small down payment and a guarantee to make a specified number of payments over a period of time. The total amount paid is the selling price plus the finance charges.

Real Estate Loans   Real estate is also frequently used in asset-based financing. This mortgage financing is usually easily obtained to finance a company's land, plant, or another building, often up to 75 percent of its value.

Cash Flow Financing

The other type of debt financing frequently provided by commercial banks and other financial institutions is cash flow financing. These *conventional bank loans* include lines of credit, installment loans, straight commercial loans, long-term loans, and character loans. Lines of credit financing is perhaps the form of cash flow financing most frequently used by entrepreneurs. In arranging for a line of credit to be used as needed, the company pays a "commitment fee" to ensure that the commercial bank will make the loan when requested and then pays interest on any outstanding funds borrowed from the bank. Frequently, the loan must be repaid or reduced to a certain agreed-upon level on a periodic basis.

conventional bank loan   Standard way banks lend money to companies

Installment Loans   Installment loans can also be obtained by a venture with a track record of sales and profits. These short-term funds are frequently used to cover working capital needs for a period of time, such as when seasonal financing is needed. These loans are usually for 30 to 40 days.

Straight Commercial Loans   A hybrid of the installment loan is the straight commercial loan, by which funds are advanced to the company for 30 to 90 days.

These self-liquidating loans are frequently used for seasonal financing and for building up inventories.

Long-Term Loans   When a longer time period for use of the money is required, long-term loans are used. These loans (usually available only to strong, more mature companies) can make funds available for up to 10 years. The debt incurred is usually repaid according to a fixed interest and principal schedule. The principal, however, can sometimes start being repaid in the second or third year of the loan, with only interest paid the first year.

Character Loans   When the business itself does not have the assets to support a loan, the entrepreneur may need a character (personal) loan. These loans frequently must have the assets of the entrepreneur or other individual pledged as collateral or the loan cosigned by another individual. Assets that are frequently pledged include cars, homes, land, and securities. One entrepreneur's father pledged a $50,000 certificate of deposit as collateral for his son's $40,000 loan. In extremely rare instances, the entrepreneur can obtain money on an unsecured basis for a short time when a high credit standing has been established.

Bank Lending Decisions

One problem for the entrepreneur is determining how to successfully secure a loan from the bank. Banks are generally cautious in lending money, particularly to new ventures, since they do not want to incur bad loans. Regardless of geographic location, commercial loan decisions are made only after the loan officer and loan committee do a careful review of the borrower and the financial track record of the business. These decisions are based on both quantifiable information and subjective judgments.[1]

The bank-lending decisions are made according to the five Cs of lending: character, capacity, capital, collateral, and conditions. Past financial statements (balance sheets and income statements) are reviewed in terms of key profitability and credit ratios, inventory turnover, aging of accounts receivable, the entrepreneur's capital invested, and commitment to the business. Future projections on market size, sales, and profitability are also evaluated to determine the ability to repay the loan. Several questions are usually raised regarding this ability. Does the entrepreneur expect to be carried by the loan for an extended period of time? If problems occur, is the entrepreneur committed enough to spend the effort necessary to make the business a success? Does the business have a unique differential advantage in a growth market? What are the downside risks? Is there protection (such as life insurance on key personnel and insurance on the plant and equipment) against disasters?

Although the answers to these questions and the analysis of the company's records allow the loan officer to assess the quantitative aspects of the loan decision, the intuitive factors, particularly the first two Cs—character and capacity—are also taken into account. This part of the loan decision—the gut feeling—is the most difficult part to assess. The entrepreneur must present his or her capabilities and the prospects for the company in a way that elicits a positive response from the lender. This intuitive part of the loan decision becomes even more important when there is little or no track record, limited experience in financial management, a nonproprietary product or service (one not protected by a patent or license), or few assets available.

Some of the concerns of the loan officer and the loan committee can be reduced by providing a good loan application. While the specific loan application format of each bank differs to some extent, generally the application format is a "mini" business plan that consists of an executive summary, business description, owner/manager profiles, business projections, financial statements, amount and use of the loan, and repayment schedule. This information provides the loan officer and loan committee with insight into the creditworthiness of the individual and the venture as well as the ability of the venture to make enough sales and profit to repay the loan and the interest. The entrepreneur should evaluate several alternative banks, select the one that has had positive loan experience in the particular business area, call for an appointment, and then carefully present the case for the loan to the loan officer. Presenting a positive business image and following the established protocol are necessary to obtain a loan from a commercial bank.

Generally, the entrepreneur should borrow the maximum amount that can possibly be repaid as long as the prevailing interest rates and the terms, conditions, and restrictions of the loan are satisfactory. It is essential that the venture generate enough cash flow to repay the interest and principal on the loan in a timely manner. The entrepreneur should evaluate the track record and lending procedures of several banks in order to secure the money needed on the most favorable terms available. This "bank shopping procedure" will provide the needed funds at the most favorable rates.

SMALL BUSINESS ADMINISTRATION LOANS

Frequently, an entrepreneur is missing the necessary track record, assets, or some other ingredient to obtain a commercial bank loan. When the entrepreneur is unable to secure a regular commercial bank loan, an alternative is a Small Business Administration (SBA) Guaranty Loan. In this loan, the SBA guarantees that 80 percent of the amount loaned to the entrepreneur's business will be repaid by the SBA if the company cannot make payment. This guarantee allows the bank to make a loan that has a higher risk than loans it would otherwise make. The process for securing such a loan is outlined in Table 11.2. This procedure is the same as the one used for securing a regular loan, except there are government forms and documentation required. Usually, some banks in a city will specialize in these loans and are better able to assist the entrepreneur in filling out the appropriate forms correctly, thereby minimizing the time involved in the government's processing and approving (or disapproving) the loan.

Both long- and short-term loans can be guaranteed by the SBA. If the collateral is of a lasting nature, such as land and buildings, a maximum loan period of 15 years on existing buildings and 20 years on new construction can be obtained. If the loan is for inventory, machinery, equipment, or working capital, a maximum loan period of 10 years is available, although the usual length is 5 years. Once the application has been completed and includes all the required supporting materials, it is generally processed within 15 days if no backlog exists. If an SBA Guaranty Loan is granted, additional reporting practices are required beyond those that exist with a conventional bank loan. Since there is typically no difference in the interest rates charged between a commercial bank loan and an SBA guaranteed loan, a commercial bank loan is usually better, as it has fewer reporting requirements and provides the opportunity to establish a good banking relationship based on the merits of the busi-

TABLE 11.2   Required Papers For SBA/Bank Financing

1. Application for Loan: SBA form 4, 4I.
2. Statement of Personal History: SBA form 912.
3. Personal Financial Statement: SBA form 413.
4. Detailed, signed Balance Sheet and Profit and Loss Statements current (within 90 days of application) and last three (3) fiscal years Supplementary Schedules required on Current Financial Statements.
5. Detailed one (1) year projection of Income & Finances (please attach written explanation as to how you expect to achieve same).
6. A list of names and addresses of any subsidiaries and affiliates, including concerns in which the applicant holds a controlling (but not necessarily a majority) interest and other concerns that may be affiliated by stock ownership, franchise, proposed merger, or otherwise with the applicant.
7. Certificate of Doing Business (if a corporation, stamp corporate seals on SBA form 4 section 12).
8. By law, the agency may not guarantee a loan if a business can obtain funds on reasonable terms from a bank or other private source. A borrower therefore must first seek private financing. A company must be independently owned and operated, not dominant in its field, and must meet certain standards of size in terms of employees or annual receipts. Loans cannot be made to speculative businesses, newspapers, or businesses engaged in gambling. Applicants for loans must also agree to comply with SBA regulation that there will be no discrimination in employment or services to the public, based on race, color, religion, national origin, sex, or marital status.
9. Signed Business Federal Income Tax Returns for previous three (3) years.
10. Signed Personal Federal Income Tax Returns of principals for previous three (3) years.
11. Personal Resume including business experience of each principal.
12. Brief history of the business and its problems: include an explanation of why the SBA loan is needed and how it will help the business.
13. Copy of Business Lease (or note from landlord giving terms of proposed lease).

Source: Small Business Administration— www.sba.gov/gopher/Financial-Assistance/rego.txt

ness. A good banking relationship is very valuable as the venture grows and more bank financing is needed.

For most SBA loans, there is no established limit to the amount of money requested in the loan. However, unless it is a specialized loan program, the maximum amount the SBA can guarantee is $750,000. Since the SBA guarantees 80 percent of loans of $100,000 or less, and 75 percent of loans of higher amounts up to the $750,000 limit, this effectively makes the loan limited to $1 million. The vast majority of small businesses and entrepreneurs are eligible for financial assistance from the SBA. What constitutes a small business as defined by the Small Business Act is one that is independently owned and operated and not dominant in its field of operation. The size limits of a small business vary from industry to industry. Some maximum size standards are retail and service ($3.5 to $13.5 million); construction ($7.0 to $17.0 million); agriculture ($0.5 to $3.5 million); wholesale (no more than 100 employees); and manufacturing (500 to 1500 employees). The proceeds of the loans can be used for almost any business purpose, including the purchase of real estate to house the business; construction, renovation, or leasehold improvements; acquisition of furniture, fixtures, equipment, and machinery; inventory; and working capital. While the interest rates are negotiated between the borrower and the bank, they are subject to SBA maximums, which are pegged to the prime rate. Fixed rate loans must not exceed prime rate plus 2.25 percent for loan maturity less than seven years and prime rate plus 2.75 percent for loan maturity of seven years or more. Variable rate loans are also available that are pegged to the lowest prime rate or the SBA optional peg rate. While it is expected that the information provided (see Table 11.2) will indicate that the loan will be repaid from the cash flow of the business, good character, management capability, collateral, and owner's equity contribution are also important considerations in the loan-granting decision. Each individual who owns 20 percent or more of the business is required to personally guarantee SBA loans.

RESEARCH AND DEVELOPMENT LIMITED PARTNERSHIPS

Research and development limited partnerships are another possible source of funds for entrepreneurs in high-technology areas. This method of financing provides funds from investors looking for tax shelters. A typical R&D partnership arrangement involves a sponsoring company developing the technology with funds being provided by a limited partnership of individual investors. R&D limited partnerships are particularly good when the project involves a high degree of risk and significant expense in doing the basic research and development, since the risks, as well as the ensuing rewards, are shared.

research and development limited partnerships
Money given to a firm for developing a technology that involves a tax shelter

Major Elements

The three major components of any R&D limited partnership are the contract, the sponsoring company, and the limited partnership. The contract specifies the agreement between the sponsoring company and the limited partnership, whereby the sponsoring company agrees to use the funds provided to conduct the proposed research and development that hopefully will result in a marketable technology for the partnership. The sponsoring company does not guarantee results but rather performs the work on a best-effort basis, being compensated by the partnership on either a fixed-fee or cost-plus arrangement. The typical contract has several key features. The first is that the liability for any loss incurred is borne by the limited partners. Second, there are some tax advantages to both the limited partnership and the sponsoring company. This tax deduction is based on two authorizations: Section 174 of the Internal Revenue Code and the *Snow v. Commissioner* case of 1974. Section 174 allows a taxpayer to deduct R&D costs as incurred expenses rather than have these costs capitalized as part of the final cost of the product. This regulation was supported by the U.S. Supreme Court ruling in *Snow v. Commissioner,* which said that it was sufficient for the taxpayer to incur the expenses of research and development in connection with a trade or business in order to treat the investment as an expense as opposed to a cost. Limited partners may deduct their investments in the R&D contract under Section 174 in the year their investments are made. Depending on the tax bracket of the limited partner (the higher the bracket, the more significant the effect), this deduction significantly increases the rate of return of the investment in the limited partnership, thereby increasing the compensation for the risk involved.

The second component involved in this contract is the limited partners. Similar to the stockholders of a corporation, the *limited partners* have limited liability but are not a total taxable entity. Consequently, any tax benefits of the losses in the early stages of the R&D limited partnership are passed directly to the limited partners, offsetting other income and reducing the partners' total taxable incomes. When the technology is successfully developed in later years, the partners

limited partner   A party in a partnership agreement that usually supplies money and has a few responsibilities

share in the profits. In some instances, these profits for tax purposes are at the lower capital gains tax rate as opposed to the ordinary income rate.

The final component, the sponsoring company, acts as the *general partner* developing the technology. The sponsoring company usually has the base technology but needs to secure limited partners to further develop and modify it for commercial success. It is this base technology that the company is offering to the partnership in exchange for money. The sponsoring company usually retains the rights to use this base technology to develop other products and the right to use the developed technology in the future for a license fee. Otherwise, a cross-licensing agreement is established whereby the partnership allows the company to use the technology for developing other products.

general partner   The overall coordinating party in a partnership agreement

Procedure

An R&D limited partnership generally progresses through three stages: the funding stage, the development stage, and the exit stage. In the funding stage, a contract is established between the sponsoring company and limited partners, and the money is invested for the proposed research and development effort. All the terms and conditions of ownership, as well as the scope of the research, are carefully documented.

In the development stage, the sponsoring company performs the actual research, using the funds from the limited partners. If the technology is subsequently successfully developed, the exit stage commences, in which the sponsoring company and the limited partners commercially reap the benefits of the effort. There are three basic types of arrangements for doing this: equity partnerships, royalty partnerships, and joint ventures.

In the typical equity partnership arrangement, the sponsoring company and the limited partners form a new, jointly owned corporation. On the basis of the formula established in the original agreement, the limited partners' interest can be transferred to equity in the new corporation on a tax-free basis. An alternative is to incorporate the R&D limited partnership itself and then either merge it into the sponsoring company or continue as a new entity.

Another possible exit to the equity partnership arrangement is a royalty partnership. In this situation, a royalty based on the sale of the products developed from the technology is paid by the sponsoring company to the R&D limited partnership. The royalty rates typically range from 6 to 10 percent of gross sales and often decrease at certain established sales levels. Frequently, an upper limit, or cap, is placed on the cumulative royalties paid.

A final exit arrangement is through a joint venture. Here the sponsoring company and the partners form a joint venture to manufacture and market the products developed from the technology. Usually, the agreement allows the company to buy out the partnership interest in the joint venture at a specified time or when a specified volume of sales and profit has been reached.

Benefits and Costs

As with any financing arrangement, the entrepreneur must carefully assess the appropriateness of establishing an R&D limited partnership in terms of the benefits and costs involved. Among the several benefits is that an R&D limited partnership provides the funds needed with a minimum amount of equity dilution while reducing the risks involved. In addition, the sponsoring company's financial statements are strengthened through the attraction of outside capital.

There are some costs involved in this financial arrangement. First, time and money are expended. An R&D limited partnership frequently takes a minimum of six months to establish and $50,000 in professional fees. Typically, it is more expensive to establish than conventional financing. These can increase to a year and $400,000 in costs for a major effort. And the track record is not as good, as most R&D limited partnerships offered are unsuccessful. Second, the restrictions placed on the technology can be substantial. To give up the technology developed as a by-product of the primary effort may be too high a price to pay for the funds. Third, the exit from the partnership may be too complex and involve too much fiduciary responsibility. These costs and benefits need to be evaluated in light of other financial alternatives available before a research and development limited partnership is chosen as the funding vehicle.

Examples

In spite of the many costs involved, there are numerous examples of successful R&D limited partnerships. Syntex Corporation raised $23.5 million in an R&D limited partnership to develop five medical diagnostic products. Genentech was so successful in developing human growth hormone and gamma Interferon products from its first $55 million R&D limited partnership that it raised $32 million through a second partnership six months later to develop a tissue-type plasminogen activator. Trilogy Limited raised $55 million to develop a high-performance computer. And the list goes on. Indeed, R&D limited partnerships offer one financial alternative to fund the development of a venture's technology.

GOVERNMENT GRANTS

The entrepreneur can sometimes obtain federal grant money to develop and launch an innovative idea. A program of particular interest designed for the small business is the Small Business Innovation Development Act. The act requires that all federal agencies with R&D budgets in excess of $100 million award a portion of their R&D funds to small businesses through the *SBIR grants program*.

SBIR grants program   Grants from the U.S. government to small technology-based businesses

This act not only provides an opportunity for small businesses to obtain research and development money but also offers a uniform method by which each participating agency solicits, evaluates, and selects the research proposals for funding.

Eleven federal agencies are involved in the program (see Table 11.3). Each agency develops topics and publishes solicitations describing the R&D topic it will fund. Small businesses submit proposals directly to each agency using the required format, which is somewhat standardized, regardless of the agency. Each agency, using its established evaluation criteria, evaluates each proposal on a competitive basis and makes awards through a contract, grant, or cooperative agreement.

The SBIR grant program has three phases. Phase I awards are up to $50,000 for six months of feasibility-related experimental or theoretical research. The objective here is to determine the technical feasibility of the research effort and assess the quality of the company's performance through a relatively small monetary commitment. Successful projects are then considered for further federal funding support in Phase II.

Phase II is the principal R&D effort for those projects showing the most promise at the end of Phase I. Phase II awards are up to $500,000 for 24 months of further

TABLE 11.3   Federal Agencies Participating in Small Business Innovation Research Program

- Department of Defense (DOD)
- National Aeronautics and Space Administration (NASA)
- Department of Energy (DOE)
- Health and Human Services (HHS)
- National Science Foundation (NSF)
- U.S. Department of Agriculture (USDA)
- Department of Transportation (DOT)
- Nuclear Regulatory Commission (NRC)
- Environmental Protection Agency (EPA)
- Department of Interior (DOI)
- Department of Education (DOED)

research and development. The money is to be used to develop prototype products or services. A small business receiving a Phase II award has demonstrated good research results in Phase I, developed a proposal of sound scientific and technical merit, and obtained a commitment for follow-on private-sector financing in Phase III for commercialization.

Phase III does not involve any direct funding from the SBIR program. Funds from the private sector or regular government procurement contracts are needed to commercialize the developed technologies in Phase III.

Procedure

Applying for an SBIR grant is a straightforward process. The government agencies participating (indicated in Table 11.3) publish solicitations describing the areas of research they will fund. Each of these annual solicitations contains documentation on the agency's R&D objectives, proposal format, due dates, deadlines, and selection and evaluation criteria. The second step involves the submission of the proposal by a company or individual. The proposal, which is 25 pages maximum, follows the standard proposal format. Each agency screens the proposals it receives. Knowledgeable scientists or engineers then evaluate those that pass the screening on a technological basis. Finally, awards are granted to those projects that have the best potential for commercialization. Any patent rights, research data, technical data, and software generated in the research are owned by the company or individual, not by the government.

The SBIR grant program is one viable method of obtaining funds for a technically based entrepreneurial company that is independently owned and operated, employs 500 or fewer individuals, and has any organizational structure (corporation, partnership, sole proprietorship).

PRIVATE PLACEMENT

A final source of funds for the entrepreneur is private investors, who may be family and friends or wealthy individuals. Individuals who handle their own sizable investments frequently use advisors such as accountants, technical experts, financial planners, or lawyers in making their investment decisions.

Types of Investors

An investor usually takes an equity position in the company, can influence the nature and direction of the business to some extent, and may even be involved to some degree in the business operation. The degree of involvement in the direction of the day-to-day operations of the venture is an important point for the entrepreneur to consider in selecting an investor. Some investors want to be actively involved in the business; others desire at least an advisory role in the direction and operation of the venture and want to share in its profits. Still others are more passive in nature, desiring no active involvement in the venture at all. Each investor is primarily interested in recovering his or her investment plus a good rate of return.

Private Offerings

A formalized approach for obtaining funds from private investors is through a *private offering*. A private offering is different from a public offering or going public (the focus of Chapter 16) in several ways. Public offerings involve a great deal of time and expense, in large part due to the numerous regulations and requirements involved. The process of registering the securities with the Securities and Exchange Commission (SEC) is an arduous task requiring a significant number of reporting procedures once the firm has gone public. Since this process was established primarily to protect unsophisticated investors, a private offering is faster and less costly when a limited number of sophisticated investors are involved who have the necessary business acumen and ability to absorb risk. These sophisticated investors still need access to material information about the company and its management. What constitutes material information? Who is a sophisticated investor? How many is a limited number? Answers to these questions are provided in Regulation D.

private offering   A formalized method for obtaining funds from private investors

Regulation D

Regulation D contains (1) broad provisions designed to simplify private offerings, (2) general definitions of what constitutes a private offering, and (3) specific operating rules—Rule 504, Rule 505, and Rule 506. Regulation D requires the issuer of a private offering to file five copies of Form D with the Securities and Exchange Commission (SEC) 15 days after the first sale, every 6 months thereafter, and 30 days after the final sale. It also provides rules governing the notices of sale and the payment of any commissions involved.

Regulation D   Laws governing a private offering

The entrepreneur issuing the private offering carries the burden of proving that the exemptions granted have been met. This involves completing the necessary documentation on the degree of sophistication of each potential investor. Each offering memorandum presented to an investor needs to be numbered and must contain instructions that the document should not be reproduced or disclosed to any other individual. The date that the investor (or the designated representative) reviews the company's information—that is, its books and records—as well as the date(s) of any discussion between the company and the investor need to be recorded. At the close of the offering, the offering company needs to verify and note that no persons other than those recorded were contacted regarding the offering. The book documenting all the specifics of the offering needs to be placed in the company's permanent file. The general procedures of Regulation D are further broadened by the three rules—504, 505, and 506. Rule 504 provides the first exemption to a company seeking to raise a small amount of capital from numerous investors. Under Rule 504, a company can sell up to $500,000 of securities to any number of investors, regardless of their sophistication, in any 12-month period. While there is no specific form of disclosure required, the issuing company cannot engage in any general solicitation or advertising. Some states do not allow investors to resell their shares unless the security is registered.

Rule 505 changes both the investors and the dollar amount of the offering. This rule permits the sale of $5 million of unregistered securities in the private offering in any 12-month period. These securities can be sold to any 35 investors and to an unlimited number of accredited investors. This eliminates the need for the sophistication test and disclosure requirements called for by Rule 504. What constitutes an "accredited investor"? Accredited investors include (1) institutional investors, like banks, insurance companies, investment companies, employee benefit plans containing over $5 million in assets, tax-exempt organizations with endowment funds of over $25 million, and private business development companies; (2) investors who purchase over $150,000 of the issuer's securities; (3) investors whose net worth is $1 million or more at the time of sale; (4) investors with incomes in excess of $200,000 in each of the last two years; and (5) directors, executive officers, and general partners of the issuing company.

Like Rule 504, Rule 505 permits no general advertising or solicitation through public media. When only accredited investors are involved, no disclosure is required under Rule 505 (similar to the issuance under Rule 504). However, if the issuance involves any unaccredited investors, additional information must be disclosed. Regardless of the amount of the offering, two-year financial statements for the two most recent years must be available unless such a disclosure requires "undue effort and expense." When this occurs for any issuing company other than a limited partnership, a balance sheet as of 120 days before the offering can be used instead. All companies selling private-placement securities to both accredited and unaccredited investors must furnish appropriate company information to both and allow any questions to be asked before the sale. Rule 506 goes one step further than Rule 505 by allowing an issuing company to sell an unlimited number of securities to 35 investors and an unlimited number of accredited investors and relatives of issuers. Still, no general advertising or solicitation through public media can be involved.

In securing any outside funding, the entrepreneur must take great care to disclose all information as accurately as possible. Investors generally have no problem with the company as long as its operations continue successfully and this success is reflected in the valuation. But if the business turns sour, both investors and regulators scrutinize the company's disclosures in minute detail to determine if any technical or securities law violations occurred. When any violation of securities law is discovered, management and sometimes the company's principal equity holders can be held liable as a corporation and as individuals. When this occurs, the individual is no longer shielded by the corporation and is open to significant liability and potential lawsuits. Lawsuits under securities law by damaged investors have almost no statute of limitations, as the time does not begin until the person harmed discovers or should reasonably be expected to discover the improper disclosure. The suit may be brought in federal court in any jurisdiction in which the defendant is found or lives or transacts business. An individual can file suit as a single plaintiff or as a class action on behalf of all persons similarly affected. Courts have awarded large attorney's fees as well as settlements when any security law violation occurs. Given the number of lawsuits and the litigious nature of U.S. society, the entrepreneur needs to be extremely

As Seen in *Business Week* . . .
A Fund Even Your Pet Could Love

Here's an investment that won't send anyone's fur flying. Salomon Brothers Asset Management is set to roll out a mutual fund, The Humane Equity Fund, that won't invest in companies not deemed animal-friendly by the Humane Society of the United States.

The society, which claims 7 million supporters, approached Salomon Brothers a year ago about establishing the fund. Says Humane Society CFO Tom Waite: "We felt a need for an investment vehicle underwritten by a major company with an animal-friendly bent." The group made its case. The society will kick in $8 million to start up the fund. Investors can buy in for $1,000.

Some investors believe that funds with both social and investment agendas underperform other funds. But manager Chad Graves says that a model looking at the three- and five-year performance of portfolios screened for animal friendliness did better than more broadly based funds. Graves isn't necessarily interested in companies that make pet products. He's looking for any good investment, but not in such animal-unfriendly sectors as pharmaceuticals, consumer products, and, naturally, hunting gear.

Source: Roy Furchgott, "A Fund Even Your Pet Could Love," *Business Week* (January 24, 2000), p. 8.

careful to make sure that any and all disclosures are accurate. If this is not enough of an incentive, it should be kept in mind that the SEC can take administrative, civil, or criminal action as well, without any individual lawsuit involved. This action can result in fine, imprisonment, or the restoration of the monies involved.

BOOTSTRAP FINANCING

One alternative to acquiring outside capital that should be considered is bootstrap financing.[2] This approach is particularly important at start-up and in the early years of the venture when capital from debt financing (i.e., in terms of higher interest rates) or from equity financing (i.e., in terms of loss of ownership) is more expensive.

In addition to the monetary costs, outside capital has other costs as well. First, it usually takes between three and six months to raise outside capital or to find out that there is no outside capital available. During this time, the entrepreneur may not be paying enough attention to the important areas of marketing, sales, product development, and operating costs. When a business needs capital, it is usually when it can least afford the time to raise it. One company's CEO spent so much time raising capital that sales and marketing were neglected to such an extent that the forecasted sales and profit figures on the pro forma income statements were not met for the first three years after the capital infusion. This led to investor concern and irritation that, in turn, required more of the CEO's time.

Second, outside capital often decreases a firm's drive for sales and profits. One successful manager would never hire a person as one of his commission salespeople if he or she "looked too prosperous." He felt that if a person was not hungry, he or she would not push hard to sell. The same concept could apply to outside funded companies that may have the tendency to substitute outside capital for income.

Third, the availability of capital increases the impulse to spend. It can cause a company to hire more staff before they are needed and to move into more costly facilities. A company can easily forget the basic axiom of venture creation: staying lean and mean. Examples of companies successfully growing by staying lean and mean and using internal capital instead of outside capital include Civco Medical Instruments and Metrographics Printing and Computer Services. Civco Medical Instruments, a manufacturer of medical accessories, was founded by Victor Wedel, formerly chief technologist at the University of Iowa in 1982. The company started with $100 and had a bank loan as an early capital source. The company achieved sales of $3.2 million and $800,000 pretax profits with 35 employees. Similar results occurred for Metrographics, which was founded in 1987 by Andrew Duke, Jeff Bernstein, and Patrick Neltri with $100 from each. The company, which distributes printing and computer services, has grown to over $2.5 million in sales with 12 employees.[3]

Fourth, outside capital can decrease the company's flexibility. This can hamper the direction, drive, and creativity of the entrepreneur. Unsophisticated investors are particularly a problem as they often object to a company moving away from the focus and direction outlined in the business plan that attracted their investment. This attitude can encumber a company to such an extent that the needed change cannot be implemented or else is implemented very slowly after a great deal of time and effort have been spent in consensus building. This can substantially demoralize the entrepreneur who likes the freedom of not working for someone else.

Finally, outside capital may cause more disruption and problems in the venture than was present without it. Capital is not provided without the expectation of a return, sometimes before the business should be giving one. Also, particularly if certain equity investors are involved, the entrepreneur is under pressure to continuously grow the company so that an initial public offering can occur as soon as possible. This emphasis on short-term performance can be at the expense of the long-term success of the company.

In spite of these potential problems, an entrepreneur at times needs some capital to finance growth, which would be too slow or nonexistent if internal sources of funds were used. Outside capital should only be sought after all possible internal sources of funds have been explored. And when outside funds are needed and obtained, the entrepreneur should not forget to stay intimately involved with the basics of the business.

IN REVIEW

Summary

All business ventures require capital. While capital is needed throughout the life of a business, the new entrepreneur faces significant difficulties in acquiring capital at start-up. Before seeking outside financing, an entrepreneur should first explore all methods of internal financing, such as using profits, selling unused assets, reducing working capital, obtaining credit from suppliers, and collecting accounts receivable promptly. After all internal sources have been exhausted, the entrepreneur may find it necessary to seek additional funds through external financing. External financing can be in the form of debt or equity. When considering external financing, the entrepreneur needs to consider the length of time, cost, and amount of control of each alternative financial arrangement.

Commercial bank loans are the most frequently used source of short-term external debt financing. This source of funding requires collateral, which may be asset-based or may take the form of cash flow financing. In either case, banks tend to be cautious about lending and carefully weigh the five Cs: character, capacity, capital, collateral, and condition. Not every entrepreneur will qualify under the bank's careful scrutiny. When this occurs, an alternative for an entrepreneur is the Small Business Administration Guaranty Loan. The SBA guarantees 80 percent of the loan, allowing banks to lend money to businesses that might otherwise be refused.

A special method of raising capital for high-technology firms is a research and development (R&D) limited partnership. A contract is formed between a sponsoring company and a limited partnership. The partnership bears the risk of the research, receiving some tax advantages and sharing in future profits, including a fee to use the research in developing any future products. The entrepreneur has the advantage of acquiring needed funds for a minimum amount of equity dilution while reducing his or her own risk in the venture. However, setting up an R&D limited partnership is expensive, and the time factor (at least six months) may be too long for some ventures. Restrictions placed on the technology as well as the complexities of exiting the partnership need careful evaluation.

Government grants are another alternative available to small businesses through the SBIR program. Businesses can apply for grants from 11 agencies. Phase I awards carry a stipend of up to $50,000 for six months of initial research. The most promising Phase I projects may qualify for Phase II support of up to $500,000 for 24 months of research.

Finally, the entrepreneur can seek private funding. Individual investors frequently require an equity position in the company and some degree of control. A less-expensive and less-complicated alternative to a public offering of stock is found in a private offering. By following the procedures of Regulation D and three of its specific rules—504, 505, and 506—an entrepreneur can sell private securities. When making a private offering, the entrepreneur must exercise care in accurately disclosing information and adhering precisely to the requirements of the SEC. Securities violations can lead to lawsuits against individuals as well as the corporation.

The entrepreneur needs to consider all possible sources of capital and select the one that will provide the needed funds with minimal cost and loss of control. Usually, different sources of funds are used at various stages in the growth and development of the venture, as occurred in the case of Walt Disney, a successful entrepreneur indeed.

Questions for Discussion

1. Why is it important for an entrepreneur to generate financing internally as much as possible rather than depending entirely on external financing? How does the entrepreneur accomplish this?

2. In order to retain as much control as possible in your company, what sources of capital would you first investigate? Refer to Table 11.1.

3. Which of the commercial bank loans described in this chapter might be available for starting up a new business?

4. Under what circumstances would you form an R&D limited partnership rather than using other funding sources? How might this create problems for you once your research is successful, and how might you solve those problems?

5. Describe the process you would follow to pursue an SBIR grant. Would this be a good avenue for an individual with a great idea but no funds or company? Why or why not?

6. What criteria must be adhered to in obtaining funds through a private offering?

Key Terms

asset base for loans

conventional bank loan

debt financing

equity financing

general partner

limited partner

private offering

Regulation D

research and development limited partnerships

SBIR grants program

More Information—Net Addresses in This Chapter

ABC
www.abc.com

Department of Defense (DOD)
www.dtic.dla.mil/defenselnk

Department of Education (DOED)
www.ed.gov

Department of Energy (DOE)
www.doe.gov

Department of Health and Human Services (HHS)
www.os.dhhs.gov

Department of Transportation (DOT)
www.dot.gov

Environmental Protection Agency (EPA)
www.epa.gov

Genentech
www.genentech.com

National Science Foundation (NSF)
www.nsf.gov

Nuclear Regulatory Commission (NRC)
www.nrc.gov

Spring Street Brewery
plaza.interport.net/witbeer

U.S. Department of Agriculture (USDA)
www.usda.gov

U.S. Supreme Court
www.law.cornell.edu/rules/supct/overview.html

Selected Readings

Alamgir, Dewan A. H. (2000). Financing the Microcredit Programs of Non-Governmental Organizations (Ngos): A Case Study. *Journal of Developmental Entrepreneurship*, vol. 5, no. 2, pp. 157–68.

Author describes a government-sponsored financial institution that provides loans to organizations to expand outreach of successful microedit programs and assists to enhance organizational capacity.

Berger, Allen N.; and Gregory F. Udell. (1998). The Economics of Small Business Finance: The Roles of Private Equity and Debt Markets in the Financial Growth Cycle. *Journal of Banking & Finance*, vol. 22, no. 6–8, pp. 613–73.

The article examines the economics of financing small business in private equity and debt markets. Firms are viewed through a financial growth cycle paradigm in which different capital structures are optimal at different points in the cycle. The analysis shows the sources of small business finance and how capital structure varies with the firm size and age.

Chirinko, Robert S.; and C. Morris. (1994). Fiscal Policies Aimed at Spurring Capital Formation: A Framework for Analysis. *Economic Review*, vol. 79, no. 1, pp. 59–73.

The article consists of four sections: (1) why capital formation is an important determinate of economic growth, (2) how the optimal amount of capital formation (therefore economic growth) is determined, (3) nature of economic distortions and how they cause capital formation to be suboptimal, and (4) impact of various fiscal policies. Highlights interaction among markets and uncertainties of the responsiveness of investment and saving to interest rates and other factors. Conclusion is that policy should focus on distortions that disrupt the capital formation process.

George, Gerard; and Ganesh N. Prabhu. (2000). Developmental Financial Institutions as Catalysts of Entrepreneurship in Emerging Economies. *The Academy of Management Review,* vol. 25, no. 3, pp. 620–29.

With ongoing privatization efforts in emerging economies, governments have supported developmental financial institutions to spur entrepreneurial activity.

Hutchinson, Robert W. (1995). The Capital Structure and Investment Decisions of the Small Owner-Managed Firm: Some Exploratory Issues. *Small Business Economics,* vol. 7, pp. 231–9.

Discussion of the merits and drawbacks of equity versus debt financing. Primarily applicable to second- or third-stage financing. Owner-managers of small firms (because of either control or risk issues) may have a tendency to underuse both equity and debt, choosing to adopt interdependent investment and finance strategies that do not fully exploit their firm's economic potential.

Jackson, Marvin; and V. Bilsen. (1994). *Company Management and Capital Market Development in the Transition.* Aldershot, England: Avebury Publishing.

Compilation of essays pertaining to Eastern Europe privatization, highlighting the "interenterprise" debt (substitutes for a well-functioning capital market) and the "queuing" problem. Will the creation of a more or less efficient and well-capitalized capital market eliminate queuing? Many enterprises, although exposed to domestic capital markets in many cases, cannot find adequate financing on these markets.

Mamis, Robert A. (1994). Seed Capital: The 12-Step Program. *Inc.,* vol. 16, no. 2, pp. 34–6.

Anecdotal review of an entrepreneur's steps in financing a temporary-employment venture. Steps were (1) using severance pay, (2) using personal savings, (3) using line of credit by overdrawing checking account (following loan refusal), (4) redemption of retirement account, (5) using charge cards, (6) using informal investors (since he could show "personal investment"), (7) reducing cost of living expenses, (8) maintaining his old vehicle, (9) bargaining further with the seller, (10) begging and borrowing from friends, (11) appealing to customers for quicker payments, and (12) establishing a formal line of credit from the bank. Critical note on growth was that the venture's cash needs were always "just beyond the reach of its internally generated finances."

Martinelli, Cesar. (1997). Small Firms, Borrowing Constraints, and Reputation. *Journal of Economic Behavior and Organization,* vol. 33, pp. 91–105.

This study tests a model relating firm age with firm size and access to credit markets. Lending to new firms is risky, so interest rates are high and loans are small. Credit markets impose a limit on the scale of operation of new firms. Firm reputation building allows markets to overcome such difficulties over time.

Meyer, James E.; and John Shao. (1995). International Venture Capital Portfolio Diversification and Agency Costs. *Multinational Business Review,* vol. 3, no. 1, pp. 53–8.

Utilizes agency cost theory to analyze the international flow of funds as it affects U.S. entrepreneurs seeking venture-capital funds on the international market. Due to the potential conflicts of interest that may arise between the investors and the entrepreneur, recommendation is that a government-sponsored agency similar to Fannie Mae be formed to reduce agency costs by providing market rate financing.

Michaelas, Nicos; Francis Chittenden; and Panikkos Poutziouris. (1999). Financial Policy and Capital Structure Choice in U.K. SMEs: Empirical Evidence from Company Panel Data. *Small Business Economics,* vol. 12, no. 2, pp. 113–30.

The study used financial panel data for investigation of the capital structure of small and medium-sized enterprises (SMEs) in the United Kingdom. Findings suggest that most of the determinants of capital structure presented by the theory of finance appear to be relevant for the

U.K. small business sector (size, age, profitability, growth and future growth opportunities, oper-ating risk, asset structure, stock turnover, and net debtors have an effect on the level of both short- and long-term debt in small firms). Evidence suggests that the capital structure of small firms is time and industry dependent.

Scholtens, Bert. (1999). Analytical Issues in External Financing Alternatives for SBEs. *Small Business Economics,* vol. 12, no. 2, pp. 137–48.

The article analyzes the ways in which various control mechanisms (ownership, collateral, re-lationship, and reputation) are fit to reduce the size-related information problem about an en-terprise borrowing risk and the ways in which various types of capital suppliers are endowed to finance small business enterprises.

Tuller, Lawrence W. (1994). *The Complete Book of Raising Capital.* New York: McGraw-Hill.

How-to book covering debt capital, special-purpose capital, raising capital when overleveraged, and tax strategies. Includes discussions on lease-buy decisions, going public, employee stock op-tions, and methods of raising capital for debt-laden organizations.

Wachtel, Howard M. (1995). Taming Global Money. *Challenge,* vol. 38, no. 1, pp. 36–40.

Argues for the creation of a new exchange rate regimen combining the best of the fixed and market floating systems, while recognizing that a globalized money system without geographic boundaries threatens the sovereignty of a country's ability to control its money supply and to influence the value of its currency.

Wasny, Garrett. (1996). A (Venture) Capital Idea from Canada. *World Trade,* vol. 9, no. 4, pp. 36–38.

Investigates the Canadian venture-capital industry, comparing it to the industry in the United States. While smaller in both total disbursal and number of venture-capital firms, Canadian firms disburse 53 percent more than their U.S. counterparts on average. In addition, Cana-dian firms differ in investment preference, preferring smaller start-up companies.

Endnotes

1. For a discussion of bank-lending decisions, see A. D. Jankowicz and R. D. Hisrich, "Insti-tution in Small Business Lending Decisions," *Journal of Small Business Management* (July 1987), pp. 45–52; N. C. Churchill and V. L. Lewis, "Bank Lending to New and Growing Enterprises," *Journal of Business Venturing* (Spring 1986), pp. 193–206; R. T. Justis, "Starting a Small Business: An Investigation of the Borrowing Procedure," *Journal of Small Business Management* (October 1982), pp. 22–32; and L. Fertuck, "Survey of Small Business Lending Practices," *Journal of Small Business Management* (October 1982), pp. 42–48.
2. Bootstrap financing is discussed in Anne Murphy, "Capital Punishment," *Inc.* (November 1993), pp. 38–42; and Michael P. Cronin, "Paradise Lost," *Inc.* (November 1993), pp. 48–53.
3. Anne Murphy, "Capital Punishment," *Inc.* (November 1993), p. 42.

12

Informal Risk Capital and Venture Capital

LEARNING OBJECTIVES

1. To explain the basic stages of venture funding.

2. To discuss the informal risk-capital market.

3. To discuss the nature of the venture-capital industry and the venture-capital decision process.

4. To explain all aspects of valuing a company.

5. To identify several valuation approaches.

DAVID WETHERELL

Where does an entrepreneur interested in starting or growing an Internet venture get funds? While there are a variety of sources, many have turned to David Wetherell and his Internet venture company CMGI.

Born in a rural section of Connecticut north of Hartford, David Wetherell, the youngest of six children, spent the first years of his life on his family's 100-acre farm raising cattle and chickens. When the farm began to fail, Wetherell's parents moved to northern Vermont to try their hand at potato farming and later to Florida for a job opportunity in construction. When in Florida, David had the opportunity to work on his curve ball for his Little League team. A fanatical baseball player, David threw so hard in games that his parents were concerned he would injure his pitching arm. He displayed this same degree of intensity in pursuing his two talents—math and music.

After graduating from an elite private school, David went to Ohio Wesleyan University where he experienced difficulty in completing his first computer programming course. David majored in mathematics but would rediscover computers later on in his academic career and devote significant time to writing code.

Following graduation from Ohio Wesleyan in 1976, David held a variety of software programming jobs. In a software position at Boston and Main Railroad Co., he developed a system to manage thousands of freight cars. Later, after starting and selling a small software company, David became the head of College Marketing Group where for eight years he developed his skills in direct marketing. In this position, his charisma, high energy level, and quick thinking were often needed to compensate for his lack of business experience. In one instance, David quickly purchased another direct-mail company without doing the necessary research that would have uncovered its poor accounting practices and losses. He managed to avoid bankruptcy in this situation by charming the bank into providing the needed support. After tripling the business to revenues of $9 million and developing a smoothly operating company, David became bored and started looking for something new to do.

When the first signs of electronic publishing emerged in 1993, David Wetherell persuaded the board of the College Marketing Group to fund Brookline Technologies, a company aimed at selling books to college professors through their PCs. This was accomplished by hiring a team of software engineers to build a Web browser four months before Netscape launched Navigator. After spending six months and $900,000 on the Booklink browser, the company was sold in 1994 to AOL for stock worth $30 million, which quickly grew in value to $75 million.

From this point on, David Wetherell devoted all his passion and energy to the Internet by immediately setting up the @Ventures fund using half the proceeds from the sale of his last company. The purpose of the fund was to take a leading share position in Internet start-ups. Following the first investment in Lycos, the fund targeted numerous subsidiaries to provide the all-important infrastructure for emerging e-commerce companies. These included Engage Technologies (a company to develop targeted direct-marketing tools for the Internet); AOSmart (a company to sell online advertising); Planet Direct, now MyWay.com (a company to provide customized news and information to Internet service providers); and NaviSite (a company to provide computer gear and links to manage the websites of other businesses).

The directors of CMGI were concerned about the burn rate of $5 million per month that was attributed to the company's money-losing ventures as well as its negative operating cash flow of $4.7 million at the end of fiscal 1996. A hot IPO in 1996, Lycos plummeted 73 percent in early 1997, but then rebounded later in the same year. This rebound generated enough institutional investor support to allow for CMGI's readiness for significant growth and acquisitions. Today, David Wetherell's CMGI has main holdings in Internet content companies such as Altavista (second tier Web portal); Lycos (number four Web portal); MyWay (creates custom-built portals with localized news and e-commerce links); ICAST (creates online audio and video programming); Magnitude Network (software that helps radio stations broadcast over the Web and link information to on-air promotional spots); Zinezone.com (multimedia site mixing video, text, and Web links to profile cutting-edge cultural figures); Raging Bull (online investor forum); and WEBCT (software for putting college courses online). CMGI also has sizable shares in online infrastructure and e-commerce companies that include CHEMDEX (marketplace for biotech and pharmaceutical supplies); SHOPPING.COM (sells almost everything); MOTHERNATURE.COM (sells vitamins, health supplements, and minerals); THINGWORLD.COM (sells online collectibles); FURNITURE.COM (sells sofas, beds, and furnishings); NEXTMONEY.COM (a gallery showing the works of undiscovered artists); CARPARTS.COM (auto parts site); BIZBUYER.COM (small business entertain bids); MONDERA.COM (provides expert advice and service from parenting to pets); NEXT PLANET OVER.COM (online comic books merchant); and UBID.COM (online auction site).

Presently, David Wetherell is directing his company to a new level by turning its current collection of stock in Internet companies into a conglomerate capable of supplying a large array of Internet services to customers and corporations. This conglomerate is a network of interlocking Net companies that work together, each one feeding its users into the other companies in the network.

ƒ❧

FINANCING THE BUSINESS

In evaluating the appropriateness of venture-capital financing, an entrepreneur must determine the amount and the timing of the funds required, as well as the projected company sales and growth rates. Conventional small businesses and privately held middle-market companies tend to have a difficult time obtaining external equity

TABLE 12.1 Stages of Business Development Funding

Early-Stage Financing

• Seed capital	Relatively small amounts to prove concepts and finance feasibility studies
• Start-up	Product development and initial marketing, but with no commercial sales yet; funding to actually get company operations started

Expansion or Development Financing

• Second stage	Working capital for initial growth phase, but no clear profitability or cash flow yet
• Third stage	Major expansion for company with rapid sales growth, at breakeven or positive profit levels but still private company
• Fourth stage	Bridge financing to prepare company for public offering

Acquisitions and Leveraged Buyout Financing

• Traditional acquisitions	Assuming ownership and control of another company
• Leveraged buyouts (LBOs)	Management of a company acquiring company control by buying out the present owners
• Going private	Some of the owners/managers of a company buying all the outstanding stock, making the company privately held again

capital, especially from the venture-capital industry. Venture capitalists like David Wetherell want to invest in software, biotechnology, or Internet companies, or in high-potential ventures like Fred Smith's Federal Express. The three types of funding as the business develops are indicated in Table 12.1. The funding problems, as well as the cost of the funds, differ for each type. *Early-stage financing* is usually the most difficult and costly to obtain. Two types of financing are available during this stage: seed capital and start-up capital. Seed capital, the most difficult financing to obtain through outside funds, is usually a relatively small amount of funds needed to prove concepts and finance feasibility studies. Since venture capitalists usually have a minimum funding level of above $500,000, they are rarely involved in this type of funding, except in the case of high-technology ventures of entrepreneurs who have a successful track record and need a significant amount of capital. The second type of funding is start-up financing. As the name implies, start-up financing is involved in developing and selling some initial products to determine if commercial sales are feasible. These funds are also difficult to obtain.

early-stage financing One of the first financings obtained by a company

Expansion or *development financing* (the second basic financing type) is easier to obtain than early-stage financing. Venture capitalists play an active role in providing funds here. As the firm develops in each stage, the funds for expansion are less costly. Generally, funds in the second stage are used as working capital to support initial growth. In the third stage, the company is at breakeven or a positive profit level and uses

development financing Financing to rapidly expand the business

the funds for major sales expansion. Funds in the fourth stage are usually used as bridge financing in the interim period as the company prepares to go public.

Acquisition financing or leveraged buyout financing (the third type) is more specific in nature. It is issued for such activities as traditional acquisitions, leveraged buyouts (management buying out the present owners), and going private (a publicly held firm buying out existing stockholders, thereby becoming a private company).

acquisition financing   Financing to buy own or another company

There are three *risk-capital markets* that can be involved in financing a firm's growth: the *informal risk-capital market*, the *venture-capital market*, and the *public-equity market*. Although all three risk-capital markets can be a source of funds for stage-one financing, the public-equity market is available only for high-potential ventures, particularly when high technology is involved. Recently, some biotechnology companies raised their first-stage financing through the public-equity market since investors were excited about the potential prospects and returns in this high-interest area. This also occurred in the areas of oceanography and fuel alternatives when there was a high level of interest. Although venture-capital firms also provide some first-stage funding, the venture must require the minimum level of capital ($500,000). A venture-capital company establishes this minimum level of investment due to the high costs in evaluating and monitoring a deal. By far the best source of funds for first-stage financing is the informal risk-capital market—the third type of risk-capital market.

risk-capital markets   Markets providing debt and equity to nonsecure financing situations

informal risk-capital market   Area of risk-capital markets consisting mainly of individuals

venture-capital market   One of the risk-capital markets consisting of formal firms

public-equity market   One of the risk-capital markets consisting of publicly owned stocks of companies

INFORMAL RISK-CAPITAL MARKET

The informal risk-capital market is the most misunderstood and inefficient type of risk capital. It consists of a virtually invisible group of wealthy investors, often called *business angels*, who are looking for equity-type investment opportunities in a wide variety of entrepreneurial ventures. Typically investing anywhere from $10,000 to $500,000, these angels provide the funds needed in all stages of financing, but particularly in start-up (first-stage) financing. Firms funded from the informal risk-capital market frequently raise second- and third-round financing from professional venture-capital firms or the public-equity market.

business angels   A name for individuals in the informal risk-capital market

Despite being misunderstood by, and virtually inaccessible to, many entrepreneurs, the informal investment market contains the largest pool of risk capital in the United States and consists of about $80 billion. Although there is no verification of the size of this pool or the total amount of financing provided by these business angels, related statistics provide some indication. A 1980 survey of a sample of issuers of private placements by corporations, reported to the Securities and Exchange Commission under Rule 146, found that 87 percent of those buying these issues were individual investors or personal trusts, investing an average of $74,000.[1] Private placements filed under Rule 145 average over $1 billion per year. Another indication becomes apparent on examination of the filings under Regulation D—the regulation exempting certain private and limited offerings from the registration requirements of the Securities Act of 1933 discussed in Chapter 11. In its first year, over 7200 filings, worth $15.5 billion, were made under Regulation D. Corporations accounted for 43 percent of the value ($6.7 billion), or 32 percent of the total number of offerings (2304). Corporations filing limited offerings (under $500,000) raised $220 million, an average of $200,000 per firm. The typical corporate issuers tended to be small, with fewer than 10 stockholders, revenues and assets less than $500,000, stockholders' equity of $50,000 or less, and five or fewer employees.[2]

Similar results were found in an examination of the funds raised by small technology-based firms prior to their initial public offerings. The study revealed that unaffiliated individuals (the informal investment market) accounted for 15 percent of these funds, while venture capitalists accounted for only 12 to 15 percent. During the start-up year, unaffiliated individuals provided 17 percent of the external capital.[3]

A study of angels in New England again yielded similar results. The 133 individual investors studied reported risk-capital investments totaling over $16 million in 320 ventures between 1976 and 1980. These investors averaged one deal every two years, with an average size of $50,000. Although 36 percent of these investments averaged less than $10,000, 24 percent averaged over $50,000. While 40 percent of these investments were start-ups, 80 percent involved ventures less than five years old.[4]

The size and number of these investors have increased dramatically, due in part to the rapid accumulation of wealth in various sectors of the economy. One study of consumer finances found that the net worth of 1.3 million U.S. families was over $1 million.[5] These families, representing about 2 percent of the population, accumulated most of their wealth from earnings, not inheritance, and invested over $151 billion in nonpublic businesses in which they have no management interest. Each year, over 100,000 individual investors finance between 30,000 and 50,000 firms, with a total dollar investment of between $7 billion and $10 billion. Given their investment capability, it is important to know the characteristics of these angels.

One article determined that the angel money available for investment each year was about $20 billion.[6] This amount was confirmed by another study indicating that there are about 250,000 angel investors who invest an amount of $10 billion to $20 billion annually in about 30,000 firms.[7]

The characteristics of these informal investors, or angels, are indicated in Table 12.2. They tend to be well educated; many have graduate degrees. Although they will finance firms anywhere in the United States (and a few in other parts of the world), most of the firms that receive funding are within one day's travel. Business angels will make one to two deals each year, with individual firm investments ranging from $10,000 to $500,000 and the average being $175,000. If the opportunity is right, angels might invest from $500,000 to $1 million. In some cases, angels will join with other angels, usually from a common circle of friends, to finance larger deals.

Is there a preference in the type of ventures in which they invest? While angels invest in every type of investment opportunity, from small retail stores to large oil exploration operations, they generally prefer manufacturing of both industrial and consumer products, energy, service, and the retail/wholesale trade. The returns expected decrease as the number of years the firm has been in business increases, from a median five-year capital gain of 10 times for start-ups to 3 times for established firms over five years old. These investing angels are more patient in their investment horizons and do not have a problem waiting for a period of 7 to 10 years before cashing out. This is in contrast to the more predominant five-year time horizon in the formal venture-capital industry. Investment opportunities are rejected when there is an inadequate risk/return ratio, a subpar management team, a lack

TABLE 12.2   Characteristics of Informal Investors

Demographic Patterns and Relationships

- Well-educated, with many having graduate degrees
- Will finance firms anywhere in the United States
- Most firms financed within one day's travel
- Majority expect to play an active role in ventures financed
- Have clusters of 9 to 12 other investors

Investment Record

- Range of investment: $10,000–$500,000
- Average investment: $175,000
- One to two deals each year

Venture Preference

- Most financings in start-ups or ventures less than 5 years old
- Most interest in financing:
    - Manufacturing—industrial/commercial products
    - Manufacturing—consumer products
    - Energy/natural resources
    - Services
    - Retail/wholesale trade

Risk/Reward Expectations

- Median 5-year capital gains of 10 times for start-ups
- Median 5-year capital gains of 6 times for firms under 1 year old
- Median 5-year capital gains of 5 times for firms 1–5 years old
- Median 5-year capital gains of 3 times for established firms over 5 years old

Reasons for Rejecting Proposals

- Risk/return ratio not adequate
- Inadequate management team
- Not interested in proposed business area
- Unable to agree on price
- Principals not sufficiently committed
- Unfamiliar with area of business

of interest in the business area, or insufficient commitment to the venture from the principals.

Where do these angel investors generally find their deals? Deals are found through referrals by business associates, friends, active personal research, investment bankers, and business brokers. However, even though these *referral sources* provide some deals, most angel investors are not satisfied with the number and type of investment referrals.

referral sources Ways individual investors find out about potential deals

Fifty-one percent of the investors surveyed were either partially or totally dissatisfied with their referral systems and indicated that at least moderate improvement is needed.

As Seen in *Business Week*
Where Venture Capital Ventures

It's hardly a surprise that the U.S. economy and the nation's venture capitalists are both on a roll. For it is the latter group, lured by the specter of huge stock market gains, that has funded the new technologies that many experts think have led the economy into the promised land of strong, inflation-free growth.

What many people may not appreciate, however, notes economist Steven G. Cochrane of RFA/Dismal Sciences, an economics consultancy, is how concentrated venture investment is becoming. "California and the Northeast are benefiting enormously," he says, "while most other areas are being ignored." Similarly, knowledge-intensive industries are garnering the lion's share of funds, while other industries are left out in the cold.

The investment pace is little short of breathtaking. PricewaterhouseCoopers reports that U.S. venture-capital firms shelled out a record $9.04 billion in 1999's third quarter, up 138 percent from the year-earlier level. That brought the nine-month total to $21 billion, 50 percent more than funds invested in all of 1998 and nearly four times the 1995 tally.

Unfortunately, many regions aren't sharing in the bonanza. At last count, only half the states had garnered more venture capital in 1999 than 1998, and six—California, Massachusetts, New York, Texas, Washington, and Colorado—were accounting for nearly 75 percent of the total, compared with just over half as recently as 1995.

Cochrane attributes the increasing regional focus to several factors. First, technology advances, as measured by new patent activity, are highly concentrated in the Northeast and West. Second, venture capital often comes from wealth created by earlier high-tech entrepreneurs. And these techie millionaires and billionaires tend to reside in such areas as Silicon Valley and Boston and to favor investing in nearby companies, which they can readily monitor and advise.

Venturing's stress on cutting-edge technology is also enabling these regions to overcome a number of relative competitive disadvantages. While fast-growing areas, such as the Southeast and Mountain West, can offer businesses lower taxes and lower energy and housing costs, California and the Northeast can supply the skilled workers and research produced by their college and university systems.

Meanwhile, the industry focus of venture capital is becoming increasingly concentrated—as Internet-related companies claim an ever-larger piece of the investment pie. By late 1999, communications, software, and information-processing businesses were garnering nearly 60 percent of venture funding, up from 41 percent in 1995. At the same time, the shares going to health care and biotechnology have fallen sharply, from 12 percent and 8 percent, respectively, to 4 percent and 3 percent.

Can venture capital maintain its momentum? Continuing rapid technological advances and the buoyant stock market say yes. But Cochrane warns that a sustained stock market correction or the failure of current ventures to pay off (as the biotech industry found in the early 1990s) could quickly upset the apple cart. In that case, the regions and industries riding the current venture boom could face a rude awakening.

Leaders of the Pack in Attracting Investment
Shares of $61 Billion in U.S. Venture Capital Invested from Jan. '95 to Sept. '99

California	41.3%	Colorado	3.2%
Massachusetts	10.8	New Jersey	2.8
Texas	5.3	Illinois	2.7
New York	4.1	Virginia	2.5
Washington	3.4	Florida	2.4

Source: Data from PricewaterhouseCoopers.
Source: Gene Koretz, "Where Venture Capital Ventures," *Business Week* (February 7, 2000), p. 30.

One method for improving this referral process has proved successful at the Massachusetts Institute of Technology (MIT) and the Oklahoma Investment Forum. Each of these has a sort of computer dating service for money—a computerized system that matches entrepreneurs with investing angels on a confidential basis. The two institutions previously made this resource available to affiliated universities. Entrepreneurs enter the system via the Venture Capital Network (VCN) at MIT and the Venture Capital Exchange (VCE) at the Oklahoma Investment Forum by filling out questionnaires on their business and funding needs. These requests are matched with the investors on each system who have indicated an interest in the entrepreneur's area of business. After reviewing the information provided by the entrepreneur (the answers to the questions and supporting material), the investor decides whether to be identified to him or her so that more in-depth discussion between the two parties can take place. The Securities and Exchange Commission's rules and regulations prohibit the systems from advising either the investor or the entrepreneur or from having any involvement in the final negotiations between the two parties.

Both the VCE and VCN have linked entrepreneurs to their investment capital in a wide variety of companies.[8] These two computer-matching systems served as the basis of Ace-Net, a system that matches angels with businesses of interest throughout the United States. Angels register on the system at a local access organization—such as the office of Enterprise Development, Inc. (EDI) of the Weatherhead School of Management at Case Western Reserve University—as do businesses in that area of the country. These angels are then matched with businesses that fit their interest criteria and have registered on the system at various sites throughout the United States, as well as regionally registered businesses. Angel confidentiality is protected.

VENTURE CAPITAL

The important and little-understood area of venture capital will be discussed in terms of its nature, the venture-capital industry in the United States, and the venture-capital process.

Nature of Venture Capital

Venture capital is one of the least understood areas in entrepreneurship. Some think that venture capitalists do the early-stage financing of relatively small, rapidly growing technology companies. It is more accurate to view venture capital broadly as a professionally managed pool of equity capital. Frequently, the *equity pool* is formed from the resources of wealthy limited partners. Other principal investors in venture-capital limited partnerships are pension funds, endowment funds, and other institutions, including foreign investors. The pool is managed by a general partner—that is, the venture-capital firm—in exchange for a percentage of the gain realized on the investment and a fee. The investments are in early-stage deals as well as second- and third-stage deals and leveraged buyouts. In fact, venture capital can best be characterized as a long-term investment discipline, usually occurring over a five-year period, that is found in the creation of early-stage companies, the expansion and revitalization of existing businesses, and the financing of leveraged buyouts of existing divisions of major corporations or privately owned businesses. In each investment, the venture capitalist takes an *equity participation* through stock, warrants, and/or convertible securities and has an active involvement in the monitoring of each portfolio company bringing investment, financing planning, and business skills to the firm.[9]

equity pool   Money raised by venture capitalists to invest

equity participation   Taking an ownership position

Overview of the Venture-Capital Industry

Although the role of venture capital was instrumental throughout the industrialization of the United States, it did not become institutionalized until after World War

II. Before World War II, venture investment activity was a monopoly led by wealthy individuals, investment banking syndicates, and a few family organizations with a professional manager. The first step toward institutionalizing the venture-capital industry took place in 1946 with the formation of the American Research and Development Corporation (ARD) in Boston. The ARD was a small pool of capital from individuals and institutions put together by General Georges Doriot to make active investments in selected emerging businesses.

The next major development, the Small Business Investment Company Act of 1958, married private capital with government funds to be used by professionally managed small business investment companies (*SBIC firms*) to infuse capital into start-up and growing small businesses. With the tax advantages, government funds for leverage, and a private capital company, SBICs were the start of the now formal venture-capital industry. The 1960s saw a significant expansion of SBICs with the approval of approximately 585 SBIC licenses that involved more than $205 million in private capital. Many of these early SBICs failed due to inexperienced portfolio managers, unreasonable expectations, a focus on short-term profitability, and an excess of government regulations. These early failures caused the SBIC program to be restructured, which in turn eliminated some of the unnecessary government regulations and increased the amount of capitalization needed. There are approximately 360 SBICs operating today, of which 130 are minority small business investment companies (MESBICs) funding minority enterprises.

SBIC firms   Small companies with some government money that invest in other companies

During the late 1960s, small *private venture-capital firms* emerged.[10] These were usually formed as limited partnerships, with the venture-capital company acting as the general partner that received a management fee and a percentage of the profits earned on a deal. The limited partners, who supplied the funding, were frequently institutional investors such as insurance companies, endowment funds, bank trust departments, pension funds, and wealthy individuals and families. There are about 980 venture-capital establishments in the United States today.

private venture-capital firms   A type of venture-capital firm having general and limited partners

Another type of venture-capital firm also developed during this time: the venture-capital division of major corporations. These firms, of which there are approximately 100, are usually associated with banks and insurance companies, although companies such as 3M, Monsanto, and Xerox house such firms as well. Corporate venture-capital firms are more prone to invest in windows on technology or new market acquisitions than private venture-capital firms or SBICs. Some of these corporate venture-capital firms have not had strong results.

In response to the need for economic development, a fourth type of venture-capital firm has emerged in the form of the *state-sponsored venture-capital fund*. These state-sponsored funds have a variety of formats. While the size and investment focus and industry orientation vary from state to state, each fund typically is required to invest a certain percentage of its capital in the particular state. Generally, the funds that are professionally managed by the private sector, outside the states' bureaucracy and political processes, have performed better.

state-sponsored venture-capital fund   A fund containing state government money that invests in companies mostly in the state

There has been significant growth in the venture-capital industry in both the size and the number of firms. The total of venture capital dollars invested has increased steadily from $2.9 billion in 1991 to $6.0 billion in 1995, to $13.6 billion in 1997, and to $16.7 billion in 1998, as indicated in Table 12.3.[11] The $16.7 billion invested in 1998 represents about a 68 percent growth rate over a two-year period.

TABLE 12.3   Total Venture Dollars Invested

Year	$ Billions
1991	2.9
1992	5.2
1993	5.3
1994	5.5
1995	6.0
1996	9.9
1997	13.6
1998	16.7

Source: National Venture Capital Association, 1999
National Venture Association Yearbook, p. 3.

TABLE 12.4   Total Amount Invested ($ Billions) and Number of Deals

	1991	1992	1993	1994	1995	1996	1997	1998
$ invested	2.9	5.2	5.3	5.5	6.0	9.9	13.6	16.7
# of deals	1191	1478	1299	1351	1526	2255	2828	3115

Source: National Venture Capital Association, 1999 National Venture Association Yearbook, p. 24.

This increase in the amount of venture capital invested has been disseminated across an increasing number of deals. As indicated in Table 12.4, the number of deals done by venture capitalists increased from 1191 in 1991 to 2828 in 1997 to 3115 deals in 1998. This number of deals completed in 1998 (3115) constituted an increase of about 34 percent over the number of deals done in 1996. However, the increase in total dollars invested was about 68 percent during the same period, indicating that venture capitalists are investing more money than ever before.

The deals venture capitalists have completed have been concentrated largely in the field of information technology. This has significantly impacted the formation and growth of firms in this industry sector. The information technology group accounts for 60 percent of the total venture dollars invested in 1998, while its closest competitor, life sciences, accounts for only 20 percent (see Figure 12.1).

At what stage of venture development was this money invested? The percentage of money raised by each type is indicated in Figure 12.2. As has traditionally been the pattern, the largest amount of money raised was for expansion (56 percent). However, a percentage higher than in previous years (29 percent) was raised for early-stage development reflecting a strong interest in e-commerce and the formation of .com companies. In fact, this interest is so strong that there are venture-capital companies focusing only on this industry segment.

The money invested from 1991 to 1998 is broken down by stage and year in Table 12.5. Interestingly, between 1991 and 1998, the percentage of deals in the area of expansion increased from 43.9 percent to 55.8 percent, while the percentage of deals in early-stage development remained about the same. The percentage in later-stage deals decreased significantly.

FIGURE 12.1 Percentage of Venture Dollars Invested in 1998 by Industry Group

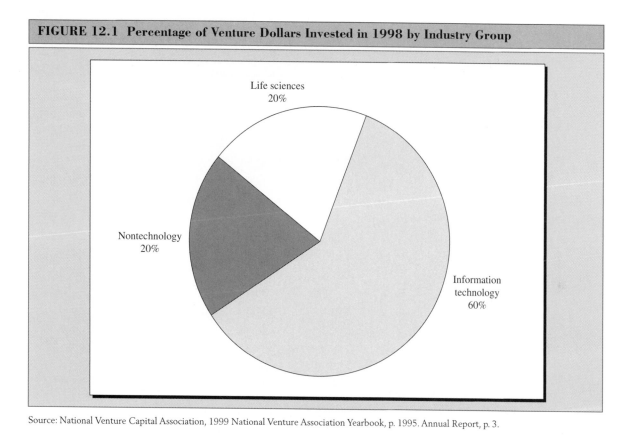

Source: National Venture Capital Association, 1999 National Venture Association Yearbook, p. 1995. Annual Report, p. 3.

FIGURE 12.2 Percentage Raised by Round Type for 1998

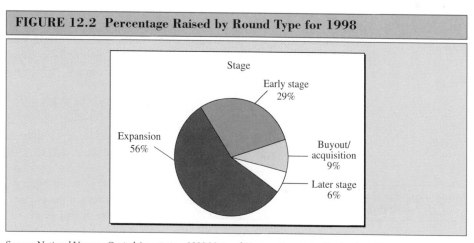

Source: National Venture Capital Association, 1999 National Venture Association Yearbook, p. 22.

Where are the deals done? In terms of the number of companies financed, 10 states accounted for 72 percent of the deals in 1998. The deals in these states accounted for $12.9 billion, or 77 percent, of the total dollars invested (see Table 12.6). Following the trend of previous years, California with 1021 companies financed (36 percent) and Massachusetts with 308 companies financed (11 percent), accounted

TABLE 12.5   Venture Investment by Round Type ($ Millions)

Year		Expansion	Early Stage	Buyout/ Acquisition	Early Stage	TOTAL
1991	$	1,262.7	842.8	184.0	585.9	2,875.4
	%	43.9%	29.3%	6.4%	20.4%	100.0%
1992	$	2,014.7	1,197.8	731.3	1,297.7	5,241.4
	%	38.4%	22.9%	14.0%	24.8%	100.0%
1993	$	1,672.1	2,106.8	449.4	1,041.4	5,269.7
	%	31.7%	40.0%	8.5%	19.8%	100.0%
1994	$	1,697.3	1,629.0	776.7	1,387.7	5,490.8
	%	30.9%	29.7%	14.1%	25.3%	100.0%
1995	$	2,085.5	2,151.5	612.4	1,118.9	5,968.3
	%	34.9%	36.0%	10.3%	18.7%	100.0%
1996	$	3,684.5	2,653.0	1,166.7	2,403.3	9,907.5
	%	37.2%	26.8%	11.8%	24.3%	100.0%
1997	$	5,843.9	3,424.0	1,524.8	2,764.6	13,557.2
	%	43.1%	25.3%	11.2%	20.4%	100.0%
1998	$	9,304.8	4,824.1	1,558.1	985.9	16,672.9
	%	55.8%	28.9%	9.3%	5.9%	100.0%

Source: National Venture Capital Association, 1999 National Venture Association Yearbook, p. 22.

for 47 percent of all companies financed by venture capital throughout the United States. Other leading states where companies received venture financing include Texas (151 companies—5 percent), New York (130 companies—5 percent), Colorado (88 companies—3 percent), and Washington (83 companies—3 percent).

Venture-Capital Process

To be in a position to secure the funds needed, an entrepreneur must understand the philosophy and objectives of a venture-capital firm, as well as the *venture-capital process*. The objective of a venture-capital firm is to generate long-term capital appreciation through debt and equity investments. To achieve this objective, the venture capitalist is willing to make any changes or modifications necessary in the business investment. Since the objective of the entrepreneur is the survival of the business, the objectives of the two are frequently at odds, particularly when problems occur.

venture-capital process The decision procedure of a venture-capital firm

A typical portfolio objective of typical venture-capital firms in terms of return criteria and risk involved is shown in Figure 12.3. Since there is more risk involved in financing a business earlier in its development, more return is expected from early-stage financing (50 percent ROI) than from acquisitions or leveraged buyouts (30 percent ROI), the late stage in development. The significant risk involved and the pressure that venture-capital firms feel from their investors (limited partners) to make safer investments with higher rates of return have caused these firms to invest

TABLE 12.6 Leading Venture-Capital States

State	Investments # of Companies	%	$ Billion	%	Fund Commitments $ Billion	%
California	1,021	36	6.5	39	5.2	21
Massachusetts	308	11	1.9	11	4.4	17
Texas	151	5	0.9	5	1.3	5
New York	130	5	0.8	5	7.8	31
Colorado	88	3	0.6	4	0.1	1
Wahington	83	3	0.5	3	0.4	1
Illinois	65	2	0.5	3	0.8	3
New Jersey	70	2	0.4	3	1.0	4
Virginia	68	2	0.4	2	0.3	1
Georgia	85	3	0.4	2	0.3	1
Total	2,069	72	12.9	77	21.5	85
All U.S.	2,859	100	16.7	100	25.3	100

Source: National Venture Capital Association, 1999 National Venture Association Yearbook, pp. 4, 17.

FIGURE 12.3 Venture-Capital Financing: Risk and Return Criteria

even greater amounts of their funds in later stages of financing. In these late-stage investments, there are lower risks, faster returns, less managerial assistance needed, and fewer deals to be evaluated.

The venture capitalist does not necessarily seek control of a company, but would rather have the firm and the entrepreneur at the most risk. The venture capitalist will want at least one seat on the board of directors. Once the decision to invest is made, the venture capitalist will do anything necessary to support the management team so that the business and the investment prosper. Whereas the venture capitalist expects to provide guidance as a member of the board of directors, the management team is expected to direct and run the daily operations of the company. A venture capitalist will support the management team with investment dollars, financial skills, planning, and expertise in any area needed.

Since the venture capitalist provides long-term investment (typically five years or more), it is important that there is mutual trust and understanding between the entrepreneur and the venture capitalist. There should be no surprises in the firm's performance. Both good and bad news should be shared, with the objective of taking the necessary action to allow the company to grow and develop in the long run. The venture capitalist should be available to the entrepreneur to discuss problems and develop strategic plans.

The venture capitalist expects a company to satisfy three general criteria before he or she will commit to the venture. First, the company must have a strong management team that consists of individuals with solid experience and backgrounds, a strong commitment to the company, capabilities in their specific areas of expertise, the ability to meet challenges, and the flexibility to scramble wherever necessary. A venture capitalist would rather invest in a first-rate management team and a second-rate product than the reverse. The management team's commitment should be reflected in dollars invested in the company. Although the amount of the investment is important, more telling is the size of this investment relative to the management team's ability to invest. The commitment of the management team should be backed by the support of the family, particularly the spouse, of each key team player. A positive family environment and spousal support allow team members to spend the 60 to 70 hours per week necessary to start and grow the company. One successful venture capitalist makes it a point to have dinner with the entrepreneur and spouse and even visit the entrepreneur's home before making an investment decision. According to the venture capitalist, "I find it difficult to believe an entrepreneur can successfully run and manage a business and put in the necessary time when the home environment is out of control."

The second criterion is that the product/market opportunity must be unique, having a differential advantage in a growing market. Securing a unique market niche is essential since the product or service must be able to compete and grow during the investment period. This uniqueness needs to be carefully spelled out in the marketing portion of the business plan and is even better when it is protected by a patent or a trade secret.

The final criterion for investment is that the business opportunity must have *significant capital appreciation*. The exact amount of capital appreciation varies, depending on such factors as the size of the deal, the stage of development of the company, the upside potential, the downside risks, and the available exits. The venture capitalist typically expects a 40 to 60 percent return on investment in most investment situations.

The venture-capital process that implements these criteria is both an art and a science.[12] The element of art is illustrated in the venture capitalist's intuition, gut feeling, and creative thinking that guide the process. The process is scientific due to the systematic approach and data-gathering techniques involved in the assessment.

The process starts with the venture-capital firm establishing its philosophy and investment objectives. The firm must decide on the following: the composition of its portfolio mix, including the number of start-ups, expansion companies, and management buyouts; the types of industries; the geographic region for investment; and any product or industry specializations.

The venture-capital process can be broken down into four primary stages: preliminary screening, agreement on principal terms, due diligence, and final approval. The *preliminary screening* begins with the receipt of the business plan. A good business plan is essential in the venture-capital process. Most venture capitalists will not even talk to an entrepreneur who doesn't have one. As the starting point, the business plan must have a clear-cut mission and clearly stated objectives that are supported by an in-depth industry and market analysis and pro forma income statements. The executive summary is an important part of this business plan, as it is used for initial screening in this preliminary evaluation. Many business plans are never evaluated beyond the executive summary. When evaluating the business, the venture capitalist first determines if the deal or similar deals have been seen previously. The investor then determines if the proposal fits his or her long-term policy and short-term needs in developing a portfolio balance. In this preliminary screening, the venture capitalist investigates the economy of the industry and evaluates whether he or she has the appropriate knowledge and ability to invest in that industry. The investor reviews the numbers presented to determine if the business can reasonably deliver the ROI required. In addition, the credentials and capability of the management team are evaluated to determine if they can carry out the plan presented.

preliminary screening   Initial evaluation of a deal

The second stage is the agreement on principal terms between the entrepreneur and the venture capitalist. The venture capitalist wants a basic understanding of the principal terms of the deal at this stage of the process before making the major commitment of time and effort involved in the formal due diligence process.

The third stage, detailed review and *due diligence*, is the longest stage, involving anywhere from one to three months. There is a detailed review of the company's history, the business plan, the resumes of the individuals, their financial history, and target market customers. The upside potential and downside risk are assessed; and there is a thorough evaluation of the markets, industry, finances, suppliers, customers, and management.

due diligence   The process of deal evaluation

In the last stage, *final approval*, a comprehensive, internal investment memorandum is prepared. This document reviews the venture capitalist's findings and details the investment terms and conditions of the investment transaction. This information is used to prepare the formal legal documents that both the entrepreneur and venture capitalist will sign to finalize the deal.[13]

Locating Venture Capitalists

One of the most important decisions for the entrepreneur lies in selecting which venture-capital firm to approach. Since venture capitalists tend to specialize either geographically by industry (manufacturing industrial products or consumer products, high technology, or service) or by size and type of investment, the entrepreneur should approach only those that may have an interest in the investment opportunity. Where do you find this venture capitalist?

Although venture capitalists are located throughout the United States, the traditional areas of concentration are found in Los Angeles, New York, Chicago, Boston, and San Francisco.[14] An entrepreneur should carefully research the names and addresses of prospective venture-capital firms that might have an interest in the particular investment opportunity. There are also regional and national venture-capital associations. For a nominal fee or none at all, these associations will frequently send the entrepreneur a directory that lists their members, the types of businesses their members invest in, and any investment restrictions. Whenever possible, the entrepreneur should be introduced to the venture capitalist. Bankers, accountants, lawyers, and professors are good sources for introductions.

Approaching a Venture Capitalist

The entrepreneur should approach a venture capitalist in a professional business manner. Since venture capitalists receive hundreds of inquiries and are frequently out of the office working with portfolio companies or investigating potential investment opportunities, it is important to begin the relationship positively. The entrepreneur should call any potential venture capitalist to ensure that the business is in an area of investment interest. Then the business plan should be sent, accompanied by a short professional letter.

Since venture capitalists receive many more plans than they are capable of funding, many plans are screened out as soon as possible. Venture capitalists tend to focus and put more time and effort on those plans that are referred. In fact, one venture-capital group said that 80 percent of their investments over the last five years were in referred companies. Consequently, it is well worth the entrepreneur's time to seek out an introduction to the venture capitalist. Typically this can be obtained from an executive of a portfolio company, an accountant, lawyer, banker, or business school professor.

The entrepreneur should be aware of some basic rules of thumb before implementing the actual approach and should follow the detailed guidelines presented in Table 12.7. First, great care should be taken in selecting the right venture capitalist to approach. Venture capitalists tend to specialize in certain industries and will rarely invest in a business outside these areas, regardless of the merits of the business proposal and plan. Second, recognize that venture capitalists know each other, particularly in a specific region of the country. When a large amount of money is involved, they will invest in the deal together, with one venture-capital firm taking the lead. Since this degree of familiarity is present, a venture-capital firm will probably find out if others have seen your business plan. Do not shop among venture capitalists, as even a good business plan can quickly become "shopworn." Third, when meeting the venture capitalist, particularly for the first time, bring only one or two key members of the management team. A venture capitalist is investing in you and your management team and its track record, not on outside consultants and experts. Any experts can be called in as needed.

Finally, be sure to develop a succinct, well-thought-out oral presentation. This should cover the company's business, the uniqueness of the product or service, the prospects for growth, the major factors behind achieving the sales and profits indicated, the backgrounds and track records of the key managers, the amount of financing required, and the returns anticipated. This first presentation is critical, as is indicated in the comment of one venture capitalist: "I need to sense a competency, a capability, a chemistry within the first half hour of our initial meeting. The entrepreneur needs to look me in the eye and present his story clearly and logically. If a chemistry does not start to develop, I start looking for reasons not to do the deal."

Following a favorable initial meeting, the venture capitalist will do some preliminary investigation of the plan. If favorable, another meeting between the management

> ### TABLE 12.7 Guidelines for Dealing with Venture Capitalists
>
> - Carefully determine the venture capitalist to approach for funding the particular type of deal. Screen and target the approach. Venture capitalists do not like deals that have been excessively "shopped."
>
> - Once a discussion is started with a venture capitalist, do not discuss the deal with other venture capitalists. Working several deals in parallel can create problems unless the venture capitalists are working together. Time and resource limitations may require a cautious simultaneous approach to several funding sources.
>
> - It is better to approach a venture capitalist through an intermediary who is respected and has a preexisting relationship with the venture capitalist. Limit and carefully define the role and compensation of the intermediary.
>
> - The entrepreneur or manager, not an intermediary, should lead the discussions with the venture capitalist. Do not bring a lawyer, accountant, or other advisors to the first meeting. Since there are no negotiations during this first meeting, it is a chance for the venture capitalist to get to know the entrepreneur without interference from others.
>
> - Be very careful about what is projected or promised. The entrepreneur will probably be held accountable for these projections in the pricing, deal structure, or compensation.
>
> - Disclose any significant problems or negative situations in this initial meeting. Trust is a fundamental part of the long-term relationship with the venture capitalist; subsequent discovery by the venture capitalist of an undisclosed problem will cause a loss of confidence and probably prevent a deal.
>
> - Reach a flexible, reasonable understanding with the venture capitalist regarding the timing of a response to the proposal and the accomplishment of the various steps in the financing transaction. Patience is needed, as the process is complex and time consuming. Too much pressure for a rapid decision can cause problems with the venture capitalist.
>
> - Do not sell the project on the basis that other venture capitalists have committed themselves. Most venture capitalists are independent and take pride in their own decision making.
>
> - Be careful about glib statements such as "There is no competition for this product" or "There is nothing like this technology available today." These statements can indicate a lack of homework or that a perfect product has been designed for a nonexistent market.
>
> - Do not indicate an inordinate concern for salary, benefits, or other forms of current compensation. Dollars are precious in a new venture. The venture capitalist wants the entrepreneur committed to an equity appreciation similar to that of the venture capitalist.
>
> - Eliminate to the extent possible any use of new dollars to take care of past problems, such as payment of past debts or deferred salaries of management. New dollars of the venture capitalist are for growth, to move the business forward.

team and venture capitalist will be scheduled so that both parties can assess the other and determine if a good working relationship can be established and if a feeling of trust and confidence is evolving. During this mutual evaluation, the entrepreneur should be careful not to be too inflexible about the amount of company equity he or she is willing to share. If the entrepreneur is too inflexible, the venture capitalist might end negotiations. During this meeting, initial agreement of terms is established. If you are turned down by one venture capitalist, do not become discouraged. Instead, select another venture-capitalist candidate and repeat the procedure. A significant number of companies denied funding by one venture capitalist are able to obtain funds from other outside sources, including other venture capitalists.[15]

Summary of Beliefs and Problems in the Five Major Ethical Systems

	Nature of Ethical Belief	Problems in the Ethical System
Eternal Law	Moral standards are given in an Eternal Law, which is revealed in Scripture or apparent in nature and then interpreted by religious leaders or humanist philosophers; the belief is that everyone should act in accordance with the interpretation.	There are multiple interpretations of the Law, but no method to choose among them beyond human rationality, and human rationality needs an absolute principle or value as the basis for choice.
Utilitarian Theory	Moral standards are applied to the outcome of an action or decision; the principle is that everyone should act to generate the greatest benefits for the largest number of people.	Immoral acts can be justified if they provide substantial benefits for the majority, even at an unbearable cost or harm to the minority; an additional principle or value is needed to balance the benefit-cost equation.
Universalist Theory	Moral standards are applied to the intent of an action or decision; the principle is that everyone should act to ensure that similar decisions would be reached by others, given similar circumstances.	Immoral acts can be justified by persons who are prone to self-deception or self-importance, and there is no scale to judge between "wills": additional principle or value is needed to refine the Categorical Imperative concept.
Distributive Justice	Moral standards are based upon the primacy of a single value, which is justice. Everyone should act to ensure a more equitable distribution of benefits, for this promotes individual self-respect, which is essential for social cooperation.	The primacy of the value of justice is dependent upon acceptance of the proposition that an equitable distribution of benefits ensures social cooperation.
Personal Liberty	Moral standards are based upon the primacy of a single value, which is liberty. Everyone should act to ensure greater freedom of choice, for this promotes market exchange, which is essential for social productivity.	The primacy of the value of liberty is dependent upon acceptance of the proposition that a market system of exchange ensures social productivity.

Source: Larue Hosmer; *The Ethics of Management* (Boston: Richard D. Irwin, 1996), p. 99.

VALUING YOUR COMPANY

A problem confronting the entrepreneur when obtaining outside equity funds, whether from the informal investor market (the angels) or the formal venture-capital industry, is determining the value of the company. This valuation is at the core of determining how much ownership an investor is entitled to for funding the venture. This is determined by considering the *factors in valuation*. This, as well as other aspects of securing funding, has a potential for ethical conflicts that must be carefully handled. Different problems that occur in five major ethical systems are indicated in the Ethics box.

Factors in Valuation

There are eight factors that, although they vary by situation, the entrepreneur should consider when valuing the venture. The first factor, and the starting point in any valuation, is the nature and history of the business. The characteristics of the venture and the industry in which it operates are fundamental to every evaluation process. The history of the company from its inception provides information on the strength and diversity of the company's operations, the risks involved, and the company's ability to withstand any adverse conditions.

The valuation process must also consider the outlook of the economy in general as well as the outlook for the particular industry. This, the second factor, involves an examination of the financial data of the venture compared with that of other companies in the industry. Management's capability now and in the future is assessed, as well as the future market for the company's products. Will these markets grow, decline, or stabilize, and in what economic conditions?

The third factor is the book value (net value) of the stock of the company and the overall financial condition of the business. The book value (often called owner's equity) is the acquisition cost (less accumulated depreciation) minus liabilities. Frequently, the book value is not a good indication of fair market value, as balance sheet items are almost always carried at cost, not market value. The value of plant and equipment, for example, carried on the books at cost less depreciation may be low due to the use of an accelerated depreciation method or other market factors, making the assets more valuable than indicated in the book value figures. Land, particularly, is usually reflected lower than fair market value. For valuation, the balance sheet must be adjusted to reflect the higher values of the assets, particularly land, so that a more realistic company worth is determined. A good valuation should also value operating and nonoperating assets separately and then combine the two into the total fair market value. A thorough valuation involves comparing balance sheets and profit and loss statements for the past three years when available.

While book value develops the benchmark, the future earning capacity of the company, the fourth factor, is the most important factor in valuation. Previous years' earnings are generally not simply averaged but weighted, with the most recent earnings receiving the highest weighting. Income by product line should be analyzed to judge future profitability and value. Special attention should be paid to depreciation, nonrecurring expense, officers' salaries, rental expense, and historical trends.

The fifth valuation factor is the dividend-paying capacity of the venture. Since the entrepreneur in a new venture typically pays little if any dividends, it is the future capacity to pay dividends rather than actual dividend payments made that is important. The dividend-paying capacity should be capitalized.

An assessment of goodwill and other intangibles of the venture is the sixth valuation factor. These intangible assets usually cannot be valued without reference to the tangible assets of the venture.

The seventh factor in valuation involves assessing any previous sale of stock. Previous stock sales accurately represent future sales if the stock sales are recent. Motives regarding the new sale (if other than arriving at a fair price) and any change in economic or financial conditions during the intermittent period should be considered.

The final valuation factor is the market price of the stocks of companies engaged in the same or similar lines of business. This factor is used in the specific valuation method discussed later in this section. The critical issue is the degree of similarity between the publicly traded company and the company being valued.

As Seen in *Business Week*
A Bad Case of Venture-Capital Envy

The world of leveraged buyouts has never been glamorous. It's about finding down-on-their-luck companies, piling them up with debt, siphoning off cash flow, refocusing management, and flipping them to make a bundle. Mundane, maybe, but a formula that has worked like a charm: Annual returns, after fees, for top-drawer funds averaged 22.7 percent over the past 20 years versus 19.7 percent for the Standard & Poor's 500-stock index.

These days, though, the funds are seeking, well, sex appeal. LBO houses from Hicks, Muse, Tate & Furst Inc. to Forstmann Little & Co. are starting to pile into high-risk Internet deals. But it's no mystery why they're changing tack: In 1999, LBO returns were just 15 percent compared with 90 percent for early-stage venture capitalists. And the trend will accelerate. "More and more funds are making Internet investing a part of their portfolio, adding to the confusion of their investors," says Jesse Reyes, managing director of Venture Economics, a Newark (New Jersey) firm specializing in private-equity research.

Indeed, some LBO investors are more than just confused: They're downright nervous. "My primary concern is whether LBO funds have the (necessary) expertise, or are they learning on our nickel?" says David Locke, senior investment officer of the Los Angeles County Employees Retirement Association, which invests $1 billion in LBO funds.

The LBO guys, of course, insist they can switch readily from Old Economy industries to the Internet. But their wildly differing strategies suggest they they're still feeling their way.

The most zealous of the new breed is Thomas H. Lee Co. in Boston, a $5 billion LBO shop that has just raised over $600 million to start a separate Internet fund. The firm hired eight Net specialists from General Electric Capital Services Inc. to oversee the fund. "While we are not constrained by our LBO charter, smaller, early-stage investments are more appropriate for a different fund," says founder Thomas H. Lee.

At private-equity fund Kohlberg Kravis Roberts & Co., however, Henry R. Kravis and some of his top execs have made several early-stage investments out of their own pockets rather than use their funds' cash for riskier deals. But the LBO fund has also made Net and telecom investments—albeit in bigger, more mature companies such as CAIS Internet, a provider of broadband Net access.

Some LBO players have few qualms about mingling higher-risk Net deals with traditional buyouts. Dallas's Hicks, Muse's private-equity fund, invests about 75 percent of the $7.5 billion it manages in LBOs. But over the past three years, it has made $100 million in early-stage Net investments—though all of them have been in partnership with traditional venture-capital firms.

However, many LBO funds remain leery of the latest fad and how customers would react should they follow it. Vestar Capital Partners, a $2.5 billion buyout fund, for instance, has foresworn Internet investing. "That's stretching our charter beyond what investors intended," says CEO Dan O'Connell.

Skeptics such as Lawrence Schloss—head of Donaldson, Lufkin & Jenrette Inc.'s merchant banking activities, who oversees $6 billion of LBO funds—doubt that the LBO world and Net investing will ever really meld. "The sun doesn't shine on the same dog every day," he says. When the stock market corrects, he forecasts, the LBO guys who strayed will quickly return to business as usual.

Maybe so. But, for now, LBO players are scrambling to find their place in the Internet sun while it lasts.

Source: Debra Sparks, "A Bad Case of Venture Capital Envy," *Business Week* (February 7, 2000), p. 30.

General Valuation Approaches

There are several valuation approaches that can be used in valuing the venture. One of the most widely used approaches assesses *comparable publicly held companies* and the prices of these companies' securities. This search for a similar company is both an art and a science. First, the company must be classified in a certain industry, since

general valuation approaches Methods for determining the worth of a company

companies in the same industry share similar markets, problems, economies, and potential of sales and earnings. The review of all publicly traded companies in this industry classification should evaluate size, amount of diversity, dividends, leverage, and growth potential until the most similar company is identified. This method is inaccurate when a truly comparable company is not found.

A second widely used valuation approach is the *present value of future cash flow.* This method adjusts the value of the cash flow of the business for the time value of money and the business and economic risks. Since only cash (or cash equivalents) can

present value of future cash flow Valuing a company based on its future sales and profits

be used in reinvestment, this valuation approach generally gives more accurate results than profits. In using this method, the sales and earnings are projected back to the time of the valuation decision when shares of the company are offered for sale. The period between the valuation and sale dates is determined, and the potential dividend payout and expected price/earnings ratio or liquidation value at the end of the period are calculated. Finally, a rate of return desired by investors is established, less a discount rate for failure to meet these expectations.

Another valuation method, used only for insurance purposes or in very unique circumstances, is known as *replacement value.* This method is used when, for example, there is a unique asset involved that the buyer really wants. The valuation of the

replacement value The cost of replacing all assets of a company

venture is based on the amount of money it would take to replace (or reproduce) that asset or another important asset or system of the venture.

book value The indicated worth of the assets of a company

The *book value* approach uses the adjusted book value, or net tangible asset value, to determine the firm's worth. Adjusted book value is obtained by making the necessary adjustments to the stated book value by taking into account any depreciation (or appreciation) of plant and equipment and real estate, as well as necessary inventory adjustments that result from the accounting methods employed. The following basic procedure can be used:

Book value	$_____
Add (or subtract) any adjustments such as appreciation or depreciation to arrive at figure on next line—the fair market value	$_____
Fair market value (the sale value of the company's assets)	$_____
Subtract all intangibles that cannot be sold, such as goodwill	$_____
Adjusted book value	$_____

Since the book valuation approach involves simple calculations, its use is particularly good in relatively new businesses, in businesses where the sole owner has died or is disabled, and in businesses with speculative or highly unstable earnings.

The *earnings approach* is the most widely used method of valuing a company since it provides the potential investor with the best estimate of the probable return on investment. The potential earnings are calculated by weighting the most recent operat-

earnings approach Determining the worth of a company by looking at its present and future earnings

ing year's earnings after they have been adjusted for any extraordinary expenses that would not have normally occurred in the operations of a publicly traded company. An appropriate price-earnings multiple is then selected based on norms of the industry and the investment risk. A higher multiple will be used for a high-risk business and a lower multiple for a low-risk business. For example, a low-risk business in an industry with a seven-times-earnings multiple would be valued at $4.2 million if the weighted average earnings over the past three years were $0.6 million (seven times $0.6 million).

factor approach   Using the major aspects of a company to determine its worth

An extension of this method is the *factor approach*, wherein the following three major factors are used to determine value: earnings, dividend-paying capacity, and book value. Appropriate weights for the particular company being valued are developed and multiplied by the capitalized value, resulting in an overall weighted valuation. An example is indicated below:

Approach (in 000s)	Capitalized Value	Weight	Weighted Value
Earnings: $40 × 10	$400	0.4	$160
Dividends: $15 × 20	$300	0.4	$120
Book value: $600 × 0.4	$240	0.2	$48
Average $328			
10% discount $33			
Per share value $295			

liquidation value   Worth of a company if everything was sold today

A final valuation approach that gives the lowest value of the business is *liquidation value*. Liquidation value is often difficult to obtain, particularly when cost and losses must be estimated for selling the inventory, terminating employees, collecting accounts receivable, selling assets, and other closing-down activities. Nevertheless, it is also good for an investor to obtain a downside risk value in appraising a company.

General Valuation Method

One approach an entrepreneur can use to determine how much of the company a venture capitalist will want for a given amount of investment is indicated below:

$$\text{Venture capitalist ownership (\%)} = \frac{\text{VC \$ investment} \times \text{VC investment multiple desired}}{\text{Company's projected profits in year 5} \times \text{price earnings multiple of comparable company}}$$

Consider the following example:

A company needs $500,000 of venture-capital money.

The company is anticipating profits of $650,000.

The venture capitalist wants an investment multiple of 5 times.

The price earnings multiple of a similar company is 12.

According to the calculations below, the company would have to give up 32 percent ownership to obtain the needed funds as calculated below:

$$\frac{\$500,000 \times 5}{\$650,000 \times 12} = 32\%$$

A more accurate method for determining this percentage is given in Table 12.8. The step-by-step approach takes into account the time value of money in determining the appropriate investor's share. The following hypothetical example uses this step-by-step procedure. H&B Associates, a start-up manufacturing company, estimates it will earn $1 million after taxes on sales of $10 million. The company needs $800,000 now to reach that goal in five years. A similar company in the same industry is selling at 15 times earnings. A venture-capital firm, Davis Venture Partners, is interested in investing in the deal and requires a 50 percent compound rate of return on investment. What percentage of the company will have to be given up to obtain the needed capital?

$$\text{Present value} = \frac{\$1,000,000 \times 15 \text{ times earning multiple}}{(1 + 0.50)^5}$$

$$= \$1,975,000$$

$$\frac{\$800,000}{\$1,975,000} = 41\% \text{ will have to be given up}$$

Evaluation of an Internet Company

The valuation process for early-stage Internet companies is quite different from the traditional valuation process.[16] Traditionally, private-equity companies would examine historical financials and operations as part of a very quantitative process using such things as DCF, comparables, and/or multiples of EBITDA. Following this, the culture and management are examined in a more qualitative way. When institutional investors focus on earlier-stage companies—in particular Internet companies that have little or no history, no historical financials, and no comparables—a different approach has to be taken in the valuation process.

For these companies, the qualitative portion of due diligence carries much more weight than in other evaluations. The focus is more on the market itself. How big is

---

TABLE 12.8   Steps in Valuing Your Business and Determining Investors' Share

1. Estimate the earnings after taxes based on sales in the fifth year.
2. Determine an appropriate earnings multiple based on what similar companies are selling for in terms of their current earnings.
3. Determine the required rate of return.
4. Determine the funding needed.
5. Calculate, using the following formulas

$$\text{Present value} = \frac{\text{Future valuation}}{(1 + i)^n}$$

where:

$$\text{future valuation} = \text{total estimate value of company in 5 years}$$
$$i = \text{required rate of return}$$
$$n = \text{number of years}$$

$$\text{Investors' share} = \frac{\text{Initial funding}}{\text{Present value}}$$

it? How is it segmented? Who are the players? How will it evolve? Once these questions are resolved, the potential entrepreneurial company's financial projections are compared with the future market in terms of fit, realism, and opportunity. After getting comfortable with the market size and potential revenues of a company, the investor examines the management team. Is this a management team that will take the company "all the way"? Who will they need to bring in? How much should be set aside for ESOP? The more complete the management team is, the higher the valuation. If the management team is still thin, then a substantial portion of the company needs to be set aside to attract and retain good employees. It is difficult to generalize in terms of the product or service as different industries demand different valuations. For example, an infrastructure business is viewed very differently from a business-to-business firm.

After going through the process of deriving a value, the investor looks at all the opportunities available in the investor market. In today's market, there is a lot of money chasing high-quality deals, which is then guided by basic economic supply and demand. With more firms going after a deal, the price of a good deal gets bid up in favor of the entrepreneur. Overall, the value in early-stage technology companies is driven by a combination of market structure and management team maturity, modified by the supply and demand forces that exist in a market that is highly competitive for good, solid companies.

An entrepreneur seeking financing should keep in mind that this is a revolution quite similar to the industrial revolution 100 years ago and the biotechnology industry funding between 1978 and 1992. Markets are changing, and traditional systems are being turned upside down. Investors and entrepreneurs who have a sense of how this is going to occur and can predict the impact new technologies will have on traditional and newly formed markets are the ones who will be highly rewarded by the market.

DEAL STRUCTURE

In addition to valuating the company and determining the percentage of the company that may have to be given up to obtain funding, a critical concern for the entrepreneur is the *deal structure*, or the terms of the transaction between the entrepreneur

deal structure   The form of the transaction when money is obtained by a company

and the funding source.[17] In order to make the venture look as attractive as possible to potential sources of funds, the entrepreneur must understand the needs of the investors as well as his or her own needs. The needs of the funding sources include the rate of return required, the timing and form of return, the amount of control desired, and the perception of the risks involved in the particular funding opportunity. Whereas certain investors are willing to bear a significant amount of risk to obtain a significant rate of return, others want less risk and less return. Still other investors are more concerned about their amount of influence and control once the investment has been made.

The entrepreneur's needs revolve around similar concerns, such as the degree and mechanisms of control, the amount of financing needed, and the goals for the particular firm. Before negotiating the terms and structure of the deal with the venture capitalist, the entrepreneur should assess the relative importance of these concerns in order to negotiate where needed. Both the venture capitalist and entrepreneur should feel comfortable with the final deal structure, and a good working relationship needs to be established to deal with any future problems.

IN REVIEW

Summary

In financing a business, the entrepreneur determines the amount and timing of funds needed. Seed or start-up capital is the most difficult to obtain, with the most likely source being the informal risk-capital market (angels). These investors, who are wealthy individuals, average one or two deals per year, ranging from $10,000 to $500,000, and generally find their deals through referrals.

Although venture capital may be used in the first stage, it is primarily used in the second or third stage to provide working capital for growth or expansion. Venture capital is broadly defined as a professionally managed pool of equity capital. Since 1958, small business investment companies (SBICs) have combined private capital and government funds to finance the growth and start-up of small businesses. Private venture-capital firms have developed since the 1960s, with limited partners supplying the funding. At the same time, venture-capital divisions operating within major corporations began appearing. States also sponsor venture-capital funds to foster economic development.

In order to achieve the venture capitalist's primary goal of generating long-term capital appreciation through investments in business, three criteria are used: The company must have strong management; the product/marketing opportunity must be unique; and the capital appreciation must be significant, offering a 40 to 60 percent return on investment. The process of obtaining venture capital includes a preliminary screening, agreement on principal terms, due diligence, and final approval. Through a referral, entrepreneurs need to approach a potential venture capitalist with a professional business plan and a good oral presentation. After a successful initial presentation, the entrepreneur and investor agree on principal terms before the due diligence process is begun. Due diligence involves a detailed analysis of the markets, industry, and finances and can take up to three months. The final stage requires comprehensive documentation of the details of the transaction.

Valuing the company is of concern to the entrepreneur. Eight factors can be used as a basis for valuation: the nature and history of the business, the economic outlook, book value, future earnings, dividend-paying capacity, intangible assets, sales of stock, and market price of stocks of similar companies. Numerous valuation approaches can be used and include an assessment of comparable publicly held companies, present value of future cash flow, replacement value, book value, earnings approach, factor approach, and liquidation value.

In the end, the entrepreneur and investor must agree on the terms of the transaction, known as the deal. When care is taken in structuring the deal, both the entrepreneur and investor will maintain a good relationship while achieving their goals through the growth and profitability of the business.

Questions for Discussion

1. As an entrepreneur seeking venture capital, what factors would you take into account before approaching a venture-capital company?

2. Why would an entrepreneur look for an "angel" rather than approach a venture-capital company?
3. Given the angel's dissatisfaction with referral sources, what other methods might facilitate investment referrals?
4. Why is it important for the entrepreneur to establish a high degree of trust with the potential investor?
5. Study Table 12.8. What conclusions can you make regarding the investor's required percentage of ownership?

Key Terms

acquisition financing	liquidation value
book value	preliminary screening
business angels	present value of future cash flow
deal structure	private venture-capital firms
development financing	public-equity market
due diligence	referral sources
early-stage financing	replacement value
earnings approach	risk-capital markets
equity participation	SBIC firms
equity pool	state-sponsored venture-capital fund
factor approach	venture-capital market
general valuation approaches	venture-capital process
informal risk-capital market	

More Information—Net Addresses in This Chapter

Federal Express
www.fedex.com

General Dynamics
www.gdls.com

Monsanto
www.enviro-chem.com

New York Stock Exchange
www.nyse.com

University of Texas
www.utexas.edu

Selected Readings

Acs, Zoltan J.; and Fred A. Tarpley, Jr. (1998). The Angel Capital Electronic Network (ACE-Net). *Journal of Banking & Finance*, vol. 22, no. 6–8, pp. 793–97.

The article describes the ACE-Net—a listing service providing a network where small corporate offerings may be viewed over the Internet by accredited, high net-worth investors (angels).

Bergemann, Dirk; and Ulrich Hege. (1998). Venture Capital Financing, Moral Hazard, and Learning. *Journal of Banking & Finance*, vol. 22, no. 6–8, pp. 703–35.

Provision of venture capital in a dynamic agency model is considered. The value of the venture project is initially uncertain, and more information arrives by developing the project. The funds allocation and the learning process are subject to moral hazard. The optimal contract is a time-

varying share contract that provides intertemporal risk sharing between venture capitalist and entrepreneur. Relationship financing, including monitoring and the occasional replacement of the management, improves the efficiency of the financial contracting.

Bruton, Garry; Vance Fried, and Robert D. Hisrich. (1997). Venture Capitalist and CEO Dismissal. *Entrepreneurship Theory and Practice*, vol. 21, no. 3, pp. 41–54.

Recent exploratory research examined CEO dismissals by boards of directors on which venture capitalists serve. The findings demonstrate that it is a CEO's failure in strategic concerns, rather than operational ones, that can lead to CEO dismissal. In addition, replacing a CEO typically has a strong positive effect on new venture performance, whether replacement CEOs are internal or external to the venture.

Cable, Daniel M.; and Scott Shane. (1997). A Prisoner's Dilemma Approach to Entrepreneur-Venture Capitalist Relationships. *Academy of Management Review*, vol. 22, no. 1, pp. 142–76.

The article considers the implicit similarities between entrepreneur–venture capitalist relationships and the Prisoner's Dilemma framework. This paradigm is used to develop a conceptual model of entrepreneurs' and venture capitalists' decisions to cooperate.

Fried, V. H.; and R. D. Hisrich. (Fall 1988). Venture Capital Research: Past, Present, and Future. *Entrepreneurship: Theory and Practice*, vol. 13, no. 1, pp. 15–28.

Since 1980, venture capital has become an important source of funding for entrepreneurs. For this reason, it has also emerged as an area of research activity and academic interest. This paper surveys the current efforts being made in this field of research and suggests ideas for further research about venture capital. A model of the venture capital process is derived, and advice is given to improve the technology of future research.

Hisrich, R. D.; and A. D. Jankowicz. (January 1990). Intuition in Venture Capital Decisions: An Exploratory Study Using a New Technique. *Journal of Business Venturing*, vol. 5, no. 1, pp. 49–63.

Discusses a study that used the repertory grid to examine the intuition involved in entrepreneurial decision making. Investment decisions can be grouped into one of three areas: management, unique opportunity, and appropriate return. Despite the general trends listed, it was shown by cluster analysis that each venture capitalist had a different way of structuring the intuition needed for an investment decision.

Lerner, Joshua. (1998). "Angel" Financing and Public Policy: An Overview. *Journal of Banking & Finance*, vol. 22, no. 6–8, pp. 773–83.

The article provides an overview of the motivations for efforts to encourage individual (angel) investors. It assesses the underlying challenges that the financing of young growth firms poses, the ways that specialized financial intermediaries address them, and the rationales for public efforts to encourage angel investors.

Mitra, Devashis. (2000). The Venture Capital Industry in India. *Journal of Small Business Management*, vol. 38, no. 2, pp. 67–79.

The venture capital industry in India is examined using information gathered from several sources.

Prowse, Stephen. (1998). Angel Investors and the Market for Angel Investments. *Journal of Banking & Finance*, vol. 22, pp. 785–92.

This study finds that the angel market can be very heterogeneous and localized. Some common characteristics of angels and their ways of selecting and monitoring investments are identified. Their behavior is compared to venture capital limited partnerships in the more formal market for venture capital.

Shepherd, Dean A.; Richard Ettenson; and Andrew Croch. (2000). The Venture Strategy and Profitability: A Venture Capitalist's Assessment. *Journal of Business Venturing*, vol. 15, no. 5–6, pp. 449–67.

This study used theoretically justified criteria from industrial organization strategy research and applies it to a new domain, namely, venture capitalists' decision making in the assessment of new venture profitability.

Wright, Mike; and Ken Robbie. (1998). Venture Capital and Private Equity: A Review and Synthesis. *Journal of Business Finance & Accounting*, vol. 25, no. 5–6, pp. 521–70.

Literature on venture capital and private equity is reviewed by adopting a framework that combines industry/market and firm levels of analysis. Industry level issues relate to rivalry between firms, the power of suppliers and customers, and the threats from new entrants and substitutes. Firm level issues concern deal generation, initial and second screening, valuation and due diligence, deal approval and structuring, postcontractual monitoring, investment realization, and entrepreneurs' exit and recontracting with venture capitalists.

Endnotes

1. *Report of the Use of the Rule 146 Exemption in Capital Formation* (Washington, DC: Directorate of Economic Policy Analysis, Securities and Exchange Commission, 1983).
2. *An Analysis of Regulation D* (Washington, DC: Directorate of Economic Policy Analysis, Securities and Exchange Commission, 1984).
3. Charles River Associates, Inc., *An Analysis of Capital Market Imperfections* (Washington, DC: National Bureau of Standards, February 1976).
4. W. E. Wetzel, Jr., "Entrepreneurs, Angels, and Economic Renaissance," in *Entrepreneurship, Intrapreneurship, and Venture Capital* R. D. Hisrich, ed., (Lexington, MA: Lexington Books, 1986), pp. 119–40. Other information on angels and their investments can be found in W. E. Wetzel, Jr., "Angels and Informal Risk Capital," *Sloan Management Review* 24 (Summer 1983), pp. 23–24; and W. E. Wetzel, Jr., "The Informal Venture Capital Market: Aspects of Scale and Market Efficiency," *Journal of Business Venturing* (Fall 1987), pp. 299–314.
5. R. B. Avery and G. E. Elliehausen, "Financial Characteristics of High Income Families," *Federal Reserve Bulletin*, Washington, DC (March 1986).
6. M. Gannon, "Financing Purgatory: An Emerging Class of Investors Is Beginning to Fill the Nether Regions of Start-Up Financing—the Murky World between the Angels and the Venture Capitalists," *Venture Capital Journal* (May 1999), pp. 40–42.
7. S. Prowse, "Angel Investors and the Market for Angel Investments," *Journal of Banking and Finance* 23 (1998), pp. 785–92.
8. D. C. Foss, "Venture Capital Network: The First Six Months of the Experiment," *Proceedings*, Babson Entrepreneurial Research Conference, Philadelphia (April 1985), pp. 314–24.
9. Aspects of venture capital are discussed in J. Timmons and W. D. Bygrave, "Venture Capital's Role in Financing Innovation for Economic Growth," *Journal of Business Venturing 1* (Spring 1986), pp. 161–76; R. B. Robinson, Jr., "Emerging Strategies in the Venture Capital Industry," *Journal of Business Venturing* 2 (Winter 1987), pp. 53–78; and H. H. Stevenson, D. F. Muzyka, and J. A. Timmons, "Venture Capital in Transition: A Monte Carlo Simulation of Changes in Investment Patterns," *Journal of Business Venturing* 2 (Winter 1987), pp. 103–22.
10. For the role of SBICs, see Farrell K. Slower, "Growth Looms for SBICs," *Venture* (October 1985), pp. 46–47; and M. H. Fleischer, "The SBIC 100—More Deals for the Bucks," *Venture* (October 1985), pp. 50–54.
11. Most of the information in this section, as well as a much more detailed breakdown, can be found in the National Venture Capital Association, 1999 National Venture Association Yearbook.
12. For a thorough discussion of the venture-capital process, see B. Davis, "Role of Venture Capital in the Economic Renaissance of an Area," in R. D. Hisrich, ed., *Entrepreneurship, Intrapreneurship, and Venture Capital* (Lexington, MA: Lexington Books, 1986),

pp. 107–18; Robert D. Hisrich and A. D. Jankowicz, "Intuition in Venture Capital Decisions: An Exploratory Study Using a New Technique," *Journal of Business Venturing* 5 (January 1990), pp. 49–63; Robert D. Hisrich and Vance H. Fried, "The Role of the Venture Capitalist in the Management of Entrepreneurial Enterprises," *Journal of International Business and Entrepreneurship* 1, no. 1 (June 1992), pp. 75–106; Vance H. Fried, Robert D. Hisrich, and Amy Polonchek, "Research Note: Venture Capitalists' Investment Criteria: A Replication," *Journal of Small Business Finance* 3, no. 1 (Fall 1993), pp. 37–42; and Vance H. Fried and Robert D. Hisrich, "The Venture Capitalist: A Relationship Investor," *California Management Review* 37, no. 2 (Winter 1995), pp. 101–13.

13. A discussion of some of the important sectors in this decision process can be found in I. MacMillan, L. Zemann, and Subba Narasimba, "Criteria Distinguishing Successful from Unsuccessful Ventures in the Venture Screening Process," *Journal of Business Venturing* 2 (Spring 1987), pp. 123–38; Robert D. Hisrich and Vance H. Fried, "Towards a Model of Venture Capital Investment Decision-Making," *Financial Management* 23, no. 3 (Fall 1994), pp. 28–37; and Vance H. Fried, B. Elonso, and Robert D. Hisrich, "How Venture Capital Firms Differ," *Journal of Business Venturing* 10, no. 2 (March 1995), pp. 157–79.

14. A complete listing of venture-capitalist firms in the United States and throughout the world can be found in *Venture's Guide to International Venture Capital* (New York: Simon and Schuster, 1985); and E. S. Pratt, *Guide to Venture Capital Sources* (Wellesley, MA: Capital Publishing Corporation, 1995).

15. A. V. Bruno and T. T. Tyebjee, "The One That Got Away: A Study of Ventures Rejected by Venture Capitalists," *Proceedings*, 1983 Babson Research Conference, Wellesley, MA (1983), pp. 289–306.

16. The material in this section is adapted from material provided by John R. Farrall, associate, Crystal Internet Venture Funds.

17. For a discussion of some problems with venture-capital deals, see "Why Smart Companies Are Saying No to Venture Capitalists," *Inc.* (August 1984), pp. 65–75.

CASE IIIa   The Winslow Clock Company

For the third time, Dr. Winslow sat up in bed, flipped on the light, and reached for The Winslow Clock Company business plan. Maybe reading through it again would calm his growing fears. As he flipped through the pages, he recalled again all the years of thinking, tinkering, and discovery that had gone into the development of his alarm clock. How could something he spent so much time and energy on be wrong? It was such a good idea, this "throwable" alarm clock: Millions of Americans would want to get this kind of revenge on their daily call to the rat race. And, in its final design, it contained all kinds of computer-age technology. Surely, the investors tomorrow will love it!

What had happened to his confidence? He had been sure enough to invest all his savings in the clock's development. What a time to get second thoughts! Didn't he use the best technical help available to design the clock and plan the production and marketing? Maybe that was his problem—too much dependence on "experts." Being a practicing psychiatrist, he considered himself a good judge of character and motivation, but maybe his obsession with his clock had clouded his perception. Should he take more time to personally study the different production and marketing scenarios? He didn't have any more time, if he wanted to get production started in time to hit the Christmas season. Should he wait another year, or risk going to market at a slow time of year, or. . . ?

The more he thought, the more the doubts and worries grew. He had to put a stop to this pointless mental exercise. The business plan he held in his hands was what he had to sell tomorrow at the meeting, so he'd better have confidence in it. If things went badly, then he could think about changes. For now, he would read over the business plan for the Winslow Clock Company (which follows) just once more, concentrating on the favorable arguments his business "experts" had made.

SUMMARY

The attached five-year business plan for The Winslow Clock Company is based primarily on the estimated potential of the company's first product, an alarm clock designed and patented by Dr. Michael Winslow, a psychiatrist by profession. He expected the sales and profits generated by this product to reach $8.5 million and $1.5 million, respectively, within three years, which would provide sufficient resources to enable the company to expand its line into related products now under consideration.

History of the Product

Under development for 10 years, the concept for the clock stems from Dr. Winslow's thought that it would be fun to have the liberty to "get back at" the alarm that so readily awakens everyone each morning. The "fun" part—and what makes the alarm unique—is that you throw it to turn it off.

Development of the microchip and related technology in recent years has made the design of such a clock possible at a reasonable cost. The technical assistance on the clock was provided by students at the MIT Innovation Center under the guidance of its director. The business and marketing planning for the clock was done with the help of Boston College MBA candidates at the Small Business Development Center under the direction of its faculty associate.

In addition, Dr. Winslow has contracted with a number of professional consultants in the areas of product design, product engineering, marketing and advertising, production, legal matters, and accounting.

Market Acceptance

Early reaction from such major retailers as Bloomingdale's and Hammacher Schlemmer in New York has been very positive, thus supporting the belief that the targeted levels of sales are achievable.

Thus, in what might otherwise be considered a mature market, new design and technology are eagerly sought by retailers and customers anxious to provide or find a refreshing selection of alternatives. The company's projected level of sales in its first year represents less than 1 percent of this growing segment of the U.S. clock market.

Competition

Although several major manufacturers account for most clock sales (with Japanese manufacturers dominating the sale of quartz movements), there is nevertheless a significant annual volume attributable to smaller specialty designers, most of whom purchase the clock movements on an OEM (original equipment manufacturer) basis from the larger producers and concentrate on unique housing designs.

Seiko, the company supplying the movement for Dr. Winslow's clock, has made impressive strides in the United States in the last four years by increasing its annual OEM business from 400,000 to 2 million units. Besides selling its own Seiko and Picco brands, it is developing a reputable supplier business. This strategy allows Seiko to enjoy some of the profit opportunity created by an expanded market without all the marketing costs and risks.

In addition, a number of large retailers contract with the major manufacturers for private-label production. This somewhat fragmented structure has created profitable opportunities for products designed for niches within the large clock market.

The question arises, If the product is attractive enough to create a niche in the market, how soon will it have competition? The concept of a "throwable" alarm and several components designed specifically for the product are patented. In addition, it would require some time and expense for potential competitors to develop the impact switch and the microchip used in Dr. Winslow's clock.

Financial Projections: Opportunities and Risks

Financial projections for the first five years of the company are summarized below. (Sales are based on only the first product, to be introduced in 1986.)

	Year 1	Year 2	Year 3	Year 4	Year 5
Unit sales (000s)	50	150	200	150	125
Selling price	$42.50	$42.50	$42.50	$40.00	$40.00
Net sales (000s)	$2125	$6375	$8500	$6000	$5000
Net profit (000s)	$333	$823*	$1503	$781	$496
Profit ratio	16.0%	13.0%	17.7%	13.0%	10.0%

*Assuming $650,000 term loan (plus interest) paid back in December.

Since components and subassemblies would be purchased rather than manufactured by the company, and then assembled and shipped by an outside contractor, the capital investment required is minimal, estimated at less than $50,000, the majority of which would be for tooling. Another $50,000 for start-up expenses, prototypes, and preproduction operating expenses would also be required in the first two months of 2000.

By March, however, the commitment increases. Because of the company's lack of credit history, all indications suggest that suppliers will require letters of credit to accompany the $814,000 in parts orders placed between March and September of 2000, when shipments are expected to begin. In addition, operating expenses between March and October are forecasted at $176,000.

Given the projected level of sales in the first two years, the company is seeking equity capital of $600,000 as early as possible in 2000. An additional term loan of

EXHIBIT 1

THE WINSLOW CLOCK COMPANY
Pro Forma Income Statements
Five-Year Projection

	Year 1	Year 2	Year 3	Year 4	Year 5
Unit Sales	50,000	150,000	200,000	150,000	125,000
Price	$42.50	$42.50	$42.50	$40.00	$40.00
Net sales (000s)	$2,125	$6,375	$8,500	$6,000	$5,000
Bad debt allowance (2%)	43	128	170	120	100
Adjusted net sales	2,082	6,247	8,330	5,880	4,900
Cost of goods sold	1,093	3,253	4,630	3,655	3,267
Gross margin	989	2,994	3,700	2,225	1,633
Operating costs	323	552	695	663	642
E.B.I.T.	666	2,442	3,005	1,562	991
Taxes (50%)	333	1,221	1,502	781	495
Net income	$ 333	$1,221	$1,503	$ 781	$ 496

approximately $650,000 would be needed by June to carry financing and operating costs through year's end.

It should be emphasized that although this combined cash injection of $1.2 million is at apparent risk for at least the six to eight months prior to the beginning of shipments (and, of course, beyond), two factors diminish this risk. First, the initial selling effort in the spring of 2000 to secure orders for the Christmas season should provide a clear indication of market acceptance by the end of April. The long lead time required to order components then becomes a positive factor. Orders for 40,000 of the first season's production of 50,000 units could be canceled without penalty a month in advance on standard items such as the clock movement. This alone would save almost $730,000. In addition, many operating expenses could be curtailed accordingly and alternative marketing plans put into place. (Direct mail-order marketing, for example, is an approach that will be explored from the beginning anyway and, in a downside case, certainly would be a viable alternative.)

The second factor that diminishes the risk is that low fixed costs allow the break-even point to be projected at 16,000 units, which should be achieved in October, the second month of actual shipments.

EXHIBIT 2

THE WINSLOW CLOCK COMPANY
Pro Forma Balance Sheet
As of December 31 ($000s)

	Year 1	Year 2	Year 3	Year 4	Year 5	Year 6
Assets						
Cash	5	203	256	1,019	2,722	3,539
Accounts receivable	—	1,345	2,044	2,726	1,924	1,283
Inventory						
Finished goods	—	73	44	48	53	58
Work-in-process	—	106	—	78	—	—
Raw materials	55	—	141	155	171	188
Net fixed assets	40	36	32	29	26	24
Total assets	100	1,763	2,517	4,055	4,896	5,092
Liabilities						
Accounts payable	40	50	141	155	171	181
Accrued liabilities	—	—	560	581	626	309
Est'd tax liability	—	70	—	—	—	—
Short-term debt	—	650	—	—	—	—
Long-term debt	—	—	—	—	—	—
Common stock	—	600	600	600	600	600
Paid-in capital						
(M. Winslow)	60	60	60	60	60	60
Retained earnings	—	333	1,156	2,659	3,439	3,935
Total liabilities	100	1,763	2,517	4,055	4,896	5,092

According to its projected cash flow, the company should be able to repay its term loan in full within 18 months. From that point on, it can fund its continuing operations from the generated working capital.

The returns on investment are calculated at 19, 33, and 37 percent in the first three years, respectively, with returns on net worth at 34, 46, and 45 percent. Net present value for the original investors would be $1.7 million, based on five years of net cash flow and not including the salable value of the firm or its continuing earning power after that time. Payback is expected in one year, based on the forecast of sales and profits. Specific financial details are found in Exhibits 1 through 7.

EXHIBIT 3

THE WINSLOW CLOCK COMPANY

Statement of Sources and Uses of Funds*
Year Ended December 31 ($000s)

	Year 1	Year 2	Year 3	Year 4	Year 5
Sources					
Funds provided by operations					
Net income after taxes	333	823	1,503	780	496
Plus depreciation	4	4	3	3	2
Inc.—accounts payable	10	91	14	16	17
Inc.—accrued liabilities	—	560	21	45	—
Inc.—taxes payable	70	—	—	—	—
Inc.—common stock	600	—	—	—	—
Inc.—short-term debt	650				
Dec.—accounts receivable	—	—	—	802	641
Dec.—inventories	—	—	—	57	—
Total sources	1,667	1,478	1,541	1,703	1,156
Uses					
Inc.—cash	198	53	763	1,703	817
Inc.—accounts receivable	1,345	699	682	—	—
Inc.—inventories	124	6	96	—	22
Dec.—accrued liabilities	—	—	—	—	317
Dec.—taxes payable	—	70	—	—	—
Dec.—short-term debt	—	640	—	—	—
Total uses	1,667	1,478	1,541	1,703	1,156

*Based on pro forma balance sheets and income statements

EXHIBIT 4   Break-Even Quantity Calculation

1. Contribution margin per unit is estimated to be $20.81 in 2000 and 2001. (See unit sales, cost, margin analysis.)

2. Fixed costs for unit sales in the first year of 50,000 units are estimated to be $332,910, including $10,200 paid for prototype development in 1999. Break-even quantity would be $332,910/20.81 = 16,000 units.

3. Based on the expected seasonality of sales in the first year of selling, the break-even point should be reached in mid-October 2000, in the second full month of product shipments.

INDUSTRY INFORMATION

The clock market in the United States has been growing at a rate of between 8 and 10 percent per year, with significantly higher growth (three times the industry average) recorded in the segments where innovative design or a technological change has been offered. The recent introduction of battery-operated quartz mechanisms combined with sleek styling to create lightweight, portable, wireless clocks has led to at least a 25 percent annual growth rate for decorative or kitchen wall clocks and to almost a 29 percent increase for alarm clocks.

Clocks are in most households and constitute an enduring and important retail gift category. As with many items that are so inherently useful that they might be considered a household necessity, the greater the opportunity to differentiate the product, the greater the ability to segment the market by appealing to consumers through unique designs that are fashioned to suit a wide variety of tastes and income levels.

A handful of major competitors serve as the dominant force in the industry and often not only sell their own brands but make private-label brands for large retailers as well. (Seiko, for example, produces the private-label quartz alarm clocks for both JCPenney and Sears.) As a result, clock movements are inexpensive and readily available, which in turn spawns a significant opportunity for a number of smaller companies to specialize in unique designs that range from the very inexpensive to one-of-a-kind collector's items.

Clocks are sold through a variety of retail outlets that include mass merchandisers, department and specialty stores, furniture and interior design stores, jewelry stores, shops that deal exclusively in clocks, and museum gift stores.

Catalog sales are also an important means of reaching the clock consumer. Furthermore, within a department store, clocks can be found in various departments

---

EXHIBIT 5   Financial Data Backup

Unit sales, cost, margin analysis	
Retail suggested list	$85.00
Dealer margin	42.50
Mfr. selling price (dealer cost)	42.50
Cost of goods sold*	14.60
Gross margin	$27.90
Other variable costs*	
Warranty	.05
Quality control allowance	.29
Shipping & handling contribution	.20
Co-op advertising allowance	2.13
Selling commissions	4.25
Designer/developer fee	.17
Subtotal variable costs	7.09
Net margin	$20.81
Note: Total cost of goods	$21.69

*Backup detail provided.

that include gifts, luggage, electronics, fine collectibles, furniture, jewelry, and occasionally even in their own clock department.

This diversity of product as well as placement makes the clock market a natural arena in which independent sales representatives may operate. This fact simplifies, to some extent, the problems that the smaller producers face in trying to get their product to the national marketplace without incurring a disproportionate expense for the hiring, training, and support of a sales force.

It is apparent, then, that the market for clocks has ample room for product differentiation. Dr. Winslow's clock, we believe, presents an exciting opportunity to capitalize on a segment of this significant market.

EXHIBIT 6   Financial Data Backup

Cost of goods sold analysis		
Item		
Movement*	$2.77	$ 3.87
(and circuit board)	$1.10	
Chip (production model)		$ .79
Capacitors (3)		.30
Impact switch		1.03
Battery holder		.20
Photo transistor		.30
Ball		.87
Molded sphere		.20
Velcro®		.07
Molded cube (housing)		2.00
Batteries		.95
Face, crystal, hands, etc.		.60
Board		.40
Board assembly		1.00
Feet		.05
Speaker, lamp, socket		1.08
Assembly		.50
Product subtotal		$14.21
Package (inc. inside corrugated)		.24
Printed inserts		.05
Portion (1/6) master carton		.10
Package subtotal		$14.60

*Add $0.30 premium per unit for air shipments.

Note: Tooling not amortized in these calculations because first production run estimated to be 10K units; all other costs listed here based on runs of 100K.
Tooling at this point treated as a capital expenditure and listed under fixed costs.

THE PRODUCT: PRESENT AND FUTURE

The product will first be described and then discussed in terms of its future potential.

Product Description

The battery-operated quartz alarm clock consists of two basic parts, the first of which is a lightweight black foam ball, approximately 4 inches in diameter, that contains the "brains" of the clock—a microchip, circuit board, impact switch, small batteries, and the audio device for the alarm. These are held inside a plastic capsule that is secured by a Velcro enclosure within the larger foam ball. The second part of the clock is the quartz movement that is housed in a handsomely styled cube of molded plastic.

What makes the clock functionally unique is that throwing the ball turns off the alarm. Great care was taken to use materials that have virtually no chance of damaging the wall or any other object. The specifically designed impact switch is sensitive enough that even a light impact will stop the alarm. On the other hand, a throw of considerable force will not disturb the contents of the inner capsule. Two insurance companies specializing in product liability testing have been consulted. They both feel that the product is safe and free enough from liability risk that they have quoted The Winslow Clock Company the minimum premium for liability insurance.

EXHIBIT 7   Critical Risks and Problems

Listed below are those areas of particular concern and importance to the management.

1. *Timing* will play a critical role in the success of this venture. The key variables are:
   - Product readiness
   - Financing
   - Approach to the marketplace
   - Production, from delivery of components to assembly, inventory, and shipping procedures

2. *Projections* used are "best" estimates, and all financial needs and operating costs have been based on what is considered to be the most likely volume of sales achievable. Because selling activities will begin early in 2000, reaction from the marketplace should be clear by late spring. Decisions can still be made to cut back—or to gear up—for the 2000 season.

    The first commitment to Seiko for 10,000 units (cost of $4.17 each) will have been made by mid-March, and estimates for the entire year will be in their production plan by then. While cutbacks can be made as late as a month in advance, increased production might be a problem since it would bump into Seiko's heaviest production season.

3. *Financing* would be another major consideration if sales were much in excess of expectations, particularly because we must assume that early orders are going to require an accompanying letter of credit. For this and other reasons, the marketing plan is meant to guard against some of these problems and is specifically geared to reach upscale stores and catalogs that will commit early to carry the "limited production" of the first year.

4. *Ironing out production* and assembly problems will be of major importance in June and July. Although the process is not complex, it will be totally new, and the production rate is currently scheduled at 5,000 units in July and 10,000 in August in order to meet anticipated shipping requirements in September and to build minimal inventory requirements. For these reasons, selection of an experienced production manager will be critical.

Several achievements have made the clock technologically possible. There is no need for an electrical connection between the clock base and the ball because an ultrasound device signals the alarm to go off. A receiver in the inner capsule "reads" the signal and triggers the humorous crescendo of the alarm; upon "advice" from the impact switch, a satisfying tone of demise is produced when the alarm hits the wall. In addition, a timing device has been built into the circuitry that automatically shuts off the alarm after one minute if the ball is not thrown.

The overall design and finish of the clock are clean and sophisticated in order to eliminate any sense of gimmickry that might lessen the perceived value of the clock. This elegant styling and the sophisticated electronics, combined with both the psychological satisfaction and the sense of fun and playfulness inherent in being able to throw one's alarm clock, should appeal to a significant cross section of consumers, from executives to athletes. The product has a strong appeal to retailers as well, who, in the words of a Bloomingdale's executive, look for "something refreshing and new to pull people into the stores."

Technical specifications of the product are as follows:

Dimensions: Base—$4\frac{1}{2}'' \times 4\frac{1}{2}'' \times 4\frac{1}{2}''$ Ball—$4\frac{1}{2}''$ diameter

Color: Model A—white clock housing with black face, charcoal ball, white, yellow, and red hands

Model B—black housing with other colors in Model A

Accuracy of movement: $+/-$ 20 seconds per month

Hands: Luminescent minute and hour hands

Foam ball: 35 ppi Crest Foam

Future Potential

The new technologic innovations that have emerged during the development of this first product have significance for the future of the company as well. First, extensions of the basic concept are possible in a variety of clocks with other features. Obvious examples are clock radios and snooze alarms. In addition, as production quantities increase, specialty designs for the premium market become possible at reasonable cost.

A family of related products such as posters, a wall-mountable target, and other clocks—all dealing with the frustration people feel with time, alarm clocks, and schedules—are natural offshoots of the throwable alarm, and their development is currently being explored.

MARKETING PLAN AND STRATEGY

Given the clock's unique function, design, and appeal, the first year's marketing plan will focus on placing the clock in upscale department stores, clock specialty stores, and catalogs that reach upper-middle-income and upper-income executives and families. The early strategy is to keep the clock out of the mass market and discounters' trade, instead making it readily available to consumers more interested in its characteristics and uniqueness than its suggested list price of $85. The sales, cost, and margin analysis is based on the assumption that the suggested list price of $85 and dealer price of $42.50 will be held constant for three years. The goal is to introduce the product with a large enough margin for the dealer in the higher-end retail and catalog business to make an adequate return and to allow the company to recapture its fixed costs as quickly as possible.

While the suggested list and dealer prices at this time are expected to remain the same in the second and third years, part of the strategy will be to refine the production and assembly costs, negotiate volume discounts with suppliers, and devise other cost-saving measures in order to offer more marketing support to the expanded dealer base without sacrificing profitability. If necessary, cost-saving measures will be adopted that will make it possible to lower the price dramatically as a means of defense against competitors in years 3 and 4 of the product's life.

Sales Tactics

The principals of the firm will contact potential buyers directly at first, beginning in early 2000 when there are still budgets available for merchandise for the 2000 Christmas season. Sales in 2000 are planned at 50,000 units, on a first-come, first-served basis, unless a retailer will commit for a guaranteed order prior to June 1. A sales rep organization will also be retained to continue these early sales efforts and to expand distribution after the first season. A commission averaging 10 percent of the dealer price per unit has been incorporated into the cost of sales to cover the activities of these sales reps.

In addition, an experienced, full-time, in-house sales manager will coordinate the selling and promotional activities of the independent rep organization. Other responsibilities of the sales manager will include (1) making direct contact with buyers, (2) making direct contact with sales reps and evaluating their performance, (3) coordinating the marketing support and promotional activities of the sales rep force, and (4) developing other possible avenues for marketing the company's products. The direct marketing approach referred to earlier is an obvious example of this.

Advertising and Publicity

A publicity campaign aimed at generating interest in the clock's development, its state-of-the-art technology, and its founder's concept of "functional fun" will be launched in early fall 2000. This publicity and accompanying new product announcements will target the "executive toy" purchaser.

In addition, a print ad campaign slated for the 2000 Christmas retail market and a cooperative advertising plan to help participating dealers are expected to aid sell-through in the clock's first major season on the market.

Expanded advertising marketing support for the second season will include the following: attendance at trade shows (notably the Consumer Electronics Show, the National Hardwares Show, and at least one of the major gift shows); an in-store promotion plan highlighted by a 90-second video spot designed and produced by a Clio-award-winning studio based in Cambridge, Massachusetts; continuation of the co-op advertising plan; and an overall advertising budget slated at 5 percent of anticipated sales for the year.

OPERATIONS MANAGEMENT

Since all assembly and subassembly operations will be handled by independent contractors, with final shipment emanating from the final point of assembly, the need for an office, a production staff, and overhead would be kept to a minimum.

Although Dr. Winslow will oversee all operations, his regular staff will supervise the critical functions of marketing and business development, administration (including office management, billing, accounts receivable and payable), and production management (the control of all facets of outside assembly and vendor supplies and relations).

Marketing and business development (including sales in the initial stages) would be managed by Ms. Kristen Jones, who has 15 years of experience in marketing and finance in both domestic and international operations for Polaroid Corporation. She has an MBA from Boston College and a BA from Brown University.

The production management area (including product engineering) is currently handled in an advisory capacity by several consultants, including Mr. Steve Canon (see enclosed profile). As the company approaches actual production (now slated for June/July 2000 start-up), a full-time production manager will be hired. Several candidates are presently being considered for this position.

Strong relationships with highly responsible subcontractors have already been established. These include Seiko, for the precision quartz movement and related technology; Rogers Foam in Somerville, Massachusetts, for the ball; Aerodyne Control Corporation in Farmingdale, New York, for the switch; and Santin Engineering in Beverly, Massachusetts, for the plastic molding.

An outside contractor in the Boston area will handle the assembly operation, which includes packaging and shipment to fulfill sales orders. Several companies are being considered and will be submitting quotes on the specifications early in 2000. A decision is expected to be made by the beginning of February. The possibility of an assembly operation outside the United States will be investigated as a cost-saving measure once production is being handled efficiently here.

The administrative position will have the responsibility of handling all office functions, including billing, receivables, credit, and payables. Two candidates are now being considered. It will be important to fill this function as soon as possible, even if it is on a part-time basis for the first few months. The candidates are available for such a schedule, if necessary.

Other critical areas that are now, and will continue to be, handled by consultants are advertising (including sales promotion and publicity)—Bill Barlow—and product design—John Edwards.

MANAGEMENT

Dr. Michael Winslow is the inventor of the clock and founder and president of the company. His profession is psychiatric medicine, and he is currently practicing at the Boston Evening Medical Center in Boston, Massachusetts, as well as at the Matthew Thornton Health Plan in Nashua, New Hampshire. He also maintains his own private practice. Dr. Winslow earned his undergraduate BS degree at the University of Michigan and his medical degree at Boston University Medical School.

It was while he was a resident in psychiatry that he conceived of the idea for the clock. He first pursued the concept as a hobby, trying to find a way to throw the clock without damaging either it or the surface it hit. Within the last two years, as it became apparent that it would be possible to create and produce such a clock at a reasonable cost, further development of the idea became another full-time occupation for Dr. Winslow.

Though he is a man of great energy, part of Dr. Winslow's success in bringing the product from the initial concept to the prototype stage lies in his effectiveness in finding and utilizing the outside resources he has needed. He has also had enough confidence in, and received enough encouragement about, the ultimate marketability of the product that he has invested his own savings in development costs, a sum of approximately $60,000 to date.

Because his profession is very important to him, Dr. Winslow intends to continue his private medical practice. But he will also serve as president of Winslow Clocks, hiring professional managers to run the day-to-day operations for him and using consultants in those aspects of the business where a particular expertise is needed.

Kristen Jones—following a year at the Museum of Fine Arts, Boston, as an assistant to the head of research—joined Polaroid Corporation, Cambridge, Massachusetts, where her experience and responsibilities grew over a broad range of marketing and finance assignments.

During the years in which Polaroid's International Division grew from $30 million to $350 million in annual sales, Jones was responsible for sales planning and forecasting for all its amateur photographic products. Later, as a financial analyst, her job was to assess the company's 130 distributor markets around the world for potential as profitable wholly owned subsidiaries, as well as to carry out new product profitability analyses.

She then joined the domestic marketing division, where her assignments ranged from sales administration to marketing manager in charge of a test program to assess the potential of selling the company's instant movie system on a direct basis. In her last position as national merchandising manager, she created and managed the merchandising programs to support the national sales efforts for all consumer products.

In February 1982, she took advantage of the company's voluntary severance program to complete work on her master's degree in business administration at Boston College. Ms. Jones earned her BA degree at Brown University in Providence, Rhode Island.

Steve Canon is a consultant, teacher, and businessman whose broad range of experience covers many aspects of new product design, development, and marketing. He presently has over 35 products of his own on the market and also teaches marketing and business law at the Rhode Island School of Design. In addition, he published a book in the spring of 1986 that deals with invention, product development, and marketing.

Among his numerous accomplishments, he has taught product design at Harvard, Yale, Princeton, and the Rhode Island School of Design. He has won awards for his contributions to the field, including two from Ford Motor Company for innovative product development. Canon has appeared on television talk shows, as both guest and host, discussing product marketing.

Although his primary contributions to The Winslow Clock Company are in the fields of product development and manufacturing/production, his knowledge of new product introductions has been very helpful in a number of other areas as well.

Bill Barlow has been president and creative director of Bill Barlow Advertising since 1978. Prior to establishing his own company, Barlow was director of advertising for Bose Corporation in Framingham, Massachusetts, a national sales promotion manager and creative director at Polaroid Corporation, and a creative supervisor for New York Telephone in New York City.

In his four years as an entrepreneur, Barlow has built an impressive list of clients and has won numerous awards and honors for excellence in advertising. His current list of clients includes Polaroid Corporation, Hewlett-Packard, Data General, Bose, and Anaconda-Ericsson Telecommunications.

He will be responsible for advertising, promotional support materials, and publicity for The Winslow Clock Company.

John Edwards is the founder of Edwards Design Associates, Inc., a firm that specializes in industrial design, product development, and graphic design. For the past seven years, this company has provided an integrated approach to the design of both products and the packaging and collateral materials to support the products.

Among his clients, primarily in the fields of consumer products and finance, are Polaroid, Bose, Revlon, Chaps, Helena Rubinstein, Avco, Putnam Funds, and Hallmark.

Edwards has a BS degree in mechanical engineering from Worcester Polytechnic Institute and an MS degree in industrial design from the Illinois Institute of Technology.

In addition to designing Dr. Winslow's product, Edwards has also provided invaluable help in finding sources for the manufacture of several components, for injection molding and for packaging.

CASE IIIb   Airview Mapping Inc.

In early March 1994, Rick Tanner, the principal of Airview Mapping Inc., started drafting plans for the upcoming summer season. For him, late winter typically involved making sales calls on the company's established and potential clients for the purpose of determining the expected demand for his services and then drafting his sales forecasts for the upcoming year.

Airview had traditionally dominated the aerial surveying markets of Central and Eastern Canada until recently being faced with increasing competition in its traditional territories presented by other air surveyors from across Canada. The protracted recession of the early 1990s, combined with the antideficit measures introduced by all levels of government, had reduced the overall demand for geomatic services in Canada, thereby producing significant overcapacity in the industry, including the particular markets in which Airview was involved.

This situation had already reduced the company's profits, but the real threat lay in the fact that the new competitors, once established in Airview's region, would stay there, permanently capturing a significant share of the Central Canadian market. These competitors, typically larger than Airview, could expand their market coverage, even if it meant creating a temporary operating base in a distant location. At the same time, their home markets were extremely difficult for small companies from other regions to penetrate due to their fierce price competition.

Rick realized that his company might face difficult times if he could not redirect his attention to some new areas of opportunity. His view was that these opportunities had to be found in international markets. He had already gathered some information on several foreign markets that looked promising from the company's perspective. The time was now appropriate to review the overall situation and decide whether to attempt penetrating any of the identified foreign markets and, if so, what entry strategy to choose.

THE COMPANY

Airview Mapping Inc. was incorporated in November 1979 by a group of former employees of Aerosurvey Corporation Ltd., with Tom Denning and Rick Tanner as the principal shareholders of the new entity. For the first two years, the company operated without an aircraft, providing mapping services based on externally developed photogrammetric images to clients in Central Canada. Airview's early success provided sufficient capital to acquire an aircraft and a photographic processing laboratory, which in 1981 was initially placed under the company's subsidiary, Airtech Services Ltd. The two operations were amalgamated in November 1983 under the parent company's name.

When Tom Denning retired in 1990, Rick took over his duties as president. He acquired Tom's shares in the company and offered 40 percent of them to his employees.

Airview's sales grew steadily throughout the 1980s, from an annual level of $500,000 in 1981 to $1.2 million in 1989. Sales stabilized during the 1990s at a level of just over $1.1 million.

Airview had traditionally maintained an advanced level of technical capabilities, investing in the most up-to-date photographic, film processing, data analysis, and plotting equipment. This, combined with the technical expertise of the company's staff, had enabled them to build an excellent reputation for the quality, reliability, and professionalism of their services.

PRODUCT LINE

With its extensive technologic capabilities, Airview provided a range of services associated with the development of spatial images of terrain, referred to (in Canada) as geomatics. The company's primary specialization was to make, process, and analyze airborne photographs of the earth's surface.

The major groups of services provided by Airview included:

Aerial Photography and Photogrammetry

Aerial photography occupied a pivotal place in Airview's business. The majority of the complex services provided by Airview were initiated by taking photographs from the air. However, aerial photography was also a separate product that, depending on the light spectrum applied in taking the photograph, could provide information on forest growth and diseases, quality of water resources, wildlife migration, land erosion, and other physical features.

Photogrammetry involved a number of image-processing techniques using aerial photographs as a basis for the development of maps, composite views, or spatially referenced databases. Photogrammetry was distinguished from aerial photography by its capability to identify three-dimensional coordinates for each point on the captured image.

Aerial photography/photogrammetry was very capital intensive, requiring a specially prepared aircraft with specialized cameras and sophisticated photo-laboratory equipment. Airview was considered one of the best-equipped aerial photography companies in Canada. Its Cessna 310 L aircraft with 25,000 feet photo ceiling was capable of producing photographs at scales of up to 1:10,000. A recently (1992) acquired Leica camera represented the latest in optical technology, meeting all calibration and accuracy requirements set by North American mapping agencies and accommodating a wide variety of specialized aerial film. Finally, Airview's photo laboratory, which was certified by the National Research Council, processed all types of aerial film used by the company.

Aerial Surveying

Aerial surveying involved taking photographs with the purpose of defining and measuring boundaries and the configuration of particular areas on the earth's surface for a variety of uses, such as establishing ownership rights (cadastre); triangulation;[1] locating and appraising mineral resources, forests, and wildlife habitat; and detecting earth and water movements.

Mapping

This service group's work consisted of the development of maps from either internally or externally acquired photographic images. Before the 1980s, map making had largely been a manual process of drawing the terrain's contours and elevations, and then inserting the accompanying descriptive information. From the early 1980s, however, the process had been increasingly computer driven. This resulted in a reduction in the manual labor required and the increased accuracy of the images produced. The new technology also permitted the storage of maps in an easily accessible, digital format that created demand for converting maps from the traditional, analog format into a computer-based format.

CADD

This area also dealt with map making, but was based on computer-operated scanners supported by CADD/CAM (computer-aided-design and drafting/computer-aided-mapping) software. With this technology, the digitizing of analog images, such as existing maps or photographs, was fully automated. The scanners interpreted the subject image as a series of dots identified by their coordinates, colors, and illuminance, and then produced their digital presentation. The computer-stored images could then be enhanced by adding descriptive information, using a process still performed manually by the CADD operators.

Consulting

Over its 15-year history, Airview had developed a multidisciplinary team of specialists whose expertise was also employed in providing consulting services associated with the planning and execution of comprehensive mapping projects. Consulting involved advising clients on the optimal method of gathering spatial information, the interpretation of client-provided data, and supervising data-gathering projects conducted by the client or his or her subcontractors.

Data capture (aerial photography/photogrammetry) and data processing (mapping and CADD) projects had traditionally generated (in equal proportions) around 90 percent of Airview's sales. The remainder had come from consulting projects (9 percent) and surveying (1 percent).

By 1994, this distribution of sales did not reflect the changing structure of the marketplace, where data capture had become a relatively small part of the overall scope of geomatic activities.

CUSTOMER BASE

Airview Mapping Inc. provided services to a variety of clients locally and nationally. The majority of the company's sales had traditionally come from the public sector. In the period 1991–1993, government agencies (both federal and provincial), local municipalities, and regional utilities in Ontario, Manitoba, and Saskatchewan had accounted for 65 to 75 percent of the company's total dollar sales.

Energy, Mines, and Resources Canada; Transport Canada; the Department of Indian Affairs; Manitoba Hydro; and Manitoba Telephone System were Airview's most significant clients. Procurement by public tender, the significant size of individual contracts (from $50,000 to $100,000+), and clear specifications of requirements characterized these clients' approach to project management.

The private sector, accounting for the remaining 25 to 35 percent of sales, was represented predominantly by clients from the mining industry, such as Hudson Bay Mining and Smelting Company, Inco, Delcan, Noranda, and Placer Dome, whose contracts were typically in the range of $20,000 to $40,000. Companies representing such diverse areas as construction, recreation, and environmental protection provided projects valued at up to $20,000 each. Companies from the private sector did not apply a rigorous procurement procedure and frequently needed guidance in defining (or redefining) project requirements.

GEOGRAPHIC COVERAGE

Airview concentrated its activities within a 1,200-mile radius of its Brandon, Manitoba, headquarters. This was the area in which the company was able to deal directly with its clients and had a cost advantage over its competitors from other provinces. It included northwestern Ontario, Manitoba, Saskatchewan, and Alberta, each contributing equally to the company's revenues.

The company had never attempted to expand beyond the national market, even though the sizable market south of the U.S.–Canada border was well within its defined geographic radius. In the past, this was justified by the abundance of opportunities available in Canada as well as restrictions on foreign access to the U.S. market. However, this situation had recently changed on both counts, which caused Rick to consider changing his company's geographic orientation.

ORGANIZATION AND STAFF

The production process associated with the services provided by Airview involved grouping activities into three functional areas: airplane operation and maintenance (2 staff members), film development (2 staff members), and image processing/output (10 staff members). Managerial, marketing, and administrative activities required 4 additional staff members.

Each production area (aircraft operations, photo lab, data capture, and data conversion) was assigned a coordinator who was responsible for quality assurance and overall coordination of the workload. These coordinators also provided expert advice to their staff and were responsible for individual projects within their respective production areas.

Airview's production activities were characterized by the relatively small number of concurrent projects (4 to 6) and their modest size. This, combined with the well-trained staff (13 out of 18 had completed postsecondary education in geomatics-related fields), enabled the company to apply a skeleton project management structure.

Coordination of project work among different production areas was the responsibility of the production coordinator, Sean Coleman. Garry Howell was in charge of marketing. Tim Connors, who occupied the position of vice president, also acted as the general manager responsible for all projects. Rick, who was the company's president, oversaw general administration and communication with customers.

PRICING

Each price quotation was based on Garry Howell's assessment of the scope of work required to complete a project. This was broken down according to category of activity (aircraft operation, film processing, digitization of images, or image analysis). For each of these activity categories, a budget hourly rate was developed, based on historical cost figures (both direct and fixed), the budgeted number of hours for a given planning period, and the company's profit targets. Recently, rates had ranged from $25 for the digitization of images to over $900 for aircraft flying time, with an overall average of $70. The initial price was determined by multiplying the estimated number of hours required in each category by its budgeted rate and then adding these figures for all activity categories involved in the project. This price was later adjusted according to Rick's assessment of the competitive situation (in the case of a tendered bid) or his negotiations with the customer.

Generally, Airview's budgeted rates and, consequently, prices were within prevailing average values in Canada. This situation reflected Airview's general knowledge of the cost structure of the industry. Any undercutting of price tended to raise suspicions of lower standards. This being the case, the competition between bidders had severely squeezed profit margins, with many firms trying to survive by quoting their services on a break-even basis.

FINANCIAL RESULTS

In the late 1980s and early 1990s, Airview had acquired advanced photographic and mapping equipment and computer hardware and software with a total value of close to $900,000. Financing for these acquisitions had been provided by bank loans and capital leases at interest rates ranging from 12.25 to 17.25 percent.

During the past two years, the cost of servicing this debt load had created a real strain on the company's cash flow, requiring an annual outlay of $200,000 to be split evenly between interest expenses and repayment of the principal. This was extremely difficult for a company traditionally generating a free annual cash flow in the range of only $100,000 to $150,000. Airview's operating cost structure was characterized by a high proportion of fixed costs. At this time, some 75 percent of direct costs and 83 percent of total costs did not vary with changes in its sales levels. This cost structure might seem surprising for a business with some 60 percent of its direct expenses associated with wages and salaries. However, considering the unique nature of the professional qualifications of the company's staff, it was extremely difficult, if not impossible, to adjust the number of staff according to fluctuations in sales levels.

This situation reduced the company's profitability at its current sales level, but simultaneously created significant profit potential with the possibility of a sales increase. It was estimated that the company, barely breaking even at its current sales of $1.1 million, could make over $200,000 in profits by increasing sales to $1.4 million.

OVERALL STRATEGIC PROFILE

Viewed from a strategic perspective, Airview could be characterized as a locally based company with strong technical capabilities, but limited expertise in marketing, particularly outside its traditional markets. Rick recognized the importance of having a clear view of his company's current position, as well as its goals for the next few years.

Analysis of Airview's structure and performance led him to develop the corporate profile presented in Exhibit 1.

EXHIBIT 1	Airview's Corporate Profile Current versus Target (five-year perspective)	
	Current	**Target**
Rank and size	$1,100,000 sales	$2,000,000+ sales
	$0–$25,000 profits	$300,000+ profits
	18 employees	30+ employees
	Medium-sized aerial surveying company	Medium-sized GIS company
	No export sales	$700,000+ export sales
Product line	Aerial photography—40%	Aerial photography—30%
	Mapping—30%	GIS—40%
	Surveying—1%	Mapping—20%
	CADD—20%	Commercial/Consulting—10%
	Commercial—9%	3–5 concurrent projects
	5–10 concurrent projects	
Geographic coverage	Canada—100%	Canada—60%
		International—40%
Performance goals	Maintenance of cash flow	Sales/profit growth
	Profit margin	Market penetration
	Protecting market share	Technology adoption
		New product development
		Productivity
Strengths	Customer goodwill	Customer goodwill
	Technologic expertise	Active marketing
	• Aerial photography	Geographical diversification
	• Digital imaging	Flexible offer
		Technologic expertise
		• Digital imaging
		• Aerial photography
		• System development
Weaknesses	Marketing	International exposure
	Narrow product line	
	Balance sheet	
Strategy	Passive	Active

INDUSTRY TRENDS

The term "geomatics" was widely used in Canada to describe a variety of fields that acquired, managed, and distributed spatially referenced data. The term was applied to several disciplines, including the following:

- Aerial photography.
- Ground-based (geodetic) and aerial surveying, that is, assessing and delimiting boundaries of land.
- Mapping—that is, cartography (map making based on ground measurements)—and photogrammetry (converting photographic images and measurements into maps).
- Geographic information systems (GIS), that is, computer-based systems for the storage and processing of spatial information.
- Remote sensing, that is, satellite-borne images and measurements; quite often, airborne images were included in the remote sensing category.

The use of this general term, however, was limited to Canada. In other countries these disciplines were referred to by their individual names. On the other hand, the term *remote sensing* was frequently used to describe all satellite and airborne observations of the earth's surface, regardless of their purpose or the techniques applied.

Although traditionally distinct, these disciplines were becoming increasingly integrated due to the commonality of the computer tools employed to acquire and process spatial information and generate the final product.

The emergence of satellite-based remote sensing had also affected the geomatics industry worldwide. Its impact on air-based services had been largely positive, despite the fact that both technologies served the same user segments. Advances in satellite technology had received a lot of publicity, which sensitized users of geomatic services to the cost advantages of remote sensing in general and aerial photography/photogrammetry in particular. Consequently, those users who could not use satellite-based services turned to airborne imagery. In many cases, satellite trajectories limited the frequency at which information on a particular earth location could be gathered. This problem was further exacerbated by the prevalence of cloud cover over certain territories. It was expected that, despite recent plans to increase the overall number of remote sensing satellites, aerial photography/photogrammetry would maintain its advantage in applications requiring high-resolution capabilities; aerial images could produce resolutions in a 2- to 3-inch range versus a 10-meter range available from most satellites, and they also had full color capabilities.

AIRVIEW'S MARKETS

In the first half of the 1990s, the Canadian geomatics industry consisted of over 1,300 firms from all geomatic disciplines employing some 12,000 people. The largest number of firms were located in Quebec and Ontario, followed by British Columbia. The distribution of primary activities within the industry was as follows:

Major Line of Business	Percent of Establishments	Percent of Billing
Geodetic (ground) surveying	65%	53%
Mapping	9	16
Remote sensing	5	11
Consulting	10	4.5
GIS	7	12
Other	4	3.5

The vast majority (86 percent) of geomatic firms consisted of small establishments generating sales of less than $1 million. However, the remaining small number of larger firms generated the majority (68 percent) of the industry's revenues. Airview belonged to the growing category of medium-sized businesses (10 percent of all establishments) with sales between $1 million and $2 million.

The overall market size in Canada was estimated at $630 million to $650 million and was dominated by local companies. The industry also generated some $120 million in foreign billings (mainly GIS hardware and software). Interestingly, the export of services had traditionally been directed outside of North America and Europe and was concentrated in Africa, Asia, and the Middle East.

COMPETITION

Competition in the Canadian geomatics industry was on the increase. The overall economic climate, characterized by fiscal restraint in both the private and government sectors, had reduced the growth rate of the demand for services provided by the industry. As a result, geomatic companies, with their increased production capacities and reduced costs, had become more active in competing for the constant volume of business. This had resulted in a decrease in profitability. Overall industry profit levels were the same as in the early 1980s despite a doubling of overall industry demand.

GLOBAL OPPORTUNITIES OVERVIEW

By March 1994, Rick had spent a considerable amount of time reviewing global market opportunities for his company. He had taken a general look at several foreign markets, identifying such major factors as their overall size and growth prospects, political stability and entry barriers, competition, and the availability of funding for geomatic projects.

This step had resulted in rejecting the possibility of entering Western European markets, which, despite their size, were characterized by ferocious competition and limited growth prospects. Eastern Europe was felt to be too unstable politically (the countries of the former U.S.S.R.), lacked funding, and was fragmented along national borders.

Rick also felt that the distances associated with dealing with markets in Southeast Asia and Oceania would put a significant strain on the company's financial and human resources, particularly in view of increasing competition from locally based companies. On the other hand, other Asian markets lacked either the size or financing required to support Airview's long-term involvement.

Finally, he decided that Sub-Saharan Africa, although in dire need of the services offered by Airview, was either dominated by companies from its former colonial powers or could not afford any significant level of geomatics-related development, particularly in view of the declining level of support received from international financial institutions like the World Bank.

On the other hand, Rick found the characteristics of some of the remaining regions quite interesting. Consequently, he decided to concentrate his deliberations on these markets, which included North America (the United States and Mexico), Latin America, and the Arab world (North Africa and the Middle East).

AMERICAN MARKET

The U.S. market was somewhat different from its Canadian counterpart in that it had a larger proportion of geodetic and GIS firms among the 6,300 businesses in its geomatic industry. The larger proportion of geodetic firms in the United States was due to its higher population density that increased the need for cadastral surveying. At the same time, faster adaptation of computers in a variety of industrial applications in the United States had stimulated demand for GIS applications and related services.

On the other hand, in view of the relative size of the U.S. and Canadian economies, the Canadian market was disproportionately large. The American market was estimated at $3 billion in 1994, only five times the size of its Canadian counterpart, or only half the relative difference in the size of the economies between the two countries. This disparity could be largely attributed to structural differences between the economies of the two countries. Canada's economy was largely dependent on the mineral and forestry sectors; both industries supported a high level of geomatic activity.

The demand for geomatics services in the U.S. market was growing at a 15 percent annual rate and was particularly dynamic in the areas of airborne photography and (satellite) remote sensing, digital conversion of existing data, and consulting.

Access to U.S. Markets

In 1994, there were few tariff obstacles when entering the U.S. market. Previously existing barriers related to licensing and local presence requirements were being removed as a result of the passage of the North American Free Trade Agreement. In some cases, Canadian companies that had succeeded in penetrating the U.S. market indicated that it had been easier for them to cross the national border than to overcome provincial barriers within their home country.

Although there had been some opportunities in the U.S. geomatics market during the 1980s, Canadian firms had traditionally been reluctant to pursue them. For aerial surveying companies like Airview, one of the reasons was the fact that aircraft maintenance and licensing requirements were much more lenient in the United States than they were in Canada. As a result, a company operating an aircraft out of Canada was not able to compete with American firms on price if there was a significant amount of flying time involved. Although these differences still remained, the recently falling value of the Canadian dollar had all but nullified the cost advantage previously enjoyed by U.S. companies.

In general, the level of competition in the United States was not much different from that in Canada except that the American firms, particularly the larger ones, marketed their services much more aggressively than their Canadian counterparts.

User Segments

It was estimated that local and state governments accounted for some 25 percent of the total U.S. market for geomatics products and services, and close to half of all local/state budgets allocated to the acquisition of geomatic services was earmarked for data capture purposes.

The greatest potential lay with the 39,000 municipal/county governments. A trend to modernize land records and registration systems that document the 118 million land parcels in the United States was the most significant factor in stimulating the demand for data capture, their conversion into a digital format, their subsequent analysis, and graphical presentation.

The average contract performed for local/state governments ranged from $60,000 to $190,000 for aerial photography/photogrammetry services. Although the Northeast, Southeast, Southwest, and states bordering the Pacific Ocean accounted for the greatest demand, there was also an abundance of opportunities in the states closer to Airview's base, such as Minnesota (3,529 local government units), North Dakota (2,795), and South Dakota (1,767).

Federal government agencies represented the second largest user group, accounting for slightly less than 25 percent of the total U.S. geomatic market. Digital mapping was the major area of demand within this segment. This corresponded closely to Airview's principal area of expertise.

Contracts with the federal government ranged from $30,000 for surveying projects to $1.5 million for data digitizing projects. On average, they tended to be larger in size than those with state and local governments and were typically awarded to larger firms. As a result of the U.S. federal government policy of decentralizing contracting for services, the demand from this user sector was spread across the country.

The third largest segment in the U.S. geomatic market was the demand from regulated industries, such as communication firms and gas and electric utility companies, which traditionally generated between 20 and 25 percent of the overall U.S. demand for geomatic services. Customers from this category were interested in more cost-efficient management of the large infrastructures under their administration. Consequently, they had been among the early adopters of GIS technology, and their major thrust was in implementing AM/FM (automated mapping and facilities management) systems that combined digital maps with information on the operation of their facilities.

The utilities market for geomatic services was spread across the United States with the size closely related to the population density of individual regions. These regional markets were dominated by large companies such as Baymont Engineering and AT&T, which—due to economies of scale—became very price competitive in catering to the utility sector.

Finally, the rest of the demand for geomatic services came from the private sector, with the most significant segments being the resource industries of mining and forestry. The rate of adoption of GIS technology in this sector was rather slow, and remote sensing of data and basic mapping were the primary services contracted out by resource companies.

THE MEXICAN GEOMATICS MARKET

Overview

By the early 1990s, Mexico had developed significant capabilities in geomatics. Between 40,000 and 50,000 people were employed in all surveying- and mapping-related disciplines. Yet, in view of the country's problems with rapid urbanization, deforestation, and land use change, local demand for geomatics products and services in the early 1990s exceeded the available supply in some product and service categories.

The primary demand for geomatics services in Mexico was created by cartographic agencies of the federal and state governments. The National Institute of Statistics, Geography, and Informatics (INEGI) was primarily responsible for integrating the country's geographic data, carrying out the national mapping project, and developing the National Geographic Information System.

Each state in Mexico was responsible for undertaking and maintaining a land survey of its territory and maintaining land cadastre. Therefore, state markets were the second largest in volume after the federal market.

Several large municipalities also purchased geomatics products and services. From 1993 to 1994, they were in the process of establishing databases of property boundaries, partly in cooperation with SEDESOL (Directorate of Cartography and Photogrammetry) under the One Hundred Cities Program.

The private sector was also a significant user of spatially referenced information. PEMEX, the state oil monopoly, was by far the largest of those users. It was also in the strongest position to acquire the most technologically advanced products and services in this area.

The total size of the Mexican market for geomatics services in 1993 was estimated at between $160 million and $200 million.

There were two cycles that affected the volume of geomatics work available in Mexico. First, there was the annual rainy season (June through September) during which the inclement weather had a negative impact on aerial surveying. Second, there was the change in Mexico's presidency every six years. As government agencies were the main purchasers of geomatic services, the political environment had a profound effect on business. In general, the first three years of any presidency resulted in minor projects, while the final three years were noted for major works.

The demand for geomatics services in Mexico was increasing. In addition, most Mexican companies competing for this business were interested in foreign participation, particularly if these relationships carried with them better technology and more modern equipment.

Mexico offered a significant operating benefit to Canadian aerial photography firms in that its weather patterns (the rainy season between June and September) counterbalanced those in Canada. This could enable Canadian exporters to utilize their aircraft and photographic equipment during the slow season in Canada (December through March).

Competition

The Mexican geomatics industry was well developed in the traditional areas of ground surveying and cartography. However, its technologic and human resources capabilities in the more technical areas, such as digital mapping and GIS, were generally limited.

In the area of aerial mapping and surveying, there were about 20 competing companies, located principally in Mexico City. Six of these companies owned their own aircraft and dominated the national market. The remaining 14 were quite small, did not have their own aircraft, and were fairly new to the industry.

Market Access

Public tender was the normal method of obtaining projects in Mexico. Most tenders were open to all companies, but some were by invitation only. The tendency was for contracts to go to those companies that had their own aircraft and the proper equipment. Subcontracting was a popular way for smaller companies to obtain a portion of larger projects.

If a foreign company was awarded a contract, it had to obtain permission to complete the project from the state geography department and from the Mexican Defense Department. In addition, until 1996, foreign companies were not allowed to operate aircraft over Mexican territory without local participation.

THE LATIN AMERICAN GEOMATICS MARKET

In the early 1990s, the geomatics market in Latin America was at an early stage of transition from traditional to digital technologies for data capture, analysis, and storage. Although general awareness of GIS and remote sensing was widespread, their adoption was largely limited to international resource exploration companies and some public institutions.

The market for geomatics products and services was dominated by the public sector on both the supply and demand sides. However, the private sector was becoming the primary growth area, particularly in the resource sector (agriculture, forestry, mining, and energy), where significant investment programs created demand for cadastral surveying, mapping, and GIS. This demand potential, in turn, was providing a growth opportunity for the local surveying and mapping industry. This industry had traditionally been dominated by government organizations (mostly military controlled), which over the previous few years had gained a significant degree of business autonomy and were actively competing in both local and international markets.

International financial institutions (IFIs), such as the World Bank and the Inter-American Development Bank, were very active in Latin America. Their major concern was economic development of the region, and they concentrated on the less-developed nations. The IFIs recognized the importance of infrastructure projects and their geomatics components and therefore provided financial support for such basic services as topographic and property mapping and cadastral information systems. As a result of this fundamental focus, the geomatics contract activity was not confined to the more economically advanced countries of the region. From the point of view of foreign-based geomatics companies attempting to enter the Latin American market, the IFI-sponsored contracts provided a very attractive opportunity since they were open for public tender.

It was anticipated that the Latin American market for geomatics products and services would grow significantly in the near term. Over the 1993–1998 period, the total demand for geomatics products and services in the region was anticipated to be in the range of U.S. $650 million to $1500 million (the low and high estimates).

The provision of spatial information and its conversion to a digital format, as well as the delivery of GIS applications and the provision of training to local staffs, constituted the major demand area, or about three-quarters of the region's market.

Geographic Distribution

Brazil was by far the largest market for geomatics products and services, with an estimated 50 percent of the total demand in the region.

Argentina, with the second largest territory and population in the region, was also the second largest market for geomatics products and services, accounting for 20 percent of Latin American demand.

Chile, with its significant resource sector, was the third significant geomatics market in the region with a 5 percent share of total demand.

Interestingly, Bolivia, with its relatively small population and economy, had a disproportionately large market for geomatics products and services (4 percent of the overall demand).

The other 13 countries of the region shared the remaining 21 percent of the Latin American market, with Venezuela and Colombia leading the group.

Competition

By the 1990s, Latin American companies had developed substantial capabilities in the areas of surveying and mapping. The mapping sector in the region had originated from the military and until recent years had been protected from foreign competition by trade barriers. Consequently, the capabilities of local firms were significant, particularly in larger countries such as Brazil and Argentina. More significantly, larger surveying and mapping companies had already invested in digital mapping technology and remote sensing. With their developed expertise and low labor and overhead costs, these firms had a significant advantage over their competitors from North America, Europe, and Australia. Their knowledge of the local market was an additional factor that placed them ahead of competitors from other continents.

Larger Brazilian and Argentinean firms had used this advantage to penetrate the markets of the smaller countries of the region. Since each national market was characterized by wide fluctuations in demand, the markets in other countries provided them with an opportunity to stabilize and, possibly, expand their sales.

In view of this situation, service firms from outside the region had to compete on the basis of their technological and managerial advantage. Large-scale projects, possibly involving digital imaging, provided the best opportunity to compete with local companies.

Despite all these impediments to foreign participation in the Latin American market, European companies had succeeded in capturing a significant share of the region's business. Their success was built on the strong business network established in the region by their home countries. Their penetration strategy was to establish their presence initially (through international assistance programs and the provision of training and education) and then develop ties with local government agencies and companies from the private sector. European firms were also characterized by their ability to form consortia to pursue larger contracts. These consortia combined European technology and equipment with local labor and market experience.

American firms had obtained a significant degree of penetration of these markets for GIS hardware and software. However, their presence in the other sectors was less pronounced, probably due to their uncompetitive cost structure.

Australian geomatics firms involved in Latin America were typically affiliated with Australia's mining and forestry companies that were active in resource exploration activities in the region.

THE ARAB WORLD (NORTH AFRICA AND THE MIDDLE EAST)

Countries of the Arab world were characterized by the dominance of their oil and gas industries as the market for geomatics-related projects. Their economies and political systems were relatively stable and provided a good foundation for establishing long-term penetration plans by a foreign geomatics company. In terms of economic development, countries in this region were less dependent on international aid than was the case in Latin America. Consequently, their approach to the development of topographic, cadastral, and administrative mapping was based more on long-term planning.

With generally higher levels of resource allocation, countries of this region had developed their own companies, typically originating from the national cartographic agencies. In the early 1990s, these agencies still dominated the industry in the region, employing from 30 to 60 percent of the total number of personnel working in the geomatics field. However, their role had been steadily declining over the past few years.

At the same time, the level of saturation of the industry with locally based personnel differed significantly among individual countries. Egypt, Iran, Jordan, Kuwait, Lebanon, Qatar, Syria, and Tunisia each had a substantial number of local specialists in the field (relative to their populations and territory); whereas Algeria, Libya, Iraq, Saudi Arabia, and Yemen had rather limited geomatics capabilities. Even more significantly, this latter group also had a relatively low proportion of geomatics specialists who were university educated.

The combined market size for geomatics services in the region was estimated at between $400 million and $600 million in the commercial sector. Some of the markets restricted foreign access. Libya and Iraq, for example, were not open to Canadian companies. Also Syria, with its militarized economy, was of limited attractiveness to Canadian firms.

Iran was the country with the best opportunity for geomatics firms. The climate for Canadian companies was favorable because of Canada's position as a politically noninvolved country and the technological advancement of the Canadian geomatics industry.

Major opportunities in Iran were associated with several national development programs in the following areas: energy production (construction of hydroelectric and nuclear power stations and upgrading the country's power distribution system); expansion of the mining industry (production of iron ore, copper, aluminum, lead/zinc, and coal); the oil and gas sectors; and construction of the country's railway system.

Kuwait and Saudi Arabia had traditionally been the target markets for several Canadian geomatics firms. The expansion of the two countries' oil production and refining capacities had triggered major investment outlays in both countries (for a total of over $20 billion between 1992 and 1994) that would continue, albeit at a slower rate, for a number of years. These two national markets were dominated by American companies, and any penetration effort there would require cooperation with Canadian firms from the construction, mining, or oil and gas sectors.

Tunisia had developed its own expertise in the area of cartography, which in turn had created demand for external assistance in the provision of more sophisticated products and services, such as digital mapping and GIS applications.

Egypt represented yet another type of geomatics market in the region. Its major thrust was now on environmental concerns. The country had developed an environmental action plan that addressed problems with water and land resources management, air pollution, marine and coastal resources, and global heritage preservation, all of which had a significant geomatic component. The cost of implementing phase 1 of the plan was estimated at some $300 million over the period 1993–1995. Egypt also provided opportunities created by a $3 billion power generation and distribution project, as well as some $2 billion in construction projects associated with the expansion of the country's gas production and oil processing capacity. Although the majority of work in the geomatics-related field was conducted by local companies, subcontracting opportunities were significant.

Egypt was also a significant market from another perspective. Historically, Egypt had exported its geomatics expertise to other Arab states. Consequently, penetration of this market could be used to leverage access to other markets in the region, particularly in conjunction with Egyptian partners.

MARKET EVALUATION

In order to evaluate each of the four geographic regions from Airview's perspective, Rick Tanner developed a summary of the primary characteristics of each market under consideration. This summary is presented in Exhibit 2. He also reviewed several ways of establishing Airview's presence in the regional/national markets, as indicated in Exhibit 3.

Discussion

Regarding the choice of Airview's optimum target area, Rick Tanner assumed that once he had arrived at a sensible, coherent marketing plan, Airview could apply for financial support from the government. In fact, he had already discussed this possibility with Western Economic Diversification (WED) and the Federal Business Development Bank (FBDB). In addition, he could expect some assistance from the Program for Export Market Development if he chose to establish an office or participate in bidding for projects in a selected market. This assistance could cover 50 percent of the cost of travel and the setup of a permanent foreign office.

His overall concerns included not only the immediate costs of implementing his marketing plan but also the process he should use to select the best market in view of its salient characteristics and the company's goals.

Rick's view of the American market was generally positive. His major concern was with price competition from local firms and possible fluctuations in the exchange rate that might, over a short period of time, undermine Airview's cost structure. At the same time, he felt that Airview's technological advantage in the United States was less significant than in other markets. Finally, he assumed that his best opportunity south of the border would be in GIS-related areas, which would require either a substantial investment in obtaining greater expertise in this area or a joint effort with a GIS company.

The Mexican market was also viewed positively, particularly after the lifting of restrictions in 1996. However, Rick felt that due to the high cost of his staff, Airview would probably be competitive only in complex projects involving both data capture and their conversion into a computer format. At the same time, he was attracted by the operating advantages of having the company's flying season extended beyond the current few summer months.

Latin America seemed to be too competitive to support Airview's solo entry. On the other hand, the region's fragmentation into many small national markets could prove challenging from an operating point of view. Rick felt that seeking an alliance with Canadian mining and resource companies, thereby successfully establishing their operations, might prove to be attractive, particularly if Airview's entry could be supported by the provision of some elements of GIS. As in Mexico's case, the countries of Latin America provided the possibility of operating the company's aircraft during the Canadian off-season.

Finally, Rick regarded the markets of the Arab world with particular interest. Airview would definitely have a technical advantage over its local competitors in these markets. At the same time, pricing in this region seemed to be generally less competitive than in the other areas, whereas the similarity of the individual national markets, in most cases based on the demand created by the resource sector, would allow for gradual penetration of the region. At the same time, Rick realized that Airview's lack of experience in international markets in general, and in the Arab world in particular, would create a very challenging situation for the company's staff.

EXHIBIT 2 Market Review

Characteristics	Market			
	United States	Mexico	Latin America	North Africa and the Middle East
Economic and political environment	Stable	Stabilizing	Stabilizing	Fluctuating
Access restrictions	None	Local agent required, no flying in Mexico	All mapping on-site in Brazil	Language, culture
Market size	Large	Small	Medium	Medium and large
Entry and operating costs	Low	Medium	Medium	Medium and high
Growth	Slow, stable	High	High	High
Financing	Cash, immediate	Transfer, delays	Transfer problems, IFI	Ranging from cash to IFI financing
Contract procurement	Transparent, fair	Ambiguous, improving	Frequently ambiguous	Ambiguous
Major products	Digital mapping, GIS	Cadastral mapping, GIS	Topographic and cadastral mapping	Topographic mapping, surveying
Long-term advantage (technology, expertise)	Limited advantage	Diminishing, but not disappearing	Slowly diminishing	Sustainable
Primary customers	State and municipal governments	Federal and state governments	Federal governments, resource sector	Central cartographic agencies, resource sector
Pricing	Competitive, but based on high local costs	Competitive, based on low local costs	Extremely competitive, based on low local costs	Relatively high
Competition	Local, very high	Local, U.S., high	Local, international, extremely high	Local, international, moderate
Entry strategies	Direct bidding, local partner	Local partner or subsidiary	Network of agents or local partner, IFI projects	Local partner or agent, IFI projects
Strategic advantages	Close, similar to the Canadian market	Entry to South America, technologic advantage, active during Canadian slack	Technologic fit, active during Canadian slack	Technologic advantage, growing, less competition, long-term prospects
Expansion opportunities	GIS consulting systems, integration	Acquisition of local subsidiary	Training	CIDA project, Libya (with restrictions)

Endnote

1. A specialized technique for defining an accurate three-dimensional coordinate system for determining the location and dimensions of objects on the earth's surface.

EXHIBIT 3 Airview Entry Strategies

Project-Oriented Penetration

This is a strategy suitable for small, niche-oriented firms. The company would have to target a specific area and seek a specific contract. Involvement would be limited to the scope of the specific contract. The main barrier to this approach could be associated with local presence requirements.

Establishing a network of local agents in the countries of interest in the region may provide access to information on upcoming tenders and allow for participation in the bidding process. Bidding for local contracts may serve as a foundation for establishing the company's presence in the region and could be treated as part of an entry strategy.

Subcontracting to Local Firms

This strategy offered the advantage of overcoming local presence restrictions.

Strategic Alliances

An alliance with a Canadian or foreign partner can work quite effectively provided the firms complement one another in resources and business philosophies.

Establishment of a Branch Office

This could be an effective way of overcoming local presence restrictions provided the firm was sufficiently financed to undertake the costs of setting up such an operation. The choice of location would also be crucial in determining the success of such a venture.

A Corporate Buyout

This seemed a somewhat risky proposition, requiring adequate financing, business acumen to succeed, and lack of restrictions on foreign ownership of local companies. If successful, however, the result would be an immediate presence in the selected market.

Establishment of Head Office Outside of Canada

Although this could enable a company to access the selected market, this possibility could be considered only for large and stable markets, such as the United States.

Foreign Ownership

Like the strategic alliance option, this could offer opportunities, particularly with U.S. firms, provided this route is in keeping with the long-term goals of the firm and the two firms are compatible.

Alliances with Local Geomatics Firms

An alliance with a local partner could be beneficial if based on the combination of local experience and inexpensive labor with Airview's equipment and data processing and mapping capabilities.

Joint Ownership of a Local Company

Acquiring a local company in partnership with another Canadian company may provide some advantages if the partners' product lines complement each other. A provider of GIS software or system integrator may be a good candidate for joint ownership with Airview.

CASE IIIc   Rug Bug Corporation

A. L. Young has come a long way with his latest invention, the Rug Bug, a motorized wheelchair made especially for children. His lightweight, relatively inexpensive model has no direct competition in a field dominated by companies that produce scaled-down versions of adult models that are inappropriate to the needs of children. A working prototype has been built, office space and manufacturing capacity contracted, and an initial sales force recruited. The only element Young lacks is enough capital to produce the first 200 units. A business plan has been drawn up describing the product, its manufacture, and the marketing plan. After several fruitless months seeking financing, Young was contacted by a group of investors who had seen a summary of his proposal. Feeling that this might be his only chance, Young has contacted you for advice on how to present his plan. He has sent you the following copy of his business plan and a list of questions. What recommendations would you make?

Young's questions:

1. I'm not much of a writer: Do you think my descriptions of the product, competition, marketing, and so forth, are adequate? Could it be improved easily without additional outside information (my meeting is in two days!)?
2. The pro forma income and cash flow statements were developed from a model I found in a book. Did I leave anything out?
3. I think $150,000 is a good amount to ask for—big enough to show we are serious about creating a growing business but not large enough to scare them away. Are they going to want to know what I plan to do with every penny? What should I do if they are only willing to invest less?
4. I really don't know what to expect from these investors. I have my own idea of how much of the company I want to give up for the $150,000, but I don't know what they would consider reasonable. Can you give me any suggestions?

Mr. and Mrs. A. L. Young established the Rug Bug Corporation on October 23, 1985, as a Delaware corporation. The sole purpose is to manufacture and distribute a revolutionary motorized wheelchair, designed for children under the age of 10. The Rug Bug motorized wheelchair will retail for approximately one-half the cost of any other motorized wheelchair for this age group. It will weigh almost 50 percent less than the standard motorized wheelchair. The unique design of the Rug Bug accounts for the differences in the retail cost and weight of the chair. In addition, the Rug Bug has numerous safety features that are not found on other available motorized wheelchairs. These three features of cost, weight, and safety allow the Rug Bug to fill a special niche in the market. It is an appropriate time to introduce this product in light of the current trend in the medical field to recommend the use of motorized wheelchairs for children. This recommendation of medical professionals arises from their determination that the spatial relations and sense of movement offered by a motorized chair provide a handicapped child with sensory experiences normal for young children. The target market for this product will be greatly increased due to this philosophical change. In order to establish the company, the Rug Bug Corporation will need $150,000. This will finance the production of the molds for various parts, the manufacture of 200 units (of which 190 will be sold), and initial marketing efforts. In addition, the company will use the funds for product liability insurance, legal fees, and continued research and development.

DESCRIPTION OF THE BUSINESS

The Rug Bug Corporation is primarily a manufacturing and distribution company in the start-up phase of operation. The inventor's initial research led to the development of a prototype. Marketing research shows the Rug Bug to be the only vacuum-molded, plastic, motorized wheelchair with unique safety features available today. The owners of the Rug Bug Corporation believe the company will be successful because of low production costs, reasonable retail costs, safety factors, low weight, and visual appeal. The use of motorized chairs by the target age group has been limited primarily for two reasons. First, the current cost of motorized wheelchairs for children ranges from $3,000 to $8,000. It has been difficult to justify such an investment for a chair since a child's growth is typically rapid, therefore limiting the time the chair can be utilized. The Rug Bug will retail for $1,850. This is a significant price differential, especially for a chair that offers additional features such as safety control. The second limitation was the medical community's view that muscle use was of primary concern in a handicapped child's development. They have recently shifted away from that stance, with many professionals now emphasizing the development of spatial skills, spatial relations, and sense of movement—all areas that the motorized chair can help strengthen.

DESCRIPTION OF THE PRODUCT

The Rug Bug is a vacuum-molded, plastic-body wheelchair powered by a rechargeable battery. The 25-pound chair has the following safety features as standard equipment:

1. A pressure-sensitive bumper strip surrounding the vehicle allows the unit to move away from any obstruction it might encounter.
2. Dual front antennae extend upward to prevent the chair from moving under low objects, such as a coffee table.
3. In the case of a confrontation with an uneven surface, an electric eye located under the front of the chair will deactivate power in that direction. The power remains operative in other directions, allowing the occupant to move away from the potential hazard.
4. A handheld remote control unit enables an adult to take over control of the chair from the occupant.
5. A variable speed control is built into the unit beyond reach of the occupant. As the ability of the occupant to maneuver the chair increases, so may the speed.
6. Though built with a very low center of gravity, the chair is designed with a roll bar.

The computerized control panel defines the Rug Bug as a technical machine; however, in appearance, the Rug Bug is more similar to a currently popular battery-operated riding toy. The visual appeal immediately distinguishes the Rug Bug from any other motorized wheelchair on the market today.

MARKETING COMPONENT

1. *Market Size.* According to the Frost and Sullivan Report No. 1468, the market for supplies and services for rehabilitation will increase to $1.36 billion in 1990 from $774.5 million in 1985. This figure includes exercise equipment increasing to $477.4 million (1990) from $302.6 million (1985); and manual powered wheelchairs, carts, and scooters increasing to $362.4 million (1990) from $197.4 million (1985). Powered wheelchairs will have 24 percent of the market in 1990 ($86.9 million) versus 17 percent of the market in 1985 ($33.6 million). According to a U.S. government report, Youth and Children Coordinate for Kids, there are 668,340 orthopedically impaired children and children with cerebral palsy, ages two to seven, in this country who might have need of a motorized wheelchair. This figure does not reflect any other potential users in this age bracket, such as the muscular dystrophy population.

2. *Competition.* Everest and Jennings is the industry leader in motorized wheelchairs, with 1983 sales of $158 million. The company's business has grown steadily in spite of charges that the company's chairs were not as good as they were in the 1950s. Poor design caused some faltering, and the frequency of breakdowns resulted in repairs that took months. Although the Veterans Administration spends more than $7 million a year for wheelchairs, performance standards are still being refined, and there are no federal wheelchair regulations. Most of Everest and Jennings' chairs are still manual, but their power market is growing. Currently, this company lists motorized wheelchairs for children, ranging in cost from $3,000 to $8,000 per unit. No other company has been found that offers a motorized wheelchair for less. It is significant to note that none of Everest and Jennings' chairs have safety features. These steel-frame motorized wheelchairs weigh approximately 50 pounds per unit. Following a 1978 accident that left her a paraplegic, M. Hamilton formed Motion Designs to make a lightweight wheelchair when Everest and Jennings indicated no interest in the project. Overall, the wheelchair has not been modified essentially since its inception in 1933, except, of course, by wheelchair sports enthusiasts. However, some 25,000 people every year suffer auto, motorcycle, and swimming accidents that put them into wheelchairs, and the disabled population today is generally much more mobile and independent than its earlier counterparts. Motion Designs introduced its first rigid, but lightweight, chairs in 1980; and in 1982 it produced the Quickie-2, a 24-pound foldable chair. Finally, Everest and Jennings brought out its own line of lightweight sports and everyday chairs, which put pressure on the new competitors to keep up. Motion Designs responded by making its chair completely modular, with interchangeable accessories. Users can adjust or mix the parts to attain a perfect fit. The newest entry into the market is a motorized stand-up wheelchair, retailing for $8,000.

3. *Distribution.* Since there are distinct and different methods for purchasing wheelchairs, Rug Bug will establish two different distribution systems. A direct system, initially employing individuals connected with the company, will call on hospitals, the Veterans Administration, Shriners, and organizations connected with the care and development of handicapped children. Of the initial 200 products, 190 will be sold in these outlets in order to generate sales without paying retail markups. This will also give the product good exposure. Manufacturers' representatives will make direct sales for subsequent production runs. A 15 percent commission on the selling price will be paid on all direct sales. After the initial 190 units have been sold (with 10 units being kept for demonstration purposes), the company will add a retail distribution system. Several retail outlets will be used in each of the major markets, including drugstores, bicycle shops, and medical supply stores. Drugstores accounted for $117.6 million in wheelchair sales in 1983 and are an important outlet for the company. Bicycle shops, while not usually a source for the purchase of wheelchairs, are an important outlet, as they will provide any service needed in addition to sales. Company-authorized service outlets will be established in each market for ease of repair, an aspect the consumer should appreciate. Retail margins will be 30 percent off the established retail selling price of $1,850.

4. *Price*. The company will sell the product to the stores for $1,850, which includes a retail markup of 30 percent of the established retail selling price. This price will position the product favorably against competition and allow for significant growth in market share as well as profit.

5. *Promotion*. Quality brochures describing the product and its characteristics will be developed and distributed as point-of-purchase sale materials in the retail outlets as well as in all hospitals, clinics, and other organizations working with handicapped children. In addition, sales material, including a price list indicating markups and return per square foot of selling space required, will be developed for use in the company's direct sales effort.

LOCATION OF THE BUSINESS

The office section of the Rug Bug will be located at Barn Bicycle on East 61st Street, Tulsa, Oklahoma. The molded plastic body will be manufactured and the product assembled at the Inter-Ocean Oil Company, located at 2630 Mohawk Boulevard, Tulsa, Oklahoma. The Rug Bug Corporation will not be charged for usage of either facility, although it will pay for utilities and telephones at both.

MANAGEMENT/OPERATIONS

Inventor Al Young will serve as the president of Rug Bug Corporation. In addition, Young will concentrate on the research and development section of operations. Mr. Young's past experience with electronics and computers fits well with the needs of the company. His ability to transform a concept into a viable product is shown through the prototype that Rug Bug currently has in existence.

Wayne Dunn and Dwaine Farrill will continue to operate in the marketing component of the company. Their extensive knowledge of and profound belief in the product make both Dunn and Farrill ideal people to initially market it on a commissioned basis.

Linda Bryant will initially serve as the unpaid controller of the company. Ms. Bryant will serve as single signatory on the banking account and prepare and monitor monthly financial reports. She has served as a cash management officer at The Fourth National Bank of Tulsa for over two years and is currently its director of business development.

FINANCIAL INFORMATION

To ramp up, the Rug Bug Corporation needs $150,000. The funds will be used to develop the molds for various parts, manufacture 200 units (of which 190 will be sold), start the initial marketing effort, and pay employee salaries, product liability insurance, legal fees, and other expenses of the organization (see Exhibit 1). The company will achieve significant sales and profits starting in the first year, as indicated in the various pro forma income statements (see Exhibits 1 to 3). The pro forma income cash flow statements (Exhibits 4 to 6) and balance sheets (Exhibits 7 to 9) further indicate the tremendous growth and profit potential.

EXHIBIT 1

THE RUG BUG CORPORATION
Pro Forma Income Statement
First Year, by Month
1987/1988

	May 87	June 87	July 87	Aug 87	Sept 87	Oct 87	Nov 87	Dec 87	Jan 88	Feb 88	Mar 88	Apr 88	Total
Sales	0	0	0	$37,000	$55,500	$55,500	$74,000	$74,000	$74,000	$74,000	$92,500	$92,500	$629,000
Less: Cost of goods sold	0	0	0	8,710	13,066	13,066	17,421	17,421	17,421	17,421	21,776	21,776	148,077
Commission	0	0	0	5,550	8,325	9,325	11,100	11,100	11,100	13,875	13,875	13,875	94,350
Gross profit	0	0	0	$22,740	$34,109	$34,109	$45,479	$45,479	$45,479	$45,479	$56,849	$56,849	$386,573
Operating expenses													
President salary	$2,000	$2,000	$2,000	$2,000	$2,000	$2,000	$2,000	$2,000	$2,000	$2,000	$2,000	$2,000	$24,000
Secretary salary	0	0	0	0	0	1,167	1,167	1,167	1,167	1,167	1,167	1,167	8,169
Employee insurance	42	42	42	42	42	42	42	42	42	42	42	38	500
Product liability insurance				763	1,145	1,145	3,638	3,638	3,638	3,638	4,548	4,548	30,926
Research and development	417	417	417	1,819	2,729	2,729	1,526	1,526	1,526	1,526	1,908	1,908	12,973
Advertising/printing	417	417	417	417	417	417	417	417	417	417	413	417	5,000
Travel expenses	625	625	625	625	625	625	625	625	625	625	625	625	7,500
Organization expenses	850	850	850	850	850	850	850	850	850	850	850	850	10,200
Total operating expenses	$ 3,934	$ 3,934	$3,934	$ 6,516	$ 7,807	$ 8,974	$10,266	$10,266	$10,266	$10,266	$11,553	$11,553	$ 99,269
Profit (loss) before tax	(3,934)	(3,934)	(3,934)	16,223	26,302	25,135	35,214	35,214	35,214	35,214	45,296	45,296	287,304
Taxes	(1,574)	(1,574)	(1,574)	6,489	10,521	10,054	14,085	14,085	14,085	14,085	18,119	18,119	114,922
Net profit (loss)	$(2,360)	$(2,360)	$(2,360)	$ 9,734	$15,781	$15,081	$21,128	$21,128	$21,128	$21,128	$27,178	$27,178	$172,382
Quantity sold	0	0	0	20	30	30	40	40	40	40	50	50	340
Price	1,850	1,850	1,850	1,850	1,850	1,850	1,850	1,850	1,850	1,850	1,850	1,850	
DL-DM-MAGF cost	436	436	436	436	436	436	436	436	436	436	436	436	
Commission percent	15	15	15	15	15	15	15	15	15	15	15	15	
Tax rate	40	40	40	40	40	40	40	40	40	40	40	40	

(1) President salary at $24,000 per year
(2) Secretary salary begins on the 6th month
(3) Product liability is proportionate to quantity sold
(4) Organization expenses (registration fee, legal fee, etc.) are amortized over the first year

EXHIBIT 2

THE RUG BUG CORPORATION

Pro Forma Income Statement

Second Year, by Quarter

1988/1989

	Qtr 1	Qtr 2	Qtr 3	Qtr 4	Total
Sales—Direct	$555,000	$1,110,000	$2,220,000	$3,330,000	$7,215,000
—Retail	194,250	388,500	582,750	777,000	1,942,500
Total sales	749,250	1,498,500	2,802,750	4,107,000	9,157,500
Cost of good sold—Direct	130,656	261,312	522,624	783,936	1,698,528
—Retail	65,328	130,656	195,984	261,312	653,280
Commission—Direct	83,250	166,500	333,000	499,500	1,082,250
—Retail	29,138	58,275	87,413	116,550	291,375
Gross profit	$440,879	$ 881,757	$1,663,730	$2,445,702	$5,432,067
Operating expenses					
President salary	$ 7,200	$ 7,200	$ 7,200	$ 7,200	$ 28,800
Secretary salary	3,500	3,500	3,500	3,500	14,000
VP—Finance salary			12,500	12,500	25,000
Employee insurance	125	125	125	125	500
Product liability insurance	7,425	14,050	25,092	36,133	82,700
Research and development	35,270	70,541	133,098	195,656	434,565
Advertising/printing	2,500	2,500	2,500	2,500	10,000
Travel expenses	1,875	1,875	1,875	1,875	7,500
Accounting services	2,500	2,500	2,500	2,500	10,000
Depreciation—computer	750	750	750	750	3,000
Bad debt expense	5,828	11,655	17,483	23,310	58,275
Total operating expenses	$ 57,895	$ 99,791	$ 185,890	$ 259,489	$ 603,065
Profit (loss) before tax	382,983	781,966	1,477,839	2,186,213	4,829,002
Taxes	153,193	312,787	591,136	874,485	1,931,601
Net profit (loss)	$229,790	$ 469,180	$ 886,704	$1,311,728	$2,897,401
Quantity sold—Direct	300	600	1,200	1,800	3,900
—Retail	150	300	450	600	1,500
Price—Direct	1,850	1,850	1,850	1,850	
—Retail	1,295	1,295	1,295	1,295	
DL-DM-MAFG cost	436	436	436	436	
Commission percent	15	15	15	15	
Tax rate	40	40	40	40	

(1) Product liability insurance = ($7,500 − 6% tax)/5,400 − $3,200

(2) Personal computer depreciated at straight line over a 5-year life with no salvage value

(3) Bad debt expense provision at 3% of retail sales

(4) Taxes (federal and state) provided at 40%

EXHIBIT 3

THE RUG BUG CORPORATION

Pro Forma Income Statement

Third Year, by Quarter

1989/1990

	Qtr 1	Qtr 2	Qtr 3	Qtr 4	Total
Sales—Direct	3,700,000	5,550,000	7,400,000	9,250,000	25,900,000
—Retail	1,554,000	2,331,000	3,108,000	3,885,000	10,878,000
Total sales	5,254,000	7,881,000	10,508,000	13,135,000	36,778,000
Cost of good sold—Direct	$ 871,040	$1,306,560	$1,742,080	$2,177,600	$ 6,097,280
—Retail	522,624	783,936	1,045,248	1,306,560	3,658,368
Commission—Direct	555,000	832,500	1,110,000	1,387,500	3,885,000
—Retail	233,100	349,650	466,200	582,750	1,631,700
Gross profit	$3,072,236	$4,608,354	$6,144,472	$7,680,590	$21,505,652
Operating expenses					
President salary	$ 8,640	$ 8,640	$ 8,640	$ 8,640	$ 34,560
Secretary salary	3,500	3,500	3,500	3,500	14,000
VP—Finance salary	15,000	15,000	15,000	15,000	60,000
Employee insurance	125	125	125	125	500
Research and development	245,779	368,668	491,558	614,447	1,720,452
Product liability insurance	31,086	46,229	61,371	76,514	215,200
Advertising printing	3,125	3,125	3,125	3,125	12,500
Travel expenses	1,875	1,875	1,875	1,875	7,500
Accounting services	2,500	2,500	2,500	2,500	10,000
Depreciation—computer	750	750	750	750	3,000
Bad debt expense	66,600	99,900	133,200	166,500	466,200
Total operating expenses	$ 378,980	$ 550,312	$ 721,644	$ 892,976	$ 2,543,912
Profit (loss) before tax	2,693,256	4,058,042	5,422,828	6,787,614	18,961,740
Taxes	1,077,303	1,623,217	2,169,131	2,715,045	7,584,696
Net profit (loss)	$1,615,954	$2,434,825	$3,253,697	$4,072,568	$11,377,044
Quantity sold—Direct	2,000	3,000	4,000	5,000	14,000
—Retail	1,200	1,800	2,400	3,000	8,400
Price—Direct	1,850	1,850	1,850	1,850	
—Retail	1,295	1,295	1,295	1,295	
DL-DM-MAFG cost	436	436	436	436	
Discount percent	30	30	30	30	
Commission percent	15	15	15	15	
Tax rate	40	40	40	40	

(1)Product liability insurance = ($200,000 − 6% tax) − $3,200

EXHIBIT 4

THE RUG BUG CORPORATION
Pro Forma Cash Flow Statement
First Year, by Month
1987/1988

	May 87	June 87	July 87	Aug 87	Sept 97	Oct 87	Nov 87	Dec 87	Jan 88	Feb 88	Mar 88	Apr 88
Cash receipts												
Sales	0	0	0	$37,000	$55,500	$55,500	$74,000	$74,000	$74,000	$74,000	$92,500	$92,500
Others	$75,000	$75,000	$ 0	$ 0								
Total cash receipts	$75,000	$75,000	0	$37,000	$55,500	$55,500	$74,000	$74,000	$74,000	$74,000	$92,500	$92,500
Cash disbursements												
Salaries												
President	$ 2,000	$ 2,000	$ 2,000	$ 2,000	$ 2,000	$ 2,000	2,000	2,000	2,000	2,000	2,000	2,000
Secretary					1,167	1,167	1,167	1,167	1,167	1,167	1,167	1,167
Employee insurance	100	150	250	1,819	2,729	2,729	638	3,638	3,638	3,638	4,548	4,548
Product liability insurance	12,973											
Research and development	0	0	0									
Advertising	2,500	1,500	1,000									
Travel expense	3,750	2,250	1,500									
Organization fees	5,100	3,060	2,040									
Commissions				5,500	8,325	8,325	11,100	11,100	11,100	11,100	13,875	13,875
Inventory	17,421	26,131	43,552				10,900	10,900	21,800	21,800	65,400	65,400
Total disbursements	$43,844	$35,091	$50,342	$9,369	$13,054	$14,221	$28,805	$28,805	$ 39,705	$ 39,705	$ 86,990	$ 86,990
Net cash flow	31,156	39,909	(50,342)	27,631	42,446	41,279	45,195	45,195	34,295	34,295	5,510	5,510
Cumulative cash flow	31,156	71,065	20,723	48,354	90,800	124,685	45,195	90,390	124,685	158,980	164,490	170,000

EXHIBIT 5

THE RUG BUG CORPORATION
Pro Forma Cash Flow Statement
Second Year, by Quarter
1988/1989

	Qtr 1	Qtr 2	Qtr 3	Qtr 4	Total
Cash receipts					
Sales	$680,615	$1,424,038	$2,722,460	$4,020,883	$8,847,996
Others					
Total cash receipts	$680,615	$1,424,038	$2,722,460	$4,020,883	$8,847,996
Cash disbursements	$ 7,200	$ 7,200	$ 7,200	$ 7,200	$ 28,800
Salaries					
President					
Secretary	3,500	3,500	3,500	3,500	14,000
VP—Finance			12,500	12,500	25,000
Employee insurance	125	125	125	125	500
Research and development	35,270	70,541	133,098	195,636	434,565
Product liability insurance	82,700				82,700
Advertising	1,250	1,250	1,250	1,250	5,000
Travel expenses	1,875	1,875	1,875	1,875	7,500
Accounting services	2,500	2,500	2,500	2,500	10,000
Commissions	102,092	213,606	408,369	603,132	1,327,199
Inventory cost	327,000	610,400	937,400	1,308,000	3,182,800
Taxes	114,922				114,922
Personal computer	15,000				15,000
Total cash disbursements	$693,434	$ 910,997	$1,507,817	$ 2,135,738	$5,247,986
Net cash flow	(12,819)	513,041	1,214,643	1,885,145	3,600,010
Cumulative cash flow	(12,819)	500,222	1,714,865	3,600,010	
Units produced	750	1,400	2,150	3,000	7,300
Unit cost	436	436	436	436	

EXHIBIT 6

THE RUG BUG CORPORATION
Pro Forma Cash Flow Statement
Third Year, by Quarter
1989/1990

	Qtr 1	Qtr 2	Qtr 3	Qtr 4	Total
Cash receipts					
Sales	$4,956,150	$7,559,840	$10,163,530	$12,767,220	$35,446,740
Others					
Total cash receipts	$4,956,150	$7,559,840	$10,163,530	$12,767,220	$35,446,740
Cash disbursements					
Salaries					
President	$ 8,640	$ 8,640	$ 8,640	$ 8,640	$ 34,560
Secretary	3,500	3,500	3,500	3,500	14,000
VP—Finance	12,500	12,500	15,000	15,000	55,000
Employee insurance	125	125	125	125	500
Research and development	245,779	368,668	491,558	614,447	1,720,452
Product liability insurance	30,743	46,114	61,486	76,857	215,200
Advertising	1,250	1,250	1,250	1,250	5,000
Travel expenses	3,750	3,750	3,750	3,750	15,000
Accounting services	2,500	2,500	2,500	2,500	10,000
Commissions	743,423	1,133,976	1,524,530	1,915,083	5,317,011
Inventory cost	1,831,200	2,528,800	3,313,600	3,749,600	11,423,200
Taxes	1,931,601				1,931,601
Total cash disbursements	$4,815,010	$4,109,823	$ 5,425,938	$ 6,390,752	$20,741,524
Net cash flow	141,140	3,450,017	4,737,592	6,376,468	14,705,216
Cumulative cash flow	141,140	3,591,156	8,328,748	14,705,216	
Units produced	4,200	5,800	7,600	8,600	26,200
Unit cost	436	436	436	436	

EXHIBIT 7

THE RUG BUG CORPORATION
Pro Forma Balance Sheet
As of 4/30/88

Cash	$302,079
Inventory	135,225
Accounts receivable	0
Total assets	$437,304
Commissions payable	0
Taxes payable	114,922
Retained earnings	172,382
Common stock	150,000
	$437,304

EXHIBIT 8

THE RUG BUG CORPORATION
Pro Forma Balance Sheet
As of 4/30/89

Cash	$3,902,089
Computer	12,000
Inventory	1,017,145
Accounts receivable	259,000
Total assets	$5,190,234
Commissions payable	38,850
Taxes payable	1,931,601
Retained earnings	3,069,783
Common stock	150,000
	$5,190,234

EXHIBIT 9

THE RUG BUG CORPORATION	
Pro Forma Balance Sheet	
As of 4/30/90	
Cash	$18,607,305
Computer	9,000
Inventory	1,541,938
Accounts receivable	1,259,000
Total assets	$21,453,243
Commissions payable	195,250
Taxes payable	7,584,696
Retained earnings	13,523,297
Contributed capital	150,000
	$21,453,243

CASE IIId   Nature Bros. Ltd.

BACKGROUND

Thanksgiving Day 1976 is the day that Dale Morris remembers as the "public debut" of his creation, a new seasoned salt mix. Although he was a salesman by temperament and career, his hobby was cooking. Having experimented with both traditional home cooking and more exotic gourmet cooking, Morris had developed an appreciation for many herbs and spices. He had also done a lot of reading about the health hazards of the typical American diet. When his mother learned that she had high blood pressure, Morris decided it was time for some action. He created a low-salt seasoning mix, based on a nutritive yeast extract, that could be used to replace salt in most cases. This Thanksgiving dinner, prepared for 25 family members and friends, would be his final testing ground. He used his mix in all the recipes except the pumpkin pie—everything from the turkey and dressing to the vegetables and even the rolls. As the meal progressed, the verdict was unanimously in favor of his secret ingredient, although he had a hard time convincing them that it was his invention and was only 10 percent salt. Everyone wanted a sample to try at home.

Over the next two years, Morris perfected his product. Experiments in new uses led to "tasting parties" for friends and neighbors, and the holiday season found the Morris kitchen transformed into a miniature assembly line producing gift-wrapped bottles of the mix. Morris became something of a celebrity in his small town, but it wasn't until the Ladies' Mission Society at his church approached him with the idea of allowing them to sell his mix as a fund-raiser that he realized the possibilities of his creation. His kitchen-scale operation could support the sales effort of the church women for a short time, but if he wanted to take advantage of a truly marketable product, he would have to make other arrangements.

Morris agreed to "test-market" his product through the church group while he looked for ways to expand and commercialize his operation. The charity sale was a huge success (the best the women had ever experienced), and, based on this success, Morris moved to create his own company. Naming his product "Nature Bros. Old Fashioned Seasoning," he incorporated the company in 1978 as Nature Bros. Ltd. Morris used most of his savings to develop and register the trademarks, for packaging, and for product displays. He researched the cost of manufacturing and bottling his product in large quantities and concluded that he just didn't have the cash to get started. His first attempts to raise money, in the form of a personal bank loan, were unsuccessful, and he was forced to abandon the project.

For several years he concentrated on his career, becoming a regional vice president of the insurance company he worked for. He continued to make "Nature Bros. Seasoning" in small batches, mainly for his mother and business associates. These users eventually enabled Morris to get financial support for his company. To raise $65,000 to lease manufacturing equipment and building space, he sold stock to his mother and to two other regional vice presidents of the insurance company. For their contributions, each became owners of 15 percent of Nature Bros. Ltd. The process of getting the product to the retail market began in August 1985, and the first grocery store sales started in March 1986. The initial marketing plan was fairly simple—to get the product in the hands of the consumer. Morris personally visited the managers of individual supermarkets, both chains and independents, and convinced many to allow a tasting demonstration booth to be set up in their stores. These demonstrations proved as popular as the first Thanksgiving dinner trial nearly 10 years earlier. Dale Morris's product was a hit, and in a short time he was able to contract with food brokerage firms to place his product in stores in a 10-state region.

PRESENT SITUATION

As indicated in the balance sheet (see Exhibit 1), more capital is needed to support the current markets and expand both markets and products. Two new products are being developed: a salt-free version of the original product and an MSG-based flavor enhancer that will compete with Accent. Morris worked with a business consultant in drawing up a business plan to describe his company, its future growth, and its capital needs. Portions of this plan are included below.

OVERALL PROJECTIONS

The first section discusses the objectives and sales projections for 1987 and 1988 (Exhibits 2 and 3). The resulting pro forma income statements for 1987 to 1991 are in Exhibits 4 and 5.

1987 OBJECTIVES

The company's objectives for 1987 are to stabilize its existing markets and to achieve a 10 percent market share in the category of seasoned salt, a 20 percent market share in salt substitutes, and a 10 percent market share in MSG products. Although the original product contains less than 10 percent salt, the company has developed a salt-free product to compete with other such products, such as the one shown in the advertisement in Exhibit 6. The dollar volume for the seasoned salt category in the seven markets the company is in will amount to $3,965,942 in 1987. In 1986, sales

EXHIBIT 1

NATURE BROS. LTD.
Balance Sheet
As of September 30, 1986

Unaudited
Current assets

110 Cash—American Bank	$ 527.11
112 Cash—Bank of Okla-Pryor	31.86
115 Cash on hand	24.95
120 Accounts receivable	21,512.75
125 Employee advances	327.37
140 Inventory—Shipping	940.43
141 Inventory—Raw materials	1,082.29
142 Inventory—Work-in-progress	803.70
143 Inventory—Packaging	4,548.41
144 Inventory—Promotional	2,114.95
Total current assets	$31,913.82

Fixed assets

160 Leasehold improvements	$ 2,402.25
165 Fixtures and furniture	1,222.46
167 Equipment	18,768.21
169 Office equipment	.00
170 1986 Lincoln town car	15,000.00
180 Less: Accumulated depreciation	(7,800.01)
181 Less: Amortization	(502.50)
Total fixed assets	$29,090.41

Other assets

193 Organizational cost	$ 4,083.36
194 Prepaid interest	2,849.69
195 Utility deposits	.00
Total fixed and other assets	$36,023.46
Total assets	$67,937.28

Current liabilities

205 Accounts payable	$15,239.41
210 Note payable-premium finances	88.26
220 Federal tax withheld	150.00
225 F.I.C.A. tax withheld	937.92
230 State tax withheld	266.49
231 State and federal employment taxes	230.92
Total current liabilities	$16,913.00

Long-term liabilities

245 Note payable—All fill	$ 2,734.86
246 Note payable—American Bank	23,740.00
247 Note payable—Sikeston Leasing	15,126.66
Total long-term liabilities	$41,601.52
Total liabilities	$58,514.52

Capital account

290 Original capital stock	$ 1,000.00
291 Additional paid-in capital	$41,580.00
292 Treasury stock	(70.00)
295 Retained earnings	(3,819.71)
298 Net profit or loss	(29,267.53)
Total owner's equity account	$ 9,422.76
Total liabilities and equity	$67,937.28

EXHIBIT 2   1987 Sales Projection

Category	Seasoned Salt	Salt Substitute	MSG
Our Product	Old Fashioned Seasoning	Salt-Free Old Fashioned Seasoning	Enhance
Existing markets #1			
Oklahoma	$ 550,922	$ 357,819	$118,889
Nebraska	399,630	302,769	100,958
Springfield, MO	254,310	192,671	64,017
Arkansas	217,980	165,147	54,871
Houston	835,590	633,064	210,342
Dallas	1,162,560	880,785	292,649
Albuquerque	544,950	412,868	137,179
	$3,965,942	$2,945,123	$978,545
Market share (%)	×10%	×20%	×10%
1st year sales	$ 396,594	$ 589,024	$ 97,854
		396,594	
		589,024	
		97,854	
Total 1st year sales volume		$1,083,472	

of the company in the Oklahoma market were 11 percent of the total sales for that market for the eight-month period that the company was operational. Since these sales were accomplished with absolutely no advertising, the company can be even more successful in the future in all seven current markets with a fully developed and funded advertising campaign. The marketing approach will include advertisements in the print media, with ads on "food day" offering cents-off coupons. This program will take place in all seven markets, while stores will continue to use floor displays for demonstrations. Nearly 100 percent warehouse penetration should be achieved in 1987 in these markets.

The goal for the category of salt substitutes for 1987 is 20 percent of the market share. This larger market share can be achieved since there is only one main competitor, Mrs. Dash, and the company is already outselling that product in Oklahoma. The company's product is superior in all respects and has a retail price advantage of 10 to 20 cents per can over Mrs. Dash. In addition, the company's product is much more versatile than Mrs. Dash. Aggressive marketing and advertising will emphasize the tremendous versatility of usage as well as the great taste and health benefits of the product. The informal consumer surveys at demonstrations indicated that consumers prefer Nature Bros. to Mrs. Dash by a wide margin.

A new product, which is already developed, will be added during this time. Called "Enhance," it is also a dry-mixed, noncooked, low-overhead, high-profit food product. Its category of MSG products has a dollar volume of $978,545 in these markets. This category includes only one main competitor, Accent, made by Pet Inc. Accent

EXHIBIT 3   1988 Sales Projection

Category	Seasoned Salt	Salt Substitute	MSG
Our Product	Old Fashioned Seasoning	Salt-Free Old Fashioned Seasoning	Enhance
Existing markets #1			
Oklahoma	$578,468	$375,709	$124,889
Nebraska	489,473	317,908	105,675
Springfield, MO	311,483	202,305	67,248
Arkansas	266,985	173,404	57,641
Houston	1,023,443	664,716	220,957
Dallas	1,423,921	942,822	307,419
Albuquerque	667,463	433,510	144,103
Existing markets total	$4,761,236	$3,110,374	$1,027,932
Market share	×15%	×25%	×15%
Existing markets $ volume	$714,185	$775,593	$154,189
New markets:			
Los Angeles	$2,892,339	$1,878,544	$624,444
Phoenix	622,965	404,609	134,495
Portland	578,647	375,709	124,888
Sacramento	845,453	549,113	182,530
Salt Lake	578,647	375,708	124,888
San Francisco	1,156,935	751,419	249,777
Seattle	578,647	375,708	124,888
Spokane	355,980	231,206	76,854
New markets total	$7,609,443	$5,032,014	$1,642,764
Market share	×10%	×20%	×10%
New markets $ volume	$760,943	$1,006,420	$164,276
New markets $ total	$760,943	$1,006,420	$164,276
Existing markets $ total +	714,185	777,593	154,189
Total volume	$1,475,128	$1,784,013	$318,465

Old Fashioned Seasoning sales	$1,475,128
Salt-Free Old Fashioned Seasoning sales	1,784,013
Enhance sales (a new product)	318,465
Total 1988 sales	$3,557,606

has not been heavily advertised, and it is a one-line product with little initial name recognition. The company's new product will have a 30- to 40-cent per can retail price advantage to help achieve a 10 percent share of this category. In summary, 1987 will be spent solidifying the company's present market positions, which make up 10.7 percent of the total U.S. grocery market, resulting in a 1987 sales volume of $1,083,472.

EXHIBIT 4   1987 Pro Forma Totals

	1987	Percent
Sales	$1,083,472	100
Cost of goods		
Packaging	129,444	11.9
Ingredients	175,668	16.2
Plant labor	35,580	3.2
Freight in	24,036	2.2
Shipping materials	924	.08
Total cost of goods sold	365,004	33.68
Gross profit	718,468	66.31
Operating expenses		
President's salary	43,200	
Sales manager	30,000	
Secretary	14,400	
Employee benefits	2,400	
Insurance	1,992	
Rent	3,000	
Utilities	1,800	
Phone	7,200	
Office supplies	1,200	
Postage	1,200	
Car lease	5,640	
Professional services	3,000	
Travel and entertainment	24,000	
Freight out	59,088	5.4
Advertising	216,684	20.0
Promotion	12,036	1.1
Brokerage	54,168	5.0
Incentives	7,500	.6
Cash discounts	21,660	2.0
Total expenses	$ 510,168	47.0
Cash flow		
Taxes	207,648	19.1
Net profit before debt service	155,736	14.3

1988 OBJECTIVES

The company intends to open eight new markets in 1988 that include Los Angeles, Phoenix, Portland, Sacramento, Salt Lake City, San Francisco, Seattle, and Spokane. These new markets make up 17.1 percent of grocery store sales, according to the *Progressive Grocer's Marketing Guidebook*, the industry standard. In the

EXHIBIT 5

NATURE BROS. LTD.
Pro Forma Income Statement
1988–1991

	1988	1989	1990	1991
Sales	$3,557,606	$6,136,224	$10,089,863	$18,506,302
Cost of goods				
Packaging	423,355	730,210	1,200,693	2,202,249
Ingredients	572,774	987,932	1,624,467	2,979,514
Plant labor	37,359	48,826	60,867	63,910
Freight in	72,930	125,793	206,842	379,379
Shipping materials	2,960	4,908	8,071	14,805
Total cost of goods sold	$1,106,575	$1,897,618	$ 3,100,240	$ 5,639,858
Percent of sales	31.36%	31.41%	30.90%	30.65%
Gross profit	2,451,031	4,238,606	6,988,923	12,866,444
Operating expense				
President's salary	43,200	51,840	62,208	74,649
Sales manager	30,000	36,000	39,000	45,000
Sales rep	25,000	30,000	34,000	38,000
Sales rep		25,000	30,000	34,000
Sales rep			26,000	30,000
Sales rep				28,000
Secretary	16,000	18,000	20,000	22,000
Secretary				15,000
Employee benefits	2,400	4,000	10,000	15,000
Insurance	3,000	4,000	5,000	5,000
Rent	3,600	3,600	3,600	3,600
Utilities	2,400	3,000	3,500	4,500
Phone	12,000	14,000	15,000	18,000
Office supplies	2,000	2,500	3,000	5,000
Postage	2,000	2,500	3,000	4,000
Car lease	5,640	5,640	5,640	5,640
Car lease	3,600	3,600	4,000	4,000
Car lease		3,600	3,600	4,000
Car lease			4,000	4,000
Professional services	6,000	8,000	8,000	10,000
Travel and entertainment	48,000	72,000	96,000	120,000
New equipment	4,000	14,000	14,000	24,000
Freight out	197,269	334,424	549,897	1,000,859
Advertising	711,521	1,227,244	2,017,972	3,701,260
Promotion	40,000	68,112	111,997	205,419
Brokerage	177,880	306,811	504,493	925,315
Incentives	24,547	42,399	69,680	205,419
Cash discounts	71,152	122,724	201,792	370,126
Total expenses	$1,431,209	$2,402,994	$ 3,845,192	$ 6,921,787
Cash flow before taxes	1,019,822	1,835,612	3,845,192	6,921,787
Taxes	209,063	458,903	785,932	1,486,164
Net profit before debt service	$ 810,759	$1,376,709	$ 2,357,799	$ 4,458,493
Percent of sales	22.78%	22.43%	23.36%	24.09%

EXHIBIT 6

Source: *Tulsa World*, June 17, 1987.

category of seasoned salt, these markets have a dollar volume of $7,609,443 a year. Salt substitutes sell at a volume of $5,032,014, and the MSG category $1,642,764. With proper advertising, the company's shares forecast in our current markets will also be realized.

A 10 percent penetration of the seasoned salt category is a very conservative projection considering the strong health consciousness of the West Coast. The products will be introduced in shippers, used in store demonstrations, and supported with media advertising to achieve at least a 10 percent market share. This would result in sales of $760,943 in that category.

A 20 percent penetration is targeted in the salt-free category. Using aggressive marketing, price advantage at retail, and better packaging, the company will be well positioned against the lower-quality products of our competitors. With the dollar volume of this category at $5,032,014, a conservative estimate of our share would be $1,006,420. In the category of MSG, a 10 percent share will be achieved. The main competitor in this category does very little advertising. Again, attractive packaging, aggressive marketing, high quality, and a retail price advantage of 30 to 40 cents per unit will enable the company to realize a 10 percent market penetration. This share of the West Coast markets will generate sales of $164,276. Total sales of all three products in these eight new markets will be around $1,931,639. The company plans to continue to solidify the markets previously established through the use of coupons, co-op advertising, quality promotions, and word-of-mouth advertising. Market share in these original markets should increase by another 5 percent in 1988. The dollar volume of the seasoned salt category in 1988 should be around $4,761,236, and our market share at 15 percent would amount to $714,185. The dollar volume for the salt substitute category would be $3,110,374, giving sales at

25 percent of $775,593. In the MSG category, a 15 percent market share of the $1,027,932 volume would give sales of $154,189. The company's total sales for the existing markets in 1988 will be in excess of $1,643,967. The totals for 1988 sales of Nature Bros. Old Fashioned Seasoning will be $1,475,128. Nature Bros. Salt-Free volume should be $1,784,013. The sales of Enhance, our MSG product, should be $318,465. This will give us a total sales volume of $3,557,606 for all three products in 1988.

FINANCIAL NEEDS AND PROJECTIONS

In this plan, Morris indicated a need for $100,000 equity infusion to expand sales, increase markets, and add new products. The money would be used to secure warehouse stocking space, do cooperative print advertising, give point-of-purchase display allowances, and pay operating expenses.

NEW PRODUCT DEVELOPMENT

The company plans to continue an ongoing research and development program to introduce new and winning products. Four products are already developed that will be highly marketable and easily produced. Personnel are dedicated to building a large and profitable company and attracting quality brokers. The next new product targets a different market segment but can be brought online for about $25,000 by using our existing machinery, types of containers, and display pieces. A highly respected broker felt that the product would be a big success. The broker previously represented the only major producer of a similar product, Pet Inc., which had sales of $4.36 million in 1985. The company can achieve at least a 10 percent market share with this product in the first year. The company's product will be at least equal in quality and offer a 17 percent price advantage to the consumer, while still making an excellent profit.

Another new product would require slightly different equipment. This product would be initially produced by a private-label manufacturer. The product would be established before any major machinery was purchased. Many large companies use private-label manufacturers, or co-packers, as they are called in the trade. Consumer tests at demonstrations and food shows have indicated that each of these products will be strong.

PLANT AND EQUIPMENT

The company's plant is located in a nearly new metal building in Rose, Oklahoma. The lease on the building limits payments to no more than $300 per month for the next seven years. The new computer-controlled filling equipment will be paid off in two months, and the seaming equipment is leased from the company's container manufacturer for only $1 per year. The company has the capability of producing about 300,000 units a month with an additional $15,000 investment for an automatic conveyer system and a bigger product mixer. This production level would require two additional plant personnel, working one shift with no overtime. The company could double this production if needed with the addition of another shift. One of the main advantages of the company's business is the very small overhead required to produce the products. The company can generate enough product to reach sales of approximately $4 million a year while maintaining a production payroll of only $37,000 a year.

To meet the previously outlined production goals, the company will need to purchase another filling machine in 1988. This machine will be capable of filling two cans at once with an overall speed of 75 cans per minute, which would increase capacity to 720,000 units a month. A higher-speed seaming machine will also need to be purchased. The filling machine would cost approximately $22,000; a rebuilt seamer would cost $25,000, while a new one would cost $50,000. With the addition of these two machines, the company would have a capacity of 1,020,000 units per month on one shift.

By 1989, the company will have to decide whether to continue the lease or buy the property where located and expand the facilities. The property has plenty of land for expansion for the next five years. The company has the flexibility to produce other types of products with the same equipment and can react quickly to changes in customer preferences and modify its production line to meet such demands as needed.

Source: Prepared by Kris Opalinski and Walter S. Good of the University of Manitoba, Canada, as a basis for classroom discussion rather than to illustrate either effective or ineffective handling of an administrative situation.
The name of the company and the names its officers have been disguised. Support for the development of this case was provided by the Centre for International Business Studies, University of Manitoba, Canada.

MANAGING, GROWING, AND ENDING THE NEW VENTURE

Preparing for the New Venture Launch: Early Management Decisions

1. To learn effective strategies in recruiting and interviewing potential employees.

2. To understand how to motivate employees, provide leadership, and create the optimum work environment.

3. To describe the important procedures for effective record keeping and financial control during the early stages of the new venture's operation.

4. To discuss the important issues in managing cash, expenses, assets, debt, profits, and taxes.

5. To understand how ratios can be used to assess the financial strengths and weaknesses of a new venture.

6. To illustrate control processes for marketing and sales plans.

7. To understand how to effectively promote the new venture through publicity, the Internet, and advertising.

BRIAN AND JENNIFER MAXWELL

Brian Maxwell, an internationally ranked marathon runner and coach at the University of California, Berkeley, was leading a marathon race in England when at the 21-mile mark he began to experience dizziness and tunnel vision, which forced

olympics.powerbar.com

him to quit the race. His consumption of energy drinks on the day of the race had failed and motivated him to find a solution for a better energy source. Teaming with Jennifer Biddulph, a student studying nutrition and food science (now a PhD chemist), they began the quest for an energy bar that would taste good, be healthy and nutritious, and provide the appropriate ingredients to optimize performance. With $50,000 gathered from savings they were determined to find a solution.[1]

During their three years of research, experts indicated to them that it would be impossible to produce a healthy product because of the large amounts of saturated fats necessary for lubricating machinery in the food bar manufacturing process. However, after many failures they found the solution. They understood that their efforts required developing a food bar manufacturing process that would not require adding fats for lubrication of machinery and would produce a product that would meet the above desired attributes. The product needed to provide a balance of simple carbohydrates for quick energy, complex carbohydrates for longer lasting energy, and low fat for easy digestion. Hundreds of recipes were tested with athletes until the most effective and best-tasting product was found. Continued requests among these athletes to have more of those "power bars" led to the final brand name, and in 1986 they officially formed the company, PowerBar Inc.

Initially the company was operated from Brian and Jennifer's basement. The first products, which went on sale in 1987, were the Malt-Nut and Chocolate flavors. After their marriage in 1988 they moved to a new facility and began hiring employees to meet the growing demand.

Their vision of finding a solution to a serious runner's energy source wasn't the only factor in forming this new venture. Both Brian and Jennifer were determined to create a work environment where employees would feel important and have a strong sense of pride in the company. They wanted a company that did not have all the things that they hated about jobs they had held previously. Thus, they created a work environment where employees are called team members, the dress is casual, and the atmosphere is on sports. To Brian and Jennifer it was important that their employees enjoyed the workplace and developed an important loyalty and commitment to the company's mission.

In the early part of the 1990s sales for the new venture increased by 50 to 60 percent. In 1997 sales began to slow and increased by only 23 percent. In 1995 Brian and Jennifer turned down an opportunity to purchase Balance Bar, a producer of an energy bar that targeted the more casual athlete and those who were looking for a nutritious snack. They had believed that their company did not need to add any new products and could continue to grow with the one product. In retrospect, they realized this mistake in strategy and that the venture could not survive on the one product, especially when they saw sales begin to stall in 1995. At that time there were many new competitors who recognized the opportunities in a larger market by introducing energy bars for the casual exercisers and snackers. So in 1997 Brian and Jennifer began efforts to find new products. In 1998 they launched PowerBar Harvest, a crunchy, textured energy bar available in a number of flavors that would target the more casual athlete and those consumers looking for a nutritious snack. In 1999 a new creamy bar called Essentials and a new line of sports drinks were launched.

Today PowerBar is still the leader in the more serious athlete market, and Harvest has just passed Clif bar to become the number three brand in this category. Sales in 1999 reached $135 million. The company also opened a state-of-the-art manufacturing facility in Idaho and two distribution centers in Idaho and North Carolina. They have also established two subsidiaries in Canada and Germany as opportunities for sales growth in international markets occur.

Brian still runs 40 to 50 miles per week. Jennifer was recently recognized in the first annual Working Women Entrepreneurial Excellence Awards competition by winning for Harvest in the Best Innovation category. In 2000, PowerBar was purchased by Nestle Foods, which intends to grow and expand it globally. Brian Maxwell will continue to play an integral role in the company.

In this chapter, important management decision areas are reviewed and discussed. Building a solid management team and loyal employee base as well as financial and marketing control decisions, recognized by entrepreneurs like Brian and Jennifer Maxwell as being very important during the early years, are discussed in detail.

ࢬ

RECORD KEEPING

Before discussing the important control issues for the new venture in its early stages, it is necessary to understand what records are necessary for the entrepreneur to maintain and some simple techniques for maintaining good records. It is necessary to have good records not only for effective control but also for tax purposes. Regardless of the sophistication of the record-keeping method, the entrepreneur should be comfortable and, more important, able to understand what is going on in the business. With the availability of new software packages that are user friendly, much of the record keeping can be easily maintained on a personal computer. Some examples of these software packages were discussed in Chapter 9. Since the long-term future of the new venture depends on profits and a positive cash flow, we can simplify the goals of a good record-keeping system by identifying key incoming and outgoing revenues that can be more effectively controlled with good records.

Sales (Incoming Revenue)

Depending on the nature of the business, it is useful to have knowledge of sales by customer in terms of both units and dollars. If you were operating a catalog business, you would find value in maintaining information about how often and how much any particular customer buys in any given time period. The types of products purchased will also be relevant, especially when and if the catalog venture wishes to notify the customer that there are special sale prices on items in which the customer has shown interest in the past. For example, a person who has shown interest in do-it-yourself products (tools or household accessories) may want to receive flyers or special sale notices on these types of products.

For a retail store it is more difficult, and perhaps less important than for a catalog business, to know every customer's buying history or behavior. However, the entrepreneur in this type of venture should try to identify the profile of the type of customer who patronizes the store. This can be done by having customers fill out a short questionnaire that identifies demographic information as well as their product and service interests, which could be translated into merchandise decisions for the entrepreneur. There are also occasions when retailers do like to have information on specific customers, such as when they are attempting to develop good mailing lists for sale notices or flyers. Credit card customers are easier to track since initial data on the customer would have been collected when the customer applied for the card. Credit card purchases for merchandise can be tracked for information on the type and amount of merchandise purchased.

The Internet venture can also utilize similar procedures to track customers. Purchase history data should be maintained on the types of products or services purchased. Customers' e-mail addresses can be requested as part of the payment transaction so that the customer can be notified of impending sales on important merchandise. Some Internet firms have established a free membership as a means of following up with sale merchandise either electronically or through the mail.

In a service venture such as a day-care center, sales would be defined as fees for service. In this case, customers pay a monthly fee for the service. The day-care center would need to maintain records on when or whether a customer paid the monthly fee. These records are important in this type of business so that customers can be politely notified with the first late payment notice. It is also not unusual to charge a fee for any late payments, commensurate with the amount due (typically this would be 1 to 2 percent of the amount due). The existence of the late fee sometimes acts as an incentive for customers to pay their bills on time. As we will see later in this chapter, cash flow problems are probably the most significant cause of new venture failure. Thus, good records regarding customer payments are necessary to maintain sufficient incoming cash so that the entrepreneur in turn can make payments of his or her bills on time.

Record keeping of customer payments can be handled either by a simple computer software package, such as Quicken, or with a simple card file system. The software package requires the entrepreneur to enter all payments to an account with a date of payment. At any time, the entrepreneur can output the payments by customer. The software can also print out a list of nonpayees for any month at any time so that late notices can be sent out the day after payments were due. The card file works in the same fashion as the computer program but would be done manually by the entrepreneur. Each customer would be listed on a card file. On the card would be recorded all payments including check number and date of payment. As customers pay each month, their card would be transferred to another card file. Thus, at any time the entrepreneur would have two card files, one for customers paid and the other for customers not paid. This is a simple method of maintaining records for ventures with a fixed number of customers who are paying by the month.

If payments of customers in any business are late beyond a reasonable time, it may be necessary for the entrepreneur to hire a collection agency. This should be done as a last resort after at least two contacts have been made over the telephone and by mail. Collection agencies will usually charge a fixed fee and then may charge a percentage for all additional revenues they collect. Other agencies may charge a single fixed fee, depending on the number of delinquent accounts and amount of money. Generally, it is more cost beneficial to choose an agency that charges by the amount collected. It is also important for the entrepreneur to make sure that the agency is reliable and professional.

Expenses/Costs (Outgoing Revenue)

Records of expenses or outgoing revenue can usually be maintained quite easily through the checking account. It is good business practice for the entrepreneur to use checks as payment for all expenses in order to maintain records for tax purposes. On those occasions where cash is used, a receipt should be requested and filed for future reference.

Canceled checks provide the entrepreneur with proof of payment and hence should be kept in order (by number and date) and then stored. The length of time they should be kept is generally a function of Internal Revenue Service requirements. In a small venture invoices that are due can be sorted by date due. Checks can then be written once a week to maintain a clean slate with no late payments. Entrepreneurs may find it necessary in the early stages of a new venture to do everything possible to make payments on time. This establishes good credibility with suppliers and can be helpful to ensure prompt deliveries and good service.

In addition to the above items, the entrepreneur should maintain information about employees, such as address, social security number, date of birth, date hired, date fired or released, and so on. This can also be maintained in either a software program or a card file. Also, it may be necessary to maintain records on all assets owned by the business. If there are significant assets, they should be identified with a date of purchase. This will be helpful in determining depreciation for tax purposes.

Once a good record-keeping system is in place, the entrepreneur will find it easier to maintain controls over cash, disbursements, inventory, and assets. In general, it is advised to establish a control process for financial variables—such as cash, assets, and costs—and for marketing and sales goals. These areas will be discussed below.

RECRUITING AND HIRING NEW EMPLOYEES

Recruiting and hiring new employees may occur at both the entry and senior management level. Strategy and procedures may differ somewhat depending on the level for which the individual is being hired. The entrepreneur will generally need to establish procedures for hiring any new employees. Many of these hiring decisions will be important, and thus, the entrepreneur should establish some criteria as to what characteristics will be considered in evaluating potential employees.

Recruiting new employees can be accomplished in many different ways. Advertising in local newspapers and using a network of friends and business associates are probably most effective for hiring entry level and less skilled positions. For senior management the most effective strategy is networking with friends and business associates such as bankers, venture capitalists, private investors, or any of the external advisors to the new venture. Personnel agencies may also be considered but may result in an expense for the entrepreneur. However, this cost may be worth it if there are no other effective options. Discussing these options with other entrepreneurs or through some of the sources indicated in Chapter 7 would probably be very helpful since many of these sources would have had experience with these alternatives.

Once resumes have been collected, especially for the entry-level employee, some basis of determining each candidate's strengths should be made. To do this will necessitate some criteria being used in the resume evaluation. Typically, such factors as education, experience, entrepreneurial activities, and interests that are common in most resumes can be used to assess the potential quality of candidates. It is helpful to sometimes rate each candidate on a scale of one to five on each of the important criteria. If more than one person is evaluating resumes, these ratings can be compared and discussed in a meeting. From the initial screening of resumes, a few agreed upon candidates would then be invited in for an interview. Again, it is important to establish an interviewing strategy and to know before the interviewing process begins what questions will be asked and how the responses will be evaluated in order to provide meaningful information for making the final hiring decision. Most firms will use a form with critical factors listed for evaluating the interviewed candidates. This is helpful if there are a number of candidates being interviewed and will avoid any confusion or recall problems for the interviewer. The goal should be to hire not only the best candidate but also someone who will perform well in the entrepreneurial environment and provide a long-term solution to the available position.

The interviewer should ask all of his or her questions at the beginning of the interview. This accomplishes two things. First, it allows the interviewer to evaluate the candidate's behavior; and second, it avoids one of the most common problems in the interview, which is talking too much and not listening. Prepared questions may include (a) what would your former employer indicate about your work performance? (b) what would your former coworkers say about you personally and your work performance? (c) what weaknesses do you have that you would like to improve? and (d) what specific work experiences have you had that have given you the most self-satisfaction? If this is a new graduate from college, the interviewer can substitute "teachers" for employer and "classmates" for coworkers. Upon completion of the interview the firm should be sure to check all of the candidate's references.

Acquiring senior talent can be critical to the ability of the new venture to successfully meet its growth goals. New evidence indicates that start-up companies are not having as much difficulty filling senior management positions as was once believed. Diana Edwards left a management position to become the vice president of corporate development at a start-up airline, Community Air. She not only took a large pay cut but had no guarantee that the airline would even be around very long. She took the position because her priorities, as for many senior managers, were based on more than salary. She saw the enthusiasm and vision of the founders, liked the business plan, and was given complete autonomy to coordinate the launch of the airline. In addition, she was given options on more than 100,000 shares of stock. Minoj Tripathi left a senior executive position with Body Shop to join a small growing start-up, Jamba Juice. He received a comparable salary but joined the new venture because of the excitement and challenge of the start-up and because the 1 percent equity could become substantial if the firm continued to grow and went public at some future date.[2]

These examples are more common today as executives choose to become part of the entrepreneurial process rather than to continue working in the structured, less-exciting environment of big business. These individuals are not just looking for significant equity but are also interested in the challenge of working for a growing new venture.

Where does an entrepreneur find this senior talent? In the examples above, one person was contacted by a recruiter and the other through a business associate. The most critical conclusion for the entrepreneur is to use all of his or her contacts and to recognize that every potential candidate is different. Thus, the package offered should be based somewhat on the candidate's needs whether it be flextime, stock options, or bonuses tied to performance.

MOTIVATING AND LEADING THE TEAM

The entrepreneur or founder of the new venture will usually be a role model for other employees. A good work ethic—being organized, being prepared for meetings, being on time, giving praise to employees, and good communication within the venture—will go a long way toward achieving financial and emotional success. If employees sense that the entrepreneur is not committed to the venture or has given up hope for success, they will act accordingly and probably seek other employment. During these early stages employees need incentives to remain committed and loyal to the long-run success of the new venture. As mentioned above, stock options or cash rewards for good performance can also be used to maintain a quality workforce.

Many entrepreneurs find the role of leader to the management team and employees very difficult. Even in very small start-up companies it is important that the founder assume this role. Leadership is not just assuming responsibility; it is also influencing and inspiring others in the organization to strive to meet the mission of the venture. Leadership can be addressed in many different ways. However, there are a number of behaviors listed below that can exhibit the leadership qualities necessary for the new venture.

- Set an example with an ethical set of values for other managers and employees.
- Show respect and concern for the personal well-being of employees.
- Don't try to do everything yourself. Give managers and employees the autonomy and flexibility to make decisions on their own.
- Recognize the diversity of employees and how they should be treated.
- Encourage and praise others in the organization when deserved.
- Provide incentives and awards for quality work effort and new ideas.
- Recognize the importance of employees having fun at their jobs.
- Be aware of the need for future strategic planning by encouraging everyone to participate.

Communication with managers and employees is one of the most important underlying attributes of all the above listed leadership qualities. Communication is more than just sending messages or telling others what needs to be done. It's also being a good listener.

Brian and Jennifer Maxwell are only one example of how start-ups are attracting quality employees by building an organization that is based on the above behaviors. Paula Lawlor, the founder of Medi-Health Outsourcing, which she describes as an unglamorous business, has been able to bring out the best in her employees. Managers are given all the venture's financials and told to define their budgets and grow their business. Other hourly employees are given every opportunity to climb the corporate ladder and move around the company until they find their niche. The personal lives of employees are important to Paula, and she accommodates their problems by letting them work out of their home or work flexible hours. Employees are given complete autonomy in how they manage their personal lives and work responsibilities. She doesn't care how or when employees get their work done as long as they meet their goals and deadlines. Behind this system is a motivated, loyal, and committed group of employees who enjoy their work environment but also understand that they are accountable for their actions.[3]

FINANCIAL CONTROL

The financial plan, as an inherent part of the business plan, was discussed in Chapter 9. Just as we outlined how to prepare pro forma income and cash flow statements for the first three years, the entrepreneur will need some knowledge of how to provide appropriate controls to ensure that projections and goals are met. Some financial skills are thus necessary for the entrepreneur to manage the venture during these early years. Cash flows, the income statement, and the balance sheet are the key financial areas that will need careful management and control. Since Chapter 9 explains how to prepare these pro forma statements, the focus in this section will be controls and management of these elements.

Managing Cash Flow

Since cash outflow may exceed cash inflow, the entrepreneur should try to have an up-to-date assessment of his or her cash position. This can be accomplished by preparing monthly cash flow statements, such as that found in Figure 13.1, and comparing the budgeted or pro forma statements with the actual results. The July budgeted amounts are taken from the pro forma cash flow statement of MPP Plastics (see Figure 9.5). The entrepreneur can indicate the actual amounts next to the budgeted amounts. This will be useful for adjusting the pro forma for the remaining months, as well as for providing some indication as to where cash flow problems may exist.

Figure 13.1 shows a few potential problem areas. First, sales receipts were less than anticipated. Whether this was due to nonpayment by some customers or to an increase in credit sales needs to be assessed. If the lower amount is due to nonpayment by customers, the entrepreneur may need to try enforcing faster payment by sending reminder letters or making telephone calls to delinquent customers. Bounced checks from customers can also affect cash flow since the entrepreneur has likely credited the amount to the account and assumed that the cash is readily available. If the lower receipts are resulting from higher credit sales, the entrepreneur may need to either consider short-term financing from a bank or try to extend the terms of payment to his or her suppliers.[4]

Cash disbursements for some items were greater than budgeted and may indicate a need for tighter cost controls. For example, cost of goods was $22,500, which was $1,700 more than budgeted. The entrepreneur may find that suppliers increased their prices, which may require a search for alternative sources or even raising the prices of the products/services offered by the new venture. If the higher cost of goods resulted from the purchase of more supplies, then the entrepreneur should assess the

FIGURE 13.1 MPP Plastics Inc. (Statement of Cash Flow) July, Year 1 (000s)

	July Budgeted	July Actual
Receipts		
Sales	$ 24.0	$ 22.0
Disbursements		
Equipment	100.0	100.0
Cost of goods	20.8	22.5
Selling expenses	1.5	2.5
Salaries	6.5	6.5
Advertising	1.5	1.5
Office supplies	0.3	0.3
Rent	2.0	2.0
Utilities	0.3	0.5
Insurance	0.8	0.8
Taxes	0.8	0.8
Loan principal and interest	2.6	2.6
Total disbursements	$ 137.0	$ 140.0
Cash flow	(113.1)	(118.0)
Beginning balance	275.0	275.0
Ending balance	161.9	157.0

inventory costs from the income statement. It is possible that the increased cost of goods resulted from the purchase of more supplies because sales were higher than expected. However, if these additional sales resulted in more credit sales, the entrepreneur may need to plan to borrow money to meet short-term cash needs. Conclusions can be made once the credit sales and inventory costs are evaluated.

The higher-selling expenses may also need to be assessed. If the additional selling expenses were incurred in order to support increased sales (even if they were credit sales), then there is no immediate concern. However, if no additional sales were generated, the entrepreneur may need to review all of these expenses and perhaps institute tighter controls.

A cash flow crisis can occur suddenly and unexpectedly as evidenced by Anchor Communications, a Providence magazine publisher that incurred a shortfall of $350,000. The chief operating officer enlisted the assistance of all the employees by training them on the significance of cash flow and asking for their help in improving it. A goal was established to reduce the shortfall with the incentive of prizes in return for any cash savings. Ideas flowed to the company on how to save money on utilities, along with cash-generating ideas on selling magazine-sponsored gift certificates for local restaurants. The company sold the certificates to subscribers and reimbursed restaurants only when they were redeemed. The result was dramatic, and in one year the company surpassed its goals and eliminated the cash shortfall.[5]

Projecting cash flow in the early stages can also benefit by conducting sensitivity analysis. For each monthly expected cash flow the entrepreneur can use a +/− of

As Seen in *Business Week*:
Surviving a Cash-Flow Crunch from Slow-Paying Clients
Here's How to Find Bridge Financing While You Wait for Your Money

Q: Our nonprofit organization offers shelter for homeless people. We are funded by federal grants. But the money does not come in until after we provide services and submit invoices. How do we survive financially until we get paid?

—O.F.S., Bayamon, Puerto Rico

A: Your problem is common to both profit-making companies and nonprofit agencies that do business with local, state, and federal government agencies, hospitals, and educational institutions—all of which can be slow at paying. Between lengthy approval processes, budget shortfalls, political power struggles, and red tape, it may be as long as eight months before you get funds for work done or goods delivered. Or payment might be delayed at the beginning of a long-term contract.

Any time billing is done on credit terms, business owners face the problem of liquidity. This is an issue that crops up in many situations—not just when you're working on a government contract. Often, small-business owners turn to home equity loans or personal credit cards to fill the gap. But there are other solutions you may prefer.

Since you're a not-for-profit providing shelter, you ought to first contact a local government housing or redevelopment agency and ask whether it would offer bridge funding for you out of its budget. If no municipal agency is willing to help, try a local lending institution. The federal money you get down the line could be assigned to you and the bank or regional agency that's helping you out. Therefore, repayment would be virtually guaranteed. "The government is a good payer. So all you need is a big brother who's got some ready cash, which sounds like a city or county agency or a bank," says Kent J. Burnes of Burnes Consulting, a small-business and economic development adviser in Grass Valley, California. "A lending institution will make sure that

their payments don't get ahead of the service delivery schedule. But they should feel pretty easy about up-fronting you the money. Then you can do some fund-raising to help pay the interest."

As you are a nonprofit, there may also be local philanthropists or businesses to help you with funding and to tide you through this cash-flow crunch, Burnes says.

For businesses, there's another option—factors, says Miles Stuchin, founder and president of Access Capital Inc. (www.accesscapitalinc.com) in New York. In a factoring deal, you sell your accounts receivable at a discount to a third party at the time you send the invoices for your goods or services, giving you immediate cash and someone to manage your accounts receivable. When the underlying bill is paid, the funds will go to the factor, who will typically also charge you interest.

"Factoring is done across all industries," says Stuchin. "Traditional factoring is concentrated in the apparel, textiles, and furniture industries. Non-traditional factoring involves virtually any industry you can imagine, anywhere there are credit terms and sales by businesses to institutional customers like governments and schools."

A good place to find a factor is through the Commercial Finance Association, which has a roster of members ranging from asset-based lenders and huge commercial finance corporations to independent, one- or two-person operations. The CFA, based in New York (212 594–3490), provides information, lists, and a monthly newsletter on its website, www.cfa.com. A subset of its membership specializes in working with government contractors and small businesses, Stuchin says.

Source: Karen E. Klein, "Surviving a Cash Flow Crunch from Slow-Paying Clients," *Business Week* (April 1, 1999).

5 percent that would provide a pessimistic and optimistic cash estimate. Thus, our MPP Plastics example (Figure 13.1) might have projected in the prior month sales receipts of $24,000 and, using the +/− of 5 percent, would have a column indicating a pessimistic amount of $22,800 and an optimistic amount of $25,200. This

FIGURE 13.2 Daily Cash Activity (Date)

Beginning day's cash balance:	$XXX	
Add:		
Day's cash sales (cash, charges, checks)	$XXX	
Collection of receivables	$XXX	
Total		$XXX
Less:		
Charge account sales (from day's cash sales)		$XXX
Total cash collected		$XXX
Cash disbursed:		
Cash refunds	$XXX	
Cash returns	$XXX	
Petty cash expenses (such as postage, travel, supplies, or repairs)	$XXX	
Total cash disbursed (subtract from total cash collected)		$XXX
Amount of cash that should be on hand		$XXX
Actual count of cash on hand		$XXX
Difference between what should be on hand and actual		$XXX

If the final number is negative or positive, then an error has occurred in collections or payments.

sensitivity analysis would then be computed for all disbursements as well. In this manner the entrepreneur would be able to ascertain the maximum cash needs given a pessimistic outcome and could prepare for any cash needs.

For the very new venture it may be necessary to prepare a daily cash sheet. This might be particularly beneficial to a retail store, restaurant, or service business. Figure 13.2 provides an illustration of the cash available at the beginning of the day with additions and deletions of cash recorded as indicated. This would provide an effective indication of any daily shortfall and give a clear sense of where problems exist or where errors have occurred.

Comparison of budgeted or expected cash flows with actual cash flows can provide the entrepreneur with an important assessment of potential immediate cash needs and indicate possible problems in the management of assets or control of costs. These items are discussed further in the next sections.[6]

Managing Assets

Figure 13.3 illustrates the balance sheet for MPP Plastics after the first three months of operation. In the asset section of the balance sheet are items that need to be managed carefully by the entrepreneur in the early months of the new venture. We have already discussed the importance of cash management using cash flow projections. Other items—such as the accounts receivable, inventory, and supplies—also need to be controlled to ensure maximum cash flow and effective use of funds by the new venture.

With the increasing use and number of credit cards, it is likely that many consumers will consider buying on credit. Some ventures may even consider providing

FIGURE 13.3 MPP Plastics Inc., Balance Sheet, First Quarter Year 1

Assets

Current assets

Cash	$ 13,350	
Accounts receivable (40% of 60,000 in sales the previous month)	24,000	
Merchandise inventory	12,850	
Supplies	2,100	
Total fixed assets		$ 51,300
Fixed assets	$240,000	
Equipment		
Less depreciation	9,900	
Total fixed assets		$230,100
Total assets		281,400

Liabilities and Owner's Equity

Current liabilities

Accounts payable (20% of 40 CGS)	$ 8,000	
Current portion of L-T debt	13,600	
Total current liabilities		$ 21,600
Long-term liabilities		
Notes payable		223,200
Total liabilities		244,800
Owner's equity		
C. Peter's capital	$25,000	
K. Peter's capital	25,000	
Retained earnings	(13,400)	
Total owner's equity		$ 36,600
Total liabilities and owner's equity		281,400

their own credit to avoid paying fees to the credit card company. There are some trade-offs in determining whether credit cards such as Mastercard, Visa, American Express, and Discover are acceptable or whether other credit options will be made available.

If credit cards are acceptable to the new venture, then the risk for accounts receivable collections will be shifted to the credit card companies. Shifting the risk, however, costs the entrepreneur a fee of about 3 to 4 percent. More often, firms are offering customers lower prices for cash sales. Those opting for credit cards will pay a higher price for the privilege of using their cards, thereby offsetting the fee paid by the company.

If customers are allowed to buy on internal credit, the entrepreneur will be responsible for collecting any delinquent payments. Delays in payments can also be problematic since, as we have seen in cash flow analysis, these delays can cause negative cash flows. Any nonpayment of accounts receivable will become an expense (bad debt) on the income statement at the end of the fiscal year. In any event, the entrepreneur will need to be sensitive to major changes in accounts receivable and should always compare actual with budgeted amounts (generally estimated to be a percentage of gross sales) as a means for controlling and managing this important asset.

Inventory control is also important to the entrepreneur. This is an expensive asset and requires careful balancing of just enough inventory to meet demand for finished goods. If inventory is low and the firm cannot meet demand on time, sales could be lost. On the other hand, carrying excess inventory can be costly, either because of excessive handling and storage costs or because it becomes obsolete before being sold. Growing ventures typically tie up more cash in their inventory than in any other part of the business. Skolnik Industries, a $10 million manufacturer of steel containers for storage and disposal of hazardous materials, recently developed an inventory control system that allows it to ship products to its customers within 24 to 48 hours. This was accomplished with a very lean inventory, thanks to the installation of a computerized inventory-control system that allows the firm to maintain records of inventory on a product-by-product basis. In addition to this capability, the system allows the company to monitor gross margin return on investment, inventory turnover, percentage of orders shipped on time, length of time to fill back orders, and percentage of customer complaints to shipped orders. Software to accomplish these goals is readily available and in many cases can even be modified to meet the exact needs of the business. The reports from this system are generated every two to four weeks in normal sales periods and weekly in heavy sales periods. This system not only provides Skolnik with an early warning system but also frees up cash normally invested in inventory and improves the overall profitability of the firm.[7]

From an accounting point of view, the entrepreneur will need to determine the value of inventory and how it affects the cost of goods sold (income statement). For example, assume that an entrepreneur made three purchases of inventory for manufacturing a finished product. Each purchase of inventory involved a different price. The issue will be what to use as a cost of goods sold. Generally, either a *FIFO* (first-in, first-out) or *LIFO* (last-in, first-out) will be used. Most firms use a FIFO system since it reflects truer inventory and cost of goods sold values. However, there are good arguments for using the LIFO method in times of inflation, as will be seen later in this section.

FIFO   Inventory costing method whereby first items into inventory are first items out

LIFO   Inventory costing method whereby last items into inventory are first items out

The differences between using FIFO or LIFO are shown below. We can see how inventory affects cost of goods sold. Using either FIFO or LIFO, the first 800 units sold would be valued at $1. The next 600 units sold under FIFO would result in a cost of goods sold of $640: 200 units sold at $1, and 400 units sold at $1.10. Under the LIFO method, the 600 units would have a cost of goods of $650. This is determined by 500 units at $1.10 and 100 units at $1. The next 950 units sold under FIFO would have a cost of goods sold of $1,037.50, or 100 units at $1.10 and 850 units at $1.15. For LIFO, cost of goods sold would be $1,092.50, which results from 950 units costed at $1.15.

Cost of Goods Inventory	Units Sold	FIFO	LIFO
1000 units @ $1.00	800	$ 800.00	$ 800.00
500 units @ $1.10	600	$ 640.00	$ 650.00
1000 units @ $1.15	950	$1037.50	$1092.50

As stated above, there are occasions where the entrepreneur might find that the LIFO method can actually increase cash flow. A case in point was the Dacor Corporation, a manufacturer of scuba diving equipment. In the early 1980s, the venture switched from FIFO to LIFO and incurred average annual increases in cash flow of 10 percent, until the early 1990s, when inflation increased so much that the company showed an increase of 25 percent in its cash flow. This decision was timely for Dacor and was implemented in the following manner.

First, it was necessary to decide if inventory was to be grouped into categories or to cost each item individually. These costs must also be pinpointed at the beginning of the year, at the end, or must be based on an annual average. For a very large inventory, the entrepreneur should categorize or pool the inventory. For those ventures with limited product lines, each item or product can be costed individually. Because of the wide variety of products sold, Dacor chose to categorize or pool its inventory for costing purposes. These options in stage one should be assessed carefully, because once the decision is made, it is very difficult to change back without incurring penalties from the IRS.

In stage two, all inventory must be costed by searching through historical records. The amount of effort required for a venture will depend again on the breadth of the product line.

Once the inventory cost has been ascertained for each category or product, an average inventory cost must be calculated. For a new venture with only one or a few products, this would be relatively easy. For Dacor, with a wide product line, this required the assistance of an accounting firm. After all the calculations are made, management must notify the IRS (Form 970) that it is converting to the LIFO method.

The decision to convert from a FIFO to a LIFO system is not simple; thus it is important for the entrepreneur to carefully evaluate his or her goals before making any commitment. Conversion to LIFO can typically be beneficial if the following conditions exist.[8]

1. Rising labor, materials, and other production costs are anticipated.
2. The business and inventory are growing.
3. The business has some computer-assisted inventory control method capability.
4. The business is profitable. If the start-up is losing money, there is no point in converting methods.

Regardless of the inventory costing method used, it is important for the entrepreneur to keep careful records of inventory. Perpetual inventory systems can be structured using computers or a manual system. As items are sold, inventory should be reduced. To check the inventory balance, it may be necessary to physically count inventory periodically.

Fixed assets generally involve long-term commitments and large investments for the new venture. These fixed assets, such as the equipment appearing in Figure 13.3, will have certain costs related to them. Equipment will require servicing and insurance and will affect utility costs. The equipment will also be depreciated over time, which will be reflected in the value of the asset over time.

If the entrepreneur cannot afford to buy equipment or fixed assets, leasing could be considered as an alternative. Leasing may be a good alternative to buying depending on the terms of the lease, the type of asset to be leased, and the usage demand on the asset. For example, leases for automobiles may contain a large down payment and possible usage or mileage fees that can make the lease much more expensive than a purchase. On the other hand, lease payments represent an expense to the venture and can be used as a tax deduction. Leases are also valuable for equipment that becomes obsolete quickly. The entrepreneur can take a lease for short periods, reducing the long-term obligation to any specific asset. As with any other make or buy decision, the entrepreneur should consider all costs associated with a lease or buy decision as well as the impact on cash flows.

Long-Term versus Short-Term Debt

To finance the assets and ensure that the new venture can meet its cash needs, it may be necessary for the entrepreneur to consider borrowing funds. Generally, to finance fixed assets the entrepreneur will assume long-term debt by borrowing from a bank. The bank's collateral for such a loan will be the fixed asset itself. The alternatives to borrowing from a bank are to borrow from a family member, friend, or, in the case of a partnership, having each partner contribute more funds to the business. A corporation may sell stock to raise funds for the new venture. This decision, however, may require the entrepreneur(s) to give up some equity in the business. Whatever the option chosen, the entrepreneur should consider the pros and cons of each.

Managing Costs and Profits

Although the cash flow analysis discussed earlier in the chapter can assist the entrepreneur in assessing and controlling costs, it is also useful to compute the net income for interim periods during the year. The most effective use of the interim income statement is to establish cost standards and compare the actual with the budgeted amount for that time period. Costs are budgeted based on percentages of net sales. These percentages can then be compared with actual percentages and can be assessed over time to ascertain where tighter cost controls may be necessary.

Figure 13.4 compares actual and expected (standard) percentages on MPP Plastic's income statement for its first quarter of operation. This analysis gives the entrepreneur the opportunity to manage and control costs before it is too late. Figure 13.3 shows that cost of goods sold is higher than standard. Part of this may result from the initial small purchases of inventory, which did not provide any quantity discounts. If this is not the case, the entrepreneur should consider finding other sources or raising prices.

Most of the expenses appear to be reasonably close to standard or expected percentages. The entrepreneur should assess each item to determine whether these costs can be reduced or whether it will be necessary to raise prices to ensure future positive profits. As the venture begins to evolve into the second and third years of operation, the entrepreneur should also compare current actual costs with prior incurred costs. For example, in the second year of operation, the entrepreneur may find it useful to look back at the selling expenses incurred in the first year of operation. Such comparisons can be done on a month-to-month basis (i.e., January, year 1, to January, year 2) or even quarterly or yearly, depending on the volatility of the costs in this particular business.

Where expenses or costs have been much higher than budgeted, it may be necessary for the entrepreneur to carefully analyze the account to determine what the exact cause of the overrun is. For example, utilities represent a single expense account yet may include a number of specific payments for such things as heat, electricity, gas, hot water, and so on. Thus, the entrepreneur should retain a running balance of all these payments to ascertain the cause of an unusually large utility expense. In Figure 13.1 we see that

FIGURE 13.4 MPP Plastics Inc., Income Statement, First Quarter Year 1 (000s)

		Actual (%)	Standard (%)
Net sales	$150.0	100.0	100.0
Less cost of goods sold	100.0	66.7	60.0
Gross margin	(50.0)	32.3	40.0
Operating expenses			
Selling expenses	11.7	7.8	8.0
Salaries	19.8	13.2	12.0
Advertising	5.2	3.5	4.0
Office supplies	1.9	1.3	1.0
Rent	6.0	4.0	3.0
Utilities	1.3	0.9	1.0
Insurance	0.6	0.4	0.5
Taxes	3.4	2.3	2.0
Interest	3.6	2.4	2.0
Depreciation	9.9	6.6	5.0
Miscellaneous	0.3	0.2	0.2
Total operating expenses	$ 66.3	42.6	38.7
Net profit (loss)	(13.3)	(9.3)	1.3

the utility expense was $500, which was $200 over the budgeted amount, or a 67 percent increase. What caused the increase? Was any particular utility responsible for the overrun, or was it a result of higher oil costs, which affected all the utility expenses? These questions need to be resolved before the entrepreneur accepts the results and makes any needed adjustments for the next period.

Comparisons of the actual and budgeted expenses in the income statement can be misleading for those new ventures where there are multiple products or services. For financial reporting purposes to shareholders, bankers, or other investors, the income statement would summarize expenses across all products and services. This information, although helpful to get an overview of the success of the venture, does not indicate the marketing cost for each product, the performance of particular managers in controlling costs, or the most profitable product(s). For example, selling expenses for MPP Plastics Inc. (Figure 13.4) were $11,700. These selling expenses may apply to more than one product, in which case the entrepreneur would need to ascertain the amount of selling expense for each product. He or she may be tempted to pro rate the expense across each product, which would not provide a realistic picture of the relative success of each product. Thus, if MPP Plastics Inc. produced three different products, the selling expense for each might be assumed to be $3,900 per product, when the actual selling expenses could be much more or less.

Some products may require more advertising, insurance, administrative time, transportation, storage, and so on, which could be misleading if the entrepreneur chooses to allocate these expenses equally across all products. In response to this problem, it is recommended that the entrepreneur allocate expenses as effectively as possible, by product. Not only is it important to evaluate these costs across each product, but it is also important to evaluate them by region, customer, distribution channel, department, and so on. Arbitrary allocation of costs should be avoided in order to get a real profit perspective of every product marketed by the new venture.

Taxes

The entrepreneur will be required to withhold federal and state taxes for his or her employees. Each month or quarter (depending on the size of the payroll), deposits or payments will need to be made to the appropriate agency for funds withheld from wages. Generally, federal taxes, state taxes, Social Security, and Medicare are withheld from employees' salaries and are deposited later. The entrepreneur should be careful not to use these funds since, if payments are late, there will be high interest and penalties assessed. In addition to withholding taxes, the new venture may be required to pay a number of taxes, such as state and federal unemployment taxes, a matching FICA and Medicare tax, and other business taxes. These taxes will need to be part of any budget since they will affect cash flow and profits. To determine the exact amount, dates due, and procedures, the unemployment agency for the federal government and the appropriate state or the IRS can be contacted.

The federal and state governments will also require the entrepreneur to file end-of-year returns of the business. If the venture is incorporated, there may be state corporation taxes to be paid regardless of whether the venture earned a profit. The filing periods and tax responsibilities will vary for other types of organizations. Chapter 10 provides some insights about the tax responsibilities of proprietorships, partnerships, and corporations. As stated earlier, a tax accountant should also be considered to avoid any errors and provide advice in handling these expenses. The accountant can also assist the entrepreneur in planning or budgeting appropriate funds to meet any of these expenses.

Ratio Analysis

Calculations of *financial ratios* can also be extremely valuable as an analytical and control mechanism to test the financial well-being of a new venture during its early stages. These ratios serve as a measure of the financial strengths and weaknesses of the venture,

financial ratios   Control mechanisms to test financial strength of new venture

but should be used with caution since they are only one control measure for interpreting the financial success of the venture. There is no single set of ratios that must be used, nor are there standard definitions for all ratios. However, there are industry rules of thumb that the entrepreneur can use to interpret the financial data. For purposes of demonstration we will use the financial statements illustrated in Chapter 9. Even though these are pro forma statements, we can assume for the analysis that they actually occurred. Ratio analysis is typically used on actual financial results but could also provide the entrepreneur with some sense of where problems exist even in the pro forma statements as well.

Liquidity Ratios

Current Ratio   This ratio is commonly used to measure the short-term solvency of the venture or its ability to meet its short-term debts. The current liabilities must be covered from cash or its equivalent, otherwise the entrepreneur will need to borrow money to meet these obligations. The formula and calculation of this ratio from the data in Figure 9.6 are as follows:

$$\frac{\text{Current assets}}{\text{Current liabilities}} = \frac{108,050}{40,500} = 2.67 \text{ times}$$

While a ratio of 2:1 is generally considered favorable, the entrepreneur should also compare this ratio with any industry standards. One interpretation of this result is that for every dollar of current debt, the company has $2.67 of current assets to cover it. This ratio indicates that MPP Plastics is liquid and can likely meet any of its obligations even if there was a sudden emergency that drained existing cash.

Acid Test Ratio   This is a more rigorous test of the short-term liquidity of the venture because it eliminates inventory, which is the least liquid current asset. The formula and calculation for MPP Plastics from Figure 9.9 are as follows:

$$\frac{\text{Current assets} - \text{inventory}}{\text{Current liabilities}} = \frac{108,050\text{-}10,450}{40,500} = 2.40 \text{ times}$$

The result from this ratio suggests that the venture is very liquid since it has assets convertible to cash of $2.40 for every dollar of short-term obligations. Usually a 1:1 ratio would be considered favorable in most industries.

Activity Ratios

Average Collection Period   This ratio indicates the average number of days it takes to convert accounts receivable into cash. This ratio helps the entrepreneur to gauge the liquidity of accounts receivable or the ability of the venture to collect from its customers. The formula and data using Figures 9.3 and 9.6 are as follows:

$$\frac{\text{Accounts receivable}}{\text{Avg. daily sales}} = \frac{46,000}{995,000/360} = 17 \text{ days}$$

This particular result needs to be compared with industry standards since collection will vary considerably. However, if the invoices indicate a 20-day payment required, then one could conclude that most customers pay on time.

Inventory Turnover   This ratio measures the efficiency of the venture in managing and selling its inventory. A high turnover is a favorable sign indicating that the venture is able to sell its inventory quickly. There could be a danger with a very high turnover that the venture is understocked, which could result in lost orders. Managing inventory is very important to the cash flow and profitability of a new venture. The calculations of this ratio for MPP Plastics using Figures 9.3 and 9.6 are as follows:

$$\frac{\text{Cost of goods sold}}{\text{Inventory}} = \frac{645,000}{10,450} = 61.7 \text{ times}$$

This would appear to be an excellent turnover as long as the entrepreneur feels that he or she is not losing sales because of understocking inventory.

Leverage Ratios

Debt Ratio   Many new ventures will incur debt as a means of financing the start-up. The debt ratio helps the entrepreneur to assess the firm's ability to meet all of its obligations (short and long term). It is also a measure of risk because debt also consists of a fixed commitment in the form of interest and principal repayments. The calculation of this ratio for MPP Plastics using the data in Figure 9.6 is as follows:

$$\frac{\text{Total liabilities}}{\text{Total assets}} = \frac{249{,}700}{308{,}450} = 81\%$$

This result indicates that the venture has financed about 81 percent of its assets with debt. On paper this looks very reasonable but would also need to be compared with industry data.

Debt to Equity   This ratio assesses the firm's capital structure. It provides a measure of risk to creditors by considering the funds invested by creditors (debt) and investors (equity). The higher the percentage of debt, the greater the degree of risk to any of the creditors. The calculation of this ratio using the data from Figure 9.6 is as follows:

$$\frac{\text{Total liabilities}}{\text{Stockholder's equity}} = \frac{249{,}700}{58{,}750} = 4.25 \text{ times}$$

This result indicates that this venture has been financed mostly from debt. The actual investment of the entrepreneurs or the equity base is about one-fourth of what is owed. Thus, the equity portion represents a cushion to the creditors. For MPP Plastics this is not a serious problem because of its short-term cash position.

Profitability Ratios

Net Profit Margin   This ratio represents the venture's ability to translate sales into profits. You can also use gross profit instead of net profit to provide another measure of profitability. In either case it is important to know what is reasonable in your industry as well as to measure these ratios over time. The ratio and calculation for MPP Plastics using data from Figure 9.3 are as follows:

$$\frac{\text{Net profit}}{\text{Net sales}} = \frac{8{,}750}{995{,}000} = 88\%$$

The net profit margin for MPP Plastics, although low for an established firm, would not be of great concern for a new venture. Many new ventures do not incur profits until the second or third year. In this case we have a favorable profit situation.

Return on Investment   The return on investment measures the ability of the venture to manage its total investment in assets. You can also calculate a return on equity, which substitutes stockholders' equity for total assets in the formula below and indicates the ability of the venture in generating a return to the stockholders. The formula and calculation of the return on investment for MPP Plastics using Figures 9.3 and 9.6 are as follows:

$$\frac{\text{Net profit}}{\text{Total assets}} = \frac{8{,}750}{200{,}400} = 4.4\%$$

The result of this calculation will also need to be compared with industry data. However, the positive conclusion is that the firm has earned a profit in its first year and has returned 4.4 percent on its asset investment.

There are many other ratios that could also be calculated. However, for a start-up these would probably suffice for an entrepreneur in assessing the venture's financial strengths and weaknesses. As the firm grows, it will be important to use these ratios in conjunction with all other financial statements to provide an understanding of how the firm is performing financially.

MARKETING AND SALES CONTROLS

In addition to financial controls, the early stages of the new venture will also require *marketing and sales controls*. These controls usually focus on key variables that reflect per-

marketing and sales controls Key variables used to reflect performance results of marketing plan

formance results established in the annual marketing plan. Some of these key variables might be market share, distribution, promotion, pricing, customer satisfaction, and sales.[9]

Market Share Market share is often difficult to measure unless the market is easily defined. However, it is often possible to ascertain the total industry sales from trade publications. The entrepreneur can then determine his or her market share by taking the venture's sales as a percentage of total industry sales. Where the venture is geographically limited, it may be possible to find out sales by state or region. If that data is not available, the best option would be to try to estimate state or regional sales by population of customers in the area as a percentage of the population of the entire market. For example, a new venture marketing a liquid grill cleaner to restaurants may know the number of restaurants in the United States but not for a specific state. The entrepreneur may be able to find out from a business directory the number of restaurants in a state or may simply estimate based on the state's population.

Market share control may be important when the market is new and competitors are entering the market, and when the market is growing rapidly. Thus, if a market is growing by 20 percent and the venture's sales are growing by only 10 percent, there may be cause for concern unless there are many new competitors in the market, which would dilute the shares of individual firms. In this case, other variables, such as sales, should be considered.

Sales Where the new venture involves sales personnel, it is important to monitor sales information such as the following:

- Average sales calls per week per salesperson.
- Average dollar sales per contact per salesperson.
- Average cost per sales call and/or per sales transaction.
- Number of new accounts established per salesperson.
- Number of lost accounts per salesperson.
- Number of customer contacts per salesperson.
- Total selling costs.

Each of the above items can provide important information over time regarding the activity of the sales force. Changes in any of these numbers would require action by the entrepreneur, who might intercept a problem that could become more serious if left unattended.

Distribution   One of the common problems for the new venture during the growth stage is being out of stock. In this case, customers will usually buy a substitute. In addition, it upsets retailers since they may lose sales to another retailer that may have more or different alternatives. The best approach besides using an effective inventory control system is to have a toll-free number for the customer to call so that merchandise can be rushed to that account.

Besides inventory issues, the entrepreneur may also need to evaluate sales by retail account and by distributor and even the increase or decrease in the number of actual distributors and retailers carrying the product. Monitoring this information can be helpful in determining trade promotions and strategy regarding sales contacts.

Promotion   Many entrepreneurs do not monitor the effectiveness of a promotion effort. It is important to know why a customer buys. Is it because of the ad that appeared in the newspaper? advertising on television or radio? a coupon? a point-of-purchase display? the special low price? a yellow pages ad? This information can be collected in many different ways, such as having sales personnel ask customers where they heard about the product or service. In the case of a print ad or mailing, it is possible to use a coupon that might provide some savings to the customer. The number of coupons redeemed would thus be a useful measure of the effectiveness of the particular ad. Understanding what promotion strategies are effective is important in controlling marketing costs and enhancing the sales volume of the new venture.

Customer Satisfaction   The use of marketing research described in Chapter 8 can be extremely important in ascertaining the satisfaction levels of existing customers. Information can also be obtained from either a customer 800 number, telephone complaints, or complaint letters. All complaints should be monitored and followed up to ensure that the customer is satisfied. Some firms have also found that the use of a suggestion box can be helpful in monitoring problems as well as identifying new ideas for the business.

Effective marketing and sales controls in the early stages of the operation of a new venture can help the entrepreneur to identify problems before they become too serious and to take corrective actions where appropriate to ensure that marketing goals are met. Often the entrepreneur incurs more serious marketing and sales problems when the business is in a rapid growth stage. Because of the strain on management and resources during the growth stage, it is more difficult to be aware of all the key variables in the day-to-day operations. If everyone in the organization manages and controls his or her area of responsibility, it is possible to avoid any serious problems.

RAPID GROWTH AND MANAGEMENT CONTROLS

As we saw above, when the new venture begins to reach a rapid growth phase, the entrepreneur needs to be sensitive to some of the resultant management problems. Usually, rapid growth is seen as a positive sign of success, and any attempt to establish important financial or management controls that were discussed above is abandoned for the sake of doing more and more business. However, rapid growth can quickly change the status of a new venture from profitable to bankrupt if the entrepreneur is not sensitive to certain growth issues. What are these issues? How can growth quickly turn a business into a failure? How should growth be managed? Although this topic is discussed in more detail in the next chapter, some issues need to be addressed in the early stages of a new venture and thus will be discussed in this section.

> **TABLE 13.1 Problems of Rapid Growth**
>
> - It can cover up weak management, poor planning, or wasted resources.
> - It dilutes effective leadership.
> - It causes the venture to stray from its goals and objectives.
> - It leads to communication barriers between departments and individuals.
> - Training and employee development are given little attention.
> - It can lead to stress and burnout.
> - Delegation is avoided and control is maintained by only the founders, creating bottlenecks in management decision making.
> - Quality control is not maintained.

Some growth problems that can affect the management of the new venture are summarized in Table 13.1. Before rapid growth occurs, the new venture is usually operating with a small staff and a limited budget.

Hence, less time is spent in evaluating management, personnel planning, and cost controls because cash seems to be plentiful.

Rapid growth can also dilute the leadership abilities of the entrepreneur. Shared vision and purpose become difficult as the entrepreneur has to devote much time to the short-term growth demands. As a result, communication begins to diminish and more compartmentalization of goals develops. Training and development of personnel are overlooked, and eventually the entrepreneur and the employees begin to feel pressure and stress. The entrepreneur's unwillingness to delegate responsibility can lead to even greater delays in decision making and less emphasis on the long-term survival of the business.

The entrepreneur can avoid these problems with preparation and sensitivity about handling early rapid growth when it occurs. If the entrepreneur finds that these issues cannot be internally resolved, then an outside consultant should be hired to provide an objective view of how to manage the venture during this stage of the venture life cycle. The board of advisors discussed in Chapter 10 can also be an important resource to assist the entrepreneur in the early stages.

It may also be necessary to put a limit on the venture's growth. This may sound like blasphemy to a new venture, but it is important to try to stay within the capabilities of the firm. Standing back and reflecting on the goals and objectives of the venture may be an important part of the control of growth. The future financial well-being of the venture may necessitate a more controlled growth rate. The limits to the growth of any venture will depend on the availability of a market, capital, and management talent. Too-rapid growth can stretch these limits and lead to serious financial problems and possible bankruptcy.

CREATING AWARENESS OF THE NEW VENTURE

publicity Public interest free advertising in any major media

In the early stages of a new venture, the entrepreneur should focus his or her effort on trying to develop an awareness of the products or services offered. Thus, the initial emphasis of a new venture should be to get some *publicity* in local media.

Publicity is free advertising provided by a trade magazine, newspaper, magazine, radio, or TV program that finds it of public interest to do a story on a new venture. Local media such as newspapers, radio, or cable TV encourage entrepreneurs to participate in their programs or stories. The entrepreneur can increase the opportunity for getting this exposure by preparing a news release and sending it to as many possible media sources as he or she can.

In order to issue a news release it is important to follow these steps:[10]

1. Identify the news release as such when mailing it to the editor.
2. Begin the release with the service or product to be marketed.
3. List the features and benefits of the product or service to the customer.
4. Make the written news release about 100 to 150 words. This is especially important for print media.
5. Include a high-quality, glossy photograph of the product or of the service being performed.

For radio or TV, the entrepreneur should identify programs that may encourage local entrepreneurs to participate. A telephone call and follow-up with written information enhance the opportunity to appear on any of these programs.

Free publicity can only introduce the company and its services in a general format. Advertising, however, can be focused to inform specific potential customers of the service—what they will receive, why they should buy it, where they can buy it, and how much it may cost. If the advertising program is to be effectively developed, it may be necessary to hire an advertising agency.

Internet Advertising

There are new opportunities for start-ups to advertise using the World Wide Web. This is an excellent medium to create awareness and to effectively support early launch strategies. Creating a website is the most important first stage. Software packages available to support the early efforts of the entrepreneur are common and can be located through a browser such as Netscape, Yahoo, Lycos, or Excite, to name a few. In the search box, typing "website software" will identify a number of these options. If the entrepreneur feels that the website requirements are complex, then a website consultant may be hired. Many of these consultants offer online website design that can be directly accessed on the Web.

The website should indicate background on the company, its products, officers, address, telephone and fax numbers, and contact names for potential sales. Depending on the nature of the business direct sales from the website may also be available. Website addresses for those ventures conducting direct sales on the Web will require advertising to create interest and awareness of the existence of the website. For example, Computer.Com, a start-up venture, spent about $3 million on television advertising during the recent Superbowl Game. This significant expenditure was believed to be necessary to create the awareness of the site to attract customers.

It is important to change the content of the website as necessary. Old or out-of-date information can be frustrating for potential consumers and can create negative results. Requests made over the Web should be responded to quickly. Websites have also become very creative with animation and quality illustrations to grab potential consumers' attention.

In addition to the website the entrepreneur may consider using a banner ad. Banner ads are small rectangular ads similar to billboard ads that appear on browser websites. The cost of these ads on the more popular browser sites such as Yahoo can be prohibitive (approximately $15,000) for a local or regional start-up. However, there are low-cost alternatives that involve exchanges or co-marketing deals with other local or regional websites. There are also firms that offer matching services for these co-marketing deals for a very small fee. You can exchange a banner ad on your site for one on another site that attracts the same target market. For example, Prairie Frontier, a wildflower and prairie grass seed venture, contacted LinkExchange, one of these co-marketing deal makers, and with its assistance was able to place banner ads with several dozen gardening and photographic sites. The company now attracts up to 1,700 hits a day on their website as a result of this exchange or co-marketing deal.[11]

Trade Shows

Another excellent method to create awareness of the new venture and build a customer base is to participate in important trade shows. Every industry has a trade or professional association that offers members the opportunity to attend and or participate in annual trade shows. These are good opportunities to demonstrate products or to just begin to network to identify quality sources of supplies, meet potential brokers or reps, or just collect business cards of potential clients.

To set up a booth at a trade show can cost as much as $15,000 to $20,000, particularly for national shows that are widely attended. In addition to travel, room, and board this could be a prohibitive expense. However, it is where hundreds or thousands of people attend to observe or identify trends in their industry. In addition to displaying information about the new venture it is also an opportunity to conduct some simple observation research on the competition.

There are some simple rules to follow:

1. Develop a preshow plan that identifies goals and objectives.
2. If necessary, train employees to make sure everyone is on the same page.
3. Bring lots of materials to distribute including any free gifts to those who visit the booth.
4. Sometimes preshow advertising can be useful to give notice that you will be in attendance and will be offering a free gift or launching a new product.
5. Collect business cards of anyone interested in your products or services or anyone who has services or products that you need.
6. Walk around observing and taking notes on competitor strategies.
7. Have a debriefing meeting with all attendees to get their observations, notes, and conclusions.
8. After the show it is imperative to follow up with all contacts made even if you are not prepared to sell them your product just yet.

Even though some of the national trade shows can be expensive, there are often local and regional shows that are not. Overall there is strong evidence to indicate that the cost per sale from a trade show is significantly less than the cost per sale from a personal sales call.[12]

Selecting an Advertising Agency

An advertising agency can provide many promotional services to the entrepreneur. The advertising agency itself may even cater to new ventures or specialize in the specific market the entrepreneur is trying to target. Traditionally, the advertising agency has been perceived as an independent business organization composed of creative people and businesspeople who develop, prepare, and place advertising in media for its customers. The agency can even provide the entrepreneur with assistance in marketing research or in some of the strategies needed to market the product or service.

Before selecting an agency, it might be useful to check with friends or agencies such as the Small Business Administration to obtain recommendations. Local chambers of commerce or trade associations can also be of some assistance. In any event, regardless of what agency is considered, it is important to determine whether the agency can fulfill all the needs of the new venture. Many smaller agencies now target small businesses and can thus provide more personalized service at lower costs than the large advertising agency.

Table 13.2 provides a checklist of items that the entrepreneur may consider in evaluating an agency. It is especially important to meet the agency staff and to talk with some of its clients to be sure that it is the right choice. All items in the checklist could be evaluated subjectively or by assigning some scale value (i.e., 1 to 7) in order to identify the best agency for the new venture.[13]

The advertising agency should support the marketing program and assist the entrepreneur in getting the product or service effectively launched. The costs or budget for advertising may be small initially, but certain agencies are willing to make their investment because of the potential growth of the venture and hence the advertising budget.

TABLE 13.2 Checklist for Selecting an Advertising Agency

Item	Value
1. Location of agency	_____
2. Organizational structure of agency	_____
3. Public relations department services	_____
4. Research department and facilities	_____
5. Creativity of agency's staff	_____
6. Education and professional qualifications of agency's top management	_____
7. Media department's qualifications and experience	_____
8. Qualifications and experience of account executives (if identifiable)	_____
9. Interest or enthusiasm shown toward firm and new product	_____
10. Copywriters' qualifications and experience	_____
11. Art director's qualifications and experience	_____
12. Recommendations by other clients	_____
13. Experience and success with new products	_____
14. Ability of agency to work with the company's advertising department	_____
15. Extra services provided	_____
16. Accounting and billing procedures	_____
17. Overall formal presentation	_____

What Is Truth, Deception, or Exaggeration in Advertising?

Some people argue that advertising influences people to buy goods and services they don't need through exaggeration of product or service benefits. Others argue that without advertising and promotion there would be no mechanism to inform consumers about the alternatives that exist.

New ventures will often find it necessary to develop promotional strategies that may use newspapers, magazines, or direct mail. The real issue involves a determination of what is truth, exaggeration, or deception. At one extreme we have the advertisement that offers a product that can extend your life span. Is this exaggeration or deception? What about advertisements suggesting that a new venture's product can outperform a competitor's product without any substantiation? Is this exaggeration or deception? In some cases there may not be any question of the ethical integrity of the advertisement. However, there are many cases where companies insist that their claims are true, although there is no real proof as to the integrity of the information.

Unethical and illegal promotion issues are the responsibility of the Federal Communications Commission or the Federal Trade Commission. However, these agencies, because of resources, only police large-scale advertising and do not police advertising by small companies.

Because of the difficulty in determining what is truth, deception, or exaggeration, the entrepreneur should consider the following before designing an ad:

1. Whether the consumer is being treated as a means to an end or as an end.

2. Whether the consumer is being told all the facts or, by leaving out some of the facts, is being misled or harmed.

3. How the entrepreneur would react to his or her own advertisement.

HIRING EXPERTS

Most of this chapter involves areas such as financial and marketing analysis that may require expertise that the entrepreneur is unable to contribute. In those instances where the entrepreneur does not have the expertise, it is recommended that outside experts be hired. Trying to save money by performing these tasks alone could end up costing the entrepreneur more than the experts' fees.

There are usually accountants or financial experts, marketing consultants, and advertising agencies that cater to new ventures and small businesses. These firms can usually be identified from local business contacts, the Small Business Administration, trade associations, or even the yellow pages.

IN REVIEW

Summary

This chapter deals with the key managerial areas of expertise that will be required to keep the business going in the early months and growth phases of the start-up. These areas—such as financial analysis, marketing and sales analysis, and advertising—may necessitate the hiring of outside experts if the entrepreneur cannot fulfill these managerial needs.

In the area of financial analysis, the entrepreneur must be concerned with managing cash, assets, debt, and profits. Cash flow must be monitored on a regular basis (usually monthly). Budgeted and actual cash flows should be evaluated when they vary significantly. Providing sensitivity analysis to monthly cash flow projections can be accomplished by calculating pessimistic and optimistic amounts for all receipts and disbursements using an amount that is +/− 5 percent from the expected amount. For some very small ventures such as a restaurant, retail store, or service it may be helpful to compute a daily cash activity table to determine where errors or problems occurred.

Assets can be managed by using the balance sheet. Besides cash, the entrepreneur will need to control accounts receivable and inventory. If accounts receivable are late or delinquent, the entrepreneur will need to tighten collection procedures. Increases in accounts receivable because of increased credit sales may require short-term financing of receivables to meet short-term cash needs.

Expenses need to be controlled in two ways. First, it is important to understand that expenses should be allocated by product, region, department, and so on. Otherwise, the entrepreneur may inaccurately evaluate the profitability of any product or service. Accuracy can improve the ability of the entrepreneur to understand which products or services are a problem, and perhaps to even explain which department, region, or manager is responsible.

Inventory must also be controlled. Too much inventory can be costly to the venture; too little can result in fewer sales because delivery dates cannot be met. FIFO or LIFO accounting may be used to cost inventory (cost of goods). FIFO will generally provide a more realistic value of cost of goods sold, unless the cost of inventory is increasing by an abnormal rate or the economy is in a cycle of inflation.

Fixed assets such as equipment may require long-term debt. Long-term debt can be obtained from bank loans, loans from friends or relatives, or, in the case of a corporation, the sale of stock. The sale of stock may require the entrepreneur to give up some equity in the business and hence must be weighed carefully.

Comparing actual costs from the income statement with standard percentages (percentages related to net sales) will be useful in managing the costs and profits of the new venture. Higher costs than anticipated should be carefully evaluated so that they do not surprise the entrepreneur later.

One method to help interpret and analyze the financial statements of the new venture is ratio analysis. There are many different ratios that can be calculated to help understand the financial picture of the new venture. The most important ratios to a start-up venture would involve liquidity, asset management, and performance. Ratios should, however, be used with other measures and pro formas in order to have a complete and accurate picture of the financial well-being of the venture.

Marketing and sales controls require careful monitoring of key market information as well as an effective reporting system by sales personnel. Key variables such as market share, sales, distribution, promotion, and customer satisfaction require monitoring to ensure that marketing plan goals and objectives are being achieved. If problems are identified, corrective action can be taken before the problem becomes too serious.

One of the most important problems an entrepreneur faces during the early stages of start-up is creating awareness of the venture and its products and services. Creating a quality website or designing advertisements on other websites can be an effective method to reaching the target market. Finding creative ways to take advantage of free advertising or publicity can save the entrepreneur significant amounts of money. In addition to publicity, the entrepreneur may need to consider some traditional media advertising. Trade shows can also be an effective means to conduct marketing research, create awareness, and identify and collect names of potential customers. Generally, the decision to advertise will require the hiring of an agency unless the entrepreneur has expertise in this area.

Questions for Discussion

1. What effect would each of the following have on (a) cash flow and (b) profits?
   a. Repayment of $5,000 personal loan.
   b. Purchase of $8,000 worth of inventory payable in 30 days.
   c. Purchase of equipment for $15,000.
   d. Increase of salaries by $4,000.
2. Why is it important to manage assets such as accounts receivable and inventory?
3. What is the effect on cash flow of FIFO and LIFO when the cost of goods is (a) increasing or (b) decreasing?
4. What possible internal problems might exist if (a) the current asset ratio is below 1, and (b) the debt-to-equity ratio has increased in each of the past three years?
5. Identify important marketing control variables for a new venture that markets baby toys. Discuss how this venture might control each of these variables.
6. Consider a new sporting goods retail store. What Internet strategies would you recommend for this venture?
7. What is the significance of publicity to a new venture? What procedure would you recommend to take advantage of any publicity opportunities?
8. What are some of the major problems that are created by rapid growth of sales in the new venture?

Key Terms

FIFO	marketing and sales controls
financial ratios	publicity
LIFO	

More Information—Net Addresses in This Chapter

Advertising Age Magazine
www.adage.com

Biz Women
www.bizwomen.com

Business Resource Center
www.morebusiness.com

Data Merge—guide on cash flow
www.datamerge.com/resources/
cashflow. html

Dun & Bradstreet Information Service
www.dnb.com

Entrepreneurs on the Web
www.entrepreneur-web.com/

Foundation for Enterprise Development
www.fed.org

Idea Cafe
www.ideacafe.com

Inc. Magazine and free download software
www.inc.com

Small Business Administration
www.sbaonline.sba.gov/

Small Business Advancement National Center
www.sbanet.uca.edu/

Smart Business Supersite (SBS)
www.smartbiz.com

Trade Show Central
www.tscentral.com

World Wide Yellow Pages
www.yellow.com

Selected Readings

Burck, C. (April 5, 1993). The Real World of the Entrepreneur. *Fortune*, pp. 62–81.

This article reflects a several-month study of over 100 new ventures conducted across the United States. The focus of the study was to identify some of the effective strategies used to grow the businesses. Issues such as specialization, preparing employees for constant change during growth, keeping good employees, and keeping management down to earth are a few of the topics discussed.

Dennis, A. (December 1996). Navigating Uncharted Waters: Accounting Services for Start-Up Businesses. *Journal of Accountancy*, pp. 81–85.

This article provides a case history of Arctic Clear Products, a manufacturer of a portable water purification system for emergency situations. It particularly focuses on some of the important managerial and financial control issues that helped to keep this company using a successful growth strategy.

Emerick D.; and K. Round. (January 2000). *Exploring Web Marketing and Project Management.* Upper Saddle River, NJ: Prentice Hall, Inc.

This new paperback provides basic coverage of Web development and use of the Internet for marketing goods and services. It is particularly useful for the entrepreneur who lacks skills in developing a website and is not clear on how the website can be used to enhance marketing programs.

Fraser, L. (1998). *Understanding Financial Statements*, 5th ed. Upper Saddle River, NJ: Prentice Hall, Inc.

This paperback provides a good conceptual understanding of financial statements. Using a variety of examples, it covers analysis and control issues and provides a simple explanation of the applications of financial ratios.

Gaston, Noel. (1997). Efficiency Wages, Managerial Discretion, and the Fear of Bankruptcy. *Journal of Economic Behavior & Organization*, vol. 33, no. 1, pp. 41–59.

A firm's shareholders may be unable to credibly commit to honor performance-contingent rewards to workers when complete contracts are absent. Managers usually administer compensation contracts and ensure that implicit commitments are fulfilled. The separation of ownership and control can increase the value of labor's specific investments in the firm. Departing from previous work on delegation, managers are allowed to transfer wealth from shareholders to workers, which creates a beneficial role for debt and a fear of bankruptcy that ensures managers take an appropriate view of the effect that the payments they make to workers have on the financial health of the firm.

Lewis, H. G. (1977). *How to Handle Your Own Public Relations.* Chicago, IL: Nelson Hall.

Although written more than 20 years ago, this book is available in most business libraries and provides a concise, step-by-step explanation of how to handle your own public relations.

McGarvey, R. (June 1995). High Hopes. *Entrepreneur*, pp. 76–79.

This article provides advice on how to keep employees motivated. Suggestions are made as to how to get employees to share the entrepreneur's vision.

Potts, A. J. (Fall 1993). Cash Flow: The Oil That Keeps the Small and Family Business Organization Running Smoothly. *Journal of Small Business Strategy*, pp. 69–80.

The emphasis in this paper is on the purposes and uses of the statement of cash flows. Two different methods of calculating cash flows are presented. Explanations are provided as to how to interpret cash flow, considering different outcomes of the venture.

Tadjer, R. (January 2000). If You Market They Will Come. *Success*, pp. 50–54.

Designing a website does not automatically mean that consumers will buy your products or services. It's important to build awareness of the site to attract customers. Three important steps that can be used by a new venture to attract people to the website are discussed.

Van Auken, Howard E.; and Lynn Neeley. (2000). Pre-Launch Preparations and the Acquisition of Start-Up Capital by Small Firms. *Journal of Developmental Entrepreneurship*, vol. 25 no. 2, pp. 169–182.

Authors examine the relationships between pre-launch preparations and the acquisition of start-up capital for small firms.

Endnotes

1. See, "PowerBar Reaps Bounty with New Harvest Bar; Crunched for Time, Americans Devour Energy Bars," *Business Wire* (August 4, 1998), p. 1; C. Adams, "A Lesson from PowerBar's Slow Start to Diversity," *Wall Street Journal* (June 14, 1999), p. 4; and "The PowerBar Story," Company website; www.powerbar.com.
2. S. Greco, "Hire the Best," *Inc.* (June 1999), pp. 32–52.
3. D. Fenn, "Personnel Best," *Inc.* (February 2000), pp. 75–83.
4. E. Pofeldt, "Collect Calls," *Success* (March 1998), pp. 22–23.
5. C. Caggiano, "Help! We're Facing a Cash Flow Crisis," *Inc.* (June 1, 1997), p. 97.
6. D. Grebler, "Entrepreneur—Focus on Cash Flow or Fail," *The Reuter Business Report* (March 13, 1996), p. 1.
7. J. Fraser, "Hidden Cash," *Inc.* (February 1991), pp. 81–82.
8. J. Fraser, "Taking Stock," *Inc.* (November 1989), pp. 161–2.
9. P. Kotler, *Marketing Management*, 10th ed. (Upper Saddle River, NJ: Prentice Hall, Inc., 1997), pp. 765–76.
10. T. Shimp, *Advertising Promotion*, 5th ed. (Fort Worth, TX: The Dryden Press, 2000), pp. 608–18.
11. B. Fryer, "Your Message Here," *Inc Tech No.* 1 (March 16, 1999), pp. 76–79.
12. S. Friedman, *Exhibiting at Trade Shows* (Menlo Park, CA: Crisp Publications, 1992), pp. 22–26.
13. R. D. Hisrich and M. P. Peters, *Marketing Decisions for New and Mature Products*, 2nd ed. (New York: Macmillan Publishing Company, 1991), pp. 392–4.

14

Managing Early Growth of the New Venture

ॐ

LEARNING OBJECTIVES

1. To understand the meaning of controlled growth.

2. To understand the importance of an effective organization culture to meet the challenges during business growth.

3. To identify the critical entrepreneurial and strategic skills that are needed to effectively manage the growth of the new venture.

4. To learn how to prepare a long-term strategic plan and how it is distinct from other types of plans.

5. To understand the benefits of time management to an entrepreneur.

6. To learn important negotiation techniques and strategies, important skills not usually well developed by entrepreneurs.

7. To identify customer satisfaction and service tracking techniques.

BILL GROSS

How does a start-up company take advantage of the seemingly endless opportunities of the Internet by using the creative talents of one person and then letting other selected entrepreneurs take over the responsibility of running these businesses? It sounds like a repeat of history when Thomas Edison made invention a business. But the new kid on the block is Bill Gross, whose vision is to grow his Idealab by nurturing and monitoring other Internet businesses that have resulted because of his ingenuity. He refers to Idealab as Internet start-ups in a box. Basically the concept is simple. Bill comes up with an idea for an Internet start-up. He locates someone, either a former executive or even an engineering student who he thinks is right for the job. That person is then given the reins to start this venture all under the roof of an incubator-like operation, where Bill provides the structure and services necessary to make these start-ups rapidly grow into successful enterprises.

www.idealab.com

Bill describes Idealab as a combination of incubator, venture capitalist, and creative think tank. Like an incubator it provides shared space and administrative services, it offers seed financing for a minority equity position (up to 49 percent), and it uses everyone to brainstorm on the most opportune technology applications. Started in 1996 in Pasadena, California, the company has to date created 30 Internet ventures, all at various stages of development. Each idea came from Gross or one of his Idealab staff managers. For each firm a CEO was found and hired using Bill's networking skills in the Internet industry and at Caltech, his alma mater. Then the core expert staff become involved to get these ventures up and running as quickly as possible. This involves developing the technology, marketing research, preparing a business plan, hiring management, launching the venture, and finally either going public or selling the business. The seed financing that Idealab provides to these start-ups does not exceed $250,000. Bill believes that Internet start-ups do not need large amounts of capital to get started but, more importantly, need knowledge, intelligence, and speed. Knowledge and intelligence are provided by Bill and the Idealab's staff experts, and speed focuses on the ability to quickly grow a start-up, but with few mistakes. According to Bill these two elements are much more important in the successful launch and growth of an Internet company than money.

Bill Gross personifies the real meaning of an entrepreneur. He probably holds the unique distinction in the field of entrepreneurship of not only starting many businesses but also turning all of them into successful enterprises. As an enterprising 12-year-old he noticed that the corner drugstore was selling candy at 9 cents and at the Sav-On nearby it was selling for 7 cents. He quickly figured out that with no overhead he could make an easy profit on the price spread. Bill then moved on to his next successful enterprise by placing ads in *Popular Mechanics*, where he sold $25,000 worth of solar devices and plans. The proceeds from this effort were used to finance his freshman year's tuition at Caltech. While at Caltech he proceeded to launch GNP Inc., a stereo equipment maker. This enterprise not only was very successful but was recognized as one of *Inc.* magazine's top 500 growth ventures in 1982 and 1985. His next enterprise was created when Bill and his brother found a way to make Lotus 1-2-3 obey simple commands. Mitch Kapor, the founder of Lotus, was impressed with their software and purchased their business for $10 million.

The success streak continued with the launch of Knowledge Adventure in 1991. This venture developed and marketed educational software. Considered to be his most successful venture to date, he sold the business in 1997 for $100 million. Idealab actually was created in 1996 when Bill was stepping down from Knowledge Adventures and negotiating the sale.

A sample of some of the companies launched by Idealab include CitySearch, which competes with Microsoft and provides online services for urban communities; EntertainNet, an Internet broadcaster that provides news and related information; and Answer.com, a website that will answer any question you might have and which was already acquired by another company. Last year Bill expanded his operations into Silicon Valley. He wanted to close to the action and take advantage of Idealab's ability to quickly transform some of these Internet opportunities into successful ventures.

Growing these start-ups is a challenge to Bill Gross, and although there is high risk in the Internet industry, Bill feels that Idealab will continue to stay focused on its mission.[1]

TO GROW OR NOT TO GROW

As we have seen in earlier chapters, the entrepreneur, through efficient planning and control, can have an important effect on the direction a venture takes. To grow or not to grow should be an important part of the entrepreneur's strategic plan, which is discussed later in this chapter. The plan will reflect the future goals and the strategies needed to meet these goals. For those who choose to grow their venture, it is necessary to be prepared for growth and to understand its implications. In many cases growth may not be entirely voluntary. Customers may demand more volume, better service, and even better prices. Colleen Barton found a solution to uncontrolled growth. Her oil drilling consulting and software development venture, Geo-Mechanics, faced this dilemma. Strategically the company planned to use its low-margin consulting to market its high-margin software. Unfortunately, customers were demanding more and more consulting from her employees, which took time away from developing and marketing the software products. To keep the company focused on technology with controlled growth, she decided to license the technology. One of her competitors that also sells equipment now markets her software for a licensing fee, and the two firms split revenues on consulting services. In Colleen's mind this was a good way to expand sales without adding employees, who were difficult to find, and without investing in new facilities to meet demand.[2]

Pearce Jones, founder and president of Design Edge, found a different solution to controlling growth. His company simply put all growth to a halt for one full year. The company realized that if it did not get control over growth, more serious problems were likely. At this point in 1998, the company had quadrupled the number of employees and had invested in a new building. Even though each new employee was contributing an increase of $150,000 in sales, the margins were small. Having the additional debt from the new facility and the additional costs for employees led to his abrupt decision to cease hiring, deactivate marketing and sales, refuse any new business, and basically focus only on its existing customers. Although Pearce admits this decision was emotionally painful, it led to dramatic changes as profits actually doubled and no employee turnover was experienced.[3]

We thus find two examples of how entrepreneurs found a way to manage growth rather than allow the growth to manage them. The important conclusion here is that there are controls and self-evaluation tools that can help the entrepreneur to manage growth. Some of these control issues and a discussion of typical weaknesses in rapidly growing ventures are included in this chapter. To begin, it is first important to understand the typical growth cycle of a new venture.

Figure 14.1 illustrates the typical growth cycle of a new venture. It can be seen that in the first few years of a new venture's existence revenues are relatively small with little growth. This initial phase typically lasts for about five to seven years, although it will vary significantly by industry. In the next phase, which typically lasts for another five years, revenues begin to grow at an increasing rate. Then the venture reaches a more stable phase when revenues and growth stabilize. What occurs after this stage would depend on the firm's ability to rejuvenate sales and begin another growth cycle. At this stage the decision in a highly competitive market may be to maintain and protect market share with little or no growth. It is also possible that revenues may even decrease during this stage as the demand for the product declines due to substitute products or changes in consumers' needs. The firm may choose to control costs and harvest the business or look for new products or new strategies to revitalize the growth of the enterprise.

Not all new ventures will enter into the rapid growth phase. Many will continue to exist at some satisfying level of sales with little or no growth. These enterprises would typically be proprietorships or partnerships that are home-based, family-owned service (particularly personal services) or craft businesses. For example, a self-employed consultant may be satisfied working alone and serving a client base without any rapid growth. This person's revenue base would be limited because of the time available and the decision not to add more people to the business. On the other hand, you could just as easily find a self-employed consultant who begins to see opportunity for growth and hires new people and expands the business into new market segments. In each instance the decision to grow

FIGURE 14.1 Growth Cycle of a New Venture

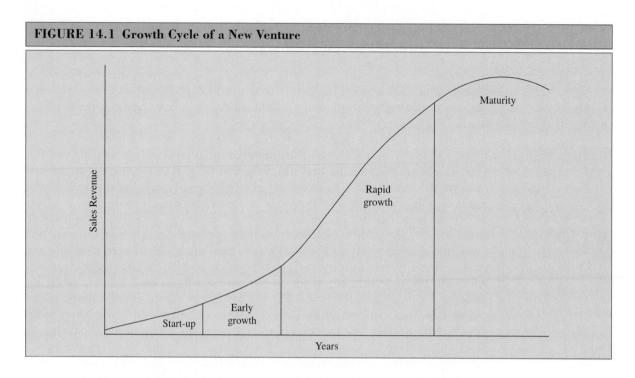

would be dictated by the entrepreneur's interest and the response of the market to the venture's product or service.

Internet start-ups may reflect a different growth cycle. For example, Amazon.com exhibited rapid growth in the first years of existence and continued with double growth over its first five years. In 2000 sales jumped to $2.7 billion from $1.4 billion in 1999 continuing its rise to be one of the fastest growing Internet companies in the world.[4] Other Internet companies such as eBay and Yahoo are also representative of this distinctive growth pattern.

Too often the entrepreneur forgets the basic axiom in every business: The only constant is change. Thus, every entrepreneur needs to understand what it takes to grow the venture and must decide whether this is the desired strategy. If the choice is growth, then the entrepreneur will need to be prepared by understanding some of the important management skills and strategies discussed in this chapter that are necessary to successfully meet the growth challenge.

ECONOMIC IMPLICATIONS OF GROWTH

In 1996 *Inc.* magazine conducted a study of its 500 fastest-growing ventures in 1984 to ascertain what happens to those ventures that are entering a growth phase.[5] In 1984 these 500 fastest-growing ventures had aggregate sales of $7.4 billion and 64,000 full-time employees, and were all experiencing the beginning of the rapid growth described above. By 1995, among the original 500 ventures, there had been 95 failures or shutdowns and 135 had been sold to new owners. The 233 companies that were willing to report earnings, however, more than made up for the failures in jobs created and revenue generated. These 233 companies had reached sales of $29 billion and employed 127,000 people full time. Thus, these 233 firms represented revenue and total numbers of employees that were significantly larger than the original list of 500 ventures.

FIGURE 14.2 A Follow-Up of *Inc.* Magazine's 1984 Fastest-Growing Ventures

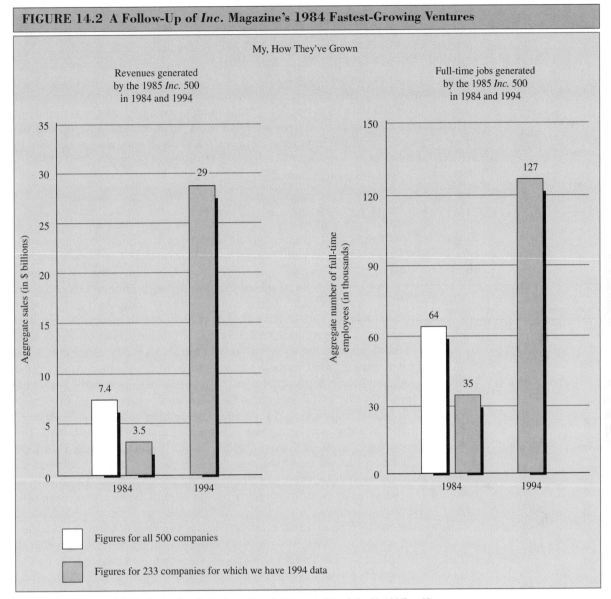

My, How They've Grown

Revenues generated
by the 1985 *Inc.* 500
in 1984 and 1994

Full-time jobs generated
by the 1985 *Inc.* 500
in 1984 and 1994

Figures for all 500 companies

Figures for 233 companies for which we have 1994 data

Source: Martha E. Mangelsdorf, "The Startling Truth about Growth Companies," *Inc.* (May 21, 1996), p. 85.

Figure 14.2 compares the 1984 results with the reported 1994 revenues and full-time employees. It can be seen how significant the growth has been when you compare the 1994 sales and numbers of employees of the 233 companies that participated with the 1984 sales and numbers of employees of the same 233 companies.

In addition to the sales and employees, it was reported that 48 percent were still privately held under the same ownership and only 6 percent had actually gone public. The fact that there were so few ventures that had gone public probably defies conventional thinking in entrepreneurship that becoming a big business required you to go public to finance the growth. A comparison of the ventures that did go public, however, revealed that they had achieved much larger growth than those that did not go public. These 32 companies from the 1984 list grew by $18.9 billion in revenues, which was an average growth rate of 32 percent. As a group these 32 firms included some of the top entrepreneurial performers in the United States, such as Microsoft, Merisel, and Tech Data. Many of these companies had also retained the original founder of the company as CEO.

The sample of *Inc.* magazine ventures does not represent small proprietorships or partnerships that do not grow but does provide some interesting insight as to the implications of a rapid growth strategy. Many of these firms were able to succeed because they understood the important management skills and strategies necessary to achieve success. Future studies by *Inc.* that include Internet companies will likely reflect even higher sales growth patterns.

HITTING THE GROWTH WALL

Researchers and authors in entrepreneurship often refer to a phase in the new venture's life as *"hitting the growth wall,"* where operations reach out-of-control proportions, cash runs out, and key employees leave for more stable jobs. For example, James L. Bildner, the founder of J. Bildner & Sons Inc., a specialty food business, had his company reach a point where he ran out of cash, he found employees leaving, and operations becoming unmanageable.[6] After achieving sales in 1988 of $48 million with more than 20 retail units and a public offering in 1986 that fueled rapid growth, the company hit the wall. With the symptoms described above, the company began to incur large profit losses, inventory control problems, and loss of loyal customers. Too many new locations, ineffective new products, new people, lack of capital, and lack of controls made everything worse.

"hitting the growth wall"   Rapid growth phase where operations are out of control

Typically ventures that are facing this situation are living day-to-day with the hope that future performance will carry them through the difficult times. This hope rests on unrealistic anticipation of that new contract, the new product that can inject new sales, or the unique sales plan that will turn things around. The reality of these unlikely scenarios is clear to everyone but the entrepreneur, who continues to expect better performance.

The tragedy of this type of scenario is that when it happens, it usually ends in disaster. The only way to survive it is to probably avoid it altogether by being prepared to manage growth up front with effective management skills and controls. When and if it occurs, the results do not have to be fatal. A clear assessment of the situation can go a long way to ensuring survival.

Bildner survived hitting the wall by conducting focus groups to learn more about the problems. Employees were included in the assessment and were assured that with good planning the company could survive. Today the company is significantly scaled down with a small presence in the Boston market and has survived hitting the wall for more than seven years.

FINANCIAL STRATEGIES TO SUPPORT GROWTH

We have repeated often in this text the importance of managing the cash flow of a business. This does not change during the growth stage but, in fact, becomes even more critical since it is often difficult to maintain close scrutiny of where cash is going. In particular the entrepreneur will need to determine how much cash will be needed to accommodate the rapid sales growth.

We have stated in Chapter 9 that sales projections are an important function in the planning process. One of the critical decisions that must be made by the entrepreneur each year is a forecast of sales. In Chapter 9 we discuss in more detail how sales forecasts may be computed. In a rapid growth company the forecasts of sales may be even more important because of its drain on cash. Sales growth costs money, and therefore the entrepreneur needs to assess how much additional cash will be needed to support the new sales in the next period. This cash amount can be determined from a simple formula.[7]

$$((Sn - GP) + OH / Td) \times Tar = \text{cash needed}$$

Where: Sn = new sales in next period

GP = gross profit (based on existing or projected percent)

OH = additional overhead in next period

Td = time frame of sales forecast in days

Tar = average collection period for accounts receivable in days

Thus, if an entrepreneur projects an increase of sales of $2 million in the next six months with a gross profit margin of 40 percent, an average collection cycle of 50 days, additional overhead of $100,000, and—to provide a safety margin of cash flow—assumes that all purchases (accounts payable) are made in cash, we can calculate the cash needed to support this increase in sales as ($2M − $800,000) + $100,000/180 days = $7222 × 50 days = $361,111. Thus, the entrepreneur will need an additional $361,111 to support the additional growth in sales over the next six months. This amount is conservative since we assumed that the entrepreneur will pay for all purchases in cash. If accounts payable or payments of these bills reflect a 50-day cycle as well, the venture will actually require less than the calculated amount. However, since the cost of growth is so difficult to determine, it is recommended that the entrepreneur use the conservative approach.

Management of cash strategies has been discussed in detail in Chapters 9 and 13 and will not be repeated here. Entrepreneurs, as noted in our example above, should be aware that during growth, financial controls are even more critical than at any other time in the life of a new venture.

ORGANIZATIONAL CHANGES DURING GROWTH

Many entrepreneurs find that as the venture reaches the growth stage, they need to change the *organization culture*. Management decision making in the hands of only the entrepreneur can be dangerous to the success of the venture during this stage. This is sometimes difficult for the entrepreneur to realize since he or she has been so involved in all important decisions. However, in order to survive, the entrepreneur will need to consider some organizational changes.

organization culture Internal venture atmosphere based on employee attitudes

Some of the important guidelines to cultural change during growth involve the following:

- Communicate all matters to key employees. Trust and understanding by employees are important so that their roles and responsibilities during this stage of business are clear.

- Be a good listener. Learn what's on the minds of your employees and what they would do if they ran the company.

- Be willing to delegate responsibility. The entrepreneur cannot always be available to assess every management decision. Give key employees the flexibility to make decisions without the fear of failure.
- Provide feedback consistently and regularly.
- Provide continuous training of key employees. They in turn will be able to train others in the organization. Seminars, course work, or internal training programs can be very important in enhancing the capability of employees as the venture grows.
- Emphasize results to key managers with incentives built in to encourage them to train and delegate within their roles.
- Maintain a focus by establishing a mission with goals and using consensus in management decision making.
- Establish a "we" spirit—not a "me" spirit—in meetings and memoranda to employees.

Creating a positive culture in the venture can enhance the opportunities to achieve success during difficult times as the venture begins to grow. The entrepreneur with a well-developed working organization can then devote more time to longer-term strategic issues. Creating the efficient organization can be enhanced with a strong board of directors and board of advisors. We see in our *Business Week* box that if you have a board of directors in place, a board of advisors can support some of the management areas noted below that are typically weak in a rapid growth venture. The criteria should be to find the best talent that will provide the management areas or skills that you feel are the weakest.

ENTREPRENEURIAL SKILLS AND STRATEGIES

During the growth stage of a venture the entrepreneur will need to consider some important management skills that often contribute to venture failure. Studies have shown that during the growth of a new venture, management skills and strategies in such areas as record keeping and financial control, inventory control, human resources, marketing, and planning are critical to achieving long-term success.[8] Each of these areas is discussed in the following paragraphs.

Record Keeping and Financial Control

Maintaining good records and financial controls over such activities as cash flow, inventory, receivables, customer data, and costs should be a priority of every growing venture. In order to support this effort it is helpful to consider using a software package to enhance the flow of this type of information. Examples of these software packages, as well as how to establish good financial record keeping and controls, are discussed in Chapters 9 and 13.

With a growing venture it is sometimes necessary to enlist the support and services of an accountant or consultant to support record keeping and financial control. These external service firms can also help train employees using the latest and most appropriate technology that can meet the needs of the venture.

Customer information should be retained in a database and defined as active or inactive. In addition, information on a contact person, telephone number, address, as

As Seen in *Business Week*...
Where's Emily Post When a Young Company Needs Her?
The Etiquette of Choosing, Using, and Paying an Advisory Board

Q: We are a communications and Web company with about 20 employees. The company is three years old. As we grow, we find ourselves facing numerous challenges relating to growth, strategy, employees, and so forth. At the same time, we are making a number of alliances to strengthen our offerings. We have thought about forming an advisory board made up of executives who have seen companies through stages like ours and companies with which we may want to form working relationships (e.g., a programming house, process engineers, etc.). Are there ground rules or protocols for this? Fees?

—A.S., Toronto, Ontario

A: An advisory board can be a great supplement to a board of directors, but it's no replacement for the fiduciary responsibility assumed by directors. That's why many practitioners recommend establishing an outside board of directors first.

Having considered that, an advisory board is ideally made up of functional or technical specialists who can complement the more general experience of your directors. Many young companies, for instance, are weak in such areas as financial planning, cash flow management, and international distribution development, where advisors can fill in the gaps. So your first criterion in selecting advisors is to find world-class talent in areas where you're weak, says Michael Gonnerman, a Boston-area financial consultant and former Arthur Andersen accountant who has sat on eight boards of advisors or directors in as many years.

What can you expect of them? From older advisors who have been around the block, you get help structuring contracts, sizing up market demand, and crafting channel strategies—skills that come only with experience. A caution: Although they may lead you to some lucrative deals, don't expect them to build your sales by leveraging their contacts on your behalf. By the same token, Gonnerman says, don't select advisors from companies simply because you want to do business with them. The litmus test should be whether you'd want them regardless of a business opportunity.

In an industry as fickle as the Internet, make sure you pick advisors who "get it." Not everyone can roll with the constantly changing business models or pick up on what drives electronic commerce. Also, assess potential advisors for their time commitment and motivation. You should expect them to attend a meeting once or twice per quarter for a few hours (outside of regular business hours) to review an agenda of specific issues, with telephone consultation as needed. In other words, don't expect heavy lifting, but demand their best effort.

In compensation, cash is not generally required (some advisors might ask for it on philosophical principle), but equity is. A rough rule of thumb: Offer 1 percent of common stock to each advisor, vested over perhaps three to four years.

Source: Jonathan B. Levine, "Where's Emily Post When a Young Company Needs Her?" Business Week Frontier (September 9, 1998).

well as important data on the amount of units and dollars of business transacted by each account should be maintained. New accounts should also be designated for follow-up, such as welcoming customers and providing them with important information about your company and its products and services.

A good example of the importance of customer information to a growth venture involved an engineering firm that was having difficulty communicating information from one engineer to another either on-site or in the office. Requests or complaints conveyed to the on-site engineer were not communicated to the home office until the engineer returned. When clients called the home office, they found that the request or complaint had not been communicated to other engineers. To resolve this problem a manual system was first employed. Each engineer on-site maintained a logbook in which notes such as client requests or complaints were recorded. These notes would then be faxed daily to the home office and kept in a client folder. Thus, when a client spoke to someone at the home office, there would be a file containing any important information about the client and project. This manual system could then be upgraded using e-mail or laptop computers, which would contain software such as Maximizer to maintain customer information using online technology.

Inventory Control

During the growth of a new venture the management of inventory is an important cost control and customer service activity that needs to be carefully monitored. Too much inventory to meet customer needs can be a drain on cash flow since manufacturing, transportation, and storage costs would be assumed by the venture. On the other hand, too little inventory can also cost the venture in lost sales, or it can create unhappy customers who may choose another firm if their needs are not efficiently met.

Efficient electronic data interchanges (EDI) among producers, wholesalers, and retailers can enable these firms to communicate with one another. Linking the needs of a retailer to the wholesaler and producer allows for fast order entry and response. These systems also allow the firm to track shipments internationally.[9]

Linking firms in a computerized system has also been developed by the grocery and pharmaceutical industries using a software system called ECR (efficient consumer response). Supply chain members work together in this system to manage demand, distribution, and marketing such that minimum inventory levels are necessary to meet consumer needs. Computerized checkout machines are usually part of these systems such that linked members are able to anticipate inventory needs before stockouts occur.[10]

Transportation mode selection can also be important in inventory management. Some transportation modes, such as the use of air, are very expensive. Rail and truck are the most often used sources of transportation when a next-day delivery for a customer is not necessary. Careful management of inventory through a computerized system and by working with customers and other channel members can minimize these transportation costs. Anticipating customer needs can avoid stockouts and the unexpected costs of having to meet a customer's immediate need by shipping a product by next-day air. These mistakes can be costly and are likely to significantly reduce the margins on any transaction.

Human Resources

Generally the new venture does not have the luxury of a human resource department that can interview, hire, and evaluate employees. Most of these decisions will be the responsibility of the entrepreneur and perhaps one or two other key employees. As the firm grows, there will almost always be a need to hire new employees. The process should not be any different from what was previously discussed in Chapters 10 and 13, where we outline some of the important procedures for interviewing, hiring, evaluating, and preparing job descriptions for new employees. Instituting an effective organizational culture such as that discussed earlier in this chapter is also useful in human resource management.

One of the difficult decisions for an entrepreneur to make is the firing of incompetent employees. Having a fair employee evaluation process is primary in justifying the firing of an employee. Employees should be given feedback on a regular basis, and any problems should be identified, with a proposed solution agreeable to the employee and the entrepreneur. In this manner, continued problems with the employee that necessitated a firing decision would be well documented.

Often during the growth of a new venture, some employees will tend to be constant complainers because of the heavier workload. Because these individuals typically require the most time of the entrepreneur, and threaten the general attitude of all employees, they need to be warned and, if the behavior is not stopped, moved out quickly.

In the late 1990s and into the new millennium many new ventures, because of the economic boom in the United States, are finding it more and more time consuming not only to find new employees but to then manage the human resource process. What some entrepreneurs are doing is using professional employer organizations (PEOs). One such company is TriNet Employer Group Inc., which came to the rescue of Robert Teal, cofounder of a Silicon Valley start-up, Quinta Corporation. Robert had found it time consuming and costly to hire and retain employees. His banker suggested he consider TriNet. After an assessment of their services he hired them to assume most of the human resource tasks of the new venture. This involved such things as recruiting, hiring, setting up benefit programs, payroll, and even firing decisions. This has given Robert more time to devote to his growing start-up.[11]

Marketing Skills

Marketing skills in the growth stage of a new venture are also critical to a venture's continued success. As the company grows, it will need to develop new products and services to maintain its distinctiveness in a competitive market. This should be an ongoing process based on information regarding changing customer needs and competitive strategies. This information can be obtained formally using surveys or focus groups, or informally by direct contact with customers by the entrepreneur or his or her sales force. Some entrepreneurs have found that occasional travel with the sales force to key accounts can be very revealing and often lead to ideas for new products.

In a small entrepreneurial growing venture it is difficult to engage in some of the more formal procedures for developing new products because of the lack of people and financial resources. Universities, however, frequently offer the opportunity to small businesses to participate as part of a student project in a marketing research class at little or no cost. In Chapter 8 we discussed some of the low-cost methods of gathering market data. The Internet, described in Chapter 7, can also be a good resource to provide market information.

The marketing plan discussed in Chapter 8 as part of the business plan should be prepared on an annual basis. The marketing plan would follow the same outline as illustrated in Chapter 8 but would designate goals and objectives and action programs for the next year. Key employees, customers, and channel members should be utilized in the preparation of this plan. Once the plan is prepared, it needs to be implemented and monitored to ensure that the goals and objectives will be met. Sharing the marketing plan with employees, particularly sales representatives, is important in getting it implemented effectively.

Strategic Planning Skills

In this textbook planning has been discussed in great detail, particularly as it relates to the start-up. It is also important for the entrepreneur to continue to plan for both the short term and the long term. Planning is a continual process, particularly in a rapidly changing environment. It is unlikely that a plan that worked yesterday will be

---

TABLE 14.1 Outline for a Strategic Plan

- Business mission
- Situation analysis
- Internal environmental analysis—includes a discussion of the venture's strengths and weaknesses
- External environmental analysis—includes a discussion of the venture's opportunities and threats (industry and competitive analysis) in the marketplace
- Goal formulation
- Strategy formulation
- Formulation of programs to meet goals
- Implementation
- Feedback and control

---

effective in today's marketplace. We mentioned the importance of developing annual marketing plans that establish short-term goals and objectives based on specific marketing activities. In addition to these short-term plans, the entrepreneur needs to continually address the long-term perspective of the venture. Typically this would involve goals and objectives for the next three to five years. A typical outline of a *strategic plan* is illustrated in Table 14.1.

strategic plan   Three- to five-year plan that includes all functions of an organization

Strategic or long-range planning begins with a restatement of the mission of the venture. This mission statement should be evaluated to ensure that it reflects the long-term vision of the entrepreneur. If it does not, then it should be modified to do so. Next is the situation analysis, which should reflect such issues as:

- What is the present business situation? What is the state of the industry? What is the state of the economy? What products or services are most profitable? Why do people buy (or not buy) our products or services? Who are our major competitors?
- What are the strengths, weaknesses, opportunities, and threats to the venture in the long term (three to five years)? This is often referred to as a SWOT analysis.

Hamish Hafter, CEO of Mishi Apparel, found that distributing a questionnaire to each of the employees of his firm was a meaningful task to understand the situation and to launch the strategic planning process. Questions were asked such as, What is working well in your department? What systems could be improved? What happens when conflict arises? Responses were collected, summarized, and distributed to help launch the strategic planning process. This is an effective method to learn more about internal and external issues that are anonymous and shared by everyone. Further meetings would then be used to prepare the situation analysis and begin the next step in the strategic planning process.[12]

After completing the situation analysis, the long-term goals and objectives of the venture will be addressed. Unlike the marketing plan, which focuses only on marketing goals and objectives for the next 12 months, the strategic plan focuses on the longer-term goals and objectives for the entire organization. These goals and objectives can address such issues as profitability, people, company image, customer relations, growth, new products and services, new markets, new financing, or timing for a public offering.

The next step in the strategic plan is the strategy formulation. At this point the entrepreneur needs to address how and when the goals and objectives will be achieved. Will the strategy involve new segments? Will it involve new markets such as international? Will the focus be on cost reduction to be price competitive? Will the focus be on quality and service to maintain higher margins?

These strategies will then be reflected in specific projects or programs. For example, a three-year new product strategy may require projects such as marketing research, engineering and design, business analysis, and testing before launch in the marketplace. These programs or projects would need to be identified in the program formulation section of the strategic plan.

Once the programs and projects have been identified, the strategic plan then describes their implementation. Who will be responsible for each program? What will be the expectation at the end of the first year, second year, third year? How much will the program cost?

Feedback and control is the final step in the strategic planning process. As we indicated above, the strategic planning process is a three- or five-year planning cycle. However, this plan needs to be evaluated at the end of each year, and decisions made to either continue or discontinue programs, or develop new goals, objectives, strategies, and programs to reflect new opportunities or threats in the marketplace. In this section, the entrepreneur identifies the key variables that will be evaluated at the end of each year and what would be expected out of each program. Thus, a comparison is made at this juncture of the actual results with the expected results to ascertain what should be done with the program. For example, an entrepreneur may be concerned about the replacement of independent sales representatives with full-time company-employed salespeople. This program is expected to take about three years to complete in the eastern United States. At the end of the first year, the entrepreneur finds that the program is going well and that five new hires have provided coverage of key states such that the transition will be completed in year 2, giving the entrepreneur the opportunity to begin implementing the same program in the western United States beginning in year 3. On the other hand, if the program was not progressing well and the company was finding it very difficult to hire quality salespeople, a new program strategy would be developed and goals and objectives accordingly modified.

Strategic planning like all other planning is an iterative process. Changes are made over time, if necessary, with the purpose of establishing an important long-term focus.

TIME MANAGEMENT

One of the biggest problems in growing the venture is encapsulated in the phrase, "If I only had more time." While this is a common problem for all busy people, it is particularly acute for the entrepreneur when business begins to grow. Time is the entrepreneur's most precious yet limited resource. It is a unique quantity: An entrepreneur cannot store it, rent it, hire it, or buy it. It is also totally perishable and irreplaceable. Everything requires it, and it passes at the same rate for everyone. Although important throughout the life of the venture, time is particularly critical during the growth stage of the venture. No matter what an entrepreneur does, today's ration of time is 24 hours, and yesterday's time is already history.

Few entrepreneurs use time effectively, and none of them ever reaches perfection. Entrepreneurs can always make better use of their time, and the more they strive to do so, the more it will enrich their venture as well as their personal lives.

Most individuals can be three or four times more productive without ever increasing the number of working hours, which reflects the basic principle that it is more important to do the right things than to do things right. This principle implies that the key to effective time management is prioritizing the items that should be accomplished in any particular time period. Instead, an entrepreneur typically establishes priorities that reflect his or her personality and values.

How does one get more out of the time spent? How does one effectively manage time? *Time management* involves investing time to determine what you want out of life, including what you want out of the venture. This implies that entrepreneurs have focused values about their ventures, work, family, social activities, possessions, and selves.

time management   Process of improving individual's productivity through more efficient use of time

Why does the problem of time management exist for the entrepreneur? It is basically due to a lack of information and a lack of motivation. The entrepreneur must want to manage his or her time effectively and then spend the time necessary to acquire the information needed to accomplish this. Effective time management starts with an understanding of some benefits that will result.

Benefits of Time Management

The entrepreneur reaps numerous benefits from effectively managing his or her time, some of which are listed in Table 14.2. One of these—increased productivity—reflects the fact that there is always enough time to accomplish the most important things. Through a conscious effort and increased focus, the entrepreneur can determine what is most important to the success and growth of the venture and focus on these things rather than on less important or more enjoyable things; an entrepreneur must learn to focus on the majors, not the minors.

TABLE 14.2 Time Management for the Entrepreneur

Typical Payoffs from Time Management

Increased productivity

More job satisfaction

Improved interpersonal relations

Reduced time anxiety and tension

Better health

Basic Principles of Time Management

The Principle of Desire

The Principle of Effectiveness

The Principle of Analysis

The Principle of Teamwork

The Principle of Prioritized Planning

The Principle of Reanalysis

This overt action will lead to the second benefit: increased job satisfaction. Getting more important things done and being more successful in growing and developing the venture will give more job satisfaction to the entrepreneur.

There will also be an improvement in the esprit de corps of the venture as the entrepreneur and others in the company experience less time pressure, better results, and more job satisfaction. Although the total time the entrepreneur spends with other individuals in the company may in fact decrease, the time spent will be of better quality, allowing him or her to improve interrelations. This also makes more time available for the entrepreneur to spend with family and friends.

A fourth benefit is that the entrepreneur will experience less anxiety and tension. Worry, guilt, and other emotions tend to reduce mental effectiveness and efficiency, making decisions less effective. Effective time management reduces concerns and anxieties, allowing better and faster decisions to be made.

All of these benefits culminate in a final one for the entrepreneur: better health. Large amounts of energy and persistence are needed for the start-up and growth of a venture, as was discussed in Chapter 1. High energy levels and long working hours require good health, and poor management of time often leads to mental and physical fatigue, poor eating habits, and curtailment of exercise. If there is one thing an entrepreneur needs to help the venture grow, it is good health. And good health is a by-product of good time management.

Basic Principles of Time Management

How does an entrepreneur develop good time management? By first recognizing that he or she is a time waster. This insight leads the entrepreneur to value time and to change any personal attitudes and habits as needed. This is embodied in the Principle of Desire (see Table 14.2). Effective time management depends on willpower and self-discipline and requires that the entrepreneur have a strong desire to optimize his or her time.

Second, the entrepreneur should adhere to the Principle of Effectiveness; that is, he or she should automatically focus on the most important issues, even when under pressure. Whenever possible, an entrepreneur should try to complete each task in a single session. This requires that enough time be set aside to accomplish the task. Although quality is of course important, perfectionism is not and often leads only to procrastination. The entrepreneur must not take excessive time trying to make a small improvement in one area when time could be better spent in another.

To manage time effectively, the entrepreneur needs to know how his or her time is presently being spent. Following the Principle of Analysis will help accomplish this. Using a time sheet with 15-minute intervals, the entrepreneur should record and analyze the time spent during the past two weeks. This analysis will reveal some areas of wasted time and provide the basis for prioritizing the tasks to be accomplished. It is particularly important for the entrepreneur to develop methods for handling recurrent situations. Checklists should be developed and kept handy. Handouts on the company and its operation should be prepared for visitors and the press. Standardized forms and procedures should be developed for all recurrent events and operations.

The essence of time management is embodied in an important principle that most entrepreneurs had to employ in starting the venture: the Principle of Teamwork. During the time analysis, one thing will become very apparent to the entrepreneur— the small amount of time that is totally under his or her control. The entrepreneur needs to help members of the management team become more sensitive to the time management concept when dealing with other individuals in the company. Each member of the management team needs to employ effective time management in dealing with other team members.

The Principle of Prioritized Planning includes elements of all the previously mentioned principles of effective time management. Each day, an entrepreneur needs to list the things to be accomplished and indicate their degree of importance. One method may be to use a scale from 1 to 3, with 1 being most important, 2 somewhat important, and 3 moderately important. By indicating on a 3 × 5 card the most important items to be accomplished that day, the entrepreneur can focus on getting to the ones of lesser importance as time permits. This prioritizing, planning, and focus on the key issues are fundamental to time management, as they allow each individual to accomplish the most important tasks. Also, some entrepreneurs are most efficient in the morning, some during the afternoon, and some at night. The most efficient period of the day should be used to address the most important issues.

As with any implemented procedure, the entrepreneur should periodically review the objectives and the degree to which these have been achieved. This is the Principle of Reanalysis. Tasks should be delegated whenever possible. The clerical staff and close assistants should be well trained and encouraged to take initiative. The clerical staff should sort out all correspondence and draft routine letters for the entrepreneur's signature. The office system should be well organized with a daily diary, card index, reminder list, operation board, and efficient pending file. All incoming calls should be filtered, and a time set for making and receiving calls except for those most critical. All meetings should be analyzed to see if they are being run effectively. If not, the person who runs the meetings should be trained in how to conduct them. Finally, any committee in the venture should be carefully scrutinized in terms of its results. Committees tend to tie up personnel, slow down decisions, and have the habit of multiplying themselves beyond their need. Through all these effects, the entrepreneur can become a time-saver, not a timeserver. This efficient use of time enables the entrepreneur to expand and grow the venture properly, increasing productivity and lessening encroachment of the venture on his or her private life.

NEGOTIATION

Growing an enterprise requires the ability to negotiate. Even though it is important, negotiation is usually not a skill well developed by the entrepreneur. As one woman entrepreneur stated, "A woman entrepreneur should develop her negotiating skills as quickly as possible. It is so important in starting and particularly in expanding a business. Women tend to be weaker in negotiating skills than men. This may reflect the level of issues typically negotiated at home versus in a business situation. These skills can be learned and then must be practiced."

negotiation   Process of resolving conflict between two or more parties

distributive bargaining   Process of resolving conflict by keeping other parties from meeting their goals

integrative bargaining   Allowing other parties to meet their goals while still maintaining commitment to own goals

What is negotiation? *Negotiation* is the process by which parties attempt to resolve a conflict by agreement. Although a resolution is not always possible, the process of negotiation identifies the critical issues in the disagreement and is therefore central to business dealings. In learning and developing negotiation skills, it is important to understand the two types of negotiation (*distributive bargaining* and *integrative bargaining*), the tactics involved in each type, and the skills required.[13]

Negotiation often involves one party attempting to get another to do something the first desires. At times, this second party will not act unless obtaining something of interest in return. This motive for a return must be understood in the negotiation process, whether the negotiation is cooperative or competitive.

Cooperative Negotiation—Integrative Bargaining

Integrative bargaining involves *cooperative negotiation* between the negotiating parties. In this situation, the entrepreneur is willing to let the other side achieve its desired outcome while maintaining a commitment to his or her own goals. In one sense, integrative bargaining is joint problem solving based on the concept of rational decision making. A model of this process depicts the negotiation flow moving from establishing objectives, to establishing criteria, to analyzing the cause-and-effect relationships involved, to developing and evaluating alternatives, to selecting an alternative and an action plan (see Figure 14.3). To be complete, this process requires that the outcomes be measured once implementation begins. The effectiveness of the decisions made through this process depends on the adequacy of the information and the commitment of the parties involved to implement the decision reached.

Several steps are involved in implementing this *rational decision model*. First, the problem must be clearly identified with all parties in the negotiation exchanging views without blaming the other parties or demanding a specific outcome. Each party involved must be genuinely interested in solving the problem and understanding the underlying concerns of the others involved. Meetings need to be scheduled frequently with advance notice of each meeting given to allow all participants to prepare. Each meeting should have an agenda, with a majority of the items having a high probability of resolution. Each agenda item should be so stated so that open discussion and integrative bargaining to reach a mutually agreeable solution occur.

rational decision model   Method of resolving conflict through objectives, analysis of alternatives, and action

The second step in effective integrative bargaining is searching for alternative solutions. In so doing, the entrepreneur and other parties involved should try to uncover areas of agreement in order to realize areas of divergence. This requires that concrete terms be used and appropriate ground rules that encourage trust and

---

FIGURE 14.3 The "Rational" Model for Decision Making

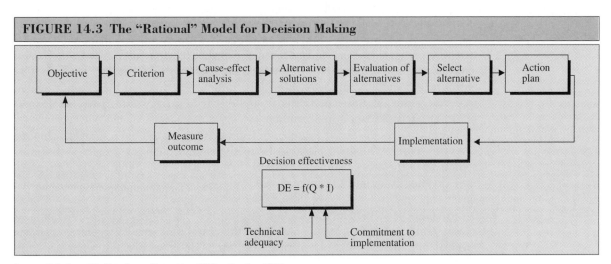

Source: C. Jackson, Working Paper, University of Tulsa, October 1987.

respect be established. Through frequent preliminary discussions, tentative solutions and ideas can be brought up and refined before being formally considered. This informal, exploratory discussion of a possible solution reduces the likelihood of immediate rejection. The techniques and frameworks used should differ depending on the specific problem at hand. Integrative bargaining occurs more quickly when the parties involved sense a greater likelihood of success. This requires that easier items be dealt with first, with any difficult items laid aside temporarily if an impasse is reached. No rigid formula should be used, since creative solutions do not come from following a systematic procedure, as we discussed in Chapter 5.

Finally, as indicated in the model of rational decision making, the best alternative solution should be selected. This requires the establishment of an open, honest relationship that allows each party to indicate when something is wrong and to report preferences and range of latitude in each problem area. This is the area most susceptible to distortion and further problems.

Competitive Negotiation—Distributive Bargaining

Even more important for the successful expansion of a business is the entrepreneur's effectiveness in distributive bargaining. In contrast to integrative bargaining, distributive bargaining does not allow the other party to achieve his or her goals. There is a fixed pie to be divided, which means that the larger the opponent's share, the smaller the entrepreneur's. Since there is no trust between the parties, a solution can be reached only through a series of modified positions of compromise and concession. In this competitive adversarial bargaining arena, each party tries to discover the other's goals, values, and perceptions. The amount of conflict usually revolves around the differing economic objectives and attitudes of the parties involved. When the entrepreneur and the other party have conflicting economic objectives, distributive bargaining can be successful only if each party compromises his or her objectives to some extent. Directly competing claims on a fixed, limited economic resource (such as the amount of the 100 percent equity in the venture) require concessions in allocating the shares.

The key to successful distributive bargaining is for the entrepreneur to discover the goals and perceptions of the other party through direct and/or indirect methods. Indirect methods include discussing the person with anyone who has had previous contact, such as your own employees, the party's employees, or outside individuals; carefully reviewing all previous written and verbal correspondence with the party; and walking around the party's business to get a feel of its vitality and direction. The entrepreneur should employ each of these indirect methods to the extent possible to get a feel for the other party's goals and drives so that a strategy can be planned before the actual negotiation commences.

The entrepreneur should also use more direct methods to obtain some insight into the other party. Whenever possible, he or she should meet informally with representatives of the other company, probing them to determine their levels of preparation. Frequently, insight can be obtained from responses to relaxed, almost innocent questions.

Several other direct methods employed during the negotiation process can also reveal significant clues. One of these is for the entrepreneur to exaggerate his or her level of impatience. This often forces the other party to prematurely reveal the amount of bargaining room left. Another method employs the principle of "nonsequiturization." In other words, at a crucial moment in the negotiation, the entrepreneur should take an entirely different posture than what has been employed throughout. This can be accomplished by making a sudden shift in manners, argument, or demands. For example, this shift can take the form of an attack if a laid-back approach has been adopted previously.

Whether direct or indirect methods are used, an entrepreneur skillful at negotiation attempts to determine the *settlement range* of the other party. The settlement range is the area of values in which a mutually agreeable solution can be reached. This area is between the resistance points of the parties involved and can be either positive or negative, as indicated in the example in Figure 14.4. In the positive settlement range, the resistance points of the two parties are compatible. In this situation, both parties would rather be involved in the deal than have a work stoppage, as would occur in the union settlement (Figure 14.4). The opposite is true when a negative settlement range exists. In this situation, the resistance points are not compatible, indicating that it will be difficult to reach an agreement that would be even minimally acceptable to the two parties.

settlement range Agreeable solution area for parties in conflict

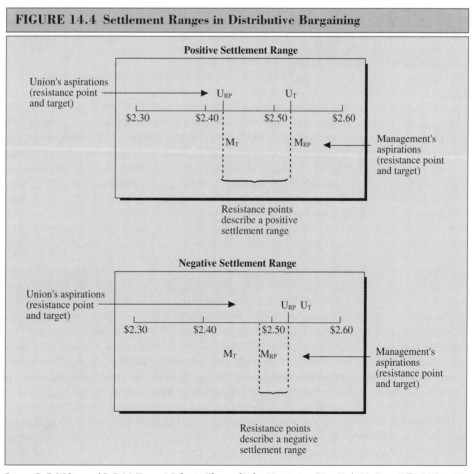

FIGURE 14.4 Settlement Ranges in Distributive Bargaining

Positive Settlement Range

Union's aspirations (resistance point and target) → U_{RP} U_T

$2.30 $2.40 $2.50 $2.60

M_T M_{RP}

Management's aspirations (resistance point and target)

Resistance points describe a positive settlement range

Negative Settlement Range

Union's aspirations (resistance point and target) → U_{RP} U_T

$2.30 $2.40 $2.50 $2.60

M_T M_{RP}

Management's aspirations (resistance point and target)

Resistance points describe a negative settlement range

Source: R. E. Walton and R. B. McKerse, *A Behavior Theory of Labor Negotiations* (New York: McGraw-Hill, 1965), p. 43.

The key to good negotiations lies in the entrepreneur's ability to manipulate the other party's perception of a likely settlement point so that this point results in a more favorable position for the entrepreneur. This can be accomplished through indicating higher initial demands, indicating an overly strong commitment to a particular position, or focusing on the other party by either minimizing his or her opportunity to develop a fixed position or enabling the party to easily revise a previously committed position.

Perhaps the best strategy for the entrepreneur is to bargain in good faith—indicating a willingness to bargain and be flexible. This will mean that the entrepreneur will make concessions throughout the negotiation process where warranted, particularly when his or her position is further away from a possible solution than the other party's. Any concessions should be linked to the other party's change or at least to an understanding that certain issues are critical in securing an agreement. This strategy often leads to obtaining a settlement point that is acceptable to both parties, completing the negotiation faster than by using other strategies.

Negotiation Approach

Although many strategies can be used in negotiations, it is important that the entrepreneur select one approach. One negotiation approach that is easy to implement has eight steps: prepare, discuss, signal, propose, respond, bargain, close, and agree.[14]

Probably the most critical and yet the most often overlooked step in this process of negotiation is preparation. With all the time pressures, an entrepreneur frequently fails to set aside the necessary time to define what has to be done and to develop objectives, the settlement range, and alternative strategies before the negotiation commences. The objectives need to be prioritized and back-off positions developed.

The second step is the initial meeting. Here, as well as throughout the negotiation process, it is critical that the entrepreneur listen carefully to the other party.

Signaling is one aspect of negotiation that tests the other party's willingness to move toward a solution. Through signaling, the entrepreneur can discern real objections and assess the other party's willingness to change his or her original position. This is accomplished through using a phrase such as "I could never agree to that the way it is stated." The entrepreneur must carefully develop the art of signaling and of reading the other party's signals.

Once an agreement to move forward to a closure is reached, a proposition must be laid out for discussion. The proposition serves as the basis for developing the final agreement.

Any negotiation approach involves responses to the other party's suggestions. These responses are particularly important once a proposition has been put forth. Although a response should take into account the interest and limitations of the other party, it does not necessarily contain concessions. Any concessions granted should reflect the priorities and points of inflexibility of the other party.

Besides response and signaling, another difficult aspect of the negotiation approach is bargaining. In bargaining, the entrepreneur gives up something for something. At first, to help develop this ability, an entrepreneur can state all bargaining items on a conditional basis: "If I . . . then you. . . ."

Every negotiation needs a closure. Closing the agreement frequently is based on a concession or on a summary. A summary is used when a multitude of issues have been discussed and resolved.

The ideal closing ends in a mutually satisfactory agreement—the ultimate goal of negotiation. Reaching an agreement is, after all, the objective of most negotiations. Any verbal agreement should be detailed in writing as specifically as possible.

Through negotiation, an entrepreneur can expand the original venture. The actual expansion and growth of the venture can take the form of a joint venture, merger, acquisition, leveraged buyout, or franchising.

INFORMATION PLANNING AND CONTROL

Throughout this text we have repeated the importance of maintaining management and financial controls to evaluate cash flows, profits, costs, inventory, and sales. The importance of, and systematic approaches to, establishing these controls are discussed in Chapters 8, 9, and 13. In this chapter we have also reiterated the importance of these control systems during the growth stage of a venture. In addition to financial and management control, the entrepreneur needs to establish information/customer service tracking systems or controls.

Customer Service/Satisfaction Tracking

In Chapter 8 we discussed the importance in marketing of meeting customer needs. Small and large companies are paying more attention to their customers and establishing processes that track and monitor *customer service and satisfaction*. Unlike financial, inventory, and sales controls, the monitoring of customer satisfaction involves more qualitative measures that can provide early warnings to the entrepreneur of impending customer problems. These problems can affect financial results as well as sales revenue, and are thus important as a preliminary process. Monitoring and tracking customer satisfaction can be performed in a number of ways that are not costly to the new venture.

customer service and satisfaction Tracking and monitoring customer complaints and suggestions

Complaint and Suggestion Programs All complaints, suggestions, and comments that come from customers either orally or in writing need to be recorded and assessed on a regular basis. These should be kept in a folder and summarized by one of the staff. The entrepreneur should plan regular meetings to discuss with his or her staff why the complaints are occurring and what solutions can be enacted to resolve any problems. It should be remembered that random complaints may not need any special attention, since it is difficult to always please every customer. However, the entrepreneur may find that a random or isolated complaint is an impending problem or is a cause of other related problems.

Focus Groups Focus groups, discussed in Chapter 8 as a technique for conducting marketing research, are a low-cost method to monitor and track customer satisfaction and service. These focus groups of 8 to 10 people can represent a particular segment of the market, member of the channel of distribution, or noncustomers of the venture. The focus group should be led or moderated by someone other than the entrepreneur and should involve an open forum on some aspect of the venture's business. For example, a focus group may be used to test customer reactions to a promotion program, a new product, sales strategies, or product service. Participant responses would be recorded (on audio- and/or videotape) and reviewed at a later date.

As mentioned earlier in this chapter, there may be a local university that would welcome companies to participate in a marketing research class project.

Customer Surveys   An entrepreneur should also periodically consider conducting a customer survey. These can be conducted by mail, telephone, or in person. These surveys should include a questionnaire that will allow the entrepreneur to standardize measured responses regarding customer service or satisfaction. Once the responses are tabulated and summarized, they should be reviewed by the entrepreneur and discussed at a management meeting. Again, it may be possible to have such a survey designed and implemented by students at a local university. Once the first survey has been implemented, future surveys can simply duplicate the process, which will save time and money.

As in any of the quantitative control systems involving finances, sales, or inventory, the process for customer service and satisfaction controls is the same. Information is gathered and reviewed and compared with what is expected. Any deviation from expectations would then involve some type of action. In the process of customer service or satisfaction controls we rely on more interpretation of the data since they involve customer opinions, complaints, or suggestions. However, an entrepreneur should have a certain acceptable expectation regarding service that, if not met, should involve some consideration of change. The fact that the entrepreneur shows the customer that the firm cares about his or her opinion can go a long way to establish more favorable customer relations.

IN REVIEW

Summary

This chapter deals with issues that need to be addressed by the entrepreneur during the growth stage of a new venture. Probably first and foremost should be whether the entrepreneur will even choose a growth strategy, since it is conceivable, in certain types of business, that the strategy may be no growth.

For those ventures that choose a growth strategy there are some impending risks or dangers. Too-fast growth or uncontrolled growth can lead to a situation known as "hitting the wall." This is when a venture grows too fast and loses control of cash, inventory, customers, and eventually profits. Although the situation does not always result in bankruptcy or disaster, it is something that the entrepreneur can be prepared for by establishing good controls and managing growth rather than letting it just run rampant.

One of the important roles of an entrepreneur during a venture's growth stage is to establish an effective organization culture. This can be accomplished through good communication, being a good listener, delegating responsibility, providing employees with consistent and regular feedback, establishing employee incentives, maintaining a focus on the mission and goals set in the plan, and establishing a "we" spirit rather than a "me" spirit.

During the growth stage there are certain critical skills and strategies that the entrepreneur will need to recognize. Management skills and strategies involving such areas as record keeping and financial control, inventory control, human resources, marketing, strategic management, time management, and negotiation are critical during the growth stage of a new venture.

Time management is critical, as it can lead to increased job satisfaction, increased productivity, less anxiety and tension, and better health. An entrepreneur should recognize that he or she is very likely a time-waster. Through a procedure described in this chapter, the entrepreneur can develop the skills necessary to manage time more effectively.

Negotiation is another important skill that the entrepreneur will use in dealing with employees, investors, advisors, and customers. Two types of negotiation are discussed—cooperative and competitive. In addition, the approach to negotiation proposed for an entrepreneur involves eight steps: prepare, discuss, signal, propose, respond, bargain, close, and agree.

The chapter closes with more discussion of controls. In particular, we focus on information and customer satisfaction and techniques for monitoring them.

Questions for Discussion

1. What is meant by the concept "hitting the wall"? Review recent business magazines and newspapers and identify an example of a venture reaching this stage. What happened to the venture? How did it survive, if at all?

2. Under what circumstances would an entrepreneur choose not to grow his or her venture? Provide examples.

3. What are some of the cultural changes or strategies in the organization that should be in place to ensure employee satisfaction and harmony? What could happen if any one or all of these did not exist in a growing venture?

4. Why is strategic planning important to a new venture? Describe the important steps in preparing a strategic plan.

5. What are the benefits of time management to an entrepreneur? What are the basic principles of time management? How can technology assist in the time management process?

6. What is the difference between cooperative and competitive negotiation? What are some of the situations in which an entrepreneur would utilize these negotiation skills?

7. Describe some of the techniques that an entrepreneur can implement to monitor customer satisfaction and service. What role can the Internet play in this process?

Key Terms

customer service and satisfaction	organization culture
distributive bargaining	rational decision model
"hitting the growth wall"	settlement range
integrative bargaining	strategic plan
negotiation	time management

More Information—Net Addresses in This Chapter

Business Resource Center
  www.morebusiness.com

Dun & Bradstreet Information Service
  www.dbisna.com

Entrepreneurs on the Web
  www.entrepreneurs-web.com

Small Business Advisor
  www.isquare.com

Small Business Help Center
  www.helpbizowners.com

Small Business News
  www.sbnpub.com

Small Business Resource Center
  www.webcom.com/seaquest/sbrc

Smart Business Supersite (SBS)
  www.smartbiz.com

Women's Business Center
  www.onlinewbc.org

Yahoo's small business site
  http://smallbusiness.yahoo.com

Selected Readings

Barringer, Bruce R.; and Daniel W. Greening. (1998). Small Business Growth through Geographic Expansion: A Comparative Case Study. *Journal of Business Venturing*, vol. 13, no. 6, pp. 467–92.

A theoretical model of the antecedents of effective small business geographic expansion is developed by using a comparative case study methodology. Findings indicated that effective small business geographic expansion involves six major areas of concern: planning for growth, managing growth, reasons for growth, expansion site characteristics, a set of moderator variables, and expansion performance. The unique nature of the geographic expansion process adds a layer of complexity to firm growth. Planning helps attenuate these challenges. The recruitment and selection of qualified personnel to staff expansion sites is also a critical activity, along with networking in the expansion site locations to establish organizational legitimacy.

Beal, Reginald M. (2000). Competing Effectively: Environmental Scanning, Competitive Strategy, and Organizational Performance in Small Manufacturing Firms. *Journal of Small Business Management*, vol. 38, no. 1, pp. 24–47.

The study of small manufacturing firms competing in a wide variety of industries examines the effects of the frequency in scope of environmental scanning on environment-competitive strategy alignment.

Bhide, A. (November/December 1996). The Questions Every Entrepreneur Must Answer. *Harvard Business Review*, pp. 120–32.

Based on the observation of several hundred ventures, the author addresses some key decisions that an entrepreneur must make as the firm begins to evolve. The focus of the article is on such questions as, What are my goals? Do I have the right strategy? Can I execute the strategy?

Chaston, I.; and T. Mangles. (January 1997). Core Capabilities as Predictors of Growth Potential in Small Manufacturing Firms. *Journal of Small Business Management*, pp. 47–57.

This research paper analyzes the growth characteristics that will contribute to a successful growth strategy. Such factors as commitment to growth, a well-defined market niche, a formal plan, and sufficient financial resources are some of the key characteristics identified.

Gartner, William B.; Jennifer A. Starr; and Subodh Bhat. (1999). Predicting New Venture Survival: An Analysis of "Anatomy of a Startup." Cases from *Inc.* magazine. *Journal of Business Venturing*, vol. 14, no. 2, pp. 215–32.

Predictions of venture success as offered by reporters and experts in Inc. *magazine are contrasted to the predictions generated from an analysis of data from a venture screening questionnaire. The venture screening questionnaire covering four categories (individual characteristics, entrepreneurial behaviors, strategy, and environment) was used to evaluate 27 "Anatomy of a Start-Up" articles from Inc. magazine. New ventures that survived were more likely to have entrepreneurs who gained knowledge and ability during the founding process, who devoted greater efforts to dealing with suppliers and analyzing potential new entrants and less time to determining identity of the business.*

Philips, D. (September 1996). Leaders of the Pack. *Entrepreneur,* pp. 124–8.

Examples of entrepreneurs who have been able to grow their ventures in light of an intense competitive environment are discussed. Growing ventures usually attract other ventures, which can increase the importance of good planning and controls.

Wasilczuk, Julita. (2000). Advantageous Competence of Owner/Managers to Grow the Firm in Poland: Empirical Evidence. *Journal of Small Business Management,* vol. 38, no. 2, pp. 88–94.

The competencies of Polish owners/managers are defined. Experience, previous occupation, and personal traits are positively correlated with growth perspectives. Motivation for starting a business is also very important.

West, G. Page III; and G. Dale Meyer. (1998). To Agree or Not to Agree? Consensus and Performance in New Ventures. *Journal of Business Venturing,* vol. 13, no. 5, pp. 395–422.

Top management consensus on issues perceived to be important by the CEOs of technology-based entrepreneurial companies bears no relationship to firm performance. In contrast, in dynamic environments and in earlier life cycle stages, disagreement on strategic issues of lesser importance to the CEO is significantly and negatively related to perceived performance.

Williamson, Ian O. (2000). Employer Legitimacy and Recruitment Success in Small Businesses. *Entrepreneurship Theory & Practice,* vol. 25, no. 1, pp. 27–42.

Recruiting new employees is one of the biggest challenges facing small businesses and a key component of organizational success.

Endnotes

1. See J. Useem, "The Start-Up Factory," *Inc.* (February 9,1997), pp. 40–52; E. Matson, "He Turns Ideas into Companies—at Net Speed," *Fast Company* (December 1996), p. 34; and Idealab website www.idealab.com.
2. D. Berman, "Relentless Prosperity Is Forcing a Choice on Many Small Companies: Expand or Die," *Business Week* (November 8, 1999), pp. 62–66.
3. I. Mochari, "Too Much, Too Soon," *Inc.* (November 1999), p. 119.
4. R. D. Hof and S. Hamm, "Amazon.com Throws Open the Doors," *Business Week* (October 11, 1999), p. 44.
5. Martha E. Mangelsdorf, "Growth Companies," *Inc.* (May 21, 1996), pp. 85–92.
6. James L. Bildner, "Hitting the Wall," *Inc.* (July 1995), pp. 21–22.
7. N. Brodsky, "Paying for Growth," *Inc.* (October 1, 1996), pp. 48–49.
8. See R. N. Lussier, "Startup Business Advice from Business Owners to Would-Be Entrepreneurs," *SAM Advanced Management Journal* (Winter 1995), pp. 10–13; M. Peters, "Surviving Success," *Banker & Tradesman* (February 10, 1997), pp. 29, 32; and W. Sommers and A. Kroc, "Why Most New Ventures Fail (and How Others Don't)," *Management Review* (September 1987), pp. 35–39.
9. Ivan T. Hoffman, "Current Trends in Small Package Shipping," *International Business* (March 1994), p. 33.
10. "Unlocking the Secrets of ECR," *Progressive Grocer* (January 1994), p. 3.
11. "You Do the Work, They Do the Paperwork," *Business Week* (November 17, 1997), p. 54.
12. K. Carney, "Strategic Planning: Ground Zero," *Open-Book Management Bulletin* (November 11, 1998), p. 3.
13. A thorough discussion of negotiation can be found in R. E. Walton and R. B. McKersie, *A Behavioral Theory of Labor Negotiations* (New York: McGraw-Hill, 1965).
14. This process is adapted from G. Kennedy, J. Benson, and J. McMillan, *Managing Negotiations* (London: Business Books Ltd., 1980); and is discussed in R. D. Hisrich and C. G. Brush, *The Woman Entrepreneur* (Lexington, MA: Lexington Books, 1986), pp. 150–5.

15

New Venture Expansion Strategies and Issues

LEARNING OBJECTIVES

1. To explain the methods for expanding the venture.

2. To discuss the types of joint ventures and their uses.

3. To discuss the concepts of acquisitions and mergers.

4. To discuss the appropriateness and uses of leveraged buyouts.

5. To discuss the different types of franchises.

6. To identify the steps in evaluating a franchise opportunity.

TOM KITCHIN

Thomas Kitchin was born in 1941 in Kansas City, Missouri, to parents who survived the Great Depression. Witnesses to the endemic unemployment that characterized the Depression, Kitchin's parents strongly instilled in him the importance of having a job. His mother in particular taught Kitchin the value of employment by encouraging him to obtain work during vacations from his Catholic school. He performed in a wide variety of jobs that included stocking shelves, bagging groceries, selling shoes, unloading grain cars at a railroad company, and working on an assembly line in an automobile factory. Kitchin's mother further promoted his pursuits by throwing parties to celebrate each new job. Although his parents' support gave Kitchin pride in his efforts, the greatest benefit he enjoyed was having money to spend on dates, entertainment, clothing, and, eventually, to buy and maintain his own car.

Kitchin studied business courses in college, a decision that set him on the path to becoming the first businessman in his family. His first position following graduation was in the area of finance and required the completion of an intensive management-training program in addition to night classes. This in turn led Kitchin into a commercial banking position as a commercial lender. By the age of 36, Kitchin had cultivated an expertise in banking and finance and was president and chief operating officer of a bank. Although he was very challenged by his work, Kitchin could not quiet his desire to start his own business.

In March 1977, Kitchin finally struck out on his own, leaving the security of his banking career to begin an oil and gas company. The new venture enjoyed early success that Kitchin attributes to his hiring of extremely competent professional geologists and engineers. A mere three years following its inception, the company had a solid track record and sufficiently strong growth plan to accomplish an initial public offering of common stock. The company went on to raise over $100 million from Wall Street to finance its exploration and acquisition projects.

Kitchin decided in December 1986 to sell his controlling interest in the company and—in 1987, in an effort to expand his professional interests—began searching for the right business to acquire. Kitchin soon found a new business to explore in his purchase of a small hotel in Georgia. Kitchin had been doing research in the hotel business and learned that the general public, especially the business traveler, clearly desired travel lodging that was consistent and predictable. He also determined that most of the hotel industry consists of franchise owners whose management practices vary from excellent to terrible. This discontinuity in service left customers confused when trying to choose a hotel.

Kitchin's due diligence in researching the hotel industry led him to the conclusion that the public was ready for a new and consistent hotel brand that would offer limited service with clean, safe, and affordable rooms in small industrialized markets.

The newly designed Jameson Inn opened for business in November 1988. Eventually, Kitchin commenced expansion of Jameson Inns according to the following guidelines: building properties consistent in appearance, expanding in a contiguous fashion to existing properties and states to ensure brand awareness, and providing service to a growing customer base. In 1994, Jameson Inns completed an initial public offering of common stock that generated capital for growth. Jameson Inns' desire to expand is exemplified by its utilization of this capital to finance its expansion across the United States as well as by its January 27, 1999, merger with Signature Inns. Jameson Inns was left the sole surviving entity of this merger after the company absorbed the 25 hotels owned by Signature Inns, as well as one hotel managed by Signature, located in the midwestern United States.

By 2001, the company owned 121 hotels in 15 states, with 7700 hotel rooms, and had 22 hotels under development. Jameson Inns' workforce has increased exponentially from 3 employees in 1987 to over 3000 today.

Unlike Tom Kitchin, many entrepreneurs find it difficult to both manage and expand the venture they have created. In order to expand the venture, an entrepreneur must first assess his or her abilities in the management area, identifying methods for expansion and determining when it may be necessary to turn the reins over to someone else. As a new venture grows and matures, a need can develop for more administration as well as a new infusion of entrepreneurial spirit called intrapreneurship.

Some entrepreneurs tend to forget the basic business axiom that the only constant is change. Entrepreneurs who understand this axiom, like Tom Kitchin, will effectively manage change by continually adapting organizational culture, structure, procedures, strategic direction, and products in both a domestic and an international orientation. This chapter looks at some of the issues and methods involved in expanding a venture. These include negotiation, joint ventures, acquisitions and mergers, leveraged buyouts, and franchising.

JOINT VENTURES

With the increase in business risks, hypercompetition, and failures, joint ventures have occurred with increased regularity and often involve a wide variety of players.[1] Joint ventures are not a new concept, but rather have been used as a means of expansion by entrepreneurial firms for a long time.

What is a joint venture? A *joint venture* is a separate entity that involves a partnership between two or more active participants. Sometimes called strategic alliances, joint ventures involve a wide variety of partners that include universities, not-for-profit organizations, businesses, and the public sector.[2] Joint ventures have occurred between such rivals as General Motors and Toyota as well as General Electric and

joint venture   Two or more companies forming a new company

Westinghouse. They have occurred between the United States and foreign concerns in order to penetrate an international market, and they have been a good conduit by which an entrepreneur can enter an international market.

Whenever close relationships between two companies are being developed, concerns about the ethics and ethical behavior of the potential partner arise. Some ethical problems among stakeholders are indicated in the two Ethics boxes.

Historical Perspective

Although the ancient merchants of Babylon used joint ventures, in the United States joint ventures were first used for large-scale projects in mining and the railroads in the 1800s. This type of venture continued in the 1900s in the shipping, oil exploration, and gold industries. Probably the best-known and largest joint venture in this period was the formation of ARAMCO by four oil companies to develop crude oil reserves in the Middle East. By 1959, about 345 joint ventures were being operated in the United States by some of the largest corporations in the country.[3] Frequently, these domestic joint ventures are vertical arrangements made between competitors. A joint venture of this type (such as the sharing of a primary aluminum reduction plant as a supply facility) allows for the large economies of scale needed for cost-effective plant operation. From 1960 to 1968, the Federal Trade Commission reported that over 520 domestic joint ventures were formed, primarily in the manufacturing sector, by over 1131 U.S. firms.[4] In the 1980s, there was an increase in the formation of joint ventures of various types, particularly of international ventures.

The increase in the number of joint ventures, particularly involving smaller entrepreneurial firms, has been significant throughout the 1990s.

Types of Joint Ventures

Although there are many different types of joint venture arrangements, the most common is still between two or more private-sector companies. For example, Boeing/Mitsubishi/Fuji/Kawasaki entered into a joint venture for the production of small aircraft in order to share technology and cut costs. To cut costs, agreements were made between Ford and Mesasurex in the area of factory automation and between General Motors and Toyota in the area of automobile production. Other private-sector joint ventures have had different objectives, such as entering new markets (Corning and Ciba-Geigy as well as Kodak and Cetus), entering foreign markets (AT&T and Olivetti), and raising capital and expanding markets (U.S. Steel and Phong Iron and Steel).

Some joint ventures are formed to do cooperative research. Probably the best known of these is the Microelectronics and Computer Technology Corporation (MCC) formed in 1983 in Austin, Texas. Supported by 13 major U.S. companies, this for-profit venture does long-range research with scientists who are loaned to MCC for up to four years before returning to their competing companies to apply the results of their research activities. MCC retains title to all the resulting knowledge and patents, making them available for license to the companies participating in the program. Another type of joint venture for research development is the Semi-Conductor Research Corporation, located in Triangle Park, North Carolina. A not-for-profit research organization, it began with the participation of 11 U.S. chip manufacturers and computer companies. The number has grown to over 35 since its inception in 1981. The goal of the corporation is to sponsor basic research and train professional scientists and engineers to be future industry leaders.

Industry-university agreements created for the purpose of doing research are another type of joint venture that has seen increasing usage. However, two major problems have kept these types of joint ventures from proliferating even faster. A profit corporation has the objective of obtaining tangible results, such as a patent, from its research investment and wants all proprietary rights. Universities want to share in the possible financial returns from the patent, but the university researchers want to make the knowledge available through research papers. In spite of these problems, numerous industry-university teams have been established. In one joint venture agreement in robotics, for example, Westinghouse retains patent rights while Carnegie-Mellon receives a percentage of any license royalties. The university also has the right to publish the research results as long as it withholds from publication any critical information that might adversely affect the patent.

The joint venture agreement between Celanese Corporation and Yale University, created for researching the composition and synthesis of enzymes, took a somewhat different form—cost sharing. Although Celanese assumes the expense of any needed supplies and equipment for the research, as well as the salaries of the postdoctoral researchers, Yale pays the salaries of the professors involved. The research results can be published only after a 45-day waiting period.

W. R. Grace Company and the Massachusetts Institute of Technology (MIT) developed a joint research effort to study microbiology. Under this joint venture agreement, researchers at MIT propose research projects for funding to a committee consisting of four managers from W. R. Grace and four MIT professors. W. R. Grace established the research fund and covers all the expenses, and MIT can publish the results of the research after a review by W. R. Grace managers for proprietary information. MIT retains the patents, while W. R. Grace gets a royalty-free license on the research results.

International joint ventures, discussed in Chapter 4, are rapidly increasing in number due to their relative advantages. Not only can both companies share in the earnings and growth, but the joint venture can have a low cash requirement if the knowledge or patents are capitalized as a contribution to the venture. Also, the joint venture provides ready access to new international markets that otherwise may not

There are certain virtues, both to the individual and to the society at large, of encouraging people to act in socially appropriate ways because they believe it is the "right thing" to do, rather than because (and thus, perhaps, only to the extent that) they are ordered to do so. What seems needed as a "remedy" is some institutional analogue to the role that responsibility plays in the human being, building action toward certain values where the ordinary legislative prohibitors are unavailable or, on balance, unwise.

At your company's annual social event, you overhear several of your production workers commenting that they have cramped hand muscles because of the design of the tools that they are using at work. The following week you contact an expert, who tells you that ergonomically designed tools would significantly reduce the discomfort experienced by the workers. The cost of the new tools is quite significant, but changing the tools would not affect production output in any way. How likely are you to buy the ergonomically designed tools?

You have recently purchased some new automated equipment that will displace 20 of your employees. You have the option of laying off these employees or retraining and absorbing them in another location. The cost of retraining and absorbing the employees in your other location will be 20 percent more than the cost of a generous severance package. How likely are you to offer the retraining option to the displaced employees?

Sources: The first paragraph is from Christopher Stone, "Where the Law Ends," in Robert C. Solomon, *Ethics and Excellence* (New York: Oxford University Press, 1993), p. 112. The second and third paragraphs are from E. Solymossy and R. D. Hisrich, "Entrepreneurial Ethics: The Impact of Accountability and Independence," Babson Research Conference, March 1996, forthcoming.

be easily attained. Finally, since talent and financing come from all parties involved, an international joint venture causes less drain on a company's managerial and financial resources than a wholly owned subsidiary.

There are several drawbacks to establishing an international joint venture. First, the business objectives of the joint venture partners can be quite different, which can result in problems in the direction and growth of the new entity. In addition, cultural differences in each company can create managerial difficulties in the new joint venture. Finally, government policies can sometimes have a negative impact on the direction and operation of the international joint venture.

In spite of these problems, the benefits usually outweigh the drawbacks, as evidenced by the frequency rate of establishing international joint ventures. For example, an international joint venture between General Motors and Fanuc Ltd., a Japanese firm, was established to develop the 20,000 robots needed by GM to automate its plants. In this 50–50 joint venture partnership, GM supplies the initial design and Fanuc supplies the engineering and technology needed to develop and produce the car-painting robots.

Cy/Ro is an international joint venture between Cyamid (United States) and Rochm (Germany) in the area of acrylic plastics. Cyamid supplies the distribution network and plant space for the new acrylic plastic technology of Rochm. Even though Cy/Ro has a high degree of operational autonomy, a high turnover rate has occurred, a situation that is particularly problematic for German executives.

Another type of international joint venture was established between Dow Chemical (United States) and Asaki Chemicals (Japan) to develop and market chemicals on an international basis. While Asaki provided the raw materials and was a sole distributor, Dow provided the technology and obtained distribution in the Japanese market. The arrangement eventually dissolved because of the concerns of the Japanese government and the fundamental difference in motives between the two partners: Dow was primarily concerned with the profits of the joint venture, whereas Asaki was primarily concerned with having a purchaser for its basic petrochemicals.

Factors in Joint Venture Success

Clearly, not all joint ventures succeed. An entrepreneur needs to assess this method of growth carefully and understand the factors that help ensure success as well as the problems involved before using it. One of the most critical factors for success is the accurate assessment of the parties and how best to manage the new entity in light of the ensuing relationships. The joint venture will be more effective if the managers can work well together. Without this chemistry, the joint venture has a high probability of difficulty or even failure.

A second factor that determines success involves the symmetry between the partners. This symmetry goes beyond chemistry to objectives and resource capabilities. When one partner feels that he or she is bringing more to the table, or when one partner wants profits and the other desires product outlet (as in the case of the Asaki-Dow international joint venture), problems arise. For a joint venture to be successful, the managers in each parent company, as well as those in the new entity, must concur on the objectives of the joint venture and the level of resources that will be provided. Good relationships must be nurtured between the managers in the joint venture and those in each parent company.

A third factor for success is that the expectations of the results of the joint venture must be reasonable. Far too often, at least one of the partners feels that a joint venture will be the cure-all for other corporate problems. Expectations of a joint venture must be realistic.

The final factor in the successful establishment of a joint venture is also essential for the successful start-up of any new business entity: timing. With environments constantly changing, industrial conditions being modified, and markets evolving, a particular joint venture could be a success one year and a failure the next. Intense competition leads to a hostile environment and increases the risks of establishing a joint venture. Some environments are just not conducive to success. An entrepreneur must determine whether the joint venture will offer opportunities for growth or will penalize the company, for example, by preventing it from entering certain markets.

A joint venture is not a panacea for expanding the entrepreneurial venture. Rather, it should be considered one of many options for supplementing the resources of the firm and responding more quickly to competitive challenges and market opportunities. The effective use of joint ventures as a strategy for expansion requires the entrepreneur to carefully appraise the situation and the potential partner(s). Other strategic alternatives to the joint venture—such as acquisitions, mergers, and leveraged buyouts—should also be considered.

ACQUISITIONS

Another way the entrepreneur can expand the venture is by acquiring an existing business. Acquisitions provide an excellent means of expanding a business by entering new markets or new product areas. One entrepreneur acquired a chemical manufacturing company after becoming familiar with its problems and operations as a

As Seen in *Business Week:*
Earthlink to AOL: Watch Your Rearview Mirror

Talk about your hot home-based business. In a mere five years, Charles M. Brewer has turned Atlanta-based MindSpring Enterprises Inc. from a desk in his studio apartment into one of the nation's largest Internet service providers. And thanks to his September 23 merge with EarthLink Network Inc., of Pasadena, California, Brewer has vaulted over the likes of Microsoft, AT&T, and Prodigy to become the nation's second-largest ISP behind America Online, Inc.

Next? Brewer and his scrappy team used their merger news as a chance to pick a public fight with their far bigger rival for supremacy of the Internet-access business. "The message to AOL is that objects in the rearview mirror are a lot closer than they may appear," says Michael S. McQuary, who will serve as president of the combined company, which will be known as EarthLink.

That may be a bit of bravado. Although the merger doubles Brewer's customer count to 3 million, and revenues to $650 million, that's a far cry from AOL, which boasts 20 million subscribers and $4.8 billion in sales. And given AOL's marketing muscle and masterful use of messaging and chat technologies to give users a sense of community, analysts give Brewer & Co. long odds of catching up. "I don't see anything in the merger that enables EarthLink to attack AOL's strength—its ease of use and its reputation as the place to go for your first Internet experience," says Jupiter Communications Inc. analyst Joseph Laszlo.

Brewer is banking on partnerships to help close the gap with AOL. As more local and long-distance providers scramble to offer one-stop shopping, EarthLink officials hope to provide the Internet component for telecom companies looking to expand. Indeed, when Sprint Corp. unveils a new bundled service plan next year, the Internet-access component will be provided largely by EarthLink.

Still, even on the Internet where overnight sensations routinely leapfrog leaders, analysts wonder if EarthLink is too late to catch AOL. With nearly half of U.S. homes already on the Net, "companies will have to start stealing customers from other ISPs to keep growing," says Strategis Group analyst David Eiswert. That suits Brewer, who relishes the role of David. The question is whether his stone can slay or even wound this Goliath.

Source: Dean Foust and Catherine Yeng, "EarthLink to AOL: Watch Your Rearview Mirror," *Business Week* (October 11, 1999), p. 130.

---

acquisition Purchasing all or part of a company

---

supplier of the entrepreneur's company. An *acquisition* is the purchase of an entire company, or part of a company; by definition, the company is completely absorbed and no longer exists independently. An acquisition can take many forms, depending on the goals and position of the parties involved in the transactions, the amount of money involved, and the type of company.

Although one of the key issues in buying a business is agreeing on a price, successful acquisition of a business actually involves much, much more. In fact, often the structure of the deal can be more important to the resultant success of the transaction than the actual price. One radio station was successful after being acquired by a company primarily because the previous owner loaned the money and took no principal payment (only interest) on the loan until the third year of operation.

From a strategic viewpoint, a prime concern of the entrepreneurial firm is maintaining the focus of the new venture as a whole. Whether the acquisition will become the core of the new business or rather represents a needed capability—such as a distribution outlet, sales force, or production facility—the entrepreneur must ensure that it fits into the overall direction and structure of the strategic plan of the present venture.

Advantages of an Acquisition

For an entrepreneur, there are many advantages to acquiring an existing business, as indicated below:

1. *Established Business.* The most significant advantage in acquiring an existing business is that the acquired firm has an established image and track record. If the firm has been profitable, the entrepreneur would need only to continue its current strategy to be successful with the existing customer base.

2. *Location.* In the case of acquiring an existing business, there is no question concerning the new customers since they are already familiar with the location.

3. *Established Marketing Structure.* One of the most important factors that affects the value of an acquired firm is its existing channel and sales structure. Known suppliers, wholesalers, retailers, and manufacturers' reps are important assets to an entrepreneur. With this structure already in place, the entrepreneur can concentrate on improving or expanding the acquired business.

4. *Cost.* The actual cost of acquiring a business can be lower than other methods of expansion.

5. *Existing Employees.* The employees of an existing business can be an important asset to the acquisition process. They know how to run the business and can help ensure that the business will continue in its successful mode. They already have established relationships with customers, suppliers, and channel members and can reassure these groups when a new owner takes over the business.

6. *More Opportunity to Be Creative.* Since the entrepreneur does not have to be concerned with finding suppliers, channel members, hiring new employees, or creating customer awareness, more time can be spent assessing opportunities to expand or strengthen the existing business.

Disadvantages of an Acquisition

Although we can see that there are many advantages to acquiring an existing business, there are also disadvantages. The importance of each of the advantages and disadvantages should be weighed carefully with other expansion options.

1. *Marginal Success Record.* Most ventures that are for sale have an erratic, marginally successful, or even unprofitable track record. It is important to review the records and meet with important constituents to assess the marginal record in terms of future potential. For example, if the store layout is poor, this factor can be rectified; but if the location is poor, the entrepreneur might do better using some other expansion method.

2. *Overconfidence in Ability.* Sometimes an entrepreneur may assume that he or she can succeed where others have failed. This is why a self-evaluation is so important before entering into any purchase agreement. Even though the entrepreneur brings new ideas and management qualities, the venture may never be successful for reasons that are not possible to correct.

3. *Key Employee Loss.* Often, when a business changes hands, key employees also leave. Key employee loss can be devastating to an entrepreneur who is acquiring a business since the value of the business is often a reflection of the efforts

of the employees. This is particularly evident in a service business, where it is difficult to separate the actual service from the person who performs it. In the acquisition negotiations, it is helpful for the entrepreneur to speak to all employees individually to get some assurance of their intentions as well as to inform them of how important they will be to the future of the business. Incentives can sometimes be used to ensure that key employees will remain with the business.

4. *Overevaluated.* It is possible that the actual purchase price is inflated due to the established image, customer base, channel members, or suppliers. If the entrepreneur has to pay too much for a business, it is possible that the return on investment will be unacceptable. It is important to look at the investment required in purchasing a business and at the potential profit and establish a reasonable payback to justify the investment.

After balancing the pros and cons of the acquisition, the entrepreneur needs to determine a fair price for the business.

Determining the Price for an Acquisition

Some of the key factors used in determining price are earnings (past and future potential), assets, owner's equity, stock value, customer base, strength of distribution network, personnel, and image. When these factors are difficult to value, the entrepreneur may want to get outside help. The price paid should provide the opportunity to get a reasonable payback and good return on the investment.

There are three widely used valuation approaches—asset, cash flow, and earnings—that the entrepreneur can use to determine a fair price (or value) of an acquisition. Some important factors that are helpful in the evaluation process to measure profitability, activity, and liquidity are indicated in Table 15.1. In addition, a glossary of terms used in financial analysis and evaluation is found at the end of this chapter. When using the asset valuation method, the entrepreneur is valuing the underlying worth of the business based on its assets. The four methods that can be used to obtain this valuation are book value, adjusted book value, liquidation value, or replacement value. Although the easiest method for assessing the value of the firm is book value,

---

TABLE 15.1 Key Factors in Evaluating a Firm

- One-person management
- Poor corporate communications
- Few management tools being used
- Insufficient financial controls
- Highly leveraged—thinly capitalized
- Variations and poorly prepared financial statements
- Sales growth with no increase in bottom line
- Dated and poorly managed inventory
- Aging accounts receivable
- No change in products or customers

the figure obtained should be only a starting point since it reflects the accounting practices of the company. A better refinement of this figure is adjusted book value, where
the stated book value is adjusted to reflect the actual market value. Another method
of valuing the assets of a potential acquisition company is to determine the amount
that could be realized if the assets of the company were sold or liquidated and the proceeds used to settle all liabilities. This liquidation value reflects the valuation at a specific point in time. If the company continues operations successfully, the calculated
value is low compared with the contribution of the assets. If the company encounters
difficulties, the actual liquidation would probably yield significantly less than the
amount calculated. The final method for valuing assets is the determination of replacement value, or the current cost of replacing the tangible assets of the business.

Another way of evaluating a firm—which is particularly relevant for an entrepreneur who is attempting to appraise a return on investment and on time—is to calculate the prospective cash flow from the business. The following cash flows are important: positive cash flow, negative cash flow, and terminal value. Positive cash flow
is cash received from the operation of the business minus costs except depreciation.
A negative cash flow (indicating the possible acquisition is losing money) can even
be a benefit to the taxes of the business or individuals. The final cash flow value, the
terminal value, is a source of cash resulting from an entrepreneur selling the business.

A final evaluation method is earnings valuation. This method capitalizes earnings of
a company by multiplying the earnings by the appropriate factor (the price earnings
multiple). Two critical issues in this evaluation procedure are the earnings and the multiple. The question of earnings involves determining the appropriate earnings period as
well as the type of earnings. The earnings period can involve either historical earnings,
future earnings under the present management and ownership, or future earnings under new management and ownership. The type of earnings used during the selected period can be earnings before interest and taxes (EBIT), operating income, profit before
tax, or profit after tax. The EBIT is used more frequently, since it indicates the earning
power and value of the basic business without the effects of financing.

After the time period and type of earnings have been established, the final step in
earnings evaluation is to select the appropriate price earnings multiple. If the primary
return from the investment will be in the form of stock sale at some future time, it
is appropriate to select a price earnings multiple of a publicly traded stock similar to
the company being evaluated in terms of the product, nature of the industry, anticipated earnings, growth, and likely stage of the stock market. Although this can be
difficult, usually a value or at least a range of values can be ascertained.

Whether the valuation of assets, cash flow, or earnings is used, determining the
price is vitally important in evaluating the feasibility of an acquisition. Other important considerations in the acquisition decision process include synergy, a specific
valuation method, structuring the deal, legal considerations, and the plan for managing the acquired entity.

Synergy

The concept that "the whole is greater than the sum of its parts" applies to the integration of an acquisition into the entrepreneur's venture. The synergy should occur in
both the business concept, with the acquisition functioning as a vehicle to move toward overall goals, and the financial performance. The acquisition should positively impact the bottom line, affecting both long-term gains and future growth. Lack of synergy is one of the most frequent causes of an acquisition's failure to meet its objectives.

Evaluation in today's changing environment focuses not only on management and market potential but also on the company's upside potential, downside risks, and vulnerability to changes in markets and technology. Some warning signs the entrepreneur should consider in evaluating an acquisition candidate include poor corporate communications, the utilization of few management tools, poorly prepared financial statements, and few changes in products and markets (see Table 15.1).

The evaluation process begins with a financial analysis of the profit and loss figures, operating statements, and balance sheets for the years of the company's operation, concentrating on the more recent years. Past operating results, particularly those that have occurred in the last three years, indicate the potential for future performance of the company. Ratios and operating figures indicate whether the company is healthy and has been well managed. Areas of weakness—such as too much leverage, too little financial control, dated and slow-turning inventory, poor credit ratings, and bad debts—should also be carefully evaluated.

The past, present, and future of a firm's product lines should also be examined. The strengths and weaknesses of the firm's products should be evaluated in terms of design features, quality, reliability, unique differential advantage, and proprietary position. The life cycle and present market share of each of the firm's products should also be considered. Is this market share diversified or concentrated among a small number of customers? How do past, present, and potential customers regard the firm's products? What is happening with the market with respect to competition, prices, and margins? The entrepreneur must carefully consider the compatibility of the firm's product lines from a marketing, engineering, and manufacturing perspective. The future of the firm's product lines must be assessed as to their rate of market growth or contraction. What are the developing trends in the number of competitors, what is the degree of competition, the number of new products being introduced, and the rate of technology? Is there any vulnerability to business cycle changes?

One method for evaluating the product line is to plot sales and margins for each product over time. Known as S or life-cycle curves, these indicate the life expectancy of the product and any developing gaps. The S-curve analysis could reveal that all products of this firm are at, or near, their period of peak profitability.

The future of the firm's products and market position is affected by its research and development. The entrepreneur should carefully probe the nature and depth of the candidate firm's research and development and engineering capability, assessing the strengths and weaknesses of each. Although the total amount of dollars spent on research and development should be examined, it is more important to determine if these expenditures and programs are directed by the firm's long-range plans. The outputs and success of the new products developed should be compared with the expenditures. What is the quantity and quality of the patents produced? How much has R&D contributed to increased sales and profits?

Similarly, the entrepreneur should carefully evaluate the entire marketing program and capabilities of the possible acquisition. Although all areas of marketing should be assessed, particular care should be taken in evaluating the quality and capability of the established distribution system, sales force, and manufacturers' representatives. One entrepreneur acquired a firm primarily due to the quality of its sales force. Another acquired a firm to obtain its established distribution system, which allowed access to new markets. The entrepreneur can gain insight into the market orientation and sensitivity of the firm by looking at its marketing research efforts. Does the firm have facts about customer satisfaction, trends in the market, and technology of the industry? Is this and other information forwarded to the appropriate managers in a timely manner? Is there a marketing information system in place?

The nature of the manufacturing process, or the facilities and skills available, is also important in deciding whether to acquire a particular firm. Are the facilities obsolete? Are they flexible, and can they produce output at a quality and a price that will compete over the next three years?

Finally, the entrepreneur should rate the management and key personnel of the candidate firm. The individuals who have contributed positively to past success in sales and profits of the firm should be identified. Will they stay once the acquisition occurs? Have they established good objectives and then implemented plans to successfully reach these objectives? Insight into management capability and the firm's morale can be gained through an examination of the turnover in executive ranks. Is it large or concentrated in a given area or type of individual? Has the firm implemented any executive development programs? Is there a strong management team in place?

Specific Valuation Method

One specific valuation method focuses on determining the present value of the acquisition candidate. As an example, let us assume that the following information has been obtained on the company:

- The current revenue level (R) is $2 million.
- The expected annual rate of growth of revenue (r) is 50 percent.
- The expected amount of required capital (K) is $2.5 million.
- The expected number of years between now and the liquidity date (n), also called the holding period, is 5 years.
- The expected after-tax profit margin at the time of liquidity (a) is 11 percent.
- The expected price/earnings ratio as of the liquidity date (P) is 15. The appropriate discount rate (d) for a VC investment of this stage, risk, and liquidity is 40 percent.

With this information, the present value of the company can be obtained using the following formula and sequence of steps:

$$\text{Present value of company} = V = \frac{R(1 + r)^n aP}{\text{Present value factor}}$$

$$V = \frac{R(1 + r)^n aP}{(1 + d)^n}$$

Step 1. Compound the current revenue level of $2 million forward at an annual rate of 50 percent for 5 years to yield a revenue level at the time of liquidity of $15.19 million.

Step 2. Multiply the future revenue level of $15.19 million by the expected after-tax profit margin at the time of liquidity of 11 percent to produce an expected earnings level of $1.67 million as of the date of liquidity.

Step 3. Multiply the estimated earnings level of $1.67 million at the time of liquidity by the expected price/earnings ratio of 15 to yield a future market valuation of the company of $25.06 million.

Step 4. To obtain a present value factor, raise the quantity 1.40 (that is, 1 + the discount rate of 40 percent) to the power of 5 (the holding period of 5 years), to yield a present value factor of 5.378.

Step 5. Divide the future company value of $25.06 by the present value factor of 5.378 to produce a present value of the company of $4.66 million.

Step 6. To price the deal, divide the required capital of $2.5 million by the present company value of $4.66 million to obtain a minimum ownership of 53.7 percent for the investment required.

While yielding a present value for an acquisition candidate, the method assumes a constant rate for revenue growth and does not adequately treat future tax savings.

Structuring the Deal

Once the entrepreneur has identified a good candidate for acquisition, an appropriate deal must be structured. Many techniques are available for acquiring a firm, each having a distinct set of advantages to both the buyer and seller. The deal structure involves the parties, the assets, the payment form, and the timing of the payment. For example, all or part of the assets of one firm can be acquired by another for some combination of cash, notes, stock, and/or employment contract. This payment can be made at the time of acquisition, throughout the first year, or extended over several years.

The two most common means of acquisition are the entrepreneur's direct purchase of the firm's entire stock or assets or the bootstrap purchase of these assets. In the direct purchase of the firm, the entrepreneur often obtains funds from an outside lender or the seller of the company being purchased. The money is repaid over time from the cash flow generated from the operations. Although this is a relatively simple and clear transaction, it usually results in a long-term capital gain to the seller and double taxation on the funds used to repay the money borrowed to acquire the company.

In order to avoid these problems, the entrepreneur can make a bootstrap purchase, acquiring a small amount of the firm, such as 20 to 30 percent, for cash. He or she then purchases the remainder of the company with a long-term note that is paid off over time out of the acquired company's earnings. This type of deal often results in more favorable tax advantages to both the buyer and the seller.

Locating Acquisition Candidates

If an entrepreneur is seriously planning to buy a business, there are some sources of assistance. There are professional business *brokers* that operate in a fashion similar to a real estate broker. They represent the seller and will sometimes aggressively find buyers through either referrals, advertising, or direct sales. Since these brokers are paid a commission on the sale, they often expend more effort on their best deals.

---

brokers People who sell companies

Accountants, attorneys, bankers, business associates, and consultants may also know of good acquisition candidates. Many of these professionals have a good working knowledge of the business, which can be helpful in the negotiations.

It is also possible to find business opportunities in the classified sections of the newspaper or in a trade magazine. Since these listings are usually completely unknown, they may involve more risk but can be purchased at a lower price.

Determining the best option for an entrepreneur involves significant time and effort. The entrepreneur should gather as much information as possible, read it carefully, consult with advisors and experts, consider his or her own situation, and then make a constructive decision.

A profile containing acquisition criteria and prospect data can help guide the search and initial screening. For a good profile, the entrepreneur must construct a checklist that identifies a prospective company, its history, management, product (or service), finances, marketing, production, and labor relations and then briefly evaluates the prospect. Prospects can be identified through internal referrals and external sources such as accountants, brokers, investment bankers, and lawyers. Once the prospect passes the initial checklist, more rigorous analysis can further evaluate the viability of the acquisition.

MERGERS

A *merger*—or a transaction involving two, or possibly more, companies in which only one company survives—is another method of expanding a venture. Acquisitions are so similar to mergers that at times the two terms are used interchangeably. A key concern in any merger (or acquisition) is the legality of the purchase. The Department of Justice frequently issues guidelines for horizontal, vertical, and conglomerate mergers which further define the interpretation that will be made in enforcing the Sherman Act and Clayton Act. Since the guidelines are extensive and technical, the entrepreneur should secure adequate legal advice when any issues arise.

merger   Joining two or more companies

Why should an entrepreneur merge? There are both defensive and offensive strategies for a merger, as indicated in Figure 15.1. Merger motivations range from survival to protection to diversification to growth. When some technical obsolescence, market or raw material loss, or deterioration of the capital structure has occurred in the entrepreneur's venture, a merger may be the only means for survival. The merger can also protect against market encroachment, product innovation, or an

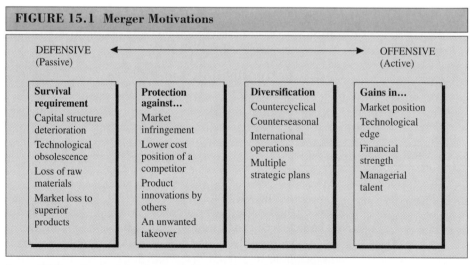

FIGURE 15.1 Merger Motivations

DEFENSIVE (Passive)			OFFENSIVE (Active)
Survival requirement	**Protection against...**	**Diversification**	**Gains in...**
Capital structure deterioration	Market infringement	Countercyclical	Market position
Technological obsolescence	Lower cost position of a competitor	Counterseasonal	Technological edge
Loss of raw materials	Product innovations by others	International operations	Financial strength
Market loss to superior products	An unwanted takeover	Multiple strategic plans	Managerial talent

Source: F. T. Haner, *Business Policy, Planning, and Strategy* (Cambridge, MA: Winthrop, 1976), p. 399.

unwarranted takeover. A merger can provide a great deal of diversification as well as growth in market, technology, and financial and managerial strength.

How does a merger take place? It requires sound planning by the entrepreneur. The merger objectives, particularly those dealing with earnings, must be spelled out with the resulting gains for the owners of both companies delineated. Also, the entrepreneur must carefully evaluate the other company's management to ensure that, if retained, it would be competent in developing the growth and future of the combined entity. The value and appropriateness of the existing resources should also be determined. In essence, this involves a careful analysis of both companies to ensure that the weaknesses of one do not compound those of the other. Finally, the entrepreneur should work toward establishing a climate of mutual trust to help minimize any possible management threat or turbulence.

The same methods for valuing an acquisition candidate can be used to determine the value of a merger candidate. The process involves the entrepreneur looking at the synergistic product/market position, the new domestic or international market position, any undervalued financial strength, whether or not the company is skilled in a related industry, and any underexploited company asset. A common procedure for determining value is to estimate the present value of discounted cash flows and the expected after-tax earnings attributable to the merger. This should be done on optimistic, pessimistic, and probable scenarios of cash flows and earnings using various acceptable rates of return.

HOSTILE TAKEOVERS

One form of acquisition, the *hostile takeover,* has received increased attention through the activities of such corporate raiders as Carl Icahn and T. Boone Pickens. Three items make a hostile takeover possible: (1) a low stock evaluation coupled with a strong performance, (2) a low debt/equity ratio, allowing the entrepreneur to use the assets of the company to fund the takeover, and (3) a high percentage of institutional investors holding the company's stock. Since the objective of these institutional investors is to make a profit, they will frequently vote in favor of the hostile takeover due to the anticipated gain in stock price and firm evaluation.

hostile takeover   A company acquiring another company against its will

The most effective method for an entrepreneur's acquisition of a company in a hostile takeover is by using a multiple-step junk bond offer. Here the raiding entrepreneur acquires a small percentage of the company (around 5 percent), lines up financial backers, and makes a very attractive offer for 51 percent of the company financed through the use of junk bonds. This enables current shareholders to sell their stock and obtain their fair share of the value. If a stockholder does not tender his or her shares, that individual's stock has less value once the takeover occurs because the greater value of the company has been used to acquire 51 percent of the stock.

An entrepreneur can also execute a hostile takeover through shareholder action by consent. This less publicized takeover format occurs when the majority of the shareholders are not pleased with the performance of the present management. They agree to back the entrepreneur in voting out the current management and electing a new management team.

As might be expected, the increase in hostile takeovers has prompted companies to use a variety of defensive measures. One defensive weapon is to stagger the terms of the board of directors by electing only one-third of the board each year. This requires the raiding entrepreneur to go through two annual elections to obtain board control. Another more direct measure is for the company to alter the corporate character, thereby eliminating shareholder action by consent.

poison pill   A method to protect the value of a company for its shareholders

A third defensive measure is for the company to institute a *poison pill*, a mechanism that protects the values of existing shareholders. With a poison pill in place at the time of an attempted hostile takeover, existing shareholders have the right to additional values. This additional value could be in the form of a provision that automatically increases the value of a current shareholder's stock in the event of a hostile takeover bid. Tendering stock to the raiding entrepreneur would then decrease the shareholder's value.

A fourth defensive measure is to institute *covenants* governing the level of allowable debt debentures. Covenants such as this would totally prohibit or dramatically reduce the additional debt that can be incurred by the company, which makes it very difficult for a raider to use the assets of the company for the leverage needed to finance the takeover.

covenants   Restrictions limiting the size of company debt

poison puts   Provisions allowing bondholders to cash in if the insurer of the bond (the company) is taken over

A final defensive weapon against hostile takeovers is *poison puts*. These are provisions in a company's bonds that allow the bond's holders to cash in if the insurer of the bond (the company) is taken over. This provision not only discourages takeovers but also helps maintain the price of the bonds. These bonds tend to decrease in a takeover activity due to the lower bond ratings that usually occur in the case of a hostile takeover.

Even if an entrepreneur does not use the hostile takeover mechanism for acquiring a venture, he or she should be aware of the activity, particularly the defensive weapons available; holding such knowledge might prove useful once the entrepreneur's own venture is successful. Perhaps one or more of these defensive measures can be incorporated into the original structure of the new venture to prevent a hostile takeover later.

LEVERAGED BUYOUTS

A *leveraged buyout (LBO)* occurs when an entrepreneur (or any employee group) uses borrowed funds to purchase an existing venture for cash. Most LBOs occur because the entrepreneur purchasing the venture believes that he or she could run the company more efficiently than the current owners. The current owner is frequently an entrepreneur or other owner who wants to retire. The owner may also be a large corporation desiring to divest itself of a subsidiary that is too small or that does not fit its long-term strategic plans.

leveraged buyout (LBO)   Purchasing an existing venture by any employee group

The purchaser needs a great amount of external funding since the personal financial resources needed to acquire the firm directly are frequently limited. Since the issuance of additional equity as a means of funding is usually not possible, capital is acquired in the form of long-term debt financing (five years or more), and the assets of the firm being acquired serve as collateral. Who usually provides this long-term debt financing? Banks, venture capitalists, and insurance companies have been the most active providers of the debt needed in LBOs.

The actual financial package used in an LBO reflects the lender's risk-reward profile. Whereas banks tend to use senior-debt issues, venture capitalists usually use subordinated debt issues with warrants or options. Regardless of the instrument used, the repayment plan established must be in line with the pro forma cash flows that the company expects to be generated. The interest rates are usually variable and are consistent with the current yields of comparable risk investment.

In most LBOs, the debt capital usually exceeds the equity by a ratio of 5 to 1, with some ratios as high as 10 to 1. Given this high debt load and the accompanying high level of risk, successful LBOs usually involve a financially sound and stable company. In an LBO, there is significantly more debt relative to equity than in a typical firm's capital structure. Although this makes the financial risk great, the key to a successful LBO is not the relative debt-to-equity ratio but rather the ability of the entrepreneur taking over to cover the principal and interest payments through increased sales and profits. The ability depends on the skills of the entrepreneur and the strength and stability of the firm.

Most LBOs involve companies with a long track record of solid earnings, a strong management team, and a strong market share position. These factors help reduce the risk of the LBO failing. This risk can be further reduced by requiring the entrepreneur to invest most of his or her personal assets in the equity of the new firm.

How does the entrepreneur determine whether a specific company is a good candidate for an LBO? This determination can be made through the following evaluation procedure. First, the entrepreneur must determine whether the present owner's asking price is reasonable. Many subjective and quantitative techniques can be used in this determination. Subjective evaluations need to be made of the following: the competitiveness of the industry and the competitive position of the firm in that industry, the uniqueness of the offering of the firm and the stage in the product life cycle, and the abilities of management and other key personnel remaining with the firm.

Also, quantitative techniques previously discussed are used to evaluate the fairness of the asking price. The price-earnings ratio of the LBO prospect should be calculated and compared with those of comparable companies, as well as the present value of future earnings of the prospect and its book value.

After a reasonable purchase price is determined, the entrepreneur must assess the firm's debt capacity. This is particularly critical since the entrepreneur wants to raise as much of the capital needed as possible in the form of long-term debt. How much long-term debt can a prospective LBO carry? It depends on the prospect's business risk and the stability of its future cash flows. The cash flow must cover the long-term debt required to finance the LBO. Any financial amount that cannot be secured by long-term debt, due to the inadequacy of the cash flow, will need to be in the form of equity from the entrepreneur or other investors.

Once the level of long-term debt financing is determined, the third step of developing the appropriate financial package takes place. The financial package must meet the needs and objectives of the providers of the funds as well as the company's and the entrepreneur's situation. Although each LBO financial package is tailored to the specific situation, there are usually some restrictions, such as no payment of dividends. Frequently, an LBO agreement with venture capitalists has warrants that are convertible into common stock at a later date. A sinking fund repayment of the long-term debt is frequently required.

There are many instances of both successful and unsuccessful LBOs. One of the most publicized involved R. H. Macy and Co., a well-known department store chain. Macy's was not in bad condition in terms of the traditional measures of sales per square foot, profitability, and return on assets. However, it had experienced a significant drop in profits and was losing talented middle executives. The LBO was accomplished by some 345 executives participating and sharing a 20 percent ownership in the $4.7 billion retailer. Ultimately, the LBO provided the following benefits: a new entrepreneurial spirit in management that fostered more loyalty in the employees; increased motivation among employees, with middle managers actually selling and earning sales floor bonuses during slack time; and a long-term planning direction for the board of directors that meets five times a year instead of once a month.

FRANCHISING

Franchising also represents an opportunity for an entrepreneur to expand the business. In the context of franchising, the entrepreneur will be trained and supported in the marketing by the franchisor and will be using a name that has an established image. Franchising is also an alternative means by which an entrepreneur may expand his or her business by having others pay for the use of the name, process, product, service, and so on. In January 1980, Jim Fowler decided to franchise his housecleaning venture, Merry Maids. The concept of a housecleaning service provided on a weekly or biweekly basis was difficult for the public to understand. Through franchising, the venture achieved more credibility, which in turn helped to facilitate franchise sales. Now operating in 48 states and in a number of foreign countries, Merry Maids has grown to a 560-location, $80 million business. Fowler's attention to image—which included required, standardized employee uniforms, quality training for franchisees, and the use of a line of pretested cleaning products—has allowed him to impressively expand a simple housecleaning business and to offer opportunities for entrepreneurs to become successful businessmen and businesswomen.[5]

Franchising may be defined as "an arrangement whereby the manufacturer or sole distributor of a trademarked product or service gives exclusive rights of local distribution to independent retailers in return for their payment of royalties and conformance to standardized operating procedures."[6] The person offering the franchise is known as the *franchisor.* The *franchisee* is the person who purchases the franchise and is given the opportunity to enter a new business with a better chance to succeed than if he or she were to start a new business from scratch.

franchising   Allowing another party to use a product or service under the owner's name

franchisor   Person offering the franchise

franchisee   Person obtaining the franchise

Advantages of Franchising—to the Franchisee

One of the most important advantages of buying a franchise is that the entrepreneur does not have to incur all the risks associated with creating a new business. Table 15.2 summarizes the important advantages of a franchise. Typically, the areas that entrepreneurs have problems with in starting a new venture are product acceptance, management expertise, meeting capital requirements, knowledge of the market, and operating and structural controls. In franchising, the risks associated with each are minimized through the franchise relationship, as discussed below.

Product Acceptance   The franchisee usually enters into a business that has an accepted name, product, or service. In the case of Subway, any person buying a franchise will be using the Subway name, which is well known and established throughout the United States. The franchisee does not have to spend resources trying to establish the credibility of the business. That credibility already exists based on the years the franchise has existed. Subway has also spent millions of dollars in advertising, thus building a favorable image of the products and services offered.

TABLE 15.2 What You May Buy in a Franchise

1. A product or service with established market and favorable image
2. A patented formula or design
3. Trade names or trademarks
4. A financial management system for controlling the financial revenues
5. Managerial advice from experts in the field
6. Economies of scale for advertising and purchasing
7. Head office services
8. A tested business concept

An entrepreneur who tries to start a sandwich shop would be unknown to the potential customers and would require significant effort and resources to build credibility and a reputation in the market.

Management Expertise   Another important advantage to the franchisee is the managerial assistance provided by the franchisor. Each new franchisee is often required to take a training program on all aspects of operating the franchise. This training could include classes in accounting, personnel management, marketing, and production. McDonald's, for example, requires all of its franchisees to spend time at its school, where everyone takes classes in these areas. In addition, some franchisors require their new franchisees to actually work with an existing franchise owner or at a company-owned store or facility to get on-the-job training. Once the franchise has been started, most franchisors will offer managerial assistance on the basis of need. Toll-free numbers are also available so that the franchisee can ask questions anytime. Local offices for the larger franchises continually visit the local franchisees to offer advice and keep owners informed of new developments.

The training and education offered is actually an important criterion that the entrepreneur should consider in evaluating any franchise opportunity. If the assistance in start-up is not good, the entrepreneur should probably look elsewhere for opportunities unless he or she already has extensive experience in the field.

Capital Requirements   As we've seen in previous chapters, starting a new venture can be costly in terms of both time and money. The franchise offers an opportunity to start a new venture with up-front support that could save the entrepreneur significant time and possibly capital. Some franchisors conduct location analysis and market research of the area that might include an assessment of traffic, demographics, business conditions, and competition. In some cases, the franchisor will also finance the initial investment to start the franchise operation. The initial capital required to purchase a franchise generally reflects a fee for the franchise, construction costs, and the purchase of equipment.

The layout of the facility, control of stock and inventory, and the potential buying power of the entire franchise operation can save the entrepreneur significant funds. The size of the parent company can be advantageous in the purchase of health care and business insurance, since the entrepreneur would be considered a participant of the entire franchise organization. Savings in start-up are also reflected in the pooling of monies by individual franchisees for advertising and sales promotion. The contribution by each franchisee is usually a function of the volume and the number of franchises owned. This allows advertising on both a local and national scale to enhance the image and credibility of the business, something that would be impossible for a single operation.

Knowledge of the Market   Any established franchise business offers the entrepreneur years of experience in the business and knowledge of the market. This knowledge is usually reflected in a plan offered to the franchisee that details the profile of the target customer and the strategies that should be implemented once the operation has begun. This is particularly important because of regional and local differences in markets. Competition, media effectiveness, and tastes can vary widely from one market to another. Given their experience, franchisors can provide advice and assistance in accommodating any of these differences.

Most franchisors will be constantly evaluating market conditions and determining the most effective strategies to be communicated to the franchisees. Newsletters and other publications that reflect new ideas and developments in the overall market are continually sent to franchisees.

Operating and Structural Controls   Two problems that many entrepreneurs have in starting a new venture are maintaining quality control of products and services and establishing effective managerial controls. The franchisor, particularly in the food business, will identify purveyors and suppliers that meet the quality standards established. In some instances, the supplies are actually provided by the franchisor, such as in the Merry Maids example described earlier in this chapter. Standardization in the supplies, products, and services provided helps ensure that the entrepreneur will maintain quality standards that are so important. Standardization also supports a consistent image on which the franchise business depends for expansion.

Administrative controls usually involve financial decisions relating to costs, inventory, and cash flow, and personnel issues such as criteria for hiring/firing, scheduling, and training to ensure consistent service to the customer. These controls will usually be outlined in a manual supplied to the franchisee upon completion of the franchise deal.

Although all of the above are advantages to the franchisee, they also represent important strategic considerations for an entrepreneur who is considering growing the business by selling franchises. Since there are so many franchise options for an entrepreneur, the franchisor will need to offer all of the above services in order to succeed in the sale of franchises. One of the reasons for the success of such franchises as McDonald's, Burger King, KFC, Boston Chicken, Subway, Midas, Jiffy Lube, Holiday Inn, Mail Boxes Etc., and Merry Maids is that all these firms have established an excellent franchise system that effectively provides the necessary services to the franchisee.

Advantages of Franchising—to the Franchisor

The advantages a franchisor gains through franchising are related to expansion risk, capital requirements, and cost advantages that result from extensive buying power. It is clear from the Subway example that Fred DeLuca would not have been able to achieve the size and scope of his business without franchising it. In order to use franchising as an expansion method, the franchisor must have established value and credibility that someone else is willing to buy.

Expansion Risk   The most obvious advantage of franchising for an entrepreneur is that it allows the venture to expand quickly using little capital. This advantage is significant when we reflect on the problems and issues that an entrepreneur faces in trying to manage and grow a new venture (see Chapter 14). A franchisor can expand a business nationally and even internationally by authorizing and selling franchises in selected locations. The capital necessary for this expansion is much less than it would be without franchising. Just think of the capital needed by DeLuca to build 8,300 Subway sandwich shops.

The value of the franchise depends on the to-date track record of the franchisor and on the services offered to the entrepreneur or franchisee. Subway's low franchise fee has enhanced expansion opportunities, as more people can afford it.

Operating a franchised business requires fewer employees than a nonfranchised business. Headquarters and regional offices can be lightly staffed, primarily to support the needs of the franchisees. This allows the franchisor to maintain low payrolls and minimizes personnel issues and problems.

Cost Advantages   The mere size of a franchised company offers many advantages to the franchisees. The franchisor can purchase supplies in large quantities, thus achieving economies of scale that would not have been possible otherwise. Many franchise businesses produce parts, accessories, packaging, and raw materials in large quantities, then in turn sell these to the franchisees. The franchisee is usually required to purchase these items as part of the franchise agreement, and they usually benefit from lower prices.

One of the biggest cost advantages of franchising a business is the ability to commit larger sums of money to advertising. Each franchisee contributes a percentage of sales (1 to 2 percent) to an advertising pool. This pooling of resources allows the franchisor to conduct advertising in major media across a wide geographic area. If the business had not been franchised, the company would have had to provide funds for the entire advertising budget.

Disadvantages of Franchising

Franchising is not always the best option for an entrepreneur. Anyone investing in a franchise should investigate the opportunity thoroughly. Problems between the franchisor and franchisee are common and have recently begun to receive more attention from the government and trade associations.

The disadvantages to the franchisee usually center on the inability of the franchisor to provide services, advertising, and location. When promises made in the franchise agreement are not kept, the franchisee may be left without any support in important areas. For example, Curtis Bean bought a dozen franchises in Checkers of America Inc., a firm that provides auto inspection services. After losing $200,000, Bean and other franchisees filed a lawsuit claiming that the franchisor had misrepresented advertising costs and had made false claims including that no experience was necessary to own a franchise.[7]

The franchisee may also face the problem of a franchisor failing or being bought out by another company. No one knows this better than Vincent Niagra, an owner of three Window Works franchises. Niagra had invested about $1 million in these franchises when the franchise was sold in 1988 to Apogee Enterprises and then resold in 1992 to a group of investors. This caused many franchises to fail, leaving a total of 50. The failure of these franchises has made it difficult for Niagra to continue because customers are apprehensive about doing business with him for fear that he will go out of business. No support services that had been promised were available.[8]

The franchisor also incurs certain risks and disadvantages in choosing this expansion alternative. In some cases, the franchisor may find it very difficult to find quality franchisees. Poor management, in spite of all the training and controls, can still cause individual franchise failures and, therefore, can reflect negatively on the entire franchise system. As the number of franchises increases, the ability to maintain tight controls becomes more difficult.

Types of Franchises

There are three available types of franchises.[9] The first type is the dealership, a form commonly found in the automobile industry. Here, manufacturers use franchises to distribute their product lines. These dealerships act as the retail stores for the manufacturer. In some instances, they are required to meet quotas established by the manufacturers, but as is the case for any franchise, they benefit from the advertising and management support provided by the franchisor.

The most common type of franchise is the type that offers a name, image, and method of doing business, such as McDonald's, Subway, KFC, Midas, Dunkin Donuts, and Holiday Inn. There are many of these types of franchises, and their listings, with pertinent information, can be found in various sources.[10]

A third type of franchise offers services. These include personnel agencies, income tax preparation companies, and real estate agencies. These franchises have established names and reputations and methods of doing business. In some instances, such as real estate, the franchisee has actually been operating a business and then applies to become a member of the franchise.

Franchising opportunities have often evolved from changes in the environment as well as important social trends. Several of these are discussed below.[11]

- *Good Health*. Today people are eating healthier food and spending more time keeping fit. Many franchises have developed in response to this trend. For example, Bassett's Original Turkey was created in 1983 in response to consumer interest in eating foods lower in cholesterol. Frozen yogurt franchises, such as TCBY in New England and Nibble-Lo's in Florida, also responded to the same trend. In Los Angeles, a unique restaurant, The Health Express, offers its customers a 100 percent vegetarian menu.

- *Time Saving or Convenience*. More and more consumers prefer to have things delivered to them as opposed to going out of their way to buy them. In fact, many food stores now offer home delivery services. In 1990, Auto Critic of America Inc. was started as a mobile car inspection service. About the same time, Ronald Tosh started Tubs To Go, a company that delivers Jacuzzis to almost any location for an average of $100 to $200 per night.

- *Environmental Consciousness*. Radon testing service franchises have grown as a response to consumers' need to protect themselves and their families from dangerous radon gas. In 1987, Ecology House, a gift store, began to add consumer products such as water-saving devices, rechargeable batteries, and energy-saving light fixtures.

- *The Second Baby Boom*. Today's baby boomers have had babies themselves, which has resulted in the need for a number of child-related service franchises.

Child care franchises such as Kinder Care and Living and Learning are thriving. In 1989, two attorneys, David Pickus and Lee Sandoloski, opened Jungle Jim's Playland. This is an indoor amusement park with small-scale rides in a 20,000- to 27,000-square-foot facility. One franchise, Computertots, teaches classes on computers to preschoolers. This franchise has spread to 25 locations in 15 states.

INVESTING IN A FRANCHISE

Franchising involves many risks to an entrepreneur. Although we read about the success of McDonald's or Burger King, for every one of these successes there are many failures. Franchising, like any other venture, is not for the passive person. It requires effort and long hours, as any business does, since duties such as hiring, scheduling, buying, accounting, and so on, are still the franchisee's responsibility. Certain steps that can be taken to minimize the risks in investing in a franchise are discussed below.

The entrepreneur should conduct a self-evaluation to be sure that using a franchise venture is right. Answering the following questions can help you determine if this is the correct decision:

- Are you a self-starter?
- Do you enjoy working with other people?
- Do you have the ability to provide leadership to those who will work for you?
- Are you able to organize your time?
- Can you take risks and make good business decisions?
- Do you have the initiative to continue the business during its ups and downs?
- Are you in good health?

If you answered yes or maybe to most of the above questions, chances are you are making the right decision to enter a new franchise venture.

Not every franchise is right for every entrepreneur. He or she must evaluate the franchise alternatives to decide which one is most appropriate. A number of factors should be assessed before making the final decision.

1. *Unproven versus Proven Franchise.* There are some trade-offs when investing in a proven or unproven franchise business. Whereas an unproven franchise will be a less-expensive investment, the lower investment is offset by more risk. In an unproven franchise, the franchisor is likely to make mistakes as the business grows. These mistakes could inevitably lead to failure. Constant reorganization of a new franchise can result in confusion and mismanagement. Yet, a new and unproven franchise can offer more excitement and challenge and can lead to significant opportunities for large profits should the business grow rapidly. A proven franchise offers lower risk but requires more financial investment.

2. *Financial Stability of Franchise.* The purchase of a franchise should entail an assessment of the financial stability of the franchisor. A potential franchisee should develop answers to the following questions:

- How many franchises are in the organization?
- How successful is each of the members of the franchise organization?
- Are most of the profits of the franchise a function of fees from the sale of franchises or from royalties based on profits of franchisees?

- Does the franchisor have management expertise in production, finance, and marketing?

Some of the above information can be obtained from profit-and-loss statements of the franchise organization. Face-to-face contact with the franchisor can also indicate the success of the organization. It is also worthwhile to contact some of the franchisees directly to determine their success and to identify any problems that have occurred. If financial information of the franchisor is unavailable, the entrepreneur may purchase a financial rating from a source such as Dun & Bradstreet. Generally, the following are good external sources of information:

- Franchise association
- Other franchisees
- Government
- Accountants and lawyers
- Libraries
- Franchise directories and journals
- Business exhibitions

3. *Potential Market for the New Franchise.* It is important for the entrepreneur to evaluate the market that the franchise will attract. A starting point is evaluating the traffic flow and demographics of the residents from a map of the area. Traffic flow information may be observed by visiting the area. Direction of traffic flow, ease of entry to the business, and the amount of traffic (pedestrian and automobile) can be estimated by observation. The demographics of the area can be determined from census data, which can be obtained from local libraries or the town hall. It can also be advantageous to locate competitors on the map to determine their potential effect on the franchise business. Marketing research in the market area is helpful. Attitudes about and interest in the new business can be assessed in the market research. In some instances, the franchisor will conduct a market study as a selling point to the franchisee.

4. *Profit Potential for a New Franchise.* As in any start-up business, it is important to develop pro forma income and cash flow statements. The franchisor should provide projections in order to calculate the needed information.

In general, most of the above information should be provided in the disclosure statement or the prospectus. The Federal Trade Commission's Franchise Rule requires franchisors to make full presale disclosure in a document that provides information about 20 separate aspects of a franchise offering.[12] The information required in this disclosure is summarized in Table 15.3. Some of the information will be comprehensive and some will be sketchy. There are always weaknesses that must be evaluated before making a commitment. The disclosure statement represents a good resource, but it is also important to evaluate the other services mentioned earlier in this chapter.

Front-end procedure fees, royalty payments, expenses, and other information should be compared with those of franchises in the same field, as well as in different business areas. If a franchise looks good as an investment, the entrepreneur may request a franchise package from the franchisor, which usually contains a draft franchise agreement or contract. Generally, this package will require a deposit of $300 to $500, which should be fully refundable.

TABLE 15.3 Information Required in Disclosure Statement

1. Identification of the franchisor and its affiliates and their business experience.
2. The business experience of each of the franchisor's officers, directors, and management personnel responsible for franchise services, training, and other aspects of the franchise programs.
3. The lawsuits in which the franchisor and its officers, directors, and management personnel have been involved.
4. Any previous bankruptcies in which the franchisor and its officers, directors, and management personnel have been involved.
5. The initial franchise fee and other initial payments that are required to obtain the franchise.
6. The continuing payments that franchisees are required to make after the franchise opens.
7. Any restrictions on the quality of goods and services used in the franchise and where they may be purchased, including restrictions requiring purchases from the franchisor or its affiliates.
8. Any assistance available from the franchisor or its affiliates in financing the purchase of the franchise.
9. Restrictions on the goods or services franchises are permitted to sell.
10. Any restrictions on the customers with whom franchises may deal.
11. Any territorial protection that will be granted to the franchisee.
12. The conditions under which the franchise may be repurchased or refused renewal by the franchisor, transferred to a third party by the franchisee, and terminated or modified by either party.
13. The training programs provided to franchisees.
14. The involvement of any celebrities or public figures in the franchise.
15. Any assistance in selecting a site for the franchise that will be provided by the franchisor.
16. Statistical information about the present number of franchises; the number of franchises projected for the future; and the number of franchises terminated, the number the franchisor has decided not to renew, and the number repurchased in the past.
17. The financial statement of the franchisor.
18. The extent to which the franchisees must personally participate in the operation of the franchise.
19. A complete statement of the basis of any earnings claims made to the franchisee, including the percentage of existing franchises that have actually achieved the results that are claimed.
20. A list of the names and addresses of other franchises.

The contract or franchise agreement is the final step in establishing a franchise arrangement. Here a lawyer experienced in franchising should be used. The franchise agreement contains all the specific requirements and obligations of the franchisee. Things such as the exclusivity of territory coverage will protect against the franchisor's granting another franchise within a certain radius of the business. The renewable terms will indicate the length of the contract and the requirements. Financial requirements will stipulate the initial price for the franchise, the schedule of payments, and the royalties to be paid. Termination of franchise requirements should indicate what will happen if the franchisee becomes disabled or dies and what provisions are made for the family. Terminating a franchise generally results in more lawsuits than any other issue in franchising. These terms should also allow the franchisee to obtain fair market value should the franchise be sold. Even though the agreement may be standard, the franchisee should try to negotiate important items to reduce the investment risk.

What would be a good franchise in this new millennium? The top five franchises started since 1995 are Curves for Women (www.curvesforwomen.com—women's fitness and weight loss centers); Ace America's Cash Express (www.acecashexpress.com—check cashing and related financial services); Home Instead Senior Care (www.homeinstead.com—nonmedical senior care services); Cash Converters International Franchise Group (www.cashconverters.com—preowned merchandise stores); and The Mad Science Group (www.madscience.org—science activities for children).[13]

IN REVIEW

Summary

There are various skills needed to expand a venture through joint ventures, acquisitions, mergers, leveraged buyouts, and franchising.

Joint ventures are separate entities formed by two or more partners. Although the most common joint ventures are between private-sector companies, they can involve universities, other nonprofit organizations, and the public sector. Objectives include sharing technology, cutting costs, entering new markets, and entering foreign markets. The success of joint ventures depends on the relationships of the partners, the symmetry of the partners, reasonable expectations, and timing.

Another means by which an entrepreneur can expand the business is through acquisition. An acquisition is the purchase of a company so that it is completely absorbed by the acquiring company. The acquisition process involves evaluating a candidate business and structuring a final deal. The evaluation process involves analyzing the firm's financial data, product line, research and development, marketing, manufacturing processes, and management. When a candidate passes the evaluation process, an appropriate deal needs to be structured.

A third method for expanding a company is through a merger. This transaction involves two or more companies, with only one company surviving. Motivations to engage in a merger include survival, protection, diversification, and growth.

An increasingly popular alternative for entrepreneurial expansion is the leveraged buyout. In this method, assets of the acquired company are used to finance the deal.

In the process of franchising, the entrepreneur has access to the franchisor's knowledge and experience, which can serve as a guidepost in establishing the business. A trusted name, advertising strength, and management advice all help to reduce the risk inherent to a new venture.

Before entering a franchise agreement, the entrepreneur should conduct a self-evaluation to be sure that the franchise form of business is right for him or her and to investigate the franchise carefully, especially if it is unproven. The financial stability, market potential, and profit potential need to be carefully scrutinized before using this as an expansion method.

Questions for Discussion

1. Why have many different valuation techniques been developed for determining the worth of a firm? In any given situation, is there one "right answer" for a company's value? What effects do your answers to these questions have on the entrepreneur making an acquisition?

2. Discuss the problems that can occur when universities and industry form joint ventures for research purposes. How have these problems been solved by some joint ventures?

3. The Chinese government has recently been interested in encouraging joint ventures with foreign companies. As a U.S. company, what might be your advantages to forming a joint venture in China? Discuss any drawbacks to consider.

4. Why does the valuation of a candidate business in an acquisition involve such detailed analysis?

5. What are the major advantages and disadvantages of franchising compared with an acquisition?

6. Identify a local franchise in your area and determine where the competitors are located and where other franchises from the same company are located. Evaluate the existing potential for the franchise.

7. Why is it important for the entrepreneur to conduct a self-evaluation before entering a franchise operation?

8. If you were evaluating a franchise opportunity, what would you look for and why?

Key Terms

acquisition	hostile takeover
brokers	joint venture
covenants	leveraged buyout (LBO)
franchisee	merger
franchising	poison pill
franchisor	poison puts

Glossary

A

acid-test ratio   A measure of the liquidity of a company found by dividing cash, marketable securities, and accounts receivable by current liabilities. Also called "quick ratio."

after-tax cash flow   The expected return from an investment project.

asset-based financing   Loads or capital secured by long-term assets.

asset turnover ratio   A measure of company efficiency found by dividing net sales by total assets.

average rate of return   A comparison of the average net income of a company to average investment.

B

book value   The original cost of an asset less its accumulated depreciation.

C

cash flow   Income less receipts (a proxy for this is net income plus depreciation).

cost of capital   The minimum rate of return that a company must earn on its assets to satisfy investors.

current ratio   A measure of the liquidity of a company found by current liabilities.

D

debt-to-equity ratio   The proportion of debt to equity in a firm's financial structure.

degree of financial leverage   The percentage change in earnings per share resulting from a 1 percent change in earnings before interest and taxes.

E

earnings per share   A measure of profitability derived by dividing the net income of the company by the average number of shares outstanding.

equity   The portion of the balance sheet representing ownership that includes capital stock, preferred stock, retained earnings, and certain other reserve or surplus accounts.

expected cash flow   The most likely (or weighted average) cash flow.

F

factoring   Sale of accounts receivable to a bank or finance company.

financial leverage   The relationship between borrowed funds and shareholders' equity. (When there is a high proportion of debt to equity in a company, it is highly leveraged, which increases the financial risk of the firm.)

financial risk   The risk that a firm may not be able to meet its financial obligations.

funds flow statement   A formalized statement of the funds flow cycle, incorporating all sources and uses of funds.

G

going concern   A company whose operation is expected to continue.

golden parachute   A provision to protect existing officers and directors of a company from removal in the event of a takeover. Often a large sum of money is involved on removal.

gross profit margin   The difference between net sales and the cost of goods sold, expressed as a percentage of net sales.

I

inventory turnover ratio   A ratio measuring the number of times the inventory of a company is turned (sold) each year.

investment value   The theoretic intrinsic value of an asset or company.

J

joint venture   An agreement between companies to enter into a partnership for a specific project.

L

leveraged buyout   A buyout in which the purchaser borrows funds to buy the stock of a company and then uses the resources of the company to repay the loan.

liquidity   The ability of a company to meet its current financial obligations.

M

market value   The price investors are willing to pay for the securities of a company.

merger   A combination of two or more companies in which one company survives, retaining its identity.

N

net present value   The present value of expected cash flows discounted at the cost of capital less the investment outlay.

net profit margin   The percentage of profit earned for each dollar of sales calculated by dividing net income by net sales.

O

operating leverage   The effect that a change in sales can have on the earnings of a company due to certain fixed expenses.

operating margin   A measure of return on sales of a company determined by dividing earnings from operations by net sales.

P

participating preferred stock   Stock that provides stated dividends but also shares in the earnings of the company.

payback period The number of years required to return an investment outlay.

preferred stock A type of stock representing one class of ownership of a company; generally has fixed dividends.

present value The current value of dollars that will be received in the future.

price/earnings (P/E) ratio A ratio determined by dividing the market price of stock by its earnings. A high price/earnings ratio of a company indicates that investors expect good company growth.

pro forma financial statements Projected financial statements of future periods of the operations of the company.

profit margin A measure of profitability of a company determined by dividing net income by net sales.

profitability index (PI) An index measuring the value of the expected cash flow of a company discounted at the cost of capital divided by the investment outlay.

R

return on assets The net income divided by the assets of a company.

return on equity The net income divided by the equity of a company.

S

sole proprietorship An unincorporated business owned by one person.

T

term loan A loan from a commercial bank with a usual maturity of five years or less commonly used for plant and equipment, working capital, or debt repayment.

time value of money The principle that money received in the present is worth more than the same amount received in the future.

V

variable cost Expenditures that change in direct proportion to the number of units sold.

W

working capital The dollar amount of a company's current assets.

More Information—Net Addresses in This Chapter

Ace America's Cash Express
www.acecashexpress.com

Boeing
www.boeing.com

Carnegie-Mellon
www.cmu.edu

Cash Converters International Franchise Group
www.cashconverters.com

Ciba-Geigy
www.ciba.com

Computertots
www.entremkt.com/computertots

Corning
www.corning.com

Curves for Women
www.curvesforwomen.com

Department of Justice
www.usdoj.gov

Dow Chemical
www.dow.com

Dun & Bradstreet
www.dbisna.com

Dunkin Donuts
www.franchise1.com/comp/dunkin1.html

Federal Trade Commission
www.ftc.gov

Fuji
www.fujifilm.co.jp

General Motors (GM)
www.gm.com

Home Instead Senior Care
www.homeinstead.com

Jameson Inn
www.jamesoninns.com

Kawasaki
www.kawasaki.com

KFC
www.kentuckyfriedchicken.com

Kinder Care
www.kindercare.com

Kodak
    www.kodak.com

The Mad Science Group
    www.madscience.org

Microelectronics and Computer
Technology Corporation (MCC)
    www.mcc.com

Midas
    www.midasautosystems.com

Mitsubishi
    www.mitsubishi.co.jp

NASDAQ
    www.nasdaq.com

Subway
    www.netaccess.on.ca/entrepr/subway

TCBY
    www.tcby.com.hk

Toyota
    www.toyota.com

Union Carbide
    www.unioncarbide.com

Westinghouse
    www.westinghouse.com

Yale University
    www.yale.edu

Selected Readings

Dollinger, Marc J.; Peggy A. Golden; and Todd Saxton. (1997). The Effect of Reputation on the Decision to Joint Venture. *Strategic Management Journal,* vol. 18, no. 2, pp. 127–40.

The impact that reputation has on the decision to proceed with a strategic alliance is analyzed. Findings indicate that (1) reputation is a multidimensional construct, (2) the personal information-processing characteristics of the decision maker mediate the reputation effect and may suppress the reputation information, (3) people may compensate weaker elements of reputation for stronger ones when making decisions, (4) the most important factors are product and management reputation, and (5) reputation is a factor affecting the decision regardless of whether the proposed target is a supplier or a competitor.

Falbe, Cecilia M.; Thomas C. Dandridge; and Ajith Kumar. (1999). The Effect of Organizational Context on Entrepreneurial Strategies in Franchising. *Journal of Business Venturing,* vol. 14, no. 1, pp. 125–40.

This study examines how the organizational context variables of size, age of the franchise, its growth rate, and time in franchising affect franchisee perceptions of entrepreneurial strategies of their parent franchisor, their innovation efforts, and franchisor managerial support for entrepreneurial activity and innovation by the franchisee.

Fladmoe-Lindquist, Karin. (1996). International Franchising: Capabilities and Development. *Journal of Business Venturing,* vol. 11, no. 5, pp. 419–38.

The international capabilities of franchisors are explored. These capabilities may be categorized as administrative efficiency and risk management. These capabilities are connected to a dynamic capabilities model of international franchisor types. This framework is not a stage model, but a description of different international franchisor types based on the franchisor's set of international capabilities and capacity for acquiring new skills.

Laamanen, Tomi. (1999). Option Nature of Company Acquisitions Motivated by Competence Acquisition. *Small Business Economics,* vol. 12, no. 2, pp. 149–68.

This article examines the option nature of collaboration and acquisitions of 111 small technology-based companies. Findings indicate, somewhat contrary to the earlier research, that collaborative arrangements were not found to be used as options to acquire small companies. Acquisitions, on the other hand, were used as options to enter a new technology or business area. The option nature of acquisitions was related to technology-based variables. Growth option upside realization was linked to market and cooperation-related variables.

Nicholls-Nixon, Charlene L.; Arnold C. Cooper; and Carolyn Y. Woo. (2000). Strategic Experimentation: Understanding Change And Performance in New Ventures. *Journal of Business Venturing,* vol. 15, no. 5/6, pp. 493–521.

This paper develops the concept of strategic experimentation as the organizing framework for the study of change in new ventures.

Pandit, B. L.; and N. S. Siddharthan. (1998). Technological Acquisition and Investment: Lessons from Recent Indian Experience. *Journal of Business Venturing,* vol. 13, no. 1, pp. 43–55.

Technology acquisition will decisively influence investment behavior, modernization, and expansion plans of firms. However, capability of the firms to acquire technology differs considerably. The entrepreneur's decision to invest and expand would depend on the technological opportunities available. The study examines the role of technology acquisition in influencing investment decisions of private corporate firms in India.

Shane, Scott. (1996). Hybrid Organizational Arrangements and Their Implications for Firm Growth and Survival: A Study of New Franchisers. *Academy of Management Journal,* vol. 39, no. 1, pp. 216–34.

A study proposes that hybrid organizational forms provide a way to overcome the agency problems of adverse selection and moral hazard in selecting, assimilating, and monitoring new managers. Consequently, hybrid forms allow firms to overcome managerial limits to firm growth and therefore grow faster. Specifically, the study shows empirically that the degree to which a firm emphasized franchising as its expansion strategy had a significant, positive effect on its growth and survival.

Shane, Scott A. (1996). Why Franchise Companies Expand Overseas. *Journal of Business Venturing,* vol. 11, no. 1, pp. 73–88.

A study reinforces previous research which found that international expansion is the result of factors external to the firm (in particular, diminished domestic opportunity). More important, however, the study shows that the external forces argument is incomplete. Internal firm capability plays a significant role in determining which firms facing the same environment will expand internationally. Interestingly, it finds that the capabilities linked with international expansion are different from those linked with domestic expansion.

Williams, Darrell L. (1999). Why Do Entrepreneurs Become Franchisees? An Empirical Analysis of Organizational Choice. *Journal of Business Venturing,* vol. 14, no. 1, pp. 103–24.

This study tests the proposition that the demand for franchise opportunities is derived from the demand for managerial inputs and risk sharing, which are supplied by franchisors in this cooperative form of ownership. The importance of these factors and others is explored in the context of a discrete choice model of entrepreneurs' choice between noncooperative, independent ownership and franchising. The findings indicate that franchisees would have significantly lower profits as independent owners, which is due primarily to unobservable differences between entrepreneurs who choose franchising and those who do not.

Wright, Mike; Robert E. Hoskisson; and Lowell W. Busenitz. (2001). Firm Rebirth: Buyouts as Facilitators of Strategic Growth and Entrepreneurship. *Academy of Management Executive,* vol. 15, no. 1, pp. 111–25.

This article illustrates how buyouts can create entrepreneurial opportunities and allow upside growth. In particular, it focuses on understanding the aspects and circumstances of the entrepreneurial mind-sets of managers who seek upside growth through buyouts.

Wright, Mike; Ken Robbie; and Christine Ennew. (1997). Venture Capitalists and Serial Entrepreneurs. *Journal of Business Venturing,* vol. 12, no. 3, pp. 227–49.

This article examines the importance of serial entrepreneurs to the venture capital industry from the venture capitalist's perspective, with particular emphasis on those entrepreneurs who have exited from an initial investment in the venture capitalist's portfolio. A ninefold classification of types of serial venture, ranging from start-up/start-up to buyout/buyout, is presented. Findings indicate that previous experience is only one element considered by venture capitalists in their investment criteria for serial entrepreneurs. Assets of previous experience generally exceed liabilities for serial entrepreneurs and for entrepreneurs receiving second-time venture capital financing. However, serial entrepreneurs do not appear to perform better than novice entrepreneurs in whom venture capital firms invest during the same period.

Endnotes

1. For some different perspectives on joint ventures, see R. D. Hisrich, "Joint Ventures: Research Base and Use in International Methods," in *The State of the Art of Entrepreneurship* (Boston: PWS-Kent Publishing Co.), pp. 520–79; and J. McConnell and T. J. Nantell, "Corporate Combinations and Common Stock Returns: The Case of Joint Ventures," *Journal of Finance* 40 (June 1985), pp. 519–36.

2. For a discussion of some different types of joint ventures, see R. M. Cyert, "Establishing University–Industry Joint Ventures," *Research Management* 28 (January–February 1985), pp. 27–28; F. K. Berlew, "The Joint Venturer—A Way into Foreign Markets," *Harvard Business Review* (July–August 1984), pp. 48–49 and 54; and Kathryn Rudie Harrigan, *Strategies for Joint Ventures* (Lexington, MA: Lexington Books, 1985).

3. S. E. Boyle, "The Joint Subsidiary: An Economic Appraisal," *Antitrust Bulletin* 5 (1960), pp. 303–18.

4. S. E. Boyle, "An Estimate of the Number and Size Distribution of Domestic Joint Subsidiaries," *Antitrust Law and Economics Review* 1 (1968), pp. 81–82.

5. J. Huber, "Respect," *Entrepreneur* (January 1992), pp. 117–23.

6. D. D. Seltz, *The Complete Handbook of Franchising* (Reading, MA: Addison-Wesley Publishing Co., 1982), p. 1.

7. L. Bongiorno, "Franchise Fracas," *Business Week* (March 22, 1993), pp. 68–71.

8. F. Huffman, "Under New Ownership," *Entrepreneur* (January 1993), pp. 101–5.

9. W. Siegel, *Franchising* (New York: John Wiley & Sons, 1983), p. 9.

10. *Directory of Franchising Organizations* (Babylon, NY: Pilot Industries, 1985).

11. K. Rosenburg, "Franchising, American Style," *Entrepreneur* (January 1991), pp. 86–93.

12. D. J. Kaufmann and D. E. Robbins, "Now Read This," *Entrepreneur* (January 1991), pp. 100–5.

13. L. Potter, "Brand-Spanking," *Entrepreneur* (February 2000), pp. 160–3.

16

Going Public

LEARNING OBJECTIVES

1. To identify the advantages and disadvantages of going public.

2. To identify some alternatives to going public.

3. To discuss the timing of going public and underwriter selection.

4. To explain the registration statement and timetable for going public.

5. To discuss the legal issues of going public and blue sky qualifications.

6. To discuss some important issues for a venture after going public.

SAM WALTON

Sam Walton, the Wal-Mart magnate, was frequently identified as one of the richest men in America. Although he was well known for his marketing strategy of introducing discount stores to the smaller cities and towns ignored by other chains, this is not the foundation for his success. In large part, the growth of his company and the concurrent growth of his personal wealth can be directly attributed to his judicious use of the equity markets.

www.wal-mart.com

Walton got his start in retailing in 1940 as a salesman and management trainee at JCPenney. He was one of the best shirt salesmen in the organization, but he knew that it was just a training ground for his real calling as a store owner. In 1945, along with his brother Bud, he began operating a Ben Franklin five-and-dime store in Newport, Arkansas. After five successful years, they moved to a store in Bentonville, Arkansas, where Sam would live until his death. The Walton brothers began expanding by buying other variety stores in the area. Utilizing his knowledge about sales, Sam set up his own buying office and applied the advertising and other marketing principles to his group of stores that others thought were applicable only to bigger ventures. Moving into the 1960s, the Waltons owned enough stores to be the most successful Ben Franklin franchisee in the country.

A new concept was developing in the retail business in the early 1960s: discounting. When Gibson's, a Texas-based discounter, opened a store in Fayetteville, where the Waltons had a variety store, Sam decided to try an experiment. Starting with a single department, his discounting attempt soon enveloped a complete store. Despite Walton's success with this experiment, and the growing threat of discounting to the local variety stores, the Ben Franklin executives were not receptive to changing the positioning of their chain. Sam decided to strike out on his own. After a brief tour around the country in search of new ideas, he developed a plan to begin operating his own discount stores in towns with populations of less than 25,000. The first Wal-Mart was opened in Rogers, Arkansas, in 1962. Sam's profits dictated the growth rate of his business. This make-do-with-what-you-have philosophy carried over to the new Wal-Mart stores. To open the first store, Sam and Bud pooled all their available resources and planned the size and the location of the store based on that amount of capital. There was no room in the tight budget for fancy displays or large offices if they were to offer quality merchandise at competitive prices in small towns. Evidently, the pipe-rack displays and bare floors were only a minor inconvenience to the shoppers, because Wal-Mart was a success from the start.

Early in the development of the Wal-Mart concept, Sam realized the vital role of distribution in determining profitability. He knew he needed the same low-cost, efficient delivery methods used by his larger counterparts. Rather than build warehousing to serve existing outlets, he clustered his expansion outlets around existing distribution points. Then Sam considered a public offering of stock. In 1970, after eight years in the discount store business, there were about 30 Wal-Mart Discount City stores. It became apparent to Walton that he needed his own warehouse to be able to buy in the volume necessary to support new openings. Yet he did not feel that the company could afford to incur the heavy debt burden needed. In the midst of a boom in new issues and on the strength of his impressive growth record, Walton sold a small part of his business to the public for $3.3 million. This cash helped to pay for a $5 million distribution center, big enough to serve 80 to 100 stores.

With his distribution center in place, Sam was ready to grow. Two years later, with 512 stores and $678 million in sales, Wal-Mart was listed on the New York Stock Exchange. The single share purchased by original investors in 1970 for $16.50 has seen 11 splits resulting in 2,048 shares trading at $57 per share in March 2000, for a total value of $116,736, or a total return of 707,300 percent on the initial investment. Sam tapped the public equity market several additional times when he needed to expand or upgrade his system, managing to keep his overall capital costs well below those of his competitors with his careful planning and tight budgeting. This helped sales, earnings, and dividends continue to grow. In 1987, sales were $15,879 million with earnings of $.28 and a dividend of $.03. This has increased in a progressive fashion, with 1996 sales of over $93.6 billion, earnings of $1.19, and dividends of $.20 per share posted. And the growth has continued through the end of the 20th century. According to Wal-Mart's annual report, 2000 was a record-setting year, with sales of over $165 billion, up 20 percent, or $27 billion, from 1999. Earnings per share increased by 21 percent, return on assets remained a high 9.5 percent, and the company paid dividends of almost $900 million to shareholders.

Of course, one of the more recent significant challenges to the company has been filling Sam Walton's shoes after his death. The successor, Wal-Mart president and CEO David Glass, has had to provide clear direction and leadership as the company wrestled with the problems of compounded annual growth, changing market demographics, advances in communication and technology, merchandise selection and sourcing flexibility, and a movement toward a more impersonal, bureaucratic organization due to its large size and increasing diversity. As stated by Glass, "Becoming the world's largest retailer was never considered." However, the venture has grown from the initial store in Rogers, Arkansas, to encompass 3700 Wal-Mart Stores and Supercenters and 475 Sam's Clubs, with 1,244,00 in the United States and abroad.

Sam Walton judiciously decided when to use the public equity market for money to finance the expansion of his business—Wal-Mart. To this day, the company is committed to "not invest[ing] more capital than is justified by [our] results." The decision to "go public," a phrase used to describe the transformation of a closely held corporation into one where the general public has proprietary interest, should be carefully thought out. To some entrepreneurs, going public is the ultimate rite, signaling entry into the most exclusive legitimate business community. But before doing so, there are

several issues each entrepreneur must carefully address, much the way Sam Walton did. These include assessing the advantages and disadvantages of going public, evaluating the alternatives to going public, determining the timing of doing so, selecting the underwriter, preparing the registration statement and timetable, and understanding the blue sky qualifications and the resulting reporting requirements as well as continuing to service the shareholders and increase their investment value.

ADVANTAGES AND DISADVANTAGES OF GOING PUBLIC

Going public occurs when the entrepreneur and other equity owners of the venture offer and sell some part of the company to the public through a registration statement filed with the Securities and Exchange Commission (SEC) pursuant to the Securities Act of 1933. The resulting capital infusion to the company from the increased number of stockholders and outstanding shares of stock provides the company with financial resources and a relatively liquid investment vehicle. Consequently, the company will have greater access to capital markets in the future and a more objective picture of the public's perception of the value of the business. However, given the reporting requirements, the increased number of stockholders, and the costs involved, the entrepreneur must carefully evaluate the advantages and disadvantages of going public before initiating the process. A list of these advantages and disadvantages is given in Table 16.1.

going public   Selling some part of the company through registering with the SEC

Advantages

The three primary advantages of going public are obtaining new equity capital, obtaining value and transferability of the organization's assets, and enhancing the company's ability to obtain future funds. Whether it is first-stage, second-stage, or third-stage financing that is desired, a venture is in constant need of capital. The

---

TABLE 16.1   Advantages and Disadvantages of Going Public

Advantages
- Obtaining capital with less dilution to founders
- Enhanced ability to borrow
- Enhanced ability to raise equity
- Liquidity and valuation
- Prestige
- Personal wealth

Disadvantages
- Expense
- Disclosure of information
- Pressures to maintain growth pattern
- Loss of control

new capital provides the needed working capital, plant and equipment, or inventories and supplies necessary for the venture's growth and survival. Going public is often the best way to obtain capital on the best possible terms.

Going public also provides a mechanism for valuing the company and allowing this value to be easily transferred among parties. Many family-owned or other privately held companies may need to go public so that the value of the company can be disseminated among the second and third generations. Venture capitalists view going public as the most beneficial way to attain the liquidity necessary to exit a company with the best possible return on their earlier-stage funding. Other investors benefit as well due to easier liquidation of their investment when the company's stock takes on value and transferability. Because of this liquidity, the value of a publicly traded security is sometimes higher than shares of one that is not publicly traded. In addition, publicly traded companies often find it easier to acquire other companies by using their securities in the transactions.

The third primary advantage is that publicly traded companies usually find it easier to raise additional capital, particularly debt. Money can be borrowed more easily and on more favorable terms when there is value attached to a company and that value is more easily transferred. Not only debt financing but future equity capital is more easily obtained when a company establishes a track record of increasing stock value.

Disadvantages

Although the advantages of going public are significant for a new venture, they must be carefully weighed against the numerous disadvantages. Some entrepreneurs want to keep their companies private, even in times of a hot stock market. Why do entrepreneurs avoid the supposed gold rush of an *initial public offering (IPO)*?

initial public offering (IPO) The first public registration and sale of a company's stock

Two major reasons are public exposure and the potential loss of control that can occur in a publicly traded company. To stay on the cutting edge of technology, companies frequently need to sacrifice short-term profits for long-term innovation. This can require reinvesting in technology that in itself may not produce any bottom-line results, particularly in the short run. Making long-term decisions can be difficult in publicly traded companies where sales/profit evaluations indicate the capability of management via stock values. When enough shares are sold to the public, the company can lose control of decision making, which can even result in the venture being acquired through an unfriendly tender offer.

Some of the most troublesome aspects of being public are the resulting loss of flexibility as well as increased administrative burdens. The company must make decisions with respect to the fiduciary duties owed to the public shareholder, and it is obliged to disclose to the public all material information regarding the company, its operations, and its management. One publicly traded company had to retain a more expensive investment banker than would have been required by a privately held company in order to obtain an "appropriate" fairness opinion in a desired merger. The investment banker increased the expenses of the merger by $150,000, in addition to causing a three-month delay in the merger proceedings. Management of a publicly traded company also spends a significant amount of additional time addressing queries from shareholders, press, and financial analysts.

If all these disadvantages have not caused the entrepreneur to look for alternative financing rather than an IPO, the expenses involved may. The major expenses of going public include accounting fees, legal fees, underwriter's fees, registration and blue sky filing fees, and printing costs. The accounting fees involved in going public vary greatly, depending in part on the size of the company, the availability of previously audited financial statements, and the complexity of the company's operations. Generally, the costs of going public are around $300,000 to $600,000, although they can be much greater when significant complexities are involved. Additional reporting, accounting, legal, and printing expenses can run anywhere from $50,000 to $250,000 per year, depending on the company's past practices in the areas of accounting and shareholder communications. In addition to the SEC reports that must be filed, a proxy statement and other materials must be submitted to the SEC for review before distribution to the stockholders. These materials contain certain disclosures concerning management, its compensation, and transactions with the company, as well as the items to be voted on at the meeting. Public companies must also submit an annual report to the shareholders containing the audited financial information for the prior fiscal year and a discussion of any business developments. The preparation and distribution of the proxy materials and annual report are some of the more significant items of additional expense incurred by a company after it is public.

Accounting fees for an initial public offering fluctuate widely but are typically $50,000 to $100,000. Fees are at the lower end of this range if the accounting firm has regularly audited the company over the past several years. They are at the higher end of the range if the company has no prior audits or if it engages a new accounting firm. The accounting fee covers the preparation of financial statements, the response to SEC queries, and the preparation of "cold comfort" letters for the underwriters described later in this chapter.

Legal fees will vary significantly, typically ranging from $60,000 to $175,000. These fees generally cover preparation of corporate documents, preparation and clearing of the registration statement, negotiation of the final underwriting agreement, and closing of the sale of the securities to these underwriters. Additional legal fees may also be assessed and can be extensive, particularly if a major organization is involved. A public company also pays legal fees for the work involved with the National Association of Securities Dealers, Inc. (NASD) and the state of blue sky filings. The legal fees for NASD and state blue sky filings range from $8,000 to $30,000, depending on the size of the offering and the number of states in which the securities will be offered.

The underwriter's fees include a cash discount (on commission), which usually ranges from 7 to 10 percent of the public offering price of the new issue. In some IPOs, the underwriters can also require some compensation, such as warrants to purchase stock, reimbursement for some expenses (most typically legal fees), and the right of first refusal on any future offerings. The NASD regulates the maximum amount of the underwriter's compensation and reviews the actual amount for fairness before the offering can take place. Similarly, any underwriter's compensation is also reviewed in blue sky filings.

There are other expenses in the form of SEC, NASD, and state blue sky registration fees. Of these, the SEC registration fee is quite small: one-fiftieth of 1 percent of the maximum aggregate public offering price of the security. For example, the SEC fee would be $4,000 on a $20 million offering. The minimum fee is $100. The SEC fee must be paid by certified or cashier's check. The NASD filing fee is also small in relation to the size of the offering: $100 plus one-hundredth of 1 percent of the maximum public offering price. In the above example of a $20 million offering, this would be $2,100. The maximum NASD fee is $5,100. The amount of the state blue sky fees depends on the number of states in which the offering is registered. If the initial public offering is registered in all states, the total blue sky filing fees can be more than $15,000, depending on the size of the offering.

The final major expense, printing costs, typically ranges from $50,000 to $200,000. The registration statement and prospectus discussed later in this chapter account for the largest portion of these expenses. The exact amount of expenses varies, depending on the length of the prospectus, the use of color or black and white photographs, the number of proofs and corrections, and the number printed. It is important for the company to use a good printer because accuracy and speed are required in the printing of the prospectus and other offering documents.

Not only can going public be a costly event, but the process leading up to it can be exasperating as well. Just ask Bing Yeh, who went through some trying circumstances starting when he decided to go public in July 1995 and ending when his company, Silicon Storage Technology (SST), issued its IPO on November 22.[1] While the exact process varies with each company, the goal is the same as it was for SST—make over the company so that it is seen in the best possible light and is well received by Wall Street. The many changes in a company that occur usually take place over a six-month to one-year period of time, not the 100 days it took for SST. For some companies, getting ready to go public can involve eliminating members of the management team and board, dumping marginal products, eliminating treasured perks such as the corporate jet, hiring a new accounting firm, subduing some personality traits, dressing up the senior management, and/or hiring new members of the management team. For Bing Yeh and SST, the makeover centered around four primary tasks: (1) hiring a chief financial officer, (2) reorganizing the financials, (3) writing a company biography, and (4) preparing for the road show.

Regardless of how much reading is done, like Bing Yeh, almost every entrepreneur is unprepared and wants to halt the preparations at some point in the makeover process. Yet for a successful IPO, each entrepreneur must follow Yeh's example by listening to the advice being given and then making the recommended changes swiftly.

THE ALTERNATIVES TO GOING PUBLIC

Since most of the alternatives to going public were discussed in Chapter 11, only the most widely used ones will be briefly discussed here. The two most commonly used alternatives are private placements and bank loans. A private placement of securities—particularly with institutional investors, insurance companies, investment companies, or pension funds—is one way to obtain the needed funds with less public disclosure. These funds are frequently in the form of intermediate or long-term debt, often carrying a floating interest rate, or preferred stock with specific dividend requirements. Most private placement transactions also carry certain *restrictive covenants*. These covenants are intended not to hamper the operations of the venture but to protect the investor and allow the investment to be profitably liquidated at a later date. The *liquidation covenant* usually contains a provision that allows the investor to require registration of a sale or other disposition of its securities at any time. The entrepreneur must evaluate whether this or any of the other covenants impose too many restrictions on the successful operation of the company before selecting private placement as an alternative source of funds.

restrictive covenant   Statement indicating the things that cannot be done without approval

liquidation covenant   The right of an investor to sell the interest in the company

To qualify for a private placement under the Securities and Exchange Act of 1933, a company must have a limited number of investors, each of whom has enough sophistication in financial and business matters to be capable of evaluating the risks and merits of the investment. This requires that the investors have available all the information that would be included in a public registration statement. In addition, the investors have to agree to hold the securities for a specified period following the purchase. As a rule of thumb, equity securities for a specified private placement will be sold at a discount of 20 to 30 percent less than the company might receive for the same securities in a public offering.

Besides private placement, a bank loan can be an alternative to going public. Although bank loans are a common way to raise additional funds, this additional capital is in the form of debt and therefore often must have some collateral of the company or a guaranty. This collateral is typically in the form of contracts, accounts receivable, machinery, inventory, land, or buildings, that is, some tangible asset. Even when assets are available for collateral, bank loans are typically made on a short- or, at best, medium-term basis, with a floating rate of interest. The repayment schedule and restrictive covenants of this financial alternative may also preclude its use.

Other debt financing can be obtained from nonbank lenders such as equipment leasing companies, mortgage bankers, trade suppliers, or inventory and accounts receivable financing companies. Sometimes these sources of capital offer the entrepreneur a greater degree of flexibility than bank loans, although not nearly as much as equity capital.

TIMING OF GOING PUBLIC AND UNDERWRITER SELECTION

Probably the two most critical issues in a successful public offering are the timing of the offering and the underwriting team. An entrepreneur should seek advice from several financial advisors as well as other entrepreneurs who are familiar with the process in making decisions in these two areas.

Timing

direct public offering (DPO)   A method of selling part of the company directly to investors

Am I ready to go public? This is the critical question that entrepreneurs must ask themselves before launching this effort. Some criteria to evaluate in making this decision for one form of going public, *direct public offering (DPO)*—as well as for initial public offerings—are indicated below.

First, is the company large enough? While it is not possible to establish rigid minimum-size standards that must be met before an entrepreneur can go public, New York investment banking firms prefer at least a 500,000 share offering at a minimum of $10 per share. This means that the company would have to have a past offering value of at least $12.5 million in order to support this $5 million offering, given that the company is willing to sell shares representing not more than 40 percent of the total number of shares outstanding after the offering is completed. This size of offering will occur only with past significant sales and earnings performance or a solid prospect for future growth and earnings.

Second, what is the amount of the company's earnings, and how strong is its financial performance? Not only is this performance the basis of the company valuation, but it also determines if a company can successfully go public and the type of firm willing to underwrite the offering. While the exact criteria vary from year to year, thereby reflecting market conditions, generally a company must have at least one year of good earnings and sales before its stock offering will be acceptable to the market. Larger underwriting firms have more stringent criteria, such as sales as high as $15 million to $20 million, a $1 million or more net income, and a 30 to 50 percent annual growth rate.

As Seen in *Business Week*
Is This Any Way to Dress Up For an IPO?

Taiwanese entrepreneur Daniel Chiang used to enjoy boasting that Sina.com, the hot Chinese-language portal he helped create, was different from the other Internet companies in Greater China. While most Chinese entrepreneurs are loath to surrender control of their companies to outsiders, Chiang and Chinese cofounder Wang Zhidong in March installed experienced Silicon Valley professionals in most top executive posts. "You have to play by the U.S. rules of the game," Chiang said in July, explaining why he stepped aside as chief executive officer.

That open attitude enabled Sina to line up $25 million from foreign investors, including Goldman, Sachs & Co. and Singapore's Economic Development Board. Boasting 1 million registered users, it also became the odds-on favorite to be the leading Internet content provider for the Chinese-speaking world.

But now it appears Sina wasn't as ready for the U.S. high-tech fast lane as Chiang had hoped. Most of its vaunted American execs have left in the past month, victims of a thorough management purge led by Wang and Chiang, sources say.

By putting its headquarters in Silicon Valley, Sina aimed to secure a politically neutral base. It also hoped to attract the talent needed to be a hit with investors. "Both Chiang and Wang were convinced that bringing in professional management would be the best thing and push them toward an IPO," says Bo Feng, a Shanghai-based banker and early Sina investor. So they hired Sha and other Valley veterans.

But problems arose quickly. The Asian founders and U.S. managers and advisors soon split into opposing factions. "Their visions and ways of doing things weren't quite the same," says Feng. Chiang and Wang pushed for a focus on China, where business was growing faster than first expected. The Americans wanted to focus on other markets. Before long, the factions were "constantly disagreeing and fighting," says a source close to the company.

Another major point of dispute was the timing of Sina's plan to go public. Sources say Wang felt a sense of urgency after China.com Corp., the Hong-Kong–based portal that was first to go public in the United States, successfully listed on Nasdaq in July. That whetted the appetites of many Asian Internet companies—including Sina. The Americans urged Sina to wait until management, a solid business plan, and detailed financial forecasts were all in place.

The conflict began coming to a head in late August. Sha, 49, was forced out as CEO, and Wang replaced him. CFO Riley Willcox, who had spent 15 years as a financial officer for Silicon Valley companies, was demoted. Soon after, sources say, he quit after Wang insisted over his objections on asking the board to go public quickly. When the board meeting was held on September 11 at the Menlo Park (California) offices of Venture Law Group, Sina's counsel, the proposal prompted Broad-Vision's Chen and Flatiron's Colonna to quit as directors. Wang had enough control of the board to approve his plan. Besides, says the banking source, "Wang decided he wanted control of his company back." Chiang and Wang declined to comment for this story, as did Sha and Willcox.

Sina won't say when it plans to go public. One hitch is that it again has no CFO: Willcox's replacement, Mark Fagan, quit after a few weeks. Morgan Stanley Dean Witter is the new lead underwriter, though Goldman remains a Sina investor. "We have the utmost respect for Sina.com and its vision for the Internet," says Goldman spokesman Peter Rose. Morgan Stanley won't comment.

Sina also won't discuss where the company goes next. If it presses ahead with an IPO, however, investors will want plenty of financial details—and an explanation of what became of its prized U.S. team. As investors turn more skeptical of Net players in general, it's a lesson in cross-cultural management that other Asian companies should study.

Source: Bruce Einhorn and Linda Himelstein, "Is This Any Way to Dress Up for an IPO?" *Business Week* (October 11, 1999), p. 58.

Third, are the market conditions favorable for an initial public offering? Underlying the sales and earnings, as well as the size of the offering, is the prevailing general market condition. Market conditions affect both the initial price that the entrepreneur will receive for the stock and the aftermarket, or the price performance of the stock after its initial sale. Some market conditions are more favorable for IPOs than others. Unless the need for money is so urgent that delay is impossible, the entrepreneur should attempt to take his or her company public in the most favorable market conditions.

Fourth, how urgently is the money needed? The entrepreneur must carefully appraise both the urgency of the need for new money and the availability of outside capital from other sources. Since the sale of common stock decreases the ownership position of the entrepreneur and other equity owners, the longer the time before going public, given that profits and sales growth occur, the less percentage of equity the entrepreneur will have to give up per dollar invested.

Finally, what are the needs and desires of the present owners? Sometimes the present owners lack confidence in the future viability and growth prospects of the business, or they have a need for liquidity. Going public is frequently the only method by which present stockholders may obtain the cash needed.

Underwriter Selection

managing underwriter Lead financial firm in selling stock to the public

underwriting syndicate Group of firms involved in selling stock to the public

Once the entrepreneur has determined that the timing for going public is favorable, he or she must carefully select a *managing underwriter* that will then take the lead in forming the *underwriting syndicate*. The underwriter is of critical importance in establishing the initial price for the stock of the company, supporting the stock in the aftermarket, and creating a strong following among security analysts.

Although most public offerings are conducted by a syndicate of underwriters, the entrepreneur needs to select the lead or managing underwriter(s). The managing underwriters will then develop the strongest possible syndicate of underwriters for the initial public offering. An entrepreneur should ideally develop a relationship with several potential managing underwriters (investment bankers) at least one year before going public. Frequently, this occurs during the first- or second-round financing, where the advice of an investment banker helps structure the initial financial arrangements to position the company to go public later.

Since selecting the investment banker is a major factor in the success of the public offering, the entrepreneur should approach one through a mutual contact. Commercial banks, attorneys specializing in securities work, major accounting firms, providers of the initial financing, or prominent members of the company's board of directors can usually provide the needed suggestions and introductions. Since the relationship will be ongoing and not end with the completion of the offering, the entrepreneur should employ several criteria in the selection process, such as reputation, distribution capability, advisory services, experience, and cost.

Since an initial public offering rarely involves a well-known company, the managing underwriter needs a good reputation to develop a strong syndicate team and provide confidence to potential investors. This reputation helps sell the public offering and supports the stock in the aftermarket. The ethics of the potential underwriter is an aspect that must be carefully evaluated. The balance in personal and business ethics is a problem frequently encountered, as discussed in the Ethics box.

"To argue, in the manner of Machiavelli, that there is one rule for business and another for private life, is to open the door to an orgy of unscrupulousness before which the mind recoils. To argue that there is no difference at all is to lay down a principle which few men who have faced the difficulty in practice will be prepared to endorse as of invariable application, and incidentally, to expose the ideas of morality itself to discredit by subjecting it to an almost intolerable strain."

Your venture is in a fiercely competitive industry, where technological competence and innovation are essential to survival. You have been hearing rumors that your major competitor has made an important scientific discovery that will give it a unique competitive advantage in the market. If true, this would substantially reduce the profits of your firm, but probably not force you out of business. At a social function, you are approached by one of this competitor's employees, asking you of possible openings at your firm. In the discussion, this individual mentions that by hiring him, you would obtain the secrets to this development, allowing you to neutralize the competitive advantage that may have resulted. While you are always "keeping your eyes open" for good people, you really don't need anyone now. Could you hire him to get the secret and then let him go? How would you respond to this individual?

Source: The quote is from R. H. Tawney, *Religion and the Rise of Capitalism*, as cited in Robert C. Solomon, *Ethics and Excellence* (New York: Oxford University Press, 1993), p. 145.

The success of the offering also depends on the underwriter's distribution capability. An entrepreneur wants the stock of his or her company distributed to as wide and varied a base as possible. Since each investment banking firm has a different client base, the entrepreneur should compare client bases of possible managing underwriters. Is the client base strongly institutional or individual investors? Or is it balanced between the two? Is the base more internationally or domestically oriented? Are the investors long term or speculators? What is the geographic distribution—local, regional, or nationwide? A strong managing underwriter and syndicate with a quality client base will help the stock sell and perform well in the aftermarket.

Some underwriters are better able than others to provide financial advisory services. Although this factor is not as important as the previous two in selecting an underwriter, financial counsel is frequently needed before and after the IPO. An entrepreneur should pose such questions as the following: Can the underwriter provide sound financial advice? Has the underwriter given good financial counsel to previous clients? Can the underwriter render assistance in obtaining future public or private financing? The answers to these questions will indicate the degree of ability among prospective underwriters.

As reflected in the previous questions, the experience of the investment banking firm is important. The firm should have experience in underwriting issues of companies in the same or at least similar industries. This experience will give the managing underwriter credibility, the capability to explain the company to the investing public, and the ability to price the IPO accurately.

The final factor to be considered in the choice of a managing underwriter is cost. Going public is a very costly proposition, and costs vary greatly among underwriters. The average gross spread as a percentage of the offering between underwriters can be as high as 10 percent. Costs associated with various possible managing underwriters must be carefully weighed against the other four factors. The key is to obtain the best possible underwriter and not try to cut corners, given the stakes involved in a successful initial public offering.

REGISTRATION STATEMENT AND TIMETABLE

Once the managing underwriter has been selected, a planning meeting should be held of company officials responsible for preparing the registration statement, the company's independent accountants and lawyers, and the underwriters and their counsel. At this important meeting, frequently called the "all hands" meeting, a timetable is prepared that indicates dates for each step in the registration process. This timetable establishes the effective date of the registration, which determines the date of the final financial statements to be included. The company's end of the year, when regular audited financial statements are routinely prepared, is taken into account to avoid any possible extra accounting and legal work. The timetable should indicate the individual responsible for preparing the various parts of the registration and offering statement. Problems often arise in an initial public offering due to the timetable not being carefully developed and agreed to by all parties involved.

After the completion of the preliminary preparation, the first public offering normally requires six to eight weeks to prepare, print, and file the registration statement with the SEC. Once the registration statement has been filed, the SEC generally takes four to eight weeks to declare the registration effective. Delays frequently occur in this process, especially (1) during the heavy periods of market activity; (2) during peak seasons such as March, when the SEC is reviewing a large number of proxy statements; (3) when the company's attorney is not familiar with federal or state regulations; (4) when a complete and full disclosure is resisted by the company; or (5) when the managing underwriter is inexperienced.

In reviewing the registration statement, the SEC attempts to ensure that the document makes a *full and fair disclosure* of the material reported. The SEC has no authority to withhold approval of or require any changes in the terms of an offering that it deems unfair or inequitable, so long as all material information concerning the company and the offering is fully disclosed. The National Association of Securities Dealers (NASD) will review each offering, principally to determine the fairness of the underwriting compensation and its compliance with NASD bylaw requirements.

full and fair disclosure The nature of all material submitted to the SEC for approval

Although certain states will review an application for registration in the same manner as the SEC (i.e., solely concerned with full and fair disclosure), others review it to determine whether the offering is "fair, just, and equitable" to the investors in its state. States have the authority to reject an offering on the basis of the perceived merits. Some of the matters state examiners focus on most frequently include the following: the percentage of ownership retained by the promoters and the amount of capital invested by them for those shares (the amount of "cheap stock" outstanding); the underwriting compensation; the existence of transactions between the officers, directors, or other promoters of the enterprise and the issuer itself (i.e., loans or sales to management and other sorts of self-dealing); and the financial performance and stability of the issuer. Once the effective date has been established by the SEC, the underwriters will immediately offer the shares to the public.

An example summary of the key dates for an initial public offering for KeKaKa Corporation is given in Table 16.2. The company's fiscal year ends March 31, and audited financial statements have been prepared for each prior year of the company's existence. This year's audited financial statements are being prepared in the usual timely manner.

The registration statement itself consists primarily of two parts: the *prospectus* (a legal offering document normally prepared as a brochure or booklet for distribution

TABLE 16.2   Summary of Key Dates for KeKaKa Corporation

All hands meeting	May 15
First draft of S-1 distributed	June 15
All hands meeting	June 22
All hands meeting	July 1
Registration filing date	July 15
Public offering effective	September 8
Closing of offering	September 17

to prospective buyers) and the *registration statement* (supplemental information to the prospectus, which is available for public inspection at the office of the SEC). Both parts of the registration statement are governed principally by the Securities and Exchange Act of 1933 (the "1933 Act"), a federal statute requiring the registration of securities to be offered to the public. This act also requires that the prospectus be furnished to the purchaser at or before the making of any written offer or the actual confirmation of a sale. Specific SEC forms set forth the informational requirements for a registration. Most initial public offerings will use *Form S-1* or *Form S-18* for smaller offerings. The form to be used depends on the company's business, the amount of public information already available to the company, the type of security to be offered, the company's size and past financial performance, and, in some instances, the proposed stock purchasers.

prospectus   Document for distribution to prospective buyers of a public offering

registration statement   Materials submitted to the SEC for approval to sell stock to the public

Form S-1   Form for registration of a public offering of stock

Form S-18   Form for registration of a smaller public offering of stock

The Prospectus

The prospectus portion of the registration statement is almost always written in a highly stylized narrative form, since it is the selling document of the company. While the exact format is decided by the company, the information must be presented in an organized, logical sequence and in an easy-to-read, understandable manner in order to obtain SEC approval. Some of the most common sections of a prospectus include the cover page, prospectus summary, description of the company, risk factors, use of proceeds, dividend policy, capitalization, dilution, selected financial data, the business, management, and owners, type of stock, underwriter information, and the actual financial statements.

The cover page includes such information as company name, type and number of shares to be sold, a distribution table, date of prospectus, managing underwriter(s), and syndicate of underwriters involved. There is a preliminary prospectus and then a final prospectus once it has been approved by the SEC. The cover page of a preliminary prospectus booklet and the final prospectus for a 800,000-share offering of Xeta Corporation are shown in Tables 16.3 and 16.4, respectively. The preliminary prospectus is used by the underwriters to solicit investor interest in the offering while the registration is pending. The final prospectus contains all of the changes and additions required by the SEC and blue sky examiners and the information concerning the price at which the securities will be sold. The final prospectus must be delivered with or prior to the written confirmation of purchase orders from investors participating in the offering.

The prospectus starts with a table of contents and summary. The prospectus summary highlights the important features of the offering, similar to the executive summary of a business plan that was discussed previously.

A brief introduction of the company follows, which describes the nature of the business, the company's history, major products, and location.

Then a discussion of the risk factors involved is presented. Such issues as a history of operating losses, a short track record, the importance of certain key individuals, dependence on certain customers, significant level of competition, or lack of market uncertainty are the typical risk factors revealed to ensure that the purchaser is aware of the speculative nature of the offering and the degree of risk involved in purchasing.

The next section, use of proceeds, needs to be carefully prepared since the actual use of the proceeds must be reported to the SEC after the offering. This section is of great interest to potential purchasers as it indicates the reason(s) the company is going public and its future direction.

The dividend policy section details the company's dividend history and any restrictions on future dividends. Most entrepreneurial companies have not paid any dividends but have retained their earnings to finance future growth.

The capitalization section indicates the overall capital structure of the company both before and after the public offering.

Whenever there is significant disparity between the offering price of the shares and the price paid for shares by officers, directors, or founding stockholders, a dilution section is necessary in the prospectus. This section describes the dilution, or decrease, of the purchaser's equity interest that will occur.

Form S-1 requires that, at the end, the prospectus contain selected financial data for each of the last five years of company operation to highlight significant trends in the company's financial condition. This analysis of the results of the company's operations and their impact on the financial conditions of the company should cover at least the last three years of operation. It provides information that potential purchasers can use to assess the company's cash flow from internal and external sources.

The next section, the business, is the largest part of the prospectus. It provides information on the company, its industry, and its products, and includes the following: the historical development of the company; principal products, markets, and distribution methods; new products being developed; sources and availability of raw materials; backlog orders; export sales; number of employees; and nature of any patents, trademarks, licenses, franchises, and physical property owned.

Following the business section is a discussion of management and security holders. The section covers background information, ages, business experience, total remuneration, and stock holdings of directors, nominated directors, and executive officers. Also, any stockholder (not in the above categories) who beneficially owns more than 5 percent of the company must be indicated.

The description of the capital stock section, as the name implies, indicates the par and stated value of the stock being offered, dividend rights, voting rights, liquidity, and transferability if more than one class of stock exists.

Following this, the underwriter information section explains the plans for distributing the stock offering, such as the amount of securities to be purchased by each underwriting participant involved, the underwriters' obligations, and the indemnification of the company.

The prospectus part of the registration statement concludes with the actual financial statements. Form S-1 requires audited balance sheets for the last two fiscal years, audited income statements and statements of retained earnings for the last

TABLE 16.3   Preliminary Prospectus Dated May 1, 1987

800,000 Shares

XETA CORPORATION

Common Stock

Of the 800,000 shares of Common Stock offered hereby, 600,000 shares are being offered and sold for the account of the Company and 200,000 shares are being offered and sold for the account of the Selling Shareholders. See "Principal and Selling Shareholders." The Company will not receive any of the proceeds from the sale of shares by the Selling Shareholders.

Prior to this offering, there has been no public market for the Common Stock and there can be no assurance that such a market will develop. It is anticipated that the Common Stock will be traded in the over-the-counter market and that prices will be reported on the National Association of Securities Dealers Automated Quotation System ("NASDAQ"). The initial public offering price per share will be determined by negotiations among the Company, the Selling Shareholders and the Underwriters. It is currently estimated that the initial public offering price will be in the range of $8.00 to $10.00 per share. See "Underwriting" for a description of the factors considered in determining the public offering price of the shares.

**THESE SECURITIES INVOLVE A HIGH DEGREE OF RISK.
SEE "RISK FACTORS" and "DILUTION."**

THESE SECURITIES HAVE NOT BEEN APPROVED OR DISAPPROVED BY THE SECURITIES AND EXCHANGE COMMISSION NOR HAS THE COMMISSION PASSED UPON THE ACCURACY OR ADEQUACY OF THIS PROSPECTUS. ANY REPRESENTATION TO THE CONTRARY IS A CRIMINAL OFFENSE.

	Price to Public	Underwriting Discounts(1)	Proceeds to Company(2)	Proceeds to Selling Shareholders(2)
Per Share	$	$	$	$
Total(3)	$	$	$	$

(1) See "Underwriting" for information concerning indemnification and other arrangements with the Representative and the several Underwriters.

(2) Before deducting expenses estimated at $_____, of which $_____ will be paid by the Company and $_____ will be paid by the Selling Shareholders.

(3) Certain of the Selling Shareholders have granted to the Underwriters the right to purchase, within 30 days after the date of this Prospectus, up to 120,000 additional shares of Common Stock at the initial public offering price, less the underwriting discount, to cover over-allotments, if any. If such additional shares are purchased by the Underwriters, the total Price to Public, Underwriting Discounts and Proceeds to Selling Shareholders will be $_____, $_____ and $_____, respectively. See "Underwriting."

The Common Stock is offered by the several Underwriters named herein, subject to prior sale, when, as and if delivered to and accepted by the Underwriters, subject to the right to reject orders in whole or in part and subject to certain other conditions. It is expected that certificates for the Common Stock will be available for delivery on or about June ___, 1987, at the offices of Eppler, Guerin & Turner, Inc., Dallas, Texas, or through the facilities of The Depository Trust Company, New York, New York.

Eppler, Guerin & Turner, Inc.

The date of this Prospectus is May ___ 1987.

TABLE 16.4 Final Prospectus

800,000 Shares

Common Stock

Of the 800,000 shares of Common Stock offered hereby, 600,000 shares are being offered and sold for the account of the Company and 200,000 shares are being offered and sold for the account of the Selling Shareholders. See "Principal and Selling Shareholders." The Company will not receive any of the proceeds from the sale of shares by the Selling Shareholders.

Prior to this offering, there has been no public market for the Common Stock and there can be no assurance that such a market will develop. See "Underwriting" for a description of the factors considered in determining the public offering price of the shares.

**THESE SECURITIES INVOLVE A HIGH DEGREE OF RISK.
SEE "RISK FACTORS" and "DILUTION."**

**THESE SECURITIES HAVE NOT BEEN APPROVED OR DISAPPROVED BY THE
SECURITIES AND EXCHANGE COMMISSION NOR HAS THE COMMISSION
PASSED UPON THE ACCURACY OR ADEQUACY OF THIS PROSPECTUS.
ANY REPRESENTATION TO THE CONTRARY IS A CRIMINAL OFFENSE.**

	Price to Public	Underwriting Discounts(1)	Proceeds to Company(2)	Proceeds to Selling Shareholders(2)
Per Share	$7.00	$0.56	$6.44	$6.44
Total(3)	$5,600,000	$448,000	$3,864,000	$1,288,000

(1) See "Underwriting" for information concerning indemnification and other arrangements with the Representative and the several Underwriters.

(2) Before deducting expenses estimated at $530,000, of which $450,000 will be paid by the Company and $80,000 will be paid by the Selling Shareholders.

(3) Certain of the Selling Shareholders have granted to the Underwriters the right to purchase, within 30 days after the date of this Prospectus, up to 120,000 additional shares of Common Stock at the initial public offering price, less the underwriting discount, to cover over-allotments, if any. If such additional shares are purchased by the Underwriters, the total Price to Public, Underwriting Discounts and Proceeds to Selling Shareholders will be $6,440,000, $515,200 and $2,060,800, respectively. See "Underwriting."

The Common Stock is offered by the several Underwriters named herein, subject to prior sale, when, as and if delivered to and accepted by the Underwriters, subject to the right to reject orders in whole or in part and subject to certain other conditions. It is expected that certificates for the Common Stock will be available for delivery on or about June 24, 1987, at the offices of Eppler, Guerin & Turner, Inc., Dallas, Texas, or through the facilities of The Depository Trust Company, New York, New York.

Eppler, Guerin & Turner, Inc.

June 17, 1987

three fiscal years, and unaudited interim financial statements as of 135 days prior to the date when the registration statement becomes effective. It is this requirement that makes it so important to pick a date for going public in light of year-end operations and to develop a good timetable. This will help avoid the time and costs of preparing additional interim statements.

Part II

This section of Form S-1 contains specific documentation of the issue in an answer format and exhibits such things as the articles of incorporation, the underwriting agreements, company bylaws, stock option and pension plans, and contracts. Other items presented include indemnification of directors and officers, any sale of unregistered securities within the past three years, and expenses related to going public.

Form S-18

In April 1979, the SEC adopted a simplified form of the registration statement, Form S-18, for companies planning to register no more than $7.5 million of securities. This form was designed to make going public easier and less expensive by having less-extensive reporting requirements. Form S-18 differs from Form S-1 in the following respects: It requires less detailed description of the business, officers, directors, and legal proceedings; it requires no industry segment information; it allows financial statements to be prepared in accordance with generally accepted accounting practices rather than under the guidelines of Regulation S-X; and it requires an audited balance sheet at the end of the last fiscal year (rather than the last two years) and audited change in financial positions and stockholders' equity for the last two years (rather than the last three years). Although Form S-18 can be filed for review with the SEC's Division of Corporation Finance in Washington, DC, as are all S-1 forms, it can also be filed with the SEC's regional office.

Procedure

red herring   Preliminary prospectus of a potential public offering

deficiency letter   A letter from the SEC to a company indicating corrections that need to be made in the submitted prospectus

pricing amendment   Additional information on price and distribution submitted to the SEC to develop the final prospectus

Once the preliminary prospectus is filed, it can be distributed to the underwriting group. This preliminary prospectus is called a *red herring*, because a statement printed in red ink appears on the front cover. The red herring for Xeta Corporation is shown in Table 16.3. The registration statements are then reviewed by the SEC to determine if adequate disclosures have been made. Some deficiencies are almost always found and are communicated to the company via either telephone or a *deficiency letter*. This preliminary prospectus contains all the information that will appear in the final prospectus except that which is not known until shortly before the effective date: offering price, underwriters' commission, and amount of proceeds. These items are filed through a *pricing amendment* and appear in the final prospectus (see Table 16.4). To see the difference between a red herring and a final prospectus, compare Tables 16.3 and 16.4. The time, usually around a month between the initial filing of the registration statement and its effective date, is called the waiting period, during which the underwriting syndicate is formed and briefed, and no company publicity can occur.

Since going public Xeta Corporation has expanded into two divisions (the commercial sales division and the lodging division), developed a vision to become the nation's premier source for data integration, and changed its name to Xeta Technologies to better reflect the new vision. After not increasing for a period of time, in fact decreasing, the stock split 2 for 1 and was trading in the $40 to $50 price range in March 2000.

LEGAL ISSUES AND BLUE SKY QUALIFICATIONS

Legal Issues

In addition to all the legal issues surrounding the actual preparation and filing of the prospectus, there are several other important legal concerns. Perhaps the one that is of the most concern to the entrepreneur is the *quiet period*, the period of time from when the decision to go public is made to 90 days following the date the prospectus becomes effective. Care must be taken during this period regarding any new information about the company or key personnel. Any publicity effort creating a favorable attitude about the securities to be offered is illegal. The guidelines established by the SEC regarding the information that can and cannot be released should be understood not only by the entrepreneur but by everyone in the company as well. All press releases and other printed material should be cleared with the attorneys involved as well as the underwriter. The entrepreneur and key personnel must curtail speaking engagements and television appearances to avoid any possible problematic response to interviewer or audience questions. One entrepreneur whose company was in the process of going public had to postpone a TV guest appearance on the "Today Show," where she was to discuss women entrepreneurs, not her company.

quiet period   90-day period in going public when no new company information can be released

Blue Sky Qualifications

The securities of the company going public must also be qualified under the *blue sky laws* of each state in which the securities will be offered. This is true unless the state has an exemption from the qualification requirements. These blue sky laws cause additional delays and costs to the company going public. Many states allow their state securities administrators to prevent the offering from being sold in their state on such substantive grounds as past stock issuances, too much dilution, or too much compensation to the underwriter, even though all required disclosures have been met and clearance has been granted by the SEC.

blue sky laws   Laws of each state regulating public sale of stock

It is the responsibility of the managing underwriter to determine the states and the number of securities that will be sold in each. The number of securities to be qualified in each state and the offering price are important, since the blue sky laws and qualification fees in many states vary according to the number and price. Only after the company has qualified in a particular state and the overall registration statement has been cleared by the SEC can the underwriters sell the number of shares that have been allowed in that particular state. Most states require the company to file sales reports following the offering so that the number of sales in the state can be determined and any additional fees assessed if necessary.

AFTER GOING PUBLIC

aftermarket support   Actions of underwriters to help support the price of stock following the public offering

After the initial public offering has been sold, there are still some areas of concern to the entrepreneur. These include *aftermarket support*, relationship with the financial community, and reporting requirements.

Aftermarket Support

Once issued, the price of the stock should be monitored, particularly in the initial weeks after its offering. Usually the managing underwriting firm will be the principal market maker in the company's stock and will be ready to purchase or sell stock in the interdealer market. To stabilize the market, preventing the price from going below the initial public offering price, the underwriter will usually enter bids to buy the stock in the early stages after the offers, therefore giving aftermarket support. This support is important in allowing the stock not to be adversely affected by an initial drop in price.

Relationship with the Financial Community

Once a company has gone public, the financial community usually takes a greater interest. An entrepreneur will need an increasing portion of time to develop a good relationship with this community. The relationship established has a significant effect on the market interest and the price of the company's stock. Since many investors rely on analysts and brokers for investment advice, the entrepreneur should attempt to meet as many of these individuals as possible. Regular appearances before societies of security analysts should be a part of establishing this relationship, as well as public disclosures through formal press releases. Frequently, it is best to designate one person in the company to be the information officer, ensuring that the press, public, and security analysts are dealt with in a friendly, efficient manner. There is nothing worse than a company not responding in a timely manner to information requests.

Reporting Requirements

One of the negative aspects of going public is the formal reporting requirements. One of the first requirements is the filing of a Form SR sales report, which the company must do within 10 days after the end of the first three-month period following the effective date of the registration. This report includes information on the amount of securities sold and still to be sold, and the proceeds obtained by the company and their use. A final Form SR sales report must be filed within 10 days of the completion or termination of the offering.

The company must file annual reports on Form 10-K, quarterly reports on Form 10-Q, and specific transaction reports on Form 8-K. The information in Form 10-K on the business, management, and company assets is similar to that in Form S-1 of the registration statement. Of course, audited financial statements are required.

The quarterly report on Form 10-Q primarily contains the unaudited financial information for the most recently completed fiscal quarter. No 10-Q is required for the fourth fiscal quarter.

A Form 8-K report must be filed within 15 days of such events as the acquisition or disposition of significant assets by the company outside the ordinary course of the business, the resignation or dismissal of the company's independent public accountants, or a change in control of the company.

The company must follow the proxy solicitation requirements regarding holding a meeting or obtain the written consent of security holders. The timing and type of materials involved are detailed in the Securities and Exchange Act of 1933. These are but a few of the reporting requirements of public companies. All the requirements must be carefully observed, since even inadvertent mistakes can have negative consequences on the company. The reports required must be filed on time.

MYTHS CONCERNING GOING PUBLIC

In spite of the available advice and the numerous entrepreneurial companies going public, there are still some myths about the process. The eight most commonly discussed myths are indicated in Table 16.5.[2] Each of these eight myths deals with an important issue for an entrepreneur in taking his or her venture public. Even though most IPOs occur with companies in such areas as medical, technical, and computer technologies, companies in more mundane industries, or in retail, can also go public. Borders Group, Baley Superstores, and Sunglass Hut International—three retail groups that deal primarily in books, baking items, and sunglasses, respectively—have each had successful public offerings in recent years.

Myths 2 and 3 deal with two important areas in going public. The entrepreneur should be concerned about the aftermarket, particularly the first six to nine months after the IPO, since any small disappointing news concerning performance can radically affect the price of the stock. This was the case for Diamond Multimedia's stock, which dropped from $26 per share to $16 per share nine months after the issuance upon a reported 40¢ fourth-quarter earnings versus the 42¢ to 45¢ expected. Similarly, an entrepreneur should recognize that with the large IPO market, market analysts for his or her company can easily lose interest and stop following the stock. Just because the underwriting team took the company public does not ensure continuous coverage, particularly if the company has poor results or is in an industry field that is no longer popular.

Myths 4 and 7 deal with the attention paid to your entrepreneurial company. In going public, an entrepreneur should realize that he or she is at the bottom of the pyramid, with institutional investors, underwriters and investment bankers, and venture capitalists being higher up. Similarly, young entrepreneurial companies are not always the spotlight companies in the IPO market. In 1995 and 1996, the hottest segment of the IPO market consisted of spin-offs from major corporations.

The entrepreneur should also be wary of Myths 5 and 6, which deal with valuation and profitability. With the significant amount of investment money available, particularly in mutual funds, there is a high demand and valuation, even for companies suffering losses. The most publicized example is Netscape Communications, the maker of software for the World Wide Web, which went public with operating losses of $4.6 million in the two previous quarters. In spite of the losses, Netscape was highly valued and increased in price fivefold in four months after the IPO. Although

TABLE 16.5 Eight Myths about Going Public	
Myth #1	In this market, high-tech is the name of the game.
Myth #2	If you're doing OK, don't worry about the aftermarket.
Myth #3	The analysts will follow you through thick and thin.
Myth #4	The young entrepreneurial companies will continue to be in the spotlight this year.
Myth #5	You need to be profitable to get a high valuation in this market.
Myth #6	Of course, you want to be the next Netscape.
Myth #7	During your IPO, you're the center of attention.
Myth #8	Somebody knows where the IPO market is headed.

Source: Mamis, Robert A., "No Tech, No Takers," *Inc.* (May 1996), pp. 45–49. Reprinted with permission. Copyright (1996) by Goldhirsh Group, Inc., 38 Commercial Wharf, Boston, MA 02110.

this sounds appealing, entrepreneurs should try to avoid this scenario, not emulate it, as sometimes a company has to have positive operating results and stock price increases commensurate with company performance.

Finally, when going public, the entrepreneur should remember that no one knows where the overall stock market and the IPO market are heading. If the company is ready and the market appears good, the company should proceed with the issuance of the IPO without regard to any tales or myths concerning the future.

IN REVIEW

Summary

Going public—the transformation of a closely held corporation to one where the general public has proprietary interest—is indeed arduous. An entrepreneur must carefully assess whether the company is ready to go public as well as whether the advantages outweigh the disadvantages of doing so. In assessing readiness, the entrepreneur must take into account the size of the company, its earnings and performance, market conditions, urgency of monetary need, and the desires of the current owners. The entrepreneur needs to consider the primary advantages of going public—including new capital, liquidity and valuation, enhanced ability to obtain funds, and prestige—along with the disadvantages of expense, disclosure of information, loss of control, and pressure to maintain growth.

Once the decision is made to proceed, a managing investment banking firm must be selected and the registration statement prepared. The expertise of the investment banker is a major factor in the success of the public offering. In selecting an investment banker, the entrepreneur should consider reputation, distribution capability, advisory services, experience, and cost. To prepare for the registration date, the entrepreneur must organize an "all hands" meeting of company officials, the company's independent accountants and lawyers, and the underwriters and their counsel. A timetable must be established for the effective date of registration and for the preparation of necessary financial documents, including the preliminary and final prospectus. After the registration and review of the SEC, the entrepreneur must carefully observe the 90-day quiet period and qualify under the blue sky laws of each state in which the securities will be offered.

After the initial public offering, the entrepreneur needs to maintain a good relationship with the financial community and to adhere strictly to the reported requirements of public companies. The decision to go public requires much planning and consideration. Going public, indeed, is not for every entrepreneurial venture.

Questions for Discussion

1. Explain the major reasons you might not wish to go public, even if your entrepreneurial venture met the general criteria for a public offering. If possible, give examples.
2. Why is going public often the best way to increase the growth of a successful privately held company?
3. You have decided to go public with your company, and you need to choose an investment banker. Three possibilities have been suggested by your board of di-

rectors. Firm A has the best reputation and overall experience but also has the highest cost. Firm B has excellent distribution capability but has not handled any companies similar to yours. Firm C has the lowest cost but is unlikely to distribute beyond the local area. Explain your choice of A, B, or C, and discuss under what circumstances you might choose the others.

4. In preparing a prospectus for the SEC, how would you use the help of management staff in areas other than accounting and finance?

5. Why do you think the SEC imposes a quiet period on companies that have decided to go public?

Key Terms

aftermarket support	liquidation covenant
blue sky laws	managing underwriter
deficiency letter	pricing amendment
direct public offering (DPO)	prospectus
Form S-1	quiet period
Form S-18	red herring
full and fair disclosure	registration statement
going public	restrictive covenant
initial public offering (IPO)	underwriting syndicate

More Information—Net Addresses in This Chapter

JCPenney
www.jcpenney.com

National Association of Securities Dealers, Inc. (NASD)
www.nasdr.com

Netscape Communications
www.netscape.com

Securities and Exchange Commission (SEC)
www.sec.gov

Wal-Mart
www.wal-mart.com

Xeta Corporation
www.xeta.com

Selected Readings

Andrews, Alice O.; and Theresa M. Welborne. (2000). The People/Performance Balance in IPO Firms: The Effect of the Chief Executive Officer's Financial Orientation. *Entrepreneurship Theory & Practice*, vol. 25, no. 1, pp. 93–106.

This study examines how CEO's functional background may influence the firm's choice between maximizing short-term financial performance (doing well at the IPO) or long-term performance (maximizing HR value).

Bruton, Garry D.; and Dev Prasad. (1997). Strategy and IPO Market Selection: Implications for the Entrepreneurial Firm. *Journal of Small Business Management*, vol. 35, no. 4, pp. 1–10.

This study finds that the impact of underpricing is greater on the National Association of Security Dealer's Automated Quotation (NASDAQ) system than on the New York Stock Exchange (NYSE). Additionally, the average offering price for IPOs on the NASDAQ is significantly lower than the average offering price for IPOs on the NYSE. It is suggested that small firms weigh the benefits for earlier cash through an IPO on the NASDAQ against the benefits from the higher price and the lower underpricing on the NYSE.

Chishty, Muhammad R. K.; Iftekhar Hasan; and Steven D. Smith. (1996). A Note on Underwriter Competition and Initial Public Offerings. *Journal of Business Finance and Accounting*, vol. 32, no. 5, pp. 905–14.

Investigating the short-term underpricing behavior of IPOs during the 1979–1984 period, a paper reports that actual or potential competition among underwriters provides at least as much explanatory power as the more standard reputation variable in determining the price run-ups in the postissue trading. The paper also provides evidence that the total cost to the issuer is in fact lower when larger issues are put into the market. However, these savings are not reflected, on average, in the IPO returns. Rather, they are reflected in lower underwriter compensation when measured on a per dollar basis.

Chua, Lena. (1996). A Reexamination of the Costs of Firm Commitment and Best Efforts IPOs. *Financial Review*, vol. 30, no. 2, pp. 337–65.

Two component costs of going public are analyzed: underpricing and underwriter compensation. The model, based on a disagreement about firm value between the underwriters and issuers, shows that underpricing is higher for firms using best efforts contracts as these firms, on average, are more speculative. Underwriter compensation is hypothesized to be higher for firms using best efforts contracts because of the high costs of market making for these firms in the aftermarket and the high distribution costs associated with the high risk of a failed offer. Empirical tests strongly support the propositions.

Cyr, Linda A.; Diane E. Johnson; and Theresa M. Welbourne. (2000). Human Resources in Initial Public Offering Firms: Do Venture Capitalists Make a Differernce? *Entrepreneurship Theory & Practice*, vol. 25, no. 1, pp. 79–91.

This paper tests whether or not venture capitalists backing affects the likelihood that initial public offering firms will report having a vice president of human resources. It also examines the combined effect on performance as a result of being venture capital–backed and having a vice president of human resources.

Deeds, David L.; Dona Decarolis; and Joseph E. Coombs. (1997). The Impact of Firm-Specific Capabilities on the Amount of Capital Raised in an Initial Public Offering: Evidence from the Biotechnology Industry. *Journal of Business Venturing*, vol. 12, no. 1, pp. 31–46.

A model of the total amount of capital raised by a firm through an initial public offering (IPO) tested on a sample of 92 biotechnology IPOs. Findings indicate strong support for the hypothesized positive relationship between the total amount of capital raised by a firm's IPO and the scientific capabilities of the firm.

Evanson, David R. (1996). Tales of Caution in Going Public. *Nation's Business*, vol. 84, no. 6, pp. 57–59.

An initial public offering (IPO) is the ultimate statement of entrepreneurial success. However, most companies that start the process never finish. Even so, the lessons learned along the way are often worth the aggravation and expense. The stories of three small firms—Rom Tech, Kwik Goal, and Best Programs, Inc.—that started the IPO process within the past few years and experienced its ups and downs are presented.

Kanzler, Ford. (1996). Poised for Public Offering? Start Your Public Relations Efforts Now. *Public Relations Quarterly*, vol. 41, no. 2, pp. 23–24.

A successful public offering depends as much upon the preparation of messages and communications as the financial statements themselves. These preparations should begin no later than one year before the public offering, but 18 months is not too early. Raising your communications to the maximum level will create increased awareness for the company and allow you to continue a high level of communications once you file the initial public offering with the SEC. After an IPO, a company's greatest challenge will be to maintain its level of communication to keep stock prices up and interest in the company active.

Kim, Juseong. (1999). The Relaxation of Financing Constraints by the Initial Public Offering of Small Manufacturing Firms. *Small Business Economics*, vol. 12, no. 3, pp. 191–202.

This study examines the effect of financing constraints on the investment by comparing the financial behavior of Korean firms before and after their stocks are newly listed on a stock exchange. Findings indicate that the sensitivity of investment to cash flow will be higher during the period before initial public offering (IPO) than after IPO. The effect of financing constraints relaxation by IPO is more prominent in large manufacturing firms.

Michaely, Roni; and Wayne H. Shaw. (1996). The Choice of Going Public: Spin-Offs vs. Carve-Outs. *Financial Management*, vol. 24, no. 3, pp. 5–21.

A study analyzes how firms choose between a spin-off and an equity carve-out as a way to divest assets. Using a sample of 91 master limited partnerships that were issued to the public, it is found that riskier, more leveraged, less-profitable firms choose to divest through a spin-off. This suggests that the choice is affected by a firm's access to the capital market. Greater scrutiny and more stringent disclosure are required in carve-outs relative to spin-offs. Two hypotheses—that management attempts to leave undervalued assets in the hands of current shareholders, and that parent organizations' need for cash is the driving motive behind the divestiture choice—are not supported.

Roell, Ailsa. (1996). The Decision to Go Public: An Overview. *European Economic Review*, vol. 40, no. 3–5, pp. 1071–81.

Firms' motives for going public are reviewed, and significant cross-country differences in the propensity to seek a listing are documented and discussed. One of the most striking contrasts among the financial systems of major developed economies is the differences in the propensity of firms to use publicly traded forms of finance. The importance of listed equity as a form of finance varies enormously, ranging from 17 percent of GDP in Italy to 125 percent in Switzerland.

Welbourne, Theresa M.; and Alice O. Andrews. (1996). Predicting the Performance of Initial Public Offerings: Should Human Resource Management Be in the Equation? *Academy of Management Journal*, vol. 39, no. 4, pp. 891–919.

Population ecology is used to explain the role of HR management in enhancing the performance of initial public offering companies. The determinants of structural inertia were examined, and hypotheses on the relationship between HRM and organizational performance were developed. The results indicate that two HR resource variables—HR value and organization-based rewards—predict initial investor reaction and long-term survival. The rewards variable negatively affects initial performance but positively affects survival.

Zeprun, Howard S.; and Adele C. Freedman. (May 1996). Raising Capital in the U.S. *International Financial Law Review 1995, Legal Guide to California*, pp. 23–28.

The U.S. public capital markets are the largest, most flexible, and most attractive sources of capital to companies attempting to raise money through the sale of equity or debt securities. Companies considering an IPO can benefit from an understanding of the basic market dynamics, investor expectations, the public offering process, and requirements imposed on public corporations after the offering, as well as the corresponding implications for corporate grievance, financial reporting, internal information systems, investor relations, corporate culture, and management. A discussion examines these issues that should be considered when determining whether or not to undertake an IPO.

Endnotes

1. For the full details of this story, see John Kerr, "The 100-Day Makeover," *Inc.* (May 1996), pp. 54–63.
2. For a discussion of each of these myths with examples, see Robert A. Mamis, "No Tech, No Takers," *Inc.* (May 1996), pp. 45–49.

17

Ending the Venture

ʃ❧

LEARNING OBJECTIVES

1. To illustrate differences in alternative types of bankruptcy under the Bankruptcy Act of 1978 (amended in 1984).

2. To illustrate rights of creditors and entrepreneurs in different cases of bankruptcy.

3. To provide the entrepreneur with an understanding of the typical warning signs of bankruptcy.

4. To illustrate how some entrepreneurs can turn bankruptcy into a successful business.

5. To examine the options in providing for the succession of a business to family or nonfamily members.

BETH BLOOM

Bankruptcy is something that entrepreneurs usually fear but also rarely understand. There is no easy way to avoid it, but there are certain strategies, discussed throughout this book, that an entrepreneur can develop to minimize its occurrence. Since it is misunderstood, it is important as part of any entrepreneurial text to identify what bankruptcy is and how it can in some instances actually help an entrepreneur turn a business around.

Beth Bloom is a perfect example of an entrepreneur who found herself mired in a Chapter 11 bankruptcy that actually had a favorable ending.[1] In 1985 Beth quit her job to join her fiancé, Drexel Wright, who was the founder of Quaker Siding Co., a rapidly growing contracting business that had achieved sales of $1 million in 1984. During this banner year, Drexel had initiated a rapid-growth strategy, which included diversification into new construction, doubling the staff to 32 employees, and initiating an extensive training program. However, by this time Quaker was having obvious problems. The company was generating a great deal of business and sales volume, but no profits. The resources that were needed to initiate the new strategy had raised overhead to a point where the company was losing money despite the growth in new business. The situation had gone too far and worsened before Beth could truly understand what was occurring.

Upon assessing the situation, she found that accounts payable were averaging over 120 days. The cash position was a disaster, and creditors were calling, wanting to know why they hadn't been paid. Some even threatened legal action if their money was not received immediately. Drexel tried to pacify the creditors, further delaying payments, so that he could continue to pay his employees. He even stopped making tax deposits in order to have funds available to handle immediate cash needs. He soon found that he owed more than $75,000 in back taxes. The stress level became unbelievable.

Beth's first decision was to cut the staff from 32 to 25. This was difficult because many of these employees were Drexel's good friends. However, there was no choice since the business was out of control. In addition to the above problems, Beth found that financial statements were poorly prepared and often inaccurate and the checking account overdrawn. A new accountant was hired, but it took some time before a more effective system could be comfortably in place.

Beth then began to seek assistance from a bankruptcy lawyer, a local university, and SCORE (senior core of retired executives). She searched the literature for information to try to find solutions to the company's problems. The choices were beginning to become more obvious, particularly with the largest creditor, the Internal Revenue Service, which was unwilling to negotiate any type of payment plan. The threat of a seizure of the company's assets seemed quite possible, so Beth quickly began to consider the options of bankruptcy. Bankruptcy, although it had a stigma of failure, seemed to be the only way to get immediate relief from creditors. In fact, once the documents are filed with the court, all collection efforts and legal actions are ended.

One lawyer recommended liquidation, or a Chapter 7 bankruptcy, which would allow the company to reopen after an agreement was made to sell some of the assets to pay off creditors. Beth dismissed this option, and on August 7, 1987, opted for a Chapter 11 bankruptcy, which would allow the company to reorganize its debt and prepare a plan with the approval of the court and the company's creditors.

The responsibility of Beth and Drexel, at this point, was to get the business back to basics and to turn a profit. With all debt frozen, the phones stopped ringing, allowing Beth and Drexel the time to begin a new plan to revitalize the company. More employees were cut and procedures for accounts receivable collection and inventory control were improved. Although some suppliers stopped doing business with Quaker, many stayed with them since they were now paying them C.O.D. Customers also supported them and agreed to the new payment plan of 30 percent upon signing a contract, 30 percent upon work commencement, 30 percent upon half completion, and the final 10 percent at full completion of the project. This payment program, although new for Quaker, reflected industry standards. This program hastened cash flow and enhanced Quaker's ability to pay off its creditors. In the past the company was collecting only 30 percent up front, but the remaining 70 percent was not being paid until the work was completed.

Each month Beth prepared financial statements for the court to let them know that the company was on a favorable path and to protect the company from a Chapter 7 liquidation. Beth and Drexel also reverted to a strategy of renovation business only and dropped any attempt to penetrate the new construction market. This was in keeping with the company's history and distinctive competency.

Gradually the company began to make a profit. In 1987 Quaker turned a $21,000 profit on sales of $537,000. By 1988 net profit margins increased by almost 13 percent, and net income reached $66,000 on sales of $514,000. However, the company's debt of more than $400,000 was going to need more than the small profits being generated, so Beth began to pursue a bank loan using existing company assets (land and building) as collateral. Finding a bank willing to make this loan took about a year of negotiating and many presentations of their new plan. Finally, they received a loan of $150,000, which was used to pay off the Internal Revenue Service and some of the other large creditors. By 1993 the company was making the last payments of the bank loan and had reduced the outstanding debt to $30,000. The company had made it back and would soon be out of its Chapter 11 bankruptcy status.

Many ventures are not able to survive bankruptcy, yet Quaker Siding's experience suggests that with hard work and an understanding of the bankruptcy system, bankruptcy can be an opportunity to revitalize the business.

This chapter provides a background of the various options available to entrepreneurs should bankruptcy be necessary. It also provides a discussion of some of the major causes of bankruptcy and what the entrepreneur can do to minimize its occurrence.

BANKRUPTCY—AN OVERVIEW

Failure is not uncommon in many new ventures. According to the Small Business Administration, about half of all new start-ups fail in their first years. The failures are personally painful for the entrepreneur and too often could have been prevented by paying more attention to certain critical factors in the business operation. Figure 17.1 compares business and nonbusiness bankruptcy filings from 1989 to 1998. These filings can be divided by type of bankruptcy (chapter filings), which is discussed later in this chapter. Unfortunately, it is sometimes difficult to separate the personal from business filings because many of the personal filings may be sole proprietorships. However, it can be seen from Figure 17.1 that the number of total filings has increased to a high of more than 1.4 million in 1998. The majority of these, however, are nonbusiness filings. Business bankruptcy filings have actually declined in this period from a high of more than 70,000 in 1992 to a total of a little more than 44,000 in 1998. In 1998 California had the highest number of business filings with 8,546. Texas and New York recorded 2,696 and 2,279 business filings, respectively, for 1998. For the first three quarters of 1999 there were only 8,986 business filings, indicating a further decline in this area. It is difficult to separate the chapter filings because they are all combined in published data. However, the most common type is Chapter 7 (liquidation), which accounts for about 94 percent of the total. Chapter 11 filings have declined from a high of 23,989 in 1991 to only 8,386 in 1998. This

FIGURE 17.1 Total Bankruptcy Filings 1987–1996

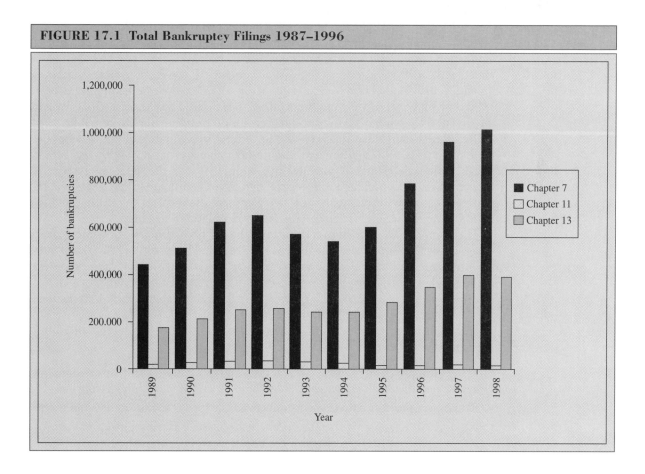

dramatic decline, however, is offset by the large increase in Chapter 7, or liquidation, bankruptcy. This may be indicative of the fact that businesses and individuals are not able to turn a situation around and hence select Chapter 7 (liquidation) bankruptcy.[2]

Bankruptcy is a term heard too often among entrepreneurs, yet it doesn't always end the ambitions of an entrepreneur or have to result in the end of the business in question. Experiences of entrepreneurs regarding the results of bankruptcy vary from situation to situation, as the following examples illustrate. Bill Lewis, founder and CEO of Federal Refunds, Inc., has filed bankruptcy twice. He now has launched a new company that assists buyers of petroleum products in recovering funds on overbilled accounts. Thus far he has not made the same mistakes he made in his earlier endeavors, and his new business has remained profitable.[3]

Eric Bruce Sr., founder of TriLogic Corporation, a computer hardware sales and networking integrator, had a series of bad breaks that led to bankruptcy. A big client ran into financial difficulty, and one of his managers left to start his own business taking other key employees with him. In addition, the federal government, which accounted for two-thirds of sales, temporarily shut down, and he could not get payment of work completed, which created a cash flow crisis. Undaunted Bruce reduced overhead (closed a few offices) and broadened his customer base by expanding his services to include setting up computer networks. The company is now out of bankruptcy and expects $100 million in sales.

Bob Farentinos had a different experience when in 1995, after the venture's first year, investors bailed out of his shoe manufacturing business, Deja Inc., because they were not satisfied with the return on investment. Farentinos saved his reputation with his creditors by selling all of the remaining assets and the name as part of a complete liquidation of the company and returning 80¢ on every dollar that he owed. He then joined with Julie Lewis to form a new shoe company, Deep E. They recently teamed up with actor Woody Harrelson to manufacture shoes made from hemp products. In 1997 they sold only 6,000 pairs, but in 1998 they booked 4,000 pairs of one style in the first quarter, moving them to secure permission from the SEC to go public.[4]

Tom Butler found that it is very easy to go from being on top of the world to being bankrupt. In 1992 he founded Q-entertainment after acquiring the Asian and North American rights to manufacture and distribute the laser-tag system of Dublin's LeisureCorp. The business grew significantly in the next few years encompassing more than 300 franchises on five continents. Franchises were being sold for $500,000, and in 1996 his venture reached $48 million in revenues.

The company went public, and Butler believed he had made it. Unfortunately things changed dramatically and quickly. He expanded by investing heavily in a family entertainment center in Mesquite, Texas. The large facility housed laser tag, bowling, and video games. However, the location prohibited the sale of liquor, which was an important service to make this profitable. A short time later in early 1998 he filed for Chapter 7 (liquidation) bankruptcy.[5]

Some lessons that can be learned from those who have experienced bankruptcy are as follows:[6]

- Many entrepreneurs spend too much time and effort trying to diversify in markets where they lack knowledge. They should focus only on known markets.
- Bankruptcy protects entrepreneurs only from the creditors, not from competitors.
- It's difficult to separate the entrepreneur from the business. Entrepreneurs put everything into the company, including worrying about the future of their employees.

- Many entrepreneurs do not think their business is going to fail until it's too late. They should file early.
- Bankruptcy is emotionally painful. Going into hiding after bankruptcy is a big mistake. Bankruptcy needs to be shared with employees and everybody else involved.

As the above examples indicate, bankruptcy is serious business and requires some important understanding of its applications. The Bankruptcy Act of 1978 (with amendments added in 1984) was designed to ensure a fair distribution of assets to creditors, to protect debtors from unfair depletion of assets, and to protect debtors from unfair demands by creditors. The act provides three alternative provisions for a firm near or at a position of insolvency. The three alternative positions are (1) reorganization, or *Chapter 11 bankruptcy;* (2) extended time payment, or *Chapter 13 bankruptcy;* and (3) liquidation, or *Chapter 7 bankruptcy.* All attempt to protect the troubled entrepreneur as well as provide a reasonable way to organize payments to debtors or to end the venture.

Chapter 11 bankruptcy Provides the opportunity to reorganize and make the venture more solvent

Chapter 13 bankruptcy Voluntarily allows individuals with regular income the opportunity to make extended time payments

Chapter 7 bankruptcy Requires the venture to liquidate, either voluntarily or involuntarily

CHAPTER 11—REORGANIZATION

This is the least severe alternative to bankruptcy. In this situation the courts try to give the venture time and "breathing room" to pay its debts. Usually, this situation results when a venture has cash flow problems, and creditors begin to pressure the firm with lawsuits. The entrepreneur feels that, with some time, the business can become more solvent and liquid in order to meet its debt requirements.

A major creditor, any party who has an interest, or a group of creditors will usually present the case to the court. Then a plan for reorganization will be prepared to indicate how the business will be turned around. The plan will divide the debt and ownership interests into two groups: Those who will be affected by the plan and those who will not. It will then specify whose interests will be affected and how payments will be made.

Once the plan is completed, it must be approved by the court. All bankruptcies are now handled by the U.S. Bankruptcy Court, whose powers were restructured under the Bankruptcy Amendments Act of 1984. Approval of the plan also requires that all creditors and owners agree to comply with the reorganization plan as presented to the courts. The decisions made in the reorganization plan generally reflect one or a combination of the following:[7]

1. *Extension.* This occurs when two or more of the largest creditors agree to postpone any claims. This acts as a stimulus for smaller creditors to also agree to the plan.
2. *Substitution.* If the future potential of the venture looks promising enough, it may be possible to exchange stock or something else for the existing debt.
3. *Composition Settlement.* The debt is prorated to the creditors as a settlement for any debt.

Even though only 20 to 25 percent of those firms that file for Chapter 11 bankruptcy will make it through the process, it does present an opportunity to find a cure for any business problems. Some of these problems are resolvable, and without the Chapter 11 protection even these 20 to 25 percent that file would never have the opportunity to succeed.

As Seen in *Business Week:*
MICHAEL ROBERTS: BLAZING A TELECOM TRAIL FOR BLACK AMERICANS A Strategic Switch Saved the Wireless Entrepreneur Millions— and Made Him a Role Model

In early 1998, entrepreneur Michael Roberts jumped at what looked like an opportunity to make millions. He shelled out $800,000 at a U.S. government auction as a down payment on seven wireless-phone licenses serving the St. Louis area. The balance of $7.2 million, plus interest, would be due in 10 years.

The auction was part of the government's plan to boost the minuscule minority ownership in telecommunications by selling licenses to small businesses. A great idea—in principle. But Roberts, an African American who had started two broadcast television stations, soon saw that this scheme to own a little cellular empire could kill him financially. He figured he would have to shell out $65 million more and knew that the government's good intentions had already backfired for a number of other black entrepreneurs: The huge cost of building a network had overwhelmed them. "A lot of [small] companies went into bankruptcy," he says. "Not me."

Instead, he approached Kansas City–based Sprint PCS, the deep-pocketed wireless carrier, which wanted small-business partners across the nation to help build and service the network that handles its calls. Sprint, which had never done business with a black-owned cellular operator before, was skeptical at first. But Roberts argued that he was their man: After all, he had started two successful companies in the TV business. Roberts said he would build the cell sites—the towers that direct calls from cellular phones—and market the service through his own retail outlets to college students and other rural consumers. Impressed, Sprint officials agreed to let him sell their service throughout most of Missouri, making Roberts' company Sprint's first black-owned affiliate. Roberts gave the licenses back to the government and signed with Sprint. That "sacrifice" gave him twice the territory his seven licenses had covered and the clout of a marquee name (Sprint handles all the billing and other paperwork). He also shook a $7.2 million debt load from his shoulders.

The St. Louis businessman expects Roberts Wireless Communications to reap $11 million in revenue this year. By 2002, he's banking on 35,000 subscribers and his first profits. He's one of just a handful of black entrepreneurs who have broken into the telecom business. "He's proactive and energized," says Thomas Mateer, vice president for affiliations at Sprint PCS.

How did he get here? Roberts' evolution as an entrepreneur has taken him from selling African goods at Lindenwood University in a St. Louis suburb to ownership of 25 companies. Excluding the telecom venture, their revenues are about $10 million now. Roberts now considers himself a capitalist, rather than an entrepreneur. "An entrepreneur's primary drive is to identify resources and make money for himself," he explains. A capitalist owns the tools of production and can spread the benefits where he wants to. Put another way: If Henry Ford had been black, his chain of managers probably would have been too, Roberts says. "In the information age, power will be in the hands of he or she who owns the backbone. I own a telephone company."

A few weeks ago, Roberts' trailblazing was recognized at the conference of the National Association

---

It is generally believed by experts that one of the primary reasons companies do not successfully come out of Chapter 11 bankruptcy is that they wait too long before filing for protection. In 1990, Yield House, a successful catalog/retailer of colonial-style furniture and accessories, filed for reorganization before its financial condition had become too severe. Its strategy during reorganization was to revamp the mail-order operation by eliminating some products that were not profitable, adding lower-cost household furnishings, refining the mailing list, and closing unprofitable stores. Although the price points went down, the company's mailing list was directed to more upscale consumers. This strategy allowed Yield House to come out of bankruptcy, with increased productivity and profitability.[8]

of Black Telecommunications Professionals in Washington, where he was given the Granville T. Woods award, named after the legendary black inventor who built the first transmitter and sold it to Bell Telephone Co. "He's a maverick," says Monica Huddleston, NABTP president. "Entrepreneurship is the single most important thing we can be doing."

Roberts hasn't forgotten his roots as a struggling entrepreneur in St. Louis. The Roberts Companies buy at least 40 percent of their equipment and services from businesses owned by people of color and women. "As I build out my business, I bring people along and give them the chance to grow in the information age," he explains.

Who gets left behind in the information age is no minor social or economic issue. The 1996 Telecommunications Act, which opened communications markets to competition for the first time, let small businesses compete where huge monopolies once reigned. The law—which affects wireless and wireline telephone service, cable programming, broadcast companies, and services to schools—has spurred tremendous growth in communications businesses. But minority companies, which lack access to capital and deep industry connections, have been stuck on the sidelines.

The NABTP is eagerly capitalizing on Roberts' success to encourage other African Americans to get into the telecom business as entrepreneurs, rather than pursue corporate careers. At the April 22–25 conference, Roberts spoke about his experience in the wireless industry. It struck a chord with another entrepreneur, James Brady, vice president at Telecon Ltd., a telecom products and services company in San Francisco. Brady, who spoke on careers, urged black telecom professionals to look beyond a nine-to-five job and toward creating companies—and to seek inspiration from their preindustrial African heritage. "Our ancestors did not look for jobs," says Brady. "They built institutions."

The 2,000-member NABTP also organized sessions on financing, introducing attendees to principals of small venture funds such as the Telecommunications Development Fund based in New York, which invests as much as $1 million a year in minority-owned telecom companies.

Procurement is another promising telecom entry point. Big companies are committed to spending billions of dollars for services from minority-owned businesses each year. Bell Atlantic, alone, says it will invest $1 billion in such ventures by 2000.

Roberts uses his growing financial clout to encourage the big fish among his business partners to make diversity a priority as well. After agreeing to pay $34 million to wireless gear maker Lucent Technologies to expand Roberts' Missouri territory, he demanded that the vendor employ people of color on the installation project. "My organization is about making sure we pass the benefits of success to others," he says. Surely, Granville T. Woods would have approved.

Source: "Michael Roberts: Blazing a Telecom Trail for Black Americans," *Business Week Frontier* (May 7, 1999).

Entrepreneurs have a tendency to ignore warning signs for bankruptcy and hold on until there is an emergency, such as running out of cash. Recognizing the signals may give an entrepreneur the opportunity to develop a strategy or plan, as Yield House did.

Surviving Bankruptcy

The most obvious way to survive bankruptcy is to avoid it altogether. However, since it is becoming such a common occurrence, it may be helpful for the entrepreneur to have a plan should he or she find it necessary to declare bankruptcy. Some of the suggestions for survival are listed below.[9]

- Bankruptcy can be used as a bargaining chip to allow the entrepreneur to voluntarily restructure and reorganize the venture.
- File before the venture runs out of cash or has no incoming revenue so that expenses not protected by bankruptcy can be paid.
- Don't file for Chapter 11 protection unless the venture has a legitimate chance of recovery.
- Be prepared to have creditors examine all financial transactions for the last 12 months, seeking possible debtor fraud.
- Maintain good records.
- Understand completely how the protection against creditors works and what is necessary to keep it in place.
- If there is any litigation in existence, transfer it to the bankruptcy court, which may be a more favorable forum for the entrepreneur.
- Focus efforts on preparing a realistic financial reorganization plan.

Following some of the above suggestions and being prepared should bankruptcy be necessary is the best advice that anyone could give to an entrepreneur. Preparation will prevent unfavorable conditions and could increase the likelihood of successfully coming out of bankruptcy.

Prepackaged Bankruptcy

In response to the poor economic environment of the early 1990s, a new type of reorganization plan emerged: the *prepackaged bankruptcy*. Basically, it warns that the entrepreneur will be declaring bankruptcy in the near future. Its intent is to make a Chapter 11 filing more predictable and thus, hopefully, a more successful process.[10]

prepackaged bankruptcy   Provides opportunity to settle debts prior to bankruptcy court legal proceedings

The prepackaged bankruptcy plan allows the entrepreneur to work with creditors to settle debts before legal proceedings begin. In this case, the entrepreneur presents all stakeholders (creditors, lenders, and owners) with a reorganization plan and a disclosure statement detailing all information about the venture's financial position. Negotiations then take place, and differences are resolved before the plan reaches the courts. In most cases, creditors are agreeable to this declaration because they have not yet had to deal with legal issues, nonpayment of debts, and expensive legal fees.

A prepackaged plan can allow a company to emerge from a bankruptcy in four to nine months rather than the more common nine months to two years via the regular route. In fact, since the process is less complicated, the entrepreneur can focus his or her attention on the business rather than on legal issues. Thus, it can save creditors and lenders significant time and money for legal fees.

However, there are shortcomings to the prepackaged bankruptcy. As soon as an entrepreneur announces a plan to reorganize, it labels the entrepreneur and the business a failure. It may thus make it difficult to sell to new customers or to contract with distributors.

The Chapter 11 bankruptcy is used when there is hope that the business can resolve its financial woes and get back on track. If this is not likely, the entrepreneur may need to consider other bankruptcy options, such as Chapter 13.

CHAPTER 13—EXTENDED TIME PAYMENT PLANS

If the entrepreneur has a regular income, it is possible to file for extended time payments as long as the unsecured debts are less than $100,000 and the secured debts are less than $350,000. This option is available only for individual propri-

Who should be made aware when a venture is in trouble? How much responsibility does the entrepreneur have to his or her employees? How much should you tell your banker? Should clients be made aware of your problems? These are all legitimate yet difficult questions that an entrepreneur may struggle with when the business is on the verge of bankruptcy. Some may feel that their only responsibility is to their family and themselves. Trying to get out of the dilemma with the least effect on your personal reputation and financial well-being could in fact make matters worse. Ethically and morally the entrepreneur is the leader of the organization, and trying to avoid responsibility will not rectify the situation. In fact, there is evidence to indicate that involving your employees, banker, or other business associates can actually improve matters. Employees may take pay cuts or stock options to stay on with the company and try to turn the business around. Bankers can be your financial best friend and can recommend ways to save money and generate more cash flow. Your clients and suppliers can also support turnaround efforts by helping to provide needed cash during the crisis. One example was an entrepreneur who ran out of cash to produce a product being sold by a large supermarket chain. A meeting with the important client that revealed the situation (brought on by a competitor's lawsuit that was settled) led to a simple solution. The supermarket appreciated the honesty of the entrepreneur and agreed to prepay for all orders so that there would be sufficient cash to produce the product. The entrepreneur needs to consider the past efforts of employees who made him or her successful in the first place. Thus, the best solution is participation. Get help rather than taking the selfish and perhaps immoral alternative. Honesty is the best strategy.

etorships, and it is strictly a voluntary form of bankruptcy. Under this plan, the entrepreneur files a plan for the installment payment of outstanding debts. If approved by the court, it binds the creditors, even if they had not originally agreed to such installment payments.

The entrepreneur must file a plan with the court that basically budgets future income with respect to any outstanding debts. The plan must provide for the payment of all claims identified as having priority under the Bankruptcy Act. In addition, the plan will outline how much is to be paid until all payments have been completed. It also allows the entrepreneur to continue to own and operate the business while Chapter 13 is pending.

The claims to be paid are in the following order of priority: (1) secured creditors, (2) administrative expenses, (3) claims arising from operation of the business, (4) wage claims up to $2,000 per person, (5) contributions to employee benefit plans, (6) claims by consumer creditors, (7) taxes, and (8) general creditors.

CHAPTER 7—LIQUIDATION

The most extreme case of bankruptcy requires the entrepreneur to liquidate, either voluntarily or involuntarily, all nonexempt assets of the business.

voluntary bankruptcy Entrepreneur's decision to file for bankruptcy

If the entrepreneur files a _voluntary bankruptcy_ petition under Chapter 7, it constitutes a determination that his or her venture is bankrupt. Usually, the courts will also require a current income and expense statement.

involuntary bankruptcy Petition of bankruptcy filed by creditors without consent of entrepreneur

Table 17.1 summarizes some of the key issues and requirements under the _involuntary bankruptcy_ petition. As the table indicates, an involuntary bankruptcy can be very

TABLE 17.1   Liquidation under Chapter 7 Involuntary Bankruptcy

Requirements	Number and Claims of Creditors	Rights and Duties of Entrepreneur	Trustee
Debts are not being paid as they become due.	If 12 or more creditors, at least 3 with unsecured claims totaling $5,000, must sign petition.	Damages may be recovered if creditor files in bad faith.	Elected by creditors. Interim trustee appointed by court.
Custodian appointed within 120 days of filing petition.	If less than 12 creditors, 1 creditor whose unsecured claim is at least $5,000, must sign the petition.	If involuntary petition is dismissed by court, costs, fees, or damages may be awarded.	Becomes by law owner of all property considered nonexempt for liquidation.
Considered insolvent when fair value of all assets is less than debts. Called a balance sheet test.	A proof of claim must be filed within 90 days of first meeting of creditors.	Must file a list of creditors with courts. Must file a current income and expense statement.	Can set aside petitions; transfer of property to a creditor under certain conditions.

complicated and can take a long time to resolve. However, liquidation is in the best interests of the entrepreneur if there is no hope of recovering from the situation.

STRATEGY DURING REORGANIZATION

Normally, reorganization under Chapter 11 or an extended payment plan under Chapter 13 takes a significant amount of time. During this period, the entrepreneur can speed up the process by taking the initiative in preparing a plan, selling the plan to secured creditors, communicating with groups of creditors, and not writing checks that cannot be covered.

The key to enhancing the bankruptcy process is keeping creditors abreast of how the business is doing and stressing the significance of their support during the process. Improving the entrepreneur's credibility with creditors will help the venture emerge from financial difficulties without the stigma of failure. But trying to meet with groups of creditors usually results in turmoil and ill will, so these meetings should be avoided.

Bankruptcy should be a last resort for the entrepreneur. Every effort should be made to avoid it and keep the business operating.

KEEPING THE VENTURE GOING

Any entrepreneur who starts a business should pay attention to, as well as learn from, the mistakes of others. There are certain requirements that can help keep a new venture going and reduce the risk of failure. We can never guarantee success, but we can learn how to avoid failure.

TABLE 17.2   Requirements for Keeping a New Venture Afloat
• Avoid excess optimism when business appears to be successful.
• Always prepare good marketing plans with clear objectives.
• Make good cash projections and avoid capitalization.
• Keep abreast of the marketplace.
• Identify stress points that can put the business in jeopardy.

Table 17.2 summarizes some of the key factors that can reduce the risk of business failure. The entrepreneur should be sensitive to each of these issues regardless of the size or type of business.

Many entrepreneurs have confidence in their abilities, which is necessary for them to be successful in their field. However, they must also be aware that the business environment changes and that they must be prepared to modify their business practices to be consistent with environmental changes. Two good examples of this need can be illustrated by the experiences of William Mow and Paula Tompkins. William Mow, founder of Bugle Boy, a manufacturer of young men's apparel, faced bankruptcy when his flagship product, the multizippered "parachute pants," became obsolete. Mow, almost too late, finally recognized the change in consumer tastes for this product and the need to change the direction of the company's product line. He immediately began to focus on moderately priced men's clothing that was more resistant to fads. The change in focus took some time, but in 1998 the company had turned the corner with sales of more than $530 million.

Paula Tompkins had a similar experience with changing market needs. Her company, SoftAd, created marketing presentations on CD-ROMs and diskettes. This market was feeling the pressure from new technology and software packages, which was making this service obsolete and creating rapidly declining revenues. Tompkins then shifted the company's focus to providing software components that could be tailored to accommodate any computer system. After making this change the company began to experience growth in revenues.[11]

Both entrepreneurs in the examples above recognized important changes and trends in the environment. They not only had to refocus their company's products and services but also had to modify critical business activities, particularly marketing and sales. We saw in Chapter 8 the importance of market planning to help prepare for contingencies such as those described above.

Preparing an effective marketing plan for a 12-month period is essential for the entrepreneur. The marketing plan helps the entrepreneur prepare for contingencies and control his or her day-to-day activities. This is now an important part of both Bugle Boy and SoftAd activities.

Good cash projections are also a serious consideration for the entrepreneur. Cash flow is one of the major causes for an entrepreneur to have to declare bankruptcy. Thus, in preparing cash projections, entrepreneurs should seek assistance from accountants, lawyers, or a federal agency such as the Small Business Administration. This may prevent the situation from reaching the point where it is too late for any hope for recovery.

Many entrepreneurs avoid gathering sufficient information about the market (see Chapter 7). Information is an important asset to any entrepreneur, especially regarding future market potential and forecasting the size of the immediate attainable market. Entrepreneurs will often try to guess what is happening in the market and ignore the changing marketplace. This could spell disaster, especially if competitors are reacting more positively to the market changes.

In the early stages of a new venture, it is helpful for the entrepreneur to be aware of stress points, that is, those points when the venture is changing in size, requiring new survival strategies. Early rapid rises in sales can be interpreted incorrectly so that the venture finds itself adding plant capacity, signing new contracts with suppliers, or increasing inventories, resulting in shrinking margins and being overleveraged. To offset this situation, prices are increased or quality weakened, leading to lower sales. This becomes a vicious circle that can lead to bankruptcy.

Stress points can be identified based on the amount of sales. For example, it may be possible to recognize that sales of $1 million, $5 million, and $25 million may represent key decision marks in terms of major capital investment and operational expenses such as hiring new key personnel. Entrepreneurs should be aware of the burden of sales levels on capital investment and operational expenses.[12]

WARNING SIGNS OF BANKRUPTCY

Entrepreneurs should be sensitive to signals in the business and the environment that may be early warnings of trouble. Often, the entrepreneur is not aware of what is going on or is not willing to accept the inevitable. Table 17.3 lists some of the key early warning signs of bankruptcy. Generally, they are interrelated, and one can often lead to another.

For example, when management of the financial affairs becomes lax, there is a tendency to do anything to generate cash, such as reducing prices, cutting back on supplies to meet orders, or releasing important personnel such as sales representatives. A new office furniture business catering to small or medium-sized businesses illustrates how this can happen. Top management of the firm decided that moving merchandise was its top priority. Sales representatives earned standard commission on each sale and were free to reduce prices where necessary to make the sale. Hence, without any cost or break-even awareness, sales representatives often reduced prices below direct costs. They still received their commissions when the price charged was below cost. Thus, the venture eventually lost substantial amounts of money and had to declare bankruptcy.

TABLE 17.3   Warning Signs of Bankruptcy

- Management of finances becomes lax, so that no one can explain how money is being spent.
- Directors cannot document or explain major transactions.
- Customers are given large discounts to enhance payments because of poor cash flow.
- Contracts are accepted below standard amounts to generate cash.
- Bank requests subordination of its loans.
- Key personnel leave the company.
- Lack of materials to meet orders.
- Payroll taxes are not paid.
- Suppliers demand payment in cash.
- Increase in customers' complaints regarding service and product quality.

When an entrepreneur sees any of the warning signs in Table 17.3, he or she should immediately seek the advice of a CPA or an attorney. It may be possible to prevent bankruptcy by making immediate changes in the operation in order to improve the cash flow and profitability of the business.

STARTING OVER

Bankruptcy and liquidation do not have to be the end for the entrepreneur. History is full of examples of entrepreneurs who have failed many times before finally succeeding.

Gail Borden's tombstone reads, "I tried and failed, and I tried again and succeeded." One of his first inventions was the Terraqueous Wagon, which was designed to travel on land or water. The invention sank on its first try. Borden also had three other inventions that failed to get patents. A fourth invention was patented but eventually wiped him out because of lack of capital and poor sales. However, Borden was persistent and convinced that his vacuum condensation process, giving milk a long shelf life, would be successful. At 56, Borden had his first success with condensed milk.

Over the years, other famous entrepreneurs have also endured many failures before finally achieving success. Rowland Hussey Macy (of Macy's retail stores), Ron Berger (of National Video), and Thomas Edison are other examples of struggling entrepreneurs who lived through many failures.

The characteristics of entrepreneurs were discussed in Chapter 3. From that chapter we know that entrepreneurs are likely to continue starting new ventures even after failing. There is evidence that they learn from their mistakes, and investors often look favorably on someone who has failed previously, assuming that he or she will not make the same mistake again.[13]

Generally, entrepreneurs in endeavors after failure tend to have a better understanding and appreciation for the need for market research, more initial capitalization, and stronger business skills. Unfortunately, not all entrepreneurs learn these skills from their experiences; many tend to fail over and over again.

However, business failure does not have to be a stigma when it comes time to seek venture capital. Past records will be revealed during subsequent start-ups, but the careful entrepreneur can explain why the failure occurred and how he or she will prevent it in the future, restoring investors' confidence. As discussed in Chapter 7, the business plan will help sell the business concept to investors. It is in the business plan that the entrepreneur, even after many failures, can illustrate how this venture will be successful.

THE REALITY OF FAILURE

Unfortunately, failure does happen, but it isn't necessarily the end. Many entrepreneurs are able to successfully turn failure into success. It is one of the important historical characteristics of entrepreneurs that we have continually identified throughout this text. Since failure can happen, there are also some important considerations that should be mentioned if it should occur.

First and foremost, the entrepreneur should consult with his or her family. As difficult as it is for the entrepreneur to deal with bankruptcy, it is even more so for spouses. Problems occur because the spouse usually has no control over the venture's operations unless it is a family-operated business. As a result, he or she may not even be aware of any bankruptcy threats. Thus, the first thing the entrepreneur should do is to sit down with his or her spouse and explain what is happening. This discussion will also help alleviate some of the stress of dealing with bankruptcy.

Second, the entrepreneur should seek outside assistance from professionals, friends, and business associates. Although not all of these people may be sympathetic, it is usually not difficult to find individuals among these groups who would be supportive. Professional support is also available from the Small Business Administration (SBA), universities, SCORE, and Small Business Development Centers.

Third, it is important to not try to hang on to a venture that will continually drain resources if the end is inevitable. It is better to consider the time spent trying to save a dying business as an opportunity cost. The time spent could be more effectively and profitably used to either start over or do something else. If a turnaround is considered possible (see discussion below), it is wise to set a time frame and, if it is not accomplished in that time frame, to simply end the venture.

BUSINESS TURNAROUNDS

Too often we hear only about the business failures and overlook those who are able to survive bankruptcy or near bankruptcy, such as Quaker Siding (Beth Bloom) or the many other examples mentioned in this chapter, and turn their business into a success. History provides some good examples of such turnarounds.

Many of the firms discussed below are large businesses that started small and grew through the efforts of their entrepreneurs. They demonstrate that Chapter 11 reorganization can give the entrepreneur time to resolve the financial problems without pressure from creditors.

In May 1990, Karl Eller resigned from Circle K, a convenience store chain that he had grown from a sleepy store chain to a $3.5 billion business that had to declare Chapter 11. Eller had grown the business too rapidly, using debt, until he lost control of the market and the business. Eller, however, broke but not undaunted, discovered that his old billboard company, which he had sold a few years before taking over Circle K, had been struggling, so he engineered a buyout with no money down (supported by a Canadian bank) and then turned around and sold 50 percent of the business to another buyer. In 1996 with the funding of a venture-capital firm, he then bought a Chicago outdoor advertising company—Patrick Media. The result was that Karl Eller was responsible for building one of the largest outdoor advertising companies in the country. In spite of the bad experience with Circle K he has redeemed himself. He considers himself a risk taker and is someone who doesn't want to go down in history as a failure.

Thomas Sawyer had to file Chapter 11 for his venture, National Applied Computer Technologies Inc. (NACT), after a financier had absconded with $35,000 from the company and the market was turned upside down from the AT&T breakup. The venture marketed switching systems that allowed entrepreneurs to hitch onto unused AT&T lines and sell long-distance telephone service to customers at very low rates. In the first year of operations the venture turned a profit on $500,000 in sales. With the breakup of AT&T customers stopped buying discounted systems until they felt the market stabilized. As a result, the company lost money two straight years and was forced to file Chapter 11. Sawyer was determined to save his company and the jobs of his employees. He convinced the judge of his reorganization plan and then gave remaining employees stock options for a penny a share. He then developed a new switch that could carry 60 phone calls at once. Working 14-hour days he eventually led the company to $7.6 million in sales in 1995 and profits of about $20 million in 1996.[14] In 1997 the company changed its name to

NACT Telecommunications and successfully went public. It is now a division of World Access Inc. and is one of the leaders in providing advanced telecommunications switching products.

Some entrepreneurs consider that an actual search for a company that is near bankruptcy can be a good way to start a business. Jim McCann purchased 1-800-FLOWERS, a near-bankrupt company, in 1983. He agreed to assume the debt, which almost caused him to declare bankruptcy. However, he expanded plans and turned the company into a successful venture with more than $300 million in sales last year.[15] As indicated in the beginning of this chapter, the total number of bankruptcy filings has continued to increase. However, the majority of these were personal or nonbusiness bankruptcies. Business bankruptcies declined in 1999. The robust economy fueled by Internet, biotech, and telecommunications start-ups has changed the playing field. The availability of venture-capital funds and the loosening of requirements by banks have enhanced the opportunities to start a new venture.

Some experts feel that this trend will have to change when the market for these ventures begins to dwindle. If it becomes necessary to file for bankruptcy, the entrepreneur should seek the advice of attorneys, accountants, and investment bankers, when appropriate. Although their fees may be high, there is often no other alternative. As stated above, with the prepackaged bankruptcy plan, the entrepreneur can minimize these fees by trying to get the creditors to preapprove any restructuring or reorganization, thus reducing the time that a firm remains under Chapter 11 and the necessity for the advisors' services.

SUCCESSION OF BUSINESS

Many new ventures will be passed onto family members. If there is no one in the family interested in the business, it is important for the entrepreneur to either sell the business or train someone within the organization to take over.

Transfer to Family Members

Successfully passing the business down to a family member faces tough odds. Experts estimate that half of these attempts fail in the transition from first- to second-generation ownership. Only about 14 percent make it to the third generation. The solution to minimize the emotional and financial turmoil that can often be created during a transfer to family members is a good succession plan.[16]

An effective succession plan needs to consider the following critical factors:

- The role of the owner in the transition stage: Will he or she continue to work full time, part time, or retire?
- Family dynamics: Are some family members unable to work together?
- Income for working family members and shareholders.
- The current business environment during the transition.
- Treatment of loyal employees.
- Tax consequences.

The transfer of a business to a family member can also create internal problems with employees. This often results when a son or daughter is handed the responsibility of running the business without sufficient training. A young family member can be more successful in taking over the business if he or she assumes various operational responsibilities early on. It is beneficial for the family member to rotate to different areas of the business in order to get a good perspective of the total operation. Other employees in these departments or areas will be able to assist in the training and get to know their future leader.

It is also helpful if the entrepreneur stays around for a while to act as an advisor to the successor. This can be helpful in the business decisions. Of course, it is also possible that this can result in major conflicts if the personalities involved are not compatible. In addition, employees who have been with the firm since start-up may resent the younger family member assuming control of the venture. However, while working in the organization during this transition period, the successor can help prove his or her abilities, justifying his or her future role.

Transfer to Nonfamily Members

Often a member of the family is not interested in assuming responsibility for the business. When this occurs, the entrepreneur has three choices: Train a key employee and retain some equity, retain control and hire a manager, or sell the business outright.

Passing the business onto an employee ensures that the new principal is familiar with the business and the market. The experience of the employee minimizes transitional problems. In addition, the entrepreneur can take some time to make the transition smoother.

The key issue when passing the business onto an employee is ownership. If the entrepreneur plans to retain some ownership, the question of how much becomes an important area of negotiation. The new principal may prefer to have control, with the original entrepreneur remaining as a minority owner, stockholder, or consultant. The financial capacity and managerial ability of the employee will be important factors in the decision on how much ownership is transferred. In many cases the transfer or succession of a venture can take many years to meet all of the requirements of the parties involved. Since evidence indicates that most entrepreneurs wait until it is too late, it is important to begin the process long before there is a need to sell or transfer the ownership of the business. The U. S. Commerce Department indicates that about 70 percent of successful ventures never make it to the second generation of ownership.

Ron Norelli was one of the exceptions because he realized the importance of a succession plan and hired a search firm to help him find a successor. Unfortunately, even though he was able to hire someone who was to be groomed as his successor, the individual decided that he did not want to take the risk. Norelli had to start the process all over again and this time conducted the search personally by using his network of trusted business associates. After a number of candidates were evaluated and interviewed by the staff, they settled on a successor who would, over a number of years, buy Norelli out. Norelli went even further by promoting one of his staff to vice president with the intent that this individual would be a good candidate to succeed his successor. The entire process took about five years, and since he began the process early enough, it gave him the opportunity to leave the business gradually with the confidence that it would successfully continue in the future.[17]

If the business has been in the family for some time and the succession to a family member may become more likely in the future, the entrepreneur may hire a manager to run the business. However, finding someone to manage the business in the same manner and with the same expertise as the entrepreneur may be difficult. If someone is found to manage the business, the likely problems are compatibility with the owners and willingness of this person to manage for any length of time without a promise of equity in the business. Executive search firms can help in the search process. It will be necessary to have a well-defined job description to assist in identifying the right person.

The last option, often referred to as *harvesting*, is to sell the business outright to either an employee or an outsider. The major considerations in this option are financial, which will likely necessitate the help of an accountant and/or lawyer. This alternative also requires that the value of the business be determined (see Chapter 12).

harvesting   Selling the business outright to either an employee or an outsider

HARVESTING STRATEGY

There are a number of alternatives available to the entrepreneur in harvesting the venture. Some of these are straightforward, and others involve more complex financial strategy. Each of these methods should be carefully considered and one selected, depending on the goals of the entrepreneur.

Direct Sale

Although this is the most common method of harvesting a venture, it does not always occur as a last resort to bankruptcy. Many entrepreneurs choose to sell so they can move on to new endeavors. Steven Rosendorf provides a good example of the considerations involved in any possible sale of the business. In 1976, his brother/partner died suddenly, leaving him alone with a $2 million costume jewelry business. At that point, Rosendorf began to plan for the eventual sale of the company. The plan included upgrading of showrooms and cost-cutting measures, as well as a reduction of his own salary. Within a few years, the company showed $2 million profits on sales of $13 million. Rosendorf felt it was time to sell the business, and within one year he did so for $16 million.[18]

Unless the entrepreneur is desperate, putting a business up for sale may require time and planning, as Rosendorf's example indicates. Successful small businesses are in demand by larger firms that wish to grow by acquisition.

One of the important considerations of any business sale is the type of payment the buyer will use. Often, buyers will purchase a business using notes based on future profits. If the new owners fail in the business, the seller may receive no cash payment and possibly find himself or herself taking back the company that is struggling to survive.

As exemplified in the Rosendorf example, preparing for a sale may necessitate serious financial reconsiderations. Many entrepreneurs give themselves big salaries and large expense accounts that obviously cut into profits. This also makes the company's earning capacity appear to be much lower than it is. Thus, if the entrepreneur must or plans to sell the business, he or she should tighten spending, avoid large personal salaries and expenses, and reinvest as much profit as possible back into the business. This formula will likely result in a much better sale agreement.

Business brokers in some instances may be helpful since trying to actually sell a business will take time away from running it. Brokers can be discreet about a sale and may have an established network to get the word around. Brokers earn a commission from the sale of a business. Generally these commissions are based on a sliding scale starting at about 10 percent for the first $200,000. The best way to communicate the business to potential buyers is through the business plan. A five-year comprehensive plan can provide buyers of the business with a future perspective and accountability of the value of the company (see Chapters 7 and 8).

Once the business is either sold or passed onto a family member or employee, the entrepreneur's role may depend on the sale agreement or contract with the new owner(s). Many buyers will want the seller to stay on for a short time to provide a smooth transition. Under these circumstances the seller (entrepreneur) should negotiate an employment contract that specifies time, salary, and responsibility. If the entrepreneur is not needed in the business, it is likely that the new owner(s) will request that the entrepreneur sign an agreement not to engage in the same business for a specified number of years. These agreements vary in scope and may require a lawyer to clarify details.

An entrepreneur may also plan to retain a business for only a specified period of time, with the intent to sell it to the employees. This may entail all employees through an employee stock option plan or through a management buyout, which allows the sale to occur to only certain managers of the venture.

Employee Stock Option Plan

Under an *employee stock option plan (ESOP)*, the business is sold to employees over a period of time. This time period may be two or three or several years, depending on the intent of the entrepreneur in exiting the business. The ESOP is often considered an alternative to a pension plan, particularly when the venture is too small to support a pension plan. Its purpose is to reward employees and to clarify early the succession decision of the new venture. The ESOP is highly regulated, where the founder creates a trust fund and he or she contributes stock or cash for buying the owner's interest in the venture. There are now more than 10,000 employee-owned companies in the United States.[19]

employee stock option plan (ESOP)   Two- to three-year plan to sell business to employees

The ESOP has a number of advantages. First, it offers a unique incentive to employees that can enhance their motivation to put in extra time or effort. Employees recognize that they are working for themselves and hence will focus their efforts on innovations that contribute to the long-term success of the venture. Second, it provides a mechanism to pay back those employees who have been loyal to the venture, particularly during more difficult times. Third, it allows the transfer of the business under a carefully planned written agreement. Finally, the company can reap the advantage of deducting the contributions to the ESOP or any dividends paid on the stock.

ESOPs, due to a new law passed in 1996, are now possible for S Corporations. David Copham's Liberty Check Printers was the first S Corporation to set up an ESOP in 1996. The company's employees now own about 6 percent of the venture.[20]

However, in spite of its favorable attributes, the ESOP has some disadvantages. This type of stock option plan is usually quite complex to establish. It requires a complete valuation of the venture in order to establish the amount of the ESOP package. In addition, it raises issues such as taxes, payout ratios, amount of equity to be transferred per year, and the amount actually invested by the employees. The agreement would also specify if the employees can buy or sell additional shares of stock once the plan has been completed. Regardless, it is clear from the complexity of this type of plan that the entrepreneur will need the advice of experts. A simpler method may be a more direct buyout by key employees of the venture.

Management Buyout

It is conceivable that the entrepreneur only wants to sell or transfer the venture to loyal, key employees. Since the ESOP described above can be rather complicated, the entrepreneur may find that a direct sale would be simpler to accomplish.

Management buyouts usually involve a direct sale of the venture for some predetermined price. This would be similar to selling one's house. To establish a price, the entrepreneur would have an appraisal of all the assets and then determine goodwill value established from past revenue.

Sale of a venture to key employees can be for cash, or it could be financed in any number of ways. A cash sale would be unlikely if the value of the business is substantial. Financing the sale of the venture can be accomplished through a bank, or the entrepreneur could also agree to carry the note. This may be desirable to the entrepreneur in that the stream of income from the sale would be spread out over a determined period of time, enhancing cash flow and lessening the tax impact. Another method of selling the venture would be to use stock as the method of transfer. The managers buying the business may sell nonvoting or voting stock to other investors. These funds would then be used as a full or partial payment for the venture. The reason that other investors would be interested in buying stock or that a bank would lend the managers money is that the business is continuing with the same management team and with its established track record.

Other methods of transferring or selling a business are through a public offering or even a merger with another business. These topics are discussed in Chapters 15 and 16. Before determining the appropriate harvesting strategy, the entrepreneur should seek the advice of outsiders. Every circumstance is different, and the actual decision will depend on the entrepreneur's goals. Case histories of each of the above methods can also be reviewed to be able to effectively determine which option is best for the given circumstances.

IN REVIEW

Summary

This chapter deals with the decisions, problems, and issues involved in ending the venture. Even though the intent of all entrepreneurs is to establish a business for a long time, many problems can cause these plans to fail. Since about one-half of all new ventures fail in their first four years of business, it is important for the entrepreneur to understand the options for either ending or salvaging a venture.

Bankruptcy offers three options for the entrepreneur. Under Chapter 11 of the Bankruptcy Act of 1978 (amended in 1984) the venture will be reorganized under a plan approved by the courts. New versions of this form of bankruptcy now allow the entrepreneur an opportunity to file a prepackaged bankruptcy plan. This plan avoids large expenses and prepares creditors in advance so that negotiations can occur before the courts become involved.

Chapter 13 provides for an extended time payment plan to cover outstanding debts. This is not involuntary and is not an alternative for partnerships or corporations. Both of these alternatives are designed to help entrepreneurs salvage the business and keep it going. Under Chapter7, the venture will be liquidated either voluntarily or involuntarily.

Keeping the business going is the primary intent of all entrepreneurs. Avoiding excessive optimism, preparing good marketing plans, making good cash projections, keeping familiar with the market, and being sensitive to stress points in the business can help keep the business operating.

Entrepreneurs can also be sensitive to key warnings of potential problems. Lax management of finances, discounting to generate cash, loss of key personnel, lack of raw materials, nonpayment of payroll taxes, demands of suppliers to be paid in cash, and increased customer complaints about service and product quality are some of the key factors that lead to bankruptcy. If the business does fail, however, the entrepreneur should always consider starting over. Failure can be a learning process as evidenced by the many famous inventors who succeeded after many failures.

One of the other venture-ending decisions that an entrepreneur may face is succession of the business. If the business is family owned, the entrepreneur would likely seek a family member to succeed. Other options, if no family member is available or interested, include transferring some or all of the business to an employee or outsider, or hiring an outsider to manage the business. Direct sale, employee stock option plan, and management buyout are alternatives for the entrepreneur in selling the venture.

Questions for Discussion

1. Describe the major differences among Chapter 7, Chapter 11, and Chapter 13 bankruptcy.
2. What advantages and disadvantages are there in presenting a prepackaged bankruptcy plan to creditors?
3. The entrepreneur can play an important role in enhancing the speed at which reorganization under bankruptcy occurs. Discuss.
4. In the early stages of a new venture, certain stress points may be critical in determining future direction. Explain these stress points and how they can affect various parts of the operation.
5. Entrepreneurs should be sensitive to certain identifying signs of bankruptcy. Using the example of an Internet company, describe some of the possible warning signs.
6. What are some of the key issues involved in providing for the succession of the business?
7. Find an article about a business in which ownership was transferred through an ESOP. How successful has this company been since the transfer? What are some of the problems that may result from using this plan?

Key Terms

Chapter 7 bankruptcy	harvesting
Chapter 11 bankruptcy	involuntary bankruptcy
Chapter 13 bankruptcy	prepackaged bankruptcy
employee stock option plan (ESOP)	voluntary bankruptcy

More Information—Net Addresses in This Chapter

American Bankruptcy Institute
www.abiworld.org

Bankruptcy Filing Online
www.bkhelp.com

Bankruptcy Forms
www.easy-bankruptcy.com

Biz Women
www.bizwomen.com

Business Resource Center
www.morebusiness.com

Dun & Bradstreet Information Service
www.dnb.com

Financial Research Associates
www.frafssb.com

Foundation for Enterprise Development
http://www.fed.org/

Robert Morris Associates
www.rmahq.com

Small Business Administration
www.sbaonline.sba.gov/

Small Business Resource Center
www.smallbizhelp.net

Selected Readings

Campbell, Steven V. (1997). An Investigation of the Direct Costs of Bankruptcy Reorganization for Closely Held Firms. *Journal of Small Business Management*, vol. 35, no. 3, pp. 21–29.

This study examines the direct administrative costs of bankruptcy reorganization by analyzing 36 closely held corporations that successfully reorganized under Chapter 11 of the federal Bankruptcy Act. Findings indicate that direct bankruptcy costs are associated with firm size and the time spent in bankruptcy and provide strong evidence that direct Chapter 11 administrative costs are not trivial for small businesses and that there are substantial scale economies in these costs.

Destefano, D. (April 1, 1996). Succession Planning. *Direct*, pp. 26–30.

Succession planning is discussed in this article as a necessity to minimize the problems and anxiety created among family members during the transfer of control or ownership of a venture. During this transfer, emotional, operational/managerial, and financial dynamics are likely to be present.

Gimeno, Javier; Timothy B. Folta; Arnold C. Cooper; and Carolyn Y. Woo. (1997). Survival of the Fittest? Entrepreneurial Human Capital and the Persistence of Underperforming Firms. *Administrative Science Quarterly*, vol. 42, no. 4, pp. 750–83.

A model is developed which explains that organizational survival is not strictly a function of economic performance but also depends on a firm's own threshold of performance. In new venture survival, the threshold is determined by the entrepreneur's human capital characteristics, such as alternative employment opportunities, psychic income from entrepreneurship, and cost of switching to other occupations. Findings indicate that firms with low thresholds may choose to continue or survive despite comparatively low performance.

Goldberg, A. (February 3, 1997). An Ideal Way to Preserve Business within the Family. *Crain's Small Business*, pp. 15–17.

In order to maintain the long-term viability of a venture it is important to consider the options for future ownership. One of the options discussed in this article is the family limited partnership (FLP). The FLP provides a business owner with the opportunity to maintain the viability of the venture, maintain control, and pay less estate taxes when passing the business over to family members.

Gutner, T. (August 12, 1996). The Best Moves If You're Broke. *Business Week*, pp. 110–3.

Well over 1 million people are expected to file for bankruptcy. Bankruptcy is not just for deadbeats but includes people in a wide range of incomes. This article provides some basic insight into what procedure to follow and what to expect should you need to file for bankruptcy.

Lussier, Robert N., and Sanja Pfeifer. (2000). A Comparison of Business Success versus Failure Variables between U.S. and Central Eastern Europe Croatian Entrepreneurs. *Entrepreneurship Theory & Practice*, vol. 24, no. 4, pp. 59–67.

Fifteen success versus failure variables were tested for differences between U.S. and Central Eastern Europe Croatian (CEEC) entrepreneurs.

Maddy, Monique. (2000). Dream Deferred: The Story of a High-Tech Entrepreneur in a Low-Tech World. *Harvard Business Review*, vol. 78, no. 3, pp. 56–69.

Monique Maddy discusses the important lessons the failure of her start-up Ademesi taught her about starting a business in an emerging-market country.

McGrath, Rita Gunther. (1999). Falling Forward: Real Options Reasoning and Entrepreneurial Failure. *Academy of Management Review*, vol. 24, no. 1, pp. 13–30.

Although failure in entrepreneurship is pervasive, theory often reflects similarly pervasive antifailure bias. This article uses real options reasoning to develop a more balanced perspective on the role of entrepreneurial failure in wealth creation. It emphasizes managing uncertainty by pursuing high-variance outcomes but investing only if conditions are favorable. In this way profit potential can be increased while containing costs.

Shepherd, Dean A.; Evan J. Douglas; and Mark Shanley. (2000). New Venture Survival: Ignorance, External Shocks, and Risk Reduction Strategies. *Journal of Business Venturing*, vol. 15, no. 5–6, pp. 393–410.

Authors develop a model to explain new venture failure. It is argued that the liability of newness is largely dependent on the degree of novelty (ignorance) associated with a new venture-novelty to the market, to the technology of production, and to management.

Shepherd, Dean A.; and Andrew Zacharakis. (2000). Structuring Family Business Succession: An Analysis of the Future Leader's Decision Making. *Entrepreneurship Theory & Practice*, vol. 24, no. 4., pp. 25–39.

This article examines the perception of potential family business leaders from a behavioral economics theory perspective. Authors argue that founders should structure succession so that the future leader incurs both financial and behavioral sunk costs as well as hold the future leader to stringent performance requirements prior to the succession.

Endnotes

1. B. Bloom Wright, with M. E. Mangelsdorf, "To Bankruptcy and Back," *Inc.* (September 1993), pp. 86–97.
2. See American Bankruptcy Institute's website: www.abiworld.org.
3. See S. Barlow, "The 11th Hour," *Entrepreneur* (April 1993), pp. 133–7; and G. Koch, "Turnarounds of the Year; Reversal of Fortune," *Profit* (Winter 1997), p. 64.
4. M. McCorriston, D. Stein, and M. Visser, "The Phoenix 50," *Success* (July 1998), pp. 37–52.
5. J. Macht, "Neglect Zaps Laser-Tag Franchiser," *Inc.* (July 1998), p. 27.
6. S. Barlow, "The 11th Hour," p. 137.
7. R. A. Anderson, I. Fox, and D. P. Twomey, *Business Law: & The Regulatory Environment: Principles & Cases*, 12th ed. (Cincinnati, OH: South-Western Publishing, 1992), pp. 744–64.
8. S. Barlow, "The 11th Hour," p. 133.
9. "Surviving Bankruptcy," *Stores* (December 1992), p. 59.
10. See D. M. Morris and E. C. Dobbs, "A Package Deal," *Small Business Reports* (March 1992), pp. 15–9; and "Prepackaged Bankruptcies: Bust Today, Back Tomorrow," *Economist* (February 15, 1992), pp. 78–80.

11. M. McCorriston et al., "The Phoenix 50s" pp. 50,71.

12. N. L. Croft, "Keeping Business Afloat," *Nation's Business* (February 1987), p. 18.

13. L. M. Lament, "What Entrepreneurs Learn from Experience," *Journal of Small Business Management*, vol. 10 (1972), p. 36.

14. See M. Warshaw, "Never Say Die," *Success* (July/August 1996), pp. 35–44; and website www.nact.com.

15. *Inc.* staff, "My Biggest Mistake: Jim McCann" (August 8, 1998), p. 72.

16. P. Brothers, "Succession Plan Vital for Family Businesses," *The Cincinnati Enquirer* (December 19, 1996), p. S11.

17. C. Dannhauser, "Will My Beloved Business Survive Me?" *Business Week Frontier* (February 12, 1999), www.businessweek.com.

18. Terri Thompson, "When It's Time to Sell Out," *U.S. News & World Report* (June 28, 1989), pp. 62–64.

19. K. Klein, "Using Stock Ownership to Motivate Workers," *Business Week Frontier* (January 21, 1999), www.businessweek.com.

20. C. Farrell and M. B. Regan, "Now, More Can Join the ESOP Game," *Business Week Frontier* (May 25, 1998), www.businessweek.com.

IV

CASE IVa Dual Pane Company

John Grayson had been in the housing restoration business for 15 years when, in 1984, he designed a machine that could remove old windows from their frames without destroying the wooden panes known as muntins and mullions that surround the glass (see Exhibit 1). One of the big advantages of the tool is that it was built around a routing drill piece that moved on a three-dimensional plane. This allowed Grayson to replace windows that up until then could not be serviced. Once the small panes were removed, they would be replaced by one large pane of double glass. The muntins and mullions would be inserted over the window to give it the same look as before.

Grayson applied for a patent as soon as he realized his machine was unique, and the patent was granted in August 1985. He has been operating the business since that time under the name of Dual Pane Company. He and his wife, Elizabeth, are the sole owners and employees of the company. She oversees the advertising and promotional aspects, and John does the actual installing. They both engage in the selling process, particularly in the colder months when the actual installation business is slower. Their current geographic market is the Boston area, although they have done business outside it. They generally have concentrated on the residential market, but have periodically completed commercial jobs.

The restoration market is affected by several factors that include the state of the overall economy, local employment levels, and the amount of a consumer's disposable income. Since the company began operations, the economy has been favorable. The GNP has been increasing, real disposable income has risen moderately, and there has been a decrease in unemployment in the Boston area. The restoration of windows is a relatively large expense, costing between $3,000 and $7,000, depending on the number of windows installed in a house. Home owners are more likely to invest in this type of restoration when their level of net disposable income is greater and when the economy is good. Today, there is a trend toward less saving on the part of many Americans, and consumers are tending to borrow for expenditures like housing restorations. Therefore, the level of interest rates affects Dual Pane's business. Fortunately, interest rates have been low recently, so consumers have been able to afford such restorations.

Another factor that affects the restoration market is the cost of energy. In the late 1970s, the energy crisis forced many people to see energy as a limited resource. Since that time, people have generally tried to conserve energy. Consumers are faced with finding alternative sources of energy to heat and cool their homes and offices. This concern with conservation gives Dual Pane an advantage in that it is replacing single-pane noninsulated windows with energy-efficient dual-pane insulated windows.

EXHIBIT 1

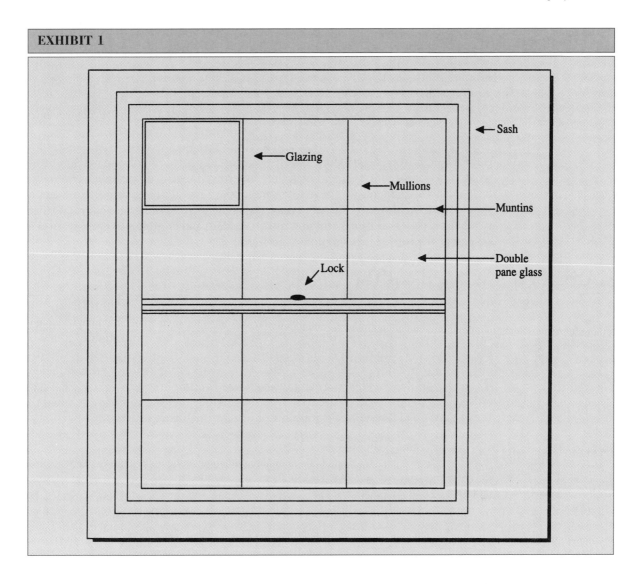

Due to the favorable economy and Dual Pane's unique method of installing double-pane glass, the Graysons have had more business than they can handle. They have advertised in the yellow pages and have sent direct mail to the subscribers of a regional home improvement magazine. Their customers have referred their friends to the Graysons, so business has expanded considerably. John has two ideas on how to handle his growing business. He could hire and train a staff of salespeople and installers, or he could franchise his business. He enjoyed the selling and the actual installing of the windows, but neither he nor his wife was interested in managing a staff of workers. Therefore, franchising was more appealing to him. He felt that one of Dual Pane's big advantages was the patented cutting tool, and he could bring the name Dual Pane to more customers if he franchised the business. Several contractors he contacted had expressed an interest in the Dual Pane machine and wondered if he was interested in franchising.

John decided that his goal was to franchise the business. There were three groups of people he could contact regarding franchising. First, he could sell the rights of the product to contractors who were in the business of restoring residential homes or commercial offices. He felt that their reach with consumers could help to broaden the exposure of the Dual Pane name. He also thought that glass companies in the Boston area might be interested in a Dual Pane franchise. Since his tool could cut odd-shaped glass, it had an advantage over existing methods, which glass companies would benefit from. Elizabeth mentioned that individuals who wanted to get into the restoration business might also be potential targets for franchising.

John needed to know how to go about franchising the business. What kind of legalities were involved? He knew that he had patent protection on the machine, but what kind of procedures should he follow in terms of setting up guidelines for owning a Dual Pane franchise? Which group should he target for franchising? How much should the franchise cost? He wanted to sell his franchise to the group or groups that would give the Dual Pane name the most exposure and continue to emphasize the quality of the work. How should he proceed?

CASE IVb   Wizards of the Coast

The excitement was high among the top managers of Wizards of the Coast, the world's leading adventure gaming company, as they sat down to review progress over the first half of 1997. The company had just completed the acquisition of a major competitor, and with the opening of its first gaming entertainment center, it was pioneering a whole new retail concept. After three years of tremendous growth fueled by one hit product, followed by an unexpected downturn in revenues in 1996, Wizards looked to be on the rebound. But everyone knew that the company still had to prove that it had a sustainable growth strategy for the future.

CREATING THE MAGIC

In 1997, Wizards of the Coast was a privately held company best known for the world's leading adventure trading-card game, *Magic: The Gathering*. Since its release in 1993, over 5 million consumers worldwide had embraced the game, which was available in nine languages and played in over 52 countries. See Exhibit 1 for a brief description of *Magic*.

The Genesis

Wizards of the Coast was founded by Peter Adkison and a group of other young professionals in 1990 to develop role-playing games. Adkison had been intrigued by strategy and role-playing games ever since his early childhood. He recalls playing games as a child all night long under the comforters of his bed using a flashlight, so that his mother would think he is asleep when she took a peek into the room during the early night hours. In high school, Peter developed a passion for the *Dungeons & Dragons* (*D&D*) adventure role-playing game (see Exhibit 2 for a brief description of *D&D*). It seemed natural to him to turn this hobby into a business. After graduating from college, Adkison was working for Boeing as a computer systems analyst, but he was eager to start his own venture. Recalls Adkison: "I was a small cog in a huge machine that itself was a small cog in a huge machine." Adkison and six of his friends kept their jobs but began developing role-playing games in their spare time.

EXHIBIT 1

Magic: The Gathering

The game *Magic: The Gathering* combines elements of chess, bridge, and the 1970s role-playing game *Dungeons & Dragons*. *Magic* is a trading card game in which the two players are rival wizards dueling for control of a magical "multiverse" called *Dominia*. Each player starts out with 20 life points or lives. The goal is to reduce the opponent's life points from 20 to zero before the opponent has reduced your life points to zero.

Before starting the game, each player builds a deck of at least 40 cards from his or her collection of cards and then plays that deck against the opponent's deck. Each player begins by shuffling his or her deck and drawing seven cards. Players alternate taking turns. Each player's turn is made up of a series of actions, such as playing cards and attacking the opponent. There are several types of elaborately illustrated cards a player can choose from. For example, lands are the most basic, providing the magical energy a player needs to play all other cards. Creatures can fight for the player either by attacking the opponent or by fighting off the opponent's creatures. Other cards represent spells that a player can cast to hurt the opponent or help his or her creatures. The basic strategy of *Magic* lies in choosing when to play what card and when to use what creatures to attack the opponent or protect yourself. More complex strategies involve combining cards to make them more powerful and choosing which cards to use in the player's deck to make it most effective. Games usually last between 15 minutes and half an hour; however, some games can last up to several hours.

One of the key features of the game is that each game played is unique since each player starts out with a deck of 40 cards individually selected from among the more than 4,000 different cards sold. It is not uncommon for a player to own several hundred or even thousands of cards. Each player tries to assemble his or her favorite 40 cards out of the pool he or she owns according to the player's intended strategy. This ingenious twist encourages players to buy or trade for new cards to enhance their powers and strategic game options.

In addition, the game is in permanent evolution since new cards are constantly released and older cards are retired by Wizards of the Coast. These retired cards gain instant status as collectibles to be bought, sold, and traded in hobby stores, in dormitories, on college campuses, and on the Internet. New cards are issued in different sets and limited editions; many cards are even printed in limited numbers. These perpetual expansions have kept the game novel and therewith contributed to the phenomenal growth as players engage in frantic buying and trading of cards in a fantasy arms race to create a competitive advantage in their individualist "starter deck." Since most of the strategy in *Magic* is assembling the unassailable deck, serious players have spent hundreds if not thousands of dollars to create their dream deck. This has led to the criticism that affluent players are more likely to win than their poorer counterparts.

In addition, with each expansion, *Dominia*, the fantasy "multiverse" where the wizards battle, also expands. "Think of *Dominia* as a beach," says Wizards spokeswoman Sue-Lane Wood. "Each expansion is a grain of sand on that beach, each its own universe." Currently, *Magic* has undergone only about a dozen extensions. However, the possible number of expansions is limited only by imagination and players' willingness to remain bewitched.

In 1991, Adkison met Richard Garfield in a chatroom on the Internet. At the time, Garfield was a doctoral student in combinational mathematics at the University of Pennsylvania and was known as an avid game player who had been designing his own games since he was a teenager. When the two got together at a game convention, the concept for *Magic* was born. Adkison had the idea that there was a need for a fantasy role-playing game that was portable and could be played anywhere in no more than an hour. He thought that maybe it should be a card game. Garfield had also been interested in fantasy games since playing a game called *Cosmic Encounter* in the 1980s. One of the pieces in *Cosmic Encounter* had special powers. By invoking these powers a player could change the rules of the game. This intrigued Garfield, and he wondered what would happen if all the pieces were magic, each one altering the game in some unique way. He believed that this idea could lead to a fantasy board game, but Adkison persuaded him to focus on cards instead and to think about a format in which players could trade cards.

EXHIBIT 2

Dungeons & Dragons

What is the *Dungeons & Dragons* role-playing game? The game commonly known as *D&D* evolved from historical war gaming, in which armchair generals lined up armies of painted miniature figurines on tabletops, decorated to look like battlefields, and staged skirmishes either historical or theoretical. Troop movements were negotiated with the help of rulers, and combat was resolved through the roll of dice and consultation of tables. *Role playing* began with an idea to put aside the role of an entire army to take up the role of an individual character, who would infiltrate a castle through the sewers below to open the drawbridge and let in the invading army. This scenario proved so popular that the designer ran it repeatedly, for numerous friends and fellow war gamers, eventually substituting fantasy monsters for castle guards as obstacles to be overcome. Ultimately, one of the players, named Gary Gygax, volunteered to create standard rules for the new game, and he added rules for playing spell-casting wizards to offer an alternative to role playing a warrior. These new rules were first published in Gygax's war-gaming periodical *Chainmail*, but in 1974 he developed a full set of rules and called them *Dungeons & Dragons*. Over the next 25 years, *D&D* would be distributed in 22 countries and translated into more than a dozen languages. The *Advanced Dungeons & Dragons* game expanded upon the original in 1978, and the second edition *AD&D* game hit the market in 1989. Over a dozen *campaign settings*—distinct worlds in which to play *D&D*—were published over the years; and novels, computer games, board games, cartoons, comic books, and other media built upon the brand. Throughout its life, the *D&D* game frequently has been misunderstood, condemned, associated with nerds, and given up for dead; yet it retains near-universal brand recognition even among people who have never played it, and sales of the game are currently rising.

How is *D&D* played? Although computer games are simulating the traditional game with increasing efficiency, *D&D* is played with paper, pencil, dice, and rule books. A character is created by rolling dice to determine his or her basic physical and mental attributes. Then the player chooses the character's profession (e.g., fighter or wizard), equips the character for the road, joins with a group of friends who also have created characters, and goes on an adventure. One of the players takes on the special role of *Dungeon Master*: this person presents the situation at hand to the rest of the players, who react in character to cooperatively tell a story and enjoy the adventure together. For example, the Dungeon Master may say something like, "You cross the drawbridge and enter the Castle of Nightmares, ready to seek and recover the famed *Staff of the Magi*, but a group of creatures step from the shadows within to block your way. What will you do?" Each of the players in turn declares what his or her character intends to do—call out a greeting or threat, draw weapon and prepare for battle, cast a spell, or anything else they imagine their character might do under the circumstances—and then dice are rolled to determine the order in which actions take place and whether or not they are successful. (The Dungeon Master plays the role of every person and creature met by the adventuring party.) Rounds of action continue until the encounter is resolved. The player-characters then move on and continue to explore the castle until they achieve their goal (in this case, finding the *Staff*) or until their characters are either captured or killed by the inhabitants of the castle. Collectively they tell the story of the adventure, and collectively they work to succeed (or fail). Assuming the party is successful, they gain *experience points*, grow more powerful, and move on to even more challenging scenarios. Ongoing campaigns may last for years, with groups playing every week for hours at a time.

Garfield came back a few weeks later with a prototype of *Magic: The Gathering*. The idea was to combine a fantasy game concept, where players controlled the acts of mystical characters, with a trading-card format, where players could buy and sell collectible cards similar to those of their sports heroes. Recalls Garfield: "The concept of a trading-card game was one of the only 'Eureka!' experiences I've had." Adkison emphasizes the point that the first prototype of *Magic* resembled very closely the later commercialized version of *Magic*: "We still have the original, hand-drawn cards, and gosh, if you know how to play *Magic*, you can play just fine with that very first game."

Operating out of the basement of Adkison's home as an eight-person company, Wizards of the Coast released *Magic: The Gathering* in August 1993. The game became an overnight success. The first printing of 10 million cards, which was expected to last a year, sold out in just six weeks. According to one game store owner, "My initial order was for 24 units, my second order was for 572, and my third was to send everything you've got in the warehouse." With its sales success also came critical acclaim and winning several game and toy industry awards.

With *Magic*'s instant splash, Garfield quit his new teaching position at Whitman College and began to pursue his true passion as a game inventor with Wizards of the Coast. Adkison made Garfield an equity partner in Wizards of the Coast and fully dedicated his then fledgling firm to creating fantasy card games. Adkison too quit his job at the Boeing Corporation to become the president and CEO of Wizards of the Coast. See the timeline in Exhibit 3.

Products and Customers

Magic cards were sold in starter decks of 60 randomly selected cards for about $8.95, and booster packs of 8 or 15 cards sold for about $2.95. Even though these were the recommended retail prices, it was not uncommon for retailers to unbundle decks and to mark up the prices of highly demanded cards. The cards featured original artwork that appealed to fantasy game players and collectors. As a consequence, *Magic* cards were both collected and traded, with a card's price determined by its strategic role and its collector value. Each deck was unique, so no two players had identical sets of cards. Players traded cards in order to create a deck with desired characteristics.

According to the chief game developer for Wizards of the Coast, 27-year-old George Skaff Elias, the typical *Magic* player is a person with a good education, disposable income, and an affinity for computers. While the game is most popular with males in their teens or twenties, the game also caught on with younger teens and with older men and women as well. College dormitories are a particular breeding ground for new "gamers." As compared to the typical player of a board game such as Monopoly, the player of *Magic* sees the game more as a hobby, something on which he or she spends a significant amount of time and money.

Manufacturing and Distribution

Wizards contracted out the design, manufacturing, and packaging of its cards and other products. Most of its *Magic* cards were designed by independent artists, who earned royalties from their sales by Wizards. The tremendous royalty payments due to the unexpected success of *Magic* were initially a problem for Wizards, which was later solved in a friendly round of renegotiations with the artists. In the beginning, the company relied on only one supplier, Carta Mundi in Belgium, since no other firm could deliver the quality needed along with the ability to do the sophisticated card sorting that was required. During the first two years of booming popularity, manufacturing capacity was the single biggest constraint on the growth of Wizards. Carta Mundi was in 1997 still the largest supplier, but other suppliers were contracted as the game grew and as they were able to meet Wizards' standards.

Wizards built a widespread network to market its cards. Most adventure games were sold through small game, comic, or hobby shops, which were often "mom and pop" stores supplied through relatively small distributors. These shops were critical for reaching the serious "gamers" and accounted for about 75 percent of the company's sales. Wizards allocated new card series to these stores, and there was often a feeding frenzy as consumers rushed to get an edge with new cards. With the increased popularity of *Magic*, Wizards was able to enter national toy

EXHIBIT 3

Timeline of Wizards of the Coast

1990	• Wizards of the Coast formed as a sole proprietorship by Peter Adkison (May) • Wizards of the Coast incorporated (December)
1991	• Peter met Richard Garfield on the Internet • First play-test version of *Magic: The Gathering* distributed • Wizards acquired the Talislanta role-playing game line from Bard Games
1992	• Wizards' first new product, *The Primal Order*, released • Six other role-playing products released • Wizards sued for trademark infringement in its product *The Primal Order* by Palladium • Garfield Games formed to launch *Magic: The Gathering*
1993	• Wizards laid off all its employees • Everyone staid on to launch *Magic*, being paid in stock • The Palladium lawsuit settled • *Magic: The Gathering* launched to record sales • The *Duelist Convocation (DCI)* started to provide tournament play for *Magic* • All employees hired back • Company moved from "the basement" to real offices • The *Duelist* magazine launched • Garfield Games and Wizards of the Coast merged
1994	• Five expansions for *Magic* released • *Jyhad*, the second trading-card game, based on the Vampire RPG, was released • First World Championships for *Magic* held in Seattle • First European office opened in Glasgow
1995	• *Netrunner*, Wizards' third trading-card game, released • The *Everyway* role-playing game released • Wizards bought Andon, a convention management company • The *Magic: The Gathering* computer game released by Microprose • Over 30 employees laid off in company's largest downsizing • All game divisions divested except for trading-card games
1996	• The *Magic: The Gathering* $1 million Pro Tour launched in New York • Wizards of the Coast tournament center opened at corporate headquarters • The *BattleTech* trading-card game released • Wizards contracted to run Origins, the second largest game convention in the United States
1997	• The Wizards of the Coast Game Center opened in Seattle • Wizards acquired TSR Inc. • Wizards acquired Five Rings Publishing Group • First Wizards retail store opened in Seattle

chains such as Toys "R" Us, bookstores such as Barnes & Noble, and discounters such as Target. These stores did not have the same atmosphere and appeal as the small retailers, but were more effective in reaching the mass market.

The Wizards Culture

Adkison was trying to preserve the creative culture that was present when the company was formed, while developing the systems needed to manage a much larger enterprise. Leading by example, for many years he refused to have his own office or even a cubicle. On his business cards and memos, his position and title was stated as "CEO and janitor." He saw the company as similar to a small software firm, with a casual, creative atmosphere that tolerated individualism and creativity, expressed, for example, in eccentric clothing, body piercing, and frequent nerf wars among employees. But over the years the atmosphere had become more reserved, and Peter now even has a corner office.

Wizards' executives and employees tended to be very committed to the gaming concept. Richard Garfield, the inventor of *Magic*, sees adventure games as the "intellectual counterpart of sports—they keep you mentally fit." He believes that with playing *Magic* comes "a lot of stealth education," whether it's art appreciation because of the beautiful cards or enhanced literacy because of the occasional quote from Shakespeare. Garfield also believes that *Magic* is a strategic game that can only be played successfully when the player has a good understanding of strategy, probability, and chance. But Adkison also recognized that devoted gamers did not always make successful executives.

> There's nobody in the company who's ever managed a company this size, including me. We're trying to balance the desire for top-notch people to take us to the next level with the desire to stay true to people who founded the company. And that is very, very tough. We faced a lot of organizational problems when hiring people on top of an existing layer. None of the people who reported to me in 1993 report to me now. Many of them are still here, but experienced managers have come into the organization between them and myself. Our board of directors has evolved also, going from a board composed mainly of founders and management to a board with several outside directors, who have a lot of gray hair.

As pointed out by Peter Adkison, the firm hired experienced managers from established toy companies, used consultants on strategy and operational issues, and brought outsiders into its board of directors. In the meantime, Adkison himself completed an MBA degree in 1997 at the University of Washington Business School. He knew that he would need to continue strengthening the organization if it was to create a sustainable strategy for growth. Some of the newly hired professionals, who came with strong credentials, did not fit well with Wizards and were asked to leave after a short time. Peter Adkison made the transition from an entrepreneur to a "traditional" CEO as he deepened his theoretical understanding of business as well as his management skills and combined both with his intuitive feel for the gaming business.

THE ADVENTURE GAMING INDUSTRY

Wizards' executives defined the company as part of the adventure gaming industry, which is itself part of the much larger toy industry. They followed publications of the *Toy Manufacturers of America*, as well as the more specialized *Comics Retailer*, a monthly publication that had in-depth reports on gaming developments. Total U.S. toy industry sales in 1996 were estimated at over $17 billion, of which the biggest single category was video games. Outside of video games, the games/puzzles category accounted for approximately $1.4 billion of sales. Role-playing, trading-card, and war games, the segments in which Wizards competed most directly, accounted for about $350 million to $500 million in 1996 according to *Comics Retailer*, while the Game Manufacturers Association estimated gaming sales at $750 million.

The adventure gaming industry began in the 1960s with the development of a number of war games. The industry was revolutionized and began rapid growth in the early 1970s with the introduction of *Dungeons & Dragons*, the first popular role-playing game. The game attracted players with its complexity and the opportunity for players to exercise their creativity. The industry was revolutionized once again in the early 1990s with the introduction of *Magic*. By 1997, *Dungeons & Dragons* and *Magic* were still the top-selling role-playing and trading-card games. The rest of the industry consisted of another major competitor, Games Workshop, a U.K.-based company with revenues over $100 million, and many smaller competitors. Industry observers estimated that the most serious potential future competition would come from companies invading adventure games from other industries.

Although there was no clear distinction between adventure and family games, what makes adventure games unique is the fact that people pursued these games as a serious "hobby," sometimes dedicating many hours a week to playing a certain game. In Peter Adkison's words: "The Magic player is a hobby gamer, meaning it is a person that would rather game than do anything else. If this person could, he or she would play all the time. The constraint people are facing is the time they have to play." This commitment of hobby-players led some critics to characterize players of *Dungeons & Dragons* and *Magic* as members of a "cult."

On the other hand, industry executives feel that this is an unfair image and see most "gamers" as devoted to the intellectual and creative challenges offered by the games. According to a survey conducted by the Game Manufacturers Association, adventure game enthusiasts are young, literate, and are doing well in scholastic endeavors. The survey indicated that a majority of them are indeed very young—about 31 percent are between 10 and 14 years of age, about 37 percent are between 15 and 18 years old, and 32 percent are 19 years or older. The survey also revealed that about 82 percent of the respondents indicated that they maintain a grade-point average of 3.0 or better in high school or college, and about 65 percent said that they read 36 or more books a year. About 80 percent describe themselves as book readers.

Another issue facing the gaming industry is the rise of the Internet and of computer-based games. While most people in the industry consider typical video games to represent completely different customer experiences, either lonely quests through fantasy worlds or "shoot-em-up" arcadelike games, the Internet offers the possibility of role playing and trading cards in a virtual world.

GROWING THE MAGIC

The success of *Magic* put Wizards on an explosive growth trajectory. Sales of about $200,000 in 1993 rocketed to $57 million in 1994 and $127 million in 1995. Peter Adkison muses: "Our margins are fantastic, just like Microsoft's on software, because we basically sell intellectual property. We have basically zero marginal cost." Wizards and Adkison had become instant entrepreneurial superstars. The company grew to about 500 employees and moved in 1996 to a new, 178,000-square-foot office complex down the street from Boeing Corporation's job center in Renton, Washington. In the meantime, Wizards had opened several international sales offices.

Growth also brought problems. Staffing became close to chaotic. In one case, Adkison found that one person who had been on the payroll for several months had never really been hired by anybody. According to Adkison, "I've made so many mistakes, it's not even funny, and that is not counting the mistakes I made last week." Many of the gamers who started with the company were not ready to move into managerial roles. On the other hand, some managers who were brought in from the outside could not work well with the gamers.

As it was already the dominant adventure trading-card game, there was not much growth potential for *Magic* in taking an increasing share of this market. Wizards focused instead on extending the *Magic* brand name into other products and in reaching the mass market to increase the overall size of the adventure trading-card industry. At the same time Wizards had become active in promoting *Magic* tournaments in an effort to give the game added legitimacy and defend it from competing games.

Extending the Brand

Adkison was now attempting to leverage the *Magic* brand name through licensing into books, computer games, and other products. With the popularity of *Magic*, Wizards was able to pick and choose its opportunities. For example, *Magic* appeared as a book series by HarperCollins, with over half a million copies sold. It was also out in two CD-ROM computer games. Wizards' executives felt that bookstores were a logical market for Wizards' products, since *Magic* players tended to be heavy readers and *Magic* itself was often played in bookstores.

Magic merchandise had been extended through licensing into prepaid phone cards, clothing, card albums and protectors, a *Magic* strategy guide and encyclopedia, and calendars. Wizards had also reached an agreement with an Internet development and design company to develop interactive CD-ROM products to serve as guides to the fantasy worlds created by Wizards. Wizards received movie and television offers, but no agreements had been reached so far. Licensing revenues were estimated to be about $1 million annually.

Going for the Mass Market

The dream of Wizards and other adventure game developers was the mass market role-playing game. Selling a normal board game was a one-shot revenue of less than $10 to a game company, but customers could spend up to $500 per year on a role-playing game. A mass market hit could easily create a billion-dollar company.

In the summer of 1997, Wizards introduced a more mainstream version of *Magic* named *Portal*. The game was targeted at a broader audience such as younger teens and families and was launched with a media campaign of close to $5 million. The aim was to move toward a consumer other than the core "gamer," who had made *Magic* a magical success. *Portal* would be distributed through mass market retailers such as Toys "R" Us and Target. Wizards also introduced the so-called Arc System games. The Arc System game is a generic trading-card game system that allows the development of card decks based on a variety of popular characters from TV, such as *Xena, the Warrior Princess*. Those decks can also be intermingled.

But Wizards saw risks with the mass market also. *Magic* gamers were attracted to the atmosphere of game stores and to the experience of the game, not just the game itself. Mass market retailers, on the other hand, saw games as "boxes." And with their tremendous buying power, Wizards would not enjoy the same margins that it did on its *Magic* sales.

Developing Tournaments

To sustain and increase *Magic* sales, Wizards was attempting to professionalize the activity of playing *Magic*, transforming it into a legitimate sport. Noted Adkison, "It's been proven that sports are very sustainable. They hold people's attention for a long time." One part of the strategy was to create players with celebrity standing who could then push the game's popularity in the mass market.

Tournaments had been organized informally in the first years of *Magic*, many held in and sponsored by the game stores selling *Magic*. And hundreds of tournaments were held each year. In 1996, the company organized a six-city professional tournament series that offered $1 million in prizes and scholarships. Wizards also created a computer-based global ranking for all professional players, accessible at the Wizards home page (www.wizards.com). In the United States, over 50,000 tournament players competed in 30 leagues.

The *Magic* World Championships generated such interest that they were carried on television by ESPN for the first time in 1997. Players from over 40 countries competed for individual and team titles, and for $250,000 in prize money. Wizards was able to attract a corporate partner, MCI Telecommunications, to sponsor the World Championships. According to one news analysis, the partnership gave legitimacy to Wizards and provided a mass audience, while MCI was able to tap an attractive audience by being associated with a "cool" event. According to the company that brokered the deal, *Magic* players were especially attractive due to their passion for the game and their desire to collect everything associated with it. "You've never seen loyalty like this. It's unrivaled across any other product or service category," states one analyst. MCI agreed to sponsor Wizards' *Magic* tournaments in exchange for exclusive worldwide rights to produce and distribute *Magic* prepaid telephone cards featuring artwork of *Magic* cards.

Wizards also published a variety of magazines connected with its games. *The Duelist* features information on upcoming *Magic* tournaments as well as articles and tips from celebrity players. The *Dragon* magazine, which came to Wizards with the recent acquisition of the *Dungeons & Dragons* game, had been published since the 1970s.

Opening Game Centers

In May 1997, Wizards of the Coast opened its first retail and gaming store, a 34,000-square-foot Wizards of the Coast Game Center located in Seattle close to the campus of the University of Washington. Designed as the first entertainment center solely aimed at adventure gamers, the center offered an extensive array of arcade video games, sold games and associated merchandise, offered food and beverages, and provided a place to meet and compete with other trading-card gamers. It was also intended to be a site for tournaments. According to Adkison,

The game center is sort of like Nike Town or Planet Hollywood. Playing is a serious hobby for the Magic player. Therefore, we decided to create the ultimate gaming and retail environment. This is a club, a hangout, a place for the devoted game players to go and know they can play any time. I was inspired by Starbucks' concept of the "third place." I wanted to create a third place for the gamer, a place between home and school or work. Starbucks inspired us but we want to make it even better.

Wizards hoped that game centers would create an even stronger game playing "community." The company also hoped that game centers could expand the interest in games and encourage people to consider games as an entertainment choice, like going to the movies or out to dinner. Just as the Cineplex concept broadened the moviegoing public, Wizards hoped that "gameplexes" could do the same thing for games. The first Wizards of the Coast Game Center carries many competitive games, but Wizards games are featured prominently.

Lisa Stevens, one of the original founders and vice president of location-based entertainment, comments: "Our strategic intent was driven by the quest "to make games as big as movies." We were all inspired by that quest. And then we ask ourselves, What made the movies big? Basically the invention of the Cineplex, where you could go as a group and see different movies. That is why we offer different games in our retail stores, even games from some of our competitors." Another objective behind game centers was to improve the retail distribution of the Wizards product line. The company was disappointed with the support given by traditional retailers to the games and felt that it knew better than retailers how to sell and support its games.

Wizards knew that the success of game centers was not a sure thing. Other companies like Gameworks had introduced family entertainment centers with very limited success. Wizards was encouraged, however, by the success of the U.K.-based Games Workshop with its gaming centers featuring the popular game *Warhammer*. Adkison pointed out: "We have the brand but we need to improve distribution. Target and other stores help sustain the sales but those stores don't create new players, that's what we do in our retail stores."

Product Development

Wizards had developed and marketed what are considered to be many great games, but none were able to replicate *Magic*'s success. Adkison remained optimistic, but at the same time realized that repeating that tremendous success would be difficult. "We have several things we're working on in R&D that could turn out to be like *Magic*. But in the gaming business, you can't bank on that success. We have to learn to make money with smaller releases."

The adventure game industry had developed largely as a result of two runaway hits, first *Dungeons & Dragons* and then *Magic*. Adkison expected that another hit would one day revolutionize the industry again. But it seemed unlikely that the same company would be responsible for the next revolution. Wizards needed to position itself to succeed even if it was not the one to develop this next hit.

In addition to aggressively promoting *Magic*, Wizards of the Coast had applied for a patent on *Magic*, covering not the design of the cards but the method of play. It was set on collecting royalty payments from imitators, which had blossomed in recent years. Entry barriers to the game industry were relatively low, and Wizards estimated that there were over 100 games trying to compete with *Magic*.

Adkison recognized that Wizards of the Coast was still a one-product company whose future was tightly linked to the success of *Magic*. "*Magic* provides over 90 percent of our cash flow. It is obviously our primary focus. The big strategic issue with *Magic* is to develop its potential to become a classic game that yields steady profits year after year. I wouldn't mind being a $500 million to $1 billion company. We want to make games as big as the movies."

Acquisitions

Wizards had recently completed two major acquisitions and was considering others. One was Five Rings Publishing, developer of the *Legends of the Five Rings* trading-card game. The other was TSR Inc., creator of the pioneering *Dungeons & Dragons* adventure game. Wizards' acquisition of TSR brought the number one (Wizards) and number three (TSR) of the adventure gaming industry under one roof in 1997. The number two of the industry is the publicly traded company Games Workshop out of the United Kingdom. Peter Adkison comments on Wizards' acquisition strategy:

> Looking at [the] hobby gaming industry means that you need to look at a horizontally narrowed focused segment. And there are only three games in the hobby category out there: (1) *Magic*®, (2) *Dungeons & Dragons*®, and (3) *Warhammer*® [owned by Games Workshop]. And the sweet thing is that we own two of those three. One thing I have learned in my competitive analysis course in MBA-School is that it may be better to be [a] big player in a small market than to be a small player in a big market. And we want to be a big player.

However, integrating these acquisitions had been a major challenge for Wizards. TSR had very serious financial difficulties, which Wizards had to sort out, and the company was in the process of moving the TSR operations and many of its staff from Wisconsin to its Seattle-area headquarters.

Wizards had also confirmed reports that it had held discussions with Westend Games, which had the license for a *Star Wars* role-playing game, and was also considering a DC Comics role-playing game. There were other small game companies that might also make attractive acquisition candidates.

Global Expansion

Wizards estimated that *Magic* was played in over 50 countries by more than 5 million players. The company now had international offices in Antwerp, London, and Paris, and had plans to open other offices in Europe and Asia soon. Adkison noted that international sales had been very important to sustaining the company during the downturn in U.S. sales in 1996. There was still a lot of expansion potential in the international market.

BEYOND MAGIC: CHALLENGES FACING PETER ADKISON

In December 1995, Wizards had the first round of downsizing as Peter Adkison was attempting to focus the company on *Magic*. Thus, Wizards divested itself of the product lines that were not primarily trading-card games. In addition, Wizards' growth came to a sudden halt in 1996, when sales fell off to $117 million. According to Adkison, while part of the cause was the inevitable leveling off of the growth of *Magic*'s customer base, the downturn was also due to the fragmentation of the retail game stores. The success of *Magic* had drawn many entrepreneurs into the game store business, but there was not enough room for all of them. The resulting shakeout caused some distributors to go under, and this hit Wizards too.

In addition, many imitators offered role-playing adventure games online. Whether this would largely replace the face-to-face experience of Wizards' *Magic* and *Dungeons & Dragons* was also a concern of Wizards' executives. Adkison commented on the Internet challenge: "Currently, we are looking at e-commerce, and how to sell online. Should we ignore it or crush it?"

While sales in 1997 were expected to be at about the 1996 level, Adkison was aiming at future growth. "We certainly can operate at a slow growth mode and make nice profits. But we are focused on growing the company more rapidly in the future." Part of the pressure for growth was coming from its original investors. Many of them were friends of the original entrepreneurs, came from modest backgrounds, and had become rich from their investment in Wizards. But this wealth was all on paper, and many wanted to cash out some of their investments. But to take the company public at an attractive price, Wizards would need to have a good growth story for new investors. Coming up with a sustainable growth strategy was critical. This was the central issue facing Wizards' executive as they sat down in mid-1997 to discuss Wizards' future strategy.

CASE IVc   Wrentham Corporation

On the morning of August 1, 1991, Hal Benning, chief executive officer of Wrentham Corporation, a large diversified manufacturing company located in Houston, Texas, picked up the phone and punched in the number of Frank Powell, chairman of the board and longtime friend and associate. The news would not be good.

"What's up, Hal?" Frank asked. "You sound troubled."

"The quarterly numbers are in and Computerstat is going to show another net loss, about $2.5 million. What's more, I've just learned that George Steele will be stepping down as division head at the end of the month to take a position with one of our competitors. He wants to move on while he is still marketable. George feels that if he stays and the division's merger with Microstat fails, his career will be damaged."

"I'm sorry to hear that but I can't say I altogether blame him," said Frank. "This merger has been an awfully messy business."

"It's been rough for all of us," interjected Hal, "but we told the stockholders when we decided on the acquisition that we could make the new combined division profitable."

"That we did, Hal," agreed Frank. "Obviously, we have quite a task in front of us. Where do we stand today?"

"We are still well behind the planned integration schedule and our costs are way over budget. I know both the Microstat people and our folks from Home Computer are trying to work together, but they just don't share a common vision for the business." Hal continued, "For example, no one seems to agree about our international strategy. The Home Computer managers view the domestic market as our bread and butter and see foreign markets as only an incremental opportunity. On the other hand, Microstat's position is that penetrating foreign markets is the key to our future growth, profitability, and even survival. Operationally, we have the same sorts of

Source: This case was written by George W. Danforth of GulfNet, Inc., USA; James J. Chrisman of the University of Calgary, Canada; and David M. Schweiger of the University of South Carolina, USA. This case is intended as a basis for class discussion rather than to illustrate either effective or ineffective handling of an administrative situation.

problems. R&D has not made significant headway on any project requiring cooperation between Wrentham and Microstat people. My feeling is that, to a large extent, we are still managing two separate organizations."

"I noticed that many of the manufacturing and financial reports are still segregated," stated Frank.

"Integrating MIS remains a problem," acknowledged Hal, "but what concerns me most is a lack of unity and trust that extends all the way down to the factory floor. Out at the Santa Clara plant, Microstat people won't follow the advice of our process engineers because they don't trust our knowledge of their products and software and systems capability, making effective R&D and marketing even more crucial to keep pace with technological change, shifting customer preferences, and increasing competition."

In response to these opportunities and threats, the president of Home Computer and his staff mapped out the following specific strategic objectives: (1) decrease dependence on the home computer market; (2) significantly increase sales to the business sector; (3) penetrate selected foreign markets such as Canada, Western Europe, Australia, and New Zealand as the first step toward securing a strong international presence; and (4) improve both product and process R&D. Management concluded, however, that it was not possible to implement the required changes rapidly enough from within the division to keep pace. Therefore, it was decided that Home Computer should seek an acquisition in order to achieve its objectives.

About that time, Microstat, a comparably sized firm located in Santa Clara, California, announced that it was looking for a buyer. It had experienced declining sales, and profit margins had been driven down by price-slashing competitors. Microstat was strapped with far too much inventory, and its cash position was weak. Faced with an approaching deadline to repay a $24 million long-term loan, it had looked without success for another lender and a buyer for its unsold inventory. To make matters worse, the company was betting its future on a new product that had yet to make it out of the design phase. Although Microstat was in trouble, Home Computer's management believed its strengths were consistent with the needs of the division.

Microstat focused on the small to medium-sized business market segment. Sales to home users accounted for only 16 percent of total sales. Moreover, Microstat had established strong distribution channels in Europe; international sales accounted for over a third of its total sales. The company was particularly strong in Germany, France, and the Benelux countries (Belgium, the Netherlands, and Luxembourg). It was also in the process of negotiating an agreement with a large Japanese electronics firm to produce computers under that company's label. Wrentham's corporate and divisional management agreed that with more emphasis on process engineering to reduce costs, and its strengths in product R&D and international marketing, Microstat would make an ideal acquisition for Home Computer.

When the acquisition was announced in January 1991, a number of teams made up of both Home Computer and Microstat managers were put together to work out the many aspects of the merger. A top management team was tasked to oversee a comprehensive integration program and to build a cohesive, unified division. Functional teams worked on the specifics of melding various operations and systems, such as R&D, sales, manufacturing, and human resource and information systems.

Six months later, it was apparent to management that the integration program had not progressed as far as it had hoped. A number of critical technical problems remain unresolved. The human resource team was finding it difficult to develop a system to determine positions, compensation, and seniority that would be perceived as fair by all employees. Management had yet to develop a usable information system, making it nearly impossible to access usable financial data in a timely fashion. Efforts to reorganize the R&D function were meeting stiff resistance; the department remained polarized along old company lines with Home Computer engineers arguing for cost control and Microstat people unwilling to budge on product design features. In addition, R&D suffered from a lack of leadership and direction as the vice presidents of R&D from both the merged businesses left after the merger. Manufacturing had experienced a similar ongoing debate over quality assurance and on-time delivery standards.

THE CANDIDATES

Two weeks later, Bill Brandt reported the results of his search for a new Computerstat president to Hal Benning and Frank Powell. He had been instructed to conduct his search without soliciting the input of George Steele, the departing president of the Computerstat division. Brandt had retired from his position as Wrentham's director of human resources the previous year but was kept on retainer as a part-time management consultant due to his experience and perspective accumulated over a career of 43 years with the corporation. Bill began:

I've narrowed the list down to three candidates, the first of whom I'm sure you are both familiar with—Tom Banks. As you know, Tom worked for one of the largest firms in the computer industry for 17 years before coming to work at Wrentham 10 years ago. For the last 8 years, he has been Home Computer's vice president of manufacturing, a position he holds today in the combined operation. He has a bachelor's degree in electrical engineering from Texas Tech and an MBA degree from Texas A&M. He's 54 years old and is married with three children. What makes Tom an attractive candidate is his years of experience in the computer industry and his ability to manage operations efficiently. Although Home Computer's products have not fared as well in the market the past few years, Tom has helped keep the division afloat by squeezing costs so that it could remain competitive with the larger companies.

Tom is known for his passionate involvement on the factory floor. It's not unusual to see Tom, sleeves rolled up, walking the manufacturing line or talking with line supervisors about part specifications or equipment maintenance. But behind the facade of a spirited, blue-collar team player is a technical genius. Tom's intellectual grasp of the intricacies of each step in the production process is unparalleled. What's more, he has an intuitive ability to recognize how any change will affect the entire process, as well as his overriding bottom line—cost.

Tom is known as upbeat, energetic, and good-natured; however, when he feels his goals are being compromised, he has been known to be very aggressive in defending his views. Some may even say that he is dogmatic and inflexible when challenged. I consider him to be a forceful advocate for quality and efficiency. In fact, many of the standards and procedures in force at the plants today were developed and implemented by Tom. He simply loves to make computers.

The second candidate is Sheila Covington. Sheila was with Microstat when it started up in 1981. Before the acquisition, she had been its vice president of marketing for three years, a position she now holds with Computerstat. She received both her bachelor's degree in marketing and MBA degree from the University of California. Sheila is only 39 years old and still single, but she has a fiancé who is a partner in a high-powered San Francisco law firm.

Sheila is known as a risk taker and an internationalist. While at Microstat before the acquisition, she was able to push through her program for headlong international expansion at a time when other smaller companies were hesitant to commit quickly and heavily to overseas markets. Her success in winning solid distribution agreements in Europe accounted for much of Microstat's success. She speaks fluent German and can hold her own in French. In fact, she was an exchange student in Frankfurt during one of her undergraduate years. She enjoys traveling and likes to mix business with pleasure during her many trips. For instance, during her 1990 vacation in Switzerland, Sheila was introduced to an executive of the Yokohama Company, which led to Microstat's negotiations to sell private label computers in Japan. Although talks have stalled since the merger, whatever hope we have of building a presence there in the next several years rests on her shoulders.

During my two weeks talking to people in the company, it became apparent that she retains quite a following from the Microstat crowd, not only in sales but also in R&D and manufacturing. While at Microstat, Sheila worked very closely with both of these functions to facilitate the production of a greater mix of products.

Sheila is a zealot for customer satisfaction, and it is this orientation that probably accounts for much of her success in opening up and expanding markets. She has not been without her detractors though. Some would say that she is either ignorant of or unconcerned with cost control. I believe this view is a gross oversimplification. Sheila understands the need to control costs as well as anyone, but she's always been more of a revenue-oriented manager. She has always tried to attack new market segments, both foreign and domestic, and has advocated increasing market share through greater product differentiation and value-added features. To Sheila, short-term inefficiencies are a necessary evil when you are creating a larger revenue base in a growth industry.

The final candidate is Carl Ferris, who I am sure you are aware is credited with much of the success of the Dynasis–Culver merger in Wrentham's communications division. He is 57 years old, and although best known for his five years at Dynasis, his real background is in network communications. Before jumping to Dynasis, he had worked for Electron Equipment Company for 25 years where he attained the status of vice president of R&D.

Carl was known as somewhat of a rogue at Electron. He spent as much time dabbling in other functions as he did in his own. Surprisingly, for someone with such a technical background, including a master's degree in computer information systems from M.I.T., he had always been a seller of ideas, a charismatic sort. I've heard the comment that Carl could sell you the sole of your own shoe and you'd thank him for it. The truth is that Carl is a leader. He has a knack for galvanizing people and gathering support.

I was able to talk to a number of my contacts at the Dynasis division over the past week, and I think I've been able to put together a pretty good picture of what has happened there. It seems that at the outset, Carl pulled together many of the best managers from both companies and formed a tightly knit team. They say that Carl presented his ideas powerfully and enthusiastically, yet listened to his people with equal interest. He cajoled top managers to advocate views different from his own. He was open and willing to compromise and absolutely demanded the same from his staff. His one firm rule was that once the team had hammered out a decision, every member was to support it 100 percent. Carl does not tolerate excessive individualism, divisiveness, or halfhearted loyalty. You're either with the team or you're not. It's been rumored that he heard one senior vice president complaining about a policy one too many times to a staff member and Carl sent him packing on the spot.

But I don't regard Carl as a hard man. He treats people with the highest dignity and respect. His praise is quick and sincere, and he abhors finger pointing. Sure, some hard decisions had to be made at Dynasis, and Carl shouldered the responsibility. One plant in South Korea was closed, other operations consolidated, and countless jobs redefined. He publicly told employees up front exactly what was going to happen and why. It was a painful transition, but Carl's reputation for integrity and his keen leadership enabled Dynasis to redirect its efforts quickly and effectively. The only problem I see is that taking over Computerstat would represent a lateral move for Carl. He has been training several men as possible successors and appears to believe he is in line to replace Jim Hamilton as COO of the corporation in a year or two. Carl is not a young man, so if you want him to take on this challenge, it will be necessary to be up front with him regarding his future here and perhaps offer him a position on the board, as well as a substantial increase in salary.

There was a pause as each man reflected on what had been said. Hal spoke up first. "I think that each of these individuals is highly capable. However, the success of the new president will be largely determined by how his or her skills and vision serve to meet Computerstat's particular strategic and operational needs."

"Whoever is chosen is going to have to get a quick handle on the situation," chimed in Frank. "There are a number of issues that must be dealt with immediately. Market demand has been lagging. The economy is in a recession, and this recent string of unprofitable quarters must be arrested and turned around in short order. This company is depending on Computerstat to generate some cash flow. Our stance has been in the past, and I believe should continue to be, that Computerstat must be able to operate successfully on its own without looking to the corporation to bail it out. The plan was that Computerstat would be in the black by the end of the year. That was the commitment George made to us and that we made to our stockholders. I am not amenable to changing these expectations at this juncture."

"I understand your position, Frank," Hal responded, "but much of Computerstat's poor performance can be explained by Microstat's initial overestimation of sales and profit projections. The company was not in the shape that we were led to believe. That said, I agree with you in substance. The turnaround must be quick. Yet the pressing short-term demands must somehow be reconciled with the implementation of a new strategic direction. I question whether either Home Computer or Microstat could have gained and held onto a competitive edge on its own. George Steele had his ideas about where this division was headed, but they haven't panned out. The new president of Computerstat will want to implement his or her own plan, regardless of what has been done in the past. I see that as a good thing."

"Well, time is short," lamented Frank, "and we are not going to get any closer to a decision by drinking coffee and speculating. We have a pool of three outstanding candidates here, and we must make a decision quickly. I suggest we notify the candidates today and ask each of them to submit a memorandum within three days outlining what actions they would take to turn Computerstat around and how they see the division competing in the future." (See Exhibits 1 through 3 for the memoranda submitted by each candidate.)

"Good idea," nodded Hal. "By the way, Bill, Frank and I have reconsidered our decision to keep George out of this process. Although we still have our concerns, we now think that it's best to get as much input as we can, including George's. I know you would have preferred to talk to George at the outset. Nevertheless, your work here reflects your customary thoroughness. I've asked George to join us here for a meeting on Friday at eight."

"That'll be fine."

EXHIBIT 1

From: Tom Banks

To: Hal Benning

It was with great satisfaction that I received your phone call telling me that I was to be considered for the position of president of Computerstat. I wholeheartedly appreciate your confidence and recognition of my past contributions to the company. Although I enjoy my present position immensely, I would readily welcome the challenge and opportunity that the position of president would offer.

As you are well aware, Computerstat has suffered losses since our acquisition of Microstat six months ago. Before the acquisition, we were maintaining marginal profitability in a tight economy and weakening market conditions. Our losses over the past two quarters can be partly explained by the company's hesitance to quickly consolidate a sufficient number of manufacturing operations to achieve the necessary lower unit costs. If such an action plan had been aggressively pursued, we could have enjoyed significant and immediate savings and been able to position ourselves to realize an adequate per-unit profit margin by now. I would implement such a plan and anticipate that Computerstat would return to profitability in two quarters, three at the most.

A second and related factor is that we are still producing the same mix of Home Computer and Microstat machines that each made before the merger. If we plan to gain a competitive edge, we can no longer afford to fragment our efforts by making a wide range of machines aimed at every market segment in the industry. We simply cannot produce the same number of models as we do now and do it at a competitive cost. We also need to be patient. I would like to see Computerstat sell more products overseas someday. But we simply cannot afford to be expending our efforts on expansion in Europe or Japan, or any other foreign market for that matter, until we have put our U.S. operations in order. While those other markets are attractive, our success or failure today, and for the foreseeable future, depends on how well we do at home.

The keys to Computerstat's success in the future are (1) strictly defining what we do best and adhering to it, and (2) understanding where the industry is headed and how Computerstat fits into that picture. What Computerstat does best is make quality, low-cost microcomputers. Microstat should be assimilated into the division so as to enhance that capability. Furthermore, such a strategy positions the company to survive and grow with the industry. Our low-cost stance enabled us to ride out the earlier industry shakeout. The industry is now approaching maturity. The days of double-digit sales growth are about over and probably will never return. The market is approaching saturation, and price competition is accelerating. A second shakeout in the near future is not unlikely. The survivors will be those companies that are structured and focused on efficiency. If I should be chosen as president of Computerstat, this is the precise direction I would take.

"And Bill," added Frank, "Hal and I don't want to walk out of this room on Friday without a recommendation for a new president for Computerstat that we can present to the full board. Time *is* of the essence here."

THE MEETING

Hal Benning closed the door to his office and turned to address the three men seated at the conference table. "First, I'd like to thank George for coming. I'm sure his insights will be quite helpful. Before we get to the matter, I'd like to tell you about an incident

EXHIBIT 2

From: Sheila Covington

To: Hal Benning

I am very excited at the prospect of serving as president of Computerstat and offer my sincere gratitude to you and to the board for selecting me for consideration.

As outlined in Home Computer's original contacts with Microstat's managers and supported to some extent by the ongoing work of the top management team, the primary aim of the Home Computer–Microstat merger was to bring Microstat's marketing strength to bear on Home Computer line of low-end computers and to continue to push forward with the enhancement of higher-end Microstat models.

The common element shared by the effective companies in the industry is that they aggressively pursue and capture market share wherever the opportunity presents itself. Concerning higher-end machines, market characteristics are changing as fast as technological advances both create and meet new needs. The range of uses for microcomputers is unlimited and expanding (e.g., multimedia, home banking, and communications). Running concurrent with this technological explosion is a greater demand for peripherals, specific capabilities, and various value-added items including service. In order to compete in this market, Computerstat must offer the customer a choice of models and assorted enhancements.

There is also considerable potential for Computerstat to sell products overseas. Our research department tells me that with our high-end machines we could achieve substantially greater penetration in Western Europe and capture a significant market share in Japan if we put forth a concerted effort.

The market for simpler machines still offers relatively untapped opportunities in many foreign areas, particularly developing countries and the emergent Eastern European states. Quick entrance will enable Computerstat to establish a firm base from which we can grow with these advancing countries; the first to the market often prevails over late arrivals, even those with better or less-expensive products.

In summary, Computerstat's recent drift from profitability is due to its failure to attack new and emergent market segments. Consistent with this reasoning, I would pursue greater product differentiation of high-end models and penetration of high-potential foreign markets with our low-end machines. Not only will this strategy set Computerstat on a highly competitive course, but it will build a larger revenue base from which the company can begin to shortly realize real and sustainable profits.

that occurred yesterday afternoon. Leo Hainsworth, the manager of our Houston plant, called. It appears that there's been a lot of speculation about who the next president will be. Anyway, Leo made it quite clear that both he and John Stearns, Computerstat's new vice president of R&D, feel they can work well with Tom Banks, but that if someone else is chosen, all hell may break loose. He didn't put it that way, but his tone was clear."

"I don't know that we are going to make everyone happy here or that we should necessarily try," interjected Frank. "After reviewing the files, I'm leaning toward Sheila Covington. I think she offers a fresh and proactive strategy for Computerstat that will enable the company to compete effectively into the next decade. She seeks

EXHIBIT 3

From: Carl Ferris

To: Hal Benning

I must say I was quite surprised when you called the other day to ask me if I would be interested in taking over the helm of Computerstat. After much thought, I have decided that if you share my vision for the company, then I would welcome such an invitation. Let me tell you how I view this challenge and precisely what I believe I can do for the firm.

My Dynasis experience has confirmed to me what I have suspected for some time. As general manager, I cannot direct the activities of an organization as a field marshal does his cavalry. I am neither that commanding nor that clever. Joining two organizations greatly disrupts conventional management processes, making the role of general manager all the more difficult. Consequently, merger situations offer a hazardous and utterly frustrating road to anyone intent on unilaterally implementing even the most ingenious strategic plan.

The fundamental purpose of any merger is to create synergies that enable one large unified firm to perform certain activities cheaper and more effectively than the two firms did apart. The reason why most companies' postmerger performance is poor is that they underestimate not only the technical difficulty associated with achieving certain synergies but also the substantial inertia demonstrated by employees of all echelons when confronted with change. The key then is to unfreeze people from the dictums and scripts of the past and to encourage and facilitate new modes of thinking and doing. This is not a matter of selling the Microstat people on the Home Computer way of thinking or vice versa. What I want to do is create a new meaning for all employees that they will feel is superior to either of the old ways; the effectiveness of any major strategic reorientation will be both dependent upon and a consequence of this.

Because future performance will be determined by the relative success of integrating the two companies, the dominant and overriding standard that Computerstat must measure itself against must be a set of goals associated with the integration program rather than those related to short-term performance. The implication of this is that if Computerstat is going to emerge as a viable and profitable going concern, it can no longer afford to continue to emphasize short-term profits at the expense of efforts that will create a long-term enhancement in competitiveness. Given the current state of the division, these objectives are not reconcilable.

As an outsider from another division, I offer the distinct advantage of not being constrained by any prior alliances or mind-set. Two polarized groups of employees are also more likely to follow my lead than that of an insider who will inevitably be associated with one of the two organizations. In sum, what I offer Computerstat is a unique set of proven skills and experience that can meld the two organizations into a stronger and more profitable company in 12 to 18 months.

out opportunities aggressively and is the only candidate who seems to understand that we are competing in an international rather than a national market. That's the sort of vision this company needs if it is to grow in this industry."

"I disagree, Frank," said Hal. "We've differed before and have come to some pretty good decisions."

"That's true, but only after I brought you to your senses," needled Frank. "You like Tom Banks."

"Yes I do. Am I that predictable?"

"Only to me," Frank laughed.

"Don't get me wrong, I like Covington, but after six months, she still owns her house in California. She rents an apartment here but flies back every weekend to be with her fiancé. Tom Banks is stable. His track record reflects a highly competent and balanced manager. He's conservative and doesn't make mistakes. His abilities and approach largely determined Home Computer's past success, and I think the course he advocates is the most responsible and reasonable for the future. Tom Banks talks about what he knows, and I trust him with the company. He's not oblivious to the changes and globalization of the marketplace, but he does understand that you can't put the cart before the horse. I sense we might be at an impasse on this one, Frank."

"Bill, what do you think?" prodded Frank, his voice rising uncharacteristically.

"Well gentlemen, I'm not sure I'm going to be of much help because my inclination is to go with Carl Ferris. I think you need to consider the priorities of the merger. Carl is the most qualified to see the integration through. He's proved he's capable of pulling off a merger, and his selection would send a clear signal that Computerstat is no longer about either the old Home Computer or Microstat. Until the two companies are truly unified, all this talk about product rationalization, costs, technologic innovation, or expansion in foreign markets is meaningless."

"But look at Tom's track record! Anyway, Ferris is not committed to the original schedule," growled Hal.

"He may be the only candidate with either enough foresight or enough courage to give the bad news," Bill responded.

"I don't see how either Banks or Ferris can provide a viable long-term focus for the company," argued Frank. "Only Sheila Covington has a clear vision for growth."

"OK, OK," called Hal. "We all agree that we disagree. George, we still haven't heard from you. How do you see it?"

"From what I've heard, I'm convinced that the reason for the lack of consensus is that the right person is not in this group of three." George cleared his throat and continued in a low but impassioned voice. "Ellis Ross has been groomed for this position for the past six years. He not only expects the position but has refused some attractive offers from the competition with the expectation that he would succeed me. Since joining us eleven years ago, Ellis has served five years as comptroller, four years heading up our strategic planning staff, and the past two as our chief financial officer."

"But Ellis is a staff man; he doesn't have any line experience," Hal challenged.

"That's true. On the other hand, he's extremely intelligent and is very well read. His analytical skills are extraordinary, and he's able to synthesize his knowledge of finance, operations, and strategic planning into cohesive action plans. That's what this division needs—a solid generalist with experience at the top, someone who understands the big picture. I'm convinced that Ellis is this person.

"It was his idea to buy out Microstat, and it was a good idea. He knows both companies intimately, and he knows how all the pieces should fit together. Any problems we've had with implementing Ellis's plan are my doing. Perhaps if I had let him run with the ball, we would be faring better."

"If he knew you were off course, then why didn't Ross assert himself more?" probed Hal.

"It's not in his nature to push his superiors toward his position, but he certainly isn't weak-willed either. He's a company man. He fully exercises the authority given him, but he respects the word of his superiors. He's a quiet, analytical type, but given the responsibility, he will see this thing through. Anyway, I told Ellis a year ago that if he stayed, he would succeed me as president."

"You did what?!" Frank said, scowling.

"The recommendation of the president has always been followed in the past," explained George, "but the point is that Ellis is the only one who really understands Computerstat as a whole. If he's passed over, you'll lose him. Besides, this is a job for a younger man. Ellis is 43 and in excellent health. He's divorced, you know. No children. He's got the vitality, drive, and singular commitment needed for this job."

"We certainly don't want to lose Ross," said Hal, "but I question whether his reserved manner makes him ideally suited for this job."

"If this discussion has shed light on anything, it's that none of the candidates can claim that distinction," Frank mused. "But I just don't feel comfortable with Ross. We need to signal to both the employees and the shareholders that we're taking a new tack."

"Computerstat needs a fresh start," conceded George, "but it also needs continuity. Ellis would serve as an effective linchpin to guide the division through transition."

"OK, maybe you're right and we should have considered Ross from the outset, but that doesn't change the fact that we need to find some common ground if we are going to be able to come to a consensus," complained Hal.

"I think you've pointed out a key issue here," observed Bill. "As things are, we could debate the merits of each candidate for a month, but one of the crucial elements of this process is that it has to be quick." Bill slid back in his chair and continued. "What I perceive is that each of us is working with a different set of assumptions. Hal, you consider past performance critical. Hence, you chose Tom Banks. Frank, you, on the other hand, believe that Sheila Covington is most capable of achieving what you think is most important, future growth. From my perspective, the overriding concern is the integration program, and, as I said, Carl Ferris is uniquely qualified in that respect. Now, we must seriously consider Ellis Ross—what he can contribute in the way of general management skills and continuity, and whether you are willing to lose him. Anyway, if we are going to reach an agreement, it will be necessary to identify some common ground, as Hal put it. In order to accomplish this, maybe we should focus less on the candidates and more on the criteria by which they should be evaluated. If we can come to agreement on that, then the logical choice should become clear."

"The best predictor of future performance is past performance," argued Hal. "Talk about vision for the future is good, but it is nothing to bet the company on. It's not real. The past we know with certainty."

"I think you're missing the point, Hal," retorted Frank. "It's a changing world, and the only thing we know with certainty is that it will continue to change. Old Man Wrentham was a legend in his time, but he would be lost today. The future is uncertain and that implies risk. A vision for the future addresses *that reality*."

"And what of the merger, gentlemen?" began Bill. "I say the ability to manage this merger is most important. If Computerstat is unable to jump this first hurdle, neither a solid track record nor a vision for future growth is going to make much difference."

"True enough, but without some solid continuity at the top, the division will muddle along regardless of what 'tack' you choose," argued George.

"Frank and I hoped to make our selection today, but it's now apparent that this decision is more difficult than we foresaw," observed Hal. "Perhaps we should think about this some more and get back together in a couple of days to decide what selection criteria are most important, why, and which candidate best fits those criteria."

CONCLUSION

What then is the most important criterion for the selection of the president of Computerstat? Is it past performance, vision for future growth, the ability to integrate the two merged companies, or a balance between top management skills and the ability to provide continuity? Given this assessment, who should be the next president of Computerstat?

CASE IVd   Doka Corporation

Russia is a radically changing country. Russian entrepreneurship is on the leading edge of the radical economic and political transformation of society that will hopefully lead to new business developments, improved quality of life, and a decline and eventual defeat of the Mafia structures. The economic vitality of Russia rests heavily on flourishing small businesses, transformed large industrial complexes, the development of financial infrastructure, and the internationalization of present businesses. This development requires high quality of management and entrepreneurship, creative thinking, and strong business ethics.

INTRODUCTION AND BACKGROUND

Russian entrepreneurship as a phenomenon is not radically different from experiences in other countries. In Russia, entrepreneurs desire economic freedom, innovations, and organizational creativity. Research indicates that the transition to a fullfledged market economy will result in an even greater diversity of entrepreneurial profiles and organizational cultures, different property forms, and a variety of corporate strategies. Not surprisingly, most Russian entrepreneurs are young, thereby allowing a new generation to achieve economic well-being. Their business activity and business mentality have been strongly influenced by (1) the country's historic heritage (state-centered structure, multicultural society, and weak middle class); (2) the Communist ideology; and (3) the absence of reliable business laws and market-oriented economic education. In spite of this, Russian entrepreneurs have much courage, as well as the ability to implement large-scale projects, to fight bureaucracy, to survive and be patient, and to be loyal personal friends.

After official acceptance of the need for economic changes for national survival and economic success in the mid-1980s and the adoption of related laws in the perestroika years, entrepreneurship in the form of cooperatives, individual labor activity, and joint ventures with foreign capital led to unprecedented growth of business activity in the former U.S.S.R. However, the absence of modern business practices and institutions resulted not only in the commodity exchange rush but also in the total breakdown of traditional economic ties. The financial speculations initiated by state-owned structures made the bankers and traders appear as superentrepreneurs in their role in economic development when compared to the industrialists.

Source: This case was written by Mikhail Gratchev, Robert D. Hisrich (both of Case Western Reserve University, USA), and Zakhar Bolshakov, Dmitri A. Popov, and Alexei B. Ilyin (all of Zelenograd Business College, Russia). This case is intended as a basis for class discussion rather than to illustrate either effective or ineffective handling of an administrative situation.

Postperestroika developments created a new national industrial structure. There are a fast-growing number of privatized enterprises and new start-ups, as well as joint ventures and foreign-owned establishments. In the post-Socialist Russia of the 1990s, there emerged a new level of economic and administrative freedom and attempts for more healthy cooperation between business companies and with the state, based on partnership and consensus in the national interests. At the same time, demonopolization of the economy has facilitated the development of entrepreneurship. To a large extent, contemporary economic creativity relates to new businesses either in the start-ups or within "incorporation by privatization" of large-scale amalgamations. Intensive networking has emerged within the entrepreneurial community. While most of the business miracles occur in trade, finance, and banking, new developments also take place in selected industries that shape the backbone of national competitiveness, such as construction, oil and gas, and aerospace. More and more private and publicly owned producers are overcoming serious economic and legal problems and benefiting from the new economy.

THE COMPANY AND LOCATION

One of the visible phenomena of such an entrepreneurial breakthrough is the fast growth of new companies in high-tech sectors of the economy, such as microelectronics, biotechnology, new materials, and software development. Doka Company, founded on May 6, 1987, in Zelenograd (Moscow), became one of the first Russian independent high-tech companies. Its founder and, later, its chairman of the board and director general is Alexander Chuenko. The company was started and continues to be located in Zelenograd, a city near Moscow with a population of about 300,000 and administratively a part of Moscow city.

The characteristics of Zelenograd as a center of the microelectronics industry of the Soviet Union (the so-called Russian Silicon Valley) were its industry-related focus and special status as a closed city (restricted to foreigners) controlled by state security officials. Zelenograd satisfied 60 percent of the demand for electronic devices in the U.S.S.R. and 70 percent of demand for many types of computer chips. Zelenograd's leading industrial facility, Angstrem, built the first satellite in the world, "Sputnik."

Founded in the late 1950s, Zelenograd remained under direct control of the state and Communist Party leaders for several decades. For a long period of time, Zelenograd was famous for its high standards of living and concentration of intellectual elite. After the breakdown of the Soviet Union and collapse of economic ties with former republics, the level of industrial production in Zelenograd dropped by more than 50 percent, thus reflecting the situation in the Russian economy in general. Having lost economic ties and many trade opportunities within the former U.S.S.R., many enterprises started seeking new international contacts. Today several Zelenograd companies have contracts with Samsung, Gold Star, IBM, and other international companies. Their experiences confirm the acceptable level of technology, quality standards, and skills required for high-tech developments.

Zelenograd itself is a technological center connecting business, production facilities, research, and higher education institutions with its Technological University (previously known as the Moscow Institute of Electronic Engineering). The Technological University focuses on preparing highly qualified young specialists in microelectronics and is ranked among the top five engineering schools in Russia. The aggressive and ambitious graduates developed a highly competitive spirit in Zelenograd even prior to perestroika. In 1987, when the government of the Soviet Union officially permitted new forms of business entities other than state-owned enterprises, many people were ready to become entrepreneurs.

May 6, 1987, is celebrated yearly by Doka as its birthday. On this date the company was officially registered as one of the first independent R&D firms in Russia, at the very beginning of the free market and private business revival in the country. This company was initiated based on the "Four Vs": volition, vitality, verve, and vigor. The founders were advanced, innovative young engineers who previously worked at state-owned enterprises. Doka was originally established as the independent "center for scientific and technical creativity of young people." This unusual form had a legal framework that allowed the company to open a banking account and act as an independent contractor. It could also establish its own guidelines in hiring people and paying individual salaries.

This new organizational concept was totally different from the traditions of the Communist state. Two years before the parliament had adopted the Law on Entrepreneurship, the first Decree was signed by the deputy prime minister allowing new independent economic firms to collaborate with the state-owned enterprises. This caused many such firms to be established by young people willing to take risks.

BUSINESS AND INVESTMENT STRATEGY

Innovations are central to the core strategy of Doka. In the current Russian high-tech environment there are many "unoccupied zones" in advancing technologies. From its start, Doka has followed a policy encouraging innovations, some of which hopefully would turn into excellent marketable products. With many new ideas and projects, Doka was in a position to launch risky initiatives.

Headquartered in Zelenograd, at the start-up Doka focused on microelectronics, applied hardware/software systems, special components, and instruments. The project groups concentrated their efforts in these fields while extending their research into new multidisciplinary areas. This strategy fit well with the conditions and available experience, as well as the intellectual and industrial abilities nearby. The company had quick financial returns and further strengthened its technological position for future growth by positioning itself when there were few competitors in the market. The revenue breakdown in 1990 is indicated in Exhibit 1, with the majority of

EXHIBIT 1   Doka's Revenue Breakdown, 1990

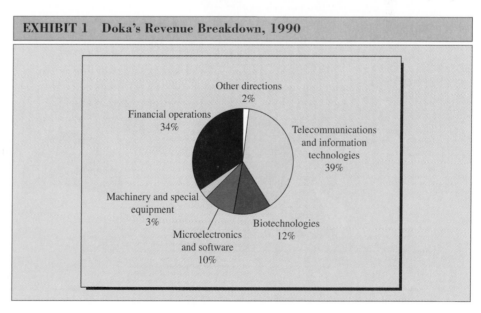

revenue coming from telecommunications and information technologies (39 percent) and financial operations (34 percent).

Doka has always had a strong strategic vision of the industry and of technology development. The company saw the need for establishing reliable links in the business environment and for developing effective information systems and telecommunication networks. Besides creating effective products in the telecommunications and information technologies as well as in engines, the company started a project that later produced original state-of-the-art machines. In the area of high-productive, virus-free agriculture plants, Doka—with a group of leading scientists in biology, algology, and chemistry developed original biotechnology and new equipment. By investing money in other innovations, similar results were achieved in pioneer investigations. These new business opportunities were approached by the company through high-tech expertise, and risks were reduced through a narrowly focused strategy in the unstable Russian economy.

One area in the Russian economy needed by the entrepreneurs was a free banking system that would facilitate innovations and business transactions in the new market economy. Doka helped fill the void by creating a banking system in the region of Zelenograd. Doka was one of the founders of Technopolis Innovation Bank, the first independent commercial bank in the region. This liaison made it easier for Doka to manage financial policy, develop investment strategy, and direct and administer funds more efficiently.

EXHIBIT 2   Doka's Investment Patterns

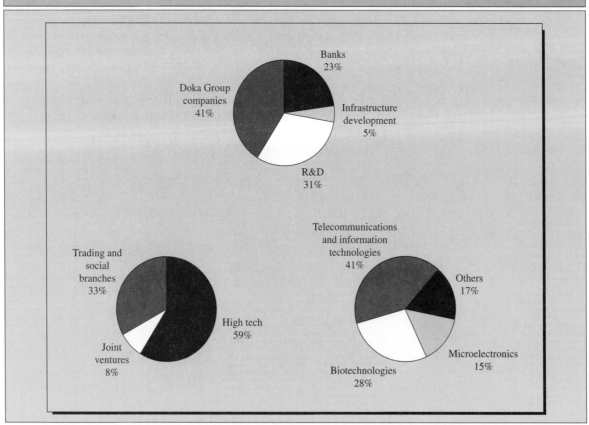

In 1991, Doka had an annual turnover of 247 million rubles ($6 million), with most of the key R&D projects and divisions being reorganized as business units under the Doka Group (see Exhibit 2). Doka was transformed into a multilateral business center with associated subsidiaries and affiliates. Each of these was engaged in separate and related innovative projects, with a clear level of autonomy and responsibility.

The affiliate members and spin-offs of the Doka Group maintain their relations with the parent company as well as with each other. This type of alliance benefits each separate group as well as the parent company. Doka was developing into a prosperous company of R&D, manufacturing, investment, and a trade system that dealt with thousands of partners and customers in different regions of Russia, other republics in the former U.S.S.R., and Western economies. According to the president, Alexander Chuenko, "Business is developing fast and the numbers (sales volume) of today do not really tell the whole story about tomorrow." For example, in 1995, Doka's sales increased in lighting equipment by 300 percent and in software by 200 percent. In addition to being one of the leading Russian software exporters, Doka is the biggest producer of virus-free potato plants in the world, with total annual production of 3 million minitubers.

CURRENT LINES OF BUSINESS

In order to be successful in business in the current unstable situation in Russia, a fast-growing business like Doka has to be extremely flexible in management and coordination. Doka had to prove its organization, marketing, analyzing, and financial potential while persisting in the core high-tech projects. A careful assessment of the developing lines of business led to the benchmarking of priorities, resulting in a number of narrowly specialized companies being detached from the Doka Group and becoming completely autonomous. Presently, Doka has several directions slated for expansion: telecommunications, software, biotechnology, lighting equipment, and culture.

Telecommunications

Doka's top management knows the importance of developing and accessing high-quality communication networks. This understanding initially led to the development of the original telecommunication system that facilitates the internal exchange of information between Doka and its suppliers, customers, and partners. It also generates additional revenues, thus reducing the costs of maintaining and operating the system. For Doka, telecommunications facilitates the internal exchange of information and the effective use of a database that contains data on 4000 customers.

One result of this effort is the Remart Telecommunication System that the company started to develop a few years ago. Doka and its partners heavily invested in Remart, which is a world-class jointly shared information medium combining a great number of separate data transferring systems and connecting them with different domestic and international networks.

Remart is a multipurpose hardware/software complex. The system has the following: a host computer that can serve up to 256 end users simultaneously, an electronic switching unit, data transmitters, and a remote workplace. Software packages include the distributed SQL-standard database support. Remart can operate as a communication server-preprocessor. The Remart database on a Sybase SQL Server is able to process a large number of simultaneous users' queries. Both hardware and software are adopted and certified for the level of quality of the telephone lines throughout the territory of the former U.S.S.R. The various data processing and communicating processes available include electronic mail, telex/telefax, databases, seminars and conferences for the remote participants, and computer advertising. One of the most important parts of the system is the Banking and Stock Exchange (Globex-analogue) module that allows bankers and dealers unlimited opportunities for contact and for making monetary transactions. There is also the Electronics Supermarket module that provides remote clients with sale/purchase information. Soon hundreds of supermarket departments all over Russia will be managed from Doka's headquarters. Today it operates in the cities of Kaluga, Kemerovo, Krasnoyarsk, Ekaterinburg, Orenburg, and St. Petersburg. The hosts of the Remart System have been installed in different regions and institutions of Russia such as the Central Bank of Russia, with the center being Doka. It also has nodes to various electronic communication networks such as Relcom e-mail, Sovam Teleport, and Sprintnet. The Remart System is technically designed and organized so that it will not be significantly impacted by any changes in the political situation. This helps Doka make sure that political cataclysms or economic turmoil does not directly affect this project.

Software

Doka is the leading Russian educational and leisure software developer and exporter. It was one of the first Russian companies selling proprietary software products, entering international markets in 1989 with the *Welltris* game. Over 200,000 copies of this game have already been sold in Western Europe, the United States, and Japan. Subsequent products have gained broad international recognition for their original ideas as well as their eloquent and intelligible graphic design. In 1992–1993, Doka created and introduced the Windows Games Set including *Magic Eraser* and a modified *Welltris*-clone game named *Tubis*.

Mass consumers' growing interest in computer dictionaries, testing, and training and educational programs led Doka to the development of easily operated multilingual software with mobile pop-up screens and mouse support. The *Doka-Tutor* program is a guide to mastering foreign languages, either to train in the lexica to check one's knowledge, or to customize the training mode to fit personal preferences. *Doka World Map* is a unique dictionary-in-pictures educational and reference package, where users can look through as many as 3000 words and expressions traveling across the world map from one picture to another and select images on the screen. And *Baby-Type* is a simple program making it possible to cope with keyboard operations playfully. About 30 of the company's educational and game titles are distributed worldwide today.

Doka is continuously expanding into new software areas. In 1994, it began developing multimedia software, which resulted in the creation of a number of CD-ROM and CD-i titles. Doka Software has regularly been exhibited at CeBIT International Fairs since 1990, and year after year several novel programs or packages are presented at this show.

Biotechnology

The management at Doka feels that biotechnology is a classic example of putting together advances in several different fields such as microelectronics, machine building, and agriculture, resulting in a unique first-class product that few in the world can develop.

The significant pollution and deterioration of the environment sparked the company's efforts to do the following: work on agricultural problems, provide future generations with a sufficient amount of food free of chemical admixture and viruses, ameliorate plantation conditions, accelerate plant growth, protect plants from diseases, and generally improve the quality of agricultural products. To fulfill this mission, Doka has cooperated with the scientists of the Institute of Plant Physiology of the Russian Academy of Sciences. This collaboration has led to the development of original technology and equipment for biosynthesis, cultivation and reproduction of plants, extension of plantation output, and other aspects of fertile bioprocessing. Some techniques for industrial photosynthesis and virus-free plants have been created, manufactured, certified, and commissioned. The industrial system for designing virus-free seed material production for potato minitubers has been developed. This has resulted in the annual production of about 500,000 minitubers, providing well-conditioned seedlings for the plantation of 1,500 hectares.

In April 1993, the Federal Program for Virus-Free Potato Minitubers Producing Development was approved by the government of the Russian federation. This program allowed technological systems like Potato Tree or Microclone designed by Doka to be purchased and used by agro-industries and farmers everywhere in Russia.

Doka's achievements in agricultural cultivation have occurred in such areas of biotechnology as microclonal propagation, regeneration in vitro, plant acclimatization, and hydroponics growth optimization. Minivit-type industrial sets were developed to make assorted greeneries (i.e., fennel, celery, parsley) rich in vitamins and other elements good for human consumption. Microalgae cultivating and organic compounds biosynthesis are also being investigated by the company. Valuable metabolites produced by Doka's unique photobioreactor are important for medicine, pharmacology, biology, and chemistry.

The company's biotechnological devices have been exhibited at international fairs and workshops in Hannover and Potsdam, Germany, and at expositions in a number of countries. These have attracted the strong interest of international experts. Since 1992, Doka has worked closely with the Prince Edward Island Potato Board of Canada, one of the world leaders in potato growing and processing. The company is looking at other international proposals on cooperation and contracts.

Lighting Equipment

Different types of leisure activities are developing rapidly in Russia. Hundreds of theaters, dance halls, night clubs, and casinos are being started throughout the country, from Moscow to the remote sites of Siberia and the Far East. The Russian people want the shows to be better and better. There is a demand in the Russian market for special stage and performance lighting systems. In 1988, Doka started production, distribution, and servicing of lighting equipment and developed its own long-term lighting program. The company developed systems and devices like lighting panels and control desks, and manufactured lamps, motors, and filters at a quality level comparable to European standards at about half the cost.

The first Doka lighting products were purchased and installed in the Moscow Ostankino TV Company. They were then installed in different clubs and discotheques in

Russia and other republics of the former U.S.S.R. This lighting equipment is still not perfected or versatile enough to satisfy the advanced requirements of more than 10,000 show centers to be reconstructed or reequipped throughout Russia. This is an opportunity, according to company managers, for Doka to import the products of Western lighting manufacturers. When Doka participated for the first time abroad as a lighting manufacturer at the specialized international forum in Siel/Paris in February 1993, people were surprised by the quality of the products displayed. This quality allowed the company to develop relationships with such firms as FAL, ADB, and JEM. Acting as their exclusive dealer within the former U.S.S.R., Doka has extended the range of lighting items available in Russia and enhanced its position as one of the leading Russian lighting companies. Doka's Western partners have obtained access to the Commonwealth of Independent States (C.I.S.) market without facing any legal, financial, or promotional problems. These Western companies have also used the opportunity to combine their products with some of the cheaper, high-quality accessories produced by Doka.

Doka decided to operate as a universal distributor by carrying a variety of products ranging from simple, small, and cheap units to complicated and expensive automated systems, complying with clients' lighting needs for shows, discotheques, and theaters, as well as entire lighting systems. This approach is unique among Russian lighting companies. In order to show all the lighting items to its customers, Doka has opened a special showroom in Zelenograd.

The lighting installations made by Doka and its foreign partners have been used by the TV Studio of the Russian State Parliament, Duma; Sergei Obraztsov's Central State Puppet Theater; Solaris Nightclub at Cosmos Hotel in Moscow; and the Mobile Lighting System of Russian State TV. Lighting systems have also been delivered to European Russia, Ural, Siberia, Ukraine, Uzbekistan, and other republics of the former U.S.S.R. International partnerships with the lighting manufacturers in England, the United States, Germany, and Taiwan have been developed. Doka's extended dealership and service network is able to reach most of the Russian regions.

Culture

Doka is also developing and promoting creative spheres such as those of architecture, theater, and music. The cultural domain provides an opportunity for cultivating and enhancing international contacts and understanding between foreign countries and Doka.

Doka's Architectural Studio professionals represent a "new wave" of modern Russian architecture and design. Besides serving as a model for good area arrangement, this architecture is used to decorate any interior. Its highest level was recognized at a special UNESCO competition and at many exhibitions in Japan, France, England, Germany, Italy, Norway, and the United States.

Doka is also sponsoring and equipping the Municipal Theater named Vedogon. This young theater has succeeded in combining the traditions of Russian realistic acting schools with the principles of medieval European commedia dell'arte. The theater company does local performances and has also toured.

Doka has also cooperated with Marina Tarasova, a well-known violin-cellist whose mastery has been highly appreciated by audiences in Russia, France, Italy, Germany, Czechoslovakia, Finland, Portugal, Hungary, Poland, Turkey, and China. The company has promoted her LPs and CDs in Europe.

INTERNATIONALIZATION STRATEGY

Doka Company is well known in Russia as an innovative and reliable manufacturer and partner. New clients and customers are constantly being developed, as are new partners in business. Doka is willing to develop initial relations on the basis of trust and friendship. This same approach is used in the company's international strategy. During the last few years, the company's products and services have been widespread throughout Russia and other territories of the former U.S.S.R., from Belarus to the Far East, as indicated in Exhibit 3. The company's goal is to match its technologies, equipment, and services to customers' requirements and expectations.

One of the features of Doka's international strategy is the development of its international dealer network. Many wholesale buyers have volunteered to become distributors of Doka in the C.I.S., thereby assisting the company to enlarge its network of qualified mounting, installing, and service outlets. By 1994 the company had established dealerships and was selling its products and services in Russia, Ukraine, Belarus, Kazakhstan, Kyrgyzstan, Tajikistan, Uzbekistan, Turkmenistan, and Georgia.

Doka is recognized by many as one of "the most aggressive" private R&D companies in the former U.S.S.R. As indicated in Exhibit 4, the company is trying to expand its business around the world.

Doka has contacts with companies on all the continents except Antarctica. Since entering international markets, a number of projects have been completed with partners from Poland, Finland, Sweden, Germany, Denmark, Belgium, France, Switzerland, Slovenia, Italy, Spain, United Kingdom, United States, Canada, South Africa, Israel, Saudi Arabia, Hong Kong, Singapore, Taiwan, Australia, and Japan. Since its foreign exhibition debut at CeBIT-1990 in Hannover, Germany, Doka has continued to participate in different international fairs and meetings, such as ECTS (London, software); Frankfurter Buch Messe (Frankfurter/Main, publishing); Biotechnica (Hannover, biotechnology); World Potato Congress (England, agriculture); SIB (Italy, lighting); and PLASA (London, leisure industries).

These projects have provided Doka the opportunity to multiply its international contacts and strengthen cooperative partnerships. That is also one reason the company promotes products in the Russian market made in Italy, Belgium, England, the United States, Taiwan, and other countries. The products and technologies developed by Doka are distributed worldwide by Doka's dealers in the United States, Canada, Japan, Germany, France, and Australia. Doka's innovations have been patented in the United States, Germany, the United Kingdom, Japan, France, and Sweden.

The international market plays a vital role for the company, especially in software development. The company's strategy for international expansion in software development is a pressing problem.

Until 1993, personal computers were not common in Russia. Workstations were bought only for business purposes, and the domestic market of home and personal computers did not exist. In 1994, a Russian market for software started as a result of large sales of personal computers (see Exhibit 5). At the end of 1994, the company started distributing its products in Russia.

At this time, the Russian government started its official fight against piracy, because in 1994, 70 percent of all software distributed in Russia was illegal. According to Deputy General Director Alexey Gritsay, "The difference between the

EXHIBIT 3   Map of Sales and Dealerships within Russia and the C.I.S. Republics, 1994

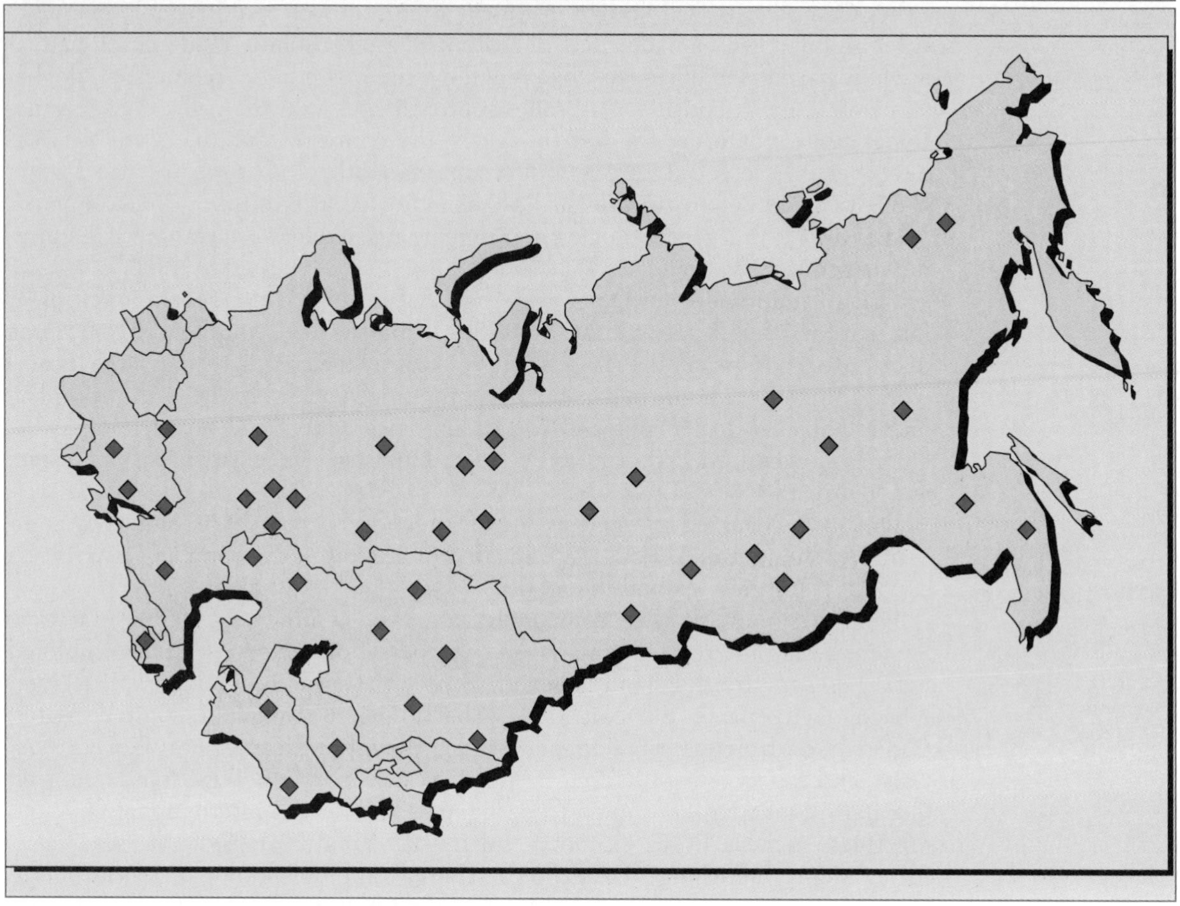

Russian and international markets is going away, and the company now has a global strategy that includes both domestic and international markets." A new game called *Total Control* was presented in Russia in December 1995, in Europe in January 1996, and in the United States in May 1996. The game could be bought in any of four languages: Russian, German, English, and French. In Russia, Doka will publish and distribute the game, and the world rights were sold to the German company Software 2000. Doka concentrates its efforts on applied, educational programs and games for IBM-compatible computers, as Apple computers represent only 2 percent of the Russian market. Internationally, the multimedia segment is growing very rapidly, a situation that is especially attractive for Doka. The multimedia segment should increase to almost $12 billion by 1996 and will increase an average of 17.3 percent a year until the year 2000 (see Exhibit 6).

Lacking a developed sales network and international marketing experience, Doka works through reliable partnerships. These partnerships include Spectrum HoloByte (U.S.); Bullet Proof Software (Japan); VIF and Infogames (France); Sybex Verlag, ZYX, and Hi/Tec (Germany); Lexicon Software (U.S.); Peruzzo Informatica (Italy); and Scandinavian CD-ROM Publishers (Denmark). Doka supplies each partner with master disks and the appropriate license to publish selected products within an

EXHIBIT 4   Doka's Worldwide Partnerships in 1994

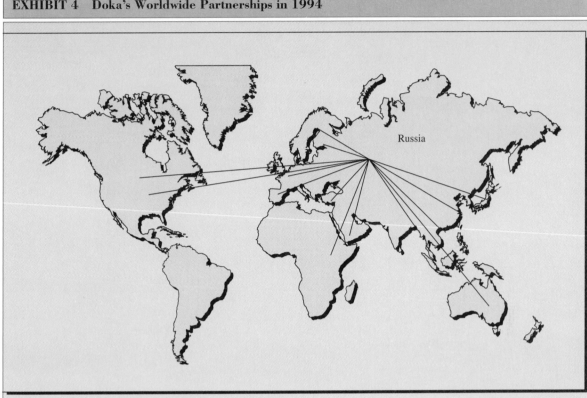

Russia

EXHIBIT 5   Russian PC Market Estimate (units × 000)

	1990	1991	1992	1993	1994	1995E
New sales	310	350	420	570	816	1,170
Growth rate	9%	13%	20%	36%	43%	44%
Retirements	15	20	25	35	45	60
Installed base	795	1125	1520	2055	2825	3935

Source: "East European Semiconductor Market Overview," *Future Horizons* (May 1996), p. 8.

agreed-upon territory. The company can also supply the packaged products on diskettes or CD-ROMs and can customize programs as well. All products are sold under the Doka brand name.

Working through partners helps Doka offset the Cold War and country-of-origin effect. The propaganda during the Cold War made Russia and Russians look very strange and wild to the world. After one presentation of Doka's products and projects in Germany, two businessmen from South Africa asked the Doka representatives if it was true that all Russians drink a glass of vodka with breakfast. Although the West usually does not doubt the quality of Russian weapons and space technologies, many people in Western countries feel that Russians cannot produce any other quality high-

EXHIBIT 6   Worldwide Multimedia Market, 1992–1996 (in 000s of units shipped except as noted)

Item	92	93*	Percent Change (1992–96) 92–93	Percent Change (1992–96) 94–96†
Total	4,815.4	10,315.1	114.2	26.9
Multimedia products	1,065.4	3,465.6	225.3	25.1
Authorizing software	728.9	1,726.1	136.8	16.2
Multimedia PCs and workstations	325.0	1,690.5	420.2	31.2
Networks	11.6	49.0	322.4	72.2
Upgrade kits	675.0	1,109.5	64.4	−4.7
Peripherals	3,075.0	5,740.0	86.7	32.5
CD-ROM drivers	825.0	1,720.0	108.5	27.6
Sound boards	1,800.0	3,200.0	77.8	28.6
Video boards	450.0	820.0	82.2	539.0

*Estimate

†Forecast of annual compound rate of exchange

Source: Dataquest, Inc. Cited in *U.S. Industrial Outlook 1994*, U.S. Department of Commerce, International Trade Administration, p. 27.

tech products. Some Western businessmen actually offered a small amount of money for the copyright to all Doka's products for the entire world and forever.

Although in 1990 Doka was the first Russian software company to take part in the CeBIT International Fair—and through displaying its products there it started searching for reliable partners—it was not until late 1991 that the first contract was signed. By 1995, Doka had 100 products and one of the highest overseas sales volumes by a Russian software company. Not all Doka's ideas and products find their customers in the West. *Lingua*, a unique program that gives the user the opportunity to choose from eight languages the language he or she wants to learn by interacting with people in different situations and hearing voices of native speakers, was not approved by the education committee in Finland. The committee complained about the unequal treatment of men and women, as all the executives simulated by the computer were men and all the tellers were women.

Doka also promotes software products made by other Russian firms that have neither the experience nor the financial capability to work directly with the West. The company offers about 10 to 15 new software products each year.

ORGANIZATIONAL STRUCTURE OF THE COMPANY

According to its statute, Doka is a closed share capital company doing its own R&D business as well as arranging a network of branch offices, associates, cooperation manufacturers, authorized dealers, and remarketers. The company is overseen by a board of directors that is responsible for the company's general directions and financial policy determination. The managing board implements the decisions of the board of di-

EXHIBIT 7 Doka Organizational Chart

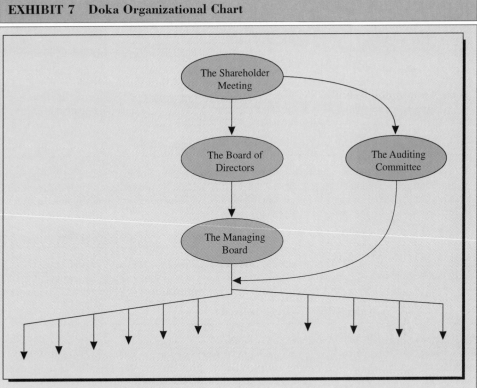

rectors and manages the overall current businesses and affairs of the company. The auditing committee provides the control of the company's finances and economy and reports to the shareholders at the shareholders' meeting. The company's organizational chart is indicated in Exhibit 7, and a description of the key individuals is shown in Exhibit 8. Exhibits 9 and 10 present the financial operations of Doka and the change in the contribution of different lines of business in the company operations for the period 1990 through 1995. The company experienced strong growth from its well-defined strategy, diversification into several high-tech areas, and access to some government-sponsored programs. The sales volume increased nearly 20 times in five years, from $1,850,000 (1990) to $34,680,000 (1995). While all the main businesses of telecommunications, biotechnology, microelectronics/software, machinery/special equipment, and financial operations had steady growth during these years (except for the decrease in financial operations in 1994–1995 due to the crisis in the Russian banking system in 1994), the role of each of the lines has changed.

In 1990, the highest sales were from telecommunications and information technologies. Their $734,000 sales volume was 39.7 percent of all the company's sales. Although the sales in this area grew over the next five years to $1,491,000, its share of total company sales dropped to 4.3 percent. This market was difficult for the company, with the larger former state-owned and now privatized companies dominating the market.

EXHIBIT 8   Members of the Board

ALEXANDER M. CHUENKO, Chairman of the Board and General Director

Chuenko was born in 1957 and graduated from the Moscow Institute of Electronic Engineering in 1979 with a diploma degree in automatics and electronics. After graduation from the institute he worked as a technology engineer at the Angstrem Microelectronics Plant in Zelenograd, which in the mid-1980s was the leading free market business establishment in the region. He was the main initiator and founder of Doka Company and has been its general director since the first day of the company's existence.

ALEXEY M. GRITSAY, Deputy General Director—International Business

Gritsay was born in 1957 and graduated from the Moscow Institute of Electronic Engineering in 1980 with a diploma degree in automatics and electronics. In the period 1980–1990 he worked as an engineer and officer at high-tech institutions in Zelenograd and Moscow. Since 1987 he has cooperated with Doka Company as a consultant. In 1990 he took the position of international business director at Doka.

EVGENY S. ZAYCHENKO, Deputy General Director, Development and Manufacturing

Zaychenko was born in 1958 and graduated from the Moscow Institute of Electronic Engineering in 1981 with a diploma degree in machinery technologies. After graduating from the institute he worked at the Elion Machinery Plant in Zelenograd. In 1988 he took a position at the Doka Company in development and manufacturing.

VYACHESLAV A. KARTASHEV, Executive Director

Kartashev was born in 1937 and graduated from the State Polytechnic Institute in 1966 with a diploma degree in radiotechnics. After graduating from the institute he worked as an engineer and department chief at microelectronics institutions and plants in Zelenograd. He elaborated the problems on economics and management in the fields of microelectronics. Since 1989 he has held the position of Doka Company executive director.

EXHIBIT 9   Doka's Assets (millions of rubles)

	1991	1992	1993	1994	1995 (9 months)
Total current assets	328.1	392.0	794.1	3201.1	6369.7
Net property, plant, and equipment	27.1	29.3	500.6	3575.7	12024.8
Total assets	355.2	421.3	1294.7	6776.8	18394.5

During this time, Doka developed other innovative areas. In biotechnology, sales grew from $218,000 (1990) to $9,969,000 (1995); in microelectronics and software, sales grew from $179,000 (1990) to $10,023,000 (1995); and in machinery and special equipment, sales grew from $63,000 (1990) to $12,173,000 (1995).

Another indicator of the company's success is its steady growth in total assets. Total assets reached 18,394,500,000 rubles in the first nine months of 1995. Net property was assessed at 12,024,800,000 rubles with total current assets of 6,369,700,000 rubles.

EXHIBIT 10   Doka's Turnover Analysis

Directions	1990 Value	%	1991 Value	%	1992 Value	%	1993 Value	%	1994 Value	%	1995 Value	%
Total	1.850	100.0	2.735	100.0	4.661	100.0	9.120	100.0	18.937	100.0	34.680	100.0
Telecommunications and information technologies	0.734	39.7	0.845	30.9	1.100	23.6	1.578	17.3	1.648	8.7	1.491	4.3
Biotechnologies	0.218	11.8	0.429	15.7	0.834	17.9	1.842	20.2	4.734	25.0	9.606	27.7
Microelectronics and software	0.179	9.7	0.336	12.3	0.853	18.3	1.915	21.0	5.302	28.0	10.023	28.9
Machinery and special equipment lighting systems	0.063	3.4	0.328	12.3	0.942	20.2	2.371	26.0	5.492	29.0	12.173	35.1
Financial operations	0.623	33.7	0.755	27.6	0.872	18.7	1.286	14.1	1.534	8.2	1.144	3.3
Other directions	0.031	1.7	0.041	1.5	0.061	1.3	0.128	1.4	0.227	1.2	0.243	0.7

One general principle is assumed in the employees' collaboration at Doka: Everyone has his or her own personality with specific characteristics, abilities, potentialities, and interests that should be taken into account and used for the welfare of Everyone and the company as a whole. The company's personnel policy keeps pace with the changing concerns and needs of its employees. This policy has minimized the company personnel turnover, which is a real problem for many other Russian companies.

Joint activities and parties help facilitate a favorable corporate climate. Events like holidays and Doka's birthday are celebrated together by employees.

Doka is an equal opportunity employer and gives all employees the same chance to succeed. Each person's opportunity to advance depends on his or her performance.

Many of Doka's managers have engineering backgrounds. These top managers do not feel that the lack of formal marketing knowledge is a disadvantage. They think business education alone does not provide the logical thinking that is so vital in a high-tech business. However, managers at Doka are taking development courses in business. Alexander Chuenko attended classes at the London School of Business, and Alexey Gritsay took some business courses at the Russian University in Germany.

Everyone in the company works hard to achieve success. Programming specialists, for example, do not complain about the lack of advanced computers. They say, "In the West, 10 specialists are writing one thing, and 10 others are writing another. We have to do everything by ourselves—what is done abroad by 10 people, here is done by only one. We have to spend more time and work harder creatively."

Executives of Doka believe in the economic success of Russia. It is just a question of time. When looking at the future, the company sees changes in Russian opportunities. The company plans to remain the leading player in three of its lines of business—software development, biotechnology, and lighting equipment—and is ready to develop new lines of business as new opportunities emerge. For example, Doka is working with some roots of different plants that can be developed to be used as a substitute for insulin. Using its competitive advantage of high scientific and technological potential, Doka wants to become a major global player in any field it enters.

CASE IVe   Executive Furniture Limited

INTRODUCTION

Paul Williams watched as the last of his employees filed out of the meeting room. They had taken the news of the buyout of the company well and seemed to be behind him. He was now the sole owner of Executive Furniture Limited ("EFL") and at long last had the freedom to run the company as he saw fit. The question now was how to turn this consistently loss making company into the profitable growing business he knew it could be.

PAUL WILLIAMS—DESIGNER

The son of a neurosurgeon and a doctor, Paul knew at an early age that he wanted to design and build furniture. However, when Paul's father had been a young boy, he had watched his own father's business collapse and had experienced the serious consequences that this had on family life. As a result, he was keen that Paul should seek the security of a professional career. Therefore, when Paul left school, he went to St. Andrews University to study English. However, three years later, upon graduating, Paul went ahead and took up an apprenticeship with a cabinetmaker in Dunblane who specialized in reproduction pieces. Here Paul learned the basic art of furniture manufacture.

Having gained the basic skills of his chosen craft, Paul craved the freedom to create his own furniture designs. To this end, at the age of 25, he went back to the student life. He completed a BA degree in furniture design at Glasgow Art College and in 1983 commenced work on a postgraduate business scholarship. As part of his coursework, Paul produced a dissertation on "Craft Furniture Businesses" and made an important discovery: The United Kingdom was at that time full of furniture makers, most of whom were starving! Paul continued with his market research on the industry and found out that things were, however, slightly better in the office furniture contract side. There was competition from Scandinavia and Italy but very little activity involving Scottish manufacturing companies. Armed with this knowledge he decided to take the plunge and started his own small business.

This case study forms part of a series of case studies developed on behalf of Scottish Enterprise to highlight the role of the entrepreneur in the creation and development of a business.
It was prepared by Karen Thornton of Price Waterhouse and Frank Martin, University of Stirling.
Copyright © Scottish Enterprise 1996.

EFL—THE EARLY DAYS

EFL was born in a workshop in Inverness, and from there Paul began to design a range of products that included boardroom tables and desks that were created specifically for the contract market. Orders came in fairly steadily.

Paul used casual labor as required, and when the need arose for more skilled workers, he was able to call on former university colleagues to plug any gaps. Paul also earned additional money from design consulting work. As he put it: "I was able to make a reasonable living—well at least I wasn't starving!" Things went smoothly for a couple of years, and Paul began to make a name for himself in the Scottish contract furniture market.

CHANCE OF A LIFETIME

In 1986 he took a stand at the Interior Design International Exhibition in London; this was to have a significant impact on the course of events. One of the items Paul had on display was a chair covered in a fabric manufactured by a Scottish textile producer. The textile company also had a stand at the exhibition, and two of the directors saw Paul's chair and approached him with an invitation to tour their factory on his return to Scotland. They also mentioned that the chairman of the Group of companies to which they belonged had been looking to invest in a furniture manufacturing company.

When Paul arrived at the textile factory, he was surprised to be shown into a meeting with the Group chairman. He offered Paul what seemed to be the chance of a lifetime. Paul would be set up in a company and provided with the necessary support, financial or otherwise, to enable EFL to develop into a successful and growing business. The chairman gave one of his senior executives the task of coming up with the most suitable vehicle for the venture. Paul sat on the sidelines and let them get on with it. "I trusted them. I thought that they must have known what they were doing!"

One of the Group's dormant companies was used to purchase a small manufacturing joinery business located in an old mill in Musselburgh. The premises, equipment, stock, and employees were all taken over by the company, which was then renamed Executive Furniture Limited. Paul became managing director of the company, and one of the directors of the textile company also sat on the board. They were to be joined by other directors in later years. The Group's Edinburgh lawyers were appointed company secretary, and the books were maintained by the Group management accountants based in Greenock. Paul was impressed.

Paul's remit was to use the cash generated by the original joinery business to fund development of his contract furniture business. The overall aim was to phase out the joinery division in two years, leaving a profitable and cash-generating furniture manufacturing business behind.

GOING NOWHERE FAST

There were a number of problems right from the outset. The joinery division did not turn out to be the profitable business anticipated. In fact the equipment was in a dreadful state of repair, and the work was beset by quality problems. There were serious difficulties estimating costs, and this led to a number of contracts being underpriced.

The company's reputation with its customers was extremely poor, and almost all of Paul's time was spent "putting out fires." This left him little time to develop the furniture division, and, as a result, this was an extremely frustrating period for Paul. Sales had reached £317,000 in 1987, but the company's financial position was poor and the Group had to invest further funds and guarantee an ever-increasing overdraft.

The board had had enough. In early 1988 the joinery division was finally laid to rest.

RECOGNITION AT LAST

Initially things began to improve. Paul at long last was able to concentrate all his efforts on furniture design and manufacture. Together with Jack Murray, a newly recruited designer and draftsman, Paul targeted Scottish architects as potential customers. He secured a number of high-profile contracts including work for the Scottish Clearing Banks and other notable industrial clients. In 1990 they won a major contract to redesign and manufacture furniture for the boardrooms of all branches of the Allied Irish Bank in Dublin.

EFL began to emerge as the leading Scottish contract furniture manufacturer, and ownership of a "Paul Williams Original" became something of a status symbol. EFL had found a niche in the furniture market with its top-of-the-line executive and boardroom furniture using modern designs coupled with traditional workmanship. In Scotland and the Republic of Ireland, the company had few competitors that operated at the top end of the market and had the same reputation for quality of design. At this time, almost all the contracts were for special one-of projects. The company seemed to have turned the corner and in 1990 made a profit, albeit a small one.

In 1991, the company moved to new premises built for them in the same business park in Musselburgh. They also had a piece of good fortune. They had occasionally outsourced some of their design work to a firm in Edinburgh that used CAD software. In that year the firm went bust. Paul was quick to spot the opportunities and time savings that CAD could offer and was able to pick up two CAD workstations relatively cheaply. He also took on one of the firm's former draftsmen. They became the first Scottish manufacturers in the very traditional furniture industry to use this technology.

With turnover having reached £473,000, Paul felt ready to launch an assault on the lucrative London markets. To that end, he developed a range of customized boardroom furniture, made possible through the use of the CAD system, and opened a showroom in London.

NOT AGAIN!

In 1992 and early 1993 things were difficult for EFL. London was an unmitigated disaster, and the anticipated sales orders never materialized. Sales levels in Scotland also began to fall with reduced orders from architects, a previously reliable source of work. Fortunately, the Group chairman had commissioned a number of items for his ancestral home, and this provided some additional work for the factory.

Staff morale was very poor. The salaried staff took pay cuts, and some had to hand back their company cars. As orders began to fall, factory employees were forced to take periods of unpaid leave, and annual pay raises were not possible. There were serious production problems in the factory: The craftsmen refused to take responsibility for their work. If all the materials down to the last nail were not there for them at the start of a job, they would sit back and wait until the production manager realized this and fetched the missing items for them.

It was a particularly frustrating time for Paul, and the constraints of being a member of a much larger group of companies were clear. In attendance at each monthly board meeting were the chairman, four directors, the group lawyer, and accountant. As a result, making major decisions was a time-consuming process.

Throughout this period the company's overdraft was worsening, and the level of indebtedness to the holding company reached £0.75 million. The financial performance of EFL over the period 1986–1993 is provided as Appendix 1. The situation could not continue, and the Group considered withdrawing its support.

A SECOND BITE AT THE CHERRY

Matters came to a head with the chairman's death in summer 1993. His son took over the chair of all of the companies in the Group, and, after spending some time reviewing the Group's portfolio, he took the decision to dispose of EFL. Just before Christmas 1993, Paul was given the chance to buy the company. For Paul this was just the opportunity he had been looking for—to become his own boss again!

Paul negotiated the deal himself without recourse to outside advisors. The prebuyout balance sheet is shown as Appendix 2. The main terms of the deal were as follows:

- Paul bought the entire share capital of EFL for £1. The lease of the premises was assigned to the Group, which in turn subleased them to Paul.
- The fixed assets were transferred to the Group and then leased back to Paul.
- Paul purchased the current assets for £35,000 (financed by remortgaging his house).
- The Group paid off the overdraft of EFL (c£200,000).
- The Group wrote off all the outstanding loans due to them by EFL (c£650,000).
- Paul renegotiated a new overdraft facility of £15,000.

On February 4, 1994, Paul signed the agreement that transferred ownership and full control of EFL to him. The first thing he did on completion of the deal was to call together all his employees and outline to them what had happened.

Starting with a blank sheet of paper, Paul started to jot down his ideas on how to transform EFL into the profitable business he knew it could be.

APPENDIX 1   Profit and Loss Accounts for 1986–1993

	1986 £000	1987 £000	1988 £000	1989 £000	1990 £000	1991 £000	1992 £000	1993 £000
Turnover	234	317	470	376	442	473	332	408
Cost of sales	(200)	(277)	(349)	(207)	(246)	(274)	(167)	(255)
Gross profit	34	40	121	169	196	199	165	153
Distribution costs	(17)	(11)	(4)	(6)	(3)	(2)	(3)	(2)
Administration expenses	(118)	(177)	(208)	(243)	(177)[1]	(293)[2]	(225)	(266)
Operating profit/(loss)	(101)	(148)	(91)	(80)	16	(96)	(63)	(115)
Interest	(15)	(17)	(57)	(20)	(15)	(18)	(21)	(14)
Loss for year	(116)	(165)	(148)	(100)	1	(114)	(84)	(129)

[1]Includes £52k credit re a consequential loss insurance claim due to flood damage
[2]Includes increased development and marketing costs for new product range

APPENDIX 2   Pre-Buyout Balance Sheet (£000)

Fixed assets	74
Current assets	
Stocks	43
Debtors	60
	103
Current liabilities	
Creditors	(69)
Bank overdraft	(205)
	(274)
Net current liabilities	(171)
Total assets less current liabilities	(97)
Long-term creditors	
Loan stock	(650)
Other parent co. loan	(103)
	(753)
	(850)
Capital & reserves	
Share capital	10
Retained losses	(860)
	(850)

Glossary

A

acquisition   Purchasing all or part of a company

acquisition financing   Financing to buy one's own or another company

administrative domain   The ways managers make decisions

aftermarket support   Actions of underwriters to help support the price of stock following the public offering

assessment of risk   Identifies potential hazards and alternative strategies to meet business plan goals and objectives

asset base for loans   Tangible collateral valued at more than the amount of money borrowed

assets   Represents items that are owned or available to be used in the venture operations

attribute listing   Developing a new idea by looking at the positives and negatives

B

balance of payments   The trade status between countries

barter   A method of payment using nonmoney items

big-dream approach   Developing a new idea by thinking about constraints

blue sky laws   Laws of each state regulating public sale of stock

book value   The indicated worth of the assets of a company

brainstorming   A group method for obtaining new ideas and solutions

breakeven   Volume of sales where the venture neither makes a profit nor incurs a loss

breakthrough innovations   A new product with some technological change

brokers   People who sell companies

business angels   A name for individuals in the informal risk-capital market

business ethics   The study of behavior and morals in a business situation

business plan   The description of the future direction of the business

business plan   Written document describing all relevant internal and external elements and strategies for starting a new venture

C

C Corporation   Most common form of corporation, regulated by statute and treated as a separate legal entity for liability and tax purposes

checklist method   Developing a new idea through a list of related issues

collective notebook method   Developing a new idea by group members regularly recording ideas

concept stage   Second stage in product development process

contract   A legally binding agreement between two parties

conventional bank loan   Standard ways banks lend money to companies

copyright   Right given to prevent others from printing, copying, or publishing any original works of authorship

corporate culture   The environment of a particular organization

corporation   Two or more individuals having unlimited liability who have pooled resources to own a business.

covenants   Restrictions limiting the size of company debt

creative problem solving   A method for obtaining new ideas focusing on the parameters

customer service and satisfaction   Tracking and monitoring customer complaints and suggestions

D

deal structure   The form of the transaction when money is obtained by a company

debt financing   Obtaining borrowed funds for the company

deficiency letter   A letter from the SEC to a company indicating corrections that need to be made in the submitted prospectus

description of the venture   Provides complete overview of product(s), services, and operations of new venture

desirability of new venture formation   Aspects of a situation that make it desirable to start a new company

development financing   Financing to rapidly expand the business

direct exporting   Selling goods to another country by taking care of the transaction

direct public offering (DPO)   A method of selling part of the company directly to investors

disclosure document   Statement to U.S. Patent and Trademark Office by inventor disclosing intent to patent idea

distributive bargaining   Process of resolving conflict by keeping other parties from meeting their goals

diversified activity merger   Combination of at least two totally unrelated firms

E

early-stage financing   One of the first financings obtained by a company

earnings approach   Determining the worth of a company by looking at its present and future earnings

entrepreneur   Individual who takes risks and starts something new

entrepreneur as an innovator   An individual developing something unique

entrepreneurial decision process   Deciding to become an entrepreneur by leaving present activity

entrepreneurial domain   The ways entrepreneurs make decisions

entrepreneurial process   The process through which a new venture is created by an entrepreneur

entrepreneurship   Process of creating something new and assuming the risks and rewards

environmental analysis   Assessment of external uncontrollable variables that may impact the business plan

equity financing   Obtaining funds for the company in exchange for ownership

equity participation   Taking an ownership position

equity pool   Money raised by venture capitalists to invest

exporting   Selling goods made in one country to another country

F

factor approach   Using the major aspects of a company to determine its worth

FIFO   Inventory costing method whereby first items into inventory are first items out

financial plan   Projections of key financial data that determine economic feasibility and necessary financial investment commitment

financial ratios   Control mechanisms to test financial strength of new venture

focus groups   Group of individuals providing information in a structured format

forced relationships   Developing a new idea by looking at product combinations

Form S-1   Form for registration of a public offering of stock

Form S-18   Form for registration of a smaller public offering of stock

foundation company   A type of company formed from research and development that usually does not go public

franchisee   Person obtaining the franchise

franchising   Allowing another party to use a product or service under the owner's name

franchisor   Person offering the franchise

free association   Developing a new idea through a chain of word associations

full and fair disclosure   The nature of all material submitted to the SEC for approval

G

gazelles   Very high growth ventures

general partner   The overall coordinating party in a partnership agreement

general valuation approaches   Methods for determining the worth of a company

going public   Selling some part of the company through registering with the SEC

Gordon method   Method for developing new ideas when the individuals are unaware of the problem

government as an innovator   A government active in commercializing technology

H

heuristics   Developing a new idea through a thought process progression

high-potential venture   A venture that has high growth potential and therefore receives great investor interest

"hitting the growth wall"   Rapid growth phase where operations are out of control

horizontal merger   Combination of at least two firms doing similar businesses at the same market level

hostile takeover   A company acquiring another company against its will

I

idea stage   First stage in product development process

indirect exporting   Selling goods to another country through a person in the entrepreneur's home country

industry analysis   Reviews industry trends and competitive strategies

informal risk-capital market   Area of risk-capital markets consisting mainly of individuals

initial public offering (IPO)   The first public registration and sale of a company's stock

integrative bargaining   Allowing other parties to meet their goals while still maintaining commitment to own goals

intellectual property   Any patents, trademarks, copyrights, or trade secrets held by the entrepreneur.

international entrepreneurship   An entrepreneur doing business across his or her national boundary

Internet   Computer online service providing important sources of information for starting a new venture

intrapreneurial culture   The environment of an entrepreneurial-oriented organization

intrapreneurship   Entrepreneurship within an existing organization

iterative synthesis   The intersection of knowledge and social need that starts the product development process

J

job descriptions   Specify details of work to be performed by an employee

job specifications   The skills and abilities needed to perform a specific job within an organization

joint venture   Two or more companies forming a new company

L

leveraged buyout (LBO)   Purchasing an existing venture by any employee group

liabilities   Represents money that is owed to creditors

licensing   Allowing someone else to use something of the company's

licensing   Contractual agreement giving rights to others to use intellectual property in return for a royalty or fee

lifestyle firm   A small venture that supports the owners and usually does not grow

LIFO   Inventory costing method whereby last items into inventory are first items out

limited liability company   Special type of partnership where liability is limited and continuity options are more flexible

limited partner   A party in a partnership agreement that usually supplies money and has a few responsibilities

liquidation covenant   The right of an investor to sell the interest in the company

liquidation value   Worth of a company if everything was sold today

M

majority interest   Having more than 50 percent ownership position

management contract   A method for doing a specific international task

managing underwriter   Lead financial firm in selling stock to the public

market extension merger   Combination of at least two firms with similar products in different geographic markets

market segmentation   Process of dividing a market into definable and measurable groups for purposes of targeting marketing strategy

marketing and sales controls   Key variables used to reflect performance results of marketing plan

marketing goals and objectives   Statements of level of performance desired by new venture

marketing mix   Combination of product, price, promotion, and distribution and other marketing activities needed to meet marketing objectives

marketing plan   Written statement of marketing objectives, strategies, and activities to be followed in business plan

marketing strategy and action plan   Specific activities outlined to meet the venture's business plan goals and objectives

marketing system   Interacting internal and external factors that affect venture's ability to provide goods and services to meet customer needs

matrix charting   Developing a new idea by listing important elements on two axes of a chart

merger   Joining two or more companies

minority interest   Having less than 50 percent ownership position

N

negotiation   Process of resolving conflict between two or more parties

nonequity arrangements   Doing international business through an arrangement that does not involve any investment

O

opportunity identification   The process by which an entrepreneur comes up with the opportunity for a new venture

opportunity parameters   Barriers to new product creation and development

ordinary innovations   A new product with little technological change

organization culture   Internal venture atmosphere based on employee attitudes

organizational plan   Describes form of ownership and lines of authority and responsibility of members of new venture

owner equity   Represents the amount owners have invested and/or retained from the venture operations

P

parameter analysis   Developing a new idea by focusing on parameter identification and creative synthesis

patent   Grants holder protection from others making, using, or selling similar idea

poison pill   A method to protect the value of a company for its shareholders

poison puts   Provisions allowing bondholders to cash in if the insurer of the bond (the company) is taken over

possibility of new venture formation   Factors making it possible to create a new venture

present value of future cash flow   Valuing a company based on its future sales and profits

pricing amendment   Additional information on price and distribution submitted to the SEC to develop the final prospectus

private offering   A formalized method for obtaining funds from private investors

private venture-capital firms   A type of venture-capital firm having general and limited partners

pro forma balance sheet   Summarizes the projected assets, liabilities, and net worth of the new venture

pro forma cash flow   Projected cash available calculated from projected cash accumulations minus projected cash disbursements

pro forma sources and applications of funds   Summarizes all the projected sources of funds available to the venture and how these funds will be disbursed

problem inventory analysis   A method for obtaining new ideas and solutions by focusing on problems

product development stage   Third stage in product development process

product extension merger   Combination of two firms with noncompeting products

product life cycle   The stages each product goes through from introduction to decline

product planning and development process   The stages in developing a new product

product safety and liability   Responsibility of company to meet any legal specifications regarding a new product covered by the Consumer Product Safety Act

product-evolution process   Process for developing and commercializing an innovation

production plan   Details how product(s) will be manufactured

proprietorship   Form of business with single owner who has unlimited liability, controls all decisions, and receives all profits

prospectus   Document for distribution to prospective buyers of a public offering

public-equity market   One of the risk-capital markets consisting of publicly owned stocks of companies

publicity   Public interest free advertising in any major media

Q

quiet period   90-day period in going public when no new company information can be released

R

rational decision model   Method of resolving conflict through objectives, analysis of alternatives, and action

red herring   Preliminary prospectus of a potential public offering

referral sources   Ways individual investors find out about potential deals

registration statement   Materials submitted to the SEC for approval to sell stock to the public

Regulation D   Laws governing a private offering

replacement value   The cost of replacing all assets of a company

research and development limited partnerships Money given to a firm for developing a technology that involves a tax shelter

restrictive covenant   Statement indicating the things that cannot be done without approval

reverse brainstorming   A group method for obtaining new ideas focusing on the negative

risk taking   Taking calculated chances in creating and running a venture

risk-capital markets   Markets providing debt and equity to nonsecure financing situations

S

S Corporation   Special type of corporation where profits are distributed to stockholders and taxed as personal income

SBIC firms   Small companies with some government money that invest in other companies

scientific method   Developing a new idea through inquiry and testing

settlement range   Agreeable solution area for parties in conflict

situation analysis   Describes past and present business achievements of new venture

state-sponsored venture-capital fund   A fund containing state government money that invests in companies mostly in the state

strategic plan   Three- to five-year plan that includes all functions of an organization

synectics   A method for individuals to solve problems through one of four mechanisms

synergy   Two parties having things in common

T

target market   Specific group of potential customers toward which venture aims its marketing plan

technological innovations   A new product with significant technological advancement

technology transfer   Commercializing the technology in the laboratories into new products

test marketing stage   Final stage before commercialization in product development process

third-party arrangements   Paying for goods indirectly through another source

time management   Process of improving individual's productivity through more efficient use of time

top management commitment   Managers in an organization strongly supporting intrapreneurship

trade barriers   Hindrances to doing international business

trade secret   Protection against others revealing or disclosing information that could be damaging to business

trademark   A distinguishing word, name, or symbol used to identify a product

traditional managers   Managers in a non-intrapreneurial-oriented organization

turn-key projects   Developing and operationalizing something in a foreign country

U

underwriting syndicate   Group of firms involved in selling stock to the public

V

value analysis   Developing a new idea by evaluating the worth of aspects of ideas

venture-capital market   One of the risk-capital markets consisting of formal firms

venture-capital process   The decision procedure of a venture-capital firm

vertical merger   Combination of at least two firms at different market levels

W

window of opportunity   The time period available for creating the new venture

Index